The
L/L Research
Channeling Archives

Transcripts of
the Meditation Sessions

Volume 2
February 22, 1976 to June 8, 1980

Don
Elkins

Jim
McCarty

Carla L.
Rueckert

Copyright © 2009 L/L Research

All rights reserved. No part of this book may be reproduced or used in any form or by any means—graphic, electronic or mechanical, including photocopying or information storage and retrieval systems—without written permission from the copyright holder.

ISBN: 978-0-945007-76-0

Published by L/L Research
Box 5195
Louisville, Kentucky 40255-0195

E-mail: contact@llresearch.org
www.llresearch.org

About the cover photo: *This photograph of Jim McCarty and Carla L. Rueckert was taken during an L/L Research channeling session on August 4, 2009, in the living room of their Louisville, Kentucky home. Jim always holds hands with Carla when she channels, following the Ra group's advice on how she can avoid any possibility of astral travel.*

Dedication

These archive volumes are dedicated to Hal and Jo Price, who faithfully and lovingly hosted this group's weekly meditation meetings from 1962 to 1975,

to Walt Rogers, whose work with the research group Man, Consciousness and Understanding of Detroit offered the information needed to begin this ongoing channeling experiment,

and to the Confederation of Angels and Planets in the Service of the Infinite Creator, for sharing their love and wisdom with us so generously through the years.

Table of Contents

Introduction 7
Year 1976 9
    February 22, 1976 10
    February 29, 1976 13
    March 28, 1976 16
    April 18, 1976 19
    May 16, 1976 23
    May 30, 1976 26
    June 6, 1976 29
    June 13, 1976 31
    June 20, 1976 37
    June 27, 1976 40
    July 18, 1976 44
    July 25, 1976 48
    August 8, 1976 51
    August 15, 1976 54
    August 22, 1976 58
    August 29, 1976 65
    September 5, 1976 68
    September 19, 1976 72
    September 26, 1976 76
    October 3, 1976 79
    October 10, 1976 82
    October 15, 1976 84
    October 17, 1976 91
    October 24, 1976 96
    October 26, 1976 99
    October 30, 1976 105
    October 31, 1976 110
    November 7, 1976 113
    November 14, 1976 116
    November 21, 1976 120
    November 28, 1976 125
    December 12, 1976 128
Year 1977 133
    April 13, 1977 134
    August 10, 1977 138
    September 26, 1977 142
    October 27, 1977 147

    November 2, 1977 152

    November 9, 1977 156

Year 1978 160

    March 11, 1978 161

    March 13, 1978 165

    March 27, 1978 169

    June 26, 1978 171

    July 3, 1978 174

    July 5, 1978 179

    August 9, 1978 181

    August 21, 1978 185

    September 4, 1978 189

    September 11, 1978 194

    October 9, 1978 198

    October 18, 1978 200

Year 1979 205

    January 29, 1979 206

    February 13, 1979 211

    February 18, 1979 213

    March 4, 1979 220

    March 18, 1979 225

    April 1, 1979 229

    April 15, 1979 233

    April 29, 1979 238

    May 6, 1979 244

    May 20, 1979 248

    June 10, 1979 254

    June 17, 1979 258

    July 5, 1979 262

    July 11, 1979 268

    July 14, 1979 271

    July 19, 1979 273

    July 26, 1979 279

    August 2, 1979 282

    August 9, 1979 286

    August 16, 1979 290

    September 6, 1979 295

    September 13, 1979 298

    September 18, 1979 304

    September 27, 1979 312

    September 27, 1979 319

    November 3, 1979 323

- November 18, 1979 328
- November 18, 1979 332
- December 2, 1979 337
- December 16, 1979 341

Year 1980 346
- January 6, 1980 347
- January 20, 1980 352
- February 3, 1980 355
- March 23, 1980 358
- March 30, 1980 361
- May 4, 1980 367
- May 11, 1980 372
- May 18, 1980 374
- May 25, 1980 380
- June 1, 1980 388
- June 7, 1980 392
- June 8, 1980 396

Introduction

Welcome to this volume of the *L/L Research Channeling Archives*. This series of publications represents the collection of channeling sessions recorded by L/L Research during the period from the early seventies to the present day. The sessions are also available on the L/L Research website, www.llresearch.org.

Starting in the mid-1950s, Don Elkins, a professor of physics and engineering at Speed Scientific School, had begun researching the paranormal in general and UFOs in particular. Elkins was a pilot as well as a professor and he flew his small plane to meet with many of the UFO contactees of the period.

Hal Price had been a part of a UFO-contactee channeling circle in Detroit called "The Detroit Group." When Price was transferred from Detroit's Ford plant to its Louisville truck plant, mutual friends discovered that Price also was a UFO researcher and put the two men together. Hal introduced Elkins to material called *The Brown Notebook* which contained instructions on how to create a group and receive UFO contactee information. In January of 1962 they decided to put the instructions to use and began holding silent meditation meetings on Sunday nights just across the Ohio River in the southern Indiana home of Hal and his wife, Jo. This was the beginning of what was called the "Louisville Group."

I was an original member of that group, along with a dozen of Elkins' physics students. However, I did not learn to channel until 1974. Before that date, almost none of our weekly channeling sessions were recorded or transcribed. After I began improving as a channel, Elkins decided for the first time to record all the sessions and transcribe them.

During the first eighteen months or so of my studying channeling and producing material, we tended to reuse the tapes as soon as the transcriptions were finished. Since those were typewriter days, we had no record of the work that could be reopened and used again, as we do now with computers. And I used up the original and the carbon copy of my transcriptions putting together a manuscript, *Voices of the Gods*, which has not yet been published. It remains as almost the only record of Don Elkins' and my channeling of that period.

We learned from this experience to retain the original tapes of all of our sessions, and during the remainder of the seventies and through the eighties, our "Louisville Group" was prolific. The "Louisville Group" became "L/L Research" after Elkins and I published a book in 1976, *Secrets of the UFO*, using that publishing name. At first we met almost every night. In later years, we met gradually less often, and the number of sessions recorded by our group in a year accordingly went down. Eventually, the group began taking three months off from channeling during the summer. And after 2000, we began having channeling meditations only twice a month. The volume of sessions dropped to its present output of eighteen or so each year.

These sessions feature channeling from sources which call themselves members of the Confederation of Planets in the Service of the Infinite Creator. At first we enjoyed hearing from many different voices: Hatonn, Laitos, Oxal, L/Leema and Yadda being just a few of them. As I improved my tuning techniques, and became the sole senior channel in L/L Research, the number of contacts dwindled. When I began asking for "the highest and best contact which I can receive of Jesus the Christ's vibration of unconditional love in a conscious and stable manner," the entity offering its thoughts through our group was almost always Q'uo. This remains true as our group continues to channel on an ongoing basis.

The channelings are always about love and unity, enunciating "The Law of One" in one aspect or another. Seekers who are working with spiritual principles often find the material a good resource. We hope that you will as well. As time has gone on the questions have shifted somewhat, but in general the content of the channeling is metaphysical and focused on helping seekers find the love in the moment and the Creator in the love.

At first, I transcribed our channeling sessions. I got busier, as our little group became more widely known, and got hopelessly behind on transcribing. Two early transcribers who took that job off my hands were Kim

Howard and Judy Dunn, both of whom masterfully transcribed literally hundreds of sessions through the eighties and early nineties.

Then Ian Jaffray volunteered to create a web site for these transcriptions, and single-handedly unified the many different formats that the transcripts were in at that time and made them available online. This additional exposure prompted more volunteers to join the ranks of our transcribers, and now there are a dozen or so who help with this. Our thanks go out to all of these kind volunteers, early and late, who have made it possible for our webguy to make these archives available.

Around the turn of the millennium, I decided to commit to editing each session after it had been transcribed. So the later transcripts have fewer errata than the earlier ones, which are quite imperfect in places. One day, perhaps, those earlier sessions will be revisited and corrections will be made to the transcripts. It would be a large task, since there are well over 1500 channeling sessions as of this date, and counting. We apologize for the imperfections in those transcripts, and trust that you can ascertain the sense of them regardless of a mistake here and there.

Blessings, dear reader! Enjoy these "humble thoughts" from the Confederation of Planets. May they prove good companions to your spiritual seeking. ☘

For all of us at L/L Research,

Carla L. Rueckert

Louisville, Kentucky

July 16, 2009

Year 1976

February 22, 1976 to December 12, 1976

Sunday Meeting
February 22, 1976

(H channeling)

I am Hatonn. Greetings, my friends, in the love and the light of our infinite Creator. It is very pleasing to see this group this evening, and to be able to speak with you. And for some whom we have not seen for a long period of time, we extend our gratitude for your presence.

These meetings, as you know, have a purpose, and that purpose is to aid you in your intellectual growth, so that your intellect may be able to keep pace with the spiritual knowledge that you gain through meditation. It is our fervent belief that the intellectual information which we share with you is of great benefit along your path. Each person must choose the path that he would wish to follow. And each person, in choosing that path, must realize that the path he has chosen shall lead to the ultimate point of interception with all other paths, the point of oneness.

Consider it, if you will, as a wheel, with an infinite number of spokes. Each spoke is an entirely different path, yet all are connected to the same center. All spokes protrude from the one center, as all paths have come from the Creator.

All paths come, and all paths go, to our Creator at all times. We of the Confederation have chosen to assist the people upon planet Earth through such means as these, for we feel that it is our most efficient means of assisting you. If we were to show physical proof of our existence, or if we were to work so-called miracles for you, then we would be proving something to you within the illusion. And, my friends, we stress that you must go beyond the illusion in which you have chosen to live at this time. Anything which appears within the illusion is that: an illusion. Though the illusion may seem to have great reality to you, and great purpose, it is nonetheless an illusion projected by your consciousness.

My friends, we wish to prove nothing. We wish only to be known; and to know us, and to know the Creator, you must transcend the illusion through the practice of meditation, and learn and know reality. Infinite reality, my friends. You shall never know all things within the intellect, yet all things, though they be infinite are known to you within your spirit. Within your spirit, you have the knowledge of all times and all experiences. Within your spirit, lies reality. And within reality there is nothing but love.

And love to you, my friends, is a concept which you have greatly misunderstood in your intellect. Yet within your spirit it is pure. It is holy and sacred and infinite. The more love which you are capable of displaying, or shall we say, the more love which you project into your present illusion, the more the illusion shall fade away, and reality appear.

Reality in itself may be an illusion, but one thing above all else can truly be known to exist. And throughout our experiences we have found only one stable aspect. That is love. It is everyone. It is around you. It is within you. It is infinite, and it is all things.

I shall transfer this communication. I am Hatonn.

(Carla channeling)

I am Hatonn. I am now with this instrument, and again I greet you, in the love and the light of the Creator. My friends, it is written in your holy works, that the man who gives all that he has to the poor and gives his body to be burned, if he has not love, then he is worth nothing. It is important, as you attempt to pursue the spiritual path, that you meditate continually on the nature of love. Love in action—that which is called service—is indeed the highest of all manifestations of light within your peoples. Yet service without love is worth nothing. And the person that attempts to serve without the heart within clear and full of light showing forth as love, is defeating his own purposes.

My friends, it is not easy to come to an understanding of what love is, for among your peoples love is already named by so many lesser emotions and states of mind—and none of these is love. When we say that love is all that there is, this begins to give you some idea of the scale on which we are speaking. If you can imagine the full force of the sun beating down upon you, and imagine that sun beating down equally, and totally, upon each entity, each blade of grass, moving each mote of air, and blessing the growth of each plant—this begins to tell you of the force and the impartiality of true love.

If you would love, my friends, neither sympathize nor judge. It is well known that you should not judge and each of you already attempts to do so. Encourage this in yourself, to the greatest degree. And also encourage yourself not to be what this instrument would call a "bleeding heart." Do not sympathize. Do not become lost in emotion, for love is not emotion, and emotional service is often a "human" service, and not the service of love.

Rather, my friends, do the following, if you would love: take the entity whom you would love, and become that entity, not to sympathize nor to condemn, but to totally become that entity. Actually allow your consciousness to reside within that person. Do this carefully, quietly, completely. If you need to, imagine your body fitting the body of the other person. Make that complete an identification. And then, move this consciousness back within your body. Let the shoulders meet your shoulders, the head meet your head. Feel the union of two entities which are truly one. Love is one.

You know that is unity, yet you sympathize, and condemn, and allow your human heart to rule that which should be free-flowing, always, without let or hindrance regardless of how you as a person within the illusion feel about another person within the illusion. Know ye not that ye are ministers, each of you? Ministers of light, as are all people. Through your eyes shines the light of the Creator. If you wish to allow your inner feelings to shutter that light, then you will only show true love to a chosen few. And in doing so, you limit that love.

This is a hard lesson to learn, but true. It can be done. And we may say to you, to the extent that you are able to do this, even partially, my friends, even very partially, you will light up a great, great deal of space within the finer spheres of the planetary vibration. You have heard of the search for one honest man, or a few righteous men, so that an entire community could be spared. My friends, this is due to the fact that one source of light can illumine a great deal of darkness.

You make a great deal of difference. It may not seem so on this plane, yet it is indeed so. That which you do is all-important, not only to you but to the planetary vibration. We come back so often to meditation, and it is because the light which you are seeking to show, that light of true love, cannot come from you, but through you. Only through you, my brothers and sisters, pouring through you like the sun pours down into the tree, so that the tree may yield its fruit up, so that all may eat of its substance. The fruit of your tree is not a physical thing, for you have a high emotional and mental and spiritual ability, and that which you can offer is within these realms. But remember that you are, indeed, a tree, and that you can be pruned. And that if you allow the sunlight to develop you, all that pass may take the fruit from your boughs.

I would close through another instrument. I am Hatonn.

(B channeling)

I am Hatonn. I am now with this instrument. Just a few more words, my friends. As I have stated earlier, if you live your existence in that of love, you all may know that by putting out, shall we say, only love, your consciousness will reach the place where all that you receive is love. Now we say, my friends, love is the strongest feeling in the whole universe. By existing in this experience, you may all, my friends, strike higher and higher. It is *(inaudible)*. And, my friends, if everyone existed in this dimension, what a wondrous existence it would be.

As always, it has been a great honor to share in your meditation. I will leave you now. I am Hatonn. Adonai. Adonai vasu borragus.

L/L Research

Sunday Meeting
February 29, 1976

(N channeling)

… I am with this group. As always, it is an honor and a privilege to be here and speak with you through these channels. My brothers and I are always glad to have new people at the meetings. And we are thankful to enter your presence.

My friends, during the course of your daily lives you reach what we could call high and low spots or areas. Sometime you hit spots that seem to bring the truth of the Creator to your understanding, and other times you have spots that make you think that there is no hope of understanding any of what is going on around you. And you ask yourself what are the things that seem to link you with the truth, and with unity. The things that sometimes emotionally affect you, as in art, or art work, where you feel as if someone has personally given you a key to higher understanding—you recognize this as beauty, my brothers, and these little conceptual awakenings are with you as you go through your daily lives.

You go through many cycles of highs and lows, but these links, as I shall call them, are to remind you of the eternal love and truth that can be within your full understanding if you desire it to be. The desire is your decision, and you will receive exactly what you desire.

This has a great deal to do with your thinking. If you can control your thoughts, my friends, you control your destiny.

At this time, I will contact through another instrument. I am Hatonn.

(Carla channeling)

I am now with this instrument. I am Hatonn, and I greet you once again in love.

You see, my friends, as you go through your daily lives, and as you are seeking the correct path for yourself, as you bend your attention to your perceptions of beauty and of ugliness, it is sometimes very helpful to remember that although you are within a physical illusion at this time, and although you are within many higher and finer illusions beyond that, yet also within you ultimately there is only one reality, and if you can observe from the point of view of this reality, your perceptions will be greatly enhanced within the illusion.

As you consider your own actions, you may well ask whether you are attached to that which is physical, or attached to that which is mental, or attached to that which is supposedly of a higher nature. We have been aware of your conversation, and we wish to say to you: to be attached, and to be detached, is to be within the illusion. You cannot be full or empty of concept without remaining within the illusion. To fill your consciousness with reality is far, far more desirable for spiritual advancement that to empty your consciousness of the illusion. Emptiness is not any special virtue. If you do not care about one thing or another within the illusion, yet still you are not full of the joy of the Creator, then you have nothing yet, no matter how detached you may be, or how attached you may be to higher things.

So seek, my friends. Seek always to fill your consciousness with that which can only be heard in silence.

The voice of the Creator: it is a still, small voice, as it has been written in your holy works; yet it is thunder, and has the power to change and transform your entire experience. Your true nature—your truest nature, my friends—cannot be expressed. It can only be felt. And when you feel it, you will become a channel in your own way, to give that light and that love that is your true essence to all those with whom you come in contact.

I would at this time transfer this contact to another instrument. I am Hatonn.

(H channeling)

I am Hatonn. I am now with this instrument and once again I greet you in the love and the light of our infinite Creator.

No matter what we say to anyone who would listen, we wish you to realize that you receive through these instruments our thoughts. These are our perceptions of the universe which we share. Much of our information we have derived from our experience, and we wish only to share with you these simple concepts.

Yet we ask that you understand that we are communicating from a level of existence which is quite different from that which you presently occupy, and upon our level of existence, understanding and knowledge are concepts which you within your present existence cannot fathom with the intellect. My friends, we must communicate to you through the use of your intellect, yet what we have to say is beyond its grasp. The true meaning of what we speak can only be found in your periods of silent meditation. It is of great importance to you to practice daily that art of meditation. Whether it be for seconds, or minutes, or hours, once each day, it is to your benefit to allow the intellect to still itself, and consciously seek within the quietness of your being the guidance of your Father, the Creator.

Above all things, this should be the desire within all of the beings of this universe: to communicate with the Creator, and to listen to the Father in silence. You upon planet Earth are presently experiencing great changes, within your social and ecological structures. You upon planet Earth are also experiencing great changes within your inner being, within your spirit. For the day has come that those upon your planet who are desirous of knowledge shall receive that which they desire. And those who desire to reject, or are blind to the presence of this knowledge, shall again experience this type of existence, until they are desirous of the knowledge, and aware of its presence.

You upon planet Earth, above all else, are spiritual beings. Though you cannot see your spiritual being, you can sense the presence of your being, and know that you are truly not as you physically appear to others. You are within your physical being. You lie within the silence. You lie within the Creator. And in order to truly understand yourself and your environment, it is necessary to practice communicating, shall we say, with your Creator. So basically what we stress above all else is the practice of meditation. This is our message. There are many things which we can say. There are even many things which we could do. Yet, my friends, unless you find for yourselves the answers, you shall be cheated, we might say. For you are responsible for your own development, and you are appreciative of your own initiative. And if you do not desire, you shall not receive.

You, my friends, are the master and the creator of your experience. And you only can decide in which area or which direction you shall go to find that which you are searching for. And, my friends, you are searching for knowledge, enlightenment, wisdom, and above all else, the thing of which these are ingredients: you seek love. This is your purpose: to seek, to know, to experience love. My friends, in all truth, there is nothing in this universe that is not love. All things have been designed to assist you in realizing the truth of the concept of love, and the truth of its omnipresence in your experience. Know in yourself love, and experience this love. It is your birthright. And if it is your desire to experience this, in due time, as all desires, it shall be experienced.

My friends, consider, if you will, that you above all else are important to the development of the entire universe. You are the center of your experience. And your development shall affect that which surrounds you. If you wish to live within harmony, then you shall, through one process or another, shall bring this about. You must dwell within the love and within the light, and listen to the guidance of the infinite Creator.

It is my desire to once again transfer this contact. I am Hatonn,

(Carla channeling)

I am again with this instrument. I will close briefly through this channel.

To seek this love, my brothers, we ask you again and again to meditate. Please know the central importance within your own spiritual growth of this centering of your consciousness. In your own way, and in your own time, your consciousness, through your own application of meditation, will begin to be centered on love. And yet we, in this application, do not say "love"; we say that you will seek the Creator. For it has been so throughout the ages that it is necessary to personalize the concept of the all-love, or the all-light, so that you may truly seek with your whole heart that which is love. It is for this purpose that the one known to you as Jesus the Christ came among your people. He came among your peoples to personify, yet another time, love.

When you seek in meditation, do not content yourself with seeking something which you call love, or light. Seek the sweet voice of the person of love. If it be not Jesus in your mind, let it be who it will be—a perfect, loving, compassionate being who cares eternally and totally about you. Give your love, and open yourself to an exceptionally pure and personal feeling of love. Do not be contented until you feel the presence of this personification of love, until this presence is so close that if you turned around, you could see it next to you.

Love is real, and within the physical you must begin to perceive it as real. Feel it, hear it, absorb it. Then, my friends, give it all away, for love is not love until you have shared it. That which you take in and do not give away will rapidly become sour. Love is a flowing and ongoing stream. Let it flow through you. In meditation, my friends, try to meet the Creator. Feel His breath on your cheek, His hand on your shoulder. Sense His loving, compassionate gaze. Know the fullness of total love. Do not be content with any less, for with any less, you will not be able to share this love with others.

We offer to you our love, and our light, and our service. We are deeply grateful for the opportunity to speak with you. We leave you in the love and the light of the infinite Creator. I am Hatonn. Adonai vasu borragus. ☥

Sunday Meeting
March 28, 1976

(The beginning of the meeting was not recorded.)

(H channeling)

[I am Hatonn.] It is, as always, a privilege to be with you. And we wish to share with you this evening a few, shall we say, points which relate to your involvement in what you would call your social structure.

My friends, those upon your planet, as they enter through the process of birth into this experience, they immediately become exposed to the programming, shall we say, of the society in which they have chosen to exist. It is each and every individual's desire to progress spiritually, whether it be a known value or not. And a portion of your spiritual progression is proper function within your social structure. Many of those today within your society who are becoming aware of the great changes which are and shall be occurring … this instrument is having some difficulty. Please be patient.

As we were saying, many of those upon your planet … this instrument is still having some difficulties due to analysis of that statement and we would transfer this contact while the instrument regains contact. I am Hatonn.

(Carla channeling)

I am now with this instrument. I am Hatonn. We will attempt to use this instrument, although the import of the message is more easily, shall we say, given through a certain type of instrument. Therefore, this particular instrument will find this portion of the message slightly awkward. But we will continue through her.

We were saying: many of those who have come into the world by incarnation have experienced in other incarnations a structure in society, as you call it, which was substantially enough different from the structure of society as it is today that there are remarkable and far-reaching conflicts. This is absolutely understandable and reasonable but only so when you understand that the problem between individuals and their so-called society is that the individuals involved do not have experience with this type of structure but with other structures, which are, may we say, perhaps more conducive to spiritual growth than this particular type of structure.

The very reason that many of those have incarnated at this time is because this will be a difficult and laborious incarnation for them, giving them a great deal of challenge, giving them a great goal. Those who are incarnated at this time, those who have incarnated into this density have chosen, not the easy way, but the way that leads to what they feel are greater rewards. For in hardship, lessons are learned much more quickly than in times of ease.

There are many who are here from your own planetary structures, from those known as planets. These people experience in their social structure *(inaudible)* yet you have understood, in that society, that the center of man's being is his spirit. It is not so on this planet. It is understood in this society that the society itself, as it touches man, is the reality. And this simple understanding within your society is the cause for all the conflict that you now feel. It is simple, and yet very difficult to penetrate, because, as we say, when you woke up as a child in this world, immediately this world began to inform your mind of its version of reality. Each of you has knowledge within you, for you came into this world with your knowledge intact. You know that this world is not correct in its speaking to you. Yet you have been very frustrated and unable to express this knowledge, because there are no words and it seems sometimes that there are no alternatives. And certainly there is no loophole, shall we say, no excuse. So you can't ignore the world as it presents itself to you and substitute your own version.

Let us back up to what we of Hatonn would perhaps say reality is. Let us look at society from that point of view. Sometimes it helps to go back to the beginning and then observe that which you see before your eyes. You know that you are as the plants and the animals and that one portion of you is of the earth and will remain with the earth. You know that many of your functions are earthly and that just as the seed grows into the plant and then *(inaudible)* and the new seed grows and the cycle goes on and goes on. So, my friends, you were once a seed. There are many things that you do that are of animal *(inaudible)*. And you fulfill your nature at this time. And this is a blessed and correct action, of instinct and of nature and of course as it should be in this world.

Yet that part of you can be laid aside while we look at the next part, which is, of course, your societal nature, that part of you which reacts with the creation of man as your animal nature reacts with the creation of the Father. You react with other men and with the creations of man, that being their ideas, their boundaries, their structures of all kinds. All things which are created in the mind of man, left to itself—that which is created in the mind of man will become more and more complicated, more and more conventionalized, until entanglements become so great that they strangle themselves. This is the inevitable end of mind without restraint.

Many of your kind have come to depend very greatly upon the powers of the mind, and upon what other people say and upon what is obviously the way things are. This phrase within this channel's mind seems to occur very often. Yet men know their animal nature and they know they are part of mankind through their thought, their speech and their actions. Yet how often they do not pull themselves through the complexity to the simplicity which lies beyond.

For your third nature, my friends, is the spiritual. You come into this world an animal *(inaudible)* you are spiritual. That which is infinite, invisible, eternal, omnipresent, omniscient, omnipotent. You are that which is. That which is, is you. The body and the mind, if properly tuned by care, may become the servants of the Creator Who dwells within your spirit. This is your proper nature and it is to this end that you came into this rather trying, rather difficult, and rather laborious environment. If you can express what you understand in spirit within this environment, my friends, what a great light you will have to shed upon the world picture.

This is a chance to express love and so move on to further knowledge. It is as simple as that. Your body and your mind are either your masters or your servants. You cannot bully either your body or your mind. They are, properly, very strong. The only way that they will become your servants is if you offer then a master which they recognize. The body and the mind recognize only that divine will which expresses through your spiritual nature.

(Inaudible)

… The master is within you. There has been much teaching among your peoples … *(long portion inaudible)*. The master, however, is not a long way away, is not hanging upon a *(inaudible)*. He has always been with you, he is within you and within me. If you allow him and his consciousness he can become the master of your frame. He will live for you and the simplicity of his nature will flow like water all about you.

(Inaudible)

There are many shadows in life but when the sunrise has reached high enough for the sun to peep over the top of the hill the shadows dissolve. Know ye not, my friends, that you are *(inaudible)* and yet the crowning spirit combines and unifies all your natures into one. *(Inaudible)* We leave you in this love. It is a precious, precious advantage which you have, for you are within a plane in which you can make great progress *(inaudible)* and we say to you what any older brother would say to a younger child who was studying. We would say, "Pay attention now, please, pay attention *now*." This is the time for paying attention not to the things that bother your mind, although you must acknowledge and adjust to them, for the mind is useful, indispensable. Pay attention to the spiritual significance of this moment and of each moment as it appears. Your signs will not be physical, my friends, *(inaudible)*.

I would like to transfer to another channel at this time. I am Hatonn.

(B channeling)

I am Hatonn. I am now with this instrument. As I was saying, pay attention, my friends. For there is a chance you will learn much and to attain much happiness. And, my friends, if you look back over the past, you will see in every instance that meditation has in some way brought you peace of mind, more, what we should say, contentment. But, my friends, it is merely, what you would say, a beginning, for there are far greater heights. Now, my friends, study on this and study the fact that there are so many brothers who are searching for something to believe in. You will find, as you obtain more knowledge, that these people will be drawn to you, not only for their advancement, my friends, but for your own. For no matter how, shall we use the term, "down" that one person may be, there is always a great opportunity to learn much.

And, my friends, as you find yourself helping these people, you will find that you need more and more energy. At this time, you will have a great amount. For, my friends, as you attempt to use this energy there is more and more stimulation of this growth. We shall be with you, my friends, for as long as you may allow us.

There is much to learn, my friends, and of what you think of as time, not much time. You have heard us say this many times, my friends. Renew your interest in meditation, my friends; you will find it to be better than before. Surround yourself with only love for, my friends, when you surround yourself in this love, it is of such a high intensity that only love may penetrate it. And, my friends, as you find yourself advancing through meditation, you will experience this and find it to be a truly great feeling. My friends, imagine yourself with this feeling completely. Now all of you, my friends, in this room, have made great progress. It is very pleasing to us. But as your progress grows you will need yet more and more help. And for this help, my friends, you need only the desire. As a rule, your first, shall we say, obstacle is to overcome your ego. For, my friends, it will slow you down to a great degree. You were not created with this ego but, through your society, it has flourished. My friends, it is indeed a very great obstacle to overcome but through your diligent trying you will finally succeed.

I shall, my friends, attempt to transfer this contact to another instrument, if he will avail himself. I am Hatonn.

(H channeling)

I am Hatonn. I am with this instrument. We are nearly at the close of our, shall we say, message. Yet before we leave, it is our desire to express to you the need within your present development for caution and clarification within your own being, towards your desires. My friends, you have come here and you indeed have a purpose or, shall we say, a mission. And this is why it is very important for you to clarify within yourself those things which you truly desire. For there are many things within this structure which you now could choose to desire. And some of these things could tend to lead you somewhat away from your chosen path. So be cautious in that which you choose to desire. And that which you choose to desire, clarify within yourself that it is truly something which you desire and feel to be of use.

Meditate upon that which you desire and if it is not proper, the desire itself shall dissipate. Discretion, you might say, is a necessity for your avenue of progression and with this thought I will leave you in the love and the light of our infinite Creator. I am Hatonn. Adonai vasu.

Sunday Meeting
April 18, 1976

(Carla channeling)

[I am Hatonn.] …We greet you tonight in the love and the light of our infinite Creator. It is indeed a privilege to speak with you tonight *(inaudible)*. There are several different requests coming from this group this evening *(inaudible)* and so we will be moving about just a bit, although we always speak on one theme and that theme is love.

Those of us who are of Hatonn, although a very small percentage of the Confederation of Planets in Service to the Infinite Creator, have many brothers and sisters, from many hundreds of locations in what you would call space and time. We manifest ourselves to you because of our understanding of what *(inaudible)*. It is our understanding that that which is real is the substance and energy and essence which you may call love. *(Inaudible)* … for there are infinite varieties of love.

There has been a request within the group for information about reported psychic predictions. Although we do not normally deal in specific information, we will attempt at this time to speak on a somewhat more specific level, due to the request, for we feel that the request was made in a spiritual manner and not in a manner of trying to find proof. Therefore, we will go to the limit of our ability to speak without infringing upon free will. We will say about the year to come: there are energies within that which you know as your planet's shell which will combine with frictions released by the changing magnetics of what you call your poles. During the warm season, at the time of dark moons, there will develop the possibility for what you would call tidal waves. We do not know at this time how serious that will be for you must know, my friends, that the energies of each of you upon the planet's surface have a profound effect upon the planet on which you dwell. However, there will no doubt be, to a certain extent, true disaster. How widespread it will be, we do not know. We do not feel that these disasters will spread to what you would call your earthquakes, for the energies have not yet apparently filled to the final level of readiness. So that those inland on the larger areas of dry land will not suffer as will those near the sea.

Very often, my friends, *(inaudible)* may have been correct either to the time, but not correct as to the intensity of the disaster or correct as to the disaster but misplaced in time. Please keep in mind that we do not dwell within your time but are forced, just as you would be in another space-time reference system, to translate, shall we say, through the use of computers *(inaudible)* our concepts into your brains, of time and space. Therefore, you see the difficulties in placing events precisely as to time. And as we have stated before, the duration and intensity of a disaster is directly linked to the vibrations of those people which are upon the surface of the planet.

We speak to groups like you and we say, over and over, that each of you is important as a source of love and light. It is difficult to see how you can be of help in your illusion, when you are just sitting in meditation. Yet we say to you, my friends, the planet upon which you live is alive.

And when you gather as a group and send your love, this intensifies it many times over and you *can* help. It is possible that the work that is already being done by many light groups upon your surface at this time will ameliorate the difficulties which we can see *(inaudible)* in the knowledge of your value to your planet. Spend a little time sending the planet upon which you live your love. Remember that you are truly going into a new age at this time. It is not any longer the period just before the new age. You have already begun the transition. I am sure that you are conscious of that. You must realize that although it may seem not to be a very incisive change, that in light of the number of years of the age which you have passed through upon your planet, the transition is taking place very quickly.

My friend, the quality of your life, by which we mean the way that you live it, will be changed in the next few years. And the more that you are able to see the underlying reality, the more that you will be able to be a positive part of that which is to come upon this planet.

I would like to transfer this contact. I will leave this instrument. I am Hatonn.

(B channeling)

I am Hatonn. I am now with this instrument. As I was saying, my friends, you are but love. Everything that you see around you, my friends, is but love. As I spoke to you earlier of the times that are ahead, you will see that this … I will rephrase. You will be, in the age ahead, my friends, in a newer and higher vibration, by which we may all grow to a greater spiritual height than before. For this vibration, my friends, intensifies all action that is generated by yourself. That is to say, my friends, for those who are seeking love, it will be more easily attained because of this vibration. Now, at the same time, my friends, it is also a time of great growth for those who are not seeking a path of love somewhat.

Now, as you know, my friends, there are many about you that you may know already, who are in great need of something, shall we say, to believe in. Through your spiritual growth, my friends, in your meditation, you will find yourselves set upon by those wishing to know the truth. Now, I am not saying, my friends, that you need to go search these people out. For, as you know, my friends, the positive charge attracts the negative. They will therefore, my friends, be drawn towards you, in the hope that you might help. You may find this hard to believe, my friends, but why are we here tonight, if not to learn the truth? For all is love, my friends, and in love there is no negativity. Therefore, love being the highest possible energy, no other negative charge can penetrate this energy. When you surround yourself in this love, my friends, you will find that when heightened to a great degree, all that you may know is love.

Now, my friends, this is, you may think, the most important lesson that you are to learn. But, my friends, due to the shortness of time it is very important that we practice our meditation. We are constantly with you, my friends, and we join with you at every time you desire. So, my friends, to see you experience this energy called love is of great satisfaction to us.

I will at this time transfer this contact to another instrument, if she will avail herself. I am Hatonn.

(T channeling)

I am Hatonn. I am now with this instrument.

(Most of the following section is inaudible.)

(Inaudible) … on the subject of love. Every great teacher who has ever visited your planet—Buddha, Jesus Christ *(inaudible)* even those who are now living—Satchidananda, Baba Ram Dass *(inaudible)* and others who *(inaudible)* all these men teach the same thing. *(Inaudible)*. Love everyone unconditionally, including yourself. Loving everyone unconditionally including yourself simply means that you never get "bummed out." When you find yourself arguing with someone over this belief or that belief, stop arguing. When you find yourself making your will prevail over another human being, stop prevailing. Love speaks not to the *(inaudible)* ear. Love speaks to the heart. *(Inaudible)*. There are many temptations. You may find yourself playing God. Loving everyone unconditionally, including

yourself, again, means never getting mad, never getting "bummed out." To live life in this manner is to live in a reality known to many upon your planet as heaven. Remain constantly loving, consciously, at all times. It is your entire purpose.

I will now transfer this contact to another instrument. I leave you in the love and the light of our infinite Creator. I am Hatonn.

(H channeling)

I am Hatonn. I am now with this instrument. As you are aware, this day which you observe in the name of the one known an Jesus, the one who represented the consciousness of Christ *(inaudible)*. As you observe this day in his name, my friends, be aware of his presence. For to observe within you this concept of Christ is to summon to yourself the consciousness which was represented by this being.

My friends, you must realize that the one known to you as Jesus was but a man, as you. He had nothing to offer other than his self and his knowledge, which he stressed many times to be that which you possess. My friends, within you is the true Christ. Within you is the true Father of all. Within you is the consciousness which was displayed by this teacher. Within you is the vision which he foresaw, a vision of love and unity, a vision of a world ruled under no other laws than those of the Creator. A vision which is to be an experience. For that which you can envision, indeed you shall experience.

Hold true to your beliefs and desires. Be assured within yourself of your guidance. And this shall be yours. All that you desire shall come to you. Therefore, be cautious and desire only those things which you know to be of love. Desire not that of the physical world, for if you fill your desires with love, then so shall you reap them. And, my friends, whatever you need, it shall be provided. And you should not spend any time being concerned with that which you feel you need upon the physical plane. For you need only one things and that is love.

And to realize how to achieve this, shall we say, state of being, we once again stress that you practice meditation. For within the silence of your meditation there shall be whispers of love from our Father, the Creator, guiding you upon the path of enlightenment which you so dearly desire.

My friends, those of you here are indeed fortunate, for you have presently the opportunity to advance rapidly in your spiritual growth. As your planet becomes more under the influence of the higher vibratory rate, all things shall increase in activity. Due to this, your desires shall be manifested more quickly. We of the Confederation are here to assist you. And you, my friends, are the masters of your own, shall we say, destiny. Reach out, my friends. Reach out and grasp unto yourself the love and light which radiates constantly in your direction. Hold unto you this love and light, allow it to fulfill you and upon the moment of fulfillment, reach for more. For, my friends, as you bring in more love and light, greater shall be your ability to disperse love and light. With practice, you can send this love and light of which we speak to those who are in need for purposes, shall we say, of enlightenment. My friends, you can help those whom you love most efficiently by surrounding them in the love and light of our Creator. For, my friends, no being shall progress unless he so chooses. And all that you may do is expose him to the love and light of the infinite Creator and allow it to penetrate and instill the desire to proceed upon the path of enlightenment.

This, my friends, brings us to a point on which we wish to speak. The moment upon which any being consciously decides to seek the path of enlightenment may be referred to as a moment of resurrection. As this day is an observance of a physical resurrection, allow yourself to realize that that which the one known as Jesus performed upon this day was only a sign, shall we say. He performed upon the physical plane a feat which was considered to be impossible. The enlightenment which was obtained by those who were aware of his action was indeed of great benefit. Yet it was but a representation upon the physical plane of what was taking place on the spiritual level. This was a moment, my friends, in which many truly decided to begin to seek and follow that path of enlightenment, that teaching, of Christ. It was indeed the day of resurrection.

Yet each and every day is, shall we say, a replay of that resurrection. For each and every day more and more of your peoples begin their search, in all honesty and with pure dedication, to seek Christ, to seek love, to seek fulfillment, to seek the Creator. Those who choose this shall indeed find that which they seek. Those within this room have arisen. Now it is time that you go forth, as did Christ, and allow those around you to see that you are indeed renewed. You need not speak of your resurrection, or renewal, if you prefer. Allow it to shine; allow it to be. Allow yourself to become the instrument of the consciousness to which we refer as Christ. Open your inner being so that you may receive and transmit clearly the love and light of Christ and of our Father, the Creator. You are the channels for the energies which are needed. Attune yourself and observe the resurrection of your planet. In these words, I leave you. I am Hatonn. Adonai vasu borragus.

Sunday Meditation
May 16, 1976

(Carla channeling)

Greetings, my friends, in the love and the light of the infinite Creator. I am Hatonn, and I am with you. I and my brothers are with you in spirit, and we are very privileged to speak with you, as always.

We have paused at the beginning of this meeting to unite the intentions of those present. As you may have noticed, it is sometimes more difficult to become one than [at another time]. It is sometimes a more distant goal to achieve an understanding of the true unity of yourself and your brothers. And so, there are many levels at which we speak, and yet at the level at which you wish us to speak this evening, it was necessary that we pause and become one.

For truly, my brothers, you are now one. Each is filled with a love, not for the humanness of your brothers and sisters, but with a love for the perfect Creator in each brother and each sister. Though your physical bodies rest within your dwelling at this time, in seeming separation, yet the hands of your spirits have reached out and closed the circle.

I would speak to you this evening of several things. First, one thing: you may have wondered, because of the recent increased activities of our craft within your skies, why our messages to you have become more, shall we say, involved not with politics and reasoning about our appearances in your skies, but on the contrary, our messages to you who have meditated together with us, have become more and more on the strictly philosophical or spiritual level. Our appearances are part of the plan which you are all aware of, to alert those upon your planet who are sleeping, in such a way that they will begin to search for a way to wake up.

You, my friends, are already waking up, and our appearances in your skies have served their purpose with you. In the days to come, we will be appearing as much as we can, and hopefully, people will be asking you questions, for they will know of your association with this type of group. And so, we are very, very interested in deepening your spiritual and philosophical understanding of our mission. That is all that matters to us. You are our physical hands on this sphere. We can give you thoughts and advice, shall we say, but it is to you, in the flesh, so to speak, to whom people will turn.

Secondly, we wish to speak with you about the circumstances of your daily lives. Again and again we have suggested meditation. There is a method of dealing with the illusion, by which you can use those happenings which are within the illusion in such a way that they become reality, and are so constructive in helping you along your spiritual journey.

The method for doing this is to remove fear from your attitude towards the illusion. Meditation is a great aid towards removing fear, for if you are confident from your meditation of the fact that all that exists is love, then whatever occurs on the outer planes, no matter whether it is pain, or death, or birth, or pleasure, you will be able to see it for what it is—that is, love—and accept pain and death, as well as pleasure and birth, so that the circumstance which is real upon the outer plane is absorbed into your being as it is, that is, as reality, and not as the illusion which your premature reactions will cause it to become.

Love casts out fear. This has been written in your holy works, and it is indeed true. If you fear any set of circumstances that may occur, you will not be able to see the reality of the love within these circumstances. It takes a good deal of resolute practice to refrain, finally, from fear of pain. But, my friends, on the outer planes, this *is* what is. Pain and pleasure. Accept both within that stillness of being which is an awareness of love.

I wish to pause again. I am Hatonn. I will leave this channel.

(Pause)

(H channeling)

I am Hatonn. I am now with this instrument. My friends, there is within your capabilities, within you, each and every, shall we say, understanding. Every individual, every being within this existence, within this creation, is, shall we say, a storehouse of infinite knowledge. For from the Father you have come, and with you, you have brought, shall we say, the files, the files of wisdom and knowledge. It is your, shall we say, privilege to go within yourself and draw out that knowledge which you seek, and examine it.

If there is an answer which you are needing, if there is a situation upon which you seek guidance, if there is a desire of love that you wish to attain, if there is an ability which you wish to manifest, then of the utmost importance to you personally is to go into this knowledge that has been given to you, and which you have brought along with you upon your path. There is within you the seed of life. There is within you the babe of creation. There is within you the Christ of consciousness. There is within you the love and the light of the Creator.

And to hold this within you, and to fail to utilize it, is to remain, shall we say, static upon your processes of growth. It is your choice, and it can be made by no other than yourself. Those within this room seek that storehouse of wisdom, for varied purposes and desires. Yet for each one, the desire which is most prevalent is to know and experience love. For within the category of love falls all things. We have said to you many times that the actual act of creation was one of pure love. From this love, you draw your energies, your life-giving forces, and your experiences. From this love, you are given all of which you are in need. From this love, you are given unto one another, and from this love, you have traveled into your present experience. And from this love, you shall attain what you seek.

In order that you may be of service to your fellow man in the days to come, it is only necessary that you see, that you see clearly, the function, the presence, the vibration of that love within your fellow man. See nothing but that love. No matter what may surround it, no matter what the person may do to you, you must recognize the love within that individual. You may choose not to be within that individual's presence, and this is your choice. But do so with the recognition of love. Pass not judgment upon your fellow man, for my friends, that which you sow, so shall ye reap. And to pass judgment is to receive it, as also to love is to receive love.

Be aware of one another. Be cautious upon your journey, yet be not withholding of the love within you. Share it freely. Project it in all directions, and once again it shall flow unto you from all directions. There was a master, whom you know as Jesus, and he gave unto you the secret of life: "Love one another as you would love yourself." This is a summation of the commandments of ten that was handed down unto your ancestors. Love one another. Be one. Come together as one, and recognize the divinity and the truth of the concept of love, and the divinity and the truth of your fellow man. It is within your capability to bring about the state of consciousness through which you can perceive the love of which we speak. Yet the tool, as you are well aware, for attaining that state, is meditation.

My friends, to meditate is to love. To meditate is to be one with the Creator and your fellow man. To meditate is your purpose. It may manifest in many physical areas, but in essence, your purpose is to be one with each other. And in order to manifest the knowledge and the truth and existence of that oneness, you must meditate.

There is to be within your present existence, a series of changes. We shall not dwell upon these changes, yet we shall dwell upon a method of alleviating the negative experiences, of which you are aware, that shall come. It is simple: love and unity. Project into each individual and each circumstance the love and the light of your infinite Creator.

Come together. Be loving, and be free. To love freely is to be in a state where suppression does not exist. No matter what may affect you upon the physical plane, no matter what any individual may do unto you, to love that individual freely is the essence of truth. To avoid suppression, project the light about each individual, and the light shall come to you. The light which you project may not prevent the individual acts of negativity. Yet what you send out is what you shall receive, and that negativity shall not affect you. For if you allow only the love and the light to flow from within you, there shall not be room for anything to come into you, other than that love and light. These laws, shall we say, are simple, yet to accomplish them seems to you to be quite difficult. And this is due to the state of consciousness in which you are presently residing. Meditate, my friends, and your consciousness shall evolve. Your love shall multiply. The flow shall increase, and the reception shall in turn enumerate greatly within you. These are not secrets that we share with you, they are simple truths.

Do not fathom within your consciousness that you are incapable of bringing about this flow of love and light. If you fathom that thought, you will stop the flow. Acknowledge that in the Father's names it is continually coming back. Allow not the stagnation of self-satisfaction. Allow not the stagnation of your own mind to replace the *(inaudible)*. Acknowledge continually that what you seek, you shall receive.

I shall transfer this communication. I am Hatonn.

(Carla channeling)

I am again with this instrument. I am Hatonn. My brothers and sisters, love one another. That is it. That is all we have to say. We have said it several times this evening; we say it once more. As you go forth into the world, you will, very soon, meet your next challenge. It will be a person whom it is difficult to conceive of on the outer planes as the Creator. You will fear him, and you will wish to put distance between yourself and him. And yet, you are one. If you can move the fear aside *(inaudible)* the reality will seep into your being, and you will reflect unto him the joy of the spirit. Rejoice that you know the Creator! And as you go forth, be of service to your fellow man. Let him know that you know that he, too, is full of joy.

My brother Laitos is with you, and sends each of you his energy. Seek us at any time, and we will be there. We pause only for one thing else before we go. There is a question. We do not know whether or not it is desired that we answer it this evening. Is a question desired? If so, please ask it.

M: Yes. I'd like the details of that "exchange of knowledge" in my '63 sighting. Could you give me details on that?

We are able to do it at this time, for the first time. It is very simple, my brother. The knowledge was not knowledge that we had and you did not, but it was an attempt which was successful to awaken within you the remembrance of who you actually are and why you are actually within this experience at this time. In the future, this knowledge will become more and more clarified, as various elements of, shall we say, your mission are recognized by you. Yet, because of your recent experience, you are now in full knowledge of the basics of your previous experiences which led you to this plane at this time. This was, basically the "knowledge." It was a communication with your greater self, saying that it was permissible to remember, and so to apply, that which you had learned.

Does this answer your question?

M: Yes.

Is there another question?

(Pause)

My friends, I leave you. Feel the love. Feel the joy in this room at this time. I leave you in this joy, and this love. I am Hatonn. Adonai vasu borragus. ☥

Sunday Meeting
May 30, 1976

(Carla channeling)

I am Hatonn. I greet you, my friends, in the love and the light of the infinite Creator. It is my pleasure, as always, to speak with you this evening. It is a special pleasure to greet those we have not meditated with in this group for a time. It is a great privilege to be with you and to share our thoughts.

We would like to begin by speaking with you about meditation. It is a technique that can be approached in endless ways. Tonight, we would like to say a few words about your physical body and its relation to meditation. Become aware, my friends, at this time of your symmetry as you sit comfortably in meditation. Your two legs, balanced. Each arm resting comfortably. Your eyes, my friends—the space between them, just balanced. That which you hear is being received symmetrically, stereophonically, by your ears. And you are in balance, each side in balance. You are a creature, in the body, of this duality—your right and your left. It is a symbol for all to see of the nature of the physical universe: that there are always two sides, two qualities, to be reconciled in balance.

As you rest in meditation now, my friends, become quite, quite reconciled to this two-sidedness of the physical. Begin to sense that point between your two sides, the point of balance, the point of stillness, the point that does not move. In between the two eyes is the point where your sight becomes one. Midway between your ears, you suddenly hear one whole sound.

You, my friends, are not creatures of duality. You simply reside in a physical body and in a physical universe which is of this nature. Therefore, you are under the illusion that you are of this nature. And it is in meditation that you seek knowledge of your true self, which is free from duality. You are not even that point of balance or stillness. You simply reside, in the physical, at that point of balance, if you have maintained a healthy awareness of who you are and that you are within your body but not of it. Many, many of your troubles in the physical arise from the fact that you've allowed that center of stillness to be moved by outward events, so that you seem to be unable to regain that balance.

Now—you find the balance of your body, and then *release* that connection. My friends, do not become so comfortable within your body that you forget that you are actually a stranger to this environment. Your essential being is unified. You not only know what this unity within yourself is, you are this unity. Coming into the knowledge of it is simply a matter of remaining still long enough to begin to know the true self. It is not a knowledge that must be pulled from far away: you *are* that knowing.

(Pause)

We are pleased, for we can see that this, shall we say, technique for understanding the way that the body may be relaxed and then moved away from has helped. I will transfer this contact. I am Hatonn.

(H channeling)

I am Hatonn. I am now with this instrument. I wish to make it evident that we are at this point conditioning those who wish to become channels of this type. Each and every individual upon the path of spiritual growth, as you may call it, shall manifest from within themselves desires for service. That which you experience at these meetings, the actual, shall we say, relay of information, is one form of service which you can render. And it is your choice, if you so desire. For those who would not desire to become instruments of this manner, we are still, through the course of this meeting, attempting to make known our presence and attempting to channel to you the love and light through us from the Creator

We have touched upon that which you would call knowledge. We wish to make it evident that knowledge, my friends, is much more than the possession of the intellect. Knowledge in its true essence is a state of being, a form of existence. It is the spiritual manifestation of the divine intellect of the Creator. Knowledge comes about upon the physical plane through a long and tedious process of development, through many years of study of the curriculum of your planet. Yet this knowledge which is accumulated upon the planet at this instant by the intellect is limited in the respect that it is contained and experienced within a limiting existence of the physical.

Your spiritual existence, my friends, is everlasting and is unlimited and from within the spiritual intellect, as you may choose to call it, there is instantaneous knowledge, there is contained all knowledge of the universe, all knowledge of the Creator. And the processes which you must utilize to bring you to the acceptance of this knowledge are simple. Yet to the inhabitants of your planet, they are quite difficult. The reason for the difficulty is because you have allowed yourself to identify with the physical form and the physical existence. Certainly it is a portion of your existence—that is true. It is but a portion. It is but a minute portion of your overall existence.

My friends, seek not identification with the world in which you exist. Seek to identify with the universe which you are and which you have experienced and which you shall remain experiencing. Seek to be one, and to be aware of it. And by one we mean the Creator and the universe. Know that it is your, shall we say, birthright to tap the knowledge of the universe, to contain the understandings and wisdoms of the great teachers that have come to demonstrate upon your planet the knowledge of which we speak. Each and every individual has the prerogative of experiencing the physical and the spiritual existence. But remember, when the physical experience is dissipated, as you all know it shall be, there remains that which you call the spiritual existence. For it, my friends, is the energy which comprises the physical. It is the energy which comprises all of existence. And as your scientists have stated, there is no possible means of destruction of energy forces. There can only be alterations in the form. But the essence is the same, my friends. The energy is omnipresent forever.

And within that energy is found the intellect, the knowledge of which we speak. The knowledge of all things. The link with the Creator. But, my friends, we could tell you not, in all truth, of the Creator. But we can tell you that He is the energy that is within all things. For from Him we have come, yet within Him we lie. It is His intellect that manifests the energies in which we flow. Flow freely with these forces and the simplicity of universal knowledge shall dawn upon you as your evolutionary processes continue.

I shall transfer this communication. I am Hatonn.

(B channeling)

I am Hatonn. I am with you. And I greet you always in His love. I will pause a moment with this instrument so that we may establish what we feel to be a unity of thought. We are pleased in each who chooses to serve as they feel the need. It has been our privilege in the past to experience such oneness in establishing contact with this instrument. And once again it is our privilege to greet you in this manner. We wish to leave our contact with all those who may desire it, who desire to serve within the capacity of their own being. We always extend our gratification for being of service to you. We wish to say we are with you at your moment of desire and always wish to share with you our love. It has been a privilege to once again speak with you through this instrument. I shall continue through another. I am Hatonn.

(H channeling)

I am Hatonn. I am once again with this instrument. We wish to express our satisfaction in having achieved contact with an instrument from whom we have been, shall we say, severed for quite some time. We wish to make it evident that we of the Confederation of Planets in Service to the Infinite Creator desire not to contact those who do not request it. It is each and every individual's freedom of choice—each person must walk upon the path which they must choose and it is not within our right to sway that choice. We only acknowledge requests and fulfill them in whatever manner is possible. Our gratitude is indeed expressed, in that we feel once again the unity of our beings. It has been our extreme privilege to speak with this group at this time and, in leaving, we ask that you seek from within yourself that which you desire. Manifest from within your consciousness that which you choose to experience. Sway not from the desires for the sought-after experiences. Be only certain that they are contained within the energies which are positive, of service not only to oneself but to all of mankind and all of the universe. Harmony with the laws of creation is your stronghold. You shall know when you are in violation if you truly seek only within yourself. In this thought I leave you and in the love and the light of the infinite Creator. I am Hatonn. Adonai vasu borragus.

(Carla channeling)

Greetings in the love and the light of the One Who is All. I am Nona. It is my privilege to ask you if there are any questions that you have at this time?

(Pause)

There is one questions on which I would speak at this time that has been requested without words. It is a subject which is shrouded in a great deal of confusion. Nor can we unravel this confusion. Yet it is my privilege to give what thoughts I can to ease the condition.

We speak at this time of the question of divorce. This is a phenomenon that is known only within certain tiny illusions. Entirely within your society it is an artificial word, for it describes what happens when one piece of paper is replaced within your society's paper records with another piece of paper. Yet this happenstance causes a great deal of pain and difficulty among your peoples.

What we wish to speak on, with compassion, is the subject of karma. You must understand, my friends, that when, within your holy works, it is recommended that marriage, as it is called among your peoples, be obtained throughout one lifetime, it is recommended for the reason that it is likelier that you will correctly apply yourself to your karma if you have a controlled circumstance throughout one experience. It is likelier, if you engage in several karmic relationships within one experience, that there will be unsatisfied karma.

Now, my friends, it is in no way necessary that because you have had an experience with more than one karmic partner, that you have in any way failed to satisfy the karma with that partner. It is simply more difficult to treat more people rightly than it is to treat one person rightly. This in a recommendation that has been chiseled upon your planet into what is known as law. Behind the "law" is the compassion of an all-loving Father.

In any experience with any karmic relationship, it is necessary within that relationship that your actions be founded in love. If an action which is founded in love results in the termination of that relationship, your karma has in no way been dissatisfied. If you remain with one person and yet your actions are not founded in love, then your karma won't be satisfied.

So you see, my friends, although the word "divorce" has great traumatic impression to give your peoples, the reality behind that word is what you make of it: you yourself, an individual upon your own path, learning through experiences with other souls. Think not of the paper but of the love. Think not of past mistakes but of your present chances to give love. We have said this before, my friends, but we will say it again. If you have gone through many years thinking that two plus two are five and then you discover that two plus two are four, you have corrected an error. Now, two plus two are no longer five in your mind. Reality—and love—and correctness—are what you make of it *now*. Right now.

I am Nona. I leave you in that love. Adonai.

Sunday Meeting
June 6, 1976

(Carla channeling)

I am Hatonn. And I greet you, my brothers and my sisters, in the love and the light of the infinite Creator. It is a great privilege to be with this group this evening. My brother Laitos is with me and will be, throughout the meeting, within the group in which you now dwell, attempting to make our vibrations available to you at your most receptive level. We are very grateful for this opportunity to share with you.

Although it is not normally our custom to open with a request for questions, we would like to do so this evening. Does anyone have a question for us at this time?

(Pause)

We are contented to refrain from answering questions which are not, shall we say, at the surface of the mind yet. There are those present who have questions upon their mind. And so we say to you: in time, with patience, the questions that are troubling you will become very clear. Questions and problems are a result of the illusion in which you are now experiencing your existence, so that what is actually a unity seems to be a process and things seem to take time. In actuality, my friends, from your birth to your death and long before your birth and long after your death, to infinity, all is one time, and one creation. Yet within the illusion, as you call your physical existence, things seem to take time and seem to unfold and develop. And because of this, it often seems that that which should be, is not, and that which should not be, is.

Yet it is the process which is the illusion. And the illusion is for the purpose of instructing you on one subject. And that subject is love. The problem that is facing you at the moment is the problem of learning how to love. Love, as it is known upon your planet, has produced many serious side effects, such as hatred, war and other negative results. We speak, as you may well imagine, of a love that is without these side effects.

Love, my brothers, is a most misunderstood term. The one known as Jesus said to you, "Not as the world gives, give I unto you." And this is very true. As what you call human love expresses itself, it is, like the illusion, a process. It has a beginning and an end and from its creation to the destruction it may take down those who feel that this is love with it, so that they become indifferent and feel that love is not all that there is, is not "it."

There is a love that is beautiful. It is not the human love, it is the love of the Creator. This love does not have limitation. It is not a process. It is simply the power that created you, the source from whence you came and the ending to which you are irresistibly drawn. And yet the end is the endless beginning.

This is love. With this love in your life you do not go down to destruction in your relationships. You do not find an end to your patience. You do not become sad. You do not become downhearted. For this love is within you and if you can allow it to flow through you, you will be able to be what you wish to be.

Such a simple thing, my friends, and yet so very difficult. And that is why you are here, to learn how to tap in to that love, even in the face of the illusion of your physical body and your physical life and the physical processes that offer you again and again a chance to show what you know—that love is infinite.

I will transfer the contact at this point. I am known to [be] Hatonn.

(Pause)

I am again with this instrument. I will continue through this instrument.

It is impossible, and in no way expected, that you can tap into this love by pretending to on the human level. We have stressed meditation each time we have ever spoken with your group and this is because the source by which you can tap into that love is within you in a spot which is reached by stilling that process of your body and your mind which is occupying your attention. When your attention has been centered not on the outer or on the mental but on the inner planes, then the door may open and love may come to you. To touch base, as it were, like this, it is not necessary to take a great deal of time. It is necessary to do it only with regularity. With regularity, that pipeline will be opened and in your life you will see the results.

There are people who do this without knowing that they are doing it. There are people who say many different things about what they are doing and believe they are doing many different things from each other. And this is a great problem within your religions, for they believe that they are different from each other. Yet the sign of one who has tapped into love, one who knows the Creator, the one Creator, this sign within your physical life is the sign of joy. That person who is joyful, no matter what he says about his joy, the person who is patient, these, my friends, are the fruits of the love that does not destroy.

If you are not at this moment experiencing the joy that is of a burning, steady nature that will not die, but will burn on, then, my friends, meditate more. Take yourself away from your humanity and get in touch with love. It has gotten a very bad name upon this planet and yet in love you were created and all that is powerful within you is of love.

I am going to leave you, and yet we will remain with you as you complete your meditation. There is healing and peace in that contact with love. Your future, my friends, not in the physical sense but in the spiritual, lies completely in your attempts to seek that love. It is a simple quest. And we are with you, to help you in any way. I leave you now. I am Hatonn. Adonai.

Sunday Meeting
June 13, 1976

(Carla channeling)

I am Hatonn. I greet you in the love and the light of the infinite Creator. It's a great pleasure to speak with your group this evening, and we greet each of you.

As you have made your way to this dwelling, my friends, each of you has witnessed an unending series of miracles this evening, for you passed through many of the creations of the Father. And this evening we would like to say a few words about this creation.

Meditation is a technique whereby the seeker may become more aware of the creation as it truly is. And yet, when you go forth from meditation, it is the world to which you now open your eyes that is to inform your knowledge gained in meditation. For if you have knowledge and cannot apply it, then you have nothing.

But you see, whatever you may see is the creation of the Father. Of course, my friends, many times you have felt within your heart the beauty of many of the creations upon your planet, those things that grow from your Earth—the trees and the flowers—and those animals that are about you. Many times you have felt how beautiful and how wonderful these creations are. And we have said to you many times, note the service that each creation is to the rest; and you have thought this many times.

But my friends, let us go beyond these intellectual perceptions of the creation. We ask you, when you are ready, to take anything that is within your illusion, whether it be a tree or something that seems to be man-made, such as a wall or cloth or something that seems to be dead, such as stone. It does not matter, my friends, what you choose to focus your attention upon, for we say to you that all things are alive. There is nothing that is without creative power and consciousness. Pay attention to whatever you choose—total attention, focused attention—for out of meditation must come the knowledge that you may apply, that all things are truly one, that all is created of love, that all exists through the power of love.

When you can perceive trees and walls and stone as love, then you will have begun to perceive things as they are. We greatly encourage this in you, my friends. For those who are beginning to meditate, it is enough to suggest that meditation will enable them to have an enhanced perception. Yet for those who are seekers of some experience, it is necessary to point further along the path, for the total end of your seeking within this illusion is to perceive the reality behind and within the illusion. And you cannot do this simply by maintaining a reasonable amount of calm, although this is greatly desirable. Your perceptions of all that you see need to become transformed.

The most central creation of the Father within your attention is of course, my friends, yourselves. Each of you is a great treasure-trove that you can observe as a creation of the Father. You can learn much from yourself. In order to do this you must focus upon yourself as if you were a tree or a stone. Not something familiar but a strange and unusual object, to be looked at and understand from a distance, from a perspective gained in meditation.

You are alive, my friends, through the power of love, and your real nature is hidden in the folds of that mystery. As you examine your thoughts and your actions, try to see what you are doing from that perspective. You have much to learn from all that you can see.

(Pause)

We are sorry for the delay, but we were having difficulty transmitting a thought to this instrument. We will continue.

You are within the creation of the Father, a very small portion of which is your perceived environment. And like all natural objects that have a birth and a death, you yourself, in your spirit, are of this nature in this environment. There is a great, great deal to learn from the creations about you and within you. Picture yourself, my friends, as a seed. It is written in your holy works that the seed depends on the soil for whether it grows or not. Your spirit is a seed within you. All that it will become is already within it. But you must put it in the correct environment. It needs darkness, by which we mean meditation. It needs light and water. It needs space to grow, the space within your life that you make for your spirit.

You must tend it—you must give it the water and the sunlight of your attention. It is good to read books and hear words such as these. And yet, my friends, the sunlight that will truly ripen the seed of your spirit is the attention that you pay to that which is happening to you: the trees that you pass, the people that you meet, the first-hand experiences of your life as you live it. You may make these things, stony ground or well-watered and warm earth, depending on where you put your attention.

You may think it strange that we who are supposedly, shall we say, more advanced than you continue to use the language of simple farmers, shall we say. And yet, my friends, the simplest things are the things that never become foolish. The universe, the creation, operates on the basis of cycles. And the life of your spirit is a bed to be nurtured just as surely as any other garden. As far as we know, that garden never gets beyond the point where it needs tending.

I would leave this instrument at this time and will return after my brother has spoken. I am Hatonn.

(H channeling)

I am Oxal. I also extend my greetings in the love and in the light of our infinite Creator. It is unusual, you might say, to interrupt and interject a message in the middle of another. Yet I wish to speak this evening through this instrument and I have found that the moment of reception is best chosen at this time.

I simply wish to share with you that we of the Confederation, as your brothers, as co-creators with you and as servants to you, are desirous of achieving these types of communications with other entities such as yourselves. We speak of many things and you have heard many messages. It may seem to you that we revolve in circles with our information. Yet you may notice that each circle through which we revolve is expanded. Those who are familiar with the processes and the evolution of these communications can verify this. As those individuals within the structure of the meetings evolve, so does the material which is received.

Yet the day shall surely come, my friends, when many of the present instruments must, shall we say, journey into other fields of service. And there is to be a need for the additional services of instruments such as those present this evening.

We of the Confederation wish not only to utilize those aspiring instruments but we also wish to communicate with you on a more personalized basis. You may choose not to be an instrument in this form of verbalization. Yet you may choose to accept our information and, shall we say, personal guidance. We wish not to make decisions for you, yet if you request it, we are willing to give information which will enlighten and assist you, so that at times you may make proper decisions.

What I am saying is that we find that there is to be a need for additional instruments and in meetings to come we shall begin to work with those that would desire this ability. We allow you time to decide and shall always allow you the choice of whether to act as an instrument or not. We have never forced our contact upon any individual, but we have always given it upon request.

This is all that I wish to say. We would desire to contact you, if it is your desire to contact us. Consider these thoughts and make your decision, for we feel that there are people in this room who have previously attempted these communications and are still desirous of them. We recognize the ability within each person to achieve this communication and we recognize your choice of whether to do so or not.

There is a reason that we discuss this, yet we shall leave it unspoken at this time. I shall return this meeting to my brother through the other instruments and I leave you in the love and light of the infinite Creator. I am Oxal.

(Carla channeling)

I am Hatonn. I am again with this instrument and I thank my brother, Oxal, for being with us and for his thoughts.

It is a very timely thought, for, my friends, we are nearer to the time when many, many questions will be asked of those who have the ability to share those answers that we can give, so that the services of those instruments will be greatly appreciated by your peoples.

The life, my friends, that has power, the life that has begun to spring from the inside, from the core of your being, so that it is an enabling life, so that the person living it is able to give with love and with energy—this life is available to the seeker who has truly sought and found that which transforms his life. Within the religion with which many of you are familiar, this experience has been called "being saved." And yet the Redeemer is your own consciousness. It is a closer thing to call it the Holy Spirit, as it is also known within the religion which has sprung up after the teachings of the master known as Jesus.

The Spirit, my friends, created all of the creations of the Father, you among them. So we say to you, yes, find the beauties and see the services but at the very core, after you have observed the laws of the Father, which are beauty and service, observe the true power—love itself—that has created all this in its perfection.

It is this spirit that can transform your life. You do not need to struggle from moment to moment, from thought to thought, from action to action. You only think you do, my friends, because you have not been taking your meditation into your life. If you cannot do it all the time, do it once. And then, do it again. Five seconds, one minute of focused concentration in the spirit to far more beneficial to you than you can imagine.

Before I leave you, my friends, I would open the meeting to questions. I would ask if there are any questions at this time?

M: What is the meaning of speaking in tongues?

Within your history, there was an experience whereby several of the so-called apostles were able to give words of truth and beauty to many of different lands who were gathered in one place. And so it was written that they spoke in many different tongues. Yet the Spirit enabled them to express their thoughts in such powerful ways that those present at that time understood within their minds, with no need for words. Therefore, the speaking of tongues, as such, is not as it is written within your holy works but is an example of that which is known among your peoples at this time as telepathy.

There is that which is known as speaking in tongues at this time. Normally, what has occurred during these modern experiences when an entity channels, as it were, a foreign tongue, is that it is an actual entity who is speaking through the person, just as the instrument at this time is speaking my thoughts.

My friends, although this is an entity rather than the Holy Spirit, it is not necessarily a bad thing. There are occasions when the being who is channeled is a highly spiritual being of your planet. And there are many other cases where that which is being channeled is a rather mischievous astral entity who is taking advantage of an offered opening, that is essentially harmless. In the third category of speaking in tongues is the person who is within himself in such a state that a portion of his own consciousness speaks.

In all three cases, it is important to the entity simply that he is able to experience a rather unusual event whereby he is, as it were, taken out of himself. This is sometimes an experience which leads a person onward on his spiritual path and although it is not the inspiration, shall we say, of the Holy Spirit itself, yet it is very helpful to the individual. If, within your modern times, someone would actually speak in tongues it would again be what is called telepathy, the force of which would be strong enough that it would seem that the person actually spoke out loud.

Don: How soon will the mass landing occur?

We had hoped at one time to land in 1965. We had to give this plan up, due to the reluctance of many of your peoples to experience the possibility of our true mission. At this time, we are seeing the possibility of a landing next year. We are attempting to give this instrument the month. It begins with "A." We cannot give a closer month to this instrument at this time. If she will relax we will attempt to condition her.

(Pause)

We will attempt a landing in August of 1977, as you know time.

Questioner: How many craft?

Approximately three million, although this is highly dependent on the success of our current mission. At present, many portions of your planet are not acceptable for landing. We are attempting at this time to widen our potential landings.

Questioner: What is your mission and purpose in landing?

I will have to use control. We have need of material within your atmosphere which enables us to store up, as it were, a power source. It is not in mineral form or any resource which your planet is lacking in abundance. We are unable to give this instrument the nature of the resource desired because she is not well-schooled in …

Questioner: Is it a gas or a liquid or a solid?

It is invisible.

Questioner: Is it in the Earth, in the water or in the atmosphere around the Earth?

It is atmospheric. We cannot say it is a gas. It is … this instrument would call it an element.

Questioner: Will your landing be visible or invisible?

It depends upon who you are. Those who are within our vibration will see us.

Questioner: Approximately what percentage of the planet will be able to see you?

We do not know. As you would say, we are working on it. There is a range of one third of your planet's population, a great, great range, which we are working on at this time. Approximately one third of your planet's peoples are at this time vibrating in such a way that they know who we are, whence we come and why we are here. They will, whether or not our mission succeeds, not only see us but go with the planet into the next vibration. We are deeply afraid that approximately one third of your planet's peoples, no matter what we do, will be lost and will have to repeat this experience. We do not know what percentage of that other third we will be able to alert in time. It is a highly tempestuous bunch of people, as you would say. Many of them are simply on the verge, just the merest shock or profound experience away from the basic realization that it is time for them to become seekers.

It is written that there will be those who go out into the harvest and it is highly, highly desirable at this time that there be as many harvesters as possible, for there are many that can be brought into the barn, as it were, at this time.

Questioner: What will be the length of time in our years of the harvesting period?

We do not have the ability to say, for it is completely dependent upon the consciousness of your peoples. That which is natural, as you may call it, is already highly advanced and nearly completed within the cycle-changing. The natural cycle will have been completed within two of your decades. The experience of your peoples has been very ragged, as you well know, and with the friction of those of your peoples who are resisting the vibration of change it may continue on for some time. Therefore, we can give you no answer.

Questioner: Do you see a possible delay past the approximate date of next August, 1977? Could there be a delay for any reason?

Oh, yes. We are at this time doubtful as to whether we will be able to complete our plan at this near date. We are simply working towards that with every thought of achieving it. But we would not be realistic if we did not say that there is every chance also that we will not be able to sway enough of your peoples by that date.

M: Do you have an optional date if that one doesn't work out?

We have an infinite number of optional dates. We cannot land among your peoples if your peoples do not want us. We do have needs which your planet can help us with but we are also capable of supplying those needs in other ways. That which we need is available, though in far smaller quantities, in many different places. So we are never in a helpless position, or as you would call it, out of gas. We are always able to satisfy the present requirements of our dwelling-craft.

(Side one of tape ends.)

(While the tape was being changed, there was a question about Bigfoot.)

(Carla channeling)

… There is a contact but it is not our contact.

Don: Whose contact is it?

There has been much talk about "dark forces." And yet there *are* dark forces. Contact with these creatures is of a somewhat, shall we say, sinister nature although it is to be remembered that, like all dark forces, these are not powerful in an ultimate sense.

Questioner: Would this be interpreted classically as a portion of the Battle of Armageddon?

Although we dislike that term, you may indeed think of darkness and light in a battle. We refrain from calling it the Battle of Armageddon due to the great fear which this term engenders, for it is a fearful story as it is written in your holy works.

Yet the forces of light and the forces of darkness have battled long and hard for this planet and, indeed, you may think of a disease entering the body. Those defenders of the body come, surrounding and destroying those diseases. In such a way may you consider those apparitions which are of the darkness, for the forces of light are many times the strength of these. And the battle is never in doubt as to its ultimate end but only as to individual, shall we say, skirmishes.

Questioner: What is the nature of the Bigfoot type of creature?

We are having difficulty giving the concept to this instrument. We can give this instrument only the image of those things which are of light but have no substance. We do not call it astral because of the nature of these beings. They are of a more crystallized nature, whereas in the astral there is a partaking of a somewhat physical form of dense matter. Within this vibration from which these creatures emerge, the structure that makes up the body is of such a nature that it is far more light and in a way more fragile.

Questioner: Can we expect an increase in the Bigfoot type of entity and possibly other entities of the same vibration or configuration in the future?

Yes. That which produces these creatures is the expectation in thought form of various peoples. That which they consider to be a menacing or frightening aspect is what they will see, if the conditions are correct. Therefore, there will be other entities, depending upon the expectation that each person has.

Questioner: Am I correct in assuming, then, the effects that are normally found when one is operating in, shall we say, astral conditions will be more manifest on this planet in what we now call the physical as the vibrational range changes? We will slowly transition?

In general you are correct, but in fact this particular aspect of what you call the Battle of Armageddon does not partake of the normal astral abilities of each of your peoples, for within the abilities which are part of the normal transition to what you would call fourth density, each person would be able to control the thought forms that were desired by himself. Yet within these, as you call it, Bigfoot and other demonstration of thought form, these thought forms are involuntarily forced upon those who are witnessing it. This is due to the imbalance between the natural environment and the minds of your peoples, making it a potential battleground for the forces of darkness.

Questioner: Where do the UFOs come from that are linked with the Bigfoot phenomenon?

You are already correct in your assumptions. We are not able to give [to] this instrument, because she doubts what we have to say, due to the fact that she has heard it from you. Yet you are correct.

Questioner: Is the instrument fatigued?

(Laughter)

I will leave this instrument, who is indeed fatigued. We are sorry for the amount of control we have had to use, yet we are very pleased to be able to answer your questions as best we can. I leave you in His love and His light. Never fear, my friends, for those who seek will never be left without the Comforter. Adonai vasu. I am Hatonn. ☥

L/L Research

L/L Research is a subsidiary of Rock Creek Research & Development Laboratories, Inc.

P.O. Box 5195
Louisville, KY 40255-0195

www.llresearch.org

Rock Creek is a non-profit corporation dedicated to discovering and sharing information which may aid in the spiritual evolution of humankind.

ABOUT THE CONTENTS OF THIS TRANSCRIPT: This telepathic channeling has been taken from transcriptions of the weekly study and meditation meetings of the Rock Creek Research & Development Laboratories and L/L Research. It is offered in the hope that it may be useful to you. As the Confederation entities always make a point of saying, please use your discrimination and judgment in assessing this material. If something rings true to you, fine. If something does not resonate, please leave it behind, for neither we nor those of the Confederation would wish to be a stumbling block for any.

CAVEAT: This transcript is being published by L/L Research in a not yet final form. It has, however, been edited and any obvious errors have been corrected. When it is in a final form, this caveat will be removed.

© 2009 L/L Research

Sunday Meeting
June 20, 1976

(Carla channeling)

I am with the instrument. I am Hatonn, and I greet each of you in the love and the light of the infinite Creator. It is my privilege to be able to speak with you.

We will not speak at great length this evening, for it is the desire of some of those present this evening that we do not, as you may say, be long-winded. We are in great appreciation to each of those who desires that we speak, for if one of you seriously wishes that we not speak, we are not able to, for we do not wish to infringe upon the free will of anyone. Therefore, we thank each of you for the permission to speak at this time.

Perhaps it would be best to say a few words about our reasons for contacting you at all and our reasons for contacting you at this time. Our mission within your skies for many years was part of our plan to enable the people of your planet to make a choice, the choice towards a progress of seeking. However, my friends, during the early years of our contact with your group we were much more concerned with, shall we say, a negative aspect of the mission, which was in a sense a kind of warning. We needed to warn those of your peoples who wished to listen that there was a crisis within the cycles' changing and that it was necessary to transform one's thinking in order to meet this crisis.

Within the last of your decades before this time, there was a very delicate, shall we say, period for those of your planet when it would have been possible several times over for your leaders to have brought your peoples into a war which would be far more devastating than any you can imagine, for the devices which your peoples now have are capable of destroying your race.

Therefore, it was necessary for us to speak very strongly on the dangers of this. At that time it seemed to us that your peoples [were] very weak in their ability to give love from within their own strength to combat this desire among many of your peoples to do war and to destroy.

I am sure that you have noticed, my friends, that within the last—perhaps two of your years, perhaps a little longer—we have ceased to speak so strongly of the negative aspects of the coming changes. The reason for that is simple. The change is now with us and instead of the negative aspect of warning, it is now possible to inform you instead of the already changing vibrations of your planet, to simply say to you, "They are within your reach now and if you meditate and if you seek them and if you add your strength to them, you may aid your planet with your love and your light, and from within help to go into this new age." You can now be full of strength, with no further need for the destructiveness.

It is a great blessing at this time that your peoples have begun to build the strength of love within themselves. You are much, much stronger as a people now than you were ten of your years ago. And with each year, your strength increases and the possibility of this destructiveness decreases. Now when we speak with you, we speak to encourage towards the positivity, as you would call them, towards the good vibrations. We speak to encourage you to help, by your love, to bring your planet into harmony with its new vibration. The new age is not coming, my friends—the new age is here.

You are all possessed of an earthly body, and within that vehicle, from the moment of your birth into this density, has been that force which you call death. Yet within you also is life and the death which you carry with you is only a minor transformation which frees the life within you to the next stage of development.

So it is with this particular cycle of your planet. Although during the cycle your planet, as it were, became ill, and called upon itself that which you would say is karma, yet you now are coming into a new cycle, where the body of your planet will be whole again. My friends, you still have the karma of your planet to alleviate, but you will find it easier and easier to do so within the new conditions of the new vibration. There has been much hatred and many things to unlearn upon your planet and with love and with light given from each of you, as individuals and as a group, you can work at this planetary karma. This is your privilege, and to a certain extent, ours. To a certain extent, it is why we are here.

At this time we will ask if there are any questions.

B: I have one. Is it right to be too passive? If pushed to the limit, is it right for a person to react to violence, if it was the only way that seems open to you, or should you allow passiveness to go beyond that?

To speak upon this subject is to speak beyond personality, to speak of the ideal. Beyond your heart, you know already the ideal that was given by the master known as Jesus. This master said that there was no end to what you call passivity. Yet it is to be remembered that the master accepted responsibility for his passivity, to the point of allowing his own death. Within your planetary sphere it is often very difficult to become a master capable of giving up one's life in order to demonstrate total love. And so we say to you, we could never recommend this choice to any person, for this choice is a private choice.

We recommend one thing only: we recommend that, faced with a situation that has you, as you would call it, in a corner, that you mentally and forcefully remove yourself from the corner and realize that you have a great deal of space about you that no one can violate; that time and space are an illusion and you do not have one second [in] a crowded situation. You have an infinite amount of time and an infinite amount of space. And you are a creative consciousness, capable of bringing to bear on this situation a creative solution which neither causes you to show a lack of love, nor causes you to betray those who depend upon you. It is not a ready solution, always, to a person who allows himself to be put in the place that someone wishes him to be put in. Yet to the person who, within himself, insists on that moment of freedom of choice where he can see himself as a dancer upon a great wide plain, with the situation a step in the dance—to this person, a creative solution will often recommend itself.

It is a difficult question to answer, for your vibration is a very intense one, and although it is easy for us to say, it is hard for you to do many of the things which we suggest and we know this. We are with you and all of the forces of light are at your disposal. Rely upon this strength, as well as your own presence of mind. We are sorry we cannot tell you a yes or no answer.

Are there any more questions? I would like to leave you now. My brother Laitos wishes to speak with you briefly. I leave you in the love and the light of the One Who is All. His blessings and mine be with you. Adonai vasu.

(H channeling)

I am Laitos. I greet you, my friends, in the love and the light of our infinite Creator. I am here briefly to discuss another question which was brought about prior to this meeting.

As most are aware, my function with this brotherhood is to assist those who would desire it, of these types and similar types of communications. We wish to say that it is within each and every individual's capabilities to achieve that which they would desire. It is within each person's capabilities to develop whatever ability that they would choose, to whatever extent that they would choose. Yet it must be noted that these abilities have remained dormant within most of your inhabitants for many, many lifetimes. And it is a simple process of communication, yet it has become foreign to you.

The most difficult, shall we say, barrier to overcome is that barrier of accepting the fact that this communication in itself is a reality. Secondly, you must overcome those intellectual analyses of the information as it is received. And thirdly, you must have within your intellectual capacities, which is brought forth from your own personal programming, the knowledges to present the concepts which are received. The presentation of certain concepts is found to be more easily done through some instruments than through others, due to their own personal intellectual programmings and processes.

In order to attain anything which is desired, the realization that it is to become is the initial step that you must take. Yet, you must meet what comes before you time after time, and practice patience, knowing that that which you have desired is in the process of manifesting and in due time, it shall be. We cannot expect whatever we choose to desire to manifest immediately. Yet the more effort which we put forward in the proper areas, the swifter that manifestation shall come into being.

For those who would choose to achieve any of the abilities, remember this: you have within you the abilities. You do not need to look outward for the assistance. Assistance, indeed, is helpful, but the knowledge that it is within you to begin with is of utmost importance. We are all Creators. We have been told this time after time and it is time that we truly realize that we indeed create that which we wish to experience.

I am with you and shall always be so. It is my choice to be with you and I am pleased that you have accepted my presence. I leave you in the love and the light of the infinite Creator. I am Laitos. Adonai vasu borragus.

(Carla channeling)

I am with this instrument. I do not identify myself except to say that I am of this planet and I come in love and peace for all mankind. I am very grateful for the opportunity to speak to this group and I use this time to ask you to send your light within your group at this time to that area known as California. I would ask you to do this at each of your meetings for the next few months of your time, as a great deal may be alleviated on the physical if harmony can be improved upon the inner planes. The inner planes function in advance of the physical and if it does not occur upon the inner planes, then it can be averted upon the physical.

I thank you very much and I send you love. ✣

Sunday Meeting
June 27, 1976

(Carla channeling)

I am Hatonn. I am with this instrument and I greet you in the love and the light of our infinite Creator. I greet each of you in the name of the Father, and thank each of you for the privilege of being able to speak with you. As always, our delight is in sharing with you our thoughts.

I would like to share with you now a little story. There was once a boy who had grown wise to the ways of the world about him, for he saw much in his daily life, and he understood much. He understood how to act, and he understood what people wished him to think. And he was a good boy.

And yet there were many things that puzzled him, as he grew, and perhaps the chief of these things was that which the grown-ups kept calling love. And he turned to his parents, and he said, "What is love?" And they said, "Love is honoring your father and your mother, and obeying them."

And he accepted this and thought on it, and attempted to show love by honoring his father and his mother. And yet he was not satisfied.

And so he went to his teacher. And he said, "Teacher, what is love?" And the teacher said, "Love is doing what the teacher tells you to do, and learning what we ask you to learn here at school."

And the boy realized that there must be some truth in this. But yet he was not satisfied.

And he went and asked his friend, "Tell me, do you know what love is?" And his friend said, "I am not sure, but I have noticed that when people want something, they say, 'I love you.'"

And the boy thought on this, and thought, "Perhaps this is closer to what love is than anything I have heard."

And he puzzled over these things a long time to himself. And one night when he went to sleep, he sailed away in a beautiful ship with wide, billowing sails. And he sailed over a rainbow bridge into the far waters, which he had seen before in his dreams, yet never so clearly as now. And his ship, seeming to know just where to go, harbored itself upon a white beach. And he went onto the glistening sand, and walked into a softly forested area. And there, he saw a beautiful entity in white robes, glistening golden, not with sunlight, but with light coming from the face of the entity itself.

And he asked the radiant being, "Sir, tell me, what is love?" And the radiant being said not a word, but he knelt down and looked into the little boy's eyes. And the little boy looked back into those luminous eyes. And suddenly his own eyes were changed, and the world was transformed wherever he looked. And he looked around the beautiful forested area. And all seemed to be transformed. All seemed to be alive with joy and love, and he knew what love was because he was seeing it. It was visible to him. Every mote of sand danced with an energy so joyful that it was indescribable to him. And yet he knew that it was love.

The being said not a word, but led him back to his ship. The boy sailed over the rainbow bridge, and back to his bed. And when he woke up in the morning, he remembered. And he looked around his room, and his room was transformed. And his mother came into the room, and he ran to her and hugged her, and said, "I love you." And he saw his mother transformed into a being that was love.

And he ran to his teacher, and said, "Teacher, I love you." And the teacher became gentle, compassionate and human, in his eyes alone.

And each thing that he looked at with his eyes of love sent love back to him, for it was all made of love. And the little boy no longer needed to ask what love was.

Love is so simple, my friends, that it cannot be described. It can only be experienced. If you will be as a child, and when you open your eyes, if you will give to the world *your* love, the world will give you back love. It is a process of recognition of what really is—nothing more.

We wish to pause at this time for a brief period of silence. And we will pick up through another instrument. I am Hatonn.

(Pause)

(H channeling)

I am now with this instrument. I once again extend my greetings to you.

We have stated that love is simple, and indeed, this is so. All things visualized within the proper perception are simplicity. The perception through which most of your peoples envision their life experiences has became distorted. The distortion is due to many things, yet one of the greatest distorters, shall we say, is the intellect through which you perceive.

You are the master of that which affects you. You are that being that is, shall we say, the helmsman of the intellect. It is at your disposal and it is for you to choose in what directions you desire focusing upon.

You as the creator of your experiences can use your intellectual processes to benefit you greatly. Yet they must be properly disciplined, and they must be open to the reception of the infinite Creator.

You are the instrument. You are the receiver of the love and of the simplicity of the Creator. It is within your ability, through the processes and practice of meditation, to attune not only the intellect, but the spirit also, to these frequencies, shall we say, on which flow the information that you seek. The clarity of the reception is affected greatly by the intellect. And through practice you may learn to control these processes and to receive that which you seek.

The intellect is indeed important to your growth. If it were not, it would not have been given to you. Yet its uses, and the extent to which you must use it, should be understood. And this is the greatest problem which you people must face. Indeed, you have begun to do this, and if you continually recognize the divinity and simplicity of all things, you have made a major step towards this goal which you are seeking to achieve. For each of you has chosen what it is that you wish to do. You may not become aware of that desire, yet if you continue, indeed you shall.

My friends, the reason for the experience of discontent, as you might call it, is due to the knowledge within you that you are not aware of that purpose. Your purpose is indeed simple, and easy to fulfill. Only rid yourself of the barriers and place yourself in those realms of meditation and thought that attune you to clear perception and reception of the guidance and of the love that is constantly offered to you. Find within yourself the jewels of enlightenment and the pearls of knowledge.

I shall transfer this communication. I am Hatonn.

(Carla channeling)

I am with this instrument. In meditation, my friends, the intellect is stilled, and the simplicity of things as they are begins to seep into your subconscious, as you would call it. Within yourself there is a sea, over which meditation does erect a rainbow bridge. On the other side of that ocean lies a part of yourself which is illumined and radiant, full of knowledge, and wishing only to bring the rest of you unto him. Contact that portion of yourself. Love is an extremely simple thing. Within this illusion that you now experience, the concept of love seems to be associated with objects, and it is felt that if one loves, then one gives "things." Yet we say to you, when one truly loves, one gives of oneself.

There are many expectations among your peoples as to the fruits of love, and when a loved one does not give you the desired things, you may say that love has failed. Yet we say to you, look to yourself, and seek to give of yourself in love, not to others' expectations, but to your own highest understanding. For what you give, you shall surely receive. All in reality is love, if you can but see it. And, most importantly, if you can but act it out. Love-in-action is the reason for which you are here. You are in an arena, a magnificent arena. And the challenge lies in your actions.

I would close through another instrument. I am Hatonn.

(B channeling)

I am Hatonn. I am with this instrument, and I greet you in the love and the light of our infinite Creator. My friends, as we have stated, love is all. But due to the complex of day-to-day living, we have gotten away from the idea that all is love. Now, my friends, there is much time to be spent on the reestablishment of what love is. For, my friends, once you have attained this knowledge, it will undoubtedly lead to many new paths, upon which many will follow.

I will leave you at this time. I leave you in the love and the light of our infinite Creator. Adonai, my friends. Adonai vasu borragus.

(After a brief pause, Carla asks H if he will be able to get a contact so that she can ask a question.)

(H channeling)

[I am Hatonn.] I am with this instrument. I once again greet you. What is the request?

Carla: S wants to know if the brothers have any thoughts to share with her at this time about her life in general?

There is indeed, you might say, contained within the life of nearly every individual a time at which questioning of one's accepted situations does occur. These questions, as a general rule, you might say, have been in some form answered this evening. That is your purpose. The enunciation, shall we say, of questions is due to the searching process that is instilled within each individual for the fulfillment of that which they have chosen to do. Often those who are even well established upon the fulfillment of that purpose shall question what it is that they are to do.

We have attempted to assist all who have requested it, both intellectually and spiritually, within the realms of understanding. It is to be known that there are many forces, shall we say, that are working hand in hand with us and the Creator, and we are at your disposal, and shall assist within those decisions. It should be known and accepted that we indeed are present and capable of giving that assistance. Yet you as the individual, and I speak with all, must choose either to accept or reject and in order to do so, must learn first to receive that which is flowing to you.

The circumstances which surround each individual are often complex and perplexing. Yet we do recommend to extensively seek, shall we say, before a decision of major importance within one's life situations is brought about. Trust within the Creator. This shall bring about the proper action.

Are there any other questions?

Carla: She also wanted to know if you were in contact with any group in Boulder, Colorado, or any near there, and if so, how could she find it?

It shall be shown to her. That is all that this instrument shall specify. But indeed it shall come about.

Carla: OK, I have a question, too. There's been a rash of sightings of kind of odd-looking, different kinds of spaceships and different kinds of entities lately, and I was wondering: can the brothers change their forms any way that they desire? And secondly, are they forming themselves into spaceships and people based on the expectations of the people they want them to see? Or just at their own whim?

It is to be understood—and we must say that we are drawing upon knowledge in both the questioner and instrument—but each individual, all of you have been told of your ability as a creator of your experience. You have touched upon realization of the realms of higher experience. Yet you are not knowledgeable of the experiences contained upon those levels. Your world is rapidly becoming aware of that which is considered to be of an out-of-the-ordinary experience or knowledge. We of the Confederation have attained through our patience and our *(inaudible)* processes to control the situations about us. Each individual is composite of divine and radiant intellect and energy and love of the Creator. The body takes upon itself the coagulation of consciousness. You are the consciousness, and you have gathered within the body. The body was energy before you entered it. You have coagulated those particles of energy and chosen to abide within them. Once you have become the master of your creation, shall we say, then you can either reside within the physical form, or within other forms of which you are not now aware.

We indeed do, shall we say, present ourselves to you in a form which you are willing to accept. It is a form we have possessed, a form that we do possess, and a form that we also are not confined to. To simplify, indeed, we choose to appear to you as yourselves, yet once you attain proper understandings, you shall evolve to a state where you also freely abide within or without physical form, as you … *(inaudible)*.

As to the numerous experiences, shall we say, we can only say that this is being brought about for the purpose of attempting to expedite the questioning processes of those who have desired and experienced that visualization of truth. Is this sufficient?

Carla: Yes. Thank you very much.

W: My writing—and focusing between the paradox of ideals *(inaudible)*.

Focus yourself upon the purpose of knowing, as we have said earlier this evening, your purpose. To focus upon the ideas within your intellect is to accept that some ideas are more relevant to your situation than are others. And to accept this is to close oneself to the reception of a more attuned, shall we say, idea. Indeed, the ideas which you possess, upon which you focus, may be of importance. And if you are properly abiding within the laws, shall we say, what you shall receive shall be only what will benefit you. Focus upon all things. Focus upon the oneness which is all things and know that you are open, and that you shall receive that love and experience that you desire.

As to your processes of relaying your thoughts and emotions which indeed are self-stimulating emotions onto pieces of paper, shall we say: it is good to exercise and to release those ideals or thoughts within your intellect. And you must realize that it has flown from that source which you seek unto you through you and to all with whom you desire to share. Then focus yourself, and the writing shall bring to you a most vivid and satisfying form for release of ideals and also for the release of frustrations of your experiences.

Are there any other questions?

(Pause)

Indeed, we sense a very strong desire yet fear to request some information. We shall not request that it be stated, yet we would like to offer something for all.

My friends, each of you are perfect beings. You have come into existence as an act of love and perfection of the Creator. And all imperfections are indeed the creations of man. Recognize your divinity, and once again, envision your perfection. Be aware of that in which you were created. Visualize it within all beings. Fear not for the reaction of others upon your actions. For you to act in all honesty, with all sincerity, to the best of your ability, and employing the best of your understanding, is what you are to do. Those to whom this is displayed shall misunderstand, yet some shall not. Yet, my friends, fear not the responses of others. Recognize only the divinity and understand that it is their confusion which they reflect in the response that is limited in its perception. Life indeed is a fulfillment. To experience it is to know what it is to be knowledgeable of the growing process through which we are traveling, and shall continue to do so.

Adonai, my friends. Adonai vasu borragus.

Sunday Meeting
July 18, 1976

(Carla channeling)

Greetings, my friends, in the love and light of the infinite Creator. I am a voice of love, known to you as Hatonn. And, as always, it is my privilege to be with you this evening.

Yes, I am love, my friends. You are love. And we are one. To give you a sense of the immediacy of that truth is very difficult and yet unless love is alive and immediate in your experience, you may search forever without truly understanding the object of your search.

There is a tree outside your dwelling, my friends. And on this tree are many, many leaves. And some of these leaves are almost perfect. Their shape is completely symmetrical and their color is beautifully green, as it should be. And there is no mark or damage and all within this particular leaf is perfect. And on the same tree, other leaves have been damaged by insects, or they have grown in a crooked manner, or their coloration is not as it is expected to be. And yet these are not good leaves and bad leaves. For within them, each, is the same perfect leaf, which is not separate from the leaf, as an ideal, but is within that leaf and is the true reality of that leaf.

Or, my friends, you may think that the many, many forms of clouds—some may bring storms and some may simply be the beautiful kind of clouds. Yet good and bad cannot be said of clouds, for they are all perfect in their cloudness.

And you yourself are in essence a perfect version of you, whether your manifestation may be good or bad, within the illusion. The ideal that created you is immediately within you. It is present within you at this time and it is informing and inspiring your every breath. And this is true of all those you meet, no matter what their manifestations.

It seems like a cliché to say this to you, my friends, and yet you will never be free of turmoil until you are able to bring into your conscious experience the knowledge of oneness in love that you can find in meditation. Without meditation, it is not likely that you would ever discover that unity with the Creator that is the wellspring of true love at all. And without repeated seeking of this unity, it is very difficult to advance at any rate in bringing love into your immediate experience.

But, my friends, in addition to the meditation you need to bring that feeling into your life as you live it, moment by moment. We have said to you before: attempt to form a personal relationship with the Creator, seek Him as you would a trusted friend, love Him as you would love the most beloved friends you could ever have. True emotion that comes from the heart, personal, deep-felt emotion, is necessary in order to bring to your consciousness the realization that in the Creator you are dealing with the single most important relationship of your life.

Allow the love for the Creator to build and become more and more personal, more and more real, more and more felt. And then, take that sweet feeling and live it day-to-day. Feel the immediacy of that Creator and share it with the people you meet. This is the secret, my friends. If you can approach each person as someone who is the Creator and whom you may be privileged to serve, your troubles will sort themselves out before you. For love is always reflected in love.

I would like to attempt to transfer this contact at this time and will return to this instrument later. I am Hatonn.

(B channeling)

I am Hatonn. I am now with this instrument. My friends, it is one thing to speak of this that we call love and yet another to understand it. For, my friends, if you think, you have spent many lifetimes upon your planet in an attempt to learn the lessons of spiritual being, so that you may reach for more understanding. My friends, do not take this lightly, for once you have learned this, there is more and more that has to be undertaken.

My friends, as we have said, love is all that there is. Now, if you understand this thing, my friends, if love is truly all that there is, then should there not be only love that is experienced? *(Inaudible)* great spiritual, shall we say, uprising that is now taking place about you. My friends, it is not always enough to be only a part, for there are so many that are looking for so much from someone who will lead them and, my friends, someone to *(inaudible)*. All of you have the ability to teach another that which has been taught to you. But, my friends, you have to truly understand that as you know, my friends, change can only take place within yourself. My friends, you have found meditation a great tool. As you continue to raise your vibrations to a higher level, you will find this tool of more use to you than ever, for truly, my friends, there is no end.

Abide, my friends, in this energy of love. You will find all that is around you acquires new aspects. And, my friends, as you know, a great part of love is understanding. Do not judge another, my friends. That is reserved for the One who has made us all. And if we look upon another to disagree, we cannot truly give a loving hand to this being's free will. I will now leave this instrument. I am Hatonn.

(Carla channeling)

I am again with this instrument. I would like to pause for a brief time in order to share with you our vibrations of love.

(Pause)

I am again with the instrument. It is a great pleasure to share with you. We ask only that you share with others as we share with you. For this is the true flower of your faith, the bloom for which you have spent so much time cultivating the plant.

We are aware that the one known as W wishes to ask a question, so at this time we will open the meeting to questions.

W: It's about the awareness of my dreams, and the bearing they might have on my feelings about reality, and how I can become more aware of the relationship.

Speaking through this instrument is easy on this subject, since this instrument has, shall we say, heard our "speech" before along these lines. The story of dreams is a simple one. Your consciousness, as you well know, has no beginning and no end and as sleep is in its way a brief foretaste of death, the consciousness has no part of sleep. It is doing something all the time, just as it is when you are awake. That "something" is as much related to itself as it always is and the circumstances only change during the period of sleep of the physical body in that the attention of the spirit is not totally drawn to the needs of the physical illusion. Therefore, it may process other levels of material which may engage its attention.

Dreams are a partial record of the activity of the spirit. They are a reliable communication from spirit to conscious self of the true development of the spirit's personality. The inability to remember what is happening during periods of sleep is very widespread among your peoples, for the spirit is hardly recognized, much less cultivated.

It is encouraged by us that you make an effort to become more in touch with your dreams. The methods of doing this are fairly simple and basically have to do with keeping a record, so that when you awaken, you immediately write down what you can remember. You will find that as you practice this, you will improve. Further, when one begins to be able to have a good consciousness of self within dreams, one will find this showing forth in a physical control of one's conscious life. In other words, as you begin to obtain control of your so-called subconscious thought, which is the manifestation of your spirit self, this will reflect inevitably in your daily life.

Does this answer your question?

W: Well, what about that relationship [with a woman]?

My friend, it is impossible for us to give you words other than love. All relationships are relationships of love. Yet, due to the illusion twisting and turning, it is difficult for you within the physical to maintain within the physical a totally unselfish attitude of pure love. If you maintain an attitude of total service and love, the difficulties which you are experiencing will vanish. If all you wish to do is offer your service, your love, the rest will simply become what it simply is in reality—the confusion of the physical illusion. This confusion is not your fault, for at your birth you began to be taught what to expect in this illusion and your expectations have been shaped and hammered into you by many, many experience, biases and impressions, all through your experiences so far. In order to cut through all the expectations and get to reality, it [is] necessary to refrain from, as you would say, reacting to expectations and hold to the one thing that is true, that is real. And that, as you know we will say, is love.

If love is to mean anything in a lasting sense, it is to manifest itself as a desire for the spiritual help and service that you can give to any whom you might love. Beyond this, we can give no comfort or advice, for all relationships are based on the need to learn this one lesson.

Is there another question?

Questioner: What is the function of homosexuality?

It is a difficulty of your language that we have trouble overcoming in that homosexuality is not understood as a type of sexuality, but is considered to be, in your language, a type of emotionally strong word.

The function of sexuality is to teach service. One is drawn to another of your species and forms a relationship and in that relationship, there are opportunities for service, or disservice, and gradually, as the spirit grows through this association, you begin to learn how to be of service. Were it not for the drive of sexuality, it is likely that there would not be these intense relationships, and therefore these strong stimulants or catalysts to learning. Those who are homosexual have had a personality difficulty which drives then in a sexual way towards their own charge, much like a positive charge being attracted to a positive charge. This is due to confusion between incarnations, the previous incarnation being of one sex, this incarnation being of another. But the function of homosexuality is the function of any type of sexuality: it is to enable a person to form an intense enough relationship that he may learn how to serve and how to love; to love others more than himself, or shall we say, to love others more than his personality, but as much as the Creator.

Does this answer your question?

Questioner: Yes.

Any other questions?

Questioner: What is the general program objective within the next twelve months?

We are attempting to intensify our program of light. We have made contact with many groups and, as you might say, the damage has already been done. Now it is time to get these groups functioning individually in such a way that they are truly light centers and their individuals are light bearers. We do not have specific objectives for this time period, although the possibility exists for increased sightings, shall we say, on demand. Are we being sufficiently obscure?

Questioner: Not any specific contact with Earth's peoples in order to stimulate events?

Not at this time. We do not know about the future. The possibility exists, as we said, on demand. It is a matter of the need for there to be, as this instrument would say, ten students in order for a class to be held. We have nowhere near that much demand. If the demand were to be generated, it would be possible, as you well know. We do not count on that much demand being generated, but are aware that it is possible that this might occur.

Questioner: Do you know of any other group planning a more general effort at contact?

Yes. However, they do not have our full approval, for we feel that they are treading on the fringes of, shall we say, being too pushy.

Questioner: Well, how do they plan to make this contact?

We are sorry, but this instrument does not have the type of contact which would enable us to control her enough to tell you this. We know of the type of contact, types of contact, we should say, that are being contemplated. We do not think that they will successfully occur.

There are those that watch and in their watching of this planet, as well as many others, set up vibrations protecting free will, which are not easily undermined. Within our own fleet there are individual groups, what we would call the "young whippersnappers" of our legion, who also advocate speedier methods. But it is our experience that it is only when one responds to a definitely requested need that any true help can be given and so we, shall we say, older heads are in the majority and prevail within the Confederation.

Questioner: Who is contacting Puharich?

The central agency of thought of our Confederation has enabled linkages which make it possible for this intrusion upon the private space/time experience of the one known as Puharich. This has been, shall we say, an experiment, as we have done others. However—we are having trouble transmitting this, but the instrument is cooperating, so we will keep giving it. Puharich has certain expectations. We have had this trouble with many contactees and Puharich [is] among the best. It is a matter of dealing in a space/time experience in such a way that you who are of [a] very rapid age do not become impatient with the expectations. Time is a very difficult thing to deal with in this contact. If I were to explain to you what time is to us, as we transmit to you, it would not be understood. For we are able to, in a single instant, speak to ten thousand people. And yet, it does not seem to us difficult.

The …

(The rest of the session was not recorded.)

Sunday Meeting
July 25, 1976

(Carla channeling)

Greetings, my friends, in the love and light of our infinite Creator. I am Hatonn, and, as always, it is a great privilege to address this group. I greet each of you and especially those who are new to our group and extend to you our love and our thoughts and our gratitude for the chance to be with you.

We of the Confederation of Planets in the Service of the Infinite Creator are about your planet in numerous crafts and we come from many, many different places within your universe. And yet we are here for one purpose and one purpose only. We are here, my friends, as a single voice of love.

Love, my friends, is the word which created all that there is. What vibration is to the physical world, love is to the consciousness that created the physical world. Love is all that there is and all that you see about you, day by day, are manifestations of love.

My friends, it may seem to you often that you are not looking at the manifestations of love when you look at your relationship with someone with whom you are having difficulty, when your nation looks at other nations with whom it is having difficulty. And yet, we offer to you the precise analogy of vibration in your physical world. It is well known to your scientists that all things are made up of vibration and energy centers. Yet to you, the manifestations of vibration seem many and varied: tables and buildings and trees and human bodies. Yet all of these, my friends, are one thing: energy in motion.

And so it is with love. Each feeling, whether it be emotional, mental or spiritual, each thought that you have is a feeling or thought that was originally purely of love. Yet man, as well as the Creator, is a creator and man has invented many complexities which take love and cause it to form many and various shapes.

In your holy works, it has been written that the way to defeat evil is to meet it with love. This is true, my friends, because the original vibration of love is always stronger than its derivative, man-made forms.

To realize that all that you see is love, is to find peace. No longer need you feel anger and distress, resentment and irritation. These are derivatives of love which can be replaced in your thinking by a consciousness of the basic true love, the all-loving, all-serving, all-creative emotion that surrounds and inspires each of you.

And how can you find this fountainhead of love, my friends? As always, we recommend meditation. For clever as man's minds are, they are often too clever and in their cleverness men have devised many strange contortions of love. And in meditation, my friends, as you lay down these man-made concepts and open yourselves to your deeper identity, the basic reality of the love that created you can make contact with you in your conscious mind. And as you come in contact with love as it really is, you gain strength to be able to look the world of man-made emotions in the face and say, "Ah, but I know a deeper and truer way to express love." If you touch base with this creative love on a regular basis, little by little your being will begin to transmit that love and you will become what you seek to become, an instrument for the love of the Creator.

You are in the world, as it has been said, but you are not of the world. You are a divine being, dwelling within the body of the so-called human. And this human will have a very short life and yet the divine being that is your true higher self will exist eternally. Seek to unify your consciousness as a human with your higher identity as a portion of the divinity of the Creator, through meditation.

I would at this time transfer this contact. I am Hatonn.

(H channeling)

I am Hatonn. I am now with this instrument. When we speak of the concept of love, we attempt to the best of our ability to bring to you our understanding of a concept which is infinite and unfolding to us and to you at all times. A concept which contains, shall we say, the explanation of all things. A concept which is much more than you shall ever realize by the utilization of your intellect. We bring to you those messages which we feel shall assist in your spiritual growth and in your intellectual understanding. We bring to you our love and our light. We offer to you an opportunity—which has been brought about by your own thinking, through your own desire—and that opportunity is for you to come into the light through understanding and experience, to come into the light of the Creator and experience His love and know the concepts of which we speak, enjoying with us and all of our universal brothers in service that which we call the Creator.

Each individual whom we are privileged to make contact with is presented with this opportunity, with our experiences, into our light. We can offer no more at the present time. But also, there is no need for there to be any more offered. For if you are open, if you are truly seeking what you refer to as the truth, then you shall recognize it as it is presented and you shall accept it and you shall do with it to the best of your ability that which you *(inaudible)*. It is you and no other who must analyze that which you receive. It is you who must accept the love. It is you who creates all that you experience. And we would not have been able to share with you our knowledge if it were not for the fact that in truth you were seeking this knowledge.

We are somewhat limited, even through this process, for we must deal with the intellect of each individual. And the individuals, all of them with whom we communicate, have accepted many limitations due to their experiences within this life and we must break not those imitations too quickly. We must offer only that which we feel can be accepted and allow it to be dealt with.

We give to you, and so also do you give to us, the love of which we speak. We cannot begin to explain the great feeling of love we have for those upon your planet and, indeed, for those who would be willing to listen. We are here for this purpose, to assist in the evolution of human thought of man upon planet Earth. Yet we cannot assist without it being requested, for within what you might call the society or upon the level on which we exist, this is a law— that you may not interfere with the free choice of any individual. And as we deal with the planet Earth as a group consciousness, we must be aware of your requests, of your needs and of your desires and of your choice.

Love, my friends, is all the things of which we speak, and it is all the things for which we have no means of expression. Love is the energy upon which you draw to bring into manifestation all that you experience. Love is to each and every individual different, yet the same. The love that permeates throughout the universe is indeed the Creator. The love that is within you is indeed the Creator. You must recognize that the love that is within all individuals is the Creator. You have heard this concept many times. There is what you would call "God" within each individual and you are constantly emanating that energy, that love, of the Creator in all directions, in all your thoughts. Be cautious, indeed, be cautious of that which you project towards your fellow man and towards the universe, for you are the Creator and that which you project shall indeed come into existence and it shall also travel back and affect you, for you are the Creator and you must live within your creation.

Through the process of meditation you may bring into focus the proper, shall we say, realization of your ability to create. Through the process of meditation you may become aware of your divinity and of the divinity of all things. We hope that through the process of meditation you may attune yourselves to the love energies that are constantly about you and that through these energies may be brought about the understanding that you seek and the experiences you desire and the purification of consciousness which is in truth the desire of all those upon your planet. This desire may not come into the realization of each person upon your planet, but as you become more aware, you shall indeed recognize that that desire is within each of us, whether they seek it consciously or not.

You are the only, shall we say, emanation of the Creator that has the ability to formulate your experience. You may share with others in your experiences and you may choose to dwell within the experiences created by others, yet no other can create for you any experience, for you are the Creator, and it is your choice.

I shall close this communication through another instrument. I am Hatonn.

(B channeling)

I am Hatonn. I am now with this instrument. My friends, we will be with you but a few minutes more, but I wish to touch on the subject of what is known to you as desire. For, my friends, truly what you desire, you shall obtain, if the desire is of a strong enough vibration. My friends, through the many years in which life has been experienced upon your planet, there have been many teachers come and go. My friends …

I am experiencing difficulty with this instrument. For that reason, I will now close this meeting. It has been an extremely great honor to share with you in your meditation, my friends. I leave you now. I am Hatonn. I leave you in the love and light of our infinite Creator. Adonai vasu borragus.

H: I received a really nice impression while I was speaking about love—at the same time I was talking I received this too and they wanted me to say it but I just went on past it. It wasn't quite clear to me, as to how to say it. But the definition of love … and it was: "Luminescence omnipresent, vacillating eternally."

Carla: That's easy for you to say!

Sunday Meeting
August 8, 1976

(B channeling)

Greetings, my friends. I am Hatonn. I greet you in the love and the light of our infinite Creator. As always, it is a great honor to share with you in your meditation.

My friends, I would speak with you tonight on the subject of progression. For, my friends, since you have started on the path, so far away now, you have sought after that knowledge which is accompanied by progression. My friends, in fact you have done well. As you know, you were all brought together in order to teach, and learn from, each other of the knowledge of love.

But, my friends, once upon the path you cannot sway from one side to another. There are many things to do, many things that must be done. And, my friends, as you know, there are many experiences along this path. In order to help you attain even more knowledge as time goes by, the vibrations will grow even stronger and you will grow to a great extent.

But, my friends, you have to keep walking upon the path. For some, it is enough to obtain knowledge of this path and to sit idly by. But, my friends, in order that you may grow ever stronger, you, like ourselves, must aid others; thus, you may gain the knowledge you would learn. Your every wish for help, my friends, is placed at your disposal. Within your experiences you have gained the knowledge of much love. My friends, walk within this path and rest within the knowledge that may be obtained.

I will leave this instrument. I am Hatonn.

(Carla channeling)

I am with the instrument. I am Hatonn, and again I greet you in love and light.

We speak to you about progression, for we know that you will progress, for that is inevitable, as all things progress. The only question open is the direction of that progression. There is a quality to experience which greatly aids progression, and ignoring this quality in your experiences will cause your progress to be minimal. Moreover, this quality of experience is one which is often ignored by your peoples, for they do not understand the need for rapid progression nor the technique for obtaining this rapidity.

Consider that experience, as you see it, is an activity such like eating a piece of fruit. The piece of fruit, being the experience, has an edible part which you immediately take into your system. When you finish with the easily eaten substances you are left with the seed of the piece of fruit, and this you throw away. You must understand, of course, that while the flesh of the fruit will feed your body for a day, if you do not plant the seeds you will not reap the long-term benefits of the living consciousness. In experience, that which you experience at the moment is much like the flesh of the fruit. It may be sweet, in which case you eat it greedily, savoring every morsel. It may be sour, in which case you will not eat it, or you will only eat part of it. In either case, whether the fruit is sweet or sour to the taste, the seed is the important part for your progress. In each experience there is a seed of wisdom, a lesson which was implicit in the experience and which you must plant in your consciousness in order to progress.

Taking your experiences into meditation is very important; offering them up to the consciousness within you, not in a judgmental way, but simply as a desire that you truly learn from each experience, not just for the day, but for the future of your spirit. On the level of your intellect, it may be helpful for you to ask yourself the following question with regard to your experiences: in this experience, was I of service? In this experience, did I want to be of service? For the seed, as we have said, which will enable you to progress rapidly, has as its key love expressed in action. And the closest we can come to giving you this concept is the concept of service.

Service, as you well know, is not always a thing, but most often an attitude. To be of service is often simply to be non-judging, to be loving, to be willing to see the possibility in another of the Christ-consciousness and its progress in that person. Insofar as you have been able to bring into this experience that attitude, you have already planted the seed as well as eaten the fruit. And as you take experiences in which you have not done this into your meditation even your failures will teach you and the seed will be planted.

The world itself, my friends, will never progress for you are the world. Only you can progress. And you can only progress by offering up your little human self to the Christ Self within you. You cannot influence the world and most especially you cannot influence the Creator. Yet this [is] not necessary, for the world is as darkness and the Creator is light. If you can ask the Creator to influence you, it will be as light turned upon darkness and the darkness will be no more.

I will transfer to another instrument after a brief pause.

(Pause)

(Carla channeling)

I am again with this instrument. I am Hatonn. We were attempting to make contact with the one known as B. However, we are satisfied that this is not a good time and we will attempt again at a later time. We would like to pause for a moment and send energy, for there are many among your group which are fatigued at this time and there are those who are not here who are thinking of this group at this time, and to all those we also would send energy

(Pause)

It to a great privilege to us to be linked in this great circle of energy, the light pouring through us and through you, to each other. We are all one.

I would at this time open the meeting to questions.

M1: Can you tell us about the second coming of Christ?

We are unable to express through this instrument this question. There are many concepts which we can speak on and a few which are so highly charged with emotion within the mind of the instrument that we have difficulty in giving a clear message. We are sorry.

Is there another question?

M2: Yes. What are your thoughts on children, especially their guidance and spiritual growth?

We find it much easier to speak on this subject through this instruments for the subject does not have highly emotional feelings about children. Therefore, we shall, as you might say, skip right ahead.

Children, as well as adults and old people, are spirits. Into this world they come, extremely vulnerable within their manifestation in the physical, yet as eternal and as complete as any one of those on the planet. What the parents do for their child is right, as long as it is an attempt to be of service. An understanding of the basic freedom of all individuals is, of course, very important.

The Father-Creator has given the family as an understandable symbol of the relationship which is between all of the children of the Father and Himself. The Nurturer and the Creator—the Spirit and the Father. In this relationship, the Nurturer—who is the Mother—and the Creator and Provider—who is the Father—grow to understand divinity and love, for the love that will flow is pure, far more pure than any love that can be discovered by other relationships. It is a deeper and simpler lesson.

And so it is for the parents. This lesson is a great lesson and we know that it will bring you much joy. Know that this is the Father, the Creator, expressing through you as instruments the love which makes up the universe.

More than what you do as your child grows, it will be what you are which affects his understanding and his progress. If you truly seek the spiritual, and if you live your lives according to the path which you seek, if every day *you* expressly make room for spiritual seeking in your meditation, in your prayer, your child will understand from the very beginning the purpose of life and the path. It is not necessary to ask him to participate. It is never necessary to encourage a small, growing being to choose one way or another. It is only necessary for a child to know that there is such a thing as the spiritual path and that it has given joy to those who are closest to him.

Beyond this, beyond the giving of love and the offering of the spiritual path, that whole and complete being which you have been given to care for will express to you himself that which he will need.

Does this answer your question?

M2: Yes.

Is there another question?

(Pause)

How many things you see, my friends, things of surpassing beauty. How many things you think that are sublime! Truly within you, there is divinity. Trust yourself, please, trust yourself, my friends—have confidence. In every sincere impulse, every honest desire to progress, let that have weight within you. Take yourselves seriously, and let that joy that you feel from time to time take root and grow, until your life itself is transformed by your knowledge and understanding of love. It will happen, my friends. Not all at once—it is a progression. And we wish you great joy upon it.

Your brothers leave you in the love and light of the infinite Creator. I am Hatonn. Adonai vasu borragus.

Sunday Meeting
August 15, 1976

(H channeling)

I am Hatonn. Greetings in the love and the light of our infinite Creator. It is pleasing to be with you once again and we welcome those that rejoin us. It is always a pleasure to see those who travel upon their path [that they] continually hold within their consciousness the values which they have gained throughout their experiences. And it is these values which have brought those who have been guided, shall we say, to once again share in this experience.

My friends, as you travel along that which you consider to be your path, you shall share with many the knowledges you have gained through all the avenues you have traveled and studied. You shall carry with you the accumulation of all the knowledge—not only gained through this experience of life, but through all experiences prior to this life. This knowledge is continually attained within you and is constantly available for your usage.

And as you know, it is through the process and practice of meditation that you may, shall we say, easily obtain access to that knowledge. As you encounter situations and people throughout your present life experience, it is your obligation to bring forth the purest and greatest manifestation. It is your obligation to share with those your knowledge, your experiences and your love. Certainly, we are aware that there are many with whom the sharing of this knowledge at the present time would be nearly useless and, at some times, would be harmful to the relationship. You as the individual carries with you the knowledge of past and present. You should be capable of recognizing those individuals with whom to share it—these experiences and this knowledge. And with those with whom you realize you should not enter into discussions, you can constantly carry with you and share with them the love which is the total manifestation of those experiences and of that knowledge.

My friends, you must realize, shall we say, the potency and the creativity of those thoughts which you place into the, what we call, the ethers. The spoken word indeed carries much power, yet the unspoken word, my friends, is even greater. As you are aware, the other realms of existence is such that verbalization of thought is no longer utilized, for it has come to those peoples' knowledge that it is simpler to utilize the natural process of thought transference or what you would call telepathy. My friends, you can send to all around you all the knowledge which you contain, by simply projecting your love to them. For as we have stated, love is the total manifestation of all your experience and knowledge. Love is the manifestation of all things.

And for you to direct that love, purely and completely, to any individual, is to share all that you contain and you contain all of the knowledge of the universe. Each one of you, my friends, are as a beacon, a beacon upon the shore to guide the ships at sea. Shine brightly! Never allow your flame to dim, to flicker, to be extinguished. Allow your flame to glow brilliantly, wherever you are, and in whatever you do, and, my friends, this indeed is enough for you to do. It is your obligation as a manifestation of the Creator to share this love. It is your opportunity to express and to learn, during this lifetime, the meaning of the concept. Do not falter, my friends, and do not be harsh upon yourself, feeling that you have faltered. For, my friends, it is your desire to become that ever-glowing fire, and it shall be done, and the experiences upon the way are indeed helpful. You cannot falter when your focus is in the right direction. You shall achieve what you have set out to do. This is the law: that which you desire you shall receive. Doubt it not and it shall be fulfilled.

I shall transfer this contact. I am Hatonn.

(Carla channeling)

I am with this instrument. I am Hatonn. Yes, my friends, that which you request, you shall receive. There is a simplicity to this which is difficult to grasp and because you are in a physical body at this time, it seems that to request something is to go, as an object of physical dimensions, and ask another physical object for some *thing*. It is this type of concept which causes love to be very difficult to understand in this place.

When you seek love, when you seek to know the source of love, it is an attempt to tabernacle, shall we say, to become one with that which is infinite and invisible, that which is nearer to you than your own body. You need go nowhere. Love is waiting for you, so close—so very close, my friends. So that the request, in its simplicity, is simply a willingness of you as individualized consciousness to become the observer in your life, to turn your life over to love, to turn your life over to Christ-consciousness. You do not have the power to show love. You can only offer your life to love, so that love can live your life. Then, as you watch, the force of love flowing through you will teach you,

You, yourself, as individualized consciousness, will never be wise to the ways of love, for the physical is a series of measurements and judgments and understandings which are limitations. Love is creative, limitless and infinite.

When love approaches a situation, love expands that situation. Love eases. Love makes possible comfort where no comfort was. Individualized consciousness cannot do this and all the will in the world cannot find the way of love.

So as you seek, seek to watch the ways of love as they flow through you. It is important to discriminate, it is important to judge. And yet, as you are functioning, allow love to flow through you, without judgment and without hindrance. And then it will teach you its ways and it will live your life. You cannot direct the Creator. As long as you attempt to direct Him, He will stand knocking, asking to be let in to your heart. Once you make the connection, then you and the consciousness of love will be together, communing and living a creative life.

Seek and ye shall find. Knock and the door shall be opened unto you. Truer words were never written. It is your responsibility—your only true responsibility—to seek and then when you have found—to share. For us to share this with you is a great pleasure. I will transfer to another instrument. I am Hatonn.

(H channeling)

I am Hatonn. I am once again with this instrument. We are having difficulty achieving contact with the instrument known as B1. We shall continue through this instrument.

My friends, it has become known to us, quite some time ago, that to reside within the state of love for all of creation is, shall we say, the only way to achieve, to gain, the happiness and the fulfillment which we seek.

You must, through your discipline, elevate yourself to a state of mind with spirit that allows no prejudices to block the free flow of your love. Allow no separations to be acknowledged, for they also cause blockages in that flow of love. Bring yourself to a state of harmony of mind, body and spirit being one with creation.

My friends, it is our responsibility to one another to love each other, without limitations of any kind. Certainly, as you reside upon this plane of experiences, there shall be those things which tend to irritate you. Yet look past them, my friends. Realize that what you see within another individual that irritates you is a projection of what you either contain or fear that you may contain within yourself.

You are the creator of your universe. You perceive within it that which you choose to perceive. You experience within it that which you choose to experience. No other can bring about the manifestation of experience or perception within your universe. You may choose to share those manifestations with others, yet no other can override your creativity. You might say it is your ship and you are the captain. You can share with the crew what you wish. But the decision is yours.

Think of this, my friends, and realize as you go along your path: you follow that which you have laid out in front of you. You experience that which you have chosen. And you are to love all that you have created.

I shall leave you at this time, in the love and the light of our infinite Creator. I am known to you as Hatonn. Adonai vasu borragus.

(Carla channeling)

I am Lattoo. I greet you in the love and the light of the infinite Creator. I have not spoken with your group very often, but there are questions within your group which it is felt that I may be most equipped to answer. So, at this time I open the meeting to questions.

B2: I'd like to know what happens to animals on this plane right now? Do they go through the same cycle as men on this plane? In their evolution towards becoming more evolved in life-forms, do they change into other life forms or do they stay animals?

This is a question which cannot be answered on the general level, due to the fact that animals begin their consciousness as a type of pool of consciousness, so that each type of animal is that animal in general. They go through many incarnations at this level, until experiences occur which mold their individual personality. It is especially common for the so-called domesticated animal to become individualized, through the love which they share with their masters. At the point at which an animal becomes individualized, he ceases, upon the physical death, to go back into animal consciousness. He will instead begin that evolution known to you as the human type of evolution. In the so-called spirit, this animal consciousness, having been individualized, will spend time dwelling upon the love of his master, and will incarnate, often in order to be with his master.

At some point, this individualized pet or animal will have become so much of an individual that his soul is ready for the step of becoming a human soul. This is a very long process, in your terms. Consciousness is a plenum, or as you may call it, a spectrum, one type of consciousness a little more articulated than the next, beginning with the most dense and still objects and going into the human, and past, into angelic consciousness. That of the animals is the step in the process which is below, next to, and merging with the human consciousness.

Does this answer your question?

B2: Yes.

W: I have a question. Concerning the artist David Bowie: was his previous incarnation—or was he brought to Earth as an alien—or is he aware of the Confederation in this incarnation? How does the way he projects as a performer relate to the evolution and possible manifestation of the Confederation?

We do not wish to invade the privacy of any of those upon your planet, and so we would not wish to speak upon the thoughts and opinions of the one of whom you speak. However, we can say without invading his privacy, that he, as well as many, many others of those who are in your public life as performers, is what this instrument has called an apple. He, and many, many others, have come in through the incarnational process and have had a normal birth and childhood upon your planet. Yet his previous experiences have not been with this planet, and so he, as with many, many others upon your planet, is rather uncomfortable at times in the vibrations which now prevail upon your Earth world. These things he expresses, as well as the understandings of which you are all aware, [have] to do with the spiritual path. It is not uncommon for those upon your planet to be aware that they are not, at heart, at home upon your planetary atmosphere. The one of whom you speak is simply in a somewhat better position, due to his renown, to, shall we say, spread the word.

Does this answer your question?

W: Yes. Is Findhorn a sort of power focus of cosmic energies? Where are various spots like this in the United States and possibly specifically in the nearby area?

The so-called magnetic anomalies which constitute such places which are known in your, shall we say, folklore, as the Bermuda triangle, are specific magnetic disturbances which can be pinpointed with fair accuracy over a period of time. However, it is best to understand that there is a great difference between the so-called window areas which indicate geographic areas whose fabric is uniquely vulnerable to interfaces with other spaces and times and the type of energy accumulation which is possible in a place, no matter where it is, in which the consciousness of people has found a niche. Findhorn is this latter type of place. Rather than being an electromagnetic phenomenon, it is a phenomenon of consciousness. The energies have been directed to this place from energies which exist everywhere.

It is true that there is a grid, shall we say, of energy which surrounds the planet. Yet these energies can be tapped off in very general and large areas. One does not have to be sitting, shall we say, on the top of the pyramid to get the energy, for with consciousness, one can move the pyramid. It is the faith of the individual which builds the energy which makes the miracles possible. Such is what has happened at Findhorn.

As you seek your place in life, seek first that seed of faith—that touching with the infinite. Then, allow your sensors, as you might say, to be touching from that sensor output. And when that center says, "This is where I wish to be," then that will be a place of power for you. It is a very personal thing, the generation of power. The place whereon you stand is holy ground. You cannot possibly develop power from an outside source on the level at which Findhorn was created. That power came and does come from the consciousness of love, which is the source of power for all things.

W: Can you give me any clues as to better care [for] and as to what precisely of sorts am I under regarding my physical strength?

We would suggest a relaxation period before you attempt to sleep. You must be stricter with yourself about putting down those intellectual worries and considerations which the day will bring. It is a matter of never relaxing. This is not good for the physical. With relaxation and meditation, then as you lie down to rest, do not allow thoughts to begin to work through, but instead allow thoughts only of a recreational nature. You must allow your brain and your body to rest. Our other suggestion is always good for anyone, and that is to allow yourself to seek the light touch. To allow yourself to remember that life as you know it is a cosmic joke. It is not good to take things too seriously. All of your busy thoughts and all of your worries are, at best, little cartoons. When you pass from this physical existence, you will spend some time laughing and some time crying. And the tears will come because you took things so seriously, that you forgot to laugh and praise the Creator that gave you this marvelous cartoon. This attitude is all-important in maintaining the balance that allows you to go through your physical experience learning and also enjoying yourself. We do not give advice as to such things as diet, etc., because it is our firm belief that these details are meaningless. That which you put into the body is an illusion. The good that you get from it is a function of your belief that it will do you good. The harm that you will get from it is also a function of your belief that harm will come from it. Nothing within the physical has power over you unless you allow it to. Do as you deem wise, and then remember, as we say, that whatever you do, it is a kind of cartoon. The greatest and noblest and most tragic things are passing fancies, my friends. Accept them for what they are, accept feelings for what they are. All are true, but all will pass. Do not forget to laugh.

Are there any other questions?

(Pause)

I am Lattoo. It's been a very great pleasure to be with you. I and my brothers seldom get a chance to speak with this group and it was indeed a privilege. I will leave you at this time. I leave you in the love and the light of the One Who is All. Adonai, my friends. Adonai vasu. ☙

L/L Research

L/L Research is a subsidiary of Rock Creek Research & Development Laboratories, Inc.

P.O. Box 5195
Louisville, KY 40255-0195

www.llresearch.org

Rock Creek is a non-profit corporation dedicated to discovering and sharing information which may aid in the spiritual evolution of humankind.

ABOUT THE CONTENTS OF THIS TRANSCRIPT: This telepathic channeling has been taken from transcriptions of the weekly study and meditation meetings of the Rock Creek Research & Development Laboratories and L/L Research. It is offered in the hope that it may be useful to you. As the Confederation entities always make a point of saying, please use your discrimination and judgment in assessing this material. If something rings true to you, fine. If something does not resonate, please leave it behind, for neither we nor those of the Confederation would wish to be a stumbling block for any.

CAVEAT: This transcript is being published by L/L Research in a not yet final form. It has, however, been edited and any obvious errors have been corrected. When it is in a final form, this caveat will be removed.

© 2009 L/L Research

Sunday Meeting
August 22, 1976

(Don channeling)

I am Hatonn. I greet you, my friends, in the love and the light of our infinite Creator. It is a very great privilege to be with you this evening. I am known to you as Hatonn. I am not of your planet, however I am deeply concerned at this time about the activities of the peoples of your planet. My friends, myself and all of my brothers at this time are very concerned about the activities upon your planet. We are limited in speaking to you, however, in that we must use this means. We are limited to this means by wisdom, for we have found that it is necessary to approach a planet such as yours in this manner. For it is very important, my friends, to give freely in such a manner that the gift cannot be misunderstood.

This is what we have for you, my friends: a gift. A gift of knowledge and understanding. This is all that we bring for you, all that there is. There is nothing more.

(Pause)

(H channeling)

I am Hatonn. I am with this instrument. Excuse us for the delay. We are certain that it is, shall we say, wondered what brings about the difficulties which you have just witnessed. We merely must say that as a radio receiver, the intellect of man can receive external energy inputs or thought forms, yet for proper and clear reception and transmission, it is necessary that analysis by the individual receiving must be refrained from, for to receive and to analyze before attempting to transmit is to cause some confusion and disjointedness in the energies received.

We shall resume communication through the other instrument in a short time. We merely wish to utilize the first portion, shall we say, of this communication to merely scan over that which has been discussed and to assist in bringing into clearer understanding some of our viewpoints and our purpose.

We of the Confederation consider man, upon the planet Earth, to be of great importance. We consider him to be our brother. For throughout our experiences and what you might call our travels, we have come to realize that there is a greater unification between all things within this universe or creation than one can realize through the processes of the intellect. Many of the philosophies which are shared among your people speak of the concept of oneness, oneness of creation. And, indeed, we have found that this concept expresses most easily the truth of the existence of our creation.

You must view all things as being merely a portion of the entire creation. Each thing is as a molecule within the overall structure of the body of the universe, or of the Creator Himself. Recognizing to some degree the functions of your own physical form, you must realize that each and every particle of your physical form is of importance to the proper functioning within that form. And so it is within the universe: each individual, each particle, is indeed of vast importance to the overall proper functioning and existence of this creation.

All of us have instilled within us the love by which we were created. There is one form of love, there is one source of love and that is the Creator. We are the projections and we are the practice of that love. And therefore contained within us is the Creator. As we are in Him, so also is He within us. All things are interdependent upon each other. All things in truth are each other, and are one.

Our purpose for being here is to assist mankind in the realization of this simple concept. Yet we must stress: to come to the realization, to the true understanding of these concepts, is, shall we say, limited, if you only employ the utilization of your intellect. My friends, you have within you the ability to know and to be all things. The intellect is contained within the physical forms and also within that form abides your essence, or your being. Your being is the manipulator of the form. You are the commander of the ship. And the intellect is a portion of that form. It is a function of that which you call the brain. "Know thyself," has been stated many times within your scriptures. Know *you*, the manipulator of your form. And from this, you shall know the Creator. You shall know the vastness and the infinite knowledges of the universe. Utilize the intellect, and learn to know thyself, for what which has created you, that which is within you, and that which you are, contains the highest form of what you might call intellect or knowledge. It is not limited to merely one plane of existence. It is omnipresent; it is omnipotent. It is all things and it is one with the Creator. It to you, it is I, and we call it love. The overall concept of all things, we call love.

I shall transfer this communication once again. I am Hatonn.

(Carla channeling)

I am with this instrument, and again I greet you in love and light. That which you know as your intellect and that which we term the intellect or the mind of the Creator are not very related concepts. We have urged this group many times to be completely aware of the uses and functions of the intellect, and so to make that very useful tool work for you, rather than you working for it. For, my friends, that is what the intellect and the physical body itself will do to you, of course, if it can.

Both the intellect and your physical form have a short stay, in an organized sense, in consciousness, and so the short-term interests of the physical form and the intellect crave instant and continuous attention. And if you, as a spiritual self, are not careful, you will be a slave to these requests of the body and of the mind. And you will not allot any time, any serious time, to your progress outside the physical.

As you seek the mind of the Creator, which is love, you are seeking something entirely different. You are not seeking something which has a limitation, which offers limitations. You are seeking just the opposite, for true knowledge and understanding gives freedom—always. And as you seek to loosen the bonds of those things which imprison your soul, you are seeking a love which is so articulated, so fastidiously realized, that it is indeed that which is a perfect knowledge, a perfect understanding, and yet the energy of this understanding, far from being a separator or divider, is a unifier. Love unites all things, love combines all things, ameliorates all difficulties, heals the wounds that you may have. A complete understanding of love, fully realized in your life, will heal you on whatever level you need to be healed—and many, many are the hurts, my friends, that do not show, yet are grievously painful within your life experiences.

To gain an understanding of love is a process which is greatly aided by what we call meditation, what you are doing now. For, my friends, within your scriptures you have heard many times that it is not a good thing to raise up graven images. This is one of your commandments within your *Holy Bible*. Yet a graven image does not have to be made of earth or stone. It can also be made of words. And all those who say, "I believe in the Father," or those who say, "Love has come into my life and will heal me," are kneeling to a graven image, for words have never done anything for anyone. To allow the experience of love to come into your life is to open yourself to it and to listen for it, to allow yourself to feel it, for the understanding without words, the experience without intellect, is what will indeed show you love.

The Creator does not speak with you in human terms. The Comforter comes to you in silence. If you wish power, to heal, to help, either yourself or your neighbors, pray only that you may listen and you may hear the voice of love. Do not expect gifts for yourself or for your loved ones; pray only that all of those upon your planet may feel this love. For as you seek for all people, both those you know and those you do not know, those who are your friends and those who are your enemies, you are bringing into being a realization of that which is true love. True love does not discriminate. It is a unifier. Sit in silence, my friends, and open yourself to the energy that flows from love itself, through you and back again, out into the creation. As you do this, the experience itself will begin to show you why it is that we suggest that you do it. We can only suggest that you give it a try.

You are seeking, my friends, you may not know what—but you know already that what you are seeking is not found in what you can see and hear with your physical instruments of perception. You know that there is something more, and we say to you that something more is not far away, but is within each individual that you meet. It is the enhancement that gives you joy in seeing each creation of the Father. Seek it in meditation, and you will see it all around you, every day. Love is with us. It may not be in the world, my friends, but you can bring it into the world, through your own eyes, and although you cannot heal the whole world, those you touch will be aided. For you are the world. For all things are one. And as you aid yourself in understanding, you have done more to help the world as it is than anything else you might do.

Indeed, you can go forth from your understanding of love, and effect changes in the physical, as you are guided to do by your own intuition. And these things are very well. Yet the basic change in your heart that gives you joy and life and love to give to others, this, my friends, is your greatest contribution.

I will open the meeting for questions, but first, I would like to conclude this message through another channel. I will transfer at this time. I am known to you as Hatonn.

(B channeling)

I am Hatonn. I am now with this instrument. My friends, but a few more words. We have spoken much of this energy called love this evening. Now, my friends, this energy is available to all who have but to ask. For, my friends, this energy is a gift from the Creator. It is of your free will to administer this energy through your daily existence. For, my friends, you may deny yourself of this great *(inaudible)* when we speak of this. Earlier we mentioned that love is all there is. My friends, if love is truly all there is, does it not sound reasonable that all that you will experience will be of the happiest vibration, constantly? My friends, this is how you were conceived. This is how it is hoped that you will return. My friends, if you look upon your own existence as a truly individual universe, you come in contact with many universes throughout your existence. Do not deny yourself the opportunity of further growth by denying yourself to look only at the love and light of each universe. For, my friends, we have evolved much, but still we must strive for only that of love. For, my friends, this energy truly exists forever and there is apparently no end to its knowledge. So, my friends, one way which you may acquire and hasten a, shall we say, attunement is through help to others. My friends, that is one of the reasons that we are with you this evening. Before opening this meeting to any questions, I will transfer this contact. It is a great honor *(inaudible)*.

(Don channeling)

(Inaudible) I am here. I am known to you as Hatonn. It is now possible to answer any questions.

H: Hatonn, can you tell me if it was your craft that was seen yesterday evening by myself and others and, possibly, what your purpose was?

I am going to use control in order to answer your question, as it is a difficult one. I was aware of your presence at a specific time. I was aware of your question at that time. I am sorry that it is impossible to specifically say what you saw. You did not see one of our craft. You saw a projection which was meant to stimulate your thinking. This projection is used in many cases. It was of a nature that would be called unreal, or an image. However, it was intended for the purpose of stimulating, as I have said, those who saw it at that particular time. I am sorry that I cannot at this time give you more information.

H: Thank you.

M: Hatonn, is the antichrist born?

There is no such concept. All of this created universe in its infinite sense is one thing. The concept of an antichrist, as it is generated by the thought of those upon your planet, is erroneous. The individual whom your peoples might call the antichrist is, in fact, the Creator, as are you and all of your peoples. To view an individual otherwise is an error in basic analysis of our universe. If this is understood in totality by the peoples of your planet, there will then be eliminated all of their problems, including the problem of the concept of what you call the antichrist.

Is this a sufficient answer?

M: Will you give the purpose of the literature relating to the antichrist in the Book of Revelation?

The Book of Revelations, in what you know as your *Holy Bible*, is stated, as are all of your intellectual communications, in a clouded or misinterpreted form. The concept of antichrist is simply the concept of individualization of thought, the concept of isolation from the Whole. It has been stated in a previous communications, "The spirit of antichrist is ever more powerful, and will be drawn closer and closer to the Earth, where it will have its final death throes. And in those death throes it will take many down with it, and they will not find the kingdom to be inherited, but must repeat over again that great cycle of time which is now culminating in the scene upon the Earth."

This, my friends, is nothing more than a parable, indicating that those who separate themselves in consciousness will find it more difficult, shall we say, to link their path back to the unity and oneness which is their actual reality.

Is this sufficient?

M: Yes, thank you.

Don: I have a question to ask through another channel.

(H channeling)

I am with this instrument.

Don: I have asked the question.

I am Hatonn. One moment.

(Pause while conditioning.)

We shall attempt through this instrument to do our best. We of the Confederation have chosen a vast amount of time ago a certain, shall we say, procedure which we follow in bringing about the awareness of not only our existence but the existence of the creative energies and of the Creator. We have chosen to utilize certain individuals, and many of these individuals are alien, shall we say, to the Earth plane of existence.

In this present time—which we find and which we stress to be of great importance to all of mankind, for it is the culmination of a cycle of experience—we have directed in great, shall we say, numbers individuals who have chosen to cooperate and to serve with us, and we have placed to the best of our ability the knowledge for bringing about the fulfillment of those agreements, shall we say. And it is each individual's opportunity and obligation to bring about a utilization of their knowledge toward that which they feel directed to do. It is difficult even for the most enlightened of your beings to continually operate, shall we say, harmoniously, when constantly bombarded by experiences of an alien or negative nature upon the Earth plane of existence. Yet if it were not for these experiences, the confusions brought about from them, and the delays—and we wish to stress, only the delay of those agreements or directions is brought about—know one thing: that which you have chosen to do shall be accomplished.

That which you desire to experienced shall be experienced, and that which you are, you are to know. You must only filter through those circumstances about you which are not harmonious to the fulfillment of your direction. What you search for may be seen through your perception in a form which is truly not proper, though it may appear to fit; it may appear to be that for which you had asked. It is only sent to tantalize you, shall we say, to test you, to see if you shall commit yourself completely under all circumstances through all trials to the fulfillment of your directions.

Faith, faith in the Creator, belief in your purpose, and continual attempt to fulfill that purpose is what is required, and patience to await its materialization is of the utmost necessity, once properly positioned within your being, these concepts, then the more expedient, the materialization of that direction and purpose. It is yours to do what you have been told you shall do. It is yours to find the proper method of bringing it into being. And it is yours to be the instrument of truths if you desire to be.

This has been somewhat difficult for this instrument, yet we truly feel we have covered the basic concept that has been desired.

Don: You'd better give it another shot—that wasn't the answer to my question. I'll try to get more clear on the question.

(Pause)

Carla: Why don't you just ask it out loud?

Don: Because I want to do it this way.

… It is … shall we say, most difficult, as you know … and the other instruments have been, shall we say, shaken. This type of experiment has been successfully achieved previously, as you are aware. And we, due to the experience of this instrument, shall attempt once again through the instrument known as Carla, if she is willing to make this attempt.

(Carla channeling)

I am Hatonn. The one known as Carla, shall we say, is scared to death, but is willing to attempt it. If she will relax. We are with this instrument. If she will refrain from analyzing what she is getting.

The Creator has shown us many things. He has not shown us ways and means of doing that which we must do. Those things are up to us. He has not shown the Earth or any other entity within creation the rhythm and tempo of its doings, for all things are free to form their own destinies.

Therefore, we cannot know the geography in time, shall we say, of those things which shall occur. Our best predictions are a function of probability curves which become more accurate as that geographical location in time draws near, at which time the prediction becomes reality upon your Earth plane. The information concerning various, as you would call it, anomalistic phenomena is a kind of aggregate which is, in general, as correct as we can make it. The probabilities are very high, on the order of, shall we say, 50 to 70 percent, that many of those disruptions of the normal magnetic rhythm of your planet will indeed take place.

The reaction of your Earth peoples to these happenings is not known at this time. Therefore, our reactions to their reactions are not known at this time. Again, we have probabilities. That, my friends, is a completely open ball game, as you would say. Your people are not predictable. We are hoping that many, many seeds which have been planted will come to fruition when people begin to view the devastation in their own geographical location. We are hoping at that point that communications with those people will be such easier. For those who know that we have spoken to the subject will be interested as to what else we have to say,

Picture a rose, as it grows on the bush. The day of its opening is not known; only its shape when it does open.

Are there any other questions?

Don: High probability points in the very near future, a few months?

There is a high probability, my friends, in that which you know as California. There are high probability points in your southern oceans. We are sorry that this instrument is very weak in geography. We are …

(Pause)

Carla: Don, I think it's Texas. Either Texas or … I don't know what else is down there, but it's in there.

We are sorry. This instrument is unable to fully understand what we are saying. There will be a great amount of suffering, yet as you all know, you may ameliorate the situation by sending light. If you will remember to do this, as this instrument would say, every little bit helps. Do not think that you are not helping, for physical suffering may be necessary, yet light will enable these souls to leave the physical to find their spirit home very quickly.

There is devastation on the coast of your European continent and again we are having great difficulty in pinpointing the location. This difficulty will be felt over a wide area.

Don: About how long from now?

We are seeing this occurring into the fall, as it grows towards the month of October.

Don: How about California?

This is very close.

Don: Closer than the other?

Much closer.

Don: That was the question, specifically. Thank you.

Are there other questions? Or may we aid further in any way with that question?

H: Yeah, I'd like to know where I got my answer.

There are many questions which dwell within those realms of mind which are below the level of the intellect. Many times these questions are deeper and more important than the question which is upon the conscious mind. You were answering a question, yet it was not the question that was intended by the requester. Yet it was a question which the one known as Don had within his being, and with which he is dealing at the present time. It is important for all of us to understand, my friends, we as well as you, that those things which we speak with to ourselves are not always to the point, but that in our progression, that which is below the level of words is a very important part of our, shall we say, baggage, that which we carry with us. Compassion and understanding of ourselves on the level below words, and the compassion and understanding of others as they deal with these things which they cannot speak of is very important in your understanding of love.

Don: I have one more question.

Very well.

Don: With respect to north or south, can you specify what portion of California would be high probability?

My friends, we cannot at this time. There is a great deal of effort being made by those within your plane and those within what you would call your spirit world to alleviate those stresses all through that which you know as the San Andreas fault. The fault extends in a very stressed manner for many hundreds of miles through the continent and out to sea. Therefore, we do not know at what point the damage will finally originate. We only know that as the rhythm of the planet is going, the critical time is very, very soon. It honestly could not be predicted at this point. However, if you asked at a time closer, it may be more possible to pinpoint.

Don: How close?

We suggest that you ask week by week. It will not be long.

Don: Thank you.

You must realize there is great danger in asking for specific information, for in specific information there dwells a great deal of nervousness on the part of the channel. Therefore, that vibration makes them more vulnerable to incorrect information.

Don: That is why I asked telepathically.

We understand. However, now that, shall we say, the secret is out, it may be more difficult to get our answers, as opposed to other beings who would, shall we say, play with your mind, if you understand what we mean.

Don: I certainly do.

My friends, are there any other questions?

M: Could you tell us what silver flecks are?

If you promise not to laugh, my friends! The silver flecks are a type of very small machine. We would not call them computers, but you would. They are communication devices.

M: Thank you.

We must add that, many times, that which you think to be a silver fleck is, in fact, a silver fleck. We advise you to examine any such thing that you may find under a magnifying glass, for the naturally earth-made item which is, this instrument calls it tinsel …

Don: What will be the shape of your silver fleck?

It will have a squareness or some form of geometrical shape. There are various types. They are easily recognizable in contrast to everyday tinsel, as you would call it. If you will take any of each type and look at it closely, you can see the difference. The factor of what this instrument would call shininess is also different.

M: How do you plant them?

We cannot tell you. In your words, they simply would appear.

My friends, this has been a very long meeting and we are very grateful to you for giving us the opportunity to speak with your group. We welcome those who are new to this group and greet them each with special love. We give you, as we give all who listen to us, our love and the love of the Creator, and our hope that you will call upon us and our energy at any time that you wish it. We are always aware of those who wish to contact us. If you do not wish us, my friends, we will never be there, for your free will is more important to us than any single consideration that we might have. We wish only to help you if you ask us.

We ask you to consider our words, not as truth, but as an interesting thought to be considered by your discriminating mind. We are in no way infallible or perfect; we are as you, foolish beings attempting to learn, striving to be a little better than we were yesterday. We are a little ahead of you on the path of evolution, and we reach a hand very gladly to give you a pull up. It's a long path, my friends, but we have found great joy in it, and we know that it is there for you also. I am Hatonn. I leave you in the love and the light of the infinite Creator. Adonai, my friends. Farewell and peace. ✤

Sunday Meeting
August 29, 1976

(H channeling)

I am Hatonn. I greet you, my friends, in the love and the light of our infinite Creator. We wish to greet those who are new to this experience, and to you we shall direct some information which will assist you in understanding this experience.

We refer to ourselves as a Confederation of Planets in Service to the Infinite Creator. We are, as you would term it, a vast number of persons who have joined together in one mind with one desire and that is to assist in the evolution, or shall we say, in the growth process of those people of your planet and many such planets as what you inhabit. It is our desire to assist you by sharing with you those knowledeges and understandings which we have achieved through our own experiences.

It is not our desire that you take what you receive from us and clutch it as being the truth and all of the truth. We only request that you simply listen and evaluate as you would wish to do so. And once you have evaluated the information, do with it as you please.

We are aware that at the present time upon your planet, many changes are occurring, not only upon the physical level with which you are so concerned, but upon those spiritual levels of consciousness and of the understanding of man. As your people go throughout their daily experiences, they encounter many circumstances through which they are given the opportunity to apply their knowledge, their understanding and their wisdoms. Through the application of these, they can overcome those circumstances which would be, shall we say, detrimental if misunderstood.

Man must learn all that he can in the time that he has, for this is his purpose for being here at this time. The purpose for the existence of all things is the unfoldment of consciousness, or to simply state, it is for the experience of love. My friends, as you are well aware, throughout your life love is a continually growing and learning process. If you allow yourself to become stagnant in that which you have discovered, you shall find yourself becoming, shall we say, eventually ill at ease with your position. So allow yourself to be continually seeking greater and greater portions of the immeasurable love which is available to you. Seek this through all of your actions, through all your thoughts. Allow this to be your goal.

My friends, all of us, working together, can overcome any difficulties which you can imagine. It is within your ability, and it is your birthright, to manifest and to control all that you experience. It is stated within your holy book that man was made unto the image and likeness of his Creator. And if you accept this as the truth, as indeed it is, this means that you, too, my friends, are that Creator. A likeness is a repetition, or a duplication. You are that: you are the extension of the Creator, individually expressed, yet universally united. From that source you have been projected, yet there is a cord, if you wish to call it that, that shall extend forever, that shall never be broken, and through that cord flows the knowledge and the being of your Creator. It comes directly to you and is lodged within you, and you, my friends, may tap the knowledge of the universe and of the Creator by going within yourself and meeting with the divinity within you. "Know thyself," has also been stated within your holy book. My friends, this does not mean that you must know the intellect, which many of yourselves consider yourselves to be. It does not mean that you know that which you refer to as the ego. It means that you know the I AM, or the God, or the Creator within you. For that you truly are, my friends. You are united and inseparable from your Creator. No matter how hard you would choose to try, you can never be out of His presence.

We of the Confederation wish to bring to man the simple knowledge, and through the application of this knowledge we hope to assist you in bringing about that which you have so long desired, a planet of a Utopian experience, one of harmony, one of unification, one of brotherhood, one unto the other serving each other and recognizing that as you serve one another, you serve your Creator's purpose, for His purpose is the expression of love, and what greater form can it take than serving those around you? Certainly you may realize that there are those that do not desire your service at the present time. Yet, my friends, the service that you can render unto those people from purely a conscious basis, without expression or action to that individual, is immense. Silently offer those who would not request your service, your love, your light, and your understanding, for they are receptive to your thoughts, whether they recognize them at the time or not. You have planted the seed of knowledge and of love within that individual. And thus, you have served him.

Service, my friends, can be done in many forms, and each individual shall seek out that service in which they know they are to function. And it is a truth that once you have, shall we say, found what you are to do, from within you, you shall know this to be, and you shall not stray. Though we are all one together within the Creator, we have chosen to express certain portions of the universal being. And without the expression of each and every portion, that being would be incomplete, and therefore, wherever one person chooses to be, you must accept their choice. Allow them the freedom to be placed within that position. Allow them the freedom to function. Allow them the freedom of being, perfection and the expression which the Creator desires [for] them and they desire to be. I shall transfer this communication. I am Hatonn.

(Carla channeling)

I am with this instrument. And I greet each of you again in love and light. As we say to you, my friends, that each of you needs to be a source of light to those around you, you must understand that we are encouraging you not as your physical selves to draw upon your resources within this illusion. We are encouraging you as spiritual beings to open the channel between your finite self and the higher self which created you, love itself. No finite entity, neither yourselves nor we, your brothers, can love, nor can we call upon our resources to show love or understanding. For those symptoms, shall we say, are much like your physical movements on the physical plane: if you think and concentrate upon your movements in attempting to perform complex tasks, it is almost certain that you will stumble in what you need to do. For in your very thinking, you will have limited the instincts of your physical being. You will have circumvented the harmony which surrounds the physical plane if it is left to its own wisdom, and the result will be that you are not coordinated, for your intellect will have borne all the limitation of this illusion, and upset the harmony.

It is also true in the purely mental sphere. If you attempt too hard to organize and concentrate and analyze your thoughts, they will disintegrate into splinters which have very little meaning and which cannot be put back together into an integrated and harmonious whole. It is very difficult sometimes to make decisions, because you are thinking too hard. Most especially on the spiritual plane, if you attempt to draw love from your own being, you will almost immediately run into very deep trouble. As you manifest upon the physical plane, your very consciousness is a consciousness made of limitations. You see that your fingers end at the tip of your fingernails; you do not see that you are one with the air that surrounds them. From the very beginning you were taught that the thoughts which originate in your mind have been created only by you. You were not taught that thought comes from a beautiful, infinite mind, and that the thoughts that pass through you, although heavily, heavily diluted, are shades of that perfect thought.

Now, my friends, to show love is simply to act as a kind of open channel through which those healing waters of love can flow—through you, not from you, to all that you touch. And how to come in contact with the spring of those waters of love? It is for the reason of coming in contact with love that we so often urge you, my friends, to meditate. As we have said many times before, the Creator is everywhere that you may go. If you go down to the doors of what you call Hell, the Creator is there. There is no thing that you can do which the Creator is not your companion while doing. You cannot close your eyes, or your fingers, or your minds, and rid yourself of the Creator. Love is within you and all about you. If you do not recognize it, yet it is still there. It has been said in your holy works, "The light shined in the darkness, but the darkness comprehended it not." Yet, my friends, if you become still, and if you open your inner eye in the darkness, it is absolutely inevitable that you will see that light and feel that love.

May we say to some of you here, it is not at all important that you have any belief or faith. This means less than nothing. Know you only that as the sun shines from heaven, there is a power in the universe that gives life. No matter how much death that you see, you see many, many times over the life that is growing, triumphant always. Light and life will always triumph. They are always there. You do not need to be faithful or believing; you need only be quiet and listen. Do not expect to hear words or voices, for most do not. Yet take these periods of silence on a daily basis, and evaluate your life after having meditated for, shall we say, a period of two of your months. It will begin to be apparent to you that the listening is producing within your being something that you are hearing, something that is making your day-to-day existence more loving.

At this time, I would like to open the meeting to questions. If anyone has a question, please ask it now.

M: Can you get an exact time on the catastrophe in California?

We still feel that there is a critical time in the near future, and that it will be before winter.

M: Thank you.

Before we leave this instrument, we would like to go very slowly around the room and give each one of you our energy. If you would desire contact with us, we would wish to send you our love and our blessing. We will pause to do this.

(Pause)

I am Hatonn. We would like to close through the instrument known as B, if he would avail himself to us.

(Pause)

We are sorry for the delay, my friends. We are having difficulty in establishing contact, and so we close through this instrument. We ask that you imagine yourself standing in a field of flowers, with the light shining down upon you, the birds singing, the beautiful fragrance of the flowers all about you. You stand in the love of the Creator, my friends, and if you open the windows of your spirit, my friends, you offer the beacon of that light to all that you meet. It may not be in very dramatic ways, my friends, that you show this. It may be in a tiny little thing. Yet, in this, shall we say, schoolhouse that you call planet Earth, it is understanding the love that resides in everything we do that is the great lesson. Love is not anywhere else, love is here, in whatever situation you are, in whomever you meet, in all emotions and in all circumstances. See the love, my friends, see the creative power, see the healing. Meditate—and then open those eyes. There is great joy upon the path of all of you, and it is very close, always.

If at any time you need the assistance of the force of spiritual love that we represent, call upon us and we will be with you, for we hear at any time that you may call. It is our nature to hear not as a single person, but as millions of ears, for to us there is no space and no time, and we are here for the specific purpose of giving you our love. I leave you now, in the love and the light of the infinite Creator. I am known to you as Hatonn. Adonai, my friends. Adonai vasu borragus.

Sunday Meeting
September 5, 1976

(B channeling)

I am Hatonn. I am now with you. I greet you in the love and the light of our infinite Creator. I am Hatonn. My friends, as you know, we usually try to cover matters which are requested for the good of this group. My friends, there are many questions within your minds this evening and we will attempt to answer them, all we may.

We are aware of the new members to this group and we bid you welcome, for you are here seeking. For that is the reason we are all gathered.

As you spiral upward in your meditations, you are more and more aware of the truly infinite amount of knowledge which you must receive in order to obtain, shall we say, a mastery of your existence and all that surrounds you.

I am experiencing difficulty with this instrument and will attempt to return to this instrument at a later time. I am Hatonn.

(Carla channeling)

I am with this instrument and I greet you once again in love and light. As I was saying, my friends, to attain mastery on the physical planet a great deal—sometimes it may seem an infinite amount—of knowledge must be gained. It is, of course, an aspect of your physical illusion that it does seem as though a certain quantity of intellectual information will constitute the knowledge that you do need to attain understanding.

We speak to you tonight to attempt to correct this impression. Yes, my friends, you are on the path, but, my friends, you are the path. You are that which the Creator may flow through. It is written in your holy works that the one known as John the Baptist cried in the wilderness, "Make straight the way of the Lord." My friends, each of you *(inaudible)* of chaotic thoughts and actions and being, memories and hopes. And your one goal, to attain understanding, is to make a pathway, as straight way, for that Creator, love, to flow through. You will never organize that which you call your self, for your physical self is in itself and of itself an unruly thing. It was born and it will die and in your physical life you will adhere to this process, whether you wish to or not, for this is the correct nature of the physical being.

Yet within you, my friends, there is a pathway, and as you meditate, you may seek and find it, and open yourself to it, and lo, the crooked will become straight and the uncrossable mountains of your life will become as plains.

You see, my friends, in our approach to knowledge we assume that that which you are seeking, you are. For that which you may be seeking, though it may seem to be, as we said, an infinite amount of knowledge, it is in fact a truth of such total simplicity, that you, sitting there now, embody it totally. A truth so simple that many, many of your kind have missed it and will continue to miss it. This truth is that all things are one. That all is love. Its understanding is the straight way.

It also helps, my friends, as you attempt to bring the straight path into your daily experience, to realize that in truth you are not living in a universe which is composed of more than one thing, and that therefore there is no such thing as power. As you attempt to bring the straight way into your chaotic existence, you can easily perceive those things with which you are having trouble as being powers against you, or as having power against you, and you can see yourself as needing a power to overcome them.

But, my friends, nothing has power. For instance, my friends, you may think that in healings the spirit overcomes the power of disease, and yet, my friends, if there were a power to disease, then there would not be a possibility of its being healed. Yet sometimes disease has power and sometimes it does not. In truth, the consciousness of love is not power. It is simply the understanding that there to no power, but that all is one. Instead of reckoning from the standpoint of power against power, attempt to keep in your consciousness the truth that there is no power, that there is only love, so that you see those things that are difficult for you as a type of love which you may understand if you contemplate it, and which you can love in return. In this way, the currents of that creative love are set up. And since you do not recognize the illusory power of your difficulties, they do indeed begin to disperse, sometimes in very unexpected ways. Sometimes you find that a situation which you felt had power against you may well stay just as it was before, yet in your consciousness you now understand that there is no power in that situation, but only love. And this understanding transforms your experience. Many things occur by interpretation only, within your mind, so that if love can be applied and the idea of power removed, you can see your interpretation in a new light, and the problem disappears.

We know that you are all here seeking, seeking something that may be true, some one thing that you do not have to dismiss as being another part of a disappointing world. And we say to you, that which you seek, you already are. Be still, my friends, and begin to discover yourself. Be very, very still. There is music within you and around you. Your own physical vehicle makes patterns of energy, tiny sounds that blend harmoniously. Love is flowing between you and those about you. Within this room, all are one. Be very still, my friends. Imagine that at the very top of your heads there is an opening, and the hunger is being filled, the hunger for light, for love, for truth. This food of the spirit is pouring into you, and going from the top of your being, spreading through each iota, each atom of your physical being and of your spiritual being, and flowing out again into the room, so that you share with all those around you in a community of love and of light.

Do not forget, my friends, in the stillness, to let that light out again to all those troubled around you, in your nation, in your world. You are all one being, my friends. You are all brothers.

At this time we would like to attempt to say just a few words through the one known as M. If he is willing, we ask that he relax and allow us to speak our thoughts through him. I am Hatonn.

(Pause)

I am again with this instrument. We are very happy for the opportunity to attempt to contact the one known as M. It is of course sometimes difficult to relax enough to achieve a first contact, and we will attempt it again in the future. I would like to transfer now to the one known as B. I am Hatonn.

(B channeling)

I am Hatonn. I am with you again in the love and light of our infinite Creator. My friends, we have touched upon what is known to you as trouble. We wish to go into this in small detail. We feel there is much understanding to be learned from this concept. My friends, as you know, everything that happens around you is caused by your desires. As you might have noticed, everything that you have desired will eventually come to pass. For, my friends, your existence is based upon this reaction, and you in turn must learn to control it. My friends, you must understand that if you were immediately given everything you desired, it would not mean anything to you for very long, for, my friends, it has been proven many, many times that you shall, we may say, appreciate only that which you have worked for. For this reason, my friends, those types of learning such as trouble and sorrow have been placed upon your paths that you, my friends, might grab hold and place it back.

Now, my friends, you must understand that although we have said love is all there is, there is, indeed, much negativity within your existence. My friends, you will see it upon your whole path, for, my friends, it has been placed in front of you that you may help yourself or those about you by dealing with these lower energies. Now, my friends, we might add this note of advice: realize that all that has happened to you is placed upon your path so that you may learn. So we say, whenever you are confronted with any type of challenge you do not understand, think first, my friends, of what the reason might be for this obstacle, what you might learn from it. My friends, if you put these sorrows in their right perspective, you will find, even in the deepest pit, that there is indeed a light up above that you may climb to, and thus dwell within the love and light of our infinite Creator.

My friends, many entities such as yourselves have allowed themselves to become stagnant because they do not face their, shall we say, troubles and deal with them. My friends, we are indeed aware that this is much easier said than accomplished. But, my friends, you must attune yourself to this train of thought so that it becomes a, shall we say, automatic occurrence. There is much to be learned, my friends. And there are many who wish to be of help. As we are here, my friends, in order to help you, that we ourselves may evolve, this opportunity is also given to you, that you may evolve through the helping of other people. My friends, this help cannot be acquired for others until you yourself have dwelt within this light and love, that you may learn.

My friends, remember also that we are with you and await your request, that we may help at any time. It has indeed been a great honor to share with you in your meditation. And as I leave this instrument, my friends, we will pass among you that you may feel this great energy we call love. For, my friends, since love is all there is, there can be no sorrow. You yourself have put this name upon the experience you are passing through. If you will but look around you, you will see many, many things to, shall we say, remind you of love. We leave you now in the love and light of our infinite Creator. Adonai, my friends. Adonai vasu borragus. I am Hatonn.

(Carla channeling)

I am Laitos. I greet you in the love and the light of our infinite Creator. I wish to speak briefly with you, my friends, about the energy that we do send to you. Each of us in the Confederation of Planets in the Service of the Infinite Creator is here for one reason only, and that is to send you our love. We do this in many ways: we speak with you intellectually through channels, we send to your planet as a whole our vibrations of love, and to specific groups and individuals, when they request it, we send a type of energy which has sometimes been called the conditioning vibration or wave.

This conditioning is one of several types of carefully beamed vibratory energy which we can send. We prefer to send this type rather than the more physical types of energy which have been used for some channels, which involve actual physical control of instruments, because other types which involve control are somewhat uncomfortable and because we do not feel that it is as important to give you specific information as it is to give you total freedom as a channel to choose at any time that which you wish or do not wish to receive.

Our conditioning wave is a wave which is designed to enhance your own meditative spiritual wave. As we have told you many times, my friends, you are very much like a radio, in that your brain is capable of receiving and sending on various frequencies of electromagnetic vibrations. These frequencies vary from what would be called lower vibrations of energy to the higher, finer or more spiritual vibrations. We enhance the vibrations that are comfortably within the spiritual realm, so that you can pick up in a much stronger sense the spiritual thoughts that may be coming to you from various spiritual sources. We, of course, are not the only voices on that particular wave-length, as you might say. You yourself have a higher self which may wish to speak with you at any time, especially when you are in some doubt as to your course of action. It is difficult for a person to come in contact with his higher self in a conscious manner. The most common way for one to become aware of his own higher self is for one to dream, and then, upon awakening, interpret that dream. Many communications are had in this way. And yet, meditating, you tune into the spiritual source closest to you, which is your own higher self. You have guides, my friends, such as you would call angels, watching over you. This has been said in scripture and is indeed true. You have not ever been, and will never be alone. You truly have those who care for you on every plane of existence.

You may tune into the brothers on this same length. This is the vibration which we send to you. If you do not wish to become a channel, there are still many uses, as you see, to this vibration, and we send it very gladly. You need only request it mentally. If you receive the vibration and for some reason it is uncomfortable to you, request mentally or aloud that it be discontinued and it will immediately be discontinued, for that which you desire is above all things important to us.

We thank you for this opportunity to explain the energy which we send to you. It is the energy of love, and yet it is a tuned energy, and this we wish to make known to you. Before I leave, I would like to ask if there are any questions?

(Pause)

If there are no questions, I will leave you now. I wish you joy upon your path, my brothers, great joy. Love one another, my friends. I am Laitos. Adonai vasu.

Sunday Meeting
September 19, 1976

(H channeling)

I am Hatonn. Greetings, my friends, in the love and in the light of our infinite Creator. It is pleasing to be with you. And indeed, it is a benefit to us to be able to share with you the knowledge that we have acquired throughout our existence and through our experience.

We, of what has been referred to as the Confederation of Planets in Service to the Infinite Creator, have come to your planet, to this planet that you call Earth, to give unto those who would request our thoughts, or shall we say, guidance and inspiration. We wish only to share with you that which we have to offer upon the intellectual and spiritual realms. We wish not to interfere. Nor shall we under any circumstances force our communications or assistance upon any individual. For we are aware of certain laws which cannot be violated without retribution and one of those is to abide by and allow any individual to choose that which they wish to experience at any time. We simply allow those who would not wish to seek out any form of enlightenment to continue their growth processes. We send them our love that we interfere not with that which they desire to do. The reason we have come is to offer our assistance. And it is pleasing to us that you have chosen to listen.

We of the Confederation have been about your planet for what you would call centuries of time. We have provided intermediaries, you might say, who have come onto your plane of existence and acted as teachers among your peoples. Many of these teachers were greatly misunderstood, even that one with whom you are so familiar who bears the name of Jesus. He taught that you are also the children of the Father that sent him. He taught the concepts of oneness and equality of all beings. He demonstrated the abilities of the consciousness of that which you would call super-intellect, or consciousness. And as he did so he informed those about him that it was within their capabilities to do likewise. And this, my friends, is one of the greatest truths which was not comprehended and which has not been utilized or taught in the proper manner throughout the centuries that have passed since he was here.

We say to you that it is you, my friends, each one of you on an individual basis has within you the ability to achieve all that you would desire. You have within you the ability to create that which you desire to experience. You are an extension of that which we call the Creator. You are His thought patterns projected throughout the infinite universe. You cannot be separated from Him, nor can you be separated from one another. Yet, you have been given the opportunity to express that creating force through your personality and individuality upon this physical plane of existence, in order that you might come to the realization that, indeed, all things are divine and unified. As you travel in different directions as projections of His thoughts, you shall find that the directions begin to mingle and that your paths begin cross with those of other individuals with whom you feel a great closeness upon contact. My friends, this is nothing other than recognizing within them the true identity of yourself.

You of the planet Earth, as we of the Confederation, are constantly working together in bringing about the elevation of all creation. And upon your Earth sphere, man is now presented with the opportunity to bring into being the highest form of what you would call civilization ever known to your planet. For you are presently ending that which is called a cycle of time of existence. All things return from whence they have come. Thus we speak of cycles. Things flow around within the universe and yet, there are dimensions of physical planes of existence which overlap and which are not recognized by those within them. And thus you can transgress into a cycle of experience of time which you would consider to be of a more elevated nature.

As your planet completes its present cycle, it is presented with the opportunity to transmute its entire physical form and all things upon it into a higher vibratory field, or a higher cycle of existence. And we say, my friends, that indeed the planet will do so. For by the abuses placed upon it by its inhabitants, it has earned the right to this opportunity. And you, as an individual, must also earn that right to be transmuted with the sphere that you occupy.

And this is done through the processes of spiritual evolution of the raising of consciousness. It is your responsibility to yourself primarily, and through thyself to the Creator, to seek out that channel of experience which is most fitting to you and gain the knowledges and the wisdom and understanding that you require to bring about this progression. It is by your efforts that you evolve. Those who do not choose to go on with their, shall we say, paths shall receive the opportunity to repeat this cycle of experience. And they shall not be aware of what is transpiring. Yet those who seek out the truth, who seek out the Creator within them, shall be aware of all things. Seek and you shall find, as the Master has said. This is an irrefutable law. Ask and you shall receive that which you desire. But be careful for what you ask, for, my friends, your very thoughts are the creation of your experience. Those thoughts of a negative form which you may label them, my friends, they shall bring to you that experience. Perhaps cloaked so that you do not recognize it. So be careful, guard your thoughts. Learn to focus your energies in the proper directions. Learn to think in the proper manner. And learn, most importantly, to go within yourself and achieve the union which is of necessity with that portion of the Creator's consciousness that lies within your being.

You are the perfect manifestation of that which you have chosen to be. And you possess the power to function properly or improperly. It is your choice. It is your evolution. It is your experience. And it is yours to do with as you would choose. Consider these thoughts. Consider your present position. Consider what it is that you desire to do, and by all means set forth the energies and achieve them for it is your birthright to have that which you desire. I shall transfer this communication. I am Hatonn.

(Carla channeling)

I am now with this instrument. And I greet you once again in the love and light of our infinite Creator.

My friends, to accomplish that which you wish to do, to gravitate, shall we say, upward on the spiritual path, may seem many times to be a very great effort. And we say to you that your will and your desire and your efforts are all-important. We cannot repeat too often to you, for truly you will get what you desire. Therefore, desire carefully and constantly. We wish to assure you, however, that it is not expected or at all natural that the effort alone will give you wisdom. For mankind can work and work, but without the spirit, the soul that is within him, that is his higher self and that is the spark of the Creator, he will achieve nothing but weariness. And many who have beaten their heads against the wall seemingly hopelessly have become heartbroken and convinced that there is no Creator and that there is no reason for living and there is no hope beyond the present physical existence.

Effort is only the seed, my friends. The fruition comes in meditation. The fruition comes when, in your desire, you stop talking and begin listening. Truly, those upon your planet are understandably bad at listening for your physical ears are beset day and night by noise and more noise, and most of it not at all important, on any level. Therefore, in order to protect yourselves from this constant noise you yourselves are constantly thinking, constantly generating a defensive wall of selfhood. But, my friends, as long as you are thinking and talking you cannot contact that wisdom that is within you, that is sleeping. You may meditate for a long time before you feel consciously that you have contacted wisdom. You may meditate for a long time before you begin to feel warmed by the presence of love. That is how hard it is to open the door that those of your people who live in this civilization have begun to experience as closed. It is a thick door. Many of your peoples do not even believe that such a door exists and that beyond it there is a reality. So we say to you, seek, and then in your seeking, meditate.

The great secret to, shall we say, getting out of the rat race, is to realize that you and only you are responsible for yourself. Let us draw you a small picture, my friends. You are an entity that has lived forever and will live forever. You are whole and you have a form that has been building and shaping itself and you are a certain way and you think certain thoughts and you are dwelling in a tiny little ball that circles a sun in a very small corner of a totally infinite universe. And you are in a classroom that is much like a circus with many things to see and many things to behold, and you are observing and you are attempting to learn. People may have attempted to tell you that this is a perfect world and that all things are of love. And you have said, "How can that be? There are horrible things in this world and they are not of love." Both are true, my friends. Your illusion is made up of many vices, some of which are so strongly on the negative side that in them exists the thought forms of what you call Satan. You know and you have felt horror and despair at the more negative of those things that those upon your planet do to others and to themselves.

This is your classroom, my friends. And we say to you that the energy that created all of these wrong thoughts was originally love. And those who were conceived in love by their free will have chosen to separate themselves into thoughts that are not of love, but are dark shadows across the face of love. But you are there, my friends, and you are to learn. See yourselves as the generators of your own destiny. If you will see your life as a work of art, you may think that life is something that happens to you, that you are the recipient of various good and bad things, but this is not so, my friends. And when you begin to take new responsibility for the way you act, no matter what happens to you, for what you are putting out, when your emotions and your words and your gestures and your actions begin to form a harvest of that which you are learning in your meditation and in your reading, then you have made the great step, my friends.

Then you may begin to become more confident of graduating from this school, of getting out of this rat race, as you would call it. When you leave your physical form, as you all will, and when you look back, you will see this life that you have lived just as you would see a work of art. And you will see whether you have written badly or well. It matters not if you make mistakes; you can but learn. And each attempt to show what you have learned will sound a chord within your lifestream that is very sweet.

The days may seem to move very slowly and many hours may seem to go on forever when you feel as if you are under fire by a hostile world. But your life is short, my friends. You are standing on a ball and you are learning. Connect with that source of love, a source which is rich in humor, a source in which you can relax and trust that there is no power on Earth, no matter how dark or dangerous it may seem to your physical eyes, that is as great as love. Your body may die and evil forces may cause you harm, but the harm is illusory. For that which you give from your inner spirit is the only reality for you. And no power can aggregate that of love within your spirit.

I would like to open the meeting to questions at this point. Are there any questions at this time?

(Pause)

I am aware of questions in the air and I would say that there is no situation in which there is not freedom. That which is bound by the Earth is only bound in illusion. That which differentiates man from the consciousness of the trees and plants and animals is his imagination. I would say never consider yourself bound, for your imagination will take you away. You must have confidence in your own ability, in your own work. You can break the bonds on any prison, not by actions where actions would be a stumbling block to others, but in your mind. Make the place for yourself that you desire in your mind and go there.

I would close through another instrument. I will leave this instrument.

(B channeling)

I am now with this instrument. I am Hatonn. I again greet you in the love and in the light of our infinite Creator.

I would give you but a few more minutes, my friends, but I feel the need to go into a bit more detail on what we have mentioned as your path. We have mentioned before there is an energy within your experience which is known as negativity. My friends, as we often said, there is no energy stronger than the energy radiating from love. Now, my friends, you may not understand the meaning of what we have mentioned as your path. My friends, as there are many, many of you upon your planet, it has been designed, my friends, by our Creator that there is yet that many paths that may bring you to an understanding of a more spiritual existence.

Now, my friends, again as I have already mentioned, it is truly a blessing from our Creator that He has bestowed us all with that which you may call free will. Now, my friends, before you can start upon your path, you must first understand what type of path you may embark upon. My friends, as your seeking has brought you here this evening it will bring you many places that you may experience what, shall we say, you may wish to. I would say in your every deed, my friends, look for the energy of love. Surround yourself in this energy, my friends, and you will find that an energy as strong as this may repel any negativity that may wish to cross in front of you.

Now, my friends, as you continue upon your path you will find many lessons. These lessons, my friends, have many times been referred to as troubles or problems. My friends, when you are met with such a situation, may we suggest that you go within. Question yourself as to what you may learn and why you are experiencing it. Now, my friends, you understand that it is very easy to speak these words. But yet it is a totally different experience when trying to act it out. But, my friends, upon initiating yourself upon this path you will find that there are many, many there to help you but they may not help you without your desire.

It has been an extremely great honor my friends, to share with you in your meditations. If you will linger but a minute, if you will linger but a moment, it has been requested that you may feel our presence. Relax, my friends, and I will leave you. I am Hatonn. I leave you in the love and the light of our infinite Creator. Adonai. Adonai vasu borragus. ♣

Sunday Meeting
September 26, 1976

(Carla channeling)

I am Hatonn, and I greet you in the love and the light of the infinite Creator. It is a great privilege to be with you and I greet each of you. We offer you our love. What we offer you, my friends, O men of Earth, what we offer you is more precious than any treasure you can imagine. And yet we mourn that so few know of the treasure of love. O men of Earth, we speak to you now in sorrow, that so many of your peoples value only those things which cost what you would call money. O men of Earth, you spend your time seeking after so many things that do not advance you on your spiritual path. How long will you sleep?

We speak to you in this manner, my friends, for we know that you, too, spend time in mourning over that soul within you that cannot be given its place in your own universe. We know that you, too, mourn for your planet. But your planet, my friends, shall we say, in general is in a very difficult position at this time, for the desire and the thought of those upon your planet have caused the situations to arise in which war and the government which provokes war seem to be a totally unchangeable set of parameters, out of which there is no way whatsoever.

Yes, O man of Earth, we do mourn with you. But, my friends—and this is what we are here to tell you—if you know who you are, at all, you can begin at this moment, at any moment, to seek out the miracle which that which you would call Christ-consciousness may do for you. It is true, my friends, you cannot save your planet. In general, the thinking has been aligned in an incorrect manner and many, many upon your planet will not achieve enough understanding of love to go on, but will have to repeat this cyclical experience.

But you, my friends, each of you, if you know at all who you are, you know that the miracle is very near, is close, and can be right now. In your holy works, it was reported many times that the one known as Jesus performed miracles. He opened ears that could not hear and allowed the blind to see. And yet, how many of you, my friends, suffer in a spiritual manner from stopped ears and blind eyes and closed hearts? Have you gone through this day in some degree unhappy? Frowning? Struggling? Then you have need of a miracle, my friends, and the miracle is very close.

What we are saying to you is simply that you can, at any time, make a change in your consciousness, not by yourself, but by what you would call the grace of the spirit of love. We have said to you so often to meditate and we say it once again. Not only is it difficult to live with a consciousness that is unhappy, irritable, frowning or afraid, lonely, in other difficulties—not only is it uncomfortable for you, but also your higher self mourns and this seeps into your consciousness, and you feel sad for your own difficulties.

Now, this moment, my friends, take your birthright! No man need change. The saints were only conscious of the reality of love. That human personality will continue on, with your encouragement or without. Yet if you seek love, by grace you shall find it. I will transfer at this time. I am Hatonn.

(H channeling)

I am Hatonn. I am now with this instrument. When we speak of the reality of that which you call love, we speak of a universal concept. We speak of a concept with which all things have been created. We speak of a concept which contains all things that you experience. And man of Earth looks about him, and he sees about him that which is disagreeable to what he would desire. And he labels it, what you would call, to be bad or negative.

Yet in essence, my friends, that too is the love of which we speak. For in order to look upon any situation, any experience, or to receive any knowledge, and to have the ability to accept or reject through your own analysis that situation, is truly a gift of love from the Creator. And in order to properly do so, it is necessary that you [have] the balance of the concept of love. For each and every experience there is that which is what you would call the opposite, and through the knowledge of each, you then have the experience of being able to bring into balance both positive and negative aspects in your learning process. Without the knowledge of each, it would be of greater difficulty, or shall we say, even impossible for you to proceed upon your path of truth and enlightenment. For, my friends, without all things that exist within the universe, our creation would be incomplete, and so would our experience.

And indeed, though it be infinite, my friends, our experiences are complete. They are complete, insomuch as they are the manifestation of the concept of love, brought forth through the Creator and His gift of creation to us.

Love, my friends, to those who truly understand, is the tool by which they create. It is the tool or the law by which they live. It is the words they speak and the thoughts that they project. Love, my friends, is that which the Creator is and always shall be. In order that you may come into a clearer understanding of this concept, it is not only necessary, as we speak, for your daily meditation, it is also necessary that you go through the experiences and lessons of your life, and that you meet that which is placed before you, whatever it may be, as a stepping stone upon which you must tread—lightly, regularly and knowledgeably. Meet that which is placed in front of you. Do within that circumstance the best that you know how. Love the experience entirely, whether it be painful or pleasurable. For, my friends, in all things there are lessons that you must learn in order to progress. And placed before you in life there is nothing of coincidence. There is only that which is intended to be learned.

There was one upon your planet with whom you are familiar, whom many call Master. And, my friends, that name can be yours. That concept that he represented, of love, can be yours. Learn to meet head-on all things in the light of love and you shall learn to master all of your emotions and thoughts, and you shall learn to generate within you a brightly luminous flame from the spark of divinity that is within you. Radiate from within the love that you learn, the love that you are, and the love that you know you shall be. For love is ever-growing and never-ending. Love never is depleted nor divided. From within you comes all things, all things that you desire. For indeed, that love within you is the creative force within the universe. You are an extension of the creation, you are the creation, and you are the Creator. You are the light. You are the way, the knowledge, wisdom and truth. You are in the Creator as He is in you, and though you do not understand it through the utilization of your intellect, in true essence you are all things.

I shall once again transfer this contact. I am Hatonn.

(Carla channeling)

I am again with this instrument. I will open the meeting now to questions, but before I do, my friends, I would answer a question which is on the minds of several, including this instrument. We are aware that some of you question how we can communicate through instruments when there are members of the group who are sleeping[1]. Very quickly, we can speak to any group of people in

---

[1] A member of the group had fallen asleep early in the meeting and was breathing heavily.

which there are people who are resting, in which there are infants who are resting. Our difficulties in speaking to groups come only when there is a person within that group, of any age, who desires not to hear what we have to say. If there is one such person, then we cannot speak.

Of course, my friends, it is not necessary that a person be fervent and faithful before hearing us. It is only necessary that he be open to hearing our words.

Are there any questions?

Questioner: Can we receive personal guidance from you when we are alone? Can you direct us in our actions?

We, as the brothers of Hatonn, will not direct or give advice at any time. However, at any time that you desire our aid, we will send to you a vibration or wave which is sometimes called the conditioning wave. This is, shall we say, a general all-purpose spiritual frequency. As we become more familiar with you, we will tune it to your own need. It is designed to intensify your own vibrational pathway to your higher self, which dwells within the Creator. This higher self, which is the Creator within you, may then speak to you, and it is the higher self which most certainly will direct and guide and give and enrich your spirit. We are only instruments, shall we say, shepherds. We can offer you the waters of wisdom and in telling you to meditate, we point out the location of the stream whence that water flows. But you, and only you, may drink and be refreshed.

Therefore, seek us, indeed, in meditation, and we will endeavor to aid you. But never in any way will we advise you. This is the prerogative only of your higher self.

Does this answer your question?

Questioner: *(Inaudible).*

Is there a further question?

M: Can meditation provide technical insights?

Each upon your planet has access to an infinite amount of knowledge. Each, through his various experiences previous to this one, is peculiarly suited to receiving certain types of information. The answer, in general, is "yes." Any type of information that is desired may be obtained. However, the knowledge of your deepest, shall we say, talents will guide you to seek that type of information that you are most well suited to receive. You may think of the repository of information as part of an infinite mind, to which you have access through meditation.

If you are seeking specific information, seek in the name of the Father, as you call Him, and seek to do service by this information. Then, become very aware of those daydreams and dreams within sleep that you may have, for the channels through which information flows from the infinite mind, through the subconscious, as you would call it, to the conscious mind, are quite often the intuitional daydream and the visionary dream. Does this answer your question?

M: Yes. Thank you.

Is there a further question?

(Pause)

We would say one more thing, and that is: to be healed of any disease or any pain, it may be necessary to understand that there is no power, none whatsoever. The Creator is not a power, for if there were one power, there could be others. The Creator is all things, in infinite quantity. It is the realization of the fact that disease of any type has no power that allows harmony to reassert itself. The basic force in the universe, if you wish to call it that, is love, and it has an infinite amount of energy, at all time, automatically attempting to adjust all things to harmony. You may see this as the power of good, and yet we say to you, it is not power: it is all that there is. In a universe that seems many times to be pulling apart, and falling into disorder, it may seem that disorder is a power, yet on the inner planes, become conscious that all that there is is the Creator. And give the disease to this "power," if you would call it that, and the healing will take place. Lift yourself off of this Earthly plane, my friends. In your mind, rise far beyond your dreams and schemes and troubles. The infinite universe, with infinite worlds and planes, awaits your consciousness.

We leave you in that consciousness, in that harmony, in love and in light. I am Hatonn. Adonai, my friends. Adonai.

Sunday Meeting
October 3, 1976

(Carla channeling)

I am Hatonn. I greet each of you in the love and the light of the infinite Creator, Whose name is great in the heavens and Whose names shall be great upon your Earth. It is our privilege, as always, to speak with each of you and we are very grateful to be a part of your meditation. We send you our love and we send you our thoughts.

Our message to you has always been simple, and yet because, my friends, your spirits are encased in flesh, our message is never understood in a simple manner, for it filters into your ears in such a way that the simplicity is lost. We tell you that all things are love, that you are love, and that your entire existence is a process whereby your whole purpose is to become aware of your true nature; that is, to become aware of the oneness of all things and of the nature of that one thing as love. It is a simple message.

Yet it is only truly simple if you are not encumbered, shall we say, by that which you call flesh, or that which you call the physical plane. It is said in your holy works that you were created a little lower than the angels. And yet, my friends, this is so, this is your particular place in the order of things. Below you is the rest of the natural creation that you can see, animals and plants as you call them, their consciousness being totally within that which you call the physical plane. They are contented and very aware within that plane, and because they are not distracted by dreams and abstractions, they are more aware within that plane than are you.

Those beings that you call angels, and we ourselves, no longer encased in physical bodies, need no longer be distracted or amazed or delighted with the various experiences of your flesh, and before us always, clear enough that we can always see it, is the Father's wish for us, so that we at all times do not have to choose between right and wrong, as you do, for always before us we see the will of the Father, because that which you would call "thought" and "wish" is visible to us, and nothing is hidden. You have a difficult way to go, my brothers. You are neither flesh nor spirit, but you are both, and it is your particular task to learn how to let your spirit rule your flesh. It is necessary for you to choose, with both choices available, before you go on into the sphere where you are spirit alone. For the Father gives free will to His children, and each of us chose at one time whether we wished to go on into the realms of spirit.

If we moved into the realms of spirit before we had chosen to leave behind both the troubles and the glory of the physical plane, then our free will would have been taken from us. This is the reason, my friends, of all of the difficulties and pleasures of the physical plane. They are there for you to enjoy and to learn from. They are there for you to be able to make a choice between seeing the world as if you were an animal, knowing only those things which you could see and feel, and seeing the world as spirits, so that all things have a religious or spiritual significance.

And so there is a choice that you make, in action and in words, which is based on your desire to seek the Creator and to be of help to all your brothers. Now the message does not seem simple any more, does it? Now it seems to become complicated, as you would call it, a metaphysical task in which all of your thoughts have to be hauled out into the open, and you must judge each of your thoughts, and you must judge each day, and it begins to seem like more trouble than it's worth!

Let us go back to the simplicity of our original statement: all things are one. All things are love. To try to describe in your daily life, so that you can see the connection between your life and love—that becomes complicated, and so we tell you to meditate, to find the simplicity within the complication. We are aware of your conversation, and we wish to say that a statement that was made is indeed true, and that statement was that you are here for one purpose only, and that is to gain knowledge, to gain understanding. This is not a selfish purpose. This is not an egoistic search. This is, indeed, your whole reason for being here. You did not create yourself in the human sense. The Creator that created you desired that each one of His children learn, of his own free will, to love Him and to [serve] each of his brothers. As each of you goes about your daily existence, the very nature within you cries out for learning and for understanding. This is your birthright, and far from being selfish, it is the whole purpose of your existence. Anything you may do for others must first spring from your understanding of yourself.

We especially wish to say to you this evening that it is very important that each of you has or begins to cultivate a feeling of confidence and faith in himself. In your holy works it has been written that there was once a father with two sons. And one son was, as you might say, "no good." The other son was excellent in every respect and stayed by his father, always working, always loyal. After many years, that son that was no good came back, and the father was incredibly happy. It is called the story of the prodigal son.

Each of you, we know, is in some ways a prodigal son, and it is written in your holy works, and you may trust that, that the Father is extremely glad to see you coming home. Each of you is a treasure beyond words to the Father. Love abides for you and in you from the Father. No one and no error can take away the fact that you are the son of the Father, and all that He has is yours.

Therefore, in all that you do, cultivate confidence in your own basic nature, for out of confidence may spring a far different degree of ability to express those things which you may know to be correct to do. Confidence causes you to relax and enjoy yourself, and we say to you that if you are enjoying yourself, then you are on the right track. The spiritual path is a narrow one, and there are many trials, but there is abundant help, for the love of the Creator is always with you. And He can lift you over the rough spots, and pick you up when you fall, bring you back when you stray.

We are high above your dwelling at this time, approximately eight miles, and the situation is slightly unusual in that we are speaking to you, shall we say, in person. Sometimes we speak to you through what you would call machines, but we happen to be able to speak to you personally this evening and we especially wish to give our love to you. Our people send our love to you always, as one being.

We will pause for a time, while our brother Laitos sends energy to you, if you will relax and open yourself to it.

(Pause)

I am again with this instrument, and I greet you once again. At this time, I would like to ask if there are any questions?

B1: Will it be possible to see you in the future?

I am unable to say. We would like to show ourselves to you, even at this time, yet because of the vibration within your particular area, it is not possible at this moment. It was more possible for us to show ourselves to you when your meetings were in a more rural atmosphere, and we could appear without violating the free will of others. However, we will see.

B1: The vibration's been getting stronger in this area?

It is somewhat difficult to explain through this instrument, for she does not fully understand the concept that we are giving her, but let us say that there are people within this particular area that are able to see within the sphere in which we would show ourselves to you, yet who do not wish to see us. Often we are able to show ourselves to those who wish to see us, and remain invisible to those who would not wish to see us. However, there are people who have enriched their ability to see into higher planes, yet who have, shall we say, forced this growth without an accompanying understanding, and they do not wish to see us. Therefore, we are in a peculiar position. It is possible that, at some time in the future, the situation will not occur. It is somewhat unusual.

Is there another question?

(Pause)

We would answer a question within the mind of the one known as G. The so-called conditioning wave, as we send it to you, is not physical in nature, although it is of an electromagnetic nature. The vibrations are such that it would not register on any of your instruments. Therefore, many of those upon your planet do not feel this energy as it reaches them, due to the fact that their receivers, shall we say, are overstimulated by more physical stimuli, such as some of your drinks such as what this instrument would call caffeine-flavored, or by smoking, or by medication, or by constant noise, or by any of the other distractions that may occur within the physical that blunt the finer senses. Those who feel this energy often have a natural talent, which is possible, just as there are natural talents for physical exercise or for music or for painting, or they have developed the ability to sense energy through a certain period of meditation. There are some people who can never physically sense the energy, although almost each person who attempts to sense it will ultimately be able to physically feel the manifestation.

In no case does this mean that the energy is not being received. Since this energy is an intensification of your own spiritual vibration, it is simply an aid to your own meditative link with the Creator. Therefore, if you do not feel that which is the conditioning wave, yet it is still working for you, shall we say, and we encourage each of you to go ahead with meditation in any way that you feel comfortable, for truly it is not for, shall we say, the show of it that we are here, but simply to help you. And those students who are distracted by various, shall we say, physical manifestations of the spiritual must simply remember that it is the underlying spiritual value of a manifestation that is important, not the manifestation itself.

I would like to attempt to transfer to the one known as B2 to close the message, if he will make himself available to our contact. I am Hatonn.

(B2 channeling)

I am Hatonn. I shall attempt a communication through this instrument *(inaudible)*. We shall go slowly with this instrument, for we feel the need, shall we say, of precaution with this particular instrument at this time. We attempted earlier to contact this instrument *(inaudible)* conditioning was apparently too *(inaudible)* one *(inaudible)* as it is in all creation *(inaudible)* of love.

(Pause)

Be patient, we shall *(inaudible)*.

(Pause)

The instrument is weak and wishes to discontinue. We leave you in the love and the light of our infinite Creator.

(Carla channeling)

I am Nona, and I greet you in love and light. My friends, I come to you on the wings of the wind that whistles through the empty space, through the countless, countless miles, as you would call them, in the universe. I come to tell you simply that the universe is a place of great wonders, infinite splendor, and it is yours to explore. Our brothers—what a wonderful, beautiful place we dwell in. All that you can imagine, you can see; the farthest reaches of your thought are places you can go. Each morning that you awaken, a wonder awaits you, if you have but the eyes to see. It has been said many times, but we say it to you, it may rain, but, my brothers, look for the rainbow, for it is truly a beautiful, beautiful universe, and the rainbows are everywhere. I send love to each of you and peace. I am Nona. Adonai vasu borragus.

Sunday Meeting
October 10, 1976

(H channeling)

[I am Hatonn.] …you have many times heard me speak. You have many times understood. Yet there have been many messages which contain great value which you have not completely comprehended. And we have given to you the clue, time and time again.

The clue, my friends, is understanding of meditation. Meditation, and the knowledge that you receive, shall be clear and unmistakable. For we can say to you, in order to penetrate that which you call your intellect we can only achieve a portion of true understanding through the intellectual processes.

You, as brothers and sisters on the planet Earth, have an obligation to one another, and that is to love one another. And you may ask, "How is it that I am able to learn to love those who would not return that love?" It is, my friends, to be known that love is something that is contained within you, in infinite abundance, and it is replenished and multiplied by sharing with others that love that is within you. Love is not of a selfish nature. Love possesses nothing. Love asks nothing in return. Love is a state of, shall we say, consciousness which is pure and unaffected by its surroundings. Once you truly understand this, then you can truly begin to know the concept of love.

You on the planet Earth have come here for this purpose: to learn, to understand the concept of what we call love. You have been given the opportunity to grow, one with the other, and you have been given the opportunity to share, one with the other, your experiences and your knowledge. As you are aware, you face a period of time in which, shall we say, your growing processes shall be speeded up. The love which you have come to realize shall now be put to the test. You, as the instrument of the infinite Creator, are to love all things constantly and infinitely. You are not to ask for the return of that love. You are to go into those situations that influence you in the world that you are in, knowing that you shall come forth after the completion of that experience still loving those with whom you have learned and experienced with.

In your life cycle you shall know many whom it shall be difficult to love. But, my friends, if you are truly to know the entire content of this concept, then it is necessary to have these experiences, for it is easy to love those who would return that love, yet it is difficult to love those who return what you would call hate.

My friends, you must realize that the love that you give shall indeed be returned. It may not come quickly, yet a portion of love, with what you call patience, will come. Be patient and you shall receive that which you have earned through your right actions, through your sharing of love. Turn to one another. Do what you can to help each other. Know that you are perfect; know that you are love. And be the exemplification of the love that you desire to receive.

For, my friends, in this universe like objects attract one another, and for you to receive the love that you desire, it is necessary that you be that love, without fault. For if your love is faulty, so shall be that love that you receive. You are the creator of your experiences. This we have stated many times. It is time that you understood the creation in which you have placed yourselves.

Guard your thoughts, my friends. Purify your thinking processes. For your thoughts are your creations, and with them you must live. And if you desire to live in a constant environment which is agreeable to you, then so must be your love. It is possible for you to achieve, and it is your birthright. You are here to learn these things. You are here to receive what you learn, and, my friends, in this lifetime you can [learn] all that you desire. Discipline yourselves. Be the masters of your environment. Receive the assistance that is being given to you, and place not barriers about you—barriers of doubt, barriers of confusion. Know that you are protected by the infinite Creator's love *(inaudible)*. Know it without doubt. Know that you shall achieve your desire. And in truly knowing these things, they shall be done.

I shall transfer this communication. I am Hatonn.

(Pause)

(H channeling)

I am once again with this instrument. We are attempting to communicate with the instrument known as B, yet there is some difficulty in that the instrument is analyzing his reception. I would once again attempt, if he would please refrain. I am Hatonn.

(B channeling)

I am Hatonn. I am now with this instrument. Again I greet you in the love and the light of our infinite Creator.

My friends, we have been together for a period of time in which we have attempted to make understood to you many new concepts. Now, on your plane, you may attempt to go to what is known as a school so that you may develop much knowledge in the hope that you may someday acquire enough of this that you may teach others.

My friends, the time flies by, to even a quicker pace. You have learned much. Now, my friends, I do not say that you have learned so much. But it is now your place to go among your people and to teach. For, my friends, many things are understood by you which cannot be put in proper phrase. As you sit and meditate, you feel this energy called love, but yet you cannot properly define it. I grant, as yourself, that it has taken us, upon many journeys, to learn the truth we have now developed.

My friends, as always, we are at your disposal, and will help you in any way you would request of us. We remind you again, my friends, that when you leave this room, you will attempt to keep this energy vibration which you now experience at a high level throughout your day. As I have said earlier, like entities attract each other. You will find this very valuable in acquiring new information that you will need. I leave this instrument now. I am the one known to you as Hatonn. Adonai, my friends. Adonai vasu borragus. ☥

L/L Research

Friday Meeting
October 15, 1976

(Carla channeling)

I am Hatonn, and I greet you in the love and the light of our infinite Creator. I am the voice of one who is with you always. As I and my brothers are very grateful for the opportunity to speak with you and to share your meditation, I especially greet each of those who are new to our thoughts. It is a great pleasure to be with you, and we hope we can be of help.

We of the Confederation of Planets in the Service of the Infinite Creator are here with you at this time to share with the people of your planet a very simple thought, a very simple concept. That concept is love. We have been here before, and we are here now, to share this concept with you.

And yet, we have had our difficulties with your peoples. For the concept, my friends, is too simple. Love, among your peoples, has become very complicated, very devious. Yet the very essence of love as we share it with you is that all things are one, that you and I are one, and that you and your brother are one. In love you were created, and your original vibration is pure and identical to the original vibration of all that is around you. And as you share this original vibration, your brotherhood becomes apparent.

This, my friends, is the way it should be, yet it is not the way your planet is functioning at this time. This you already know, but we touch on it because it is the heart of why we are here. We feel that those to whom we speak at this time know this already, and that each of you is already seeking through his life to better this understanding. My friends, we know that that path is steep and rocky, and we ask that you take confidence in your path. Take heart in your mission to be of service and to give light, for this is truly the one thing that is of importance, and you are not incorrect in attempting to direct your lives in this seeking.

We share with you the thought that through others you may see the Creator, and others may see the Creator through you. Yet of yourselves, you cannot give or receive the love of the Creator. It is only through the consciousness of the Creator Itself that you and your brother are one. Of yourself, you cannot do what you wish to do. You cannot depend upon your own resources. Yet you have infinity behind you, the storehouse of talents and power and ability so great that you can never exhaust it. Your cup may always run over with all that you need, if you can but remember whence love comes.

Love does not come from others, nor can you call it from within your own heart. The Creator that is within you, and that exists as your heart and soul, is your link to total and infinite love. Never depend upon yourself. Never shame yourself if you have been inadequate. Know only that you simply failed to ask the Creator, and next time, remember. In this way, you may meet each situation in life as a rich man who has so many assets that he cannot count them. In this quiet confidence, many, many things can be met with love and with graciousness, whereas if you were to analyze the situation in terms of your own abilities, you would say, "I cannot handle this situation," and, feeling poor in spirit, the situation would overcome you. This is never necessary, for you have all that you need from the Father. Just remember that He gives you what you need, and seek the connection with Him.

It has been written in your holy works, "I have meat that ye know not of." This was said by the master known as Jesus. And he was speaking of that connection with the infinite storehouse of the Father. Those upon your planet have put value on things that can be measured, and one is considered a rich man if one has a certain measurable amount of certain measurable items. Yet all of these things that can be measured will also rust and spoil and die. And so will your physical body. So seek, each day that you can possibly find the time, for that link between yourself and the fount of all love, and at this fount, refreshed in yourself, you may always be a blessing to others, as you wish to be.

At this time, we would like to pause in order for our brother Laitos. We will return to this instrument. I am Hatonn.

(Pause)

I am Laitos. I am with this instrument, and I greet each of you in the love and the light of the One Who is All. It is my special privilege to work with channels, as you call them, and as we have several new people here, I would like to share with each of you that which we call the conditioning wave. It is a type of energy which enhances your own spiritual vibration, so that you may the better have contact with your own spiritual sources, as well as with our thoughts, if you wish them. I would like to pause at this time and move among you and give each of you a feeling of our presence at this time.

(Pause)

I am again with this instrument. Before I leave, I would especially like to contact the one known as G. If she would relax and make herself available to our thoughts, we would like to say only a very few words through her, in order to let her know what our contact is like. We are always pleased to have potential instruments for our thoughts, for there are times when information may be needed, and our ability to speak through those who wish to be of help to others is most appreciated. I will at this time attempt to speak just a few words through the one known as G. I am Laitos.

(Pause)

I am again with this instrument. We are having a slight problem due to the fact that the instrument is not aware of how similar our thoughts are to hers. The impression that we give to an instrument is simply a thought. It is generated by us rather than the instrument, but it will not continue unless the instrument speaks it. If the one known as G will simply speak what comes into her mind, then we can speak through her. We prefer not to use the stronger conditioning wave, where there is a physical ray, for this causes physical discomfort and tension within the instrument. We prefer the more conscious and free communication of this time. We will again attempt to communicate through the one known as G. I am Laitos.

(G channeling)

All is calm. *(Inaudible)* You are kind. Thank you. We are here, we are with you *(inaudible)*. We are here.

(Carla channeling)

I am again with this instrument. We wish to give great thanks to the one known as G. We are so very pleased to speak through her. We felt that we needed to leave a little energy within the instrument known as G, for the first few times an instrument is used, it is quite a strain. But we are so happy, and we greet the new instrument with much appreciation. There will be time in the future when the flock will need its shepherds. And we are grateful to those who wish to serve in this way.

My brothers and my sisters, there is so much joy, even within the darkness that often shrouds your planet in its vibrational pattern. You can find the joy every day. We rejoice with you in all that you do, for it all is an emanation of love, and the laughter of those who understand rings throughout the universe. Do not forget to meditate, my brothers, we are always with you if you wish it, though we will never be with you if you do not. The free will of each of you is of utmost importance to us, but we are here at any time.

I leave you in love and light. I am Laitos.

(Carla channeling)

Greetings, my friends. I am Hatonn. And before I close, I would like to open the meeting to questions. Are there any questions at this time?

P: How long have you been here?

We have been coming here for thousands of your years. We have never been totally gone from your plane of existence since your history has begun to be written. But we have been here much more in force, as you would call it, much more *(inaudible)* of our craft are with you now than at any time in your history of several thousand years. At that time, there was also a situation where your peoples were at the end of what we would call a cycle of time in which spiritual learning was supposed to be completed. At that time and at this time, there was a large failure of those upon your planet to complete the lessons in time. And most of those at this time had to repeat their experiences here before they could go on. Unfortunately, many of those that repeated are not yet certain of what they have learned, and are just upon the verge between graduating and having to repeat again. Yet, this time it is more serious, for it is not only a minor cycle but a major cycle that is ending, so that the repetition this time is more of an investment for your spirit.

L: I would like to know the difference between a channel from your own higher consciousness channeling those thoughts that come from your higher consciousness and the different personality that that seems to be—the difference between channeling that and the brothers.

In one way, there is no difference at all. Those who are used to thinking in terms of space and time find it very difficult to understand that there is no space, but only vibration. The vibration in which we exist and the vibration of your higher self is one. We speak to you, and your higher self speaks to you, from a vibration which you would call a spiritual one. Our information is not ours, as such, for we are acting as conscious instruments of the Creator. We and your higher self are both imperfect. We do not pretend, nor would your higher self, to know the total truth. Yet our understanding has the benefit of more experience than your consciousness. Therefore, the contact is a valuable one.

In truth, we have come to your planet not because the information is not available to each upon your planet from your higher self, but because many of those upon your planet do not have contact with the higher self or even know of its existence. Yet many, especially within the, shall we say, society of science, are more open to the words of one who is in a so-called flying saucer than one who is in a spiritual realm of your own planet and dwells always with you. There are those, who cannot conceive of such a thing as an angel, who can fully conceive of an extraterrestrial being. We are taking advantage of this, shall we say, edge to get the information to the peoples of your planet. It is the same information. If there were any difference, one of us would be, to that extent, incorrect. You will find any spiritual source as being of the ring of truth in equal measure with other spiritual sources. Beware of those special sources which deny the correctness of other sources, or say that they are more correct.

Does this answer your question?

L: Yes, thank you.

Is there another question?

L: I would like to know if there is a correlation between the Confederation and … I know there is correlation between the Confederation and the spiritual … but I would like to have that explained a little bit more—between spiritual experiences through this past age which people have had. What is the correlation? Have I made that clear?

Not to the channel.

L: Spiritual experiences that have been gone through by, for instance, saints. Is this the same kind of communication, and in the same service? Do you understand what I am saying?

We understand what you are saying, although the instrument is not quite clear. We will be able to speak through her.

The creation, as we have said, is a vibrational, shall we say, vortex. The original Thought in all perfection has been prismed like a lens might spread light, so that the infinitude of various colors of existence, as it were, are possible. Those who have mystical insight are beginning to be able to play upon that prism, and move from one, as you would call it, reality to another. Those of us who, in this manner which we enjoy, travel through time and space, have learned to play upon that prism with some exactitude. Very few of those upon your plane have become able to travel as we; yet spontaneously, many of those who spend time cultivating the art of meditation have become able to spontaneously slip into a more satisfactory reality for gaining knowledge of the spiritual.

Those whom you call saints have frequently been able to make contact with their guides. Each of you has guides. As it is written in your holy works, each of you has angels that guard you lest your foot stumble. We are not angels, although it has been said laughingly, and in some cases not so laughingly, that we are angels. We simply are not of your planet, and your angels, as you would call then, are. Yet we are beings, and so are those guides whom your saints have seen.

When those upon your planet have seen the Creator, they have moved to a level which is of a finer vibration than the one which we enjoy. We too have our visions of the Creator, and we know, beyond a shadow of a doubt, that there are levels which we have not yet been able to attain. As far as we know, the path of knowledge goes on forever.

L: Thank you very much.

Thank you, for allowing us to share with you. Never thank us, for it is our dearest wish to be able to be with you and help those of your people who wish it in any way that we can. Is there another question?

Don: What about the California earthquake?

We have been waiting for that one! This instrument is in good shape, so we will go ahead [with] the answer.

My brothers, California is doing very well. There has been a great deal of light. We are very gratified by the fact that people have been paying attention to what we have been saying, and to what various other sources have been saying. There has been prayer on the level at which this planet has not seen prayer for some time. These forces have enabled this so-called disaster to be temporarily allayed. We have a probability curve for California now that looks better for perhaps the next eight months. There will be an eventual happening, but each, as you would say, ounce of prayer, of light, which is sent to them enables the difficulty to be ameliorated and delayed just that much more, while those souls who will be affected have that extra time to prepare themselves for that which is to come. We are not speaking of physical preparation. We are speaking of spiritual preparation. At this time we are looking at probabilities an the order of 80 per cent—which is fairly good news—that the area along that fault in California will remain stable except for tremors until early summer of '77.

Don: Okay. What about the proposed contact in a more general way?

We are not able to give through this information, but we can give her the name, Philadelphia. The probabilities on this have not changed appreciably. We will probably not be able to do it as early as summer of '77, but that is our first target date. We feel that we will be able to do a scattered bit of advertising in November and early December, but it will not be on the scale at all of which next summer would be.

Don: What form would this advertising take?

We are hoping to be able to have physical sightings paired with our effect upon your communications, and in one or two cases we are contemplating, shall we say, playing around with your power sources. We wish to emphasize that unless we have a majority of those people in any particular area that desire to see us, we will be unable to have a general display, which makes it quite unlikely that we can succeed.

Don: In Philadelphia?

Shall we say, we have a good market there. There are other locations. We were even contemplating Washington, DC. We have—the closest thing we can give to the instrument is a picture of a weather satellite on your TV program. There are areas of light that show up as we scan your globe. They shift, my friends, yet it is surprising, in your terms, where these areas of light show up. Some places you might think were very *(inaudible)* have enough polarity to be negative, that the light is somewhat canceled out. Your Washington, DC, interestingly enough, is one of your more spiritually aware areas. One would think that all of your politicians would make the area very black, but most politicians feel strongly enough that what they are doing is incorrect that they spend more time contemplating their Creator.

Don: Tell me [about] any other areas.

There are parts of many states which do not have city-names. You are dwelling within one such area. The western and central southern part of Florida is of a good vibration, and in your mountain areas, there is much lights. Where you would call Seattle area, and east and south from there is of light. There is much light in some parts of your central country, and it is very spotty.

P: Why have the only places you've named been in this country? Will you only be contacting this country or will you be contacting other …

This is worldwide. We have difficulty with this channel because this channel is very ignorant of geography. When we show the picture to her of light areas in other continents, she does not recognize them. We have attempted several times to give through her worldwide information, and she simply cannot communicate what we are giving. We will have worldwide, shall we say, ambitions in this direction, and whatever effects we will have will no doubt be scattered, as you may understand that there are some areas which are more receptive to us than others. We expect to, for instance, have some success in Australia. Rather than the whole world, we can say area by area the probability is higher or lower.

P: *(Paraphrased)* Do you have the power to move things on Earth physically through your mind?

There is a distinction which must be made between what we can do and what we will do. Not we, but we as a spiritual entity, understanding the power of the Creator. Yes, we could ameliorate the conditions completely, just as we, for instance, parted the Red Sea. Yet we have learned through experience that we must not tamper with those things which those upon your planet have brought upon themselves for their own learning. The free will of those upon your planet to experience those things which they desire, even if it be their physical death, is more valuable to them and to us than our desire to see them escape these physical difficulties. Moreover, we may say to you, you have the power through mind alone to cause that fault to disappear. If those upon your planet could only think as one, as it is written in your holy books, you too could move mountains. It is simply that those upon your planet do not know the power of the soul. We suggest that when you are concerned, in all confidence send to the object of your concern the love and the light of the Creator.

B: What, if anything, will happen to the East coast from Virginia on up? In the near future?

We have explained before, but not to you, that we have a difficulty with time. Our probabilities are as waves, the most near in time is a ripple very marked and clear in its outline, yet the ripple in the future is less clear and less easy to pin down as to location in time.

(Side one of tape ends.)

(Don is asking about why so many contactees report medical examinations.)

Don: … Why are they interested in the species? Just for an academic interest in the species?

No, this particular group is interested for a more personal reason. They feel an interest in some of the resources of this planet. They are not of a negative nature, but their interest is more acquisitive than scholarly, shall we say.

Don: You say acquisitive? Acquisitive?

That is correct.

Don: What do they want? Why?

We are attempting to speak through this channel. It is such a different type of concept that we are having difficulty.

Don: Take a crack at it.

We wish to condition the instrument for a moment.

(Pause)

Within your physical plane, within the globe which you call the Earth, there are assets which you have no need of which those of other technologies can use. That is why we say that these people, though they are acquisitive, are not destructive to you.

Don: Why are they examining the people that they take on board? What are the examinations for?

They wish to understand how we function.

Don: Are they third or fourth density?

They are fourth density. Now, you do have a very few third density beings visiting, but this is a far more scattered occurrence.

Don: Is the—do you know of any particular third-density vehicle that has been made known through our research?

Those that visited Hickson were third density. In South America—we cannot give it through this instrument, it is not in her mind—

Don: Villas-Boas?

This is correct—was third density. You do have your occasional, shall we say, weekend campers.

Don: What about the military police vehicle? Was that third or fourth density?

Third density.

Don: Betty and Barney Hill?

Fourth density.

Don: Walton?

Fourth density.

Don: Sgt. Moody?

Those two were fourth density beings. By far, the majority are fourth density.

Don: Van Tassel?

Van Tassel was visited by those of the Confederation which are not precisely fourth density. You must realize that as, shall we say, with your spies, many times we have a cover story which is acceptable to the hearer. This particular contact was one of the experiments which we tried which convinced us that hothead methods will not work.

Don: Will the Integratron work?

If we ever went ahead with it, yes. However—

Don: Was it the hotheads that gave it to Van Tassel?

That is correct. We simply found that we are no better than our instruments. You see, that is the secret. That is what we find so difficult to remember when we wish to give the gift of happiness and love, peace and brotherhood. We forget that we have no right to impress even the most beautiful of gifts upon people.

Don: Is the taking on board for a physical examination—would you consider that an infringement on free will?

We would.

Don: And the fourth density beings that are doing this are not aware of, shall we say, the infringement?

Many of your scientists know of the infringement of free will upon animals and yet they, in order to gain valuable information, cause this infringement upon these animals. It is in this spirit of a small sacrifice for a great deal of knowledge that this is being done.

Don: Will these exams have the objective of ultimately helping our species or the persons examining them?

This is correct. Not the person in particular but the species.

Don: Can you give me an idea what they're trying to gain from the examination?

If they were to tune to our atmosphere in such a way as to extract that which they need from our Earthly sphere, the vibration involved would need to be tailored to the exact make-up of our species, speaking as you. They are therefore measuring the parameters of function in what you would call your organs, and in your being, in order to discover how best to effect this transfer in such a way as to be of benefit to those of Earth while extracting from the Earth the commodity which they desire.

Don: Now, they want to do what to be of benefit to Earthman? Through the knowledge of the tuning of his organs?

They do not actually wish to be of benefit. They simply wish not to be of harm.

Don: And the harm could take place because of the close proximity of their operations?

This is correct.

Don: Would these operations be visible?

No.

Don: But, yet we could be harmed?

This is correct. Vibration would harm.

Don: And then they are planning possibly to make these invisible landings for their own purposes?

Yes.

Don: Do they need something from this planet?

In a way, I suppose all of us who are in your skies need something from your planet. But what they need is more of a physical or Earthly plane than what we need.

Don: What will they use this commodity for?

Power.

Don: What type of power? For their craft?

Yes.

Don: In other words—

Also, my friends, we are attempting to give this through the instrument, but it is different and therefore difficult—as you would take a vitamin pill, sometimes those of other atmospheres find need which they cannot fill, especially in their travels, and within your Earth there are, shall we say, cosmic vitamins which, in the body of the fourth density, are most helpful.

Don: In other word they want to be in close proximity to our surface or on it for refueling purposes in their travels?

Of ship and self, yes.

Don: And in order not to cause damage to the physical vehicles of those upon the surface, they are measuring the precise vibrations of the internal organs. Is this correct?

You have it.

Don: This, then, has [no] real function with your primary objective?

That is correct. We have not encouraged them, yet we have not banned them from this plane, for we do not see enough of a negative effect upon those of your planet to ourselves infringe upon the free will of them.

Don: Do you find it possibly a help in advertising?

We have been rather amused, you might say, at the aid it has been. However, it has played greatly into our hands, you may have noticed, by increasing the confusion factor, shall we say. This is most welcome.

Don: And you then—well, do you anticipate stepping up your advertising by a major percentage in the next year or two?

We have great hopes in this direction. Probabilities increase from 5 percent at this time to approximately 30 percent in the summer of '77.

Don: What about '78?

Our probabilities begin to fade, and we cannot give accurate determinations. If we are as successful as we have been to this point, the probabilities will go up. We are hoping that they will go up very steeply. We are hoping that the probabilities will exceed 50 percent in time for us to give information to those upon your planet before too much of the change of a natural kind has taken place, so that your population may have time for some spiritual preparation. More accurate than that we cannot be without guessing.

Does this answer your question?

Don: Well—I guess this is a long enough session, unless somebody else has a question.

The instrument is somewhat fatigued at this point, so we are just as happy to close the session. We would like to leave you with the feeling that we are with you, that the Creator speaks through us, through you, and through all. Look into your brother's eyes, my friends. He is the Creator. Listen to the voice within you, for it is the Creator. I leave you in the love and the light of our infinite Creator. I am Hatonn. Adonai vasu borragus. ✤

Sunday Meeting
October 17, 1976

(Carla channeling)

I am Oxal. I greet each of you in the love and the light of our infinite Creator. We of the Brotherhood are, as always, most privileged to be with you. The Confederation of Planets in the Service of the Infinite Creator is indeed a brotherhood, my friends, and our purpose is one: to share with you our understanding of love. We are of one purpose, although we are quite different, one from the other.

But we have learned, my friends, in our travels what brotherhood is. If we could share with the peoples of your planet this understanding, those troubles which each of you has with your brothers would be no more.

We ourselves know that we are not perfect beings, and that we cannot judge or be judged by any of our brothers. There is no way, my brothers, of judging yourself or others in a spiritual manner. You can never know precisely how you are doing along the spiritual path, for those things which signify to your eyes as being one way or the other, good or evil, positive or negative, may in the eyes of the Creator signify something quite different.

It is a difficult thing to give up, that judging of yourself and of others. It is a difficult thing to love yourself and others in a totally trusting way. Yet this is precisely the key to understanding. If we could offer you this understanding of yourself as a being who is capable of many, many imperfect acts, yet whose heart is perfect, then we would have succeeded in a great thing.

For you see, my brothers, brotherhood is only possible to be unified with your brothers through the Creator. You will never be one with your brothers on the level of man to man, or man to woman, for imperfections breed discontent, and misunderstandings always occur. Yet, by the grace of the Creator within you and within your brother, there is a link so strong and so perfect that it can make the most opposite and diverse personalities one. It can cause the most unsympathetic situation to come into harmony. And this transformation occurs when a brother stops seeking a brother in love, and seeks only to rejoice in the Creator who is in his brother, be he a friend or a foe.

There is such a confusion among your peoples, such a terrible, noisy confusion, in which you speak incessantly of right and wrong, in which your peoples judge and accept judgments and spend endless, endless time in discussion. Yet harmony will never come on that level; right and wrong will never be discovered on that level. From the smallest relationship to the greatest of your nations' relationships, brotherhood can never be achieved by reason, but only, as you would call it, by prayer and meditation.

People are not alike, yet love has created them all. And the Creator within them is lovable, is love itself, and can speak to you of love in the face of the most inharmonious aspect on the outer plane. The spiritual path is not an easy one. You have known this, my friends, for some time. And when we say to you that our message is simple, we do not for a moment think that it is a simple thing to put into action. It has been written in your holy works that the master who teaches the consciousness of Christ brought not peace, but a sword. And this is the sword we ask you to accept in your lives, the sword of not judging, the sword of even willing to be foolish in another's eyes. For when one does not judge, when one is willing to trust to the Creator, those around that person may think of him as foolish. Moreover, there is a great satisfaction on the love of a personality in, shall we say, vengeance or getting even. But what you are doing, my friends, when you answer those who judge you with an answering judgment, is collecting your karma, as you would call it, there on the spot. Yet your karma to them has not been collected, and you will answer for that karma. Far better that you allow the karma that has come to you to die, as you forgive, and in that forgiveness, the karma that is reflected from you is satisfied.

Whatever one has done to you, let it end there, my brothers. Brotherhood is never an equal partnership, for each brother will give more than half; so it will seem to him, for this is the way of learning. You *are* your brother. Do not think of equality; think of *(inaudible)* finding more room in your heart for forgiving and understanding and compassion. You are not doing this for another. You are doing this for your brother, who is you.

I am Oxal. I would like to speak through another instrument at this time.

(H channeling)

I am Oxal. I am now with this instrument. We speak often of brotherhoods and of love. We speak often of many things, yet it is most often that we speak of the need for personal, shall we say, progression through the proper utilization of your experiences, and through the advocations towards your meditations. It is for you to realize that you progress not only for yourself but for the benefit of the universe, for the fulfillment of the Creator's will. For as you have learned, and as we speak of it, all things are indeed one with each other, and one cell, shall we say, cannot live without reflecting that growth upon the others. The universe is forever expanding, and it becomes more illumined, as do you. You, my friends, are the reflectors of the light of the Creator, and as your capacity for reflection becomes greater, that reflection of light throughout the universe is enhanced, in order that it may spread to the farthest reaches in order that it may be shared by your brothers.

You are the mirror of truth and of light. Each individual must take upon himself the responsibilities of what you would call light, and that is to progress spiritually, and to allow the love to take form within you, and to be shared with those around you. It is your responsibility to refrain from those avenues of expression which will be negative, not only to yourself but to those around you. You should not indulge in mental, shall we say, activities that are harmful to you or your brother: activity such as judgment, activity such as possessing, or limiting in any way the thoughts or actions of another.

My friends, you are unlimited beings, and you lead an unlimited experience. You may accept upon yourself those limitations by which you unconsciously desire to learn, yet when you are done with them, you shall release them and realize the capacity within you to create and to become equal, or shall we say, become aware of your equality with all mankind, and all things within the universe. What you do unto yourself is not only done to you, but it is done to all around you. The Creator finds no separation between you and your brother, for your energy fields coincide and enmesh together to present a group energy field that reflects the light and the wisdom that is contained within it. Self-motivation upon your path of evolution is important. It cannot be for yourself that you desire to progress, or for your fellow man. It should be for the benefit of the Creator and all of the Creation, knowing that you are a portion, that you are important, and that you are capable of assisting [in] bringing about the love and the light in greater clarity throughout the universe.

You are instruments in many, many ways and you can choose what forms of instrumentality you desire to use. Yet know that what you choose to do to be perfected, and that in order to perfect it you must allow it to flow freely from the Creator. Do not block your instrumentality through lack of faith in

His ability to work through you and His willingness to perfect you. Fear not, my friends, for fear is the creator of that experience. Lack of fear brings about harmony in experience. Experience *(inaudible)*. The fear that we find in your people reflects about them, and draws to them what it is that they fear.

This, my friends, is one reason that we must communicate with you in this manner, for we are feared by your peoples and our presence would heighten those fears. And this is not our desire. We are servants unto ourselves and unto you, our brothers, and above all things are servants in the name of the Creator. When it is made known to us that we can dwell among you in harmony and be accepted as your brethren, we shall remain, serving in what ways that we can, and bringing forth to you, the people of Earth, our knowledge and our light. Call upon us when you will, for whatever assistance that you need, and we will provide that assistance which is of the will of the Creator. Ask nothing in your prayers, either of us or of the Creator, that is of a selfish nature. Ask to be guided as a servant and all that you need shall be provided. Seek not spiritual awareness, but a demonstration of truth; seek that spiritual awareness in order to become truth. In order [for] you [to] receive the right to demonstrate to and share with others the truth that you are, you must first become that truth and understanding, and merge entirely with it into the universal aspect of light. You must be one with the Creator, for He is the truth, and through Him, you shall reflect that truth to others.

You are not alone, my friends. You stand with the Creator and your fellow man upon the brink of a civilization which is to be brought about in your actions, a civilization in which man may draw close to one another in the ways which have been intended: in harmony and in service to one another and in tune with your Creator.

We of the Confederation give you our thanks for accepting us into your consciousness. We assure you that we shall only endeavor to do that which we feel to be of the greatest benefit to your peoples. It has been our privilege to be with you this evening, and we look forward once again to meeting with you. Yet know that we shall always be with you, within your heart. Call upon love, and we are there. In the love and the light of our infinite Creator, we leave you at this time. I am known as Oxal. Adonai vasu borragus.

(Carla channeling)

I am Laitos, and I greet you in the love and the light of the infinite Creator. It is our special privilege to work with conditioning rays in attempting to condition new instruments, and at this time, if you would be patient with us, we would like to attempt to work with the one known as B. If he would relax, we would attempt to send him a very few simple thoughts. If he will relax, and attempt to speak our thoughts as we give them to him, without analyzing them, it would be our privilege to make contact with him. I am Laitos.

(Pause)

I am again with this instrument. We are having some difficulty making contact with the one known as B, due to a very common type of difficulty with this type of communication …

(Inaudible section.)

… again, without hesitation. In this way, the flow of our thoughts will be uninterrupted. We would like to attempt once again to speak just a very few words through the one known as B. I am Laitos.

(Pause)

(Carla channeling)

I am again with this instrument. We thank the one known as B for the opportunity to condition him, and we assure him that contact will take place. It is only a matter of becoming familiar with our technique of voicing our thoughts. If you will bear with us, we will also attempt to condition and contact the one known as P. Again we say relax, and open yourself to our thoughts. As you receive a thought, simply speak it out, without regard to what you may think of it, for in this way, we can speak through you, and in no other, without using a more physical type of ray than the one we prefer to use. We wish to speak only a very few words through the one known as Paula, if she will relax and make herself available. I am Laitos.

(Pause)

(Carla channeling)

I am again with this instrument. As this instrument would say, while we are at it, we would like to condition the one known as G. We are aware that at this time he is not desirous of becoming, shall we say, a vocal channel, for he is still attempting to reassure himself as to our presence. Therefore, we will simply attempt to give him energy in such a way that he may be aware of it. If you will bear with us, we will condition him.

(Pause)

I am Laitos. I thank you again for having the patience to let us work with you. This particular contact-type of communication is somewhat boring to learn, we are aware, yet without these channels being developed, we would find ourselves sadly short on channels when needed.

Before I leave you, I would like to open the meeting to questions. Are there any questions at this time?

Questioner: Can you tell me something about the civilization, the great civilization?

Are you referring to a civilization in the present time? On this planet?

(Inaudible)

We are sorry. The instrument does not know what you are talking about, which makes it more difficult to give the answer through this channel. But we will attempt to.

(Pause)

We are having difficulty with this channel, and due to that, we would attempt to answer through the other instrument. I am Laitos.

(H channeling)

I am Laitos. As many of you are aware, civilization as you would call it upon your planet has taken many forms throughout the ages. There have been those periods which have been considered as golden eras within those civilizations. There have been golden eras known in many, shall we say, of your national civilizations. There have been empires of great magnitude throughout your histories of which you are aware. Yet there has been upon your planet, as many of you have accepted, that era which you refer to as having been that of the Atlantean, a place and time upon your planet in which man evolved hand in hand with his Creator. A time when there were no limitations as to your expressions, and there were no transmutations or implications within those expressions. A time of great, shall we say, ability, technically and spiritually.

The time is dawning upon your planet. The peoples of that era are you. That era, my friends, was brought about between an experience of destruction, because it was made known that if you had indulged, and begun the transmutation *(inaudible)* and begun the physical, shall we say, indulgences throughout the people of that time, they brought about or upon themselves what you would call a karmic liability, to once again evolve through the experiences which would bring them back to the realization of that golden era, an era of perfection upon the physical plane.

My friends, once you achieve absolute, shall we say, harmony, it is still your choice to return, and while under the influences of the sensual and physical, you are continually bombarded by this choice. This brought about, shall we say, the destruction of that golden age, yet it shall not stand in your way *(inaudible)* age. For man upon planet Earth—those who are, shall we say, of a serious nature—is dedicated to absolving those experiences which are destructive to bringing about that day of love among all on your planet. Is this sufficient?

(Side one of tape ends.)

(H channeling)

… shall we say, of what you would call telepathic communication. We initiate and send to the instrument thought. And as the instrument sits and clears his thought processes, the reception is made. And generally, upon receiving thought from us, the initial experiences of the…

(Inaudible)

… if indeed the thought is from an alien source, shall we say, or one self-initiated, and this in itself is a communion of our thoughts. Yet it brings about confusion, for there is the expression of that. In order that you may receive clearly, what communion of thought that is experienced should not be one of question, but one of receptiveness, and you should rely upon your ability to know that it is ever present to transfer the thoughts that you receive properly and promptly *(inaudible)* instrument.

And you must understand that we communicate conceptually: as you progress, and as you receive the concept, it must be filtered through your intellect, and through your storehouse of vocabulary, the expression of that concept is brought forth. And this is the communion of thought that is desired. And you must not be afraid of your own ability to discern the source from which the information has come.

You know from within yourself whether you desire to accept or reject the concepts, and you as an instrument are free to nullify any reception by purely desiring it to stop and refusing to express it. Many times, our instruments, while learning, and at times those who are well-established, interject unconsciously portions of their own thought. Yet, my friends, if those portions interjected were, shall we say, detrimental to that which we wish to express, then we would not utilize that instrument. If you should investigate that type of instrumentality of which we are speaking, you shall find that there have been many that wished to achieve the contact, and that the greatest portion no longer express this form of communication. Many have chosen upon their own to refuse that flow of information, and many, my friends, have been refused by us when they have misused that information they have received. We stand not in judgment, but we shall not allow the misuse by our instruments of that which we wish to share.

Is this sufficient?

(Inaudible)

Are there any other questions?

(Pause)

If there be no questions, we shall leave you. We are grateful to be with you, and always we shall remain. Our love and light and that of the Creator be with you. I am Laitos. Adonai. Adonai. Adonai vasu borragus. ☥

Sunday Meeting
October 24, 1976

(H channeling)

I am Hatonn. Greetings, my friends, in the love and in the light of our infinite Creator. It is, as always, a privilege to be with you and to share with you that which we have to offer in the area of, shall we say, enlightenment, on subjects which are vital to you upon your path of progression. We of the Confederation have drawn near to you at this time, for you have requested it. We are here to serve you in whatever ways that we can without violating in any form the choice of any individual.

This evening we would speak to you upon the subject of what you would call tribulations. As you are aware, those upon planet Earth are undergoing, shall we say, an experience of growth and one of learning. Your life in its entirety is an accumulation of lessons, lessons which you have designed to experience, lessons through which you can learn the truths and the application of those truths that will enable you to bring about the existence that you truly desire. And that existence, my friends, may be expressed in many words, but shall we say, [any] orthodox expression would be the existence within heaven.

Heaven, my friends, is wherever you place it. It is wherever you desire it to be. It is an eternal factor. Thus, it is not to be gained, but recognized and accepted. And in order to come to the realization that you indeed exist within that heaven which you desire, you must undergo what we have called tribulations. You have placed before you on your path circumstances which, when encountered, are somewhat difficult to comprehend. Circumstances which, shall we say, test your emotional stability, your intellectual stability, and most of all, your spiritual stability and dedication.

My friends, when confronted with situations which are incomprehensible through the processes of your intellect, accept it and face it, knowing that it has been desired by you as an experience for the opportunity of growth. Righteously confront that situation. Enter into the experience with an attitude of love, of love which contains no resentment or fear. Accept that which you have created, for indeed, you have brought it into existence. Know that, no matter how it appears, it is for the best. Know that within you is the ability to properly react to any situation.

My friends, when we say to know that this ability is within you, we cannot stress the importance of the factor known as faith at these given times. You have been taught that within you is that which you call the Creator. You are portion and particle of the creative force and vitality that permeates the universe. Attune yourself to that presence within you, through the utilization of your meditations, and learn what it is to truly know the ability within you.

Your abilities are infinite. Your love is also infinite. There are no limitations placed upon you by your Creator. They are placed upon you by yourself, in your acceptance of them. There are no situations which you, as your own personal creator would place before yourself, that you could not properly confront and overcome.

Many situations will bring you to a point, being human, shall we say, as you are, to despair. Feel not guilty, for this feeling of despair is only natural upon your planet. During your trials, you shall, shall we say, be influenced by the mortality which you have chosen to possess at this given time. It is as the negative and positive poles, the mortal and the immortal, one knowing limitation, the other knowing infinity. Yet neither is complete without the other.

My friends, your existence within the Earth plane, and within physical environment, is vital and essential to your growth, for you have desired it. You have brought it into existence. And now that you have chosen it, you must learn, you must learn how, within you, the ability can be utilized to manifest the perfect experience within the physical environment. Many great teachers have walked your Earth planet and demonstrated that, even within the physical form, they could demonstrate the unlimited abilities of the Creator within them. "The kingdom of heaven lies within you," so say your scriptures. Seek not outside of your form, deity. But know the deity that is in you. Seek not to experience those things about you which would deter that seeking of deity within you, for you are confronted with many situations, day in and day out, which titillate your senses and your desires upon the physical level. Yet these also, my friends, are trials which you have placed before you. And when you come to the day that all things may be offered you that at one time were tests to you, and you no longer even need to ask yourself if they are desired, then you shall walk with the masters and you shall teach with their assistance to your brethren on this plane.

My friends, to walk with those teachers, you must be above the influences of the physical level of existence, and yet remain in it. This is within you, the ability to bring this about. It is a long and tedious journey that you have chosen. Stamina, or shall we say, patience is of the utmost importance. And, my friends, once again: you must have faith in your Creator, and above all, in yourself. Know that you are divine. Know that you shall succeed. Know that you cannot be overcome by any negative experiences or incidents. You are the master of your universe. Go within yourself and know these things, and emerge in whatever form you would desire.

I shall transfer this contact to another instrument. I am Hatonn.

(Carla channeling)

I am with this instrument. I am Hatonn, and once again I greet you in the love and the light of the infinite Creator.

My friends, you may have asked yourself before this many times: "If indeed I chose these tribulations, whatever was on my mind when I did that? What was my higher self thinking about?" We cannot penetrate the nature of the Creator, nor would we pretend to. And if there is a reason that the white light and perfect love of the Creator was generated into what you have called the Word, so that entities may appear to people the cosmos, we do not know it. Nevertheless, that this is so, we do know. It is possible that, in infinite humility, the Creator offered to all of His infinite parts total freedom to remake that creation. This is, indeed, the option that was before you as you contemplated your entry into the physical illusion before your physical birth.

Before you came into the physical illusion, you were in an atmosphere where thoughts were obvious things, as real to you as the physical objects of your illusion are now. And the choices that you now find so difficult were not even choices. And you asked yourself, if you were put to the test, would you still know what love was? Would you still know how to serve your brother? Would you still seek the Creator with all your heart?

And so you came into this illusion. Perhaps one might think of what is in the mind of this channel: that in your armed forces, parents hope that their child will become a man. Service under these conditions is more difficult, yet under difficult conditions, one developed more rapidly.

And so it is with you, my friends. This was your motive. Whatever else you needed to do while you were here, your basic motive was to penetrate the things of this illusion with your discrimination so that you could see the love and the light, as you would call it, the heaven that penetrates all that there is. In order for you to see those things that are lasting, it is necessary for things not to always go, on the physical plane, perfectly well, for if your day-to-day existence was not at all troubled, you would perhaps be satisfied to live out your physical existence without seeking further knowledge. It is when things become difficult that you seek to know the reason.

My friends, in all space and time, wherever polarity of good and evil exists, those entities which the Creator tossed into the void have forever and ever turned back to the Creator with an instinct that cannot be denied. Whatever entities have attempted, however much separation they have attempted to put between themselves and the Creator, there is an instinct which cannot and will not be denied forever. Perhaps this is, in a nutshell, the answer to the riddle of why we are all aware beings. We are a timeless answer to a timeless question.

In your tribulation, in your difficulty, know that this is an opportunity for you to discern, to seek out that which will not rust and will not spoil, to unlock from within your heart those feelings which will long exist, while all more petty and mundane feelings pass away.

As always, we suggest meditation, for this is the kind of assignment which one cannot do by oneself. I would leave this instrument at this time, for one of my brothers, Laitos, wishes to condition several who are here. I am Hatonn.

(Carla channeling)

I am Laitos, and I greet each of you in the love and the light of the infinite Creator. I am one with you, and I thank you for the opportunity to be with you at this time. As my brother has said, it is my special privilege to work with conditioning those of you who desire it, and at this time I would like to pass among you and offer to each of you the conditioning wave.

(Pause)

We thank you for this opportunity. We would like to take just a little of your extra time, if you would be patient, and attempt to contact the one known as N. We have not used this instrument for a long time, and if he is willing, we would like to say a few words through him. I am Laitos.

(N channeling)

I am Laitos. I am now with this instrument. I greet you all again in light and love. I will not say many words through this particular instrument, but I would like to say that it has been a very great honor and privilege to speak to this group at this time. I will now leave this instrument. I leave you all in the light and love of the infinite Creator. I am Laitos.

(Carla channeling)

I am Hatonn, and I am again with this instrument. Before we leave you, we would like to open the meeting to questions. Are there any questions at this time?

(Pause)

If there are no questions, my friends, we will only leave you with the thought that you are as harps. You have the power to tune yourselves to harmony or disharmony. You cannot control the wind that blow through you. You can only control the sound that you can produce when the wind touches you.

My friends, the wind of experience can blow hot and cold, harshly and gently. Yet, you have the key: you may tune yourselves. Meditate, my beloved brethren, you are all one. You are all in harmony. It is only a matter of finding that sweet harmony.

I am Hatonn. I send you our love and the love of the Creator, and I leave you in His love and light. Adonai vasu borragus. ☙

Tuesday Meeting
October 26, 1976

(Don channeling)

… in the love and in the light of our infinite Creator.

It is a very great privilege to be with you at this time, a very great privilege. This is our mission. Yes, my friends, this is our mission: to speak to you. We have spoken to you for many, many of your years. We have spoken to many upon the surface of your planet. We have spoken primarily through instruments such as this one, and we have done this for a specific reason. You are aware of this reason.

We are limited, as you know, to provide information, shall we say, but information in such a manner so that it may be accepted as being from us or rejected, shall I say, as not being a valid communication from what you would call an extraterrestrial source. The information, my friends, must be given to the peoples of your planet. It is urgently needed. Yet we cannot do this in any manner that would prove to them beyond questionable doubt that it comes from us.

My friends, it is necessary to act in this way, because to act in any other way would destroy the primary benefit that each of you on Earth receive in your stay upon planet Earth. You are in the condition that you are in at this time, as are all those who dwell upon the surface of your planet, primarily to experience a condition of voluntary choice. Each thought that you think is yours to choose. It is necessary to choose wisely if you are to progress. But the choice must always be up to the individual and not impressed from some external source. This is the method by which the individual grows in understanding. This is the only method by which he grows.

My friends, each of you here tonight is aware enough of what we have given you to make wise choices in your thinking. All that is lacking, shall I say, is possibly diligence, diligence in choosing thoughts, my friends. This is the way of the masters.

My friends, your thinking is all that exists. The entire universe is thought. All that is necessary for any condition or any experience is thought. We extend to you simple instructions to be used in an extremely beneficial environment to create a very rapidly accelerated evolution of thought. Make use of your present condition, for it has been chosen, it has been desired, in fact, as you say, totally programmed by yourself. It is for your benefit, my friends, each of you individually. Make use of your present condition, for this is what you planned to do. Do it, to reach that goal that each of us so earnestly desires: the goal of union in thinking with our Creator. For in this union, my friends, is all that you could ever possibly express in love.

It is, shall I say, a strange and devious path to this understanding. But if it were not necessary it would not exist. Become aware of each second of your existence. Know in fullest detail the motivations of each of your actions and each of your thoughts. Meditate and become aware. Use this awareness then, to act. It is not necessary to make complex plans for future activities. It is only necessary to meditate. In your meditation, the understanding that you seek will be easily revealed.

It is necessary that the individual gain knowledge in this manner, for only in this manner can he become able to direct his own thinking. In any other manner, my friends, he is not truly evolving, but simply reacting. And, my friends, the name of this game in which you now find yourselves is evolution. That is the secret behind all the activities upon your planet: an evolution of mind. You find yourself at present in what you might term a celestial cesspool of confused thinking. This is strong language. But, my friends, we can say at this time that this is the case upon your planet. It is a condition that is not desired by any of us. However, it is a condition that exists, and it is a condition that can produce the very gods that have the responsibilities for the evolution of those who have been deprived for so long of the knowledge that they would seek.

(Pause)

I am sorry for the delay. I was having some difficulty with the instrument. I shall continue. It is difficult at times to express through an instrument using your language precisely what we wish to say. For this reason, it sometimes seems that we prolong our communications. It is necessary to attempt to express in your language that which we would wish to give to you in such a way that it will be useful to you. I am going to condition this instrument, but at this time transfer the contact to another instrument.

(Pause)

(Carla channeling)

I am with this instrument. I am Hatonn. Again, I am sorry for the delay. We are having quite a bit of difficulty with this instrument this evening. We will continue.

It has been written in your holy works that you need not ponder what your needs are, because they will be met by the Father. This is a truth which has been much misunderstood by your peoples. Truth is not something that one can consciously say, and thus be clothed in. One may hold in one's hand those words which have been spoken by the Master known as Jesus or any other of your holy words, one can know them by heart, and one can proclaim them to others, and yet if one is speaking them and not living them, they will not be true for him. The Creator will *not* guard his footsteps, will *not* give him his daily bread, for his consciousness is still dwelling in the precincts of the illusion. It is only in meditation and contemplation of that presence which is more real than your very breathing that you become aware of the actual reality of the Creator. Once for one moment in a day you have touched this reality, you walk forth bearing that reality as a cup bears the life-giving fluid within it. Then the Creator will fulfill your every need.

We have said to you many times to remove your concentration from those things which *(inaudible)* and to place that concentration upon the Creator. And the Creator will put His concentration upon what you need. Within the illusion, you ofttimes are mistaken about what you truly need. The Creator is never mistaken. Therefore, leave all high-sounding words and all appearances, and seek within yourself for the silence in which is that still, small voice, as you would say.

We are here, as have been many before us, to bring you good news[2]: to tell you that love and the thoughts that proceed from love are all that there is within the universe. We are here to ask you to claim your birthright as the creator of your thoughts and therefore of your universe. Link your thoughts with the Creator, and let Him think your life.

I would like to transfer back to the other channel at this time. I am Hatonn.

(Don channeling)

I am with the instrument. I am Hatonn. I am sorry for the delay in using this instrument. It was necessary to establish a better contact. At this time, I have established this contact.

My friends, it is very, very important to know yourself. This is your first mission upon this planet, to know your own thinking. There is only one way for you to do this and that is through meditation. Through meditation, you will be able to know

---

[2] When Hatonn said "good news," an individual on the floor above began playing soft, sweet music, as if on cue.

yourself. It is impossible to analyze in a conscious manner your own thinking. It is necessary that you become aware of yourself in meditation. For this reason, meditate each day. This is of prime importance. It is difficult sometimes. Your busy activities *(inaudible)*. However, if you are to accomplish what you have set out to accomplish, it is necessary that you do this. In no other way can you fulfill your own desire to grow, to take this splendid opportunity to grow into that form of thought, you might say, that you have chosen for your own. For that form, my friends, is a form of total love.

At this time, I would request questions.

Carla: What can you tell us about Bigfoot?

I am aware of the problem concerning Bigfoot. The problem is very simple. It is unfortunate that, at this time, this information is somewhat restricted, shall I say, as are many bits of information which we may give you. However, it is possible to say that the Bigfoot type of creature is an important part of the development of your planet.

He will increase in great numbers in the very near future, and play a very important part in the transition of your planet. He is not a malevolent form. He is docile. He is not related to another form which is not of a physical nature but of what you term an astral nature. This form is similar to what you know as the werewolf. It is not a Bigfoot creature. It is not manifesting in your physical illusion except for very short periods of time. There is nothing to fear from these creatures, for they are unable to attack those who are of the light.

B: Are they able to attack humans at all?

This is possible. It is dependent upon the vibrational situation.

B: Of the human being?

That is correct.

Carla: Are you aware of the article I was reading this afternoon? Can you see that in my mind, about the UFO with the Bigfoot-type entity inside it? Could you at all say what that guy was doing in the UFO, or what the guy was seeing on the ground that saw this, why they're in UFOs, what the connection is?

This is a vehicle of conveyance which is formed by thought on what you call an astral plane. The creature of which you speak is not physical, in your terms, but partially so. His vehicle, both physical and that conveyance which you term a UFO, partially materialized into your density. He is able to vitalize his body through the use of the blood of animals, upon which he preys, just as a bird of prey in your skies uses the blood of the animals upon which he preys. The difference, my friends, is that this entity, for most of your experience, is not physical and is a transient in your world. This is possible at this time because of the progress of your planet in transition. It was possible in the past only in very limited cases, but will become more prevalent in the future, along with many other entities which have been for many years of your time denizens of what you term the astral planes. Many of them will be for short periods of time manifesting in the physical and then, as time progresses, for longer periods. It is necessary, if one is to sustain a physical body, that body be nourished by physical substance, just as you nourish your physical body. Each of these creatures, no matter what type, if they are to maintain a physical body as you know it, will find it necessary to nourish that body. The mutilations of which you speak are simply nourishments. They are not being carried out by the variety of Bigfoot that now dwells within your plane. This variety of Bigfoot is vegetarian.

Carla: The werewolf type of Bigfoot—is its form dependent upon the thought forms of the people of this planet? Is he shaped, made like he is, because of various—

The shape of this entity is ancient. It is a formation that was brought about by the mating of a certain race in your ancient times, a race that evolved in what you would have called the second density. This race was lost in your physical world at the end of that cycle of experience but remains in thought in what you term the astral plane. As your planet makes its present transition, it is possible in a more direct manner for these earlier forms to emerge in your worlds due to the transition which is both mental and physical, the physical part having to do with a nourishment, and a polarization which is derived from the cattle which are mutilated and drained of blood.

Is this a sufficient explanation?

Carla: Yes, thank you. I would like to ask about the other Bigfoot, if that's all right. The physical Bigfoot, is that an ancient species too? How did this form evolve? How long has it been on this Earth, and how long—

This … this animal, as you might call it, is neither truly an animal or what you call a species of man. It is, as you say, of a different order. It is what you might call the missing link, the missing link between the ape-man, that you know upon your planet, and the human that you know upon your planet. There was, in many years past, an experiment that occurred upon your planet, an experiment having to do with the mating of a species that you know of as the ape and the species that you know of as human. This experiment was performed by, shall I say, the scientific community, which had a purpose somewhat unknown to your peoples today. The purpose was to produce a physical vehicle which could endure great hardships as the ape-form, as you know, can. However, it was desired that the ape-like vehicle be equipped with the intelligence of the more highly evolved human. The experiment was to create a race of human apes, a high order of intelligence but yet with vehicles which could endure great hardship. The reason for this was that a transition of planetary condition was foretold, a condition that would no longer facilitate the human because of atmospheric and environmental conditions. It was thought that if this more rugged race of creatures could be developed, that experience in the physical upon this planet could continue. This, then, was the origin of what you know as the Bigfoot creature. The human which was used in combination with what you know as the ape was not the type of individual that now inhabits your planet, but of a different variety.

Carla: Was this in Atlantis?

This was previous to the time of Atlantis, however, there were some experiments done in what you know as Atlantis.

Carla: And the Bigfoot has survived ever since then in remote places?

This is correct, however, in very sparing numbers. He has had the intelligence to maintain total aloofness, for he has realized that it would be of no benefit for him to come in contact with the race of man that is now upon your surface. However, at this time, there is a need for him in increasing numbers.

B: Will it ever be possible to communicate with this creature?

This creature can communicate with you at any time he desires. It is only necessary for him to think, for he is telepathic.

Carla: I'm not really clear about what the connection is between the UFOs and Bigfoot. I guess that's part of the restricted—

The UFOs of which you speak are vehicles created by the astral form.

Carla: Oh. They are the ones like the werewolves?

Yes, they are vehicles created by thought,

Carla: So the Pennsylvania type or the California type of Bigfoot don't have connection with UFOs? Or connection with you? Or is that a whole other story?

The UFO is a thought form created on the astral plane. It is a vehicle which transports that astral from of the entity which you might term a werewolf.

Carla: OK, but is there a connection between the Confederation and the physical UFOs? Because there have been UFOs sighted in connection with the non-werewolf type of Bigfoot, too. Or is that coincidence? Or is that restricted?

(Pause)

I am sorry for the delay. I was working this out. This instrument is having difficulty with this concept. However, I will attempt to answer your question. Physical Bigfoot has been in contact with the Confederation throughout its stay upon your planet. It has been in contact through the method of telepathy. There is a liaison which takes place. The liaison is more for maintenance than anything else.

Carla: What type?

Maintenance—food.

Carla: Oh!

There are cases when these creatures are in need of physical sustenance in the form of food. We simply supply them.

Carla: Oh. I know you're getting tired.

Don: I'm OK.

Carla: OK. One more question. There have been numerous cases—I can only think of one specifically—but I just never could figure it out. It was the case in Pennsylvania. I know the channel's familiar with it, so just get it out of his mind. And in connection with a UFO and Bigfoot, the contactee had a kind of an alarming difficulty where he fell down and was having a fit, but then he saw the—

This condition is understood at this time.

Carla: Was this an anomaly? Was this the Bigfoot attempting to communicate to man on Earth? Or was it the UFO?

It was a case of communication specifically with an entity in your world, in your race. He—the craft was a thought form created by the entities of your astral plane. It had substance and being in your world for a short time. It conveyed the bodies of creatures which are likened to what you call the werewolf. These creatures emerged upon your physical world and were drawn to the entity known to you as Stephen because of his polarity. They found, upon the physical plane, a like mind, you might say, and for that reason, came in simplest form to greet him. He in turn fired at them with a weapon which they then understood to be an act of hostility, and, for this reason, retreated. They were unable to maintain the thought form which was their vehicle, which then vanished.

They were able at a later time to, shall we say, dematerialize. However, the vision that the one known as Stephen enjoyed was impressed by, shall we say, his higher self. It was a warning not only to him, but to all men of this planet to choose carefully their path.

Carla: And that's why he was in such a traditional form—a guy with a sickle?—because of his higher self talking to him?

That is correct.

Carla: I see. OK. Thank you very much.

Are there any other questions?

B: Will there be an increasing number of these physical examinations by UFOs?

These physical examinations are not planned by us. These physical examinations are examinations done by another group. They are not meant to harm. They are meant to help. They are not for the purpose of aiding you in your developments but for the purpose of understanding your human condition, for there are entities now concerned with this planet who have not evolved through your human condition, as you call it. They are not familiar enough with your vehicles and desire this knowledge so as not to harm you, for it will be necessary for them to come within close proximity of your population. Numerous times in the past, there has been harm done to members of your population caused by proximity to their craft. It will be a valuable knowledge that they derive from these examinations. It is, I am afraid, a necessary part of the coming program having to do with what you might term the harvesting process upon your planet, for you see, my friends, at this time the harvesting process is stratified, and there will be more than one type of contact, for your planet at this time is amazingly stratified in levels of consciousness. It would not be such a complex job if it were not for the fact that you terminate, at this time, what you call a master cycle of evolution. It is a very complex sorting job, you might say, and for this reason, much information about those of your peoples who dwell here is presently needed.

We, of what you call the teaching realm, realize the Confederation of Planets in the Service of the Infinite Creator are not involved in this portion of the mission with respect to your planet. We have the job of helping you in the evolution of your own consciousness. We are, what you might say, are college professors. We are not in any common function over those who will be acting on your surface in a more direct manner. Some of them are a little more rash, shall I say, than others, and this, my friends, is basically due to the stratification of which I have previously spoken.

That there are many, many here to aid you at this time, my friends, is true. There are many levels of consciousness. Your planet goes through a transition that is monumental in its experience. There is no one single answer to any of your questions, except the question with respect to the Creator and His love. All of the other activities are very numerous in their orientation. As you know, the numbers of people upon your surface are many. The conditions of thought upon your surface range in a wide polarity of development. Consequently, those whom you meet from elsewhere may have a wide range in their methods.

Does this sufficiently answer your question?

B: Yes, thank you.

Are there any other questions?

(No further questions.)

There is but one other thing that we would wish to pass through this instrument at this time, and that is that each of you will be completely successful. You cannot help but be so, for you have chosen a path which terminates in success. The only factor in the slightest question, my friends, is the rate down which you travel this path. That rate, my friends, is a function of but one thing: a function of your thinking.

Carla: I do have one more question, if the channel is not too tired. What you said reminded me of it. Is that all right?

I am aware of the question.

Carla: You are? I will ask it if you wish.

It is not necessary. It is a very great privilege to say at this time that each of you is upon a mission that has been selected long ago. This mission very, very shortly will culminate, shall I say, in a flurry of activity, which will be unexpected. However, all of the fragments of this culmination are being brought together as planned.

Carla: That was basically my question. Basically, I wanted to know whether all the delays we are having are built in, in other words, that the people of this sphere who are helping, like Brother Philip, were attempting to time it so that it would come out at the right time. Is that why we're having these delays?

This is basically correct.

Carla: Thank you.

At this time, I will leave the instrument. It has been a very great privilege to speak with you. It is always a great privilege. Avail yourself of our contact through meditation. We will do everything that we possibly can to aid you in your seeking of that which we all seek: to understand love. Adonai. Adonai vasu.

Saturday Meeting
October 30, 1976

(Don channeling)

[I am Hatonn.] … the love and the light of our infinite Creator. It is once more a very great privilege to be with you. We of the Confederation of Planets in the Service of the Infinite Creator are always ready to serve you. Our service at this time is limited, but shortly the limitations under which we now serve you will be lessened.

However, it is necessary at this time to interact in the way that we now use to speak. We are here for one purpose: to bring to you that knowledge that is essential. There is only one essential knowledge, my friends, and that is what we bring you.

(Pause)

(Carla channeling)

I am with this instrument. I am Hatonn. We frequently, my friends, do have difficulties with channels, and it is almost always due to their desire to monitor our message. There are many reasons that this interferes with our message, but most often it is due to fear on the part of the channel, for the channel often feels that he is speaking his own thoughts. The relationship between the source of the Brotherhood and the channels who are the instruments for that source is one which is difficult to express in the concepts of your language, for we are truly one. We use those concepts which are within the channel's mind. We play on the instrument that we find. If the instrument has powerful biases, he may find himself repeating, due to the fact that we are attempting to establish better contact through the means of repeating familiar material.

We say all of this due to the fact that even the most experienced channel suffers difficulty in communication due to analysis of our message. We do wish to speak through the one known as Don. So at this time we will condition him and attempt to continue through him. I am Hatonn.

(Don channeling)

I am again with the instrument. I will continue speaking through this instrument. I was saying that we are here to give to you that which is necessary to know. There is very, very little that is really necessary to know, my friends. But it is necessary to know this very small amount very, very well. In fact, my friends, you must know it beyond any question. Then you must use it to its fullest capacity. This is actually all we have to give to anyone upon your planet—nothing more.

It, my friends, is all there is to give, anywhere, at any time. For if this gift is received in totality, you then possess the entire creation.

And why, my friends, should we give to you this gift? Because that is part of the understanding, my friends. When you possess it, you desire nothing more than to give it away. For in possessing it, you can do nothing but give it away. For this is, in truth, the real knowledge of what is behind everything that exists.

(Pause)

I will continue. In this creation, there are many, many facets, many planets, many stars about which they revolve, many galactic systems. And yet each of these things is a part of one thing. That one thing we call creation, [is] a creation of our thought, for we are parts of the Creator. Just as, if you are the parent of a child, that child is a part of you, so are we parts of the Father of this creation, this infinite creation in which we presently find ourselves,

It is possible to understand the expression that created this creation and ourselves, and act so as to reflect the completeness, the essence of this expression. Then you have all knowledge.

It is necessary, if the individual is to become aware of that knowledge, for him to meditate. There are many things in your present existence that seem complex. There are many problems that seem difficult to answer. In truth, there is no complexity, there is no problem without an answer. All that is necessary is that you avail yourself in meditation to the knowledge that is part of you. It is part of you because you are the child of the one Father, who is the Creator. If you seem at this time to be less than the total understanding of this Creation, then it is only because you have desired to be less. For this is, in truth, what was provided for you. All that is necessary for you or for anyone else, is that you become aware of this knowledge. And the method, my friends, is meditation. This meditation may be done at any time or any place. It is not necessary that you take any particular position at any particular time of day or with any particular group of people. It is not necessary for you to be in the dark or by yourself or even to close your eyes. With practice you will be able to clear the conscious mind of the trivial daily activities which constantly beset it, and become instantly aware of the real creation. The more that you practice this, the more that you will become aware of truth and reality. Presently, the population of your planet is so busy with trivial and transient qualities that very, very few of them are in any awareness at all of the real creation. This is due to an extreme lack of meditation among those peoples of your planet.

There are many answers that can be provided through the process of meditation. However, they all dissolve to a single understanding. That understanding will transcend any intellectual complexity which you may be presently aware of.

As I have said previously this evening, we of the Confederation are here to bring you one thing. That thing is understanding. If you didn't already understand we could not bring it to you. But what we wish to do, my friends, is bring to you that additional amount that you desire. It is up to you, and only to you, to receive it. Each of you may receive as much as you wish, at any time that you wish, at any place that you wish. The process of meditation is so important that we cannot overstress it.

At this time I will transfer the contact to the other channel.

(Carla channeling)

I am again with this instrument, and again I greet you in the love and the light of the infinite Creator. I will continue, my friends.

Meditation is important precisely because it is the key to what you desire. In meditation, as you become accustomed to that contact with the Creator, your identity becomes more aligned with the truth of who you really are. And in that meditation, your universe expands, for you no longer feel that you are boxed in a little room, beset on all sides with that heavy furniture of your mind, which includes your problems, your difficulties, and the biases which you hold on the subjects which are of interest only within the illusion. That furniture melts away, and suddenly you are in a very large, very beautiful, very spacious place, in which the sun is shining, in which there are sweet odors in the air, and in which that peace reigns that you seek.

We have found in speaking with your peoples that you are most apt to comprehend our meaning when we speak to you in some vivid metaphor, and it is for this reason that we have long understood why the master known as Jesus spoke so often to your peoples by telling stories. And we give you now two of these symbols of our messages that you may perhaps hold with you. We hope that they will aid you.

The first is, my friends, that it is the function of the physical illusion to, as we have said to you, box you in, to make you feel crowded, to press you into a situation in which you feel pressure.

In meditation, you release that pressure by changing your identity. You find that there is a great deal of space in which to play and rejoice. And you find that in meditation you do not perceive the crowded situation that you perceive in your daily life. Therefore, we say to you when you are feeling crowded, pressed by the difficulties of life, take hold of the image of yourself as being a completely free dancer in an infinite space which is filled with light. You can move about; you can view the situation as it really is. You are a creative person; you are a dancer. You do not walk; you dance. You are not in darkness; you are in light.

There are situations that must be dealt with: this is why you are in the physical plane. And yet there are ways in which this meditative state can be brought to bear upon your waking life.

And again we say to you, your spirit came to the physical plane, as you call it, and willingly buried itself in what you may consider to be dust, for it is so written in your holy works. Yet there was a reason. You well know the reason. And if you *(inaudible)* we ask that you think of how a pearl is made—a speck of sand that aggravates and pains the living tissue, and yet, in its pain, that which is added becomes a pearl. Your spirit may be polished and burnished until it gives light to others and to yourself. This will happen, and that it causes pain is simply the way the process works.

There is nothing physical or, as you would say, Earthly, about your emotions, your pain, or your joy. These are but the outer layers of that which will affect you eternally. That which is one thing on the physical level is transmuted through learning, so that your spirit in its real and true nature is nourished by the very thing which seems to you to be such bad medicine.

These images we offer you to hold in your mind. But know that these are only words, and that meditation itself is and should be your primary link to your Father.

Before I leave this instrument I would like to open the meeting to questions.

B: Can you say anything about *(inaudible)*?

We have spoken many times, through this instrument and others, of the harvest. May we ask what you are specifically requesting? It is a large subject.

B: Will it occur all at once, or will it be spread out over a period of time?

The latter is correct. What has been spoken of as the harvest has already begun, and will continue for several of your years, perhaps as many as would make a quarter century. In fact, time being our most difficult concept to cope with in dealing within you who are within this time continuum, we cannot say for sure that it would last any certain time. But that it will last several of your years we do know.

M: *(Inaudible)*. What is the method *(inaudible)*?

When the crop is ripe, the reaper comes among it. We understand the gist of your question. It is difficult for you to perceive that the mechanisms of a cosmic or celestial nature may be on a scale which is difficult for you to imagine. But it is truly said in your holy works that to the Creator, a thousand years is but an evening. It is through the natural cycle of physical birth and death that most will enter their new *(inaudible)*. It does not take a great many years for all of those on the planet to end their Earthly existence. It will not happen all at once, any more than any natural process happens all at once. It is simply that as you see the leaves upon the trees of your planet falling, although they do not fall all at the same time, there is a period when they are all on the tree, and there is a period when your trees are bare, and the leaves have gone on to the next cycle.

B: So it won't necessarily be *(inaudible)* as much as it may be a very natural time of change for every individual *(inaudible)*.

This is correct. There is very little chance that people will actually leave by ships. This is greatly undesirable. We are willing to consider the possibility under greatly adverse circumstances. We do not feel that the probabilities are at all high.

(Pause)

It is difficult to predict your peoples. In working with the channels we have among your peoples we find that some are hoping that we will come *(inaudible)*. Some are hoping we will not. When your people begin to become totally aware of, shall we say, the jam they are in, we do not know which way the wind will blow. We are, therefore, keeping our probabilities quite fluid.

B: Thank you.

You are most welcome. I would like to say through this channel that, as the Creator will not let His children stumble, no matter what the method of harvesting. For those who are truly seeking Him, and in this we include those to whom we are speaking, the road through the change will be straight. The way will be *(inaudible)*, for you are serving what you might call your initiation willingly on this plane. You are binding up your own wounds. Those who will be having difficulty during the harvesting will be those who have neglected the health of their spirit within this dimension, and are therefore forced to, as you might put it, go into the hospital in the next dimension. These people will be shocked, startled or otherwise disturbed by the events that occur, and will not be able to take their places immediately.

However, we wish to share with you at this time that you will be at your best at that time, in whatever dimension you may find yourself. This is true not only of you, but of each who has consciously decided to become a shepherd.

Is there another question?

Don: In the next five-year period, what changes do you see?

We have spoken through this instrument before regarding changes that are upcoming. We have spoken of the difficulty in California. There is also, as we have said, a difficulty which may take place along the coast of what you would call south Central America.

(Pause)

We have difficulty in giving world-wide information through this instrument. If it is desired by the other instrument, we will transfer this contact to him, for we are having grave difficulty in giving this information.

Don: Just one other question before the transfer: what causes these problems within the planet. How does it effect places like California?

We trust you are not referring to the apparent physical causes? Those having to do with the stresses?

Don: No—the basic cause.

We feel that you are already aware of the cause, but we will attempt to confirm through this instrument your understanding. As all things in the physical are created, so the entity which is your planet was created within an energy nexus which was in balance, in such a way that its forces were harmonious, and evolvement was without upheaval. As nothing stands still, so the entity known to you as the Earth evolves constantly and in what you might consider a gradual manner. Yet it is an even and steady progression which is allowed by the evolving nexus of vibration. When the thought of those upon the surface of this vibratory nexus becomes unbalanced, and these peoples become fragmented and inharmonious in their thinking, these people, like germs, infect the organism of the planetary vibration. The basic cause of the disease which is known to your scientists by so many scientific terms is simply, shall we say, a virus of disharmony.

Health is restored, as it is within your physical vehicle, when the vibratory nexus can cease fighting the disharmony and can restore its own natural polarity of vibration, so that the Creator's infinite strength flows in, through and out again without hindrance.

Does this answer your question?

Don: Yes. Why the California area?

We do not feel that any particular location among your peoples is an effect of those peoples, but it is an effect of many, many of your years of a planetary imbalance in discharge of polarity. For that area which you know as California has become diseased because the place is balancing that particular part of a world-wide imbalance which needed to be corrected. Wars have never reached that which you know as California, and yet the conflagrations among your peoples *(inaudible)* have caused this sickness. It is not any one people that is to blame, for many of your peoples have cooperated.

(Pause)

We cannot transmit through this instrument, for there are mathematical expressions, many which she does not know. But we say unto you that there are lines of force which exist within the ellipsoidal form of your sphere which, shall we say, predict the location of these particular difficulties. We are sorry. It is very difficult to express through this instrument. Perhaps we can impress this upon you directly. I will at this time transfer to the one known as Donald. I am Hatonn.

(Don channeling)

I am with the instrument.

(Pause)

I will leave the instrument at this time. It has been a very great privilege being with you this evening. We are constantly available. It is only necessary to desire our contact. Adonai, my friends. Adonai vasu.

L/L Research

Sunday Meeting
October 31, 1976

(Carla channeling)

I am Hatonn. And I greet you in the love and in the light of our infinite Creator. As always, it is a privilege to be able to speak with your group. And we especially send our greeting and welcome to the one who is new to our thoughts. To him and to each of you we say that it is a very great privilege to be able to serve you by sharing with you our thoughts.

I have said to [you] that I am Hatonn. Yet, I am not a person by that name but rather one of many who identify himself by that name. We are a people who have come to your planet from what you would call a planet which is far removed within space and within vibration from your planet. And we join with many, many other peoples from other locations in space and time and vibration to bring to your peoples at this time a message.

We of the Confederation of Planets in the Service of the Infinite Creator have come to your planet to share with your peoples a message. It is a very simple message. And it is much required by your peoples at this time. We come in answer to a call that has gone out from your peoples, for so many of you upon your surface are seeking at this time: are seeking to know the reason for your existence; seeking to know why you were created and who your Creator is. This call is as audible to us across what you would call vast distances as if we were right beside you. And we are here to attempt to serve those who are seeking at this time by sharing our impressions concerning the question of why each of us is here.

We of the Confederation do not set ourselves apart as the ultimate in truth and knowledge. We do not claim to be infallible. But we feel confident that as we have progressed beyond that place [at] which you now are experiencing existence, we can share with you what understanding we have gained.

It is especially important that we share this knowledge with you at this time. For you see, my friends, the reason that your peoples are so anxious at this time to discover the purpose of their existence is that at this time your planetary sphere is marking the end of a cycle of existence. And it will be necessary for your peoples to, shall we say, take a cosmic examination. And those who pass will go on to the next level, and they enter the next lesson. Those who do not pass this examination, will have to repeat this so-called Earthly grade once again.

We are here to help you with this examination. We have been here, as you have earlier spoken, for some time; as you would say, for many thousands of your years. Yet it is at this time that we are far more numerous for it is at this time that we are more needed.

And what is this message that we have come to give you, my friends? It is a simple message. We have one

Creator and we are that Creator. We have been created by love and we are love. In all things that are apparently so different there is an underlying unity and that unity is love. In all experiences that are so difficult there is an underlying understanding that unifies the disparity and that underlying essence is love. At your beginning and at your ending is love. Instinctively, those upon your surface know this and from this inner instinct has come many, many of what you would call religions and philosophies. And yet, due to those elements which are of an illusionary nature, the information becomes complicated. Distinctions and differences begin to be made between brothers and between understanding. And the unity is lost.

Again and again this has happened among your peoples. That which is begun in total love and unity is divided and set against itself by the intellectual understandings of men.

The nature of the illusion which you call physical existence is such that the intellect will, by its very nature, analyze, criticize, discern each experience with which it comes in contact. Therefore, that which you perceive with your intellect, that which you touch with your physical fingers, will forever seem to you to be of a certain type and therefore not of a more general type. This and that and not love.

It is for this reason that we have so often said to this group that the most important thing that we can say to you is that you must form a habit of meditation. It is only when you allow your intellectual mind to become quieted so that your inner self may begin to function that you may begin to realize your connection with the infinite love of the Creator. That you may begin to feel that love flowing through you and making a mind of unity between you and your brothers, be they your friends, your enemies or even total strangers. In meditation you may begin to feel that strength of that unity. You may begin to feel your own power as a perfect child of the Creator. Only in meditation can you find these things, for they are not apparent in your waking consciousness.

So often among your peoples it is assumed that in order to believe, shall we say, in order to belong to the company of the faithful, as you might put it, it is necessary to have an experience which is of a so-called emotional nature. We say to you, with or without emotions, with or without what we would call possibly insincere thrills, your birthright, not a matter of faith but of reality, is to be a child of the Creator. It is a simple thing, not necessary to be believed but to be experienced. This is another reason that meditation is important. To listen to many leaders within your so-called spiritual community, one would begin to believe it is necessary to go through various experiences or to believe certain things and to accept certain things in order to come into a so-called right relationship with one's Creator. Yet, the true spiritual fact is not one way or another. It is yours, completely, individually. You in silence, over a period of time, will form your own understanding of the Creator and His link with you, and your ability to help your brother through that link. There is no need for word or thought if you but meditate on a regular basis. It is not obvious immediately but the cumulative effect begins to seep into your waking existence as you find that you have those knowledges that you seek given unto you in a simple manner, springing from your own mind as needed.

We would like to transfer the contact at this time to the other instrument. I am Hatonn.

(Carla channeling)

We are having some difficulty with the instrument known as Don and we understand and will therefore not attempt to contact him at this time. My brother Laitos is with me at this time. And if you would be patient we would like to condition each of you in the room. We will pause at this time and move among you. If you desire contact at this time we ask that you make yourself receptive and we will indicate our presence to you.

We would first be with the instrument known as B1.

(Pause)

We move now to the one known as R.

(Pause)

We move now to the one known as M.

(Pause)

And to the one known as E.

(Pause)

We move know to the one known as B2.

(Pause)

We thank you for this opportunity to share with you. Before I go, I would like to open the meeting to questions. If you have questions, please ask them at this time.

M: How can you best send energy to someone?

We are aware of your question. Among your peoples it is not common to actually see those thought forms which are of healing or helpful nature. Therefore, it is difficult to tune, as you might say, those thought forms. Yet, the ability to send thought forms, or as some would call it, to pray, is a matter of simply, in a confident and quiet manner, visualizing that object or person whom you wish to help and then visualizing the white and perfect light and love of the Creator flowing from the Creator through you and to that object or person so that it totally surrounds the entity whom you [visualize.] This is all that is necessary. It is most helpful if, when you visualize the entity who needs help, you visualize this entity in its real condition, that is, in a perfect condition. For although within the illusion your thoughts have caused many and apparent difficulties, each true entity in its true form is perfect. Therefore, visualize that perfect image surrounded by the light.

Does this answer the question? Or there another question?

Questioner: If we have a special work to do, can it be done without actually [being] aware of it on the levels of our conscious mind?

This is deep thought, my sister. May we answer this in two parts? First, each of you who is in this plane of existence has one purpose which is of a primary nature. That purpose is to become aware of your true self and in so doing you begin to vibrate in harmony with that true self; that is, to vibrate within the harmonies of love. This one vibratory Thought created all that there is and as you come into harmony with this Thought you become a beacon of light that lights all those about you. This is your primary service. Whatever else there is for you to do it is best served by you becoming more and more able to be who you truly are. Being is always more important than doing, for one acts from the heart, for one acts very *(inaudible)*.

As to the second part of the answer, each has missions which are to accomplished. It is not necessary to understand on a conscious level what these missions are. Moreover, these missions need not be grand in any way. For it impossible for you to judge within the illusion the importance of what you do. The one who is known to you as the master Jesus was a carpenter, and yet his mission was great. It has also been said in your holy works that, "The last shall be first," and this is far truer than you can comprehend on the physical level.

In all humility, my brothers and sisters, do that which is in front of you to do and love. For this is your first mission. If you continue in your seeking and meditation you will be guided.

We would say to you, each at this time, your higher self and those whom you call angels can help you as well as we of the Confederation. It is only necessary to meditate. And these suggestions and feelings and understandings will come to you very simply. Does this answer your question?

Questioner:

(Inaudible)

Is there a further question?

(Pause)

It has been a great privilege to speak with you, my friends. Within your experience at this time love is but one of many, many descriptions of feelings and thoughts which you have. And it may seem a very distant goal to you that all could be love. Yet, that which you imagine fondly as heaven is nothing more that the final realization that all is truly love. You do not have to go far, you do not have to die a physical death to enter that Kingdom of Heaven. It is about you. Meditate and seek thy Kingdom. As always, we are here to aid you in your meditation. If you desire our presence, simply request it and we are with you. I will leave you at this time. I am known to you as Hatonn. Adonai, my friends. Adonai vasu borragus. ♣

Sunday Meeting
November 7, 1976

(H channeling)

I am Hatonn. I greet you, my friends, in the love and in the light of our infinite Creator. I have come to offer to you those directions which we feel it is of benefit to share with you. We place not judgment upon the position which you occupy within, shall we say, your spiritual life. Yet, we recognize and we constantly attempt to share with you those informations which are of the greatest benefit for what you would term to be the group consciousness of each meeting.

As you may recognize through your own abilities, there are those upon your planet who have chosen to seek out the truths and the knowledges that are available to them. And then there are those who have chosen only to seek the material, shall we say, possessions and the emotional involvements which shall provide for them temporal happiness that they seek. And then there are those who vacillate in what you might term the middle of these two: those who dwell into the material and those who dwell into the spiritual. And being aware of the desires and the directions of each individual not only within your meeting but throughout your globe assists us in bringing forth the most beneficial informations and assistances to each group or to each individual with whom we work.

As you journey throughout this life, you shall have presented to you many opportunities. Opportunities by which you may grow and opportunities by which [you may] learn and understand the composition and the operation of the universe or of the Creation. My friends, there are laws which are not written in the books of men. There are laws that override all of the, shall we say, cardinal laws of your planet. There are laws which are handed down to the people upon your planet through what you would call teachers. One of these teachers was that person whom you refer to as the Christ. One of the laws, shall we say, that he commanded to his disciples was, "To know thyself." My friends, if you wish to journey throughout this life and gain from it the greatest benefit, then you must first, above all things, know thyself. Know what it is that you desire. Know what it is that you shall do in order to attain those desires. Know how you react to all situations and leave out nothing. For many times, my friends, when one views oneself, that portion which you would call the ego of man interferes and disrupts proper and fair evaluation of oneself. For the ego itself shall continually seek out, shall we say, the enhancer or the elevation of one's opinion of oneself. And, my friends, it is not your position to be placed above or below any other individual. It is not your mission to fulfill to be the greater, to be the greater emanation of truth than any other individual. And this is what that portion of you which you refer to as the ego continually seeks after. Recognition of oneself rather than acceptance of one's true identity.

Your true identity is divine. Your true identity if perfect. Your true identity is in balance. And in order to seek out and to know thyself one must turn within and seek from within the depths of their inner being the enlightenment and knowledges available through what you might call divine inspiration or guidance, or from the words of God that are within you. There is deep within you the presence of the Creator. You have gathered about that presence density which you have termed to be yourself or your physical body. And it is within your capability to penetrate that density and to enter into the presence and the existence of the Creator, which is instilled within you. And from this presence and the allowance of it to work through you, you can know what it is you are here to do. And you shall know the areas and the directions to take in order to achieve that which you have not only come to do but that which you have chosen to do.

Many times as you travel through this life you shall experience difficulties. And each difficulty is placed before you in order that you may come to a realization. A realization that shall assist you in understanding yourself. A realization that shall assist you in understanding those about you and the world about you. As you penetrate the density and enter into the likeness and the presence of your Creator, you shall find that you shed layer by layer of those fears and doubts and anxieties that you have drawn unto yourself. And as these things are taken from you, as these things are released by you, the true existence of which you are becomes clearer and clearer. And my friends, once you have achieved the knowledge of yourself from the inner depths of your being, you shall realize that you not only know yourself but that you know your Creator. And you know the creation in which you exist. For as we have often said, as all of your great philosophies have stated, in true essence we are all one together. We all vacillate and exist within the same area of creation. And all energies continually flow together and penetrate one another. In knowing oneself, inwardly and outwardly and completely, is knowing all and knowing all people and all existence.

In order to know yourself, you must serve others. You must render unto others that love that you find within you. You must share with all around you that which you have learned in order to proceed further and further into the depths of your being. It is as though there were doors and you contain within you the key to each door. The key to one door may be service; service to a particular individual. And the key to another may be service to a group of individuals. And the key to another may [be] the discipline of willingly accepting a profession by which to acquire material needs. And the key to another may be the acceptance of the discipline of studies through your educational systems. Yet, my friends, the key, the key which is of greatest importance, the key which unlocks the door of knowledge as to what other keys to utilize, is the key which we have called many times, meditation. There is, to our knowledge, no greater way to come into the realization of one's true identity than through the proper and disciplined utilization of the art of meditation.

Certainly this can be attained through other avenues of discipline. But none, to our knowledge, are more swift in their actions and reactions upon you. We of the Confederation have been aware of the movements and of the decisions within each person upon your planet for a vast amount of your time. And we are aware that the dawning of the consciousness which you may call Christ consciousness has indeed begun upon your planet. My friends, it is your responsibility to continue feeding, shall we say, that consciousness, so that it may grow. And in order to feed it, my friends, you must know thyself. Know what your portion within the overall view and the overall raising of that consciousness contains. Know what it is that you are to do. And once again, in order to know this, you must know thyself. Love one another and you shall indeed love yourself. But love not yourself and indeed you cannot love another. For you must know what love is from within you in order to share it with others. All things lead back to the same position no matter in what direction you turn; no matter what avenue of seeking you choose, it shall lead you back to the center of your being and bring forth from within you the love and knowledge of the universe.

I shall transfer this communication. I am Hatonn.

(Carla channeling)

I am with this instrument. I am Hatonn. Again I greet you in the love and the light of our infinite

Creator. At this time, I and my brother Laitos would like to spend a little time working with you in silence. It is often very difficult to give you concepts without distorting them in some way through the use of channels such as this one. And when we have those who are accustomed to our contact we like to spend some time in direct communication. So [we] would pause at this time and work with you individually.

(Pause)

(Carla channeling)

I am again with you. I am Hatonn. My brothers, to know yourself is not a task that will end. It is simply a task that will progress. And as you progress the way will be lighted. And though your load be heavy, it will be so much easier, through understanding, to carry it.

Within your illusion, although you are in a community you seem to be always alone. And we say to you your aloneness is the key to many understandings. Until you understand [how] to be alone you will never be able to fully be a part of a group. Many among your peoples have the need to be with others and yet they find that they are not satisfied. Conversely, my brothers, it sometimes seems that to be alone would be the most precious thing because one seems to be always dealing with others in your community. Yet, until one is able to share in community, one cannot totally use the time alone. And so it is a circular problem. For to be alone is in the end impossible, for you are one with all that there is. For to be with a group is impossible for there is only one. So you are within the physical. It is a mystery. Yet, through meditation you may find the heart of being alone and the heart of being part of the community. For in both states you are inspired by the Creator and His love which you have called the Word.

In your solitude, realize first that you are in direct relation to love, and that this love is your whole existence and all else is the appearance of love. In your communion with others, realize that the blessings and the troubles are possible only through the relationship of love between you.

To know yourself, in yourself and in others, is a great task. But you are all part of the body of light which is all creation. And to know yourself in the end [will] be a continuing job.

Before we leave this instrument we would like to open the meeting to questions. If you have any questions, please ask them at this time.

(Pause)

We will leave you at this time. We leave you in the love and the light of the infinite Creator. Adonai vasu. ☥

Sunday Meeting
November 14, 1976

(H channeling)

I am Hatonn. Greetings, my friends, in the love and the light of our infinite Creator. We greet you and extend to you our appreciation for asking us to join with you this evening. It is always our privilege to share with those who would request it that knowledge which we have attained through our experience.

We wish only to share with you that which we have come to know as the truth. Yet, we do not state to have within our grasp or within our consciousness the entire picture, shall we say, for we too remain upon that ladder of progression which we have come to accept to being infinite. We too are learning day by day as we travel throughout this experience as you term as life.

We of the Confederation of Planets in the Service of the Infinite Creator have, in what we consider to be recent times, experienced similar existence to that which you experience at the present time. And being aware of those lessons which can be learned and also those pitfalls which can be experienced, we have chosen to come forth and share with those who would accept them, informations and guidances that would be to their benefit. We of the Confederation do not wish to interfere with any individual who would choose not to listen. It is only our desire to be completely open and free with knowledge and love we have come to know. And freedom, my friends, can only be found in the recognition of the choice of others.

Generally, we address these groups and share with them philosophical viewpoints. And within these viewpoints there can be found in-depth meanings and clues to assist you as you journey through this life experience. And among these clues, shall we say, the most two important which we can stress is the practice of meditation and the practice of service unto your fellow man, which is in itself is the expression of love.

Service, my friends, comes in many various forms and it is your choice as to which you would choose to utilize. You need not lift a hand. You need not render physical assistance. All that is needed, my friends, is to truly love one another. A love which is not possessive. A love that is pure from the very existence from which it has come. Love, my friends, is much more than man upon planet Earth realizes at this time. For one who truly loves can look upon disease and one who truly loves can look upon all forms of decadence and view perfection and know that underneath or within that which is viewed lies the potentiality of perfect being, perfect expression. For, my friends, within you there are both portions which are vital to bringing forth the balance of being that you seek. There is that aspect that you would label negative and that which you would call positive. And yet if it were not for both poles' existence, both sides, there would not be the knowledge of one or the other, and the true recognition of balance and the true knowledge of value. And that value, my friends, is knowing that all things are indeed balanced and in perfection. What seems to be imbalanced to you is but an experience through which you may learn.

All things are to be viewed as beneficial and it is your choice to recognize the benefits. You have entered into this life experience at a vital time in the history of your [mankind.] Lying before you is an opportunity which man has sought after for innumerable generations. You presently have the opportunity of bringing about that which you may term to be a golden era, a rebirth of the consciousness, a rebirth of the awareness, a rebirth of the knowledge of the divinity within each man.

And each individual upon your planet is important in the universal scheme, shall we call it. For, my friends, as you sit in your periods of meditation, as you love one another, and as you render service unto one another, from within your being is projected those energies which will flow throughout not only the sphere on which you live but throughout the universe. Energies of love attracting to itself like energies of love, each magnifying the other. Each blending those energy fields of all of the men upon this planet. With each little portion of love that you send out upon the ether waves, you have rendered service unto your fellow man. And you have brought unto yourself greater portions of love from those around you.

Seek not the discrepancies that you may find within each person that you view. Seek that divinity. Seek out that perfection that lies within each of us, and in doing this you have fulfilled your portion of the plan which you have assisted in bringing into manifestation of the evolution of planet Earth. There is not one person upon your planet that is not needed. All of God's children are equal and important. Whatever your role be in life, accept it willingly and do it knowing that you are fulfilling that minute portion which is necessary to bring into existence the heaven that your peoples seek. It is within your grasp. Fail to attain and you fail none but yourself. Strive to succeed and you succeed for all.

I shall transfer this communication. I am Hatonn.

(Carla channeling)

I am now with this instrument. I am Hatonn. And again I greet you in love and light. As we look down upon your peoples we cannot see you individually. We see only the shape of your sphere. It is a beautiful sphere. And yet we sense within our beings each individual who is seeking the Creator. We are sensitive to these seeking voices among your peoples for that is our mission to your world. We are to add our help to each of you who requests it.

We have in the past attempted various means of communicating with your peoples. We have attempted to describe through channels such as this one the blessings that can come from seeking through meditation the source of your existence. We have described our governmental structure, as you might call it, our peaceful society structure, all of the desirable components which lives in peace, lives in honesty, lives in order to be of service. Yet, we found that this message, while sounding very attractive, does not call many among your peoples to the practice of meditation. And so, we simply suggest meditation on a trial basis. We do not have to tell you that within your physical illusion at this time your society is not in a satisfactory state. We do not have to tell your peoples that war and hatred and what you would call bigotry and racism, what you would call greed and hunger for money are not the satisfactory goals to seek. Your peoples, to a great extent, are aware of this. We therefore suggest meditation as a means of, shall we say, getting in touch with what the alternatives are to those things which your society offers as goals which you may seek.

We can say to you, that whatever you may seek you will find. So your choice of what you are going to seek within this physical experience is all-important. If what you seek lies within the illusion, you shall have some measure of success, yet how poor you will be in those ways that even now you know exist. For in spirit, poor in the sense of peace we pass from this brief experience leaving your, shall we say, bank account behind and yet facing the spiritual banker. It is often the case when one begins to meditate on a regular basis, that one's physical problems straighten themselves out gradually, so that it looks as though meditation brings prosperity. If this is so, my friends, this is not inevitable. It is only a simple demonstration of harmony. There is no reason why one who is spiritually rich cannot also be in good health and living in comfort. The point is to seek those things of the spirit and all else will follow as is needed.

We do not promise heaven in the sense that meditation offers an easy street. For we have in our brotherhood worked upon the spiritual path for yet many more eons than you, yet within our ranks, because there always lies more than one path from one point to another, we have dissension and disagreement. We have discussion and argument. We are not without imperfections. We often do not see the total picture. It is simply that at least we are being honest in a way that we have gained by virtue of continued seeking. We are a little more in touch [with] who we are than your peoples. We have begun to see that we are all truly one in the Creator. Meditate, my friends.

At this time I would like to open the meeting to questions

M: *(M asks a question about a UFO sighting.)*

No.

M: Could you say any more about what their purpose was?

This type of experiment, shall we say, is the product of a research project, as you would call it. Although the entities were not abducted by Confederation people, they are not negative in their orientation but their purpose is benign.

M: *(Inaudible)*.

Kindly. They wish to prevent the people of Earth from having ill effects during the transition periods which is to come, when they will be using Earth plane energy for their needs.

M: Does this mean that they are themselves trying to help with the transition?

They are not helping in the transition, but they will be a part of it. The help that they will be giving will be simply to avoid harming the entities upon this planet's surface. It is difficult to explain. We are sorry that we cannot be more specific.

M: Thank you.

Don: Some information on the Second Coming?

This instrument has been aware of that question and therefore we would like to pause for just a moment to strengthen the contact.

(Pause)

I am with the instrument. Although the concept of the Second Coming is grossly in error in that the consciousness of the one known as Christ has come many times, there is an incarnation of the master in consciousness at this time among your peoples. This master is at this time a young boy. He will be among your peoples and will aid them.

Is this information of help?

Don: Yes. But I need more.

What do you wish to know?

Don: Where is he?

Carla: Don, I see a dry land. I don't know—like the Mideast or something, but I've never been there.

Don: How old is he?

Carla: I get fourteen. Fifteen. Fifteen.

Don: Can you do any better on where he is located.

Carla: Arabia? No, no better than that.

Don: How soon will he be recognized?

Carla: I get twenty-five. Within ten years.

Don: Any other information?

(Carla channeling)

I am Hatonn. As you may be aware from the atmosphere within your meeting at this time, to deal with information such as this is [a] somewhat solemn responsibility.

Questioner: Can you tell us *(inaudible)* to do?

Due to the fact that this consciousness is at this time incarnate and is subject to total free will we can only watch. This entity will attempt to be of service. But his method will be peculiar to the time and the place. As he is a teacher, he will teach. We would say at this time that it is very important that each who is tempted to follow the leader, listen always for the words of the master who leads not to himself but to the Father. Who speaks not of heavenly kingdoms—we correct this instrument—who speaks not of the kingdoms of Earth but of the Kingdom of Heaven. It has already begun that there are leaders among your peoples that are of a negative vibration. It is difficult perhaps to understand but because of the ways of power within the spiritual planes those who are negative in a strong sense have a great deal of power just as those who are positive have a great deal power. And although the light will always defeat the dark, it is very difficult for those who are not themselves sensitized to the light to easily distinguish between those who are of light and those who are of darkness. Yet, always discrimination can occur for the powers of light seek far beyond themselves and far beyond this illusion. To be true to your own light, depend ultimately on no leader, but upon the Creator that is revealed by any true leader.

Is there another question?

Questioner: I have a question. Do you know what is meant by the Tree of Life?

We will speak through this channel, although we do not need to speak at great length, for it is within this channel's mind. But we will give through this instrument our own estimate of this body of knowledge.

That which is known as the Kabbala is an extremely appropriate and accurate physiological description of the spiritual paths within this illusion. Using symbol for that which is positive or active and that which is negative or passive, that which is male and that which is female, describes in very understandable terms the process of seeking the Creator. It has been much misunderstood among philosophers. Its truths are very simple. If one is drawn to this study, we certainly encourage it—this or any other philosophical or religious study. However, we always request that above all else, dependence be placed upon communion with the Creator in meditation.

That which is known as the Kabbala is a structure made of words. Words are fallible and will break down, but communion with the Creator is without words and is beyond thought and it will preserve and sustain when nothing else will.

Does this answer your question?

Questioner: *(Inaudible).*

Is there another question?

Questioner: Are there UFO bases on Earth?

Yes.

Questioner: Could you give me a little more information?

Some of our craft are based under what you would call ocean in various locations.

Questioner: Do you know anything about the disappearances in the area we call the Bermuda Triangle?

We are sorry, but this instrument is tired. We would conclude through another instrument. I am Hatonn.

(B channeling)

I am Hatonn. Again I greet you in the love and the light of our infinite Creator. I will leave through this instrument. I encourage you all upon spending more time in meditation. In the love and light I leave you now. I am Hatonn. ✞

Sunday Meeting
November 21, 1976

(Carla channeling)

My beloved brothers and sisters, it is a great privilege to make contact with your group. And I do so only to say my blessing and my peace are with you and your world. I am known to you as Philip. And I send you all the light of my brotherhood. I have wished to give encouragement to you and I know that you have felt it.

My beloved brethren, love each other. Serve each other. Know that throughout all of those who dwell upon your Earth at this time are your brothers and sisters. With your aid all will one day live in harmony. Do not falter. I may continue in a moment.

I am Philip of the Brotherhood of the Seven Rays. I leave you in light. My peace be unto you.

(H channeling)

I am Hatonn. Greetings, my friends, in the love and in the light of our infinite Creator. We are certain that you have noticed this evening that there is indeed a great deal of what you would call conditioning of the instruments. You may have noticed that there is a great intensity of energy flowing, and as this meeting progresses we shall increase that intensity and ask that you only still your self and accept that energy, if you so desire. For, my friends, the energy that you feel is energy that will assist you. It will bring forth into you physical *(inaudible)* greater physical energies, greater emotional controls, and greater intellectual disciplines.

My friends, those rays which we so often beam upon you that you call the conditioning ray are not only to provide telepathic contact but they are to assist you in recharging those energies which you dissipate through your lack of knowledge and discipline.

We of the Brotherhood of Planets in Service to the Infinite Creator are here only to serve those who would desire it. And we are grateful to be given the opportunity to join with you in these meetings and to provide our assistance as it is requested. We ask your patience for a moment, for as you may have noticed there are some differences in the voice of the instrument. And we are attempting to utilize greater control. And require a moment to bring that control to that point which is most advantageous for bringing forth this evening's message.

(Pause)

I am Oxal. My greetings to you. Many of you have never, shall we say, heard my voice. It is rare that I am given the opportunity to speak with you. Yet I am present at all of your meetings working with those of you who are desirous of obtaining those goals in life which you may or may not be aware of.

And it is that upon which I desire to speak this evening.

Each and every individual upon your sphere of existence is an instrument of the Creator. Each instrument by choice previous to the incarnation has chosen to fulfill that which many of you would call destiny. Many of you have chosen to work with one another and to love one another in simple fashion. And some have chosen to take upon themselves the responsibilities of what one might call a teacher. Some have chosen to enter into fields of endeavor in their life. Yet, we must stress, no matter what it is that you have chosen to do, whether it seems to you to be a task of simplicity or a task of great magnitude, it cannot be measured, my friends. Your worth to the Creator, your worth to your fellow man, and your worth to the entire universe is immeasurable, as is your existence. You are an infinite being. You are instilled with divinity. You are of the utmost importance. You are a portion and particle of the divine Creator. Without your existence the creation would be incomplete.

Never, my friends, judge that which you are to do once you become aware of it. And seek out that which you are to do. Know what it is that you have come into this existence for. And proceed to do it knowing that you are going about being thy Father's business. Do not attempt to do the Creator's business. Be that business. Judge not yourself. Judge not others. Accept all things freely and lovingly, and in saying this we do not mean that you must submit yourself to the onslaught of negativity.

Learn, my friends, to control those forces which influence. For indeed you have this ability instilled within you. Learn to be able to be, shall we say, bombarded by all negativity and meet it with you own positive energies and with the love and light which resides within you and overcome that negativity, purify it, encase it in the light, and send it back from whence it has come with your blessings.

Know, my friends, that indeed you and you alone are in control of your life and all the influences within it. You can accept upon yourself anything that you desire but no one has the ability to place upon you an experience or thought or energy form that you have not allowed to come in. It is true that many people do not know the proper means by which to control that which they accept, or to distinguish between the energy flows and know their work. Yet, my friends, if you seek out with true dedication that which you have entered into this life to achieve, a portion of that will bring forth to you the knowledges that you need in order to instill, or shall we say, in order to initiate the protective measures that you will require in order to achieve that destiny that you have chosen.

Realize, my friends, that as you travel life's journey you can alter that destiny. You are not committed to fulfill that which you have chosen to do. But if you do not know that, indeed, you shall return until you have done so. For in choosing your mission, shall we say, in life, you have done so because it is something that you have needed to give and to learn from. It is a lesson that you must experience in this classroom of life in order to achieve, shall we say, the next level of existence. You cannot learn 99% and pass, my friends. You must know all things, experience all things that this plane of existence has to offer. The passing grade is 100%.

My friends, that which you endeavor to do is much more serious than you have thought. Yet, do not be discouraged, for know that the Creator would not allow you to take upon yourself a greater task than what you can achieve and fulfill righteously.

My friends, as I have said, you are divine. Know this at all times. Recognize and learn to see the divinity within those around you and know that that divinity is within all beings. No matter who you come across in your life, whether they would be what you would call criminal, evil or good, they are divine. They are either fulfilling that which they have chosen to do or they shall do so in the future. Know that each person progresses at their own rate. Know that each person has that right to choose in what direction to go. Give whatever assistance you can to those that would request it. Give whatever assistance [you can] to those [who] would not request it when you know it would not be violating their will. And, my friends, the hardest, the hardest thing to do for those truly dedicated is to render no assistance to those that they know would not accept it. For to share your energies with those who would rebuke it is to waste, shall we say, precious time and precious energy. All that you can do for those is to love them and to bless them and allow them to go their way.

Each of you, my friends, has in one form or another begun the journey; the journey that shall lead you into the knowledge of that mission you have chosen.

Advance forward and never look back, for what is behind you, my friends, is experience. Utilize it properly and continue to go forward knowing that you shall indeed achieve those goals which you have entered into life for. Indeed, you are the servant of the Creator and the servant of your fellow man as the Creator is your servant and your fellow man your servant. But service, my friends, comes only in love and love does not demand and love does not possess. Love does not criticize. Love does not place judgment. Love my friends, as this instrument has been told before, can be simply defined: the L is for luminescence, the O is for omnipresence, the V is for vacillating, the E is for eternity. Love is luminescence, the light within you; the omnipresence everywhere vacillating and flowing forever eternally within you and within all your men who walk this plane of existence. And within each particle, within each molecule, within atomic structure that your scientist's observe, this love is and this love shall always be. It cannot be smitten. It cannot be hidden. It cannot be denied. Love is the most potent energy of the universe and it shall succeed over that which you call darkness or negativity.

Take these words of wisdom. Do with them what you will. Know that I love you, that my brothers and I continually send you our love, our light. We work upon a plane of existence which is what you would consider above yours. And we do many things which you do not see to assist you, but, my friends, it is your life and it is your mission. Do with it as you will and know that we will assist you.

I am Oxal. Though I leave, my brother Hatonn shall speak through another instrument, for this instrument is growing tired. I leave you in His love and in His light. I am Oxal.

(B channeling)

It is our pleasure to be with you. We are with you always in the light and the love of our infinite Father. It is indeed a pleasure to send forth this love in many forms and in all directions. And it is indeed an honor to instill within you these words of truth to be scattered as seeds from the essence of life. From the beginning, or the origin, of all existence there has always been an eternal truth that shall exist always. For the love we send to you is not a *(inaudible)*. Yet as it passes through we send with it the love within us *(inaudible)*.

We are sorry for the interruption. We shall attempt a different communication. I am Hatonn.

(Carla channeling)

I am again with this instrument. We would like to attempt to speak just a few words through the one known as M if he would be receptive to our contact, for we feel that the one known as M would indeed be of service. Yet, we in no way desire to infringe upon his free will. We will therefore simply attempt to speak a few words, if the instrument would relax and make himself receptive. I am Hatonn.

(Carla channeling)

I am again with this instrument. We understand and sympathize with all conditions of question and doubts regarding the contact. We are extremely privileged to help each of you for there are many ways to serve. And vocal channeling, as you call it, is but one.

It is possible that at some future time events may alter the thoughts of those who are not sure about attempting to be of service in this way. Yet, whatever the service is, my friends, it matters not. For as our brother said it, within this *(inaudible)* it is not the apparent magnitude of the service that we are concerned with in learning. It is only the attitude and the intention.

It has been written in your holy works that the master known as Jesus, indicating the correct role of the teacher, knelt upon the ground and washed the feet dusty from the road of those who were his students. This he did as a lesson. My brothers, that which you call humility among your peoples is a difficult lesson to learn. Many are those among you who feel that they are stronger than their brothers and must help them. Yet, we wish to share with you an understanding of yourselves for no one, my friends, is strong. Each is a collection of the strong and the weak. And just as when you are weak and you reach your hand out, someone has helped you and you needed that help.

Just so, if someone reaches out to you, you have as much need as that weak man as you did when you were weak *(inaudible)*. For in your strength you can only stay strong by giving that strength to others. Just as in your weakness you could only change by giving your weakness.

Mankind, and by this we mean the race of those whose souls or being are filled with the Creator in consciousness, all these men are one great *(inaudible)*. The strong have need of the weak and weak need of the strong, for all together make one. It has earlier been said, too, that without each of you, my brothers, the universe would not be completed. Without the weakest of your brethren, without the most troublesome, without the most foolish, you would be lacking. Know that you have a blessing and you are asked to reach out your hand. Know that just as the master known as Jesus would stop and heal the most wretched of those along the way, stop what he was doing with thousands to heal one weak man, so it is never your great dreams that are most important, but that which is required of you at the moment.

This cannot be accomplished without meditation, for inspiration of this kind is considered words of folly by your wise men. Meditate and go within, for that which is foolish to the world is a treasure to you *(inaudible)*.

Before I leave this gathering of souls, I would ask if there are any questions.

Questioner: *(Inaudible)*.

We are with the instrument. We are aware of your question. Each of you who dwell within the physical also has at the heart of that physical body an animating spirit. And this animating spirit often becomes the starved by the active daily existence of your physical being. It is in sleep that this being refreshes itself, for it is then free of the gross physical form with its chemicals and its impurities. And it can take instruction, work out deeper difficulties which have penetrated to its existence, and store up energies with which to animate the physical being during the waking period. Dream activity is of this nature and without the dream activity the physical being would soon be unable to function. This has been proven by your scientists and this instrument is aware of the research. Therefore, we say to you upon the level of the intellect alone it is apparent that the one of whom you speak does indeed dream.

As to the blocking of the dreams from the conscious mind, this soul comes into the physical body as an inmate into a prison. Depending upon the shock of that entry, the consciousness of vital spiritual being may have various awarenesses of what the prison is like. Those who have become [aware] that they are in prison are often more able to free themselves through dreams, even though their spirits are sad within them because of their imprisonment. Those who have some degree of consciousness of their condition of entrapment find it easier to be aware of their dreams. One such as the one of whom you speak are somewhat traumatized and have been unable to put their true personality, as you might call it—that is, the system of biases that make up that individual—into the totality of their physical consciousness. They are truly in, shall we say, solitary confinement.

In order to begin to unlock the consciousness of the imprisoned soul, so that it can communicate with the conscious mind through remembering the dreams, it is suggested that since this is a desirable situation to attempt to attain meditation, be devoted first to the silence and then to a seeking of wholeness. It is suggested that within this second type of meditation the seeker become aware of the Creator's infinity and presence in all areas and in all corners. There is nothing left out of the Creator. There is nothing that needs to be known that the Creator does not know. The Creator is within each of us. This meditation makes the consciousness available, when applied patiently, that relaxes the trauma of the imprisoned soul. Memory is to a certain extent a habit and it is a matter, in this case, of changing the habit of not remembering.

We are always available to aid. And it is also to [be] said that each of you has guides within what you would call the astral planes who are able to aid you simply by giving you light and strength within your worldly sphere. Seek this help and it will be given.

Does this answer your question?

Questioner: *(Inaudible)*.

My brother, there are many different lessons to be learned within the physical plane. To most who are here it is necessary that the consciousness be fully awake to the higher, shall we say, intellectual decisions of the physical world. But there are those who need to experience sensations. In order to do this it is necessary only to be within a physical form. There are others whose karma involves this debt. However, the one of whom you speak had a need to experience the beauties, the color, the light, and the feeling of the physical plane and he was able to do this by incarnating in such a vehicle. He receives these sensations in a pure and untouched manner due to the fact that his mentality is, as you would say, retarded. This is what he needs in this experience.

It is not a cruel creation. The harmonies are sometimes difficult to understand.

Is there another question?

Questioner: *(Inaudible).*

The instrument spoke of the Brotherhood of Seven Rays and the meaning of this is simply that light as you know it in its pure form contains various basic hues of colors. All of these colors together make up the light. And all the differences within all mankind make up one being.

The brotherhood which takes its name from this *(inaudible)* has been formed to work with all of the different hues and colors of mankind's spirit so that, as the one known as Brother Philip said, one day all of mankind will move in harmony and in oneness.

Does this answer your question?

Questioner: *(Inaudible).*

If there are no more questions, I will leave this instrument.

Questioner: *(Inaudible).*

One not only can, but one almost always does. It is simply that these contacts are not often remembered. If you work towards sensitizing your memory, you will begin to remember being given instructions by your teachers. This is the life of the soul.

(Tape ends.)

Sunday Meeting
November 28, 1976

(Carla channeling)

I am Hatonn, and I greet each of you in the love and the light of our infinite Creator. I and my brothers are privileged to be with you this evening.

Before we begin we would like to spend a few moments balancing the harmonies within your group in order to more easily tune ourselves to your needs at this time. If you will relax, we will work with you at this time.

(Pause)

I am again with this instrument. I am Hatonn. We of the Confederation of Planets in the Service of the Infinite Creator have been among your peoples for many of your years. And our purpose in your skies is becoming known to more and more of your peoples. This is our objective. Not in forcing our purpose upon the people of your planet but only in making it known what their purpose might be.

To those who wonder what would bring a more advanced race, as you might call us, to do such standoffish and unrewarding work among less advanced peoples, we can only say that our peoples no longer need to employ their time and their talent in order to gain what you call money so that we may live. We are, as you might say, independently wealthy. We have all that we need. And yet, as all conscious beings do, we have the need to grow. We cannot grow in power or riches. We can grow only in knowledge. We have found that this growth in knowledge is only possible through our sharing the knowledge that we have with our brothers. We, therefore, need you in order to grow.

It is only proper that we should meet each other, for all of creation is based upon giving one element to another. All of the creation, which you may observe in your daily life as the seasons change, is a balance, a harmony, and a flux, one element giving opportunity for the other to flourish. This giving, this growing, this knowledge is within you, is within each of you. Yet, my brothers, so many of your peoples have been taught by the society in which they live that they must rush blindly from one experience to another, filling in any space of time that is left empty by another experience. Thus the flow, the harmony, the balance of your own understanding is blocked while constantly blocking your own receptions, for you are constantly thinking, you are constantly reacting.

It is very important to your peoples at this time that you seek the knowledge of who you are and what you truly want for your planet, and indeed your whole solar system is at this time progressing into a new area of space and a new vibration of experience. This has been said by so many of your own people we do but echo this truth. It has even been given a name. Many of your people speak of the Aquarian

Age, or the Golden Age. You may join the Age that is to come, that is already becoming apparent, if your vibrations are such that they are in harmony with that vibration. That is what we are here to tell you. That is our purpose here: to share with you our understanding. Our understanding is that we are all created as one being. That that one being is in a state of perfect love and harmony. And that our purpose in this and every experience is to more fully realize and understand the reality of that perfect love.

Your peoples are much like what you would call chain smokers. As the smoker smokes one cigarette after another, he loses the taste. The very experience he is seeking so hard eludes him more and more. Avoid this if you like. To space these experiences that are properly *(inaudible)*, it is by far the most advantageous way to use meditation. In whatever manner that you choose to practice this technique, silence holds the key to your understanding of yourself and the creation around you.

I would like to transfer the contact at this point. I am Hatonn.

(H channeling

I am Hatonn. I am now with this instrument. I greet you once again in the love and the light of our infinite Creator. I have said that silence is the key. My friends, in that book which you call the *Bible* the word silence is mentioned many times. And in truth, the silence of which we speak is the key to all knowledge, all understanding. That silence is the time spent listening to the voice of the Creator. And that voice may be heard through the practice of meditation. It is a voice that is not audible. Yet it is a voice that is clear and precise. It is a voice such as you have never heard. Yet, it is a voice to which you listen to at all times. My friends, to define the Creator is, for any being, incomprehensible. Yet, to begin to understand Him is indeed within your, shall we say, ability. Each and every individual, as we are aware of it, is nothing other than a projection of a pure thought from that source which we call the Creator. Each thought has taken upon itself forms of personal identities. In an essence they vacillate upon that same, shall we say, spiritual cycle of existence.

If it is true, that your existence has been brought about through none other than the thought of the Creator, and if it is true, as it has been stated in your holy scripture, that man is created in the image and likeness of his Creator, then therefore it is true, my friends, that your thought brings into existence the creation in which you live.

My friends, you have been given this opportunity, this live experience, in which to learn many lessons. And you have been given all of the abilities of your Creator for within you, He is. And working through you He shall always be. And with these abilities you truly create the experiences that you have. Not only in this life but in all existence upon all levels.

There are certain, what you would call, laws that are undeniable and unbreakable. Yet, it is your choice. It is your choice in which directions to go and what creations you wish to experience. It is necessary for man upon the planet Earth at this time, above all others that you are aware, to learn to control the thought projections, especially those which are detrimental not only to other individuals, but to your Earth sphere and its environment. Man upon planet Earth, indeed within himself, is godly in nature. You are divine and you have no limitations unless you choose to accept them. Yet, where man upon planet Earth has, shall we say, gone astray, is in the failure to recognize that that for which he searches is within him.

Those upon planet Earth—not all, but most—seek that divine intelligence that they call God. They use the intellect to search for Him in books. They search for Him in dwellings called churches. They search for Him to be working through others. And most often fail to recognize that He is working through them from within them. My friends, it has been stated that the Kingdom of Heaven lies within. And indeed these words are true. Within you is that spark of divinity. And that spark of divinity, shall we say, is a part and particle of the overall construction of that energy which is the Creator. You have not been separated from Him. You are not fallen angels, as some may think. You are creators working together whether you be aware of it or not, formulating the existence that you need.

It is so simple, my friends, that man has missed the simplicity of existence. It is not within the intellectual capabilities of man to totally understand the words which we speak. But it is indeed within the spiritual intellect of man to understand all things. And in order for both that which you call the physical intellect and the spiritual intellect to work together, closely and in harmony at all times, an attunement must be made by the individual. An attunement which takes away the barriers of limitation, the barriers of judgmentation and draws all knowledges from the sphere on which you exist within this body and this sphere, all spheres on which you exist in spirit. All are unioned; all come together; and all is known. But in order to do this there is a great need for dedication to achieving that point of knowledge. Dedication to service of your fellow men. Dedication to fulfillment of your Creator's will. And dedication to bringing about the most perfect being that you can be.

My friends, the disciplines which the masters have taken upon themselves are indeed difficult in the eyes of mortal men. But once they are accomplished, once they are internalized, they too take upon themselves the simplicity of truth. They bring forward the rewards. And those rewards, my friends, cannot be spoken of in words, for they are of the Creator and words are only a portion of this creation and of the Creator's existence.

How can man understand, how, only utilizing a portion of his abilities, the knowledge of the universe? Man must learn to utilize all that is within his capability and indeed that, my friends, is unlimited.

Divine in nature are all your fellow beings. Recognize this within them. Allow them to do that which they choose and assist them in any they may request. But place upon them no limitations or judgments for it. It is they themselves and only they who have that right to limit and judge what they are to be and what they are to do. Go through this experience of life knowing that all things are indeed the reflection of the divinity within you and accept them and learn from them what you can. And love them at all times as your Creator loves you.

I shall once again transfer this contact. I am Hatonn.

(Carla channeling)

I am again with this instrument. I am Hatonn. Before I leave this group, I would like to open the meeting to questions. If you have any at this time please ask them.

Questioner: *(Inaudible).*

I am Hatonn. We felt that to impress information at this time would be premature.

Don: *(Inaudible).*

I am with the instrument. Your group is now in harmony and at peace, so we ask that you let your hearts carry that peace out with you and into another world that may not look like what your heart looks [like] right now. All of creation speaks of harmony and it takes a very special eye to see it. That is the eye that is informed in meditation. That is the ear that is informed in meditation. That is the heart that is informed in meditation. *(Inaudible)* … and now is the time.

I leave you in the love and the light of the infinite Creator. I am Hatonn. Adonai vasu. ☙

Sunday Meeting
December 12, 1976

(Don channeling)

I greet you in the love and the light of our infinite Creator. It is a very great privilege to be with you. I have been observing *(inaudible)*. We are aware of all of your activities, all of your thoughts, which may surprise you or it may not. For as you know, we have been interested not only in your planet, but select groups *(inaudible)*. We're concerned at this time about certain activities upon your planet. We're concerned at this time that certain information reach your peoples.

We're concerned. We are helpless, you might say, in some respects for we can only give information in certain limited ways. We give information through channels such as this one simply because the channel is receptive and has allowed the information to pass through him. Had he not allowed this, we could not give this information. There would be no way available *(inaudible)*, for this is the desire of our *(inaudible)*. That, and only that which is desired will be given. Only that which is desired will be received. For this reason, those upon your planet will be receiving, as always, precisely what they desire. It is a problem, we realize, to give precisely what is desired to those who desire it and not infringe upon those who do not desire what we offer. We have to offer what we understand to be a truth/beauty far beyond that which is experienced upon your planet. Yet, we can only offer this in a very limited way.

My friends, free will must be at all times criteria for our communicating, for our contacts, for any of our peoples' contacts. For this reason, we are dependent upon those upon your surface who would reach out for us. My friends, we have much to do and yet, it is difficult, in a sense, for your peoples to understand the simple truths that we bring forward to you. These simple truths, my friends, will, as it is said in your holy works, set you free. For you are truly in bondage: bondage to an idea that is false. An idea which the peoples of your planet have clung to steadfastly for many, many of the generations. An idea which led them down a road of confusion. An idea that brought them to the present state, which is in any terms, quite *(inaudible)*.

We implore you to act with us to help those who seek our help. And yet, we realize that you yourself have limitations and barriers. We feel sad that these limitations must always be upon us. And yet, these limitations are the essence of our being here, for without them you would not exist. These limitations, my friends, are the essence of the creation. *(Inaudible)* for in His total understanding, He is creating a perfect balance, a perfect freedom of experience. For, my friends, even though that which you experience may seem to be far from what you desire, it is precisely what you desire. You would not be experiencing it, my friends, if you did not desire it. You desire it for purposes of growth. You desire it for other purposes. And yet, it is the essence of your life. Join with us to improve that essence at as fast a rate as you can possibly afford. This is our mission: to aid you on that path at an ever increasing rate and an ever increasing understanding. Give to us your time in meditation. We shall wait for all of your peoples as *(inaudible)* as yourselves to reach that which you desire: a state of understanding that lasts, a harmony, a love *(inaudible)*.

It has been a great privilege speaking through this instrument, my friends. I will transfer this contact. I am Hatonn.

(H channeling)

I am Hatonn. I am now with this instrument. My friends, as you endeavor to seek out those knowledges and truths which would assist you in your growth and in your ability to assist others in theirs, it is necessary that you recognize that that which you seek shall only come as quickly as you, shall we say, desire it. Yet, my friends, what we mean is that with the effort you put forth you determine the speed in which you receive the assistance which you seek. There are many upon your planet, and indeed you know many of them, who would wish to gain knowledge and assistance, yet who are, shall we say, unwilling to follow, shall we say, the divine bartering system. That which you receive, my friends, you are deserving of through the efforts that you put forth. And that which you receive is not to be hoarded, it is to be shared. Yet, it is only to be shared with those who are seeking that knowledge. You need not be concerned with seeking out those to who you may render your assistance for as you have seen, they have come to you.

And as you develop, and as you become, shall we say, the instrument of greater knowledge, then greater numbers shall seek from you that which you have attained. And we wish to stress that you make it clear to those who would come to you for assistance that you are indeed willing to share with them that which you have come to know, but that they also must be willing to share with others, put forth the efforts on their own to gain the knowledge that they seek. And as you are aware, the effort which is of greatest importance is that dedication to the practice and proper utilization of your daily meditation. As you have experienced, through your meditation you gain the unspoken words, the unwritten wisdoms. And through your meditations, you gain the strength to persevere [in addressing] those tests which befall you.

And as many of you have come to know, the greater your desire and your effort to attain the highest form of knowledge available, the greater the test. But all things, indeed, as you would recognize it, has a price, my friends. Even that which you seek of a spiritual nature. All things must be attained in a way that balance can be maintained in the universe. To seek knowledge is to ask to receive energies and if you draw forth from the universe any energy then you must be willing to send forth energy to replace it.

My friends, you can leave no voids in your life or in your efforts or in your attainments. You are the master of your existence. You are the co-creator of your universe. And that which you do must be done completely, for each, shall we say, error which you commit there is repercussion of a negative nature. And for each right that you perform there is the repercussion of a positive nature. So therefore, whatever energies come to you, they have come due to your projection of like energy. And as they flow throughout this universe, you must be, shall we say, open to allow the cycles of energies to continue flowing freely so that they may be shared by all.

As many of the teachers upon your Earth have told their students, the greatest step towards attaining that which they seek is to bring in focus the discipline of one's own thoughts and actions. To think properly is to create properly. To think unrighteously is to create havoc within your universe. These laws you cannot transmute. These laws are those which you must live by throughout this existence and all others which you have experienced and shall experience. As those of you here have attained certain levels of knowledge, it is your responsibility to share them when given the opportunity. And it is your responsibility to seek out greater levels so that your assistance can be of more benefit. Yet, it is your choice whether to do so. There is no energy within the universe capable of overcoming, or controlling in any way, your actions. Only you are the creator. You may accept the influences of your co-creators. That is also your choice.

As this group proceeds to grow and to learn, it shall become evident, step-by-step, to each individual, their, shall we say, mission within this organization.

Indeed, my friends, you are of great importance to those around you. And this position which you have requested, in one form or another, is one which shall bring upon you from time to time the scorn of your fellow man. For you must recognize, my friends, there shall continually be that, shall we call it, balance, between those energies of the positive nature and those of the negative. And if you are recognized by an individual as being the opposite of what they feel that they are, they shall fear you through their lack of understanding and attempt to bring upon you an air of nonacceptance through their reflections upon you. Bless these individuals, seek not to retaliate. But seek, shall we say, to remain segregated from those influences as much as possible.

As you endeavor to do that which you feel is of importance to you and to your universe, recognize that you are the individual and that you are the whole. Seek not to know the fallacies of your universe for indeed they are not existent if you do not recognize them. The plane of existence on which you are presently living, as many times we have stated, is strictly an illusion projected by the thought patterns of its inhabitants. It is your, shall we say, birthright to create it in whatever way, shape or form that you desire. It is within you to accept or reject the outer manifestations upon this plane of existence. Recognize that which is of benefit to you, and accept not that which is of detriment to you. This is indeed difficult, yet it can be attained. As you seek out the Creator within you and join with Him and use your *(inaudible)*.

I shall transfer this communication. I am Hatonn.

(H channeling)

I am Hatonn. I am once again with this instrument. We are unable to achieve contact with either of the instruments that we have attempted to communicate through due to different circumstances within each. And, as always, we recognize the freedom of choice in each individual. We would ask that you would allow our energies to flow and our love to *(inaudible)*. As we leave you, know that we shall remain with you at all times. We are aware of the difficulties and we shall work upon our plane of existence to assist you, each of you in your hour of need. Yet, it is you, as we have stated, who have manifested the difficulties that are experienced. It is you, as the creator of your universe, that contains the power *(inaudible)* through conscious projection of your creative ability.

I leave you now in the light and in the light of our infinite Creator. I am Hatonn. Adonai vasu borragus.

(Carla channeling)

(A question was asked but not recorded.)

Don: *(Inaudible)* … is of a somewhat unpredictable nature, although we feel that it is still highly probable that there will be what you call earthquake activity in the area of California and the sea on the date we have mentioned, because the Earth, as you might say, is angry and violence is very probable. It is possible, due to the increase of what you would call consciousness-raising activity directed toward alleviation of this difficulty, that it may either be put off or its intensity diminished. We do expect this activity, but nothing is ever hopeless. And your efforts to send light can and will help.

Have you further questions?

Don: *(Inaudible)*.

The area around Los Angeles has a very high probability, in the area of 85 to 100%. This probability remains high. It is at this point at about 65% and climbs steadily to 85% during the next two years. It reaches 90% within one day and remains at that level for a period of seven of your days.

Don: *(Inaudible)*.

It reaches 90% on the date which we have given you, which is the September [3 or 30.] It remains at the level of 90% for seven of your days. From that point on it is gradually more difficult to judge the percentage of the possibility for it is a high probability that it will already have happened by that time.

Don: What magnitude *(inaudible)* on the Richter Scale?

We are aware of your measurements, but we are wary of giving you these measurements due to the fact that depending upon the consciousness of light groups such as yours, the intensity may be *(inaudible)*. Your scales may indicate as high as between a 7 and an 8.

Don: *(Inaudible)*.

We are sorry that this instrument's understanding of geography is *(inaudible)*. There is a probability that extends in sort of a triangle shape from a line somewhat north of Los Angeles extending inward, cutting a long wedge of the south and out to sea south of Los Angeles and cutting upwards through the ocean to form the third side of the triangle. This is the area of greatest tension. Precisely where it will happen, we cannot state. Again there are probabilities. The highest probability, which ranks perhaps 60%, is that the worst shocks will occur somewhat south. There is probability of perhaps 30% that it will occur to the greatest extent on the northern line and there is perhaps a 10% chance that the activity will be at its most intense at sea.

Don: How many days before the event will we be able to *(inaudible)*?

We are having difficulty for we have difficulty with your time. Our accuracy varies. To be able to state at any time before an event actually occurs upon your plane, it will simply be a matter of chance, for we are constantly adjusting our understanding to your local time system. Therefore, we cannot state as gospel, as you might say, ahead of time. Although it is possible that we might be accurate ahead of time, our predictions are just that. And our predictions—much like your weather reports based upon fact. For us to be able to intercept in actuality in advance of this happening on your plane, it would be necessary for us to be in perfect coordination with those planes which are immediately adjacent to your physical plane. And we have the same problems with those planes of your system which are not bound as we do with the physical plane, in that they are local and dependent upon their time systems. Within those planes of your system which are not bound by time, this event is not also bound by time and therein lies the difficulty.

Have I by any chance made myself clear enough for your understanding?

Don: Yes. I would like to ask one more question. You have indicated that these cataclysmic effects are not completely desired. Can't this be viewed as a beneficial catalyst in the ultimate advancement of the Earth's population?

That which is necessary and that which is desirable are not necessarily the same. That your peoples must go through an inharmonious adjustment to their environment may be necessary. Yet, harmony is a desirable fact and one which is more natural to spiritual growth.

Don: My question is, is it not possible that the desired harmony be achieved more rapidly *(inaudible)*?

Are you speaking of this particular instance?

Don: *(Inaudible)*.

My brother, what is happening upon your planet now is what is necessary and therefore it is desirable. However, the physical plane is most effective when the catalyst of the physical problems is worked out entirely within the individual consciousness of each who dwells within the planet. When each who dwells within the physical plane is dealing with and coping with his path in terms of physical problems and difficulties, the harmony of the planetary sphere is maintained. This is indeed the most rapid and the most desirable rate of growth when the individual is growing at the same rate as the natural environment is growing. These cataclysms are simply evidence that the personal growth of those who dwell upon the planet have not kept pace with the natural environment's growth. Therefore, the entry into the next vibration has become difficult, making it necessary for the inharmony between consciousness and environmental consciousness to be alleviated by catastrophes such as the one you are experiencing.

Certainly, these drastic difficulties will cause some consciousnesses to open at last and thereby graduate, for drastic circumstances do encourage rapid growth. However, growth would have been much more rapid if it had been chosen on the personal level in harmony with the environment in the first place. This is why we feel that it is not particularly desirous that these difficult conditions prevail. However, we accept the necessity of it at this time due to the consciousness of your people.

Questioner: *(Inaudible)* … seems to me that the only hope for a relatively large percentage *(inaudible)* … is to experience the cataclysmic transition. Am I correct in that *(inaudible)*.

There is always a chance that those who are lost will find their way home. And this is why great efforts are being made by the Confederation and others to encourage shepherds to go out among the lost and do what they can to brief those, as you put it, on the fence into the light. Your question is difficult for us to respond to in your language, but we will attempt with this answer.

Those who dwell upon your planet have, whether they will or not, come to a time which is irrevocable. This is the time that they will either graduate or not. Your environmental difficulties are inevitable. They occur whether or not they do any good. They do not occur in order to give lessons, although they will certainly do some good. This is simply an adjustment period. For the most part, those who will graduate are already awake, for, you see, this is very late. We have been speaking to peoples for many years now. Most of those who we could collect have been collected. We understand the thrust of your question and we do assure that the catastrophes that your peoples will experience are at the most basic level part of harmony and part of a goodness and not to be feared. For …

(Side one of tape ends.)

(Carla channeling)

Does this answer this question?

Don: What can people like us do in light of this transition to best aid the master plan?

As you know, we cannot guide you in your day-to-day choices of activity. We can only encourage you to meditate and seek guidance from your higher selves, for each of you was sent by your higher selves with a job to do. You have the means to do it. And you certainly have our appreciation for your desire to help us help you. The answers will come in meditation. You know that you do have help from those upon the higher planes of your planet. We have long encouraged you to think of yourselves as shepherds and channels. And certainly we can say this is the key as service is always the key. But beyond that we cannot guide you, for that would be an infringement upon your free will. This is, above all things, your planet. You have incarnated here specifically to take that responsibility upon yourselves and to make choices for yourselves, to render your personal service.

We say only to you that we are completely with you and send our light and our love to you. You must be aware that our basic desire is to tell this planet that love is all that there is; to let this planet know that the creation is the Creator's and that many, many within its infinity praise His name. An earlier voice than ours, that of the master known as Jesus, instructed his followers to go to the ends of the Earth and tell all that they met about the Truth. This is the time honored [so] and we subscribe to it. We are instruments of the Creator and so are you. We have our limitations and so do you. But your limits are far, far more capacious than ours for you have chosen to incarnate and this gives you greater scope and greater responsibilities.

May we assist you further through this instrument?

Don: *(Inaudible).*

I leave you. I am privileged to be using this instrument and we do thank the one known as Carla. We are with you. We are your brothers. Adonai vasu. I am Hatonn. ☥

Year 1977
April 13, 1977 to November 9, 1977

Wednesday Meditation
April 13, 1977

(Don channeling)

I am Hatonn. It is a very great privilege to once more be with you. It is always a very great privilege to be able to communicate with those of the planet Earth who are receptive to our contact. We would very much appreciate contact with all of the peoples of this planet. However, this is not possible at this time.

Very shortly we will be contacting many more of the peoples on your surface than we have in the past. We will be doing this through various methods. We will create in the very near future what you would call an advertisement of our presence. This will alert very large numbers of the peoples of your planet as to our reality. At this time it will be necessary for those who believe that they know of our mission to come forth and speak of that, if they so desire. They will find, unfortunately, considerable frustrations in doing this since, as before, they will have no way of proving that which they have come to know as the truth about us. We would prefer to be able to give this understanding directly to the people of your planet. However, this is not possible. It is only possible to give to them the unproven truth of our presence and our mission. For this reason, we will maintain a continued aloofness from direct contact. However, our presence will be less aloof or less unknown. This is timed in such a way as to coincide with certain activities that have been carried out by numerous of the peoples of your planet. These activities have resulted in a partial dissemination, in a very limited fashion, of the actual purpose of our contact. We are at present planning to stimulate the seeking of knowledge about us by becoming somewhat more open in our activities. It has been thirty of your years since the activation of public contact in a very limited way. During this time, such information about us has been stored within your societies upon the surface of your planet.

The second phase, as you might call it, is now beginning. A phase that will include, as I have said, an advertisement of our presence to be followed by the dissemination of still unprovable information about us. This, my friends, is the second phase.

I will transfer this contact at this time to another instrument.

(N channeling)

Again it is a great privilege to speak to you. This second phase, as we have called it, will help many of your peoples on their way in search of truth. As I have said, it will … I will pause.

(Doorbell rings.)

We welcome the new member to the group this evening. As I was saying, this new phase will help more people in their search for the truth. They will be stimulated and will have new energy to pursue the truth. My brothers, there will be much more frustration and it will cause many to wonder deeply whether or not they are pursuing a worthwhile path. But I and my brothers will be [with] them and with you at all times if you desire it to give assistance as much as we can.

I will now transfer this contact. I am Hatonn.

(Carla channeling)

I am with this instrument. I am Hatonn, and I greet you in the love and the light of the infinite Creator. We did not wish to come to this instrument earlier for we wish to use the talent and build up the confidence of each of our instruments. Also, each instrument has his own special talents and we wished to speak through this instrument on subjects which would be of interest to the new member.

Within your universe there is a local phenomenon which is known to you as time and a local set of conditions represented to you by mass and space and your so-called Euclidean geometry. And because of this we speak to you of cycles and of timing our campaign. We are dealing with a local set of parameters and it is in this way that we communicate with you that we bridge the gap between our way of thinking and your way of thinking. There is a level on which the talk of cycles and anything of campaigns is, if anything, only partially so for this is a level of which we are far more aware than you: that all things are truly one; that all cycles truly become circles; that all corners truly become rounded into one unending globe of unity—infinite, invisible, eternal and containing all that there is.

These concepts are not graspable by your peoples and so we deal with the local, understandable frame of reference and say that you are coming to the end of a cycle and that we are attempting to help those of you who wish to be helped at this time to make progress on your cycle so that you may spiral upward in the great dance along the spiritual path. To understand your place in the universe at this time is very, very critical. Because you are within a physical body, it is important that you deal in a balanced manner with your physical existence with the demands and the responsibilities of the physical life. It is very difficult, and purposely so, to balance the physical existence and spiritual seeking. It is to test your ability to do this that you have entered this sphere. It is a great mistake, my friends, to care too much for the physical body and its needs.

Yet, we say to you also, beware of the opposite. Do not care too little for your physical vehicle and its needs. You must look upon your physical vehicle as just that: it is a vehicle. It is functioning well for you and like a good fruit tree, it has grown, it has come into its youth, it has borne truth. Perhaps it has grown a little gnarled, a little bent, and as the years go on it will become increasingly gnarled and it will [have] served its time. All of its fruit will have been given up and it will be cut down. This is your physical body. You may accept it as a good and faithful servant. The circumstances of your being here, of the type and condition of your life, are intended and are offered to you so that you make take your conditions and learn. You may take your body and be of service to others. Your body has hands with which to reach out to others; a mouth with which to smile, my friends; a mind to function well for you and to think well of others. It is not you, but it is no stranger to you. It is yours for a time. Keep this in balance, neither rejecting or being overly fond of those portions of your identity which are only temporary.

In meditation, seek your permanent identity. Within you there is a perfect body. And that body is your spirit. It is not a body as you would think of a body. And yet it is the ultimate house of your soul. To penetrate upward through the various shells of being to the final center of yourself is the goal of meditation. For within that final center is your link with all that there is. We are urging you, shall we say, to do your homework at this time. The joy, the state of joy, my friends, that you left to come into the physical existence is very greatly needed among your peoples at this time. And how few there are that understand that joy is the natural state of existence for each of those who dwell upon the surface of your sphere.

You see, my brothers, you are not on the same order of the apple tree. You are not out in the weather. You do not grow, wither and die. You are a consciousness that is not born and does not die. You are joy. To touch this place within yourself is all-important at this time, for if you can but make contact with your higher self, you can be of great comfort and of great service to many in the days to come. For in the days to come, as we have said many times, there will be many who are afraid, and many who have put off their voyage of self-discovery until the very last minute and who, when they finally realize that they must now decide who they are, will be absolutely terrified. One person, who is sure of who he and is radiating the joy of that knowledge and who can reach out with his light will be of infinite service, as people always have been when they are able to shine with the light and the love of the Creator.

Before I leave this instrument, I would like to open this meeting to questions.

M: Last week you briefly discussed the Bermuda Triangle. Can you give any more explanation on what is causing it, where people are going—disappearing in that area and in other areas that are similar?

I have no objection to sharing certain descriptions with you through this instrument as to the supposed location of people who disappear under the circumstances. However, the descriptions are very, very rough and bear little resemblance to the full truth due to the limitations of the instrument's understanding and the limits of your present technology.

In the first place, many of those who supposedly disappeared are merely on the bottom of the ocean. However, there have been some anomalistic cases where beings, and in some cases inanimate objects were, shall we say, bent through a dimension of space/time which is not space/time, but which is an analogous substance which interacts with your space/time to form, shall we say, interpenetrating spheres. These are local shunts, or time displacement tunnels, as you might call them, developed and/or discovered many centuries ago. Or in some cases, they are simply anomalistic occurrences of a natural type but of the same order. In some cases, the objects are simply crushed by the excessive power of the transformation. But in most instances, the objects are transformed into another type of vibration which, while not at all equal to your higher planes, are none the less congruent or tangent to these planes in such a way that beings can no longer exist in this local time and space, but instead exist in what you might call an alternate reality, though we do not like this term.

It is as though you take a maypole with many colors of ribbon and plaited the ribbon in an infinitely yet completely regular complexity so that many realities interpenetrate. Each of these realities have many planes. The only difference, my friends, is that there is no maypole and this we cannot explain to you. Our reluctance was in talking about the precise structure or methodology of constructing such areas because this type of power would again be wasted by your peoples if at this time if it were rediscovered. There has been enough waste already.

Does this answer your question?

M: Yes.

N: I have a question. When I channel, it seems that I can usually pick up the contact fairly easy and then after a short period of time—most of the time it is a short period of time—I just seem to lose it. I get the basic contact, or thoughts, but I can't seem to carry it for any length, but I'd like to. Do you know why I do this or have any suggestions to help me with channeling?

I am aware of your question. When an instrument such as yourself reaches the level of ability of which you speak, he has two choices. He can either remain at that level or he can consciously work to extend or to enlarge his ability to sustain an image. Basically, those who succeed in becoming a more extended type of channel are those who are willing to build up their confidence enough to continue sustaining an image beyond the first completed thought or image.

There are several ways in which to encourage yourself in this service to others. Perhaps one of the best ways is to encourage within yourself any tendency to do spiritual reading or meditation upon a spiritual thought. This, shall we say, stimulates your own higher self and provides our contact with more fuel, if you would call it that, for our own thoughts to mesh and work with.

This type of channeling that we are using with your group is not pure channeling. Very seldom do we achieve anything like a pure contact. It is a joint effort between the channel and our thought wave. The more open the channel is to being used to saying things without regard to their sense or what will come next, the more confidence the channel has that something will work out in the end, the more extended our contact through anyone channel can be. There is a delicate balance, of course, between being confident enough to sustain a contact and being so confident that you lose a contact while attempting to speak your own thoughts. However, we do not feel that you would ever have this problem due to your temperament and nature which is not prone to this type of energy.

Therefore, we simply urge you, in addition to silent meditation, [to] put aside a few minutes as often as possible for spiritual reading or meditation upon a thought or an image of a spiritual nature. Then we simply suggest that as you pray that you may be of service to others you then relax and have a quiet confidence that this prayer will be answered. It will take a while for you to build up to longer messages, yet, as you seek so shall you find. And this is true of this desire to serve as well as any other desire that you might have. We are at all times with you and encourage you in any way that we can. And above all, we wish to express our gratitude that you wish to be of service in this way.

N: Thank you.

I am with the instrument. Is there another question? I am with you. I and my brothers at all times are with. It has been said that we are a voice of love. And let me tell you, my friends, our voice is millions strong. And our voice is heard by more and more of your peoples. We thank you for letting us speak among you and share with [you] our thoughts. We ask you to lift up your voice also, for each voice that speaks of love and light to your peoples is a voice of great worth and of great beauty. Seek that love and light within yourself, my friends, and then share it. I leave you in His light and in His love. I am one of Hatonn. Adonai.

Wednesday Meditation
August 10, 1977

(Carla channeling)

I am Hatonn, and I greet you in the love and the light of the infinite Creator. We are very pleased to be with you and we greet each of you. We have a good contact tonight and this makes it easier for us to share our thoughts with you.

Your peoples, my friends, do not always have a good contact with us, or with any of those who attempt to help them to remember their true self. Why is it, my friends, that your peoples are often so unaware of the friends that they have? We have come from other worlds, shall we say, other dimensions, other times. Any of your helpers are parts of your own real self, separated from you only by your limited consciousness while within the physical illusion. Others of your helpers have been your teachers through past experiences on the soul level. You have teachers who are within the physical illusion with you at this time whose words you may read or hear; whose music you may hear; whose feelings you may come to understand on a conscious level.

Within the illusion, all of these helpers, my friends, [who] people your world—are inhabitants within the life of your true self which you call the soul. And yet, how many of your peoples, my friends, think they are alone, and the world is a jungle and they must get by the best they can? With this kind of philosophy, my friends, every day is a difficult one; every decision is a hard one; and all brothers and sisters are met with suspicion. Yet, my friends, you are truly very rich in friends, most of them unseen, most of them available only through meditation.

Your own higher self is your greatest friend. Your own higher self retains the memory of all that you have learned. Not only in this experience, but in that great sum of experience through which your true self has traveled on its path to where you are now. It has been written in your holy works that the master known as Jesus came to declare the acceptable year of the Creator, the acceptable time for understanding of unity. At the beginning of your cycle, your people were unacceptable, for there was a great darkness, a great forgetting, for all the souls that had begun in this cycle at that time had to begin with total lack of memory, had to begin in the darkness of total illusion to rediscover independently and of free will all of the truths of the Creator; all of the truths and of love and brotherhood; all of those things that separate the conscious awareness of the living soul from the instinctive rise of awareness of your animal life.

And in the instinct to conscious awareness of truth, your peoples have labored long, for thousands of your years, through many lives. You have worked to begin to express in a conscious manner your knowledge of unity.

The master known as Jesus came to declare that acceptable truth. He served as a perfect example. And those truths have become more and more acceptable to individual souls as the cycle has progressed. That acceptable year, my friends, draws nigh and is upon you. That which you are expressing at this time may well be your final expression within this cycle. It is time, as this instrument would say, to get it right. It is within the awareness of each of you within this group to understand the pressures of the one who desires to pass the test at the end of the school year. There is a studying, there is a caring, a desiring that one's level of understanding may be acceptable.

We ask, my friends, that as you turn to meditation, you turn with desire to understand fully that which is acceptable, that which is true. Many, many are the philosophies and the religions among your peoples that always, no matter what the disagreements and contradictions of what you may call dogma, always the ethical considerations remain constant. The ethics, that which is acceptable, do not seem to be in question for action is the most expressive form of truth. Therefore, we ask you to meditate and seek that truth. And then go forth and enjoy. Allow that which is acceptable to the Father to flow from you as you have received it in meditation.

Perhaps there is a greater question in back of what we speak to you about this evening. Perhaps while you are within the physical illusion you can never be totally sure that it is truly an illusion and that your real self is completely infinite and has eternal life. It is for reasons such as these that a word known as "faith" was conceived by your peoples. The word has unfortunate connotations, yet it is not foolish to have faith. There are many things which are not seen, but which you for some reason have inner conviction will come to pass. My friends, they will come to pass whether or not you have inner convictions. But your own personal progress along the lines of seeking will be much more rapid if you allow yourself to trust that intuition that tells you that our words are true. As you allow yourself to have as much faith as you may feel comfortable with, that small amount of faith will express itself to you in reflection in many privately convincing ways so that gradually you will not have to go on faith anymore for you will have been shown in ways that are clear to you that that which you had faith [in] is indeed true.

Therefore, my friends, [it] is not the tool of the fanatic or one who is mentally deficient or one who is mentally lazy. Faith is the conscious tool of the intellect used to link your intellect, which is a rather weak tool, with your intuition and your deeper awarenesses, which are very strong tools, but about which you know nothing intellectually. Many have said that there can be no link between the intellect and the intuition, or the heart. But, my friends, this is not so for all people know those things about which one has faith. All people are aware that it is possible to believe in love, in hope, in giving, in healing. All people, even the most materialistic, my friends, are aware of the legitimacy and the worth of these unseen powers. Their faith may be greatly diminished, but the words, concepts and the possibility of faith are meaningful. Ask yourself what things you have faith in; what things are of worth to you. And allow those things to expand as you bring them into your conscious, intellectual awareness. First, through meditation and then through the actions given to others in joy.

We are attempting the transformation of beings through these speeches. We can do so very little, my friends. We can only urge you to meditate; possibly, inspire you through our descriptions of those things of which we have the greatest faith, in which we feel the greatest belief. In our vibration, these are not inspiring words, these are the sober truths. In our vibrations, my friends, they must come through the mists of the material illusion. They must be filtered through your words. And all we can hope is that through the magic of your imagination and your desire to seek the truth our words will inspire you to meditate.

As we said many times, we do not know it all. We are not very wise. We have simply been a little farther up what you might call Jacob's Ladder. And we know that the journey is far, far more beautiful, more rewarding, and more deserving of faith than any possible journey to any possible place in space, in time, or in imagination. The journey for truth, my friends, is a journey for love, a journey for yourself, for you are truth and love. We hold out our hands to you on this journey and if at any time you wish our thoughts or the simple strengthening of our vibration, request it mentally, and I and my brothers will be there. That, my friends, is another thing in which you may have faith.

I would like my brother Laitos to work with you. I will return. I am Hatonn.

I am Laitos. And again I greet you in the love and the light of the infinite Creator. If you will be patient, I would like to work with each of you briefly to offer our contact to you. I would like to condition the one known as G. If she would relax, I would condition her. If she desires, I will speak a sentence or two through her. Please relax and speak up as I give you my thoughts. I am Laitos.

(Carla channeling)

I am again with this instrument. We have some adjusting to do with this instrument. If the one known as G would be patient, we would like to slightly adjust the tuning. We will again attempt contact. I am a Laitos.

(Carla channeling)

I am Laitos. We thank the one known as G for the privilege of working with her. We have a fairly stable contact and we are greatly appreciative of the opportunity. We would attempt to contact the one known as M1, if he would relax. We would like to say a sentence or two through him if he desires this service.

(M1 channeling)

I am Laitos. I …

(Carla channeling)

I am again with this instrument. I am Laitos. We are very, very pleased to make contact with the one known as M. It is an exciting thing for us and for the instrument and we assure the instrument that it gets easier to maintain contact as one becomes used to the shock of speaking one's thoughts out loud for it is very different to speak out loud than it is to hear within without having [put one's] thoughts into words. We are most pleased. I would now like to condition the one known as T and speak just one or two sentences through him if he would desire this service. I am Laitos.

(Pause)

(Carla channeling)

I am again with this instrument. We are aware of the problem. It is a great shift from the intellectual to the intuitive, as we have been speaking about this evening; to speak thoughts without knowing ahead of time the direction of the thought. Thus it is almost like, shall we say, a noise in the head which cannot be separated into words at first, and the noise blurs the words. However, if you desire this service and persist in attempting, you will eventually become able to, shall we say, decipher the signal from the noise. The noise is [the] background of your daily existence for there are many, many small thoughts and constant pressures which are attendant upon living within a chemical body and having the responsibilities and social ties through which your life within this illusion has its dynamics and within which you learn. We [are] attempting to say that this noise is not in itself evil or to be vanished, for you are here to learn, not to, shall we say, groove, entirely. Or, shall we say, you are here to learn and groove, but not one at the expense of the other. In meditation, this background noise will gradually sift away. And all of the messages will begin to come through a little better, including ours.

We thank you very much for the privilege of working with you. We would like to attempt to condition the one known as M2, the one known as R, the one known as S. If they would relax and make themselves open to our contact we will attempt to make a better contact with each life vibration. I am Laitos.

(Pause)

I am Laitos. We rejoice that we have been able to be with each of you. It is a good contact tonight. And we are very, very privileged and pleased. I will leave this instrument now and return the meeting to my brother Hatonn. I am Laitos.

I am with the instrument. I am Hatonn. And I greet you again in love and light. Before we close, I would open the meeting to questions. Does anyone have a question?

Questioner: What was the beginning? Hatonn, you talked briefly of our higher self being the sum of the knowledges of the many lives we have lived. Where did it all start? How did it all start?

This information is beyond our understanding. It is our intuitive feeling that the Father has no beginning and no ending, has no limits of any kind. It is our intuitive understanding that the conscious universe as we know it with its infinity of expressions, vibrations, times, spaces, dimensions and thoughts was an instantaneous expression of the Father in a single vibration which in your holy works has been called the Word. The Word, my friends, was love. There was one original Vibration that expressed itself out of the infinite, out of the invisible. Love then formed gradually, step-by-step, all that the individual consciousnesses which were expressed by love at that time could begin to create. The universe has been peopled more and more by the individual imaginations and thoughts of all of those infinite beings that were created as part of the love vibration. Each of you, my friends, has dwelled since the beginning of time. Before the beginning of time, there was the Father. It is our intuitive understanding that after the end of time, when all of the particles of infinite love have made the journey back to the Father, there will still be the Father. There is no beginning and there is no ending, but our universe is love.

Does this answer your question?

Questioner:

(Inaudible)

If there are no further questions we will attempt to bless each of you and thank you for the great privilege of having contact with your unique and precious life vibration. Each of you is a totally unique and precious child of the Creator. Wherever you are on your journey, my friends, we are all with you. We are all your brothers. I and my brothers leave you in the love and light. That is all that there is. Adonai vasu borragus.

Monday Meditation
September 26, 1977

(H channeling)

I am Hatonn. Greetings, my friends, in the love and in the light of our infinite Creator. I shall speak with you this evening for it has been requested and it is our purpose for being here. I shall speak upon several subjects and shall attempt to answer many of your questions as we are aware of them.

I have said that my name is Hatonn. Yet, I wish you to know that this is not a name as you would know it. It is merely a means for identifying ourselves in a way that is acceptable to you. If you were within our world, shall we say, you would understand the concept; the concept of lack, shall we say, of desire for identification. This does not mean that we do not live as individuals. But it means that we live as one, together, united for one goal, desirous not of, shall we say, boosting of our personalities and of our egotistical traits. We wish only to unite and to serve, as we have come to the realization that all men are servants to one another. And it is our obligation and our desire to serve those upon planet Earth in their time of need.

We have come from many areas as you would understand it and have traveled great distances as you would understand it. But to us the distances are nearly nonexistent. We feel that those upon planet Earth who attempt to understand, shall we say, the mechanics of the universe have somewhat erred in their pursuit of knowledge. For, my friends, to understand the physical intellect that you utilize while existing upon the planet Earth, to utilize that intellect to attempt to understand the universe, is in many ways a useless endeavor. The intellect which you utilize has been programmed to accept finite principles, meaning that you have placed limitations upon that which it shall accept. And the universe, my friends, is founded upon [the] infinite, all things being infinite and therefore having no limitations. So it is incomprehensible to us that man could understand the universe in its totality utilizing only the intellect which is many times *(inaudible)*.

We do not attempt to be scornful in any manner. We attempt only to display and to give the truth as we perceive it. Whatever we say we ask only that you listen if you would wish to and decide for yourself if it is the truth that we speak and if the truth that we speak is that which you are seeking. For, my friends, the truth may be presented in many ways. Though it shall always say the same, it can be phrased in many different [ways] and brought through many different sources.

The reason it is this way upon your planet is because your peoples are still endeavoring within their personalities and seeking means of personal identification. Therefore, each shall choose the path that is most comfortable for them to follow. In understanding this, you can see that it is not the responsibility of anyone to point the fallacy of any path out to one who is consciously following that path with love in their heart. Though the path may not be the purest in your eyes, the love within their heart is. And that love shall eventually draw all to that universal point where all is indeed one with the other.

Look not upon your brother as someone different then you. Look upon your brother as a reflection of a portion of yourself and of your Creator. The Creator, my friends, is a term which we use to signify that which we consider to be the omnipresent energy and intelligence that is, shall we say, the maker of all things. We see the presence of that Creator within each individual and within all matter. For if indeed, as many of your major philosophies have stated, all things are one, then the Creator must be within them. The greatest law which you may observe is to love and respect one another as you would yourself; to love and respect the Creator within each individual. Do not attempt to focus upon those points of personality which seem undesirable to you, but focus your attention upon those points of universality, one with the Creator, within your brothers. And in this way, you shall commune more quickly, in love and in harmony, with not only your brothers upon this planet, but with your brothers throughout the universe,

For indeed, the universe in which we all exist is infinite in size and infinite in population as you would know. We of the Confederation of Planets in Service to the Infinite Creator, as we sometimes call ourselves, have been with you throughout your history, though we are more numerous now than ever before. And each of you taking a look at the situations within your world can indeed understand why. For man upon planet Earth is caught not only in his own illusion, but in a dilemma. He has created for himself what you would term as inevitable destruction due to environmental abuse and conscious projection of negative thought forms. This is indeed evident and has in many ways been stated by your scientists. Though they do not know the true reasons why, they know the effect that is already in process.

Therefore, we have come to help, to help the people of Earth to understand what it is they have done to cause this effect and what it is they can do to alleviate to the greatest extent those effects already in process. We wish not to speak of doom. We wish not to speak of annihilation. We wish to speak of the rebirth of planet Earth. Rebirth in not only a physical sense, but more important in a sense that you would term as being spiritual. My friends, you can dwell within this type of environment as long as you choose to do so. But if you choose to advance, shall we say, upon the evolutionary scale, then it is necessary to strive spiritually to understand yourself and your ability to create the environment that you choose. Each and every one of us are the extension, as we have stated, of the Creator. And within us is planted that ability to project thought forms, and if given enough time, to manifest that thought form into physical actuality and experience. You are indeed the co-creator of your environment with those who you choose to associate with.

Man upon planet Earth looks about these days and times in many ways to experience what is termed as phenomena. But we say to you that there is no such [thing] as phenomena. All things are natural within this universe and all things are possible. Each and every one of you is the phenomena—your life, all of your experiences, are created by you and most of you do not even realize this. To us this is phenomena: your lack of understanding of your own ability.

Man of Earth, open your heart, open your mind and your spirit. Allow the truth of the universe that lies within you to radiate not only within this environment, but throughout the universe. Do not label anything or limit anything. Allow your life to flow freely as it is meant to be. Go within yourself periodically each day in what you would term meditation, and allow the God within you, that essence of the Creator within you, to calm you, to inspire you, and to fulfill your needs. Listen to the silence which you can so easily hear. And within that silence we promise to be all the knowledge of the universe if only you would reach out and accept it.

We say many things as we speak to you on Earth. But indeed the most important that we come to bear is the need for the individual to take upon himself the initiative to evolve himself or herself on a spiritual basis. And we have found the most, shall we say, expedient tool to be the practice of meditation. It is a key given to us by our Father the Creator to unlock those doors that seem to be so stubbornly bolted before us. Free yourself and free your brothers by going within yourself into the silence. This is the most necessary part.

We of the Confederation are very happy to share with you. I shall transfer this communication to another instrument. I am Hatonn.

(Carla channeling)

I am Hatonn. I am now with this instrument. And again I greet you in the love and the light of our infinite Creator. I shall continue.

Yes, my friends, we ask you to meditate in silence, each of your days. And we do this for a reason, my friends. We have said to you love is all that there is. You must love your brothers and sisters. But, my friends, the beginning of love is the love of yourself as a whole and perfect being. It is in meditation that you become aware of the true nature of yourself and therefore, my friends, the true nature of the universe, for you are inseparable, completely linked with all that there is. That is why you and we are brothers, for neither time nor space, nor all the dimensions of creation can separate the oneness of consciousness.

Consider, my friends, yourselves as physical beings who are dressed in many layers and types of attire that cover that which you call your nakedness. You have many items which you do, which you place upon yourselves, many various ways in which you arrange those portions of your body which may grow from day to day. That which you call your hair is arranged in such a way as to make a certain impression, or to please you or to please society. And when you are armored with all of the clothing and the appearance that you desire, then and only then do you meet the world as you perceive it outside yourself. With each layer of clothing, with each arrangement of your hair and your odors and the various manifestations of your physical being, you are separating yourself from the outside world and limiting the responses which you will need to receive in your turn. These are your defenses on a physical level against those things that you do not consider part of yourself. They are your definition of yourself. Perhaps this is not conscious. And perhaps your definition is very carefree. Yet it exists, my friends.

The thought of allowing your physical being to wander naked in the physical world is not one which seems very desirable. And yet, my friends, all beings are naked. All beings are unified even in their body, even on the level of physical illusion, by the total naturalness and validity of all of the functions and manifestations of their physical form. In nakedness, those differences which seem so obvious when one begins to speak, when one begins to limit oneself by clothing and by cultural differences, fall away and one can see that we are all one.

On a mental level, shall we say, or an emotional or a spiritual level—we must correct this instrument—mental, emotional and spiritual levels, those levels which are unseen, are those we would take up at this time. On these levels, you also have clothing and limitations. You have your mental and emotional limitation closely connected with your concept of who you are, and these may be considered like unto your clothing. But inside your clothing my friends, is the most terrible limitation of all. Like tight bandages, your unseen self is wrapped in a terrible stricture consisting of those feelings which you have towards others concerning those things which you feel they have done to you [for] which you have not forgiven them. And, on the other hand, my friends, your feelings of guilt for things which you have done to your brothers and sisters for which you do not feel forgiveness. You will never be whole, my friends. You will always be cripples as long as you carry these bandages about your spiritual body. Oh, my friends, this instrument has within her memory a story of a man who went home with a beautiful woman and as she undressed she took off her wig, her make-up, and her padded brassiere and her wooden leg, and suddenly she wasn't very beautiful anymore.

My friends, all those that you look at, within this group and elsewhere, all these, my friends, are cripples. They all have wooden legs. They all have wigs. On the level of your human personality, they are wrapped in the tight bandages of those things they have not forgiven and those things for which they feel they are not forgiven. And therefore they manifest within the illusion in imperfect ways. And you, my friends, manifest within the illusion in an imperfect way.

Now we return to meditation. As you begin to go into the silence, perhaps you have games you play, as we would call them, in which you attempt to carry your clothed spirit, your limited spirit into the silence. Do not do this, my friends. Picture yourself, mentally, taking guilt and discarding it as you would a piece of clothing. Taking resentment, fear—putting it aside and walking as your shining naked self into the waters of cleanliness. After you have bathed yourself in total forgiveness, total cleanliness for the moment, you can emerge and in your mind you can sit down and listen. Listen for those signals which will come to you in the silence. You are a whole and complete person. Within you is perfection, wisdom and all the attributes of love. Yes, you will come out of meditation. Yes, you will begin to wrap the bandages about yourself. But as you come again and again into meditation, strip yourself clean and allow that soothing feeling of wholeness to come into your awareness. You begin to view your brothers and your sisters with something that does approach true love, for you will see, behind whatever manifestations may occur, that whole and perfect being that dwells perhaps very far beneath, perhaps very obviously beneath the mental, the spiritual, the emotional, and the physical clothing.

We have always greeted you in love and in light, for that is all that there [is.] We can greet you in nothing else. As you go into the silence, know that you are within that which is love. There is nowhere to go. You have no outer influence to seek. All that you desire is within. Meditate, my friends. And always we will aid you in any way that we can.

At this time I would open the meeting to questions. If you have a question, please speak up.

Questioner: Could you give some thoughts on dreams and interpreting them?

We are aware of your question. My sister, you must already know that consciousness does not cease either with sleep or with death. Therefore, that which you recall from your dreams is a record that your consciousness has been keeping during your slumbers. There are many levels of consciousness below that which you call consciousness, and many are not understood by those who study dreams. The level that is most often described by those who study the importance of dreams is the level wherein you are as your higher self attempting to speak to your conscious self about the material which you have covered in your experience within the last day or short period. There may be many symbols which those who interpret dreams have fairly adequately covered which may be used within your own dreams as a kind of symbolism to, shall we say, soften the blow of the lessons that your dreams are attempting to offer you.

We do not consider this [the] most important type of dream, however. In actuality, your consciousness is being taught by your teachers during sleep. And quite often, if you are very careful to keep records of your dreams, you will begin to consciously remember at least part of these lessons. This is most valuable to you and it is worth attempting to discover by means of keeping records of your dreams.

There are some cases where [the] more advanced among your peoples have the job, shall we say, of leaving their body during sleep periods and within one of the spiritual bodies, as this instrument would call them, going to other places and working with those who may need some kind of help either with mental or physical problems. These healers, as one might call them, are rare, but they are very helpful and do exist and it is another activity that occurs in, shall we say, a dream form.

Separate from all this my sister, are visions, either of the future or of the present, in which you see in a very real sense that which is to occur. This takes place on what you would call the fifth dimension and does not have anything in common with dreaming. You are actually there and your consciousness is fully awake.

Does this answer your question?

Questioner: Yes. Thank you.

Is there another question? My friends, this has been a longer meeting than usual. And we are very grateful for your patience as we have had a good deal to impart to you. We ask you again to understand that we come to you not to give you technology—for, my friends, you would not be able to handle technology—but love. For, my friends, you badly need love.

Let us share with you this. If all of you could love each other, you would refrain from your war-like efforts and from your defensive efforts. And, my friends, that money which you now have to spend on your technology would be enough to give you the breakthroughs that your scientists would like to make. We may tell you that we are aware at this time on your planet that [there] are [those] close enough to understanding methods of propulsion, fusion power, and other helpful pieces of technological breakthrough that an application of money sufficient to fund their research would make the breakthrough. But your governments will not spend the money on research unless it has defensive abilities.

My friends, technology will come when you have love. We realize this must seem to you to be, as this instrument would say, a great cop-out. But it is not.

We can only say to you that when you have love, you are joyful and full of energy and that which has been given to you to do you will do. And the breakthroughs will come and the technologies will come. If you do not have love, as it has been written in your holy works, all that you do will be hollow.

It is especially important that we say this to you at this time, for you are at the end of a cycle, and if you had the time, you could not use it. For time is coming to a kind of ending and you are coming to a beginning. Therefore, attempt at this time to find the love within yourself, and to reach out to your brothers and sisters.

If your path takes you into science, into politics, into any manner of interaction with your brothers and sisters, so be it. Philosophers and spiritual-minded people are not off on top of a mountain. They come down from the mountain and live for the good of their brothers and sisters and for the love of the Father that gave them the life, the consciousness, the talent, and the will.

We reach out our hands to you, my friends. And we leave you in the love and the light of our infinite Creator. I am Hatonn. Adonai vasu borragus. ☥

Thursday Meditation
October 27, 1977

(Carla channeling)

I am Hatonn. I greet you in the love and the light of our infinite Creator. As always, it is a blessing to speak to this group. And above all, I would like to greet those whom I have not greeted before and to welcome back to the group one who has been absent. And to touch each of you with the love of my brothers and me. That love is always with you, my friends.

We of the Confederation of Planets in the Service of the Infinite Creator are here not to walk among you and trade with you. Not to stand in your seats of government and change your laws. Not to affect those forces which have authority over you. For as it says in your holy works, we are very willing to render unto Caesar those things which are Caesar's. We are not here to be an authority over you, for it is our understanding that you are in authority over yourself. Perhaps not, in this illusion, completely. But we are beings of reality, and we do not wish to deal with the illusions of government and society, for although they are very real to you and are necessary for your learning at this time, they are transient. And we wish to speak to that part of you that is not transient.

We would tell you a little story about a young man. We shall call him John. John was a fine young man, intelligent and well-loved by all who knew him. He was successful in his work and he achieved all that he wished to achieved very easily. But there was one thing he could not achieve. He could not achieve wisdom; he could not achieve peace of mind; he could not achieve joy. In other words, my friends, he was not free. He was not in a state of love.

And so, he collected money. Great quantities of money for he knew that with money one could buy much. And he went to one teacher after another attempting to buy wisdom. And he found beautiful tracts of land and he bought them. And he took his teachers and gave them land. He spent many years attempting somehow to, shall we say, plug himself in to freedom. He gave all that he thought he had. And all he found in the end were many, many words, many actions. But no peace, no joy, no freedom. For he was always conscious of himself. He was always figuring. He was always self-aware. He could not get free and into a space in which he was so completely himself that he was a channel for joy. Finally one day, John, who was no longer a young man, who was no longer handsome, and no longer rich for he had given all his riches away, despaired and he went into the mountains. Mountains which were no longer his. And he did not take food and he did not take bedding, for he was truly in despair.

And it came to him suddenly that he might pray as he had done often in the past. But this time, my friends, it was different. He had nothing to give.

And so he opened himself up, just a crack, and was almost blinded by the light that came through as he opened himself, no longer proud, no longer conscious of himself, but in total honesty saying, "Father, I have nothing but what I seek." Once he had opened himself, he became suddenly joyful. And after a timeless moment on his knees in the pine needles, in the gray of evening, he arose. And he reached and hugged the trees and he capered and danced and sang. And he was totally free. And he looked around and suddenly the world was whole and he had everything.

My friends, what this man, John, did with the rest of his life is not important. He had a mission which he had brought with him into this experience. And he was no longer blocking. He had a simple mission and that mission was to be. And by that being to give light. When he realized who he was, he no longer blocked the light.

My friends, each of you has his belongings, both physical and mental. Both emotional and psychic. These things are the baggage of the illusion. Some are more useful than others, but all are less than central to reality. We ask you to meditate. And in that meditation bring nothing but the simple perfection of yourself. Do not try to offer qualities and specifics. But in meditation open your heart to wisdom. Nothing less, my friends. Nothing more.

Imagine what you brought into this experience that you call your physical life. And what you will bring when you leave. And know that that and only that is what you are attempting to open within this illusion to the light of the Father, as we may call Him. Call the Creator what you will, but know that reality is very simple. And that true freedom lies not in being somebody. Not in great action. Not in great movement. But in the state of your heart at any given moment. Go in meditation to that reality and feel yourself blossom.

At this tine, I would like to pause and then allow my brother Laitos to work with the newer channels. For the present, I will leave you. I am Hatonn.

(Carla channeling)

I am Laitos. And I greet each of you in the love and the light of the infinite Creator. It is a privilege to work with you. And I would like to say to those of you who wish to experience contact such as this instrument receives, or to experience vibrations which this contact is carried upon, that it is only necessary for each of you to mentally request this contact and we will be with you.

May we say to you, my friends, not everyone experiences contact in the same way. Not everyone desires to give service by being a vocal channel. Yet, we hope and feel that it is true that our vibration, which is intended as a strengthening or underlining of your own vibrations of meditation, will be helpful to you. So if you will relax and request our presence, I and my brothers will work with each of you. We will specifically call on a few who are attempting to gain some skill in speaking our words. May we say how grateful we are for these channels, for as you know, my friends, many of your peoples desire to hear words of, shall we say, comfort or words of challenge regarding the spiritual path. And many find it difficult to accept these words from other sources but find it, perhaps, acceptable through instruments such as these. Therefore, we are very grateful, for without instruments such as you we could not fulfill our mission of making available this information without, shall we say, infringing upon your free will. For you can believe or disbelieve as you wish, for after all you are only sitting in the dark and listening to one of your brothers or sisters. This satisfies us, for we are not perfect and would never insist that we are right. We wish only to share our understanding as we know it with your peoples.

I will now attempt to speak a few words through the one known as B, if he would relax. I am Laitos.

(B channeling)

I am Laitos. *(Inaudible)*.

I am again with this instrument. The instrument is in need of further conditioning. We wish at this time …

(Carla channeling)

I am again with this channel. I am Laitos. We are grateful to use the one known as B. And we offer him this advice. We find this instrument very sensitive, and each time we begin to work with him again, we overstimulate the receptive centers. It is almost as if there were a, shall we say, psychic allergy to beginning the contact due to eagerness. Therefore, we suggest to the channel that as he accepts the contact, he allows even as long as minutes to go by during the conditioning process. Each of those in the group will be patient and in this way the oversensitivity will recede. This sensitivity is a very valuable trait in that it is akin to compassion. And compassion is extremely important as one works along the path of spiritual development, as you might call it. It is simply to be tempered with discipline. Compassion and discipline. These two in balance create wisdom.

We would like now to attempt to speak just a few words through the one known as G, if she would relax and allow us to speak through her. I am Laitos.

(Carla channeling)

I am again with this instrument. I am Laitos. We thank the one known as G. We are pleased and will continue to work with the instrument. We would like now to speak through the one known as J, if she would relax and cease analyzing any spontaneous thought and simply speak them as she receives them. I am Laitos.

(J channeling)

This is Laitos. *(Inaudible)*.

(Carla channeling)

I am Laitos. I am again with this instrument. We are very happy that we have made contact with the one known as J. And we are sorry that we, as you might say, blew her circuits. It is very difficult to monitor the contact when it is first recognized for it is a powerful vibration. It will be easier and easier. Meanwhile, we thank the one known as June. We would like to go now to the one known as M1, if she would relax and speak our thoughts as she receives them. I am Laitos.

(M1 channeling)

I am Laitos. I am now with this instrument.

(Carla channeling)

I am again with this instrument. I am Laitos. We would like to condition the one known as M1 and try to say just a couple of sentences through her before we go one. Therefore, if you will be patient we will pause and condition the instrument.

(M1 channeling)

I am Laitos. I am working with this instrument. And I would …

(Carla channeling)

I am again with this instrument. I am Laitos. And as this instrument would say, hip-hip-hooray! We are very happy for we are making good contact tonight and we appreciate and love the one known as M1 and each of you who are attempting to be our instruments, for we love those of your planet very much. And we are most grateful for your aid in sharing with the peoples of the planet.

If you would be patient just a little longer, we would like to attempt to say a couple of sentences through the one known as M2, if he would relax. We realize that it is very difficult to still the conscious mind, for our thoughts and your thoughts, my friends, are indistinguishable except for the fact that we think our thoughts and you think your thoughts. Therefore, when we place a concept within your minds it feels very much like your thought except for the fact that you did not generate it. Therefore, in order to receive these thoughts clearly, it is necessary for you to not to analyze but simply to repeat the thought that you have received. If the one known M2 would desire this discipline and service we would now attempt to say a few words through him. I am Laitos.

(Pause)

(Carla channeling)

I am again with this instrument. We would like to thank the one known as M2 and we will continue to work with him at any time he may desire. We would like to, before we leave this instrument, attempt contact with the brother known as T. It has been quite some time since we have worked with this instrument and we would very much like to, shall we say, touch base. I am Laitos.

(T channeling)

I am Laitos. We are pleased once again to speak through this channel. It is often difficult to reestablish contact *(inaudible)*.

(Carla channeling)

I am Laitos. We were attempting again to reach the one known is M1 and we tell her this so that she will know that she was not imagining or creating the contact herself. We simply wish to close and offer the meeting back to our brothers from Hatonn. We leave each of you, but not truly, my brothers and sisters. We do not leave you. We are everywhere for we are not limited as are you. We are sensitive to the vibrations of seeking and where that vibration is, there are we. You must know that you have many aids, many guides, many friends. Much strength is about you. The forces of what you call good are all about. You have only to desire. By this we mean seriously desire this contact. Not only with the brothers from the Confederation of Planets, but with, shall we say, the good guys of your own planet. For you have your guides and your angelic forces that create about your planet an extraordinary beauty. Therefore, if you seek comfort, contact, understanding from the thoughts that we can share with you, mentally re-request our presence and I and my brothers will be there. Perhaps you will not feel us physically, this varies from person to person. But where it counts, my friends, in what you call your subconscious, if you are seeking, if you open to the good, to the truth, and to the beautiful, those qualities that are not qualities but merely the names of one thing and that one thing is love, will come to you. Seek and you shall find.

We are servants of you all. I leave you in the love and the light of the infinite Creator.

(Carla channeling)

I am Hatonn. And I am again with this channel. And I greet you once again in the love and the light. Before we close the meeting, we would open the meeting to questions. If anyone has a question, please ask.

J: I had a dream about Bing Crosby. I was wondering if his spirit had visited mine.

I am aware of the question. We spoke earlier of the fact that we do not need to be limited to a physical body, but that we can be aware of everything at once. This is true of reality. There is no time and there is no place. And all things occur simultaneously. However, within your vibration you are caught in the tide of time and in the shore of space. However, from time to time there is a small hole in the veil of the illusion and you are a witness to the future or the past. It was this type of experience that you described. The, as you call it, soul, of the one known as Bing Crosby was not a visitor of yours. Rather, you became aware of that part of the record which had to do with events that would occur in the future. This is a skill which has its uses among your peoples. It can be a healing skill, for if you can begin to know that which is occurring, you can then offer your love and your light in such a way that you can mitigate the extremes of difficulty that you may have seen. For the future is not certain until it comes up on the shores of your particular moment. Therefore, until that wave of time rolls in you can change that which is to be. Perhaps not completely, but in intensity certainly.

Does this answer your question?

J: Yes, thank you.

We thank you for the privilege of speaking with you. We do wish to encourage those who have a gift of higher sense to offer that gift for good, as you may call it, and conscientiously attempt to use it and not abuse it. But certainly, my friends, not bury it, for the higher gifts are those of light and as such you should not hide them under the bushel.

Is there another question?

W: I desire to channel, and I wonder if my posture sometimes distracts me. Because sometimes during meditation I feel numb. Have you some suggestions on better posture and concentration for channeling?

There are no certain answers to your question on posture. We have said this before: the posture that aligns the physical body with the physical channel is the posture which your yogis adopt. However, there are very few people who can do this comfortably. Therefore, we often have suggested that you find that posture which is comfortable and if that be horizontal, vertical or even standing on your head—which is of course doubtful—but if it were comfortable, we would suggest that you adopt this, regardless of the biases which others may have about your posture.

For instance, the instrument through which I am talking through now is not in a very good position for the free movement of psychic energy. Consequently, she often overheats. However, were we to insist that she sat in such a way that the chakras were firing totally in a vertical line, we would lose this channel, for her discomfort would be such that we could not use her. Consequently, we prefer that she overheat.

We suggest that you experiment with the comfort factor in mind. Moreover, we would suggest that the main barrier to channeling in almost each and every channel is the working of the conscious, intellectual mind. No matter what the conscious desire of the channel, it is such an ingrained habit to analyze and judge what one says before one says it that blurting out in front of other people that which are not sure may be intelligent-sounding is completely foreign to your nature.

Thus, the thing to do is to get comfortable and then to put your concentration on the one thing that is truly keeping you from being contacted consciously; and that is the stilling of the conscious mind. When you are sending you cannot receive. It very simple but it is very difficult.

Does this answer your question?

W: Yes.

Is there another question?

(Pause)

I will leave you now, my friends. There has been much talk this evening about the damage that your peoples may wreak upon each other. You have heard from this source and from many others, we are sure, that there are very difficult times ahead. So we wish to leave you with this thought. It is written in your holy works, "Yea, though I walk through the valley of the shadow of death, I will fear no evil." Do not fear evil, my friends. You may be hurt, those about you may be hurt. This is part of your experience, no more and no less. You and all of those in your experience will die. It may be from one cause and it may be from another. Do not fear evil. But seek only to fulfill that which you came to do. We assure you that the shadow of death is as bad as it will get. The sun will shine. The skies will clear. And that which your peoples will do …

(Tape ends.)

L/L Research

Wednesday Meditation
November 2, 1977

(Inaudible portions are indicated by ellipses. In general, the entire recording is difficult to hear.)

(Carla channeling)

[I am Latwii.] … because I missed you … and it is a good opportunity to work at this time … prior to the message that we have to give. If you will all relax I and my brothers are attempting to adjust the focus of our vibrations. … they are balanced, you must understand that the spiritual energies … and if you are not properly balanced shall we say, firing off center. … … Spiritual vibrations distorting the signal … receive … and therefore … I and my brothers … balancing … should be able to feel a slight pressure in the area which you call the crown chakra.

I am Latwii.

(Pause)

I am Hatonn, and I greet you in love and light. My brother Laitos is continuing to balance the energies in this room. There is high energy group and thus it is … Be as one … we are not satisfied with this group … we wish for you to be as one. If you can allow your thoughts to embrace those who are with you. They are your brothers and your sisters. They are all here to seek. Allow that seeking to … allow the balancing to take place … you seek without selfishness … only because you are … seeking true …

We are pleased … we will continue with this instrument. We must caution you always that we can only give you what you desire to receive. If you do not desire to receive what you may call philosophy … truth … we have … no … communication becomes very difficult. So know yourself as you go into meditation and know and trust … we thank you very much for this opportunity to work with you. We are feeling better … energies now … saying … It is within rather … there is a balance … so we ask you … power is always a two-edged sword.

Let us talk to you about reality, my friends. It is important to talk about reality. We have talked with this group many times about love, many times about meditation. We wish to talk about reality. We are giving you the same truth but through a different filter. For it is this filter that you need at this time. There is in creation …

(Unknown channeling)

I am Hatonn. I am once again with you. And as it has been stated, I would now attempt to answer any questions that you would wish to speak. Are there any questions at this time?

Carla: Could you say anything about the program for the next year? Your hopes?

We of the Confederation are aware of certain patterns which have been set within the realms or shall we say the environment of planet Earth. We have great intentions of attempting to alter some of the flows of energy which have been set into motion by your peoples. Yet, we have not yet been able to distinguish or determine in which manner we would be more successful in dealing with the situations upon your planet. But we are attempting, as rapidly as possible, to educate your peoples through many sources in order that we may be accepted upon a physical form of communication. By this we mean, that as it is known, there are occasions upon which we choose individuals upon your planet and establish with them direct physical communication, and it is part of our program and part of our desire to attempt to broaden this form of experience, within what you would term your next calendar year.

It shall become evident that we are not yet aware of to what degree of an increase in direct communication we need, and we of the Confederation are willing to do this upon any scale mandated by the group desire of the inhabitants of your planet. We have been pleased recently by the upsurge of interest, in not only the existence of what you call UFO's, but the interest in the existence of life forms throughout the universe.

There are greater and more intense studies being put into process by your educators and scientists. And as they filter their findings, more and more each day to your peoples, life such as ours throughout the realms of the universe is becoming an everyday accepted fact. It is pleasing to see the upsurge of this knowledge, for it brings us closer to the day that we may work with you, hand in hand, in building in what you would term the new world. Look for this to occur. The information shall be available through your normal filtered resources, if you understand our meaning. But it is our objective to attempt to increase our assistance upon the physical plane and it shall be seen by many.

Do you request further information?

Carla: By, "being seen by many," do you mean on television or in person?

We mean by selected groups and individuals, not through the forms of communication that you would view and listen to, but in direct experience.

Carla: Do you have any feelings about what a group meditation should best focus on, whether it would be against natural disasters or against war, in other words for the planet's peace or for the peace among men? Which would be the most fruitful for the immediate present?

We of the Confederation have in previous communications expressed the fact that one of our greatest concerns is your peoples' obsession to toy with their existence by the utilization of warfare. It is one of our greatest concerns at this period of time, for as you are aware, even though there are still places of turmoil on your planet, you are living in a basically peaceful period of time, as compared to the previous years. But as you are also aware, each period of peace throughout your history was none other than a period of preparation for war.

We predict nothing, but we ask that you focus your energies upon the prevention of escalation on the physical plane of the warfare. For we of the Confederation wish not to interfere and it is you, the people of planet Earth, that are given the first opportunity to prevent the destruction of your peoples and the environment. At this point in time, the desire of some nation's leaders to substantiate and incur warfare is great. This would be your most beneficial exercise.

Are there any other questions?

Questioner: Could you tell us how many people around the world are in contact with you? Thanks.

We are in communication with the entire population of your planet, but not to all of their knowledge. To give you a number would be beyond the capability of the instrument. Though we must make you aware that this form of communication that you experience here is only one form which we utilize. It is indeed one of the most desirable. But look about you, look at your life and how it is progressed. Look at the informations brought forth through the media, look at the informations brought forth through books, movies, radios and televisions. Look at what seemed to be fantasies ten years ago; they are becoming evident realities today. We communicate through your scientists; we communicate through your doctors. We communicate through your law makers, although they are difficult to deal with. We communicate with all of your peoples.

Are there any other questions?

Questioner: I'd like to know if it may be related to my spiritual growth, the fact that my digital watch jumps ahead a few hours occasionally, and then I find [another watch?]

We would say to you that all experiences understood are beneficial to your spiritual [alignments] and growth patterns. The phenomena that you experience are only clues and indications given to you, through what you might term the grace of God, to continually remind you of that which you are dealing with; the potential that lies within you. For the experiences that you are having are none other than a barometer for you to utilize to determine the magnificence of your Creator.

Are there any other questions?

(Pause)

If there are no other questions, I would leave you with the thought just spoken in answer to the question: utilize your life's experiences as that barometer to determine not only the Creator's magnificence but your own. I leave you in the love and the light of the infinite Creator. I am Hatonn. Adonai, my friends. Adonai vasu borragus.

Carla: Guess, who came through right at the end, right at the end, really strong? "I am Monka. I am Monka. Blessings to your group." Ha! We haven't heard from Monka in about ten years. That's all I got, it was really strong.

(Carla channeling)

(Very loud static is heard on the tape. The transcription is only to give an idea of the contents and should not be considered accurate.)

I am Oxal. I and my brother Laitos would like to work with each of you for awhile. We would like at this time to work silently with each of you who desires to become a channel. Each of you will go through your minds to our contact. We will work intensively with you for … Thank you. I am …

(Pause)

I am again with this instrument. What a great privilege it is to work with you. Normally one or the other of us … additions are somewhat illusions, and felt it would be somewhat of a good idea to work with two different vibrations … some are more sensitive to the Oxal and some to the Laitos vibration … but they are, shall we say in brackets, which gives a good stable area of spiritual vibration. We would open the meeting for questions at this time. If anyone has a question …

Questioner: *(Inaudible).*

We are aware of your question. Indeed, my sister, that is our position to a great many … we have much confidence and yet, cannot give … but we can give to peoples of your planet is our presence … love … and this we give in total freedom. And this, my sister, is your best gift … may be reaped by a sister or a brother. Not the words, unless they are asked, not the gestures, unless they are needed, but a true heart and that … complete love … this is not … as you would call it … love … we use this … rather than love … for we do not wish to limit the concept of love to that of the parent of this child. But that love … wind … love is that …

… sadness … situation … without …words and gestures can only aid those … therefore, understanding sometimes … this is our distortion …

Is there another question?

Questioner: *(Inaudible).*

I am very pleased to speak through this instrument. We do not often use this instrument, for ours is a strong vibration, a very pointed contact. This instrument … quite a bit. We wish to come through because our vibration is … to this group. We want you to ground yourselves … reality. … that vibration which is Hatonn is a gentle, kind …. Oxal is a stronger one and bears more of the, shall we say, stark power of love. That which we call love is the … force, shall we say, the mathematical equation behind our force. There is no law but love … higher … you cannot understand our love without … reality … meditate … my friends, you remind me somewhat of what you would call your aborigines, stalking through virgin jungle. They know no other tribes. They are aware of no other beings. Then one day, knowing that there is no one else in their entire … they come across one footprint. All the other footprints have washed away thousands of thousands of years … Fire … suddenly they know that in some inconceivable … some creature like them stood where they are standing …

My friends you have been …. And in some inconceivable future, some day you will see … not real … you can either approach your evolution by tucking your toes in your mouth and then rolling in circles along the dusty road …

(Tape ends.)

Wednesday Meditation
November 9, 1977

(Unknown channeling)

I am Hatonn. Greetings, my friends, in the love and in the light of our infinite Creator. It is as always our privilege to be with you. And this evening it is pleasing to see so many. We of the Confederation attempt so often to communicate in many forms with your peoples, and time and time again, we find that our attempts are in somewhat what you would call, a fruitful *(inaudible)* and then there are other times when we find no ears to listen. And it joys us and it gladdens us to know that you wish to listen and to know that above that, you seek the truth, the truth upon [which] all things are founded. You seek the truth in order that you might understand not only your environment, but your own inner being. My friends, we say to you that if you do not know yourself and of your abilities, then you shall remain in ignorance until you do so. You may attempt in many ways to gain intellectual knowledge. You can earn many degrees, as you would call it. You may be accepted by the greater peers of your society, you may be recognized as what you may term a genius, but yet we say, you remain in ignorance in spite of all these things if you know not yourself.

We of the Confederation have attempted to tell your peoples throughout many, many of your years the importance of this simple knowledge of the inner being that sustains and ordains your existence. We of the Confederation have mentioned to our contacts, time and time again, the method which we feel most beneficial by which to gain this knowledge of self and of the universe. And as you are aware, that method is what we term as meditation.

Meditation, my friends, brings us the key to the universe. It is the key to the inner being that you are. It is the key to the door of the Creator's house. It is the key to the door of all truth and understanding.

Meditation is the silence which is spoken of so often within the holy works that your peoples recognize upon this planet called Earth. My friends, the silence that you enter into is a silence which may at time seem to be vast and at other times to be very minute. And this is as it should be, my friends, for within the universe, all things are both infinitely small and infinitely large. For every expansion there is that opposite, contraction; for every thing there is balance. And balance, my friends, can only be achieved by the experience of both sides of what we may call the scale. The scale of positive or negative, if you so desire. Within your meditations you may find that balance. For it shall provide you with the understanding of your experiences, whether they be of the positive or negative nature. They are to be understood, for without the understanding of that which you experience, the lessons have been overlooked; the lessons have passed you by.

Very often, as man upon planet Earth proceeds through his daily chores and activities, he becomes, shall we say, unknowledgeable of that which occurs around him, for his attention is focused in one area and his closest sensitivities in order that he may concentrate upon the performance of his duties. We say that as you go through these duties of life, concentrate if you must, in order that you do the best that you may do; but allow your sensitivities to remain in complete function, so that you may absorb the entire experience that you encounter. And as you absorb these experiences they shall register within your memory banks, there to be held in order that you may learn to understand and call upon that understanding in what you would call your future.

Man upon planet Earth is what you would consider to be the highest form of intelligence within the universe, if only he would recognize this ability. We of the Confederation have lived through your experiences. We have grown through similar experiences. And through our growth we have learned the simplicity and the magnificence of your race. For we, too, are of your race. There are some basic differences, for we have progressed the same as you and we have possessed the same forms as you.

Man upon planet Earth is residing upon a testing ground of spiritual awareness; testing grounds in which he may grow and gain all of the knowledge necessary in order to expand into the universe and spread the love and the light, the truth and the understanding of our Creator. It is indeed, shall we say, your opportunity and obligation as inhabitants of planet Earth to become the teachers and the servants of your fellow beings within this area of space in which you reside. There is around and about you, throughout your system, intelligent life; some with greater understanding than what you possess on planet Earth and some with less understanding. But in no other civilization, within your confines of space, is there the magnitude of possibility for progression that you may experience on the planet Earth. You have not been chosen idly to abide upon this planet. You have progressed throughout the evolutionary scales, throughout thousands and thousands of what you would call years and you have earned the opportunity to reside upon this particular planet, to fulfill your own particular purpose in this creation.

If man upon planet Earth was truly aware of the number of individuals, as you would consider them, throughout the universe, that would desire inhabitation upon this planet then he would begin to realize in greater detail the importance of his existence, and the special importance of this period of time and experience upon this particular planet. There is throughout the universe a structure, which we will simply call a hierarchy. They oversee your activities, they evaluate your progression, and they do many things for you to enable you to obtain the experiences that you have earned and are necessary for your growth.

You are constantly, what you might call, monitored by this hierarchy. They pass not judgment on you, but they watch with great concerns your activities. For they are aware of your purpose, and they are awaiting its fulfillment with great patience and compassion for their fellow beings upon planet Earth. They in turn send forth to you emissaries of truth and knowledge and understanding and love. We, my friends, are those emissaries. Yet, we claim not to be of any greater value than man upon planet Earth. For, my friends, we could not bring these truths to you if it were not for your presence. We could not serve you if you did not inhabit this place—in time. So we are grateful that you have come to listen. For expressing your desire to listen to our words, you have given us the only means of fulfillment of our purpose at this point in time in this universe.

We are always grateful to you, we shall always love and respect each and everyone of you, and we shall always be here to help. Whenever it is desired, this is our purpose, to assist you in the awakening of your inner self. Once this awakening has been achieved, then no longer shall you need our assistance. For you shall be with us, perhaps not in physical form but in what you would term "spiritual essence."

Earth, my friends, is the training grounds for what your mythology has termed as "gods." This has been expressed through other instruments, and it is indeed the truth. Be not discouraged if your society seems to be against you, or go against your code of morality. Do not be discouraged, my friends, because it is your opportunity to grow. It is your opportunity to learn and to understand your own power of creativity.

For we say that what you experience is the manifestation of your own thought patterns. Whether they be of a conscious or subconscious projection, they are indeed the manifestation of your own [inner] thoughts, [feelings,] emotions and understanding. So is it not logical that in order to truly know your universe and all about it, that you must first know yourself?

If the law of creation which we have given to you is indeed true, so are the words that we speak. We demand in no way that you accept what we say. We only speak it for it is what we understand and what we experience. It is your choice, my friends, to either grasp on to this understanding and to refine it or to search for another one. But we assure you that in due time, whether it be within this life experience or not, all of the peoples upon planet Earth shall come to understand the simplicity of the truth that we speak.

We of the Confederation are aware of all of the great teachers now on your planet and all of the great teachers within your past. We recognize none as being greater than the other one, only some who were known better, who experienced greater success. And of these, the most successful was the one who you would call the Christ. The Christ, my friends, was the manifestation of the desires of your peoples for the truth and for an example. Follow the words that he spoke but above all live the life that he lived. Live the truth that you find that you may speak, as did this teacher and the universe shall lay at your feet and give praise unto you, for indeed you are the risen Christ. For each and every one of you is the risen Christ the moment that you understand yourself.

I would transfer this communication. I am Hatonn.

(Carla channeling)

I am with this instrument. I am Laitos, and I greet you in the love and the light of the infinite Creator. I and my brothers ask you to pause with us at this time to work on conditioning. We are privileged to work especially with those who desire to intensify their contact with the Confederation of Planets in Service to the Infinite Creator. We will work on each of you at this time, and we ask you to relax. We ask you to envision the energy of love all about you. It permeates the air about you, my friends. You breathe it in with every breath and absorb it through the skin of your chemical body. Love is all about you. You breathe it in and you are a sentient being and you cause this love to have direction, my friends. And this love that you breathe in and absorb spirals up your energy centers—and we are aiding you and feeling this at this time—and the energy rises as smoothly as you have begun to open the doors of meditation. And as you become a purer channel, my friends, this energy rises more and more smoothly and becomes a pure love energy as you give it out as freely as it has come to you. And now this energy, my friends, leaps up like flames from each of you and becomes a beautiful white energy, and moves from one to another about the circle that you have made in your seeking this evening. We ask you to feel this energy, feel the unity of that movement of the love in the circle. Feel the potential building up. This unity of love my friends, is reality. You are experiencing love at this time. Now, relax and continue to feel the energy coming in, being directed by the wisdom of your being, being sent to the group as love energy, and feel the unity.

(Pause)

Very quickly, my friends, we will make contact with some of the newer instruments. We will not spend a great deal of time on this, but we wish to exercise the newer channels, if you will be patient. We would like to attempt to say just a couple of sentences through the one known as G, if she would relax. I am Laitos.

(Pause)

We would move now to make contact with the one known as J, if she would relax and speak freely.

(Pause)

We would move now to contact the instrument known as B and say a couple of sentences through him, if he desires to speak our thoughts. I am Laitos.

(Pause)

We would now touch on the instruments known as G and M, so that they may feel our presence.

(Pause)

I am Laitos. We are sorry we are not getting verbal contact, but we felt that it was important to let the whole group feel the energy of the group, so that those who had not previously had experience with contact could feel the energy going from place to place within the circle. This is also part of beginning to become familiar with our type of contact, our type of energy. We are aware that members of the group will be attempting to make contact in a new locality in the near future. And we wish to say to the one known as M, that we will be with you and that we will continue working with you—I, my brother Hatonn, and many others of the Confederation. Place, obviously, does not mean very much to us. And indeed, we become very, shall we say, confused about time. What we hear in any time and at any place is the desire of our brothers and sisters on planet Earth for the thoughts that we have to share.

My friends, we would ask you to become aware of the fact that you are real. It is indeed almost as though your peoples, my friends, think of themselves as one of your toys, a doll perhaps, or a stuffed animal that a child would pick up and play with, making pretend in various situations and then putting the doll aside. And so you treat yourselves, my friends, many times. And then you say, I will play the part of a wage earner, or I will play the part of a man about town, or an attractive woman, or I will play the part of a churchgoer, or I will play this or that role. And you do not believe yourselves, my friends. You do not understand the game at all.

You see, underneath the sawdust and the tinsel of everyday life, there is something in you that is real. And that reality is very precious and will outlast the tinsel and the chemical body itself. The things that happen to you daily are quite important to this real self. Not perhaps in the way they seem to be important, as you pretend to be this or that. The importance of these things comes to you in a funny way, shall we say. It comes to you depending on how you desire that it comes to you. It has been written in the holy works that you call the Holy Bible, "Seek and you shall find." Just as you desire your experience to be, so it will show itself to you.

Most people, my friends, thinking of themselves as little more than a sawdust doll, do not desire deeply that they may discover the truth in their existence. Therefore, they do not discover the truth in their existence. But, my friends, if you truly desire that each moment may teach you its lessons, then you magnetize yourself, just as though you were walking through a vast beach and looking hopefully for precious metals. Sawdust, my friends, does not attract metal. But if you have magnetized yourself, ah, the metal comes to you through all of the useless sand and it attaches itself firmly to your understanding.

Desire. Do not be afraid of that word. What you desire is up to you. The intensity of your desire is very much up to you, my friends. Do not be afraid to really want to know the truth. Not just now, but all the time. When you are eating, my friends, when you are drinking, when you are speaking, when you are watching your television; you are in there, my friends, you are real, and you are here to learn the truth. It is a simple game and you play it by magnetizing yourself with the desire.

I will turn the message back now to my brother, Hatonn, and open the meeting to questions. I am Laitos, and I thank you very, very much for the privilege of speaking with you.

(Tape ends.)

Year 1978
March 11, 1978 to October 18, 1978

L/L Research

L/L Research is a subsidiary of Rock Creek Research & Development Laboratories, Inc.

P.O. Box 5195
Louisville, KY 40255-0195

www.llresearch.org

Rock Creek is a non-profit corporation dedicated to discovering and sharing information which may aid in the spiritual evolution of humankind.

ABOUT THE CONTENTS OF THIS TRANSCRIPT: This telepathic channeling has been taken from transcriptions of the weekly study and meditation meetings of the Rock Creek Research & Development Laboratories and L/L Research. It is offered in the hope that it may be useful to you. As the Confederation entities always make a point of saying, please use your discrimination and judgment in assessing this material. If something rings true to you, fine. If something does not resonate, please leave it behind, for neither we nor those of the Confederation would wish to be a stumbling block for any.

CAVEAT: This transcript is being published by L/L Research in a not yet final form. It has, however, been edited and any obvious errors have been corrected. When it is in a final form, this caveat will be removed.

© 2009 L/L Research

Saturday Meditation
March 11, 1978

(Carla channeling)

(The first part of the tape is inaudible.)

[I am Hatonn.] … A story from the Buddhist … is known to this instrument, which emphasizes this truth. In the story, a wise old man is accused of fathering a child. And when the mother …

We are not denying in any way that each personality incarnates into the illusion with one primary, as this instrument would say, program. This program is general and can be applied in various ways. If some ways are blocked, it may or may not be possible to fulfill the program as originally intended. However, it is a frequent thing that those who plan ahead find their plans … This is true, shall we say, of the soul in an infinite sense, as well as it is true that the personality is … The ultimate program for any individual … is completely achievable …

For that goal is simple: it is to be aware of the original Thought, to be aware of love. Whether the actions that are part of, shall we say, the karmic programming, are taking place as planned … the primary goal of expressing the original Thought is always … each individual is free the whole time. Many times it seems there are circumstances [that] are far less than …

An important thing to understand about the interfacing between the ultimate program and realizing love and the action program for one personality in one life experience is this. If the individual continually grounds himself in the original Thought, a condition is thereby prepared for an interface between love and proper action. We have said to you many times, meditate. Meditate and … Do not doubt, distrust or cease in your desire to be of service. As you meditate, allow that desire to keep the vibration, the antennae let us say, of your senses on the finer planes … You have felt that you are in the wilderness, and yet it is precisely in the wilderness that you must be alone, for you have the challenge of being aware of that which is paradise totally within yourself rather than being in the position of dwelling in paradise and attempting to remember the wilderness. We say to you the experience of wilderness is extremely important to growth of what you would call your soul.

As the immortal soul plunges into a cycle of experience such as you have committed yourself to in this density, the darkness of not remembering the Creator's Thought and all … All senses are stilled. Slowly the wisdom, kept like a seed within the soul, begins to put forth tiny sprouts and through many life experiences those sprouts are encouraged to grow.

In many situations, where there is ease within a life experience, choices are not made on the part of the individual because in paradise the individual grows complacent and does not evaluate all things in the belief of the original Thought. Inconsistency, impurity of motive, causes an interruption in the vibratory pattern of growth. And that particular incarnation serves only as a resting point between other more beneficial incarnations.

We do not ask you or any individual to truly rejoice in feelings of desolation, in feelings of getting off the track, shall we say. And yet we say to you that [with] enough determination, that wandering in the wilderness can one day herald that which is described in your holy works as the voice of God crying in the wilderness to make straight the way of the Creator. When you are struggling to understand, the struggling may seem to go [on] interminably. But then, suddenly the rocky places are made smooth, the mountains are made land. In your outer life it is possible nothing might have happened to cause this breakthrough. It is your inner light that counts.

This [is] why we say that you are free. It is your thought, your choice, your understanding. Trust that understanding. And we ask you again, do not fear the wilderness. Do not fear sorrow, desolation, lack of understanding … All of these things mean nothing. Only one thing matters: that is that you continually seek the original Thought. You can not re-choose what is past. You can choose this moment at all times; to become totally conscious of the moment, to see love, to seek the Creator.

These are inner things. They may not ever be brought into action on the dramatic plane. Some paths are dramatic, some are not. And this is true with all individuals. Those who have dramatic incarnations are those who have chosen a multitude of times; those who do not are those also who have chosen. There is no predetermining … There is only one choice, my friends. The Creator is everywhere, within each choice.

We speak to the one known as Carla also, for she has had many doubts lately as to the validity of her health in this incarnation. The Creator offers to those who wish to serve, the wilderness. Those who serve will [be] forever seeking that which is … My friends, you know there is great joy in the seeking. There is joy in fellowship. And there is joy even when totally isolated from your fellow man. In fellowship … Do not ever … seek out the joy of yourself and the Creator … Love is within you. Joy is within you. And the wilderness is within you. Step forward fearlessly. Paradise is also within you.

I would like at this time to open this meeting to questions.

S: I would like to know about my dreams I have been having. Can you shed any light on them? … Is there anything I should be afraid of?

(Carla channeling)

I am aware of your question. You are one who is sensitive [to] the emanations of finer vibrations. This is not obvious to you in the waking state. However, in your, shall we say, immortal soul you are very advanced in study upon the inner planes and in other incarnations have spent most of your time in these states.

In short, this the essence of your experience. However, you are experiencing difficulty due to an incomplete, or shall we say, … of the proper methods for achieving these altered states. Therefore, when you are as consciousness moving into them, you are bypassing certain, shall we say, guardians and attempting to go directly into a more advanced vibration. It is somewhat akin to attempting to walk through the walls of a house rather than go through the door. In order to work on this, it would perhaps be helpful for you to, in a conscious state, after surrounding yourself with white light and praying to the Creator for guidance, and then attempt to project through a carefully straight line. We are not suggesting of projecting bodily consciousness, but only projecting the thought of a straight line.

There are various colors and images which should gradually come to you. And it would perhaps be well to keep notes of what you see. In this way you may perhaps by, shall we say, self-hypnosis methods, recall consciously a piece, a door, shall we say, into higher vibrations.

Does this answer your question?

S: … I'm not sure.

We are aware of your problem. It is for this reason that we spoke to you of colors and images. You are, as are most who dwell in the dimension of Earth, not sensitive to specific visual counterparts of finer plane beings. In other words, most of those upon your planet do not perceive spirit guides and ghosts. If you were to fall completely in a state of sleep, as you call it, then you would then be totally able in your well-collected spiritual essence to contact the guides, to speak to the proper guardians of each plane. And to do all that is necessary to assure proper passage for lessons.

For my sister, as you well know, … However, in the conscious, or semiconscious state you will have difficulty identifying as being guardian and your own guide. However, you will see them as images or colors. But when you are seeing these things, even faintly, you have indeed fastened into your own symbols for the reality within. You are not seeing the reality, you are seeing the symbolic representation, in simple translation of a more complex reality. However, to focus on a color or an image is the same in consciousness [as] to focus on your guide or the guardian of a plane. Therefore, as long as you are protected by prayer and visualization of white light, and as long as you do not work in this endeavor for long periods of time and thereby become weary, this endeavor will be without danger to you. Among other things, it may give you more confidence in your ability to sense psychically that which cannot be expressed …

S: The last dream that I had … And I was just trying to let it come over me so that I could understand it better. And then I heard a voice saying to get out of it. Was I in danger then? … Should I continue to get out of it, or am I in danger if I dream? I'm afraid to let it come back over me. I feel that there is danger there. How am I to handle future instances in between my trying to open the door, instead of walking through the wall, as you say?

I am aware of your question. You were not in danger from outside influences at the time of which you speak. The voice was the voice of your fear on a level of being which was not able to see the inner planes and felt the leaving … For it is indeed true that were a spirit to completely leave without any trace the physical body, death would occur. However, the spirit would never do so. However, the answer to blackness is always light. It is perhaps asking a great deal of one who seeks to become immediately conscious of behavior within a dream, or what is called a dream in your terminology. Thus, if in your dream you have spoken and requested that your guides move you to the proper orientation for permission of the guardians to enter the desired plane, and if you had asked this in the name of the Creator, the obstacle would have been removed and your quest would have been successful. As it was, you did very well to remove yourself from that state of fear.

The important thing to remember is that to call upon the name of the Creator is to orient oneself in a manner of protection. It is not particularly desirable for any individual to proceed faster than the pace that seems most promising. Therefore, it is not necessary that you set yourself the goal of overcoming this obstacle *(inaudible)*. However, we reassure all those who seek that there are no terrors of the deep, shall we say, that cannot be countered by constant repetition of that which is divine. In unity, let there be no separation.

While this is not a difficult concept, it is only when it is fused with determination and vigor, and shall we say, an emotional emphasis, that it achieves its proper function.

Does this help?

S: Yes. I guess I'm still a little leery about the whole situation, because, one, when I first know that the dream is coming on, I immediately ask for light in the infinite Creator to be with me, and yet the effects of what the dream is, the environment that is around me even with my trying desperately to hang onto the light, is so … I feel like I'm being held over a pit. I don't know how or what more I can do to reassure myself to get over it without the constant fight that I have. I have to do it. I mean, if I am already asking the infinite Creator and I've already pictured light around me, and yet the dream is still there and I am still struggling so with the darkness … and the fear is still there, then that is why I'm *(inaudible)* when I wanted, when I asked *(inaudible)* to understand it.

I thought that was the last thing that I could reach for was to understand it *(inaudible)*. I felt that I had almost lost myself. So, even though your words are encouraging, I dread experiencing another dream like that just to prove that what you say is true. Because I feel like I've already done what you have said. Because that is how I do react to a frightening situation. I immediately call on the infinite Creator, because I know *(inaudible)*. So although I am in a sense eager to move on from this and find about these other planes, and this is something that I would really like to do, only the process is so overwhelming.

I'm not sure if I understand exactly … Okay, if I sat down consciously and tried to picture the line and the door and asked for guidance through it, then would that … If I do that tomorrow, could I be assured that I won't have one of these dreams tomorrow night?

[I am Hatonn.] I am with this instrument. As we earlier said, it is not desirable that you *(inaudible)*. It is desirable that you do seek as, shall I say, you are comfortable. We suggest that as this is *(inaudible)* as you call it, you arrange to study what we have said at length. The matter of fear if greatly limited to those who endure it and when the one who does not fear calls upon the Creator with intense emotion, it is a different experience from one who fears and seeks for a straw to hold onto. It is a matter of becoming what this instrument would call a magical personality. And this is indeed what you are *(inaudible)* learning to do within the strengthening framework of your personal daily life.

Instead of repeating ourselves, we will simply allow you to say what we would say. By all means, do not plunge into fear in order to rid yourself of fear. Instead, do what seems good and beautiful and true; you are aware that you can break this chain of events and continue to do so until you feel good about following that *(inaudible)*. It is a relatively unimportant part of your understanding. As we have said, you are extremely well developed in this area in the unlimited sense and it is a matter of remembering rather than learning within this limited life experience that you [are] dealing with. Therefore, it is not *(inaudible)*.

Is there another question?

S: Yes. When Carla, B and I were being regressed, I always wondered what your thoughts were about our experience or what we said our past life was on another planet and what we are doing here. Just recently I've had a lot of doubts about my previous training and *(inaudible)* at least I thought I was being trained for service here.

I am with the instrument. I am aware of your question. It is a question that I cannot answer directly. We are supportive of all those who seek *(inaudible)*. We are supportive of those things which they do to attempt to understand their place in the creation, and their methods of following the path of the Creator. Each individual must put together his own puzzle *(inaudible)*. When the one known as Carla, and the one known as B and the one known as S discovered a bit more of …

(Side one of tape ends.)

(Carla channeling)

… in the light of the larger perspective and service to humanity.

It is important that you understand that each of you has had many, many more experiences than you have discovered and *(inaudible)* session many, many incarnations, some of which seemed to be not useful. As we said earlier, in each incarnation there is the possibility for the kind of dramatic service that puts one in the public eye as one who serves the Creator. And in many incarnations each individual does not choose that but chooses instead a path of less visibility and more inner work. This is according to the need of that incarnation, that particular moment in eternity, if you will. These incarnations are not *(inaudible)* and can be missed. An incarnation can be largely of work in the inner planes and partially of work in the public eye *(inaudible)*. It is dependent upon the desire of the individual. Again we ask you, go back and study that we have said to you *(inaudible)* this evening.

What we have said this evening is not simple. It is an advanced message far more hard and far less delightful than an introductory message. It is a message that we could only give to a dedicated seeker. We wish you much light in your pursuit of what you had to say.

Is there another question?

(Pause)

Perhaps you wish to cease at this time. I and my brothers of the Confederation *(inaudible)*. It is, my friends, as though the creation were water. What will you do, my friends? Will you simply be a sponge and soak up the creation and squeeze it out unchanged, untouched? Or will you accept the water as does the earth, filtering, giving minerals, giving taste to the creation, the very essence of your creation, mixing *(inaudible)* so that life carves in you its channels and you give to life your *(inaudible)*. You are aware that pure water has no taste, *(inaudible)*. Do not fear to become intimate in life as you *(inaudible)*.

I leave you in all the love of the creation and all the light of the creation. I am your brother. I am Hatonn. *(Inaudible)*. Adonai vasu borragus.

Monday Meditation
March 13, 1978

(B channeling)

I am the one known to you as Hatonn. As always, I greet you in the love and light of our infinite Creator.

My friends, I will speak to you this evening of what is known to you as understanding. For, my friends, this is indeed a very … I will continue. This is indeed a very important … This is very important in your spiritual growth, for, my friends, you must accept people for what they truly are. For, my friends … I am experiencing much difficulty with this instrument. I will transfer this contact and may return at a later time. I am Hatonn.

(H channeling)

I am Hatonn. We of the Confederation [are] speaking to you this evening of understanding. We feel that it is important that man upon planet Earth learn to understand that which occurs around him and that which occurs within him. For in understanding these things, man can gain a greater insight and then man can proceed forward with understanding. And with that understanding he may weigh the outcome of his actions and therefore determine the proper avenue of action for him to take. But understanding, my friends, those things that you need to understand is somewhat difficult for man on planet Earth.

Consider, if you will, when all of you attended your educational processes. In the subject that you call mathematics you are often given a problem. And for that problem you must arrive at [an] answer. Consider, if you will, to know the answer is only a portion of solving the problem. For you must understand the problem and the means by which to derive the answer. Therefore, in this situation, knowledge and understanding are two separate factors which commune together and assist you in solving the problem before you.

So it is that man proceeds through his life, knowing many times the outcome of his actions, but not precisely understanding the intricate workings of his actions. With proper understanding, man upon planet Earth could become the god on planet Earth. For indeed the difference between men and gods is understanding. Knowledge you have. It has been a portion of you always. Wisdom is the proper application of that knowledge. But understanding, understanding, my friends, is the knowing when to apply that wisdom. Understanding is knowing how to arrive at the answer. Understanding is the most important ingredient in the overall spiritual growth of mankind. Indeed, you may arrive at certain conclusions and they may be beneficial for you, but the benefit in most circumstances is less to you unless you have understood the workings of these actions.

We of the Confederation have applied many of your years, more than you've ever imagined, to just gaining understanding of the universe and the way all things function within it. And we have yet to arrive at the point of total understanding. And we feel it to be true that we shall seek greater and greater levels of understanding for eons to come as we grow within this universe. But as we have progressed in our understanding, we have seen our growth come more rapidly. For, my friends, all life within this universe is very simple, [like] that which you call mathematics. For all thought produces an energy wave and [an] energy wave produces a certain action and a reaction. Each is able to be calculated if you have gained the understanding to monitor, shall we say, these thoughts in a way that you are aware of their conclusion.

We of the Confederation know beforehand what our thoughts and actions will bring about. We understand these things to a great degree even though we have not perfected the application of the understanding that we have gained. It is as with all things, practice is needed. Man upon planet Earth needs to begin to practice. He needs to begin to practice the monitoring of his thought-actions. He needs to begin to practice in understanding knowledge and wisdom. All of these things are greatly enhanced through the process of meditation, which is perhaps the greatest thing that you may practice in your life experience.

But man upon planet Earth presently proceeds to think, shall we say, improperly, thus accumulating greater and greater degrees of misshapen conclusions to his thoughts and actions. And he continues to wonder why. But if man developed his understanding he would know why things are as they are. For he has created them and he, being the creator of his experiences, should accept upon himself the responsibility for those creations and begin to apply understanding. For understanding, my friends, is not only recognizing the functions and mechanisms of your thoughts and actions. Understanding is applying love. For in understanding your actions, you may determine whether they shed love to your fellow man, and if they do not, then we say that your actions are improper.

For whatever you do, my friends, it does indeed affect all mankind. Whether you see that effect going any further than your own personal experience or not, you have placed an energy into your atmosphere. An energy that will never die. An energy that will pass among many people and affect in some small way their own being. So whether your actions be self-centered or directed towards the peoples, you must care and love one another enough to gain the understanding so that you may create for yourself and with others the environment that man upon planet Earth desires.

We understand your difficulties within your society. We understand what may seem to be your lack of knowledge. And it is this understanding that has made us capable of reaching forth to you and sharing our knowledge and our love with you. For we would react much as the man upon planet Earth if we did not understand your actions and your circumstances. For it is the nature of man throughout the universe to question and to even judge that which he does not understand. So consider, if you will, the importance of understanding. Recognize the difference between it and knowledge and wisdom. Recognize the link between the three. And look at the actions and the thoughts within your life and attempt to understand them. Attempt to see their outcome and by seeing this you may gain a greater degree of understanding than you have now.

We of the Confederation cannot do these things for any of you. We can only share with you our thoughts, hope that you accept them and apply them and work with them. And if they prove to be of no value to you we suggest that you refrain from using the knowledge that we give. But we of the Confederation have used our methods for a great length of your time and we have found them to be beneficial to us and we know that they shall bring the same benefit to you if you apply them in your life.

We of the Confederation indeed are not a source of ultimate truth and shall never claim to be so. We are a source of limited truth and limited understanding, ever progressing, as is man upon planet Earth. We are only to some extent more fortunate than you for we have progressed through your present experience and into ours. Indeed, upon your level of existence understanding is somewhat different than upon ours. And it is one of the greatest keys to reaching any upper level that you would desire.

We of the Confederation look upon you and even we wonder at times why you do not see the simplicity of your difficulties. And the answer is immediately within our consciousness, for we [see] that man's understanding is far behind his knowledge. And only recently, unfortunately, man's wisdom has begun to flourish. Work on these things and you shall notice a change within yourself.

We of the Confederation are pleased to be with you and we shall always be with you whether you are aware of us or not. We watch over you. And we love each and every one of your peoples for we understand their situations and love the divinity within each of them.

I shall transfer this communication. I am Hatonn.

(Carla channeling)

I am with this instrument. I am Hatonn. I greet you again in love and light. My brother Laitos is working with each of those who are in the meeting this evening. I would like to pause while this process goes on.

(Pause)

I would now like to attempt to say a few sentences through the one known as M. I am Hatonn.

(M channeling)

I am Hatonn. I would like to say …

(Carla channeling)

I am again with this instrument. I am Hatonn. I would like to thank the one known as M for picking up the ball so well. Each session gets a little easier and we thank her for her service.

We continue working with each of you and we guarantee that it will get better as time goes on. I would like to speak a few words through the one known as G1, if she would relax.

(G1 channeling)

I am with this instrument. *(Inaudible).*

(Carla channeling)

I am again with this instrument. I am pleased to say that my brother of Laitos has left his chair and is kicking up his heels. We are very pleased when we have good contacts. And to the one known as G1 we would express our feelings that seeking is always appreciated. We feel most grateful for her seeking of *(inaudible).*

We would like to work with the one known as G2. If she would relax and make herself available to our contact we would speak a few words through her. I am Hatonn.

(Carla channeling)

I am again with this instrument. It is truly a great privilege to work with each new instrument. As you begin it may seem to a new instrument that the contribution would be small, but we say to you that each accomplished instrument his gone through a prolonged period of being a new instrument, a developing instrument, an inadequate and doubting instrument. As you, as an individual, and as you all, as a group, continue, the transformations will continue and the quality of the contact will continue to improve. It is your seeking as individuals and as a group that determines your experience.

When as a race you were young and *(inaudible)*, you understood with your physical bodies. The understanding of your heart beating and your lungs breathing and the stimuli to which your adrenal system reacted was your understanding. This was an unbalanced understanding.

As you climbed out of the darkness of the body, you as a race willfully entered the darkness of the mind. And now you wander as seemingly as very tiny ghosts inside a great *(inaudible)* computer, caught in endless tunings of switches.

Understanding, my friends, is understanding of only one thing: the love of the Creator/creation. If, as you see through the eyes of your physical bodies, you do not see the Creator, you have not yet acquired understanding.

Seek it, therefore. To actively seek is to live. Those who do not seek are waiting. For what are they waiting, my friends? For the most part they are waiting for the physical death so that they may remember that they do not want to wait. You already know that you do not want to wait. You are eager for the adventure of understanding.

At this time I would open the meeting to questions.

G1: *(Inaudible).*

We are aware of the question. We will attempt to answer through this instrument. Your understanding, shall we say, is consciously of a physical nature. As you well know, in addition to the physical universe there dwell within your planetary spheres finer dimensions which possess their reality and are peopled with their own characters. In the dimension which is called by some of your peoples the lower astral planes, there dwell but these same peoples but are called thought forms. These thought forms are what you may call archetypes. They include your whole array of demons and monsters, if you will, your myths, your so-called Big Foot, and vampire and werewolf and all the fantastic *(inaudible)* of bestial characters having been created by the archetypical imaginations of your peoples dwell as thoughts forms and [they] come into your reality because of the excessive and pointed emotions. The place that such entities will appear is dependent on a seemingly random energy pattern and is, in effect, not random. To explain it to you would be far too complex for easy transmission. For the energies of the planet, the race, and what you call your nations and states and cities, your individuals, all must he taken into account.

Let us say that those sightings, or sightings *(inaudible)*, are terrestrial rather than unearthly *(inaudible)*. The incident of which you speak, being a tragedy as it was, began to be known to the subconscious awareness of many people before it occurred, just as many people in many situations are aware of tragedies before they occur. Fear of such events actually hastens their eventuality, unless that fear is resolved in a positive way as *(inaudible)*.

The more who were aware of the tragedy, the more certain it was to occur. This is due to the fact that events occur on the so-called inner planes at an advanced time/space nexus to their appearance on the more dense physical plane.

Does this answer your question?

G1: *(Inaudible)*.

We are grateful for the opportunity. Is there another question?

(Pause)

If not, I will close through the one known as B. I am Hatonn.

(B channeling)

I am now with this instrument. My friends, I will leave you after a very few words, for we realize that you are all tired.

My friends, go forth at each day with that that is known to you as love, in your love, in your heart, in your mind. My friends, always remember, as you well know, that all is love. My friends, when you dwell within your physical realm you indeed dwell within the energy that is known to you as love. My friends, as you allow your intellect to, shall we say, rule your existence, my friends, you yourself cut off that flow of energy which is known as love from yourself. My friends, do not allow this to happen, for it is truly of your own making. My friends, remember, study the thing known to you as love. Treat all that you meet and, my friends, that is to say, those of which you do not already know. For, my friends, they are a concept of our Creator Who created us all.

My friends, it has been a great honor to be with you this evening and share with you in your meditation. I leave you now in the love and light. I and my brothers thank you. I leave you now. I am Hatonn. Adonai, my friends. Adonai vasu borragus. ☥

L/L Research

L/L Research is a subsidiary of Rock Creek Research & Development Laboratories, Inc.

P.O. Box 5195
Louisville, KY 40255-0195

www.llresearch.org

Rock Creek is a non-profit corporation dedicated to discovering and sharing information which may aid in the spiritual evolution of humankind.

ABOUT THE CONTENTS OF THIS TRANSCRIPT: This telepathic channeling has been taken from transcriptions of the weekly study and meditation meetings of the Rock Creek Research & Development Laboratories and L/L Research. It is offered in the hope that it may be useful to you. As the Confederation entities always make a point of saying, please use your discrimination and judgment in assessing this material. If something rings true to you, fine. If something does not resonate, please leave it behind, for neither we nor those of the Confederation would wish to be a stumbling block for any.

CAVEAT: This transcript is being published by L/L Research in a not yet final form. It has, however, been edited and any obvious errors have been corrected. When it is in a final form, this caveat will be removed.

© 2009 L/L Research

Monday Meditation
March 27, 1978

(Carla channeling)

I am Hatonn, and I greet you in the love and the light of the infinite Creator. I speak to you as a representative of the Confederation of Planets in the Service of the Infinite Creator. I also speak to you as a voice from within yourself that beckons you inward; not outward, my friends, but inward.

We hover high above your planet, offering what seems to be telepathic instruction from one being to others. But in effect, my friends, that is not true. We are one being—you and I and all that dwells in consciousness—and we speak to each other as an arm speaks to a leg, or as two brain cells communicate in the same entity. Those who are upon your planet speak to each other in such a way that, if you understood that you are one body of consciousness, you would understand that you are like a cancer or a disease to yourself: the entity attacking itself, the entity fearing itself, the entity destroying itself.

In your so-called orthodox medicine, it is understood that when a cancer attacks your physical vehicle, your attempt is to remove it, cut it out, and dispose of it. But, my friends, if your doctors could understand the true meaning of cancer, they would not cut it out but would, instead, reinstruct it so that it would become benign and proper. And this is what we are attempting to do to you. For you are conscious, and all of those on your planet are conscious and what you continue in hostility and fear—one to another, brother to brother, nation to nation—the answer, my friends, is not further violence to cut out those who are wrong. The answer, as always, is love. Love is an atmosphere in which consciousness can be reinstructed in the original Thought.

Within you, my friends, is the wisdom that is totally and completely aware that you are part of a being called the universe. As you look out into what you call outer space, know that within you is the true reality of which outer space is only a picture. Your consciousness, my friends, is an incredible and infinite geography, peopled with an infinity of creatures equipped with the collective wisdom of eons of experience; for, my friends, within some part of your being, some deep and, for the most part, hidden part of your being you have all knowledge, all power, all compassion. It is as they were in files in a room to which you have lost the key.

Do you wish, then, to explore outer space to repair the great damage of your society, or do you indeed think of it as hopeless? Take these attitudes away from the world, my friends, and turn them in to yourself, for you yourself are the great object on which to practice your own wisdom, on which to develop your own understanding. If you can solve those slums which exist within the topography of your consciousness, the slums in your cities will begin to take care of themselves.

You say, "What can one person do?" We say to you: one person can work on one person, but that one person, my friends, is a hologram of all that there is. Your consciousness is all consciousness. Work on it, and you work on your race, your planet—the vibration that speaks for Earth.

We offer you our love and our serenity and encourage you to seek those qualities in meditation. When you are upset, do not blame it upon little things which have occurred in the outer world: blame it on the lack of meditation. When you see your fellow man in a hostile manner, don't blame it on his actions but on a lack of meditation. Your environment does not have to have any power over you, for all that there is is within you. The environment is only a shadow compared to the power of love within yourself. Meditation can unlock that power.

I would like to transfer at this time to the one known as B. I am Hatonn.

(B channeling)

I am Hatonn. I am now with this instrument. My friends, we speak to you of, shall we say, improving your inner being. For, my friends, we realize that it is much easier spoken than done. So we offer you, my friends, very few suggestions.

My friends, it is very important that you realize and understand the energy which surrounds you all. Now, my friends, you gain, shall we say, a positive energy. You are, shall we say, engulfed in a great field of energy. My friends, this field may be increased through much practice. That is to say, my friends, that the harder you try, the wider your skills will become.

Now, my friends, think good of all. It is very easy to assume an opinion of another being. My friends, you are not truly aware of the ordeals of growth which is being his experience. My friends, through the help of others you are, indeed, helping yourself. And, my friends, we find it easy to … a growth that may take to *(inaudible)* a greater portion of the day. But, my friends, it is important that we experience this energy in all that we say and do, without even thinking.

My friends, as you well know, we are always available for, shall we say, support. Feel free to call upon our energy at any time; for, my friends, we truly are one.

I will leave you now. And, my friends, as we said, for as long as you try in meditation you will feel this energy *(inaudible)*; for, my friends, it is our gift to you. We wish only to share with you. And, my friends, we wish this experience [to be] that of yours.

I leave you now. I leave you in the love and light of our infinite Creator. I am Hatonn.

(Pause)

(Carla channeling)

I am Oxal. I greet you in the love and the light of the infinite Creator. I am very grateful and privileged to speak with you. I wish only to say that we of Oxal take a continuing interest in your group and send you our light at all times.

Remember, my friends, you *are* the light of the world, as are all those who have consciousness of what you would call Christ or Creator or love. Call it what you will; there is no difference. It is a feeling we are a magnetism of love that permeates those who seek it. Take confidence, and forgive all those mistakes you may make. Each day try again, and each day you will gain.

Each day is a fork in the road. Keep your eyes open, my friends. One road is lighter than the rest. Yet, whatever road you are on, you are the light.

I leave you in that love and that light. Adonai vasu borragus. I am Oxal.

Monday Meditation
June 26, 1978

(H channeling)

[I am Hatonn.] It is, as always, a pleasure to be with you. We wish it to be known that we will be among you this evening and that we will touch with you and speak with you as it has been requested.

Those within this group and those not in attendance associated with this group are all very special to us. Many of you have known of us and have sat with us a great number of times over spans which you call years. In this time we have watched over your patterns of life. We have witnessed the ebbs and tides as your life flows in the stream of consciousness and love and of the universe. Man upon planet Earth does not understand in totality the creation in which he lives. And it has often been the quest of many of the great minds upon your planet to seek out truths which would unlock doors to man upon planet Earth and assist him to understand his universe. These great minds have been inspirations to many of your peoples. Yet, they have only touched upon the brink of knowledge and of awareness. We, in our own right, have also only begun to touch upon that brink, for understanding this entire universe is not within our grasp at the present time. We have learned to understand many of things which still puzzle many of your people. Yet, there are those things which we have not yet understood that occur around each of us.

We of the Confederation have sought through our meditation, through our service to mankind, to fulfill a long goal which we had set for ourselves eons of time ago: that is to know and understand the Creator and His universe. It seems but yesterday that we began, and it seems that we will never end in our quest for this knowledge. Yet each step of the way we find relief, we find happiness, in knowing that our understanding has grown and knowing that our love has been multiplied. We of the Confederation share with you, above all things, our love. But there are those among your planet who will not accept our words of intellectual understanding. Yet, we are free to send them our love and our assistance for as they would call upon their Creator, whatever that belief may be, they call upon us. For we have realized that we are also a portion not only of the creation but of the Creator.

When one calls, whomsoever may hear that call should serve the one in need to the best of their ability using the best of their discretion.

We of the Confederation admire this group, for though you have seen your difficulties in your personal lives and within the life of the organization called Eftspan you have grown and we have grown by watching you and being with you and serving you. We wish [you] to understand that the day will come when you must be willing to freely offer your assistance in a much more demanding way than you do now. And in order to do this properly you must prepare yourselves by becoming the being that you desire to be: one of knowledge and wisdom, love and understanding, one of strength and integrity. All of you have desired this and in some ways you have gained portions of your goal.

Yet, we and all of you must understand that there is never time, as you would call it, for you to neglect the attainment of goals you have set for yourself. For man upon Earth lives within an atmosphere or an environment which is attuned to the premise of time. Your physical bodies are sustained for only a short period, therefore when you neglect the seeking and the fulfillment of your chosen mission and goal, you neglect the entire essence of this short span you live upon planet Earth. You live not for frivolity or enjoyment. You live for love and enlightenment, for the fulfillment of your role in the creation of a perfect universe. If your actions are attuned to the consciousness of the Creator, your life shall experience no difficulty, not in essence. It may appear that you do indeed have difficulties, but they are lessons. Some are difficult, others are not. Be not discouraged by your own lack of disciplines. Be not haughty about your achievements. For you are as others, all others within this universe. You are a creator, you are a part and particle of an undividable growing and consciousness universe.

We of the Confederation share these thoughts with you and commend you for what you have achieved. We also wish to somewhat warn you that you must realize that your journey has only begun. Be more determined, allow yourself not to falter. Be not discouraged with yourself when you do.

I shall transfer this communication. I am Hatonn.

(Carla channeling)

I am with this instrument. I am Hatonn. At this time, my friends, I will open the meeting to questions. Please feel free to ask any question for it is our great privilege to share our thoughts with you.

(Pause)

I am again with this instrument. We would then leave this instrument and allow a brother who has not previously spoken to this group to speak through this instrument. Therefore, with our hearts attuned with you and all our love with you, we leave you in the love that is only that of the Creator. Adonai vasu borragus.

(Carla channeling)

I am Orkan. And I speak to you this evening for the first time. It is an infinite pleasure to me and I greet you in the love and the light of the One Who is the Creator of us all.

I am a flame. I am a flame that flickers, my friends, that glows, that grows, that is eternal. I am the flame of creation; the flame of your physical sun that warms your planet and allows your food to grow on your fertile land. I am the flame of destruction that transmutes all that there is. Yes, my friends, I am a flame. I appear as the love in the heart of those who give. I appear, my friends, as the intelligence of those who think. I am the flame that creates beauty, whether it is the beauty of the Creator or the beauty of mankind; the beauty of your art or your music; the beauty of your architecture, of your statues, of your philosophy. I am a flame that may but flicker in the darkest of times, my friends. I am to be found by those who can recognize love.

I am and you are the flame, my friends, the flame of love that burns and consumes. It is not something that you reach out to find. The total freedom, the total annihilation of fire is not something that you may use, my friends. Love can only use you. It is not a tool, my friends. You are the tool for love. You have not chosen a gentle path. You have chosen the path that consumes those things about you which are not love. The rate of that consumption is completely dependent upon you. When do you wish to become the flame of love, of joy, of light, of laughter, of freedom? It is up to you, my friends, for the flame is always there inside you, inside me. My friends, the flame is not an answer. For as far as we know, we have no answers. We have only the process of love. We have only the knowledge that the flame, that the love is grace, is easiness, is strength.

If you have the discipline to seek the flame in moment, whether it be in the day or the night, in joy or sorrow, in something great or in something very small, if you have the discipline to seek it, then you become the flame. And when you have achieved this identity, this manifestation, it is not, my friends, that you become a teacher, it is only, my friends, that you become a window through which the flame can be seen.

I am Orkan. It is a great privilege to meet each of you, and I and my brothers are with you. Adonai vasu. Adonai.

(Carla channeling)

I am Laitos, and I greet you each in the love and the light of the infinite Creator. I will not speak to you long, my friends, but I wish to work with each of you. If you would open yourselves to our influence, I and my brothers wish to at this time to come into the room and work with each of you personally. If you will be patient and mentally request our presence, we will attempt to strengthen your own natural meditation. I am Laitos.

(Pause)

I am again with this instrument. It is a great privilege to use this instrument for we have not been able to use her for some weeks. And we are very grateful for the chance to work with each of our instruments.

My friends, we ask only that you meditate; five minutes, ten minutes, however long you may. Daily meditation, my friends; it is an old story but it does not lose its importance. Life as it is known by your peoples seems very normal. But we say to you, my friends, that the universe is very, very unusual. There are many, many strange things all around you. Many informative, unusual occurrences. To pick up, to understand those things that are missed by so many, it is necessary to tune the mind by meditation.

I would like to close through another channel. I am Laitos.

(H channeling)

I am Laitos. I am now with this instrument. It has also been a long time since we have spoken through this instrument. For the benefit of those who are somewhat new to the actual training of an instrument, we are utilizing a great degree of conditioning with this instrument. We are showing those interested the technique which is the least desirable. The communications which we offer which you may witness now are much more easily transmitted when the instrument allows the energy to flow, allows himself to speak the words without thought, and accepts the communication with faith.

We of the Confederation speak with your peoples and we need many instruments for, what you would term, the future. We desire in the development of channels to be accepted by the instruments at their own choosing. And we have chosen the previously witnessed form of conditioning because we have found it necessary for most to have this experience in order that they may be, shall we say, thoroughly convinced of the validity of the communication, for you may witness and believe in it but then attempt to doubt it either in its validity or your own. We say to you that the source of the message is, shall we say, irrelevant. We shall not ask or judge from [where] goodness has come, we should only accept it and use what is beneficial to you and pass the rest on into the others without concern. We press nothing upon you; we bless you for your acceptance.

We leave you in the love and in the light of the infinite Creator. I am Laitos. Adonai, my friends. Adonai vasu borragus. ✝

Monday Meditation
July 3, 1978

(Carla channeling)

I greet you in the love and the light of the One Who is All. I am Hatonn of the Confederation of Planets in the Service of the Infinite Creator. I and my brothers hover high above you in the sky. We are at this time approximately 7.3 miles above your dwelling place. Aboard our ship, as you would call it, are more than 4,000 of our brothers and sisters who bear one name, my friends, the name of our home, as you would call it, our planet, the planet of Hatonn. We come from a planet, my friends, which has come through a great death and a great birth. The kind of birth into an age in which we no longer need the artificial creations of our kind. We have come into an age, my friends, where we can dwell in the creation of the Father.

Our planet is now a sentient being. All wildlife, as you call it, is conscious in a way that most of you *(inaudible)*. And we ourselves can speak without tongue and hear without ear for we are in a vibration in which time and space are plastic, in which we can move from one level to another with conscious awareness and understanding. Our conscious awareness and understanding have led us to one awareness and one understanding. And it is for this reason that [we have] come among you and your peoples at this time.

We come bearing witness to the Creator, my friends. And yet the Creator is not as you have pictured Him. He is not a judge, He is not a man, nor, my friends, is He a woman. He is not a being. My friends, we bear witness to love. We bear witness to all that there is which is love. This is the understanding that we have come so far to share. And why, my friends, do we come among you at this time to speak of love?

You, my friends, approach a planetary death and a planetary birth. For as the cycles grow in your time and your space, in the locality of your present existence, the time and space has rolled around for a vibrational change. Not my friends, a vibrational change as you would understand it. We are not speaking of physical things but of the energy which creates physical things. It is difficult to explain to you of the vibrational change in which death and life are transformed while the physical body continues to die and live. And yet, this is what we bring to you. And we bring it [to] you because so many among your peoples, my friends, know that there is something beyond the physical body and the physical death. There is something that is more than the brief span of their lifetime and the brief span of experience in this lifetime.

My friends, the answers to the questions you seek are all about you, written in the holy works in all of what you call your religions and philosophies. Many,

many teachers walk the Earth at this time who speak the truth and yet, my friends, so disillusioned have your people become that your people no longer believe in their books, nor their leaders. They do not even believe, totally, in the inner voice that compels them towards the seeking for that which is beyond life and death.

We come mostly, my friends, because your peoples can understand our presence with more ease than they can understand books and your orthodox teachings. We have come to add our voice of truth as we know it to the many voices of the same truth as it is known already. We come by the millions, my friends. Far across the universe, across your galaxy, and across the reaches of other times and other space, there are many civilizations who have crossed into a vibration in which the truth of the Creator is obvious. Where this is so, my friends, beings have no choice except to turn to a life of service to others. With understanding of the Creator, my friends, comes the information that all your needs will be taken care of. Thus we have no more needs. We have meat and drink, as it says in your holy works, that your people know not of[3], because our vibrational change made it possible for us to create that which was needed by thought. We no longer have need of government as you know it for we can communicate our desires to a central computer which does the will of the people instantly. We are then free, my friends, to love. Love of others is much easier, my friends, when you can see the vibration of love in each of your brothers and sisters. The selection of a mate, my friends, is much easier when you can see the connection going back many, many lifetimes with your appropriate partner. One by one, my friends, those things which you call problems are solved by the application of divine love shedding light, shedding truth, shedding enablement on the so-called immobile lifespan. We are now free in spirit as a people. What we wish to do is our work of service. We have no need mentally or physically or emotionally; then our needs must become spiritual. And we find that we can only satisfy the spiritual desire for increased understanding by service to others. For this we must look outward, my friends, if you wish to use that expression. Outward across the voids between civilizations until we find one such as yours that is crying out at this time for the knowledge which we have to share. And so we are here.

We are aware, my friends, that in your daily lives you cannot see clearly that love is in everything. And without that truth the problem of finding *(inaudible)*, of knowing friends in everyone, or finding enough supply of those things which are needed for physical existence, of finding mental stimulation which is satisfying, of finding that emotional stability which among your peoples is called happiness—all of these things, my friends, are anything but easy.

But you see, my friends, you are not without a clear understanding of love. It is as though you were in a deep, underground prison to which you have the key, my friends. Your body is the prison. It is a dense, chemical *(inaudible)* which carries your spirit about. It is extremely useful, for in it you experience emotions and situations which act as a catalyst in order that the understanding of your basic spiritual self may become tempered and toughened, thus producing at the end of an experience in the physical body an intense understanding of love. It is as though, my friends, in our vibration we can never truly practice our understanding of love for we see it clearly. Anyone can see in the daylight, but you my friends, are in darkness. To see the light in the darkness is much, much more difficult.

What is the key that unlocks the prison? It is a simple key, my friends. It is the key of meditation, or as this instrument has described, the activity of inner listening. Life and love do not come to you from us, from books, from on high. No, my friends, life and love come to you from within. For within each of you is the spark of the Creator. It is a matter of becoming conscious or aware of that spark which is already there and then allowing that light within to shine through to the outside experience and thus illuminating it, thus granting supply were there was lack, healing where there was pain, friendship, brotherhood and harmony where there were enemies, disagreement and disharmony. As you breathe in and as you breathe out, my friends, you use up this mortal life that you have taken on with courage and dedication at the outset to make use of as a time of learning and *(inaudible)* under adverse

---

[3] *Holy Bible*, John 4:31-35: "Meanwhile the disciples besought him, saying, "Rabbi, eat." But he said to them, "I have food to eat of which you do not know." So the disciples said to one another, "Has anyone brought him food?" Jesus said to them, "My food is to do the will of him who sent me, and to accomplish his work."

circumstances—under the circumstance of forgetting what you knew as a spirit. Try to remember, my friends, what you already know: that all men are brothers, that love and consciousness dwell in everything, that all that is around you is alive and part of the creation which is love.

We ask you, my friends, to have faith. Not in some dogmatic repetition, but in the basic concept that you are not here aimlessly but for a purpose. In meditation, my friends, ask that you may fulfill your purpose. You need not know to the last detail what that purpose is. You need only dedicate yourself to the intention and desire to fulfill your purpose. Spirits, my friends, have a purpose which is inevitable. And that is that they should love and share.

The ideas among your people having to do with purpose are all accepted ambitions, and the ideas of greatness and dramatic accomplishment. But we say to you, my friends, that your purpose is to love and to share. The details matter not, but only the care and daily constancy of your willingness to manifest the love of the Creator. In this, my friends, you will surely fail if you attempt to do it yourself. For we are all, when cut off from love, unloving people, unloving beings, my friends, with very few resources. However, the Creator is an infinite and invisible flow of love. In meditation and in conscious thought, call upon that infinite supply.

I will pause while one of my brothers speaks through one of the other instruments. I am Hatonn.

(H channeling)

I am Laitos. Greetings, my friends, in the love and the light of our infinite Creator. It is a pleasure to be with you and I would touch with you but a short time.

I am here for one purpose and that is to assist you in sensing our presence within this room. It has been a pleasure for a great period of time to be bestowed with the duties of shall we say, conditioning new instruments within this group and within other groups. And a portion of that duty is to share our love and our energies with those who visit with us.

We are among you now and we ask that you relax. And if you can sense our presence we ask that you please allow it to flow and do not become apprehensive. For we of the Confederation are here to love and serve man on planet Earth. This is our sole purpose. We shall not instruct you how to live but we shall offer advice on how to build a better life during your short stay upon this planet.

We of the Confederation are dedicated to our service for it sustains our being. We have found through our experience that to serve another is to indeed serve oneself. For it is spoken within your holy works, "As you sow, so shall you reap." To give service in love to another is only to assure yourself that when you are in need it shall be given to you.

I am touching with you now and giving you my love and the love of all of those within the Confederation. It pleases us to see you. We ask only that you listen and take that which is of importance and use it forever and that which you find somewhat disagreeable to your accepted train of thought we ask that you dispel that from your consciousness which you so desire. We claim not to know all that there is in the universe for, to the best of our knowledge, the universe is infinite and the experiences and the knowledge within must therefore be the same. However, we do claim to have progressed through very similar circumstances as what you experience now and offer what we feel to be the greatest degree of assistance that we can presently render to your people.

We have spoken through many people upon your planet such as you are witnessing now. Many of your peoples have grown aware of us and it is pleasing to see that a few more have come to listen. And we humbly and gratefully respect your presence.

It has been my pleasure to be with you. I shall now leave you. I leave you in the love and the light of our infinite Creator. I am known to you as Laitos. Adonai.

(Carla channeling)

I am again with this instrument. I am Hatonn, and again I greet you in love and in light. At this time I would open the meeting to any questions that you may have of us, always keeping in mind that we are not infallible and only wish to share our thoughts with you in the simple way of brotherhood. If you have any questions please speak forth at this time.

M: I have a question. Is the Confederation of brothers connected with a group that is based in Florida called the Mark-Age group? And if you are connected, what is the connection?

We are aware of the question. The light center which is in that portion of the creation on planet Earth that you call Florida is in contact with the Confederation. However, due to the individual differences which reside within that group there are other entities which are in contact with them also which are of your planet and which have in the past given false information. This complicates the attempt of seekers such as yourself who wish to understand our message and seek understanding through this group. They offer much of our message, however, my friend, we do not give individual advice for that is an infringement on the free will of the individual.

We can only share our understanding of, as our brother has spoken, how to live the better life, the life of love, the life which is natural to you in a higher sense.

This group has had its temptations with what some have called lower astrals in the past and has channeled false information about landing and other natural phenomena. However, it has managed to understand what was occurring and not try to justify its mistake. Due to this, this group manages to dispense, shall we say, a fair amount of our so-called cosmic sermonettes without too much distortion. What you must do in dealing with information such as Mark-Age Metacenter is learn to separate the wheat from the chaff, as this instrument would put it. See the truth in that which is given and with compassion allow the channel to make mistakes without you being emotionally disturbed by false information. In fact, my friends, this would apply to all of your established, so-called religions of your planet where the original manifestations of universal truth and love had become clouded by the distortions of men who with their intellect and with the help of lower inspirations have muddied the waters of the original truths. These truths are there and can be recognized. What you cannot use and do not need, discard. Do not become emotionally upset if others have an emotional need for what you consider distortion. Allow them their path to understanding while knowing that it is not your path to understanding. There are infinite numbers of beings, each with his own path, each with his own recognition of truth.

Does this satisfactorily answer your question?

M: Yes, thank you.

Is there another question?

G: I have a question, a little along the same line. I am interested to know if there are any groups in western North Carolina who you are channeling through, and if so, would we be able to contact those groups if we moved there?

We are aware of your question. You must understand, my friend, that that which you need must come to you in a certain way. We cannot, shall we say, from on high, alter the course of your life, of your experience, or of your understanding. That which is needed will appear, this is the rule of the Creation. We are aware that this is not a satisfactory answer and we are sorry, but we cannot become temporal teachers, guiding you to our outposts of knowledge. If it is for you to continue in this phase of understanding, your group will appear. If your group does not appear in your new environment, consider, my sister, whether you are perhaps to begin such a group or whether you are to perhaps to find a totally new source of continued progress.

We declare at this time, as always, that these spoken messages are only the stimulants to begin and to continue in your own spiritual search. Do you understand my sister, why we cannot give the address and phone number of your contact?

G: Yes, I understand.

We are grateful for your understanding. Another question, my friends?

R: How does one recognize this group when it appears?

The thing which is right, feels right. This means that this individual must be in touch with his feelings and of course, as always, this goes back to a daily period, brief as it may be, of meditation. When the one known as G met with the entities who became the group which now sits in circle with us, they were strangers but there was a feeling of appropriateness, the feeling perhaps, shall we say, of rightness. And this feeling was shared by all those who were long intended to work together in this group. It was a natural and spontaneous feeling from within, as all spiritual stages occur. All the one known as G did was to act on her feelings. First by going to a class and then by attending a meeting that she had heard about, and then attempting in sincerity and some humility to follow what was to her and still is to her a sometimes strange discipline. This takes being in touch with what feels like the right thing to do. It is a subtle feeling, that of rightness. And we can only suggest that each of you meditate and allow harmony to reign within yourself so that you may speak to yourself and know that feeling of what is right and what is appropriate. Does this answer your question, my brother?

R: *(Inaudible).*

We wish to encourage each of you for each of you has all the stimulus that you may need. As we have said before, your lifetimes are not unplanned. You may go down many, many paths but each will be sufficient. You cannot make a totally wrong choice for all choices are within the creation of love. But there is always an optimum choice, a choice which is really right for you, not for anyone else, my friends. From small things to large there is rightness.

We ask you to meditate.

Is there another question?

(Pause)

If there are no more questions, my friends, we leave this channel although we do not leave. We are able to respond at any time you may need our presence as a comfort or as company as you go into meditation. For those of you who are not channels may find it impossible to detect our presence but if you mentally request our presence, we will be there and you will eventually be able to feel our presence, perhaps as light or some physical sensation having to do with our joining of vibrations with yours.

We offer our presence, as we said, not to dictate but only to give the brotherhood and the love of all of us to you. We are not strangers, my friends, though we come from far. We are brothers no matter what star our home revolves around. There is no doubt in our hearts that we are all part of love.

It is with joy beyond telling that I leave you in that love and that light, my brothers and my sisters. I am called Hatonn. Adonai, my friends. Adonai vasu borragus.

L/L Research

L/L Research is a subsidiary of Rock Creek Research & Development Laboratories, Inc.

P.O. Box 5195
Louisville, KY 40255-0195

www.llresearch.org

Rock Creek is a non-profit corporation dedicated to discovering and sharing information which may aid in the spiritual evolution of humankind.

ABOUT THE CONTENTS OF THIS TRANSCRIPT: This telepathic channeling has been taken from transcriptions of the weekly study and meditation meetings of the Rock Creek Research & Development Laboratories and L/L Research. It is offered in the hope that it may be useful to you. As the Confederation entities always make a point of saying, please use your discrimination and judgment in assessing this material. If something rings true to you, fine. If something does not resonate, please leave it behind, for neither we nor those of the Confederation would wish to be a stumbling block for any.

CAVEAT: This transcript is being published by L/L Research in a not yet final form. It has, however, been edited and any obvious errors have been corrected. When it is in a final form, this caveat will be removed.

© 2009 L/L Research

Wednesday Meditation
July 5, 1978

(Carla channeling)

I am Hatonn. I greet you in the love and the light of the infinite Creator. I am with the instrument. It is a blessing to speak with each of you and we greet those who have not sat with this group for awhile and offer them our love.

My friends, we always speak to you of one simple thing: the love of the Creator. We are aware that, from your horizon, this love does not seem to be accessible in many ways in your daily life. And yet we say to you, my friends, that this love is closer to you than your breathing; more easily accessible than your own hands and feet; more familiar to you than your own thoughts. This love was the pattern from which each of you was stamped. Yes, my friends, each of you stamped in complete identity. And that same love that made you each the same has touched each with a unique part in that identity so that the universe is an identity and a harmony at the same time.

Where are you going, my brothers, that you can use this information? To what can you reach out, my sisters, so that you can make use of the knowledge of love? What dramatic inquiry can you prosecute so that you can demonstrate love in the court of your daily life?

Perhaps some of you, my friends, have had the experience of having an object in your lives, some, shall we say, daily, simple, physical object such as what this instrument would call a carpet which has become dull and worn and perhaps torn in places through years of daily, careless use. And yet, my friends, if you pick it up and look on the unused side, it is still perfect.

In daily use, love becomes worn and shabby. This, my friends, is through carelessness of use. We always urge meditation and it is simply because, in meditation, you establish contact with that part of yourself that understands the nature of love.

No matter how worn and shabby your ideals, your actions, or your concepts have become, there always remains the eternally pristine side where love flourishes in its original form. It is a great trick of mental discipline to reverse your understanding of love so that the clean, new side shines forth through your actions and words but it is infinitely possible at any time for you to do so.

We are aware of the moving picture which you saw this evening and although we are aware of the many yawns and giggles which were the reaction of each of you due to the aesthetically inadequate presentation of these ideas, yet, we wish to share with you the basic truth of, as you would call it, life beyond physical death.

We are aware, my friends, that death is a transformation which seems most final and frightening. And it is because of this very nature of death that your peoples avoid contemplation of their lives in the perspective of their eventual demise. Yet, what we urge you to do—namely, to meditate, to learn, to grow, to love, and to remember the Creator—would be quite senseless were it not for a continued existence in which you would be able to reap the benefit of your growing and learning. For, indeed, my friends, we are aware that there are times when, in order to grow, to learn and to give, you must make decisions which are not as much, shall we say, fun as decisions which have little obvious spiritual advantage.

Therefore, we take this opportunity to affirm to you that you, my friends, live. Indeed "live," is not a meaningful word, for we all are. To live suggests that one dies and this is not the case. We all are. It is our understanding, my friends—in our limited understanding, we wish to stress—that we all are, regardless of time or space or dimension or mortality. All of these things are illusions and there are many, many illusions in the Father's creation; many ways of experiencing consciousness. You, my friends, experience it only one way of many.

You have experienced much, each of you, and slowly, slowly, you add to the store of experience. And slowly, slowly, that experience adds to your store of personal wisdom. And slowly, my friends, your wisdom draws you closer to the love of the Creator. It is as though you were the moth going about the flame or the planet going about the sun. The orbits seem perpetual and yet, in the fullness of time, the moth is attracted to the flame, the sun explodes and becomes one with the planets and the universe; unity is achieved.

My friends, I will pause at this time and condition each of you. My brother Laitos is with me. I am Hatonn.

(Pause)

I am Hatonn. I am again with this instrument. I am conditioning this instrument. At this time I would open the meeting to questions. Does anyone have a question?

(Pause)

I am giving the instrument an image. It is that of a sea anemone waving beneath the waters of the ocean. It moves ceaselessly with the tides and the currents, never still, always giving beauty, always responsive to its environment. You, my friends, are rooted in love. The waters move about you as it is proper for them to do, bringing you joy and sorrow. The good clean waters of experience move about you one way and then another. Rooted in love, my friends, you may bloom at full tide and empty. Rooted in love, my friends, you may always be graceful, always full of joy.

The concept of beauty is very dull upon your planet for beauty, my friends, is everywhere. Rooted in love, my friends, you may see that beauty and feel that joy and those about you may, through you, feel and see that which is true and that which is real.

My friends, we are among you as those who drop seeds. As it is said in your holy works, the seeds are dropped—from whatever source, my friends. As the seeds drop into your life, my friends, see that you welcome them and cultivate them and as you go about, if there is someone asking for a seed, a thought, a boost from you, be aware, my friends, for you are creators too.

I leave you in the love and the light of the infinite Father. I am known to you as Hatonn. Adonai, my friends. Adonai vasu borragus.

L/L Research

Wednesday Meditation
August 9, 1978

(Carla channeling)

[I am Hatonn.] I greet you in the love and the light of the infinite Creator. May we of the Confederation of Planets in the Service of the Infinite Creator extend our blessings and our love to each of you as you sit in this group this afternoon.

We [hover] *(inaudible)* in a very large and well-appointed craft with our comforts taken care of, my friends, with all our needs satisfied, the vehicles that carry our spirits totally removed from a condition of want.

This, my friends, allows our spirits a state of unlimited freedom. And as we travel without limitation from one level to another within the creation of the Father, we seek what we have always sought. We seek what you would term happiness. My friends, if happiness does not mean physical needs being satisfied, then it begins to mean something else and we, my friends, as a civilization, have traveled many more dimensions in thought than you can imagine in pursuit of that which is real and which satisfies our understandings. And we have found one understanding only that constitutes our happiness and that understanding, my friends, is very, very simple. The understanding that we are one, and that our oneness is that of love, is the complete and total message that we have come to give those of planet Earth.

That you are one, my brothers and sisters, and that the nature of unity is love, is the truth as we understand it, that we come to share. For you see, my friends, if you are not distracted by the demands of your day-to-day struggle for existence within the physical plane, then you are free to examine your existence as a being in infinite time and space. Now, because you are a being, my friends, there is always a dynamic between that which you now understand and that which you desire to know. We are as intense in our desire to progress as are you. The only difference, my friends, is that we have discovered that we can progress most effectively as a species with our minds and our hearts linked in one desire.

And what desire is it, my friends, that gives us happiness? It is the desire, my friends, to share our love with others, the desire to be of service to others. For we have found, since we have no need of the limitations of the physical dimensions, that in spirit "each of you are we" and "we are each of you." My friends, we are one being. We are not two, we are not several. Whatever the difference is in our condition, those differences are an illusion. For we are all one being formed in love. Like rays of an infinite and everlasting light, we have shot out through the prisms of our hopes and our dreams, and we are each in a unique vibratory position, relative to that great central sun of being which we call the Creator.

In meditation, my friends, you can begin to take the prism effect away. When a prism is removed from a light source, the many, many colors and shades of your rainbow become one white light. And so it is with each of you, my friends. It is as though as if you sat in love and contemplation together. Your vibrations shoot off into infinite space as a collection of harmonizing colors and yet, remove that understanding one dimension closer to the Creator, and one sees only the white light of all embracing love. Love, my friends, with a purpose. For nothing in creation exists without purpose. Each of you, my friends, has a purpose.

In the past, your contemplations of tomorrow have brought about the present. Those things that you have desired at that time have come to fruition in this time. Yes, my friends, ask and you shall receive, and those things that you have asked for you have received. The future, my friends, as you call that illusion, is yours completely, at this moment. That which you desire will form and sculpture the harmony and the arrangements of your events to come in the future. Therefore, we ask you, desire carefully, my friends. And when you have considered your desire, prosecute it, intensify it, purify it and seek it with all your heart.

In meditation, open your heart to your desire. Enter the love that is about you and is empowering you. We are not with you to inform you as to what your desire might be. We cannot suggest to your planet and to its peoples the content of their desires. Nor should you, as [you go among] your peoples, judge others on the content of their desires, so they be different than yours. But for yourself, attempt in love to seek that which you most truly desire. And the white light and love of the creation will be yours to use.

I would like to transfer at this time to the one known as N. I am Hatonn.

(N channeling)

We greet you in the light and love of the Creator. My friends, it gives me pleasure, as you might say, to be with you at this time. We feel the energy generated by your group is a most joyous occasion, limited by your senses. You are not aware of the vibrations you send out as a group. These vibrations spread unstoppingly and affect beings; some [are] conscious of this, most are not.

When you come together as a group, what you will call love is generated, my friends. You recognize it as high or good feelings or indescribable feelings within you. It is but a small, small speck, we would say, of the total picture that we consider to be reality. We do not feel superior to you, for truly we are you! We realize this can be abstract, stating that individuals are in reality not individuals but are one. If you truly desire to find the truth of what we said, we suggest meditation—as usual. This method will aid you greatly in solving the [puzzles] of not seeing reality.

My friends, we have talked to you on various occasions, and we feel there are very few times in which we have not mentioned meditation. We feel we pound it into your heads, so to speak. But only you can reach within your head. And if you feel you are not achieving this as quickly as you would like, we ask you, do not worry about it. For in reality, my friends, there is no time, there is no hurry. We are available to you because at this particular point of your journey there is an opportunity for you to become aware more quickly.

We feel very good communicating with you in this manner. But it is not necessary, for if any individual desires our thoughts, we are with you instantly; no matter the situation you are in, no matter what you are doing. It won't matter, we are with you, if you desire. We send you love, my friends; we love you, and we feel the vibrations of love within you. It is a joyous occasion. At this time I will transfer this contact. I am Hatonn.

(Pause)

(Carla channeling)

(The recording becomes difficult to hear to the end of the tape.)

I am with this instrument. I am Hatonn. As my brother Laitos … [among you] at this time to work with some of those of you who desire to become channels. I would at this time attempt to make contact and speak just a few words to the one known as Jim McCarty. If he would relax and mentally request our contact we will *(inaudible)*. I am Hatonn.

(Pause)

I am Hatonn. I am again with the instrument. We are adjusting our [beam] to make it more of a sharp and less broad [band] and then we will again attempt to contact the one known as Jim McCarty. I am Hatonn

(Pause)

I am again with this instrument. We thank you for your patience. We are having difficulty with the one known as Jim due to the large reserve of energy which lies within this instrument's aura. We are generating some, shall we say, feed back and it is not [a smooth contact] with you. However, at any time the instrument desires to work with our contact, he need only mentally request our conditioning and the one known as Laitos will [be with you.]

At this time, I and my brother would like to work with the one known as A. If she would relax, we will attempt to say a sentence or two through this instrument. I am Hatonn.

(Pause)

I am again with this instrument. We thank the one known as A for the privilege of working with her. We have barely made contact. However, there is some tension or confusion, as you might call it, on the part of the instrument, due to largeness of *(inaudible)* and again we say that we are most happy to work with each new instrument at any time it may be requested.

If you will bear with us, we would like to attempt to contact the one known as E. It is necessary that the instrument relax and speak thoughts as they float through his mind without regard to their analysis or judgment. I am Hatonn.

(Pause)

(E channeling)

I am Hatonn …

(Pause)

(Carla channeling)

I am again with this instrument. I am Hatonn, and we greatly thank the one known as E. The experience of contact somewhat blew away the channel. This is a common experience and easily overcome with practice. We are most pleased and so happy to work with each of you. If you can be patient for one moment more, we would like this opportunity to acquaint the one known as H with our vibration. We wish to do this very carefully. *(Inaudible)* the one known as Laitos will pass amongst each of you and attempt to aid you, strengthening your own spiritual vibrations. For, my friends, this is all our conditioning wave [is] and it is not, shall we say, a wave that is foreign to you but one which we attempt to tailor to yours so that the cosmic energy that we are able to tap into by our conditioning is made available to you in your own unique pattern.

At this time I would open the meeting for questions.

Questioner: Do you feel there is still a need for more channels like we have in this case?

I am aware of your question. We have a great need for channels. But it is not in a sense of an attempt to start, shall we say, an organization, which grows in numbers and converts as with the church. There is a need for the truth on your planet, a dire need which is expressed by many. The truth has in many cases become distorted by those who are the most ignorant to offer it. We ourselves are aware that we distort the truth by speaking in verbal communication rather than allowing only silence [instead of] thoughts. But we feel that you, too, see, shall we say, an archetypical method of communication, which we employ and which uses a "now" organization, or shall we say geometry[4], [so] we possibly have less distortions in our discussion of true understanding. A great part of our truth lies in the fact that we do not claim to be telling the entire truth, for it is our humble feeling that we do not know the absolute truth.

However, many of those among your peoples are [reaching out] in their day-to-day lives for a meaning which is beyond that which is experienced in the daily realm of your being. It is possible to consider, if one is a philosopher, that there may be no meaning; and many of those who seek spiritually have, sadly but honestly, come to the conclusion that all things that they hear are less than true, and therefore there is no ultimate meaning. We bring a message of love, a message of ultimate joy, meaning and brightness to the universe.

We do not say that all things are easy on a day-to-day basis. We do not turn our backs on the horrors and indignities that you experience. We say only that they are lessons and therefore a part of a journey whose end is, surely and without any error, that of total love and total joy. We say this to people who

---

[4] Referring to the concept of circular time, or all time being in one "now" moment.

are seeking that truth, but do not want to believe that life is random and that all things may be wrong. We ask people to consider our words and only if they speak to that which is already in their hearts to adopt it as something to examine and investigate on their own. Yes, my brother, there is a great need of channels. Not of the UFO message as such, but only of love. Love itself, my brother, is our only message. Does this answer your question?

Questioner: Yes, thank you.

Is there another question?

(Pause)

I am working with this instrument, if you will be patient.

(Pause)

I would like to respond briefly to a question which has not been asked, but which was earlier asked before your meditation. We refer to the question of good and evil. It is one to [record,] my friends. We ask you to understand that like all opposites, that it is the result of being in motion. When one is in motion, there is that which is ahead and that which is behind. If you could understand yourselves as beings which have been sent out from a great central source, and which are at varying speeds making a great circular return to that central source, then you can begin to understand good and evil.

At one point in your evolution, my friends, you were at the farthest point from the central source, which we call Creator for want of another word. There was nothing behind and nothing in front of you, when you began your travel. As you moved toward that great light, that great central sun, light is before you and darkness behind you. Wisdom before you and ignorance behind you. Those who wish to gain power may gain it in one of two ways—by aiding and abetting that journey towards the light which is called good, or by, shall we say, applying the brakes [in] progress and attempting to reenter that portion of the cycle [which has already been] which is called evil.

If you can understand that at the end of your journey, when you are without [motion,] there will be no good or evil. It may help you *(inaudible)* [combat]that which you see as evil at this point. The principle which drives those who are vibrating in what you would call the evil range is that of separation. They are attempting to separate themselves from the great central source. They are attempting to become more and more individualized, thereby shutting themselves off from power and love of the creation. The type of power that this generates is similar to that which is generated by the applying of brakes in one of your automobiles. It is a friction which generates a good deal of heat. Because this power is so obvious in being seen and felt, and because power in and of itself is admired on planet Earth, many vibrate in the direction of evil, for they can see that they are powerful. Those who attempt to accelerate towards the good are deliberately giving up more and more of their individuality and taking on more and more of the love and power of that central sun source.

That which is separate within them is gradually burnt away, and thus they become lights that truly [lighten the darkness up.] We wish you to understand, my friends, that there is nothing good or evil about good and evil; they are valid choices in a universe of motion.

We have found [it is] appropriate to us to accelerate our journey towards the central source for we have found that union with each other and with the Creator [is joy and happiness] and we prefer laughter to power. We can only ask that you have compassion for the great evil that is within your energy at this time. All of those who are applying the brakes will one day choose otherwise. That much is [a metaphor,] my friends. Meanwhile, monitor your own progress and make your own choice.

Are there any other questions?

(Pause)

I would close through the one known as [McCarty.] I am Hatonn.

(Jim channeling)

I am Hatonn. I am now with this instrument. My friends, you spoke to us about, shall we say, your individual path. My friends, there is much ahead in your spiritual growth, my friends. You will reap a reward well worth the path of which you think is lost. My friends, continue in your meditations. I will leave you now. I am Hatonn. Adonai, my friends. Adonai vasu borragus. ♣

Monday Meditation
August 21, 1978

(Don channeling)

I greet you, my friends, in the love and in the light of our infinite Creator. It is a very great privilege to speak to you this evening. I speak through this instrument.

I am at present in what you call a spacecraft. And yet, my friends it is not a spacecraft. For you space is a medium which surrounds your planet. It is far, far out into the heavens, farther than you could ever imagine. You see us as peoples who come to you from far distant places, unreachable and unapproachable in this vast universe. This is true, my friends, and yet it is not true. Those far distant places are within you even as you now sit within this room.

This is the paradox, my friends. The great paradox of understanding which is not yet apparent to those who dwell upon your surface [is that] all that exists in this vast universe exists in one place, in one time. Each of us, my friends, [is] in all places, and in one place. And yet we appear to be limited, [stunted], unable to move about in the vastness where all is created. My friends, this is not at all the circumstance which we experience. It is all but an illusion. In truth, you and I are all things, for all things are also you, my friends. We are all part of this vast creation and this vast creation is all part of us.

At the present you apparently are limited but this is of your own choosing. You've chosen these limitations for a purpose. For a purpose that has taken you through many experiences. You're here to *(inaudible)*, enabling you to find your way towards that which you desire. If you did not desire, my friends, you would not be here. We are here to help you with your desire. This is our only mission. In truth it is our only *(inaudible)* to help you with your desires. Desire calls us. Were it not for your desire, we could not come. Were it not for your desire, we could not speak to you this evening. Desire what you call enlightenment, desire what you call awareness. Desire like you *(inaudible)* the evolution of spirit. My friends, these are one in the same thing.

We come to point to you the single path that leads toward that which you desire. The single path is simple, my friends. The way to *(inaudible)* can only be [discovered] through meditation and by whatever name you call it, resolves itself to one simple principle: total and absolute unity and the dissolution of self.

For how is this accomplished, my friends? How is this accomplished? Painstakingly, through many experiences. This is one way. And yet this accomplishment may occur many *(inaudible)* through time and complete and total resolution. It depends, my friends, upon your desire and your desire, my friends, depends upon your meditation.

For your desires *(inaudible)* by the awareness that is generated through meditation. Only this will lead you to that which all of you ultimately seek. Only that desire, my friends, to spend time in meditation, and the desire will grow. This growth will lead you on each step of the way on the glorious plan in reunion. Reunion with your soul. For as this reunion takes place, you will recognize yourself for yourself, my friends, is all of us.

It is has been a privilege speaking through this instrument. I will now transfer this contact. I am Hatonn.

(H channeling)

I am Hatonn, and am now with this instrument. [Those of us] with the Confederation of Planets in Service to the Infinite Creator consider it a great privilege to serve men on planet Earth. We have come for one reason and one reason only. We have recognized the need for assistance to your people. We have recognized the pleas that call freely through that which you may refer to that which you may refer to as the "evils," or through the universe. For the thoughts of your peoples, as the thoughts of all beings, are energy forms which travel with great speed as they are projected by your peoples. And all of those throughout the universe who have become aware of these energies and who are capable of assisting you have either come to your planet or send their love to your peoples.

We of the Confederation have been given the opportunity to come to you and to await the moment that we may unite as one, serve one another, love one another, and then focus our energies and our love to serving those throughout the universe, as we have come to serve you. We of the Confederation recognize to a greater degree, as we see it, the natural functions, or shall we say, laws that govern man's existence on planet Earth and throughout the universe. In these sessions we attempt to assist you to understand, as best as we can, on an intellectual basis, these energies or laws that govern your existence. Yet we have found that there is truly only one law, that is love, my friends. You have been instructed—[by] all of the great teachers that have walked this plane that you call Earth—to love one another. All of the major philosophies upon your planet agree upon this point, though they may differ in many areas.

Man upon planet Earth has an infinite capability to love one another and it is only begun to open those doors and to utilize this ability. Man upon planet Earth, as he exists presently, is in what you might refer to as an infantile state. Indeed, your civilization has progressed rapidly. Especially within this period of time you call a century. Yet this progression upon the physical plane of existence is irrelevant to the progression of your ability to love one another. And indeed in many cases, it is detrimental to assist you to develop the ability of the consciousness of love, for man upon planet Earth becomes engulfed in his experiences. Man upon planet Earth is constantly bombarded by negative and positive energies flowing around him and creating within him. Man continually focuses upon the development upon his society of his technology, but unfortunately, [in] your more advanced nations there is a lesser degree of interest than there should be in the spiritual development of your race.

We of the Confederation are interested in only this portion of man upon planet Earth. Indeed, we are intrigued by your societal structure, your technological development. Yet it is irrelevant to us at what stage of development you reside upon this physical plane of life. For, my friends, as you pass through this experience, you pass beyond the veil of death as you return. You continue to exist, your energy or your spirit remains intact and planted within it is the accumulative knowledge of all the years past. Not only in your most recent experience but in all of those that have come before. And your development continues onward, time after time. You shall enter into experiences, some similar to this, others much more different. But each with the purpose of assisting you to learn how to love one another. Some have come here for certain purposes and, indeed, all have a purpose for their existence now and always. Some are to be teachers and some doctors, some simple people serving only their families, but none have come with a greater mission. For all have come for the purpose of love and the fulfillment for the desire of the Creator.

For it was His desired intent, as we understand it, that the universe be one. Indeed, it is infinite in size to the best of our knowledge. Yet, in totality, it is but one universe governed by one omnipresent energy. And we call that energy but we lack the ability to express to you through your words, the entire meaning of this concept. We of the

Confederation have watched over you for a great deal of time. We have watched you people struggle and it has saddened us to some extent. But we have witnessed great conflict and unfortunately a lack of love for one another on your planet. We wish not to chastise your civilization. We wish only to serve and love you and ask that you do so for one another.

I shall transfer this communication. I am Hatonn.

(Carla channeling)

I am Hatonn, and again greet you in love and light. If those present will be patient, I would like to work briefly with the one known as S that she may be more familiar with our contact. I and my brother Hatonn will work with the conditioning ray and I will attempt to say just a few words through her if she will react and speak freely those thoughts which come into her mind. I am Hatonn.

(Pause)

(Carla channeling)

I am again with this instrument. We are moderating our energy as we are overloading the one known as S, shall we say. We will attempt again with a finer tuning. I am Hatonn.

(Pause)

(Carla channeling)

I am again with this instrument. We thank the one known as S and are very grateful for the opportunity to work with her. Contact is very good as the instrument is very sensitive. However, we will have to work with moderating our energy to be totally comfortable. At this time we would like to condition the one known as B. I am Hatonn.

(Pause)

(Carla channeling)

May we thank each of those who are visiting this group and assure them that at any time they wish our contact we will be with them. As you become familiar with our contact it will be more and more unmistakable. And so we wish also to say that at any time that our contact is inconvenient, you need only request that we leave you and we will do so instantly. We are here only to serve you and to help you serve in the name of the Creator. At this time I would open the meeting to questions.

Questioner: I would like to know if you can tell us anything about the educational systems and how they will be changed in the future? *(Inaudible)* but we need to know at this time.

I am aware of your question. When we receive a question which involves the free will activities of those who apply their wisdom and their knowledge in an effort to improve the lot of life for those upon their planet then we must needs fall back on the principle of freedom of choice. Therefore we cannot say to you what would be the best way, for it is your planet, my sister. And you deal with those things which are known to you as limitations as well as those things which are known to you as ideas. And in this dense and chemical atmosphere, it is necessary for you to know in your heart and think out with that fine tool which is called your brain what will be the best way to serve your peoples.

You know that the great principle of love is the heart of all learning. And that all those souls who breath the atmosphere of your planet come with a certain degree of wisdom and desire to learn that is unique to them. It is therefore extremely difficult to form a system of education which is comfortable and beneficial for all. Thus you must always decide whether you wish to perfectly educate the few or gradually and imperfectly educate the many. Without the understanding of each parent that the child is a spirit born in love, without the understanding of each parent that the center of life is in appreciation of the force and the beauty of life and the love that creates it, education becomes an artificial and difficult matter instead of the joyful and spontaneous flow of information gladly asked for and gladly given.

Without mind to mind understanding it is impossible to know the great uniqueness of each soul. It is impossible to respond to the great uniqueness of each student. And so you are where you are in an arena in which those things which are true in the highest level must somehow be brought down to practice in an atmosphere in which truth can not prevail perfectly. We ask you, my sister, shall it be better for you to refrain from aiding because you cannot be perfect or shall you go forth, armed in love, and use those things which you know and those abilities of mind that you have worked upon in this incarnation and do what you can knowing that while it is imperfect …

(Tape ends.)

Monday Meditation
September 4, 1978

(Carla channeling)

I am Laitos, and I greet you in the love and in the light of the infinite Creator. It is my great privilege to speak with you, and I come to you before my brother Hatonn in order to balance the considerable energy of this group.

At this time, we ask that each of you visualize your circle as being one which is totally enclosed in a beautiful white globe of light. Visualize this globe as being created by the love in each heart and by the unity of the group. In this way your energies will come into balance, and our contact will be smoother and more helpful, we hope, to each of you. I will pause at this time. I am known to you as Laitos.

(Pause)

I am with the instrument. I am Hatonn, and I greet you in the love and the light of the infinite Creator. I greet especially each of those who is new to this group and send to each and all our love as well as that of the Creator in which we come to you. Many of you have questioned where it is that we come from and yet we say to you, that that is irrelevant. For it is not our origin or our virtues that should endear us to you but only one thing, my friends, and that is our information.

Who are we? We are a voice that speaks to you. Yes, from other dimensions, from other spaces, from other universes than that which you know. For we move in such a universe that time and space as you know it are no more. We move in a universe where the emotions of sadness and separation are to us as beacons that call us. Distances do not matter. But only the cry that we hear from those who would wish to know that which we have to give. The information that can end your separation and your sorrow.

Our information is simple, my friends. A very, very simple truth we bring to you, the highest truth that we know, although we know that there is a higher truth, for we are not perfect. And that highest truth, my friends, is that we are all one. The universe has been made up of one substance and that, my friends, is love. How can I say to you, each a beautiful being that sits within your dwelling place at this time in meditation, that you are one being, one with us, one with each other and one with your beautiful planet. It is difficult, is it not, my friends, to see the truth. For you dwell in a dense physical illusion, as we would call it, in which energy seems to you to be mass. In which emotions, as they are, are habitually masked by your peoples, so that they speak falsely. And that falseness is believed as truth. And the separation goes on and on, my friends, among your peoples.

Those who you choose to lead you, do not lead. And by choosing leaders you have somehow, my friends, given up the feeling of responsibility for yourself, the feeling of confidence that you can stand a beautiful and perfect soul upon your own two feet, figuratively speaking, and be able to do the very best that you can in clear conscience and in happiness, whatever the outcome. Choosing leaders that do not lead, and giving up your own choices to the leaders that do not lead, has left your peoples frustrated and confused.

My friends, the answers lie not in outward reforms but first in the inner reform of each person that restores self-respect and reliance upon itself, knowledge of brotherhood and sisterhood and the ability to act on what you believe. Then, and only then, my friends, can you move forth into the world in which you are now living and learning and act for right or for wrong, but in the confidence that your judgment at this time is the best that it can be. And, my friends, how do you find that confidence that your peoples are so lacking? How can you find the love that has been lost in infinite separations? Nation to nation, people to people?

We have come to tell you the truth of love and the power of unity. But we cannot do more than inspire you to find for yourself those truths. For each soul, my friends, each being, as we have said through this instrument many times, is a kingdom unto himself, a regal and imperial entity. Yes, we are all one, but the paradox is, my friends, that we are all unique and all completely necessary to the creation. And it is for each imperial entity to make the decision to seek for himself the truth of existence of consciousness. There are many truths, my friends. There are many, many levels of reality and each of your brothers that you meet may speak to you from a different level. But within yourself, my friends, you are at a unique place in your journey towards the truth. In order to seek the truth it is important that you make contact with that place within yourself which has a will to purpose, and when you make contact with your deepest purpose you will find that your deepest purpose is to seek the truth.

Why are you here, my friends? To what end are you conscious at this time? To what end do you feel and sense and respond to the many, many things that occur to you within each day. Seek the answer to this question, my friend. Our most recommended procedure for this seeking is what many call meditation. This word, my friends, has many seriously unfortunate connotations and those who would perhaps most enjoy the practice of meditation are sometimes uncomfortable with the phrase, for they feel that it may involve a complex practice. We do not recommend any practice but only the resolve to seek and the repeated attempt to quiet the outer self so that that still, small voice, as your holy works say, may be heard.

I would at this time attempt to transfer to the one known as Don. I am Hatonn.

(Pause)

I am Laitos. I am sorry for the delay. At this time, I would like to work with each of those within the meeting in order to strengthen their own spiritual vibration, shall we say, and let each feel our contact. If you would desire to experience what we call our conditioning wave, we ask that you mentally request that we will be with you at this time. I am Laitos.

(Pause)

I am with the instrument. Again we ask in order to strengthen the unity of the group's energy that each of you visualize a beautiful white ball of light that surrounds your entire dwelling place and in which you are all totally bathed in love.

(Pause)

We thank you. This is a much better flow of energy, and we can use this instrument better. At this time we would like to attempt to speak a few words through a newer instrument, and thus we would transfer to the one known as M. I am Laitos.

(Pause)

I am again with the instrument. We have good contact with the one known as M. And at this time would simply attempt to work with her conditioning wave, if you will be patient with us. I am Laitos.

(Pause)

I am again with this instrument. The one known as M has a very good contact and lacks only confidence at this time. This is extremely beneficial to us that she is so desirous of aiding us, and we emphasize often, my friends, that being a verbal channel is only one way of speaking those thoughts which our vibration offers to your peoples. For many are the questions that are asked and the seeds that can be planted, as the conversation was saying before this meeting began. Thus, channeling as you are aware of it now is only one of many avenues that you can take to be of service to your fellow beings, and yet we do need as many verbal channels, such as this one, as we can find, due to the fact that this particular type of communication is a good way of speaking to those who are seeking the truth and is for some more informative and interesting than a less formal conversation. Many are those, my friends, who desire the simple information that we have to give. At this time, if you will again be patient, I will attempt to say just a few sentences through the one known as R. I am Laitos.

(Pause)

I am again with this instrument. Thank each of you very much for your patience. It is sometimes time-consuming working with new instruments but we very much appreciate the group's willingness to help. We thank the one known as R, also. Again, we have good contact. However, if the one known as R would cease from analyzing our thoughts we would be able to let them flow to her. For when one analyzes our thoughts, they cease in their flow and therefore the channel is interrupted. This is a very common problem, and we are always happy to work with those who would request our presence. At any time you would wish to work upon the conditioning wave and becoming more aware of our presence, we simply ask that you request our presence mentally. If at any time it is inconvenient for this contact to proceed, mentally request that we leave and we will instantly obey your desires.

I am Laitos, my friends. It is a great privilege to work with each of you. And as I am in contact with each of you, I feel that you are my brother and my sister, and that we truly are the universe together. Adonai, my friends. I leave you in love and light.

(Pause)

I am again with this instrument. I am Hatonn, and again I greet you in the love and the light of the infinite One. We had wished to speak a few thoughts through the one known as Don, and if he will allow himself to be conditioned while we open the meeting to questions, we will again attempt before the close of this meeting. At this time I would open the meeting to questions. Does anyone have a question?

Questioner: I have a question. My name is J *(inaudible.)* The question boils down to this: Can you give me some sign or something so I know that it is not my subconscious or I myself talking and answering …

I am Hatonn. I am aware of your question, my brother. The answer is far from simple, but we will attempt to elucidate to you the laws that govern the seeing, shall we say, of paranormal events by witnesses within the physical illusion. Each entity, as we have stated, is striving to understand the truth of their being. There is, shall we say, a base speed of progress which approaches zero but which inevitably, over an infinite length of time, will bring that searching soul into knowledge. Many of the peoples upon your planet Earth are progressing at this pace, for they do not have any conscious desire to seek, and therefore they do not seek. Many others among your peoples are dimly or perhaps acutely aware that there is something which is beyond what is known to, shall we say, the society at large, as truth. There is a reality beyond reality. And it is peoples like yourself who are beginning to accelerate their progress by becoming aware that there is such a thing as seeking.

The more serious and dedicated one is to the seeking of truth, the more one begins to activate those forces which are beyond the limited understanding of his environment. We do not believe, if you will pardon the pun, in faith! We have no faith in belief! That which we offer to you is that which is already known to you on a level which is deep. We urge you only to make a conscious dedication towards the seeking of that which is locked within yourself, for you constitute the universe. If we are all one, then shall we say, you are a hologram of all that there is. Now, that may seem like a long preamble to a discussion of signs and wonders, but it is difficult for us to make you understand that it is not through faith or through intellectual searching, through books that you may find a sign or a happening to convince you of the reality of the metaphysical universe. It is through the conscious commitment to seeking the truth in some practice, such as meditation, which carries your knowledge in your action. This can be secret and should be secret. By this we mean it is not necessary to go begging in the streets to show your piety, as many on your planet have done. It does not make them more susceptible to information of a higher realm or more likely to witness the unlimited power of the universe. The wonders and the signs are locked within yourself.

As you meditate, seek and attempt to become consciously aware that you are an eternal being, a wondrous being, a consciousness looking out through eyes into a physical universe, but looking in through your inner eye to that which is infinite, invisible, and in the terms of your workaday world, miraculous. It is this, this turning of the consciousness that will begin to open to you the small subjective signs that your journey is beginning to take place. We ask that you keep, shall we say, your eyes open. Many signs begin as the merest coincidence. We cannot promise to give you a sighting. We tell you only that we do not wish to convince you that we are anything. We only wish to offer information that you may listen to with a discriminating ear, using that which is valuable to you and discarding the rest.

We attempt to speak the truth without distortion. But words, my friend, are a distortion. Only the unspoken concept of love is complete. We would ask not only you, my brother, but each in this room, to become aware of a universe in which signs and miracles do not signify. Because each has become aware of the incredible miracle of consciousness in which the power of a healing or a sighting or a metal bending is not a sign at all. The sign, my friends, being instead the power of one person to walk in another person's shoes; the power of love, to reach and touch when those you call your enemies are attempting to build walls.

The power of the truth to take a situation that is, my friends, truly abnormally and miraculously confused and make it whole again. The incredible thing, my friends, is that you are all attempting to think and to feel what the truth may be. Do not let signs and wonders sway you. For signs and wonders may be explained away and faith may be broken by the absence of this. Seek the truth and you will find that each moment is miraculous, and more and more those things that occur to you become signs and your life becomes an inner adventure, which perhaps you cannot explain to others. For the truth, my friends, is subjective. You can never ever share it with another in the fullness of your inner understanding. You can only love. If you can only love one another, my friends, that would be the greatest miracle of all.

Can we answer your question more clearly, my brother?

J: [No, thank you.]

We thank you that we can share our thoughts with you. May we ask if there might be another question?

R: *(Inaudible).*

I am with the instrument. We find that as a part of the growing process that you, my sister, have a mixture of occurrences and that some of your sensations are truly those of a sensitive, as this instrument would call it, and some those of you yourself speaking internally, as a part of the growing process attempting to integrate those parts of your personality that are not yet totally in harmony. It is a difficult situation for a sensitive person, and we recommend that in your meditation you pray for stability and protection and feel the love that makes us all whole. We would not recommend developing your, shall we say, psychic powers, at this time, but work instead for the stability which will stand you in good stead when you later begin to develop, both as a personality and as a sensitive, and by that we mean one who is sensitive.

(Side one of tape ends.)

(Carla channeling)

I am with the instrument. I am Hatonn. If you will be patient for a moment, we will condition the instrument to reestablish a better contact. I … I am Hatonn. I am Hatonn.

To the one known as R, may we say that our answers are not final. We are your brothers, and not, shall we say, your gods. We have gone one step further than you and have left some limitations behind. But oh, my friends, the universe is indeed infinite, and we know that we are not infallible, and with that clear understanding we shall share with you our understanding, such as it is, of the beginning of all things.

It is our understanding that that which was the Creator is infinite, and when there was a desire for self-realization, that which was one Being took energy, which we now call love, and with this infinite energy created all that there is.

Each of you my friends, and each of us, was created to lend a realizing consciousness to the Creator. In essence, we then are the Creator, realizing our self. But it is not we alone who are the Creator, or some entity somewhere else who is the Creator, but all of us together who form the Creator. Without one of you, my friends, the creation would be incomplete. We cannot lose anyone. We are all totally and completely necessary by our very being. In the infinitude that is eternity—and that is a hard concept to grasp we are aware—the polarity that was achieved by the Creator in His creation, when love came forth and made all the universes, brought about an infinite series of cycles; each beginning in comparative darkness and rising to comparative light.

Each of you has been through many cycles, becoming more and more a true reflection of the Creator. It is for this reason that we are. We are here to realize the Creator, to see and to reflect and to share the Creator with each other, and thus we are the Creator. Whenever you realize that great force of love in your dealings with others, you have given love to the Creator. For the Creator is in all that you see. Now how, my friends, can you be expected to know what love is and how to give it? This, my friends, is the question which you bring to the troubles of your life, as you experience it day by day in this physical density that you now enjoy. Each seeming difficulty is, shall we say, a quiz, a test, perhaps even, if it is a very difficult situation, the equivalent of a midterm, as this instrument would call it.

What you are is being brought to the catalyst of a situation in which you must then discover the best way of showing love. It is not an easy vibration, the one in which you now live. But it is one in which the learning is greatly intensified. We have in our vibration a greatly extended life span. This is due, my friends, to the fact that when one is aware of all one's own thoughts and all the thoughts of others, then one cannot feel separation. Therefore, the stimulus for emotional displacement by sorrow and grief, frustration and anger, is almost never felt to any great extent, and we have very little choice but to vibrate in love and in unity.

Thus, our learning comes over long periods of time, as you would call it, simply by sharing that which we know with others. In this we refine and refine ourselves, more and more purely. But it is a slow process. You on the other hand have chosen, and are appropriately placed in, a situation in which love is completely masked in some situation, and you must from your own understanding of reality find the love within each being and within each situation, dwell on it in your heart, and thus correct in your inner picture the errors in your outer picture. Many of those in your world have a strong faith that 2 plus 2 equals 5 in many situations. And you have been taught wrong information as basic as 2 plus 2 is 5, and you have absorbed it into your being. Now in your heart, when all seems awry, it is your lesson to find the harmony, to find that 2 plus 2 is 4 and thus secure in your knowledge of love.

Allow that love and that right understanding to illuminate the situation and heal what can be healed. You cannot heal other beings unless they request it or desire it. But you can heal that portion within yourself which may feel pain. And in healing yourself, in truth you heal the universe. Remember, my friends, your basic attempt is to seek for yourself, and then share with others whenever you can. But to seek for others is impossible. We are aware that we could not have responded adequately to a question as deep as yours in such a brief answer. But, may we ask if this is satisfactory for the present?

R: *(Inaudible).*

We are grateful to you, my sister, and to show you that at all times we will be with you, if you request it. It is written in your holy works that He Who is the Creator will wipe every tear from our eyes. And we say to you that such is the truth as we know it. There is no sorrow that will not be comforted. And no understanding that will not be made complete. And these are not aphorisms or empty words. Go in meditation to that place within yourself where the Creator is, and dwell in the love that is indescribable.

I would like to close through the one known as Don, if he would accept our contact. I am Hatonn.

(Pause)

I am again with this instrument. I will close through this instrument, as the one known as Don does not desire to be an instrument at this time. I leave you in love and unity. I am Hatonn. Adonai vasu borragus. ♣

Monday Meditation
September 11, 1978

(Carla channeling)

[I am Hatonn] … which is known to this instrument as the [chamber.]

As the sea creature grows [he] becomes too large for his previous shell and creates for himself a larger one. And when in the course of time he again grows, he then creates a larger shell and so on in a beautiful and unending spiral until such time as he has no need whatsoever for any physical vehicle, the consciousness having left his form. Then, my friends, all the shells are empty, having served their purpose.

There are two distinct stages to the development of your mental vehicle. In the first stage it is primarily important that you constantly be aware that in each situation there is freedom, and you are not iron-bound by any restrictions from the outside.

In order to fashion this awareness, it is in this stage necessary that you construct for yourself the larger mental shell, the larger home in which to grow. Each time that you find that a situation is impressing you as limiting or difficult, it is time for inner work, my friend, in which you explore and discover the larger and the most spacious mental atmosphere that is necessary for your balance.

There is a certain point in your development when you will find that you do not need the shell at all, but instead in the vulnerable body of consciousness you may swim out into the waters of the universe and merge with all that there is. In that moment, my friends, you will have discovered that there is no need for any vehicle whatsoever, for all things are one. And as your home is the universe and as all things are one, no protection is necessary.

We are aware that this second stage is for the most part a very distant goal. And yet, we wish you to know that it does exist and that within it is a larger reality which in good time will supersede the limitations and the difficulties of your present state of consciousness. Meanwhile, enlarge your shell, my friends, through meditation, let contemplation open yourself within. For the world without only seems to press in upon you. In reality it's pressing upon itself and you are free!

We are enjoying this contact and find that transfer of information is very smooth at this time. We would like to leave this instrument now and use the instrument known as N. I am Hatonn.

(Pause)

(N channeling)

I am Hatonn. *(Rest of N's channeling is inaudible.)*

(Carla channeling)

I am with this instrument, and again I greet you in love and light. At this time, if you have a question, I would request that you ask it.

Questioner: Hatonn, hi, it's been a while. I've been reading a book in which it states that a man named Timothy Leary has said that the discovery of the DNA was a very, very important scientific and spiritual discovery. I wonder if you could comment on its importance or non-importance.

I am with the instrument, and I greet you, my brother, and prefer that we are never away from you as you think of us and question our existence, yet always send us your love. We always send you ours, [and] we never question your existence.

Questioner: *(Laughing)* I guess I owe you one. I don't really question your existence, I question your form.

I am with the instrument. That, my brother, is a separate question. We will attempt to answer the question on DNA for it is an interesting one and indeed central to an understanding of the essential nature of evolution. For evolution is of a unitary nature and is not physical as opposed to metaphysical. For all things function in a certain way, which is the way of, shall we say, the broken circle or the spiral.

When the Creator sent all things in darkness to begin the great trip back to Him, He defined the infinite circle and yet, as we climb from cycle to cycle, we seem to be moving and indeed we are moving within the parameters of what we may call the spiritual journey. But at the end of the journey, you will find that we have been describing not a spiral but a circle. To understand the building block of your physical vehicle is to begin to get a model also for the building blocks of [the] journey towards the light.

We begin to see that which is physical as an extremely complex but completely understandable and programmable series of bits of information, which are capable of reduplication and progression in space and in time. That which is programmable is re-programmable, and so evolution on a physical level has its existence. It is a simple truth to realize that the nature of your spiritual journey, of the journey of your star system, of the journey of your galaxy, and of the journey of the universe, as you know it, progresses along a similar series of programmable and re-programmable cycles.

What your scientists have not yet discovered is that there is a purpose behind the existence of consciousness, whether it be the consciousness of a cell, the consciousness of a being, of a race, of a star system, of a galaxy, or of a universe. Without the understanding of this purpose, those of your scientific community who deal with the genetic and that what is called recombinant research, may act irresponsibly and yet, this has been done before and its consequences and planetary karma have been [reaped] and yet, my friends, the cycle goes on.

Does this answer your question?

Questioner: Actually, no, not fully. I do understand what you are saying, and I appreciate it. What I was thinking was that DNA is sort of like the cosmic telegraph office between the message of the Creator and the cells of our body. And that, I was also thinking one night, in a somewhat questionable visionary state that the DNA, that the message coming through DNA [is also better than juvenation and allows the basic drive of reproduction rather than just the creation of a cell, it would also have sort of a within a telegraph office … we deliver the message to create the DNA mind and the personal and drives … is that correct?]

I am with the instrument. That which is DNA is as a blueprint for the construction of the vehicle. Those drives which are part of the vehicle, that is, those of hunger, reproduction, desire for oxygen, and other necessary functions of the vehicle are blueprinted by DNA. However, that which makes a being a being is not DNA-oriented but rather is within the, shall we say, eternal nature of the spirit or soul which inhabits and animates the actions of this vehicle for the time in which that vehicle will remain viably conscious on the physical level.

Now there are, shall we say, blueprints which are the counterpart of DNA on the eternal or spiritual level.

Questioner: What about the mental level?

That which is mental is a matter of programming, as you no doubt are aware from what you have said, and can be reprogrammed, and this is what we were attempting to say about DNA itself. As the vehicle slowly follows evolution of a species, so your mind can be more rapidly reprogrammed by your conscious direction of will in the appropriate circumstances. However, that which is eternal within you, and which is related not to a day-to-day activity but to the personality, which expresses itself in a timeless and instant vibration at all times, is not being fully reprogrammed by a mental reprogramming but is influenced over many lifetimes and many experiences. However, a serious and concentrated effort in one incarnation can gradually make a distinct change in the vibration of the being. In fact, at any moment, if your will and desire were strong enough, you could instantly change your eternal being. It is simply that that instant of will and perfect desire is not easily come by.

Questioner: Doesn't that will and desire already influence the genetic message? And isn't it … see, what I am trying to get at … it appears to me, that people have genetic malfunctions in their bodies [that] would be karmically imposed, genetically, from … the genetic message delivered by the soul says, ah, this is karma.

Let us separate theories of karma from the genetic structure of a physical vehicle. May we say first that each case of incarnation is individual, and not all genetic malfunctions are due to what is known to your peoples as karma. However, if a soul is reliving karma by a certain situation which he chooses, he does not form a physical vehicle with that genetic imbalance, but rather chooses a physical vehicle which already has that imbalance. The imbalance itself is guided by the rules of DNA in its random combination. The parents of a particular physical vehicle might by mediation cause the randomness of DNA selection to be less random. However, this is due to the action at a distance, a fact of the mind upon physical particles, such as spermatozoa and ova. The soul and its philosophical nature must not be considered to be interacting with the physical DNA genetic code prior to incarnation. The soul chooses the vehicle which best suits it.

Questioner: Is that the secret of longevity and perhaps even immortality or a long life of the body, a conscious spiritual … meditation or … of the spiritual mind and the DNA genetic code …

That which is long life is desired by some among your peoples. But in your present vibration it is not truly desirable. There will come a time when longevity is natural. Efforts to precede this natural moment by means of scientific and technological advances may perhaps be fascinating and inspiring to your peoples. However, when longevity is a desirable tool, which you may use to good effect, learning and growing throughout a longer incarnation, the exterior vibrations will of necessity have, shall we say, ameliorated and wars and violence and other negative aspects will have lessened in their impact on the planetary vibration. The efforts of single individuals to have lives on the planet which do not take into account the utter negativity of the planetary vibration are lives, which, shall we say, are those of a hermit and may not be as rewarding to the progress of the soul. However, we realize that we are not addressing ourselves to your question, but it is not a question that we can answer simply.

Questioner: Are you saying that it would just as much behoove us not to spend a great deal of time say maybe even trying to communicate or *(inaudible)* with our genetic code, that would be pretty much a waste of our time, at this point.

Our basic feeling is that those who work in this area are great pioneers, and as their work is perfected it is greatly hoped that that Golden Age which your planet so richly deserves may come to pass, and all things will come in good time. However, while those who are working in this area continue, we have noticed that the planetary vibration itself becomes perhaps a little darker, perhaps a little brighter, but basically the same and our basic suggestion is that to help the planet grow is at least as desirable an activity as to help in an esoteric understanding which cannot be fully used until it can be used by all.

Questioner: Well, I thank you very much. As usual, I have more questions now than what I started from. I do appreciate it.

We thank you for allowing us to share our thoughts with you. Is there another question?

Questioner: *(Inaudible).*

I am aware of your question, my sister. First, let us elucidate the question for the one known as [Ra] for his description of longevity as we understood it included not nearly a long life as we now know it, but that which you would term an impossibly long life, such as one which would span two centuries or more. And, indeed, we enjoy a longer life than you by many centuries, for our whole sense of time and space have changed, as we have entered new vibratory patterns. Now secondly, let us address ourselves to your question of a normally long life being perhaps not desirable.

May we say to you that lives, as you know them, whether long or short, by any standards, are in a certain pattern, which you have chosen before you enter into the pattern. As a result of going from the beginning to the end of this pattern, your spirit hopes that it will have learned certain lessons, and thus have improved and defined the vibration which is its essence in the sphere of eternity in which all of you truly glow.

When one contemplates and then does that which is known as suicide, one cuts short before the natural end the time of learning, and more often than not the lessons which that soul had hoped to learn had not been learned. Consequently, it is often so that rather than alleviating karma, the action of taking one's life adds more karma to the burden which is already carried and which you are trying to discharge by the expression which is the lifetime which you are now living.

Thus, when you reenter incarnation you have not only the original lesson to relearn but an additional severity to that lesson which is brought on by that pain which you have caused to those who you have previously left. Many times this type of karma is alleviated by the total forgiveness of those whom you have hurt.

However, it is simply desirable to live until it is time for your lesson to be through, for your burdens to be laid down. It is a truism, we are aware, but we must repeat that you are not given those things which you cannot bear. Thus, working through what is difficult when you finished with a lifetime at its natural end, whether it be short or long, you can then go on and learn other perhaps more agreeable lessons in other perhaps more agreeable spheres or vibrations.

If you may think of your existence as having a natural rhythm and an ongoing purpose, perhaps it will be easier for you to understand that suicide, as you call it, is a stoppage of that rhythm in an arbitrary manner. Instead, it is desirable to proceed with the rhythm of your existence, always seeing the many lessons that are about you and letting the realization of love flow into you from the Father. If you can keep these realizations before you, your life in this realm and all others will be enjoyable and fruitful. Does this answer your question?

Questioner: Yes, thank you.

We thank you, my sister. Is there another question?

(Pause)

I am with you. Please, my friends, know that the love of the Father flows throughout the cosmos on the winds of all of the universe to you, through you, from you. I am Hatonn. I leave you in that love. Adonai vasu borragus. ☙

Monday Meditation
October 9, 1978

(Carla channeling)

I am Latwii, and I greet you in the love and the light of the infinite Creator. As always, we of the Confederation of Planets in the Service of the Infinite Creator send out blessings and our love to each of you, and we welcome those who have not sat with this group for awhile. We especially appreciate the opportunity to speak through this channel, for we have not used her for some time, and it is always a pleasure to use you as a channel. *(Inaudible)*.

I come to you because we of Latwii would teach you meditation. Each of us, you see, my friends, has, shall we say, a specialty. Each of us aspires—in intention, in attitude, in personality, shall we say—to *(inaudible)* planetary Earth that makes us specialists in one type of information. And we of Latwii are specialists in a type of information that has to do with a simple *(inaudible)*, one which we bring to the people of your planet, one which is centered around meditation, one which also speaks with you: time to recognize who you truly are.

In your busy lives, my friends, in all the hurly-burly of your everyday lives, when do you have time to realize who you are? And if you, indeed, think who you are, are you not then judging yourself and asking yourself to be a better person and berating yourself for your failures? *(Inaudible)*. This is not what we of Latwii will send you, for we wish to bring you only the love, the infinite and ever-present love of the Creator that pours to you like the sun pours its warmth upon your planet.

You humans, my friends, with the creation of man, have built walls between yourselves and between you and love so that you experience the winter, and you become cold in your heart and can feel that the love is limited between you and your brothers and sisters and between you and the Creator who needs you. But we say to you, my friends, there is a place that is within you in which it is always summer. It is high upon a hill, and to this hill you must climb. You must seek and gently—very gently, my friends—remove your senses from the world around you, from the world around you which may be cold and harsh in its emotions, and step-by-step walk up an inner hill in silence, leaving that part of yourself behind that may in any way feel the tiredness and the toil of your everyday life. Cleanse yourself in the waters that you may find in the pond by the hill that you will climb. Dress yourselves in clean, white garments and proceed upward. You will finally be healed in consciousness, my friends. And at the top of that hill is this place. Now sit in the meadow, and listen to the birds sing, and smell the sweet smell of the flowers, and feel the warmth of the sun. This, my friends, is the Creator's love. It is infinite. It is omnipresent. It is closer to you than your own breathing and your own thoughts. This be done to you, my friends. This is our succor. We ask you—find the key to love in yourself, in your daily life.

(Pause)

I am Latwii. The contact with this channel *(inaudible)* and to touch with each of you is our privilege. We send each of you our love and our light, and we leave you, as always, in the love and the light that is only the Creator's, for *(inaudible)*, my friends, the Creator. Adonai vasu.

(Pause)

I am Hatonn, and I greet you in the love and the light of the One Who is All. My friends, we are most pleased that you have included meditation in your plans this evening, for we were aware that your evening is full and that we have come late. We shall attempt to be brief.

We wish only to tell you tell you the story, my friends, of a seed, a small seed. This seed, my friends, grew deep in the darkness of the soil, responding to its nature and put forth one leaf, and then two, and then three, and then four, and then many, all in good time. And at a certain moment *(inaudible)* was plucked and eaten, that which was useful, by the standard of the one who planted the seed. We ask you, my friends, to remember that it is not only the seed that is planted that is *(inaudible)*. We ask you to remember that you may see tension in your own lives as you put forth your leaves, for the seed knows not when the fruit may come, it knows only that the process must go on.

We ask you to have faith in your missions, whatever they may be. We ask that you grow, not judging your leaves because they are not fruits but being in a state of complete joy that you are going forward, that you are producing your leaves, that you are alone, that you are *(inaudible)*.

There are many fruits, my friends, that have been planted by the Creator, and they will all be true and found to be good in their own time. This time is not a time that you can tell. This goodness is not a goodness that you can tell. *(Inaudible)* for your patience and your confidence in yourselves and your lives.

At this time I would ask if there are any questions.

(Pause)

If there are no questions I will leave this instrument. I am known to you as Hatonn. I send my love to you, and my light. Adonai vasu borragus. ✣

Wednesday Meditation
October 18, 1978

(Carla channeling)

I am Hatonn, and I greet you in the love and the light of our infinite Creator. This evening we are far from you and are using transmitting equipment of our own design in order to share our thoughts with you, for we have, shall we say, business elsewhere on your planet at this time, as there are some of what you would call crises, and there are times when those of the Confederation of Planets in the Service of the Infinite Creator must group together in certain patterns of thought and form in order to maximize the sending of love to those troubled peoples upon planet Earth. We say to you at this time that your planet has never been very much closer to what you would term armed conflict, and we ask that in your meditations you realize that you are the light of the world and that that which is you is of infinite help.

Each atom of love, shall we say, is infinitely strong. We do not ask you to pray for peace but only seek to be loving by yourself and as part of this group which functions as the light center, and that light will help.

We greet those who are new to this group, and we ask you this evening to declare your independence from the world of man. My friends, you live on a planet which is more beautiful than most of the other planets of your density in your entire galaxy. You have a greater variety of wildlife, of trees, of plants, of things that swim in your water and fly in your atmosphere. Each of these things, my friends, is a creation of the Father, and each act in service and love and in balance expressing that instinct, that which is love. And so, my friends, it is given to you to do and you are that which is infinite, that which is eternal, and thus you have been given that which is freedom, and you do not need to act on instinct. And thus, in your own strength and your own freedom, you have gone, as a race, and have created a world which does not, in any great extent, express the love and service that is the essence of the Creator. And as you take in those things which are about you in the creation of man, you leave the perspective that is yours by right, that is yours by nature. You leave your simplicity and become intellectual and complex, and you find yourself speaking many words and doing many, many things and expressing yourself in many, many ways that are not totally expressive of the love of the Creator.

Nor do we say, my friends, that this is a fault of yours, for this is a lesson that has been drilled into you by a race who came before you, and that was a lesson drilled into them by those who came before them. Misunderstanding piled upon misunderstanding, and so your species has gone far down the road to separation, to world building, to physical and mental—both emotional and spiritual—and the walls that separate you, my friends, seem incredibly permanent.

It is time, my friends, to understand that you can declare your independence from the world of man. This does not necessarily mean physical absence from the world of man, not physical reclusiveness from its activities. It means only that you commit yourself to understanding the lessons of the creation, those things that are true and all about you, those things that are inclusive in seed and flower, in sunshine, in harvest, and in the infinite and totally balanced cycles of your natural world.

One among you, who is a master known to you as Jesus, said that, "I and my Father are one." "I," my friends, and "my Father." Who, my friends, is "I?" Is it a man known to you as Jesus? But did he mean, instead, that all of us and the Father are one? We ask you to contemplate the oneness of the creation. I and my Father are not two, are not separate. There are no walls between us. I need only open that inner door of consciousness and listen, and in the silence, that which has been called in your holy works that still small voice, may speak to you. That which it speaks may not be expressed in words or many, many times in actions, but only in a sense of wholeness, of harmony, of balance, of that simple thing which we call love that has created not only us, my friends, but all that there is. All the stars that your greatest telescope can see. All of these things, my friends, are "I." Place, time, personalities are all one. You cannot be anywhere but in the creation. But you can act, my friends, for you have the power of eternity within you.

How shall you act, my friends? We ask you …

(Pause during the interruption of a telephone call.)

I am Hatonn. We are sorry for the interruption. We will continue.

We ask you to contemplate, my friends, those two creations—that of the Creator and that of the sons of the Creator—and you [to] ask yourselves which expresses love? And further, to ask yourselves how that love can be translated into the creation of man. For each of you, my friends, in each day, can express love in the creation of man, for there are no walls so high that love cannot express itself through. There are no doors that cannot be opened with love. And you have that love, my friends. It is not yours by personality or by heritage in the human sense. It is yours because you are part of the Creator, and the Creator created you in love, and there is that within you which is perfect and perfectly expressive of love.

We ask you to contact that part of yourself which is the whole creation, which has the wisdom of the whole creation. We ask that you do this by inner listening, by service to others, or by any means which, for you, is your own unique method of finding the truth.

We, as each of you are aware, do not consider that we ourselves are authorities on the truth but only those who have reached our hands out to you in love to generate a desire within you, a desire that may take spark, so that you desire to find out for yourselves what is the truth.

I would like to pause at this time so that my brother Laitos may speak. I am Hatonn.

(Pause)

I am Laitos, and I greet each of you in the love and light of the infinite Creator. I was attempting to contact other instruments, however, they are not receptive, and we will use this instrument. We thank you for this opportunity to share our thoughts with you and assure you that it is a very great privilege to tell you that love is what we feel for you, and that is why we are here.

It is our special privilege among the Confederation of Planets to work with those who desire what we call conditioning. We would go around the room, shall we say, and attempt with each of you to make a functioning contact with you so that you may feel our presence.

We assure you that verbal channeling is not our only reason for contact, but it is our special privilege to work with each meditator in strengthening his or her own meditative vibrations. We will start with the one known as H and, shall we say, work our way around the room, if you will be patient. We are in the room with you and will be with each of you. I am Laitos.

(Pause)

Laitos here, my friends. We thank you for being able to work with you. We have attempted to give strength to [heal] certain physical ailments, shall we say, that were bothering those in the room and hope that we have helped. Our light is with you, and we ask you to summon me any time that you may desire our contact. Let me say to you, as always, our contact is a help to achieve contact with that which is truth. We are only helpers, and it is our great, great honor to aid you.

The truth, my friends, is inside you. Inside you, my friends, lies all that there is. And with that thought, I will leave you. I am Laitos. Adonai.

(Pause)

(Carla channeling)

I am Hatonn, and I am again with this instrument known to you as Carla. Thank you for your patience. At this time I would open the meeting to questions.

(Pause)

Questioner: *(Inaudible)* my question.

Go ahead, my brother.

(Inaudible)

We are aware of your question, my brother, and we speak to you in general, although we ask you to understand that due to the free will of each person on the planet, situations are not static and are not dictated by fate but are dictated by the free will of the planetary consciousness. That is why so many of us are here, and that is why so many of those on the inner planes in your own planetary vibrations are in conscious contact with, shall we say, disciples attempting to alleviate, shall we say, the birth pangs of planet Earth.

First we would like to say—and we say this most seriously—it is a great challenge to you and, to a lesser degree, to us, to bring the planet through to 1984, so that it may have its physical changes as they occur, for there are among your peoples who are leaders [who] are most bloody-minded and jealous and are liable to destroy the planet by man-made means before nature has had its day.

That which is known to you as the physical change of planet Earth, as you well know from your previous research, has already begun taking place and is well underway. What is perhaps not known to you is that groups of people in light centers like this one, meditating in love, have managed to alleviate not one but several series of your earthquakes, especially those in your western coast, so that smaller earthquakes happened in quick succession, none of which did the great damage that one earthquake should have done.

Questioner: I understand that the worst earthquake *(inaudible)* could happen in California?

That is correct. We have for several years been alerting light groups like your own to the possibility that meditating in love could alleviate the great stresses of the Earth which are manifesting due to the built-up consciousness of the planetary mind over many generations. Thus, that which can be cataclysm has, so far, been sparing of lives while slowly alleviating the great stresses in the Earth. We go on with this work and know that you also do.

There are many stresses; that is only one. To pray, shall we say, for California is not what we ask, but rather, simply that you concentrate on being a loving person and sending your love to the planet as a whole. The planetary consciousness becomes lighter and lighter as it receives the love generated, first from that central sun which is the Creator, but then flowing through you persons of free will on planet Earth [who] have good wishes for all on your planet, and the Earth itself begins to feel it. It is perhaps, shall we say, an extreme example of what a physicist would call action at a distance where, by concentrating on small particles, changes in the material world may take place. These are very gross changes, and yet, if enough of the consciousness of your planet is alerted, even they can be alleviated. Things get worse rather than better, as you know, as you approach the new location in space. And by, perhaps shall we say, 1982 much will have become clear as to whether the natural sector of the creation—in other words, the planet itself—has begun to vibrate successfully in what so many of your poets have called the golden age to come.

Questioner: Is it possible to *(inaudible)* a specific date, about, when this can occur?

It is possible, but in order to do this we would subject this channel to a type of information which is highly precarious and which this instrument does not wish to use.

Let me take a moment and speak on this subject which is perhaps not related but important to express. We of the Confederation of Planets are many, and though we are of one spirit we are not one mind, for we are, as you, individuals. Those of the Confederation that believe that it is necessary to warn humankind of the specific dates are doing so. However, this type of information is highly, highly difficult, due to the fact that we are transmitting through time, not space; therefore, our time coordinates are not apparent to us and must be, shall we say, decoded by a computer system which is very much like a complex computer of yours. It is infinitely difficult for us to understand your time system. Therefore, even when our channel remains pure, we are capable of giving incorrect information.

Now let us complicate the picture. Unless we place extreme protection about this channel and use complete control—a type of communication with which you, my brother, are intimately familiar—we cannot protect her from the use of astrals who may or may not have the correct information. For that reason, also, we do not wish to subject an instrument to this type of information unless she desires it.

Questioner: *(Inaudible).*

We do ask only one thing, and that is that you and all of those in this room attempt to know who you are and what you wish to do, and do it with love.

There are those upon your planet who are capable of receiving specific information, and so they do, but [they] will show to you that the higher truth is far more important than earthquakes and fires and all that you may be subjected to from the physical development of the new age, will be the spiritual development of the peoples of your planet. To help them, you cannot pray for them but only attempt to become a pure vessel, shall we say, of that which we call love. Love is that which is indescribable. It is more strong and powerful than the word would suggest in your language, and certainly you have no other word which is as expressive. We have attempted at times to use the word "desire" to indicate that which communicated life to the cosmos, but desire today among your peoples expresses upon a physical level, and this we do not mean. Thus we ask that you find love within you and then open those eyes which are windows to that love, and let it shine forth to the best of your ability. Do not be sad because you have failed at any moment, but only try again. That is all that we can do.

Questioner: I understand that we have a very limited way of knowing creation, and I know that the channel you are using is probably a little tired from making contact, and I appreciate the love in which you have answered my questions. Thank you.

My brother, it is we that thank you. We are most grateful to you, for it is our only purpose to share with you that which we have learned by experience.

(Pause)

Is there another question?

Questioner: Is the holy shroud of Turin really the cloth that Jesus Christ was wrapped in?

Carla: I don't know. Everyone is totally silent.

(Pause)

Carla: As a matter of fact, they're laughing. Just a minute, let me see if I can get anything.

(Carla channeling)

I am with this instrument. We thank you, my sister, for your question. We ask you to understand that clothes are not our greatest interest, and clothes of those who are dead even less so. The one you know of as Jesus is a man of great humor and insight, and the fact that his shroud would be valuable strikes him as funny. We can only say to you that the ideas of a man are important and not that which has come in contact with his physical body. May we say further that those things which are valued among your peoples as religious relics often appear to be strangely and psychically active, thus giving internal evidence of their reality; but we ask you to understand that there could be no true evidence left by one of the vibration of the master known to you as Jesus, and that it is the thought forms of those who have come after him and elevated him to an untrue status that have invested these objects with their apparently unusual nature.

Does that answer your question?

Questioner: Yes, thank you.

We thank you, and we are sorry that we sometimes cannot take seriously those things which are taken seriously among your peoples. But love itself, my friends, we take very seriously.

Is there another question?

Questioner: I have a question. Are experiences … difficult situations … always … could be considered karmic in nature? Or just some? Not wanting them themselves, do they have to be necessarily karmically related? And is it important to know the difference, if there is a difference?

I am Hatonn. I am Hatonn. I am Hatonn. We are establishing contact. This instrument was somewhat distracted by the snoring of the one known as B. I am Hatonn. We are aware of your question.

Karma is greatly misunderstood among your peoples. There are laws which are known to you as karma, and they are are simple cause and effect, much as you would understand; but you must also understand that your lives are not completely directed by karma.

Primarily, those things which are directed by karma are certain choices that you make having to do with relationships with others and, to a lesser extent, your occupation or interest or hobby, shall we say. As an example, we would point out that this particular instrument has strong karmic ties with music and, therefore, in this incarnation she has been powerfully drawn to it for the reason that she has great desire to create beauty through music. This bias was positioned in her by actions in previous incarnations and has affected her life. You will notice that there is no other person involved in this, but it is a simple cause and effect coming through the incarnation.

Karma is often good rather than bad; but, further, it should be understood that the day-to-day incidents of your life are, rather than karma, a type of random number system which gives you a path in each situation in each day. You have your choices to make, and they have not to do with karma but with love.

Frequently, the most difficult problems are, indeed, karmic, but they have to do with a relationship which was in some way unbalanced in a previous incarnation. In that case, we ask that you attempt with all your being to stop the wheel of karma. The way to do this is to forgive. Forgiveness is another word for love of that who seems to be an enemy. To forgive completely is to remove karma from the situation. To love completely is to be free. To love, it is truly said, is to conquer. Therefore, if you find a situation especially difficult, come out of your meditation with the question, "How does this situation look now in the light of meditation?" And with that tool of yours which is perfectly good and for you to use, known as your mind, objectively and carefully search the situation for the lesson you are to learn. If you find it is karmic, then perhaps you know that which you must do. If you wish to progress as quickly as possible, seize that which you think you must do and do it, whatever pain it may cause you at the time.

In alleviating the karma of another, you have shown the greatest love one can show. To forgive is truly to love.

Does this answer your question, my sister?

Questioner: Yes, thank you.

Is there another question?

(Pause)

Due to the longness of this session, we will pause only a moment to leave you with some last thoughts.

We leave you with a few pictures, my friends, such as this instrument has just seen, drawn by the one known as R, the tiny things: the flowers and the trees, and the not so tiny things that have been through the cycle of life and death and are still beautiful. Now the great things, my friends: the mountains, the great seas. Draw back, my friends. See even the greater things; see your beautiful planet with its mists and clouds. Pull back, my friends, until all you can see is the vast creation of the Father, and let you then know that all within that creation is love.

I leave you in that love and that light.

(Tape ends.) ❦

Year 1979

January 29, 1979 to December 16, 1979

Monday Meditation
January 29, 1979

(Carla channeling)

I am with you. I am Latwii. I greet you in the love and the light of the infinite Creator. I am in station above your nation at this time—what you call your United States—as a substitute for the brothers of the sons of Hatonn, for they are on mission elsewhere and have asked us to listen for you and speak to you and share our thoughts with you as would they. It is with great pleasure, therefore, that we are here to offer you all that we have to offer. All that we have to offer, my friends, is a very simple thing: we offer love and we offer light. We would offer it in more concrete fashion to your planet if only the peoples of your planet as a whole wished it. But we wish to be of service, and that concept involves precisely assessing and supplying the needs of each of those whom we serve.

There are many among your peoples whose desires we cannot satisfy, or whose desires we do not wish to satisfy, and that is why we have not landed in public places and made ourselves known to you in an unmistakable fashion. But there are many of you who wish precisely what we have to offer, and it is for that reason that we need instruments such as this one to transmit our thoughts to you and to offer you that inspiration that we can and to pour into the circle of your meeting that feeling of love that is our gift to you, the people of Earth.

We ask you once again at this time to work inwardly for peace in yourself, for as you are, so is the world. Each of you upon your planet is the world. In a way, shall we say, a vote is taken at any particular instant in that river which you call time, that illusion that you call time, that locality you call time, and in that instant the amount of peace which each of you beings upon the surface of your planet have within your heart is the peace of the earth. It has never been more important for you to be in peace within yourself or to realize that you are responsible for mankind.

Your world is angry, your peoples fanatical in many parts of the surface of your planet. Unfortunately, my friends, that which you call religion has entered the picture, and in some cases it is believed that, as you have a way of saying, God is on one side or the other of an issue. My friends, God is on the side of peace, of forgiveness, and of brotherhood. We ask you, in your meditations, to find these virtues within yourself and to practice them as best you can, for the fate of your planet at this time lies heavy in the hands of all of us who have worked so very hard to prepare you for what you are now experiencing—transition into what has been called by some the Golden Age. My friends, the transition has, so far, been more harmonious than had been expected. This was due to the raised consciousness of many of your peoples. We ask you to continue this work. We ask you to plant seeds in others, not simply about us, for who we are is of no consequence, but about the philosophy of brotherhood.

Remember, my friends, that you are not aware in the universe, either as a person or as a planet. And those things which you do as a planet affect your solar system and, in turn, the energy grid of your galaxy. We are all one, my brothers. We ask that you care a little for yourselves, for us, for your planet. Care enough to sit in silence and open yourself to the process of seeking the truth.

We have used the terms love and light many times, and we want to consider at this time the meaning of this glib cliché, what a cynic would call this cosmic sermonette that flows so easily from her lips that she sometimes doubts that she is receiving. First, second, third—those words are meaningless to us, for all things are one. It is difficult for us to explain to you that all time and space are one and are not matched one to the other, but have infinite variations of which your time and your space is only one variation. But in your time and your space there is a first and a second and a third, and you must understand that first there was consciousness which was the Creator, and this consciousness had a will which manifested itself as that which is known in your holy work called the Bible as the Word, and this word is love. And as will imposed itself upon that which was around it, it formed that which was around it into a basic material called light.

You may think, if you wish, of love as being heat, in that it is random consciousness, consciousness everywhere without end and without beginning, without direction, but constantly in motion. When love takes form, it gains what is known in your terms as a vector, a direction, a rotation, and becomes light, and of love has been created light. All of you are made of that one substance in more and more sophisticated arrays of sophistication of energy, of light. You are all light. It is for this reason that those who are fully capable of understanding this truth have been able to defy the laws of gravity, have been able to create action at a distance, have been able to cause magnetic changes and other so-called miraculous phenomena.

We come to you, my friends, in love and light, for that's all there is. It is as simple as that. But in love there is joy and warmth, and for that we ask that you go within and meditate.

I am aware that there are questions about meditation, and I can only say that disturbances, of whatever kind, are meaningless; that the greatest ally that you can have as a being seeking the process of meditation is patience. Yes, you will fail each time, according to your own judgment, to achieve what you would term a perfect state of meditation. But you do not need to judge yourself. You need only to attempt to seek the truth. It is in the attempt that the process takes place.

We ask you to think of yourselves as you go into meditation perhaps as nature spirits, one with the world, oblivious to warmth or cold, dressed as are the flowers or the trees in bark of leaves, laughing or dancing, one with the world of nature, resting in the motherhood of the planet which is Earth, reaching out for the fatherhood which is wisdom, feeling the balance, my friends, feeling the humming. You are in balance, my friends. You are male and female. You are all that there is. You are all opposites. And in that knowing may come rest; and in that rest you may seek the truth.

If I am to be an elf, I will then gather up my bark and my leaves and take leave of this gathering so that the one known as Laitos may work with you. I am Latwii.

(Pause)

I am Laitos, and I greet you in the love and the light of the infinite Creator. I have been attempting to contact the one known as W. We were hoping that he would have the confidence to speak without being urged. However, lack of confidence is totally understandable in the new channel, and therefore we will encourage him by saying that, indeed, we were trying to contact the one known as W, and at this time again we will attempt to speak a few words through him. I am Laitos.

(Pause)

(W channeling)

I am Laitos. I am now with this instrument. I greet you in the love and the light of the infinite Creator.

(Pause)

(Carla channeling)

I am again with this instrument. I am Laitos. We thank you for your patience. We were working with the one known as W, due to the fact that he was very close to continuing and was only stopped because of the difficulties of adjusting his vibrations to our incoming concepts. As experience is gained and as the conscious mind is carefully stilled, this will cease to be a problem.

We thank the one known as W and are very happy to have established contact.

At this time I would like to continue a few words through the one known as G. I am Laitos.

(Pause)

(G channeling)

I am Laitos. I am with this instrument.

(Pause)

(Carla channeling)

I am again with this instrument. I am Laitos. In order to bolster the confidence of the one known as G, we would like to state that our next concept had to do with the nature of love. We felt that the one known as G had momentarily received this concept but had lost it. We will continue working with the one known as G at this tine and at any time that she may wish to call upon us.

If you will be patient we would like to spend a few moments working with the one known as D. If he will relax himself, and if he desires our contact and our conditioning wave, we will attempt to make contact with him and say a few words through him at this time. I am Laitos.

(Pause)

(Carla channeling)

I am again with this instrument. We would interrupt to suggest that the one known as D straighten the lower portion of his spine, as there is an energy blockage and we can tune to him more easily. This is not true of all people, but the one known as D is very sensitive, and we wish to strengthen his basic spiritual frequency. We will again attempt to contact the one known as D. I am Laitos.

(Pause)

(Carla channeling)

I am again with this instrument. We feel that good contact has been made now, and if at any time the one known as D wishes our contact at the subconscious level and work with a conditioning wave, he has only to request our presence. If at any time as we are working with him he feels it uncomfortable, he has only to make a request that we leave. This is important to understand, due to the fact that it can sometimes be inconvenient to be receiving conditioning in the company of those who are not aware of the process.

May we thank each of you new instruments for working with us for, as we have said, there are very many among your peoples who desire the exact service that we have to offer, and it is only through channels among those of your peoples who wish to serve in this way that we can offer this service, for we cannot interfere in the workings of your planet. This must be your decision, for such is the law of the Creator. You have the perfect right to do what you wish. We wish you love.

I am Laitos, and I thank you, and I leave you in the capable hands of my brother, Latwii, and in the love and the light of the infinite Creator. For now, Adonai.

(Pause)

I am Latwii, and again I am with you and thank you for your patience in attending my foolish words.

Please forgive me if I seem more full of humor than our brothers of Hatonn but, indeed, our group has its own personality and is not, perhaps, as dignified as the ones known as Hatonn. Yet we assure you, my brothers, that we are as loving and as caring. And although we laugh because you think of us as one thing or another, because you think it might be important whether we fly in silver UFOs or golden UFOs or red ones or white ones—yet, still, we are your brothers.

The truth is, my friends, we can be what you wish us to be. We are from a dimension in which that which we think becomes what we are. Ask us to be in a silver UFO, so shall it be. We live in a universe of light. All things dance in humor and in joy, for such is the truth of love.

At this time we follow the practice of the brothers and sisters of Hatonn and open the meeting to questions. If you have a question, please ask it now, for it would be our pleasure to attempt to share our thoughts with you.

(Pause)

Questioner: How can I help my brother to understand the significance of this life and for myself to understand it better also?

(Pause)

I am aware of your question. I am Latwii. To be truthful, you cannot help those about you understand by words but only by example. Thus, it is yourself who must understand.

The most efficient method of understanding is meditation. Due to the nature of your experiences it would be advisable for you to meditate within the world of nature. However, we perceive in the minds of those within this meeting that the climate which is being enjoyed by you at this time is not favorable for outdoor meditation. Thus, we ask that as you meditate and attempt to understand, you picture the starry skies. Those things which came from sightings of this nature are most often found to be helpful by those who are going through a transforming experience. Thus, the question does not become, "What is the UFO?" The question becomes, "What am I attempting to transform in myself? What is the guidance that I am attempting to express to myself by this sighting which I have seen or of which I have knowledge?"

The answer may not come immediately, but this is the track which should be followed in order to explain the significance of the sighting of your brother's.

Does this answer your question?

Questioner: Yes, indeed!

We are very happy to be of service. Is there another question?

G: I have a question. Could you explain your world?

We can explain but are not sure if we can make sense to you. In our density, which is slightly different than that of the brothers and sisters of Hatonn, we are able to perceive dimensions of time and space as they begin to flow into infinity. We are beings of light, and this we can mold ourselves to that which we wish. Our lifetimes have become what to you would seem to be infinite, although to us they are not infinite, for that which is really infinite cannot be measured, and we, though we have no beginning and no end, are still aware of ourselves, and so we know that our journey is not yet finished. We are travelers, and like those who make a living chain, we reach our hands to our brothers,

If we have learned anything in our travels, it is that there is nothing too small to matter; there is no being too insignificant to forget; there is no God so great that He is not one with all of us. We are united. You are not local beings. You are beings of the universe, of a universe in which we are truly all one, not figuratively, but literally.

You think that you are a person, with organs and blood and bones, but we say to you that you are light and that all light is one, and that all places are one, and all time is one.

We are beings; we are aware of ourselves. We are aware of you. But what is more, we *are* you. We can feel your bones, your organs, the beating of your blood. There is nothing about any being in the universe that is foreign to us.

The only thing that calls us back from complete lighthood is that we have not yet forgotten our own being and become free, truly free of self. When we do that we know that our journey will have come full circle, and it will be time for the Creator to send us out again as beings conscious only of the darkness of separation.

We are part of a cycle, and that cycle is love. Our planet is our homeland, and we love it. And yet our planet is what you would call a star, and our star is what you would call the star within the star.

There is much we cannot explain to you, for it is beyond your science and certainly beyond this instrument's ability to express herself.

Most of all we wish to say to you, I am brother, sister; I am friend. I have nothing but love for you and your people. Your planet is being born. It is an important time for you. And we care. We care a great deal, and we are here. We of Latwii and all the brothers and sisters…

(Side one of the tape ends.)

(D has asked about the healing power of Latwii.)

(Carla channeling)

I am again with this instrument. I am Latwii. My brother, there is no presumption in asking of healing. We ask only that you understand that as you call upon outside sources to aid in healing, you are simply using what you would call a crutch. Your healing power is your understanding of the truth. I am one with you, and you are one with me.

If your feelings about Latwii's brothers and sisters—love—can give you the necessary belief in the truth of perfection in being, then it is very simple for you to ask us to heal, but you must understand that healings are not created by any channel but by the Creator, Who does all things perfectly.

Let us attempt to explain the nature of those who are not well. There is perfection in what you might call a mold. We are aware that you are very familiar with this concept, due to this instrument's conversation with you. The mold itself is perfect, and the product of the mold can only become distorted by work fatigue or other distorting pressures that came to bear upon the finished product after it has been taken from the mold.

Sometimes an entity requests a certain state of what would be called limitation or lack of health so that the entity may learn certain things. Sometimes entities have only a passing misunderstanding or distortion with the truth, and healing is a matter of a very simple adjustment to thought. Each case is individual, and there is no case that is hopeless.

In healing, call upon light, for light is the material that was used to create the mold. You may gladly call upon us, and we will gladly assist you by sending you our light. But remember, within yourself you have the power to tap into the light of the universe, for you and I are one, that oneness being not in either myself or you, but in the Creator. Thus, we ask you to call in pure faith upon the Creator. You are an instrument, and you can direct love and light and healing. The will of the Creator is for the good. Ask that it be done.

The only reason that we discourage you at all from calling upon any name but the Creator's, is that names, beside the Creator's, are meaningless and false.

You yourself, my brother, are not D. You are light. You are love. And within you is a power that is so great that it contains all that there is. Find it and use it.

At this time, because of your desire, we will send you light, and you may mentally direct it as you wish. The entire group at this time will share in the circle of light. I am Latwii.

(Pause)

I am again with this instrument. May we ask the one known as D if he was able to perceive that which we have sent him?

D: Yes.

May we ask, then, my brother, if you are aware that the power is inside you?

D: I am.

We leave this with you, and we ask that you take this realization with you. Trust no outside influence. Listen to no words of wisdom, for the discriminating heart and mind of your spirit will guide you infallibly in your journey. And all that you need is yours for the asking.

Does this answer you, my brother?

D: Yes.

We are very pleased. Are there any other questions at this time?

(Pause)

We perceive that you are all considering questions and deciding to await another time, due to fatigue at the length of this session, and so will, shall we say, pack our bags and be on our way, sliding off on rays of light—mark you, my friends, on rays of light, for that is an important way of travel in the dimensions.

Harness your emotions. Find your light, and you, too, may travel among the stars. I leave you to find the wonder of love and the joy and the freedom of light. I am always with you, as are all my brothers. I am Latwii. Adonai vasu borragus. ✣

L/L Research

Tuesday Meditation
February 13, 1979

(Carla channeling)

I am Latwii. I am one with this instrument. Again I greet you in the love and the light of the infinite Creator and wish to send you the love of the brothers and sisters of Hatonn who are on duty elsewhere during this difficult evolutionary period in your planet. They have asked those of Latwii to, shall we say, cover their channels, and we are doing so to the best of our ability, which is considerable. We send you love and laughter.

We were attempting to contact the one known as R, due to the fact that he desires to remain an open channel and to have help in his creativity. However, he was analyzing our thoughts. Therefore, we will attempt again to make contact with the one known as R to build his confidence and to let him know that those of the Confederation of the Planets which are in the Service of the Infinite Creator are always with you. I am Latwii.

(Pause)

I am again with this instrument. We are aware that the instrument known as R has a brain that is jumping about like a jumping bean and, therefore, we will go ahead and speak through this instrument, assuring him that we had good contact and that when he is properly, shall we say, relaxed and peaceful within himself without worrying about time and space he will be able to contact the brothers and sisters of the Confederation at his will. We will always share our thoughts and …

R: May I ask a question, please?

We are delighted to have you ask a question.

R: Am I barking up a dead end … when I was talking to Carla about the concept of healing through neurogenetics?

We are aware of the question. To speak of barking up the wrong tree is impossible when there are a forest of correct trees. However, it must be understood that there are a million ways to approach the problem of imposing the perfection of the original idea of an entity upon that which has become distorted in your illusion.

One perfectly reasonable method of attempting to create physical perfection, as you would call it, would be that which you have spoken of. However, it must be understood that each case is an unique one, and in each illness or malfunction of emotional, spiritual or mental nature there are lessons to be learned, and there is a process which is known as learning the lesson among your peoples. We find this a ponderous concept. However, we tend to have difficulty with your concept of time, and your concept of learning the lessons is deeply tied up in your concept of time. Therefore, people upon your planet consider that it takes time to learn the lesson.

It does not take time, it takes a focusing of the will. This, however, must be done completely and freely before the new programming is attempted. The one thing that cannot be done is to reprogram before the lesson has been learned. As we said, this can be accomplished either in no time, in a small amount of time, or in what you would call a lifetime.

This particular entity has been learning a lesson and offering lessons to others through what seems to be a physical distortion of the perfection of her nature, and the lessons seem to be progressing well, shall we say. However, we do not understand progress and can only say that she is very close to achieving the point at which she is of such a disciplined nature that she no longer needs a limitation on her activities in order to stimulate the so-called mission that she has come here to perform. Her nature is so adventurous and enthusiastic that she programmed herself before this incarnation a method whereby her activities would be limited so that she could reach the goal of sharing with others those things which she knows upon a certain level, which she would not have been able to concentrate upon had she been, shall we say, working full time, as you put it among your peoples, and dealing with six children which was her conscious programming. Consequently, she was carefully maneuvered around these obstacles to her becoming a guide to others through writing and being. She has now become a being with very little of the lesson to learn. Therefore, it is quite possible that a healing will take place—if not by barking up your tree, by barking up another.

However, we may say that that which you are working on at this point is, shall we say, a seed concept and should be considered most carefully, for it has a good deal of awareness of that which is of a truer nature than most of that which is of an intellectual nature and is written down among the peoples of your planet.

One of the great graces of the one known as Timothy Leary is a sense of humor, which we find absolutely essential for the progression of the soul. We find so often in your culture that seriousness is equated with holiness, and we say to you that this is, indeed, not so and that there is a holy joy which should be connected with constant and unremitting discipline to achieve the perfect balance between joy and the carrying of that which you know in your culture as the cross. It is said in your holy works, "Peace I bring to you. My peace I give to you, not as the world gives to you." It must be remembered that joy and the cross walk hand in hand. It is not an easy path, but it is a very joyful path, and approached with a sense of humor, each lesson can be reduced to no time instead of a small time, to a small time instead of a great time, to a great time instead of a lifetime, and so on. And, thus, you may consciously take charge of your life and goal.

Does this answer your question?

R: I feel that what you're saying is that neurogenetics for the one known as Carla might possibly—in lieu of progress with her lessons—might possibly be an area to be explored and, therefore, Timothy Leary should be sought out.

You may rest assured that if this is to be it will occur in its proper time. To make an effort in this direction is not an infringement upon free will, for if it is not to be it will simply fail.

R: You do see neurogenetics as a proper field of communication for a real concept rather than just an illusory fantasy?

What you call your neurogenetics is like the alphabet—the fundamental necessity which is behind the kind of leap which must be made into the next dimension. If you do not have complete understanding of your personality at this level, you will not be able to be telepathic and to control consciousness.

Carla: I quit.

(Laughter)

R: *(Inaudible).* That was good!

(Transcript ends.)

L/L Research

Sunday Meditation
February 18, 1979

(Carla channeling)

I am with this instrument. I am Latwii, and I greet you in the love and the light of the infinite Creator and welcome each of you to this group—those who are absent from time to time and those who are new. Again we send you the love of your special friends of Hatonn.

Ah yes, my friends, we are with you, and we are aware of the many questions upon your minds this evening. But to us the questions, although we will be glad to work with them, are humorous, due to our point of view which may seem strange to you, for we are aware of that which makes all else humorous, and that is the law of the Creator.

We have said to groups such as yours many times that the law of the Creator is one, that the understanding of that law is all wisdom and truth, and that the best word for that law is love.

We can take you on a great trip to show you that your thinking is local. You can best understand this concept by considering the love within the creation of man which varies from place to place. As your cycle changes, you have seen the laws of nature, so-called, violated many times by those who are able to use a less-local illusion or reflection of the law of the Creator. Thus, metal is bent, objects are moved, people are healed. We can take you away from your time and your space, and you can see that they are, indeed, not laws at all. We can remove you from mass and show you that that, too, is an illusion and not a law.

How far can we go with you, my friends? Through how many dimensions can we take you until you are in a place of light where things begin, where things end, where things are. You see, my friends, we wish to answer your questions as best we can, but we wish you to realize more than all else that questions and answers are meaningless. Feelings and emotions are meaningless. All of the tools with which you are familiar at this time are not helpful outside your locality. You have one useful attribute, and that is the quality of your love. Have you loved today?

At this time we would like to transfer to another instrument. I am of a group of beings calling themselves Latwii.

(Pause)

(Carla channeling)

I am Latwii. My vibrations are again with this instrument. We have been about the room and greet each of you, but we are having difficulty contacting the other instrument. We will attempt to do so at a later time.

Without further ado, may we open the meeting to questions?

Questioner: I have a question.

We greet you, my brother.

Questioner: This may seem trivial, but I'm intrigued by the stone that our friend *(inaudible)* found, and I was wondering what significance of it you are aware? Or what is it?

We are aware of your question. We would ask that the stone be placed in the channel's hand.

(Pause)

We are having difficulty with this instrument, due to her lack of training. However, we can say to you that this is a natural formation untouched by man and unconnected with man. We are attempting to explain to her the processes which caused the formation of this rock. It has many layers. It was not made at once. It has been …

Carla: OK, all I can do is tell you is that I'm seeing it coming down to the Earth and then being thrown up in some kind of a volcanic … or … thrown up like a mountain being thrown up and landing and its being weathered by water.

Questioner: Is it an extraterrestrial rock?

I am with this instrument. The interior of this rock is not planetary. However, the exterior of this rock is.

Questioner: What is the significance of this rock, if any, that you are aware of?

That which it is given by its possessor. It would seem to be a good talisman, due to the fact that it signifies a transformational change to its possessor. We knock questions and answers, and yet we encourage the transformation of man.

(Laughter)

You must realize we think we are funny, too. We think everything is funny, due to the fact that we are in a position where light is all that there is, and light seen in its pure state is complete joy.

(Pause)

Questioner: I'd like some verification of an article that I read the other night that's called "The Evidence Of Homotelepathica," and I'd like to get some feedback on your feelings of its accuracy.

(Pause)

We do not find your intellectual efforts to be part of our aid to you and urge you to follow that which, according to your own free will, seems best. You must realize that to understand yourself you may not need longer and longer words but longer and longer silences.

The idea of a brain as a computer that can be reprogrammed, and the idea of planetary consciousness as a giant computer that can be reprogrammed is a manipulative idea not directly associated with the Creator's primary law which concerns the freedom of all beings. The conscious individual and the conscious planetary awareness can make conscious changes, but the strong cannot coerce those who are not ready. Thus, patience becomes your ally, and a sense of humor that which you hold dearest.

We are sorry we cannot be more responsive to your question, but we feel that you are searching so deeply in an intellectual way at this point that we do not wish to unbalance you by entering into intellectual discussion but merely encourage you to seek the discrimination that is inherent within your own faculties below the level of the conscious mind.

Does this in any way satisfy you as an answer?

Questioner: Well, it seems to me that you're saying that the intellect is getting in the way of my spiritual development rather than as a useful tool *(inaudible)*.

The key in all things is balance. Your intellect is a tool. Yours in balance with the proper amount of meditation and the contemplation of your, shall we say, emotional being in day-to-day and moment-to-moment actions—ah, there is perfection. Without such balance, the intellectual machinery will not feed you correct information, due to the fact that your intellect cannot synthesize information but only analyze. The activity of intuition must be sought out within a different type of mental activity which is below the conscious level. You may choose to do this while you are doing some familiar chore. You may choose to meditate. It does not matter how you achieve this state of unquestioning being in which you are listening for that within yourself which is below the conscious level.

It is, however, important for you to know that it is as important for you to understand those levels of yourself which are below consciousness as it is for you to understand that machine which is called the intellect. The intellect is a tool. The dreaming subconscious is a tool. The planetary consciousness, which lies below all of these things, is the greatest tool. Therefore, as you find your intellect racing after one idea and then another, pause and take a few moments to balance yourself with the search into other areas of your own ability to understand yourself, for within that understanding of yourself lies the understanding of that which is.

Does this answer your question?

Questioner: I had the impression that some of the ideas that were coming through in this particular paper were not necessarily purely intellectual but were a synthesis, and that's what I was pursuing in the question. It seems like the intellectual aspect of it is simply a symbolic translation of the intuitive knowledge.

[I am Latwii.] If you can make the leap from language to intuition within yourself, then you have become telepathic with the author and no longer need his words. However, this is not usually the case, and normally one absorbs the written word with the intellect. Thus, to accomplish that which you desire, which is to imprint these ideas in your own intuition, the thing to do is to take them into meditation with the full intention of allowing your discriminatory power to discern the wisdom within them.

Again, you see, we do not wish to be your gurus. We wish only to encourage you in your own searches, for that which lies before you is your guru, if you wish to put it that way, and we are only the voices coming from various people who have volunteered this service.

We do sound, however, as though we were down on all intellectual knowledge and, of course, without some intellectual knowledge the greatest of intuitions could not then be shared with your fellow man; therefore, always the balance.

Do you see our point, my brother?

Questioner: I see your point. I guess I had not yet groked the difference between an intellectual symbol for communicating an intrinsic concept and the purely intellectual reasoning of data.

In that case, my brother, let us demonstrate to you the difference. In one case a person reads that there is nothing so beautiful as a rose, and he sees the picture of a rose and perhaps even goes to the store and purchases such a blossom and puts it in his vase and observes it, having been told that this is a beautiful blossom. This is programming from outside.

There is, however, another way of observing this same flowers and that is with a shock of recognition as a miracle. When one sees a rose at dawn on a spring day with the dew still hanging from the tiny petals, with a bee still fluttering about it making honey, and the miracle and the wonder of this rose sink deep into your own understanding, and it is yours. It has come from inside. Perhaps it cannot be communicated. Perhaps you can write about this rose, and someone else may go to the store and grasp it and bring it home and try to duplicate that feeling.

Do you see the difference, my brother?

Questioner: Yes, I do. Well, I see the result is exactly the same though, and that is an understanding, the groking of roseness. One you get through first reading about it and then going to the store and experiencing it, and the other, you've just got to wander around in a garden until you have found one without knowing what it is.

The difference, my brother, is in the level of awareness to which that love has reached. On the one hand, it has touched that within you which will survive, that within you which is free from time and space. In the other, it may or may not have reached that far but probably has not, for it has simply become something that you have experienced.

Thus, we have often said to you: our words, hopefully, are salutary and encouraging and sometimes inspiring, but they are nothing compared to your own efforts, that [of] meditation and understanding of the existence that is about you.

(Pause)

You see, my brother, we are not crazy about words.

(Pause)

Is there a point which you would like to pursue further, my brother?

Questioner: I think I've got a lot to consider. I'll consider what you said. If I can't understand you, I'll talk with you further.

We are ready at any time, my brother.

Questioner: I understand your concept, but I also hear you saying that by reading about something before you experience it, maybe you can never really know it as deeply. And I don't know if I really agree or understand that not too clearly.

We would not agree with that either. We simply say that we are, shall we say, stacking the odds against ourselves by reading faster than we meditate.

Questioner: Oh, I see. You're saying that if your knowledge goes beyond the development of your being that you will create an imbalance in yourself.

You have penetrated our meaning.

Questioner: Oh, yeah, well, I understand that. That's what I find. I find myself longing for more development of my being as far as the experience of felicity on a one-to-one basis with my fellow humans, and I already seem to have a language, you know, symbolically explaining that, without having had as much experience, much development of it, in my opinion, as I'd like.

We suggest to you that one good exercise in achieving rapport with your fellow human beings is to gently place yourself face-to-face with them and look at them for a period of time. Most of your beings cannot do this, for it reveals too much of their true identity. However, there is a very loving link between those who can gaze upon each other for a period of time. This may help you to develop in compassion with your brothers and thus encourage that which you seek in telepathy.

You must realize that those of your planet have very poorly tuned receivers. They are not too bad at sending, but they are terrible at receiving. Therefore, to encourage yourself in receiving, it is necessary to become very relaxed, very receptive, and very trusting. This is sometimes difficult. Therefore, the gazing of eyes is a good exercise in receiving.

Questioner: I've been doing that on a one-to-one basis in meditation and making use of meditative tantric exercises, use of psychedelics, and it seems to be a really good exercise in surrender, in trying to intercept *(inaudible)*.

This is correct.

Questioner: *(Inaudible)*. Thank you.

Oh, we thank you, my brother. Without your questions we'd be flying around up here with nothing to do. May we help someone else?

Questioner: I wonder if you could speak more … You used a term which intrigued me the other night—the other day—when I first met you over here, and that was "genetic personality" and getting in touch and identifying with that. I wonder if you would talk about that a little? I've never heard that term before. OK?

As this instrument has become slightly fatigued, I will again attempt to contact the one known as Don so that he may carry on with this communication. I am Latwii.

(Pause)

(Carla channeling)

I am again with this instrument. I am Latwii. I will attempt to continue through this instrument, although she is somewhat fatigued.

The entity that is the personality is, in its true nature, a vibration which is a group of biases, shall we say, which make it unique, as unique, shall we say, as the colors which a mineral may give off when tested in a laboratory. No two compounds have the same color. So it is with the infinite number of personalities in the cosmos.

When these beings either chose or are given a physical vehicle, they take on a certain genetic, physical characteristic. Into this they must put that perfection which is their own. The bonding of these two is called the genetic personality, and it is that which comes into the incarnation, having made whatever arrangements it's necessary to make in order to accommodate that particular physical vehicle and that particular vibration.

Peculiar, of course, to working with the genetic personality is to remove oneself back to the point at which arrangements were made with the physical vehicle, which might in some way have been choices not designed to suit or please that personality throughout the incarnation, but the answer lies in working with the basic genetic program of that physical vehicle in connection with the unique vibratory nature of the personality.

Does this aid you in your understanding, my brother?

Questioner: I'd like to hear, not necessarily now but in the future sometime, more specific information on, how would you say, genetic personality engineering. That seems to be a point of interest. You know, that seems to be the next question, how specifically … because it seems like that would heal bodies *(inaudible)* step up the genetic message. I'd sure like to see the channel you're using right now get to that point.

We agree that this channel probably should not be used at this time to further go into this question. However, we suggest that you again listen to the previous communication on this subject which did shed some light on your question, and we do send you our love and our light.

We are sorry that the instrument is fatigued.

Questioner: That's OK, I appreciate everything.

We're glad. We really get a great charge out of talking to all you and of substituting for our brothers, Hatonn and Laitos, who send you their love.

Questioner: Where are they?

We are very glad you asked that question, due to the fact that this instrument is dying to know.

They are at this time in your southern waters, high above them, attempting to, shall we say, cool out, as this instrument would put it, a very bloody-minded plan that is being perpetrated by those in power, not in one country or another, but by an international economic group of those who would profit from chaos.

Questioner: Did you say southern waters?

That is correct.

Questioner: Where is this *(inaudible)*? Southern waters …

Questioner: Southeast Asia.

Questioner: Is that it?

Questioner: Southeast Asia … Vietnam.

We are attempting to give the information to this channel who is notoriously poor at geography. We're working with her, if she will … if you will be patient.

If you go to what is known as the Philippines and keep going west you will find Hatonn.

Questioner: In Vietnam.

We are aware of that statement and that is correct, although not precisely so, for Hatonn is attempting to monitor a large area. Hatonn is working through a pyramid which lies within China and is attempting to draw energy from the Earth that has been put there many, many centuries ago in your time. It is attempting to remove the effects of that which has been maddening your peoples, a lust for …

(Side one of tape ends.)

(Carla channeling)

I am Latwii. I am sorry for the interruption, but this instrument is not mechanically-minded. Please go ahead.

Don: Do you know if the Iranian riots were caused by ELF *(inaudible)*?

As this instrument would say, right on, brother.

Don: Question number two. Are the Chinese invading primarily because of the ELF knowledge?

Again, my brother, that is correct. The Russians are not being led by wise men and have a desire at this time to make good their promise to take over the Earth, and they have in their means at this time the power to do so, and they know that if they wait they will no longer have the power to do so, and they are gambling that the powers will not unleash the conventional nuclear weapons but, instead, will simply knuckle under. We, however, are aware that this is not likely, and so we are attempting to damp out these vibrations.

However, to do this without infringing upon free will is very difficult, and since it does not disturb the solar system or even the astral planes of your planet, we are having the same kind of difficulty that you would have in your court room if you were attempting to stop a murder before it was committed. We can see what is happening, but we cannot do very much about it. We hope that each of you will meditate on peace and pray that your peoples are not fooled by all of those things which occur in the weeks to come, and …

(Interruption from Don.)

Please go ahead, my brother.

Don: My question, assuming that the Chinese invasion *(inaudible)* Chinese knowledge of the ELF weapon and the need to [resolve] their own right now in a very clear-cut manner so that … because they are afraid of the use of the weapon against them by the Russians, so that on a clear-cut choosing of sides and getting us on their side …

I'm sure, my brother, it is worse than that, for at this time it has been used on China. And it is, in part, that stimulus which has made them decide to make this move, for they know that they are as vulnerable as the rest of the planet.

Questioner: Does the entire invasion have to do with the Russian ELF weapon rather than the so-called Cambodian problem?

There is no Cambodian problem.

N: *(Inaudible).*

That is correct.

N: Do you foresee a Chinese invasion of Vietnam in order to start a confrontation between the Chinese and the Russians, or do you see a Russian invasion of Iran?

This instrument believes that the Chinese have already invaded North Vietnam. Therefore, we won't speak.

N: What about Iran, the Russian invasion of Iran?

The Russians have invaded Iran, not with weapons but with psychotronic mind-control devices.

N: Is that what the ELF weapon is?

That is correct.

N: What is the exact effect …

Don: I'll tell you all about that. You don't have to get that through channels.

N: I mean upon the Chinese. What has been the effect of it?

Polarization.

Don: OK. You're tired now, aren't you?

I am fine. The instrument has sore shoulders.

Don: Is that where the pyramid is connected with the ELF weapon?

This is correct. We have buried, deep inside each pyramid that we have put along the magnetic lines of force of the Earth, crystals which are capable of dampening these vibrations. However, the magnetic lines of force of the planet have shifted, and we are having difficulty in making them work, and we may not be able to do so. However, this is our plan.

N: Is there anything we could do physically, such as helping the moving of the crystals? Is there anything of that sort that we could do that you all could not do?

Carla: Got a passport?

N: Really? It would really make a difference?

My brother, you could not do it, due to the fact that you could not get there. Yes, you could physically do it if you could get there, but …

N: You mean, it would help?

Actually, no one but a very few even knows where this pyramid is, and other pyramids around the Earth are likewise blocked by the governments that supposedly own them. Therefore, what you can basically do is on another plane, and it is, of course, just as important, and that is to be a good person within yourself, to meditate, and to love. And in that way you can add your light, and as so often said among your peoples, a little light in a great darkness shines a long way. Therefore, attempt to be a little light even though there is great darkness, and that will be the greatest help that you can be.

We have attempted to directly affect those who would be in a position to work with the pyramids and have been successful only partially. There are many pyramids that are lost or buried, due to floods and the forming of mountains.

N: Which is the closest one to this house that you're aware of?

The closest one to this house would probably be in Mexico.

N: OK. That's what I was wondering. Are you utilizing these at the present time? I mean, do you utilize all of them or just certain ones in the areas where the weapon is being used?

We would like to use them all as a belt of protection about the planet as it was designed to be used. However, we are utilizing the one in Egypt at this time, and it is not functioning properly, due to the two degree lack of unity with magnetic correctness. Therefore, the problem, shall we say, is larger than can be solved in the time we have left to solve it on your physical plane. What little can be done is being done by our thought processes working through the crystals which are in place. They are simply not properly aimed for the magnetic fluxes which are affecting your planet at this time.

N: It wouldn't help to get a hold—for Don or somebody to get down into Mexico and get hold of the crystal and, you know, move it two degrees? That wouldn't help? It seems it would certainly be worth it as far as the masses of population are …

It has already been attempted by those other than Don and it has not been properly done.

At this point, our best bet is to meditate. We are not speaking here of a passive and, shall we say, a doomsaying attitude, for by meditation many of the cataclysms which could have struck California two years ago were averted, and they were directly due to the meditation of groups such as yours, and thus no lives have been lost in comparison to what would have happened had one large earthquake occurred instead of various small ones. We hope that this continues.

This is the same sort of result we are hoping for in these tensions provoked by the Russian's weapons. We are hoping that people gradually will became able to deal with them one way or another without ever going over the edge to Armageddon. And this is what we are dealing with at this point. We are hoping that the end of the cycle will be relatively peaceful and that the birth of the new age will be easier than that of Armageddon.

N: So the ELF weapon is counterbalanced by strong goodwill energy laid upon the same population that the weapon is being used on.

That is incorrect. There is no protection against this particular weapon by means of goodwill. We are attempting to send neutralization through the crystals to the weapon. The goodwill has to do with the spiritual planes of your planet which are not affected by this weapon. And on these spiritual planes dwell the higher selves of government leaders who are responsible for decisions involving the weaponry of which we speak. This is why meditation and goodwill is our best bet at this point. We are still speaking of people here, for they are the ones that use the weapons. Goodwill cannot affect that weapon, for it is a mind control device.

N: Can people prevent the use of that weapon upon themselves through meditation?

No.

(Inaudible comments by some members of the group.)

My brothers, it has been a great pleasure to speak with you. We may not have been too inspiring tonight, but we wish to leave you in love and light. Truth cannot be overly concerned, not about anything but only about one thing—that you love. Do love. Don't fool around, my brothers. Just love. I leave you in love. It is all around you. You can feel it flowing through you. I leave you in His love and in His light. I am Latwii. Adonai vasu borragus. ☙

L/L Research

Sunday Meditation
March 4, 1979

(Carla channeling)

I am Latwii, and I greet you in the love and the light of the infinite Creator. It is a privilege and a blessing to be among you at this time, and we welcome and greet each of you and send you the love of the brothers and sisters of Hatonn who are at this time on station elsewhere and have asked us to look in on your group whenever you should ask for our presence.

We of Latwii are of a different civilization from Hatonn, but our aim and purpose in being in your skies at this time is the same—that of improving the relationship between the unknown that lies beyond the reach of your peoples and that which is known by your peoples, or, to say it another way, to improve your relationships of love to those beloved brothers and sisters of the universe that dwell upon the surface of your sphere at this time.

Yes, my friends, you have a relationship to love. The relationship is unity. Thus, you encompass that which is known and that which is not known, for love is the essence of the unknown. Thus, discovery is always a form of love, and that which is known already, that which you are weary of, is a form of separation from love and from yourself.

As we look upon the peoples of your planet we see them multiplying the details of their lives in much the same way it has been written in your holy work known as the Bible. When they were in the temple, money changers sold many items that could be bought for sacrifice. Imagine, my friends, the noise of the trading and the bleating, the chirping of the sacrificial birds, the clinking of coins as they passed from hand to hand, the confused penitence of those who came to the temple seeking to find in themselves something that they had lost, something from which they were separated, seeking to find love and wholeness in the knowledge that they were one with the Creator who loved them.

To choose an image from another of your cultures, imagine the jewel inside the many petals of the lotus. How tightly are the petals closed, my friends, about the jewel of love within you? How much do you have to peel away from your life before you come to the singular and single essence of truth that is all about you? Love is everywhere. It sings in the wind, it sings in the trees. In the season which now approaches, it will sing in the burgeoning greenery and blossoming beauty of your natural world. And within your heart, my friends, do you truly need so many details to lie between you and that same simplicity of being that lies in knowing that you are one with love, that you can give love and receive love and receive love without shame and without stint, that whatever your mistakes, whatever your difficulties, you may turn from them in a moment as you would turn from any error and be fully one with love?

There is no process involved; there is no learning or wisdom involved. It is so simple that we cannot express it, and yet we ask you: throw the details from your life at least once a day. Remove the petals from the lotus, charming as they may be and as delightful as they may smell. Find the holy ground. Find the jewel, that which is love. Upon this ground you can stand without fear of falling, losing your footing, or being cast away from your place, for this is your birthright. Love is what you are. What you think you are, if you think you are not love, is an illusion, a mass of distorted detail that can be slowly weeded or quickly weeded from your life—as you would weed from a garden those things which were not pleasant or helpful—by the process of meditation.

We realize that each of you is looking for help in finding a way to this simplicity, for truly that culture in which you now live does not promise this simplicity, much less deliver it. We realize that the temptation is great to listen to those who teach, those who prophesy, and to allow them to have influence over you, but we ask you to monitor all things that you hear, read and see, including our words, with a finely-tuned discrimination of your heart, for you yourself are the most stable thing in your universe.

There is a pattern within you which can be fulfilled in many ways, but there are shortcuts. There are easier paths and harder ones. Outside influences may confuse you, or they may enlighten you. You must discriminate, and we urge you to do so, as we say, especially with our words, for we do not mean to influence you but only to inspire you to do your own work on your own precious and immortal being, for we are brothers to you in love, and we hold our arms out to you in love.

Where we are is a very light place, and the nature of light is such that we can see the simplicity of which we speak. Therefore, we are not wise to speak of this simplicity; we are simply stating the obvious. But as you go forth in the world, my friend, it will be wisdom to you, as people ask your opinion, if you can plant the seeds of simplicity, kindness, and all the qualities of that one understanding union with the Father, which is love. Plant those seeds, taken from what you would call the heaven world, into the soil. And do not be concerned whether they grow, for that is not your business. You merely respond when asked.

We are also aware at this time that many of you are concerned about others, and we ask you again to remember that each person has a pattern for their life. In many cases this pattern has not been revealed to the person, due to his lack of meditation, or due to the necessity for the pattern being hidden in order that a lesson may be learned. Thus, if you are concerned for another we encourage you to feel at one with the person for whom you care, to feel at one with love and light, and then to allow that unity to flow.

The essence of freedom is to know that the pattern has been freely chosen by each being, is being given a chance to reveal itself to that person in its own way. Within the illusion that you call the physical life, you cannot tell what is good and what is bad, for the lessons are many, and often what seems to be a difficulty is in fact a prelude to a great learning and a great happiness. Therefore, trust in the pattern of each unique being, and trust that we are all connected, unique as we each are, in total harmony of being, so that our patterns flow together as do the waters of the sea, each atom changing and flowing until one becomes all and all is one. Yes, you are unique, but you may let the bubble burst upon the wave of your being and merge completely with the unity of all and still be unique. You cannot lose this uniqueness. Therefore, allow the beauty of the patterns in the great tapestry to emerge, treasured and loved by you, given their freedom by you, whether you understand or whether you are only trying does not matter. All that matters is that your attitude is that of love toward yourself, toward others, toward the planet on which you dwell, and toward the creation of which you are a part.

(Pause)

We would like at this time to attempt to make contact with an instrument we have not used before. Our vibrations are somewhat different from that of Hatonn's, therefore, we may have some difficulty in using this instrument. We will attempt contact with the one known as B at this time. I am Latwii.

(Pause)

(B channeling)

I am Latwii. I am now with this instrument. My friends, there is much to say about the energy known to you as love. As you know, it is all around you. But, my friends, we must ask ourselves how that we may attempt to have this energy work for ourselves.

Now, my friends, you know that the stronger love *(inaudible)* for love, the stronger the energy. So that is to say, my friends, that it may be some help to you to, shall we say, orient yourselves to places where you might find this energy.

My friends, we must attempt to cleanse ourselves and …

(Pause)

I shall try again. My friends, it is important that now that you have learned of this energy that we may share with others and, therefore, shall we say, make the vibrations of this group stronger.

My friends, it is indeed a great honor for us to speak with this group with so many in attendance.

My friends, as you see this time of year come, shall we say, portray the true look of love. My friends, allow yourselves to grow and blossom. Allow yourselves to touch others, for this energy known as love, for, my friends, if you do not learn it will indeed *(inaudible)* within yourself.

As I have already said, it is indeed a great honor for us to speak to you, and the one known to you as Carla has stated the energy that is present with us is somewhat different from that of Hatonn. My friends, as we leave you, we will indeed join in your meditation so that each may share this energy.

My friends, as Hatonn [does,] I leave you in the love and light of our infinite Creator.

I am the one known as Latuah [Latwii.]

(Pause)

(Carla channeling)

I am again with this instrument. I am Latwii, and I have been traveling about the room in a small globe of light, which is the most comfortable body, shall we say, of our peoples, and we are aware at this time that, due to the fact of interaction of our vibration with you, we have generated some heat. Therefore, if you will be patient, we will attempt, shall we say, to cool you off with a few cooler thoughts and breezes. Give us a few seconds, and we will attempt to help you adjust to our vibration.

(Pause)

We hope you are now feeling better, and we do greet you in love and light, and we please ask your forgiveness for our emphasis on light and wish you to know that the heat you are experiencing we will keep attempting to dissipate.

As we open the meeting to questions, the first question that we would answer is concerning our name. And we must confess to you that it is a name which is created, for we do not have names as you know names but only a vibration of light. Therefore, our name means in your language "the double," or "the second," and it is simply the one who is standing in for Hatonn. We are your doubles, and we send you double love and double helpings.

We would now open this meeting to questions.

(Pause)

Now, my friends, surely someone has a question, for we are [crying] to answer.

(Pause)

Questioner: I've been reading lately about gnomes that we humans don't see because we're afraid of them, and I want to know *(inaudible)*.

Yes, my sister, they do indeed appear. They are, as we, members of a vibration which is unseen among your peoples, just as—to use an analogy of which you must be aware, for this channel is aware of it—the television. You are aware of the sound of a channel coming from another domicile within this dwelling place. It is on a certain channel. At the same time there are other channels being broadcast which that particular set is not at this time picking up. However, with the simple turn of a dial it would pick up another channel, and you would see a different universe, populated largely by soap commercials, so we understand.

In our universe we have such forms which are the spirit formations of plants, animals, the thoughts of humans, the thoughts of masters, and, at the very highest levels, the discarnate entities themselves, who are the true masters of your world and who teach in the realms. There are many, many levels to this channel. It is more complex than a television channel. But what it has in common with a television channel is that it is not seen by those who are on another television channel. Thus, the dimensions directly involved with your Earth plane, which are invisible to you, are those which give the sphere of energy, which you call your planet, its life. Elves, gnomes, fairies, devas and spirits of all kinds are the elemental forms which govern the growth, the health, and the life of such things as rocks, flowers, trees, grasses and animal life.

When we come to the thoughts of man, we come to a different realm, and then above that realm is the realm of the so-called masters.

If you would improve your plant, farm, animal and mineral life, you would simply make contact in love with those things which you know to be there but which you cannot see, sending them love and asking for their help. This they will appreciate greatly, and they will give you of their bounty.

Does this answer your question, my sister?

Questioner: Yes, thank you.

We thank you!

Questioner: I have a question. I am continuously *(inaudible)* at the various and different experiences from which we all come together. I am continuously amazed at the variety of experiences that have brought us from different paths to common experiences. I opened a path myself and continue, in meditation, to use a psychoactive facilitator for my own liberation and growth, and it's always very interesting. I'm interested in knowing what significance and what role this can play in the larger planetary scheme, from your perspective, which of course is a much more detached, liberated perspective than I can achieve.

My brother, your question is somewhat scattered, so my answer will be somewhat scattered, for which we ask your forgiveness.

The complexity of your existence and the drive that each in this room feels to seek the truth send each in this room on the many different paths, and there are many levels of awareness of the reality of these paths.

Those substances which you speak of as psychoactive have unique effects upon each person. The one who is already prepared for, shall we say, the quantum leap to consciousness—in what many among your peoples have called the Golden Age—would take such substances and feel no effect, for they are already at the level at which they are, shall we say, metaprogramming their own codes of personality and growth. The disciplines of personality are such that your only permanent exit from this illusion into the next is that of personality.

The psychoactive drugs, as you call them, are a ticket to a vacation spot in which you may experience states so that you know that they are there. The chief drawback to using these substances is that when one returns to one's natural capabilities, one is perhaps disheartened at one's lack of natural ability to metaprogram one's own discipline of personality.

You must realize that you are a personality with such potential that you yourself could become a star—by which we mean a sun rather than one of those who are in the movies—or anything else you wish to be. This is the extent of your metaprogramming potential. You are not using it.

When you can attain transcendent unity with a psychoactive drug or substance, you are then on a journey which you will remember. There are, of course, dangers in dealing with states of consciousness to which you have no right by nature. That is, that you will take a wrong turning, and you will not be protected by your natural wisdom and experience in these levels. Thus, it is advisable to work with a guide with [whom] you plan to take such a journey. Otherwise, it is advisable to meditate, to explore each action and each thought and learn the discipline of personalities so that you can became transcendently one in love and thus be in that state in nature, so that when the time comes for you to progress you will have, shall we say, the window seat on that journey, and it will be yours without any substance whatever.

Questioner: I understand.

We are so pleased. Does this answer your question?

Questioner: Yes, it did.

Oh, we are glad. We thank you very much for allowing us to share our thoughts with you. Is there another question?

Questioner: Hatonn [says] there are other beings. Are there other beings with you?

This is correct. We are many. We have a civilization, and this civilization has sent a large group of us to you.

Questioner: Do you travel in space ships?

We do not travel in the same type of space ship as the one known as Hatonn. We are closely akin to light itself, and thus travel in what you would simply call light. There is a difficult concept to convey, but our personalities are complete, and the basic difference between ourselves and Hatonn is that our sense of humor has gotten outrageous, so we have trouble sometimes talking to those among your peoples, for they feel that our humor is misplaced in dealing with such serious questions as love, truth, and beauty. However, to us the joy of life is so great that we find all this seriousness very humorous.

The ones of Hatonn are of a love vibration, which is beautiful to us, and they are our brothers and sisters in Confederation, just as we are brothers and sisters. Yet, our union has become more complete, so that we would seem to you to be a great ball of light, and you would not be able to see us as individuals; whereas those of Hatonn would appear to you to be individuals, for they are, shall we say, one level closer to you in the nature of their type of physical vehicle.

Questioner: Would it be correct to say that Latwii is more of the light and less of the personality, and Hatonn is more personality?

No, my brother, we would say we are more of a light vibration, and the brothers and sisters of Hatonn are of the love vibration. The love vibration is that which you are striving for. The light vibration comes as those of the love vibration learn the lessons of light vibration and enter a vibration of great power. We have enormous power, and we have learned the lessons of love to the extent that we are incapable of misusing it; thus, we may have it. It is difficult to explain to you that which we see ahead, but we can tell you that beyond love and light there is something that we would call unity, and it is for that which we strive.

Questioner: Are you … are you all always around as [is] Hatonn?

We are always with you, as are all members of the Confederation. Yet, each group has its own personality and its own, shall we say, genesis of need. Therefore, we have not been called to this group until Hatonn had to leave in order to monitor the shenanigans of your blood-thirsty, war-mongering leaders in the South Pacific. They called upon us at that time because they thought that your group is ready for us, and we were very happy to jump right in there and do our best and send you all our love.

Questioner: I am very gratified to … I am very gratified to experience these new voices which seem to be manifesting not only in the channeling dimension but also here at home in River City, that people within Eftspan and Space Group are at last beginning to find a voice and to come forth in song, and it's very exciting for me. I hope … I hope that this is just a start of a new direction for us as a group because we have, for a long time I think, suffered from a fragmentation of goals and direction.

[I am Latwii.] We are reviewing the memory of Hatonn, and we find that your group has not suffered but, rather, has done very well. Most groups which intend to be light groups disintegrate due to personality conflicts. Yours has weathered these conflicts; therefore, you may rejoice that love has prevailed in your group and will continue to prevail. Never be disheartened by apparent disharmony, for there must be friction before something can move.

We are grateful that you are gratified and simply say that each of those in the group is truly attempting to do that which the Creator has for them, and this is all that is required. It is not an act of bravery or a great challenge, but simply as natural as getting up and doing what is to be done, and we thank this group for being natural and for staying together in the light and love of the infinite Creator.

Is there another question?

Questioner: One more question.

Go!

(Pause)

I am again with this instrument. I am again with this instrument. I am again with this instrument. I am Latwii. I …

(Tape ends.)

Sunday Meditation
March 18, 1979

(Carla channeling)

I am Laitos. We greet you in the love and the light of the infinite Creator. We will speak with you only for a moment. We will be attempting to begin first through the instrument known as S and then through the instrument known as N in order to build their confidence.

We would like to enable this group to become more unified and balanced at this time. So if you will have some patience and open yourselves to our conditioning, we will lend you our conditioning waves that you may all seek together that truth which lies beyond our poor words. I am Laitos.

(Pause)

(N channeling)

I am Laitos. I am now *(inaudible)*. I do greet you in light and love. It is a very special event for me to be with you at this time. We see there are those who are new to this type of channeling, and we say to you we come in love.

Many of your people do not realize that love is around you and permeates through you at all times. We have used the description of being asleep to describe most of the people of Earth. Some are awakening, although still groggy. Few have awakened totally, but we are with you at this time, my friends, to aid in any way possible your awakening—awakening to the fact that you are, in reality, a much higher being. The physical life as you know it is like a small grain of sand on a beach compared to the total you.

Because of the many different paths each of you take during your life, you come into contact with different methods of awakening. We hope to be helpful to you. The time has come for us to shake off this sleep and to awaken and to take its place that is rightfully … that it belongs to by right.

My friends, at this time my brothers and I will send energy to each of you who desires it, and we will attempt to make it noticeable to you that you are receiving this energy. We ask that you pause for a few minutes and just relax. I am Laitos.

(Pause)

(Unknown channeling)

I am Laitos. I am again with this instrument. We will attempt to contact another instrument. I am Laitos.

(Pause)

(B channeling)

I am Laitos. I am now with this instrument. Once again, my friends, I greet you in the love and light of our Association.

My friends, as the new season is upon us there is much to do and much to learn. So, my friends, as you always know, there is much to learn. Now, as we have told you many times, it is imperative that through your meditation you will advance your spiritual growth.

Now, my friends, as you know that there is indeed many of you who are asleep, my friends, it is important that there be someone that may recall the awakening of yet another being to their spiritual growth.

My friends, as you find, shall we say, time in which to do the many things that you have planned, my friends, we ask that you allow, shall we say, equal time for that of your spiritual growth. Now, my friends, when we say "equal time," you must realize that there is ample opportunity in which to do this throughout your daily existence. My friends, continue in your meditation, and your spiritual growth is assured.

I shall now leave this instrument. I am Laitos.

(Pause)

(Carla channeling)

I am Latwii. I greet you in the love and the light of the infinite Creator and send you the greetings and good wishes of those of Hatonn, whose emissary we are at this time, [and] who wishes you to know that he appreciates the love that you are sending him and the Confederation in its attempts to send love to the leaders of your planet at this critical time. He wishes you also to know that the crisis is not over, and so he regrets very much not being on station in your skies, and so those at Hatonn have asked us, Latwii, to remain with you as counselors and true philosophers, to share our thoughts with you, and that we will do.

My friends, this instrument has been deep in prayer in the last two minutes, for she fears, as always, that she will not speak the words that we give her. We think that this is a perfect example of what makes us laugh at the people of your planet. You are so serious, my friend; you are so sure that you will be able to tell the truth by the use of your intellect.

My friends, it is as though you have great trees growing on top of your heads with their roots very deep inside your brains, and all the while you are concerned about uprooting these great trees with their great and deep roots. You stood out in the rain and let the sun and the wind pour over these trees and nourish their growth.

My friends, why do you worry? Why do you concern yourselves with those things over which you have no control? Why can you not pray and then let it go and act? Why can you not act and then let it go, be it error or correctness?

My friends, the roots of that tree that grows within your brain, that tree which is called the intellect, cannot be uprooted by force. The intellect can only be starved. Stay out of the rain, my friend. Avoid the sunshine. Do not think too much. It is as simple as that. Do not think about not thinking. The over-use of the intellect, the over-seriousness of your people, has held back more spiritual advancement than we can tell you among your people. You who are in the vast minority among the peoples of your planet, you who are the hope of your planet, you who care to know the truth—do not think that you can think your way to the truth. Know that you can only be the truth. You can only act the truth. You can only love, for that is the heart of the truth. You can only be the original Thought, for that is the heart of love.

There is a love that created you. In that love is all light and all joy. Joining it makes you as light as a butterfly. You have no gravity. You do not need to be serious. You do not need to heap blame, or guilt, for your past incorrectnesses upon yourself. Nor need you do it for others in any way, for others are only yourself, *(inaudible)* in your mind so that you may see yourself better,

Look each person in the face—look yourself in the face—and find love. If you cannot find it, let it go. Wisdom was not ever won in a moment, until the moment comes. Peacefully await that moment. Do not think about that moment or strive toward that moment in your minds for there is a deeper faculty in your heart, and it is called the will. And we urge you, instead, to employ that. Will to know the original Thought of the Creator. Seek and ye shall find. How many times have those who have spoken to you from the Confederation of Plants in the Service of the Infinite Creator said those words, "Seek and ye shall find; knock and it shall be opened unto you"? These words are from one of your holy books, and they are true. The advice is simple. It is not, "Think and ye shall find, think and it shall be opened unto you." But think will. Use your imagination. Use your faculties of hope and desire.

And as you seek, let the journey be one of laughter as well as tears. Let yourself laugh. Let yourself enjoy that which is beautiful in each moment. Do not think too much. That tree in your head, which is your intellect, is very useful if you need firewood; and you do need a certain amount of it. You have a chemical body. You must live in a chemical world. You must make decisions having to do with your chemical personality. And the truer *(inaudible)* the intellect stokes the decision-making fires. Very well, then. Use it for that. For your spiritual thinking, stop it. Go into meditation with a free heart, not with a free mind. Let your mind do what it wishes. You are not concerned with your mind. Let it tie itself in knots. It does not concern you. It is a tool; it is not you. Shrug it off. Let it be unimportant.

We offer you these foolish sentences in the hope that you will see what is behind them—our desire to hold our hands out to you, our brothers and sisters, for we stand in [realms] where these things are apparent, where love is enjoyed and shared, where the intellect is understood and not over-emphasized. Indeed, we may say your intellect is, by far, greater than ours, for we know what we know by a process of direct intuition. We share one great body of knowledge among us, and nothing is forgotten. Thus, we need not the tree of intellect.

There is a place you can go in meditation that is a better place, my friends, a place in which you can be clean and fresh, new, just born, and free. We invite you to join us, for in meditation you are in a great company of all those in higher planes.

With these few thoughts I will end this discussion and proceed to a request for questions. May I ask if you have anything to ask?

(Pause)

We do so enjoy question time, so please feel free to ask questions.

(Pause)

N: I have a question, but I don't want to say it. *(Inaudible)* You may not really answer it, just comment. Thank you.

We will attempt to, although this instrument, we find, has a positive hatred of such, due to the fact that she has too much ego. Nevertheless, we will use her.

We find that, in the larger sense, your question is very basic and, although you are thinking specifically, the decisions you must make at this time have to do more with a basic philosophy of life than anything else, and thus we can only say to you that in mediation you can find your true feelings. It is important that you realize that right and wrong are not concepts, as such, that are valid, but only that which is subjectively, for you, comfortable and proper. Thus, as you deal with people and situations, you must first deal with yourself. Knowing where you stand and who you are, you may then act in confidence.

We urge you to recall that as a plant begins to develop it has no knowledge of its destiny, and yet it is unfolded perfectly day by day. We do not believe that the flower has the faculty, shall we say, of trust or patience. The flower simply knows that there is no time and that time is only an illusion. Thus, when it blossoms it does so in a sweet surprise that is not in time but is at the proper moment. So you human beings are. You have a destiny, you have a time to blossom, a time to be picked. You have freedom: freedom to learn, freedom to look about you, freedom to actively direct that which you will do.

Unlike the flowers, you have freedom of movement and of thought and of action. But, nonetheless, your destiny is simple and profound, and you can trust it with perfect confidence, knowing that it is, shall we say, built in, and that all things, if you are in tune with yourself, will occur in the same harmony as the maturation of a flower, so that you will find a day of sweet surprise when that which has needed to blossom will have occurred.

We of Latwii send the sunlight of our love to you at this time, my brother, and hope that our words have aided you. Is there another question?

(Pause)

If there are no other questions we will leave this instrument. This is only our second group, and we have not yet learned how to encourage you to come with questions so that we may work with you more individually. This we enjoy very much, so we have been working with the planetary consciousness, and it is a great pleasure to work with each unique individual who asks questions, for we are then able to vibrate in harmony with each unique vibration, and we enjoy the electrical union very much.

We thank each of you for listening to our humble words and ask you to realize that we know very little and that you should not take what we say too seriously but only listen to your inner voice, for that contains the wisdom, not we. We can only love you and leave you in love and light.

We are those of Latwii. Call us Latwii, or simply send us love with no name, for our vibration is truly what we call ourselves. We leave you in that vibration and assure you that we are with you at any time that you ask for us.

We will send healing to two of you in the room whose physical vehicles are not functioning properly. We will pause at this time and do so.

(Pause)

We bid you adonai. Vasu borragus. ✤

Sunday Meditation
April 1, 1979

(Carla channeling)

I am the group consciousness of Hatonn, and I greet you in the love and the light of the infinite Creator. We are very pleased to be back in personal contact with you after an absence that was necessary, but we have found that our activities are needed now in your area, and so we have been assigned back on our usual post, which has pleased us very much, for to make contact with those beings whom we love is a great pleasure to us.

Even though we are always aware of you, to speak through channels such as this one so that we may make our thoughts known to you on a conceptual, vocal level is a special privilege, for we are then able to monitor our communication in microseconds of action and reaction, as of beings fused in one exchange of love.

You see, my friends, we of the Confederation of Planets need you, just as you need us. In our reality, someone to love and cherish and help and inspire is as necessary to us as is food and drink to you. To us, those whom we have found to be serious students of the path of the Creator are as delicious as your meat and drink is to you, for you are the means whereby we can enlarge our own horizons of understanding; you are the means whereby we can learn more and more about the disciplines and interrelationships of what you may call the genetic personality. We study the Creator's arrangement of articulated love, which is manifested forth in His perfect beings, and as we see you dwelling in your heavy chemical illusion, fighting so valiantly to understand and to deal with the intensive emotions of that vibration, we are able to gain new depths of insight into the plan of the Father. We know that there is a plan, but its beginning and its end are shrouded in mystery, even for us. We only know that it is circular and that when we are fully at one with the knowledge that we seek there will be no time, space or emptiness and our own personalities will again become part of that one universal Thought of love which created all that there is. We know that we will be sent forth again, new beginnings of new universes and new cycles of growth. But there are many things about this plan, which is infinite, about which we do not yet know, and it is in helping those of you upon the planet to whom we speak that we learn by the interaction between us more and more about the basic genetic personality that is common to all of us.

We, of course, as we have said many times, have learned what we can in your illusion. We are now in another illusion, an illusion in which we can create by thought that which we need, in which we can see each other as vibrations, in which we can speak telepathically, and in which we can travel in time. But these are not goals. These are merely the marks of another step along the great line of evolution.

We have not traveled to the end of the rainbow, as you would say. We have not found the pot of gold. We have only found that the road goes on and on and that our companions became more and more loving and the road more and more delightful. And so in your day-to-day efforts to find your road and to follow it, knowing in your heart that good will come of this effort, it is a private effort, not one which you can share, not one which others will understand. So you do not use the symbols that many understand, for we do not speak in the symbols of any race or culture. We do not use the personalities of masters who have incarnated upon your planet, such as Jesus and Buddha and Lao Tse. Although we could do these things, we feel more honest in telling you that there is a road paved with love, designed with love, difficult to follow but full of rewards. It is the road of those who seek the truth. You can believe with all your heart in a master who has incarnated, such as Jesus, or Buddha, or Lao Tse—it has no bearing on the road, for those things which one uses as walking sticks on that road are all acceptable. The road is the same. We ask you, therefore, when you hear religious and philosophical discussions to know in your heart that each is correct, each is right. All disagreements are disagreements, not about the road, not about love, not about the striving for truth, but merely about that stout walking stick which many use to give them confidence. This instrument prays to the one known as Jesus. We find this provincial but acceptable. We accept and love the one known as Jesus, but we call nothing master except the way of the Creator's which is followed step-by-step in prayer or meditation, day by day.

At this time I would like to leave this instrument so that a brother may speak to this instrument. I am Hatonn.

(Pause)

I am Telonn. I have not spoken to this group for some time, and I greet you in the love and the light of the infinite Creator and express my delight at being able to be with you at this time.

I am called here by the group consciousness of this group and wish to work with you for a brief period of time.

If you will be patient, I would like to work with your imagination. I would ask you, please, to allow your being to vibrate in a higher rate of spiritual vibration by visualizing a small, white globe in the center of the room. It is very bright and round, and it is beginning to expand. Watch it expand until it has engulfed you completely, and then allow yourself to feel the zero gravity of light. We are working with you at this time.

(Pause)

We ask you at this time to allow the consciousness within your light sphere to float out of your dwelling place and move up into the sky. Move above the clouds and look down. You are now a ball of light; if you will, a UFO.

(Pause)

We must ask the one known as Carla to let go of her physical body, as she is pulling the ball of light back.

(Pause)

Very gently now, we ask you to allow the ball of light to reenter your dwelling place …

(Pause)

… and your consciousnesses … regain their seats within your physical vehicles. Feel the weight of gravity at this time and know that you will not always be so.

(Pause)

I am Telonn. I leave you in the vibration of light, of eternity, and of the love of the Creator.

(Pause)

I am Latwii. I am with you. I greet you in the love and light and am happy to tell you that my brother, Hatonn, has given us permission to speak with you, even though he is back, for he thinks we did a pretty good job while he was gone, and he says he is very surprised that we could talk with the local yokels without sounding like we were talking down. We thought we did pretty badly, so we were glad to hear that.

We greet you, and we love you, and we are very glad that we are still able to speak with you, for the one known as Hatonn has had jurisdiction over your group for many years now, and we would not go against him for anything. Therefore, hello and love from us.

We come to be buried within you, as are acorns. We come to be planted in you, as are seeds, for you are the seeds of tomorrow. And we hope to instill in you some of our thoughts and to see them bear fruit. We thank you for the privilege.

May we open the meeting to questions at this time?

(Pause, during which H enters.)

I am Latwii. We greet the one known as H and send her our love. We are aware that this is a shock to her system and will give her some time to adjust to our vibration. Therefore, we will pause for a few moments.

(Pause)

There is a question which we would like to answer that has been asked by the channel herself, and we can only say to her that she must always choose the way of love and attempt not to intellectualize but to give. That is the secret to loving. Therefore, if there is a conflict in her life, she must resolve it by loving.

To love is an activity, even if nothing is done but a rearrangement of an attitude. Therefore, we ask the one known as Carla to consider the foundations of her being, that they are love, the original Thought of the creation, which was love, and the guidance of those which are ahead of her which you may call angels, and that higher self of hers which can help her, of the Creator Itself which is love. There is nothing to which she can turn that is not love. Therefore, ask for help, seek help, and you will receive it, and that help will be in the form of the grace to love, the wisdom to love, and the understanding to love.

May we ask if there are other questions at this time?

Questioner: A few weeks ago after meditation we were discussing something I was not aware about or had heard about, but I was curious at the time, and I remember that we said we should ask questions during meditation. It had something to do with a boom, a sort of blast that seemed like a dynamite-type blast that was heard all over the city or in two or three parts of the city at the same time. Do you know about that?

We are aware of this problem, and it is this type of problem that has caused the brothers and sisters of our brother civilization, Hatonn, to come back to station at this time.

The Earth changes of which the Confederation has spoken many times have been taking place for many years, and the thinking of the people has become more and more polarized, thereby making the Earth changes more easily occur.

The sounds which you heard had to do with energies within the Earth itself which, interacting with the atmosphere, caused sharp delineations in layers of atmosphere, thereby causing these sounds which were not entirely unlike what you would call thunder but were caused not by the electrical disturbances in the air but electrical disturbances from within the Earth.

We are back in the usual pattern of, shall we say, Earth watch, which is our term for it. Due to the fact that even though the situations in the South Pacific, in the Middle East, and between Russia and China, as you call these parts of your land, are not resolved, nor are the leaders less bloody-minded than before, in …

(Side one of tape ends.)

Questioner: Another thing I want to understand clearly is what … does your explanation mean that there is some physical change in the center of the Earth, or are you saying that there are energy powers that we are exuding that can't be seen that are causing this change in the Earth?

(Carla channeling)

I am Latwii. Please be patient, for we are conditioning this instrument. I am Latwii. I am deepening this instrument's concentration at this time. I am Latwii. I am with the instrument. I am aware of your question. I am Latwii.

We may begin by saying that the sounds which your group discussed were of a fairly local nature. Your question had two parts, and the second was more complex.

The Earth's crust has a much more carefully precise name which this instrument does not know, but part of it is unstable at this time, and there are shifts which are possible in this region as well as in many others, shifts that usually happen along what you call fault lines but which can happen easily in areas where there are extensive underground openings, such as is true in your area. It simply means that there could be a geographical rearrangement of your terrain, which would involve a rearrangement of the molecules of many houses and people. It would be called a great disaster, were it to happen.

The reason that it is happening is centuries and centuries old and begins one thousand years before the birth of the master that signifies this period, or cycle, of your development. We speak of the one known as Jesus.

In this time, many came into being from the previous cycle who had much karma to alleviate. Due to improper actions, involving the use of power over other people, they were given three thousand years in order to learn the lessons of love. When a thousand years had passed and the theory that there was one Creator had barely begun to batter down the resistance of those who were not ready for the unity of all that there is, the master incarnated and gave to the people of this planet that which is the truth to be learned. It has been reported badly in your holy works. But there are enough of his words in those books in order for you to be able to understand the lessons of love, forgiveness and redemption which he encouraged his disciples to learn.

However, the people have repeatedly used this very name, not to love, but to fight; not to be peaceable, but to make war. The tensions, the disagreements, the dishonesty, the habitual lying between peoples has long involved nations, provinces, towns, communities. All levels of your civilization have been eaten by something which we would call a cancer, and that is the cancer of separation, not knowing that all beings are one and that what is done to another is done to oneself. We do those things which involve the concept of two beings. That involves the concept of an enemy or a competitor. That involves the concept of a wall between. This limits communication and increases polarity and hostility. And eventually these vibrations sink into the planet itself. That which is most sensitive to these vibrations—the crust or the mantle of the Earth—begin to move and drastically realign themselves, attempting to relieve the tensions of the planetary consciousness. Thus, yes, your people have caused these things over thousands of years.

It is not unheard of for this to happen. It is something like the birth of a child. Going from one density into another is like being born, and your planet is being born at this time. The delivery, so far, has been difficult, but the baby is alive.

There are those among you who wish to learn and wish to love, and we feel there is hope for you. Thus, we speak to you personally and not to your leaders, for we cannot deal with your nations with their concepts of competition and nationality.

Does this answer your question?

Questioner: Yes, thank you.

We thank you for our ability to share our thoughts with you. Is there another question at this time?

(Pause)

We will leave this instrument at this time. We again greet the one known as H and hope that she has not been too taken aback by this unusual activity.

We send a message to the one known as S who has requested repeatedly that she simply be given a reassurance that she is heard and loved by the Confederation. We are always with the one known as S, and we love her and her desire for the truth and encourage her in what may seem a lonely pilgrimage. That which is in the soil seems alone, but when it blooms it may see the sun and the rain and speak with the birds.

I leave this instrument now. We are so happy to be with you. We leave you in light and that which creates light—the love of the Creator. Adonai vasu borragus. I am Latwii.

L/L Research

Sunday Meditation, Easter
April 15, 1979

(Carla channeling)

I am known to you as Hatonn, and I greet you in the love and the light of the infinite Creator. I greet you especially on this day which is holy within your culture, and [we] are very, very pleased and privileged to be able to be a part of your celebration of that which lives which was thought to be dead.

Within this channel's mind there is a quote from a poet. It goes like this: "April is the cruelest month, breeding lilacs out of the dead ground." We would like you at this time to ponder those words, for you must take all things personally if you would find their inner meaning. Rather than skimming the surface of the meaning, be shameless and make those things which are general specifically about yourself and see what applies.

What is the dead ground in your life? Perhaps you know the answer to that already. Perhaps there is all too much of it: the familiar, the simple, and the easy—those things which are concerned only with the transitory experience which began when you first drew breath in a chemical vehicle on planet Earth and which end when your last breath is expelled in this experience. In the illusion—this is called life, this breathing. But in reality the experience itself is without life. And yet, my friends, you are here, and it is a precious and unusual thing that you are.

Many are the souls who have wished at this time to draw breath upon your planet and experience that which is occurring upon your planet at this time, for that which is occurring is a change, just as a change in your seasons may be called a change. You may generalize and say, 'Why, spring is the same as winter; it is the same Earth, it is the same trees." But the transformations are remarkable. Out of the dead ground there grow new things that are alive and those that blossom and bloom. That which was skeletal and brown and bare became lovely, bursting with life and hope and promise, and so is your life at this tiny point which is the present.

And why is this a cruel process, my friends? Why is April the cruelest month? Why is change difficult? Let us move our vision to another story that has held the interest of many for two thousand years. It is the story of a master among your men, called Jesus, who was taken to a tree and thereupon fixed until he was dead. Does that not seem cruel, my friends?

You are in the midst of that which is cruel. Cruelty is a part of change. Pain is the price of growth. When the one known to you as Jesus was lifted gently from that tree, he was dead—and yet it is this holiday that you now celebrate on which he blossomed into that which was, not transient, but alive, conscious and loving.

Flowers, my friends, are for a season, and many of them are only for a season—they do not regenerate themselves. But you are not flowers. You are seeds which are sown in the dead ground of a chemical body that you may experience the thunder and the lightening, the rain, the snow, and the wind that only a chemical body can give you, for it is in those circumstances that your emotional reactions are intensified, invariably. And it is through this intensification of emotions, it is through this often painful process of emotional reaction and thought and contemplation that you grow that within you which is alive, eternal and loving.

There is a curious peace to be gained from knowing that you are capable of using those things which are given you, not just those things which are transitorially joyful, but those things which are of transitory pain. This peace, indeed, passes understanding, for it means that in no circumstances are you without propriety, that those things which do not seem to have a purpose do have a purpose, and that purpose is to help you to grow—not in this life only but in the life that is real, that which extends in the infinite present in the great circle of time and space which is now and here forever.

We have often said to you that the Creator is a Creator of total love, and yet there was a pain in separation when that unity which was the Creator consciously separated Itself into an infinity of individuals. There was a wish that the Creator know Itself and a hope that the Creator might love Itself and, thus, It gave Its parts free will. As you gaze into your brother's eyes you may see the Creator or you may see your brother; it is your choice. Truly, you may love the Creator in your brother and, thus, you love the Creator.

As you see the world of nature about you at this time, you may appraise the Creator, or you may choose not to. Each moment you can make of your life as you will. And that, too, is cruel. That is the ultimate responsibility, for it is only the mature and emotionally strong personality who can remember the Creator and recognize the Creator and love Its parts. The good and the bad, so they seem—they are the Creator.

Some parts of the Creator do not know that there is One, that the Creator is He and that the definition of both is love. Thus, your love of that ignorant brother may be the blessing that helps that brother to know himself for the first time.

How many times have you been in motion today? How many times have you felt the stillness within you that is the Creator—the perfect balance that is the perfect dance of love?

This instrument today spent her morning singing hymns to the Creator. "Alleluia He is risen," she sang. We say to you, "Alleluia *you* are risen." Your body is transitory. In meditation, allow that feeling of freedom, of love, of sweet companionship, of peace to soak through your chemical body, to soothe those nerves that have been frayed by the intense emotions of your experience at this level. Let hope come into your heart, for the Creator is forever full of hope. Let love heal that which needs healing in your thoughts; let it touch your pain. The original Thought that created you is love. That union can exist again in meditation. This is not an escape, my friends. This is a centering in knowing who you are.

We have heard your discussion this evening and the conversation that perhaps meditation makes it more difficult to live among your people. Do not let this be so for you. Let love give you confidence. Let it give you a smile from the heart. Let it give you, above all, compassion. Just as the one known as Jesus finished his stay to the bitter end and triumphed over cruelty, take whatever cup is given to you and drink it unafraid. If it is yours, take it. But in meditation ask for the discrimination to know that which is yours and that which is not yours. When you feel that you know, you will be as one that has come forth in the spring, in your own way beautiful. Think of yourself as nothing less, for you are beautiful, each of you, as beautiful as the Creator, as lovely, and as loving.

At this time I will pause that my brother, Laitos, might condition each of you and offer you a strengthening wave. I am Hatonn.

(Pause)

I am again with this instrument. I am Hatonn. My brother Latwii wishes only to say a few words.

(Pause)

I am Latwii. I am with this instrument. I wish you all much love and light. We in the service of the infinite Creator thank you for allowing us in your meetings.

We are having a good time this evening. We in our light ship or plane, which are colors which are different from our identities, are enjoying the show. Your sun is most entertaining at certain times, and we thank you for the beauty of your solar system. We are enjoying it.

We only wish to say hello and to give you our love. We feel like children today and wish you the very best of childhood—laughter without fear and belief without doubt.

I am Latwii. Adonai.

(Pause)

I am known as Hatonn. At this time I would open the meeting to questions.

(Pause)

H: I have a question. As Carla and I were speaking earlier this evening, I'm concerned about reincarnation because I have a dissertation to do, and I was wondering if you can tell me if the sources I have are reliable.

(Pause)

I am conditioning this instrument. I am Hatonn. I am Hatonn. I am Hatonn. I am aware of your question.

As always among your people, those books which are written by learned men about subjects which are beyond the grasp of terrestrial science are not reliable, due to the fact that their base of data is necessarily not that of reality but is predicated upon the insistence that the scientific method, as you call it, be used to prove or disprove theses concerning spiritual subjects. The nature of a spiritual subject is such that the scientific method will fail, due to the fact that freedom of choice is paramount in spiritual growth. Consequently, it cannot be proven that there is life after death or that there is purpose to life in such a way that it cannot be refuted, for if this were done, those among your peoples would have no more freedom from ignorance and would have to realize the truth of their own function within their incarnation.

Reincarnation is an important part of the system of the evolution of spirit among beings and, thus, it cannot ever be proven in the density of your plant any more than it can be proven that the one known as Jesus was resurrected on a spring day long ago. It must be an article of faith, something that is individually and subjectively taken to be true. For this reason, those books which attempt to prove reincarnation are going to run into insurmountable difficulties. Of more use to you will be simple anecdotal books which are collections of stories concerning cases suggestive of reincarnation.

Does this answer your question?

H: Yes, thank you. But I have another, if I may. Would it serve any purpose from your viewpoint … that is to say, would it be an imposition upon you if I should ask questions about the origin of man on this planet?

Insofar as our knowledge will permit, we are delighted to share our facts with you on any subject which does not infringe on your free will. You must understand that we are not a final authority and are capable of error. However, within these limits we will be most happy to answer your question.

H: Thank you very much, and with your permission I will frame a few questions possibly for next time.

We will be delighted. You may ask questions now if you wish.

H: Well, there's one in particular I'm concerned about, in terms of intellectually knowing—which I understand is not a good thing in itself—but why are we as human beings here in the first place? Is there something that we became entrapped in, or did we choose to come here for growth, or just what?

We ask you to think in terms of cycles. There is something that you have in common with the cycle of the seasons. As seeds you were planted here without free will, due to the fact that you were ready to be planted. From that point on you had complete free will regarding the rate of your growth within a certain framework which measures growth in such a way which has been made very clear to you by various masters at various times. The one most familiar to you is the one known as Jesus the Christ.

A measure of your growth is your unselfish love for your Creator and for your fellow man. As the shoot climbs from the darkness of the soil to the sunlight, so it took you many, many incarnations to get the first inkling that there was any purpose to life other than the fulfillment of your basic bodily needs. At that level, each individual was an extremely selfish person. But the catalyst, if you will allow us to call it that, of physical existence works upon the soul of mankind in such a way that the experiences which he meets in an incarnation allow him chances to learn the lesson of love. In many, many cases in an incarnation a person makes a simple choice for his own good or for the good of another. He learns to help. He learns that to say no is sometimes of more help that to say yes. He learns that to bow one's head is often helpful. He learns that to listen is often helpful. He learns many, many things and experiences many, many things. And slowly, as he climbs toward that light which is the perfect love of the Father, instinctively drawn there through many, many incarnations, he begins to become the kind of person that is capable of becoming a seed, the seed of a new man who can be planted in a new world.

However, in the next cycle of experience you will have free will about when you are planted, for you will have enough true love within your being that it will be a real choice for you to decide [to remain] behind and help your fellow beings who are below you or whether you wish to enter a cycle of growth as a light soul.

Does this answer your question, my brother?

H: For now, yes. Thank you.

We thank you for allowing us to share our thoughts with you. Have you more questions?

Questioner: I have a question. I'm wondering if you can shed some light on the planetary alignment that's to come in 1982. I've heard about it. It concerns me, and I'm not very clear on what is to happen, since no man in recorded history has seen this.

You have us there, due to the fact that we do not ourselves know what will happen, for the free will of the planet will have a great deal to do with the severity of Earth changes that take place due to the gravitational force exerted upon the crust of the planet Earth at that time. You are incarnate on a planet which is very busy being born, going through a cycle.

The Earth changes have intensified as have the polarity of the tempers of the people of the planet. We are sure that you have observed that many have became more loving and, at the same time, many have become far less loving and more prone to the bloodiness of battle within the last thirty years.

These changes in the planetary consciousness are at one with the changes in nature, and natural catastrophes and difficulties of all kinds have increased dramatically within the last thirty years. This change will continue to worsen both on the human and physical levels for approximately the next fifteen years.

The so-called Jupiter effect, as this instrument has known of …

(Side one of tape ends.)

(A question was asked about the Shroud of Turin.)

H: Can you tell us if this is the valid shroud that Christ was garbed in when he was in the tomb?

(Pause)

We ask your patience as this instrument is not yet in a proper state.

(Pause)

I am Hatonn. We are aware of your question, my brother, and have spoken with others of your group about this very artifact. It is an interesting quirk of your peoples that you are so sentimental about clothing. Would that you were as sentimental about ideas.

The so-called shroud is an example of a phenomenon which is called an action at a distance effect in physics. Although it was not the winding sheet of the man known to you as Jesus, the belief that it is has caused imprints to appear. They have been caused by the thought forms of those who pray, and this can show to you the power of prayer and belief. Thus, although we discourage placing importance upon the clothing of those who are dead, let us encourage you to contemplate the immense power of that which you call the Holy Spirit.

In meditation, in life, that which you wish, that for which you pray, that which you desire and will, my friends, that is what you will receive. As surely as thought has imprinted the cloth, so shall your thoughts become things; so watch carefully what you desire, for it will come to you. Desire that which you truly wish.

Is there another question?

(Pause)

We leave you, my friends, floating upon the winds of change. We are aware that each of you has a feeling at this time of rootlessness, and we encourage you to know that the Creator is everywhere, that your footing need not be recognizable, for the Creator is close. Love is near. Light is all about you. Your security and your safety are never in question. You may live, and you will surely die, but that which is you will bloom anew, and your radiance of being will become evermore bright.

We, who are your humble brothers, send you our love. May you rest in the love and the light of the infinite Creator.

I am known to you as Hatonn. In the name of the Confederation of Planets in the Service of the Infinite Creator, I leave you in the love and the light. Adonai vasu borragus.

Sunday Meditation
April 29, 1979

(Carla channeling)

I am Latwii, and I greet you in the love and the light of the infinite Creator. I have not spoken through this instrument for some time, but I wish to drop in for just a few minutes to welcome each of you and greet the one known as H, for our vibration is that of peace, and we offer it to her unreservedly,

Yes, my friends, we come to your planet in peace, and we speak peace among your peoples, for we are men of peace and women of peace, and we dwell in harmony. And it is our good fortune to be able to be of service to your planet at this time when peace is so important among your peoples.

We are aware that it is a cliché among your peoples that peace is important, and many give it lip service. A few know how to achieve peace, for it is so simple that it is difficult for your peoples.

Peace is achieved when there is a state of total love between peoples. This is a state not easily achieved among your peoples. Indeed, it is not easily achieved within each of your beings, but we urge you to seek total love, first of yourselves and then of others.

In the name of the Creator I leave you in love and light, and I thank you for permitting me to speak to you. I am Latwii.

(Pause)

I am Hatonn, and I greet you again, as did my brother, in the love and the light of the infinite Creator. I would like to tell you a little story.

Once there was a gardener. Year after year he planted his seeds and learned much about his crops, knowing which seeds to plant against which, which crops to move so that the land would not be depleted. He knew the rooting of each tree and of each type of grass, and he began to feel very powerful, for he had often been told that he had the best garden in all of his territory. And one day he was asked how his seeds grew, and he began to explain by taking a seed and separating it into its parts. And as he took his knife and separated the seed and showed his students the functions of each tiny part of this tiny seed, he found that he had killed the seed, for much as he would try he could not put it back together. And so he learned that he was not the originator of the garden but only the caretaker.

My friends, we ask each of you at this time to consider that you, yourselves, are seeds, planted in the garden of Earth. We ask you to understand that you are whole and perfect. It is good to nurture yourself. It is good to understand yourself and to care for the garden that you have created for yourself to grow in. But we of the Confederation of Planets in the Service of the Infinite Creator say to you, as a kind of gardener, do not separate the parts of you too completely; do not observe so closely that you peel away something necessary for the wholeness of your growth; allow yourself to be, for in that way the instinct that is within you to become can have its way in its own time and at its own pace.

The sun rises and sets upon your planet 365 times in one of your years, and yet it is in one particular day in which a seed chooses to sprout, in which a flower chooses to bloom, in which a tree chooses to blossom, as has been the experience of each of you in seeing the beauty of the springtime that you are now experiencing. Such beauty is nothing compared to the beauty of the soul, of one who is of a likeness of the Creator, such as yourselves, my brothers and sisters, Therefore, as you observe yourself, allow yourself the freedom to be instinctual, for your instincts are good, and the love which you find in meditation will know how to direct itself as your moments come.

We are aware that you are interested in the world situation at this time, and we have been monitoring it very closely, for it has been a delicate and dangerous time for many months now. But we feel at this time that there is more of an equilibrium than there has been and that there is *(inaudible)* that your prayers for peace have succeeded to a certain extent for the present. We do, however, ask that you continue in your constant day-to-day attempts to become a focus for love on this planet, for difficulties of long standing will continue indefinitely. As far as we know, there will be need for your prayers for peace. Only remember that that peace begins within yourself.

I would at this time like to pause for a few moments for my brother, Latwii, to speak. I am Hatonn.

(Pause)

I am Latwii. I am very glad to speak with you and will not take much of your time. However, I would like to share with you the color green which we are enjoying at this time, if you will allow your vision internally to be flooded with this color. We have been enjoying your fifth dimension, and the color green in this dimension is very beautiful to us. We think that your vibration is a lovely one, and we are enjoying it tremendously. Therefore, we shall at this time send to you our vibration of green and allow it to fill the room in which you dwell on the dimension which is beyond your own. If you will allow yourself to relax, we will allow it to encompass you, for it is a healing vibration and a common one.

I am Latwii.

(Pause)

I am again with this instrument, I am Latwii, I am enjoying your density greatly, as your colors are greatly more transparent and less dense than our own, and we find it to be very much like living in a world of glass instead of liquid, The experience is stimulating, and we are happy to send our vibrations of light to your planet at this time.

We wish only to stop in and say hello, and we will be on our way, and we wish you farewell and love.

(Pause)

I am Hatonn, and I am again with this instrument. We thank you for your patience, but we were deepening this instrument's state of meditation.

We especially thank each of you, for we are aware that there was a desire for a meeting this evening on the part of this instrument, and it is always such a pleasure to speak with you and to share our thoughts.

At this time we would open the meeting to questions.

(Pause)

H: Do you have a family? Do you have a husband? Or are you a woman?

I am with the instrument. I am Hatonn. I am one of many who call themselves Hatonn, for we are a planetary consciousness encompassing a culture who has come to a oneness of thought in unison; and as we desire to serve, so we have been sent to you, called by your need.

I, myself, speaking to you at this moment, am a woman, and I am mated. However, we are not of your density, and our relationship is more that of an extended family, as you would call it, than your mated relationships which keeps walls between people, both in the generations and between friends. Thus, you may be speaking next to a man who is also Hatonn, who may be my mate or my brother, or simply one of the brothers of our clan of service.

H: Do you have children?

Yes, we do. However, there is a difference between our methods of raising children than yours, in that children are raised by the entire clan so that each child has many older people to whom he can turn. In the event that one does not understand, there is always another. This, we find, is unlike your culture in which the child has very few chances for an understanding relationship with an older person. This is due to the difference in our vibrations, for in our vibration the truth is clear to us, and we can see the thoughts of those around us, even those from whom we are separated, as you would call it, physically by space. Thus, there is no falsehood or deception in any of our relationships; and therefore, each child seeks out those who vibrate in harmony with him without feeling that he must choose one person over another because of what you would call a blood relationship.

There is, of course, a special affection for one's father or mother of the flesh, as you would call it, but it is nothing compared to the emphasis which you in your density put on this simple relationship. For in reality, you in your illusion have used this relationship to work out a great many lessons of love and service whereas we cannot use this relationship, for knowing the truth of love by the vibrations, seeing the thoughts of all those about you, we would not learn those lesson in any event, were our relationships restricted. Therefore, the restrictions are lifted, and we are free. However, we choose our friends within a vibration level which closely matches our own. And when our children are ready to mate, there is no question as to their suitability for each other, for their vibrations are obviously in harmony. Thus, our family life, as you would call it, is harmonious, and we are then free to serve others. And it is this freedom that has allowed us to come to you, for we have heard the call of your planet for help, for you desire to be as we—free and happy.

And yet, all that we can tell you is that that freedom is within yourself and not within the outer world, for the outer world is a distraction and a series of distractions which serve as a catalyst for your understanding. This catalyst you may ignore; you may become unhappy; you may become tired or you may consider these things within yourself, deciding what each lesson of your life might have to do with love. And when you see the love in a situation, then you have come one step closer to what you would call the kingdom of heaven. That is the place in which we dwell, for our dimension relates very closely to your heavenly vibration, as you would call it. In that vibration we live, and from that vibration we reach back to you to help, as it were, by inspiration, to help you want to be lifted up into a place in which there is peace and joy in reality and not only in dreams.

Does this answer your question?

H: Yes. Do you feel any other emotions besides love? Do you ever feel angry?

We feel an emotion besides love, but it is not anger. We feel an immense sorrow, a grief. We grieve for your peoples. You are not the first civilization that has approached annihilation on a planetary level, but there are not many of you. We grieve because you are separated, and we yearn and wish and hope that we can help you become one within yourselves, with love. We grieve as parents grieve when their children are unhappy, wanting to give them happiness but not knowing how. We grieve at your nations, that they are hostile to each other. For ours is a vibration of love, and when there is love there is sadness, sadness for those who do not know love; and this emotion we feel.

We speak only for the vibration of Hatonn. You must understand that we are one of many, many civilizations which make up the Confederation of Planets in the Service of the Infinite Creator. We are, shall we say, among them, not at the greatest of vibrations. Indeed, the one known to you as Latwii, and the one known to you as Telonn, are both of a light vibration which is much higher and much more full of joy than our own. And in their messages there could never be any grief. But we have not yet reached their wisdom, and we vibrate in love. Thus, we feel sadness, and we reach out to you in both love and sadness. And when you accept our love and your own sadness as a people diminishes slightly, then we feel great joy; and when you wish to fight among yourselves, then we are sad again.

(Pause)

H: Do you feel other emotions between yourselves *(inaudible)*?

May we say to you that it is difficult to express our thoughts through this channel on this subject, for she does not have a vocabulary suited to express the shadings of love. There are many, many different kinds of appreciation.

There are differences of opinion among us, but they are not inharmonious, for differences of opinion are simply differences in vibration and when that can be seen simply as that, it becomes simple to move an inharmonious vibration so that the person is better placed to be in harmony with those about him. You have an expression for this, which is a cliché among your peoples. We find it in this instrument's mind. It is called, "Birds of a feather flock together." And this is precisely what happens among our people.

Those of us who have one goal, one type of desire, spend our time pursuing it as one being. And yet, we all appreciate each other's skills and abilities. Thus, we do not leave the vibration of love, yet our emotions vary widely as we listen to the healing of one and the music of another, or the cooking skills of another, or the poetry of another, or the ability to travel through densities and bring back beautiful stories of another.

You do not know who is speaking to you, for we do not have names. You may be having a contact with a healer Hatonn, or the singer Hatonn, or the poet Hatonn. Thus, the messages vary from time to time to a certain extent, but we are enough alike in our desire that there is similarity.

In this instrument's mind there is a fact which perhaps helps to clarify the question. The word "snow" is one word in your language, but among those who live in the far, far north there are many, many words for snow. Thus it is with love. When you can see the variations and the shades of love, you can appreciate and feel an incredible variety of love.

H: Thank you very much for answering my question.

We are the ones to thank you, my sister, for without you we would be talking to ourselves. Is there another question?

Questioner: Yes. What is evil in your density? Is evil out in *(inaudible)*?

I am aware of your question, but there is some difficulty in answering it fully, for there is no evil in our particular density. We are in a density of unity. Evil, as you know it in your density, seems rather complex; but in reality it is simply the manifestation of separation—brother from brother and man from Creator.

Each man is the Creator. The lack of understanding of this principle of universal law is the source and the beginning of evil. Man, not understanding that all is one and that what man does to his brother he does to himself, decides to gain power over his brother and enslaves his brother.

Sometimes this evil is projected from individuals to larger groups. Whole nations, as you call them on your planet, can become evil. Whole planets can become evil. It is simply a measure of separation of man from the knowledge and love of the Creator. It is a type of ignorance, and this is why the best defense against evil in your illusion is the knowledge of what evil really is. Thus, faced with evil, you can find the Creator in the source of that evil. This blocks the evil from coming into your world, for one who loves is stronger, in unity, than one who does not love, in his evil.

In many situations that may seem that evil has triumphed, it must be understood that—metaphysically speaking—evil cannot triumph; it can only lose. That is the best it can do. That is what it is now doing upon your planet. It is keeping love in flight.

The difficulty is that many among your people do not care whether they are good or evil. Thus, they are a little good and a little evil—not truly good and not truly evil. They vibrate so weakly that they cannot help and they cannot hinder; and then they leave the field clear for those who wish power over others and wish to be evil. Thus, we always ask for you to know that all things are one, that love created all that there is, that the original Thought is love.

A true understanding of the unity of all that there is is a great gate into a realm of white light from which we can gaze at the cold eyes of evil without fear. For evil exists only on the lower planes, in one of which you are now enjoying an experience. It is an expression in which you can find evil, but it is only an illusion. It is an illusion which is caused by thought. That thought is the thought of separation. That which is good is the thought of the unity of love.

We do not have evil, due to the time we have spent on the evolutionary spiral, feeling the density that you now enjoy, through the next density which you will come to enjoy, into the one which we now enjoy.

In the next density which you will enjoy there will be evil, but it will be in a greatly attenuated form and will be seen to be a creature of thought only. Thus you will be able to deal with it in a more adult manner. It will not be as threatening, and it will be easier for you to become adept at loving. The lessons become easier as the path becomes lighter.

When you've reached the vibration that we now enjoy, there will be no evil; and you will find that in order to possess and to learn you must reach backward as teachers, such as we, and attempt to bring after you those who are now seeking to follow the path that you have chosen. In this way we deepen our understanding. You deepen your understanding by direct confrontation that is far more painful, but it is far quicker. And this we say to you: you have a marvelous opportunity day by day to enrich that within you which is immortal with an understanding of love.

Does this answer your question?

Questioner: Yes.

H: How many densities are there beyond your density?

We do not know. There may be a finite number, but we cannot find the end of the densities which lead to the perfect life. Therefore, we are in the position of saying that, as far as we know, the path towards the light is infinite. It is a mystery to us how a path could be infinite and yet one could reach the end. We have no knowledge of the end of this path, for it disappears into perfection. We know ...

(Side one of tape ends.)

(Carla channeling)

I am Hatonn. I am aware of your question. I am deepening this instrument's state, if you will be patient. I am aware of your question,

My sister, we must answer by giving contradictory answers. We can heal, but we may not, for the freedom of will of each individual among your peoples is the first law of our contact with you. Thus, unless it happens by accident, as has been the case from time to time, we cannot perform healing by way of proof that we are real. We must tantalize or challenge but never prove our reality.

There are many reasons for illness among your peoples, and were we to come through the process of incarnation and incarnate upon your planet with our power of healing intact in our physical body, we would then have the right to heal among your peoples. And there are many healers among your peoples that do not come from your planet but which have come because they wish to help at this time, for there is a good chance that in the generation to come there will be a great need for healers and no one of normal medical skills to help.

We are not of your density nor of your planetary consciousness but of what you would call a cosmic consciousness. Thus, we have no rights among your peoples. We can only teach. To perform among your peoples those things which are called miracles is simply going too far.

There have been entities who have attempted to break the Law of Free Will so that they could more quickly prove themselves real to humans and, thereby, help to save your planetary consciousness which is teetering on the brink of negativity. But they find that their interference, shall we say, backfired upon them, for they use channels whom they choose to be their channels [who] are most often too weak to deal with the energies. And if they work directly they cannot gauge the energies of the individual properly. Thus, we choose not to manifest physical healings or other phenomena. That we could do this goes without saying, for we can create things from what you would call thought. But we are your neighbors. We are not your God. And as neighbors we feel that we can send you our love but that you must work out your own destinies.

As we have said, there are many reasons for people to have various illnesses, and as they work these reasons out they pursue an individual course. For us to step in without being of your planet would be against cosmic law, and that law we take very seriously.

We can do one simple thing, however, and that is to send you energy to help to balance your own spiritual vibration. This is permissible, due to the fact that it is not interfering with your spiritual vibration but only, shall we say, agreeing with it, acting as, so to speak, a carrier wave for it, not interfering with your individuality but only lending it strength. Thus, at this time we would pause and send you this conditioning so that you may feel the love that we have for you.

(Pause)

I am again with you. I am Hatonn. This healing we give to you freely. It is a spiritual one. Those in the spirit may heal spiritually, and our conditioning wave is of such a nature. Those in the flesh may heal in the flesh. Such is the law of the universe of which we are a part.

Does this answer your question?

H: Yes, thank you.

May we ask if there are any more questions?

(Pause)

We have great gratitude to you for allowing us to share our thoughts with you. It is, indeed, a privilege, as always, to speak to this group. We send you our love, which is only the love of the Creator channeled to us through you[5] and out into the world.

We leave you in love and light. However, if you wish our presence you have only to mentally ask for the brothers and sisters of Hatonn, and we will share our love with you. If our vibration is not properly adjusted to you at some time, you have only to request that we leave. We never truly leave, for we are with you always in thought if you call. Adonai, my friends. Adonai vasu borragus.

(Pause)

I am Oxal. I will speak only for a moment, but I come because my brother has not spoken to you about a subject dear to our hearts. We speak of meditation. We speak of love and light. We speak of the Creator. But where do we find these things, my friends? Do we find them in our pastimes? In our work? My friends, we find them in a moment of contemplation, in a moment in which we see the beauty of the world of the Creator, in a moment of silence in which that still, small voice speaks within us, in which sweetness comes into our hearts. Seek those moments, my friends, day by day.

I leave you. I am Oxal. Adonai vasu.

---

[5] The phrase "channeled to us through you" was given. The phrase "channeled through us to you" may have been intended.

Sunday Meditation
May 6, 1979

(Carla channeling)

I am Hatonn, and I greet you in the love and the light of the infinite Creator.

We are having some difficulty contacting this group at this time, due to the concern of the one known as M, which is causing an ambivalence, and if she will be patient we will attempt to deepen contact with this instrument while conditioning each of you. I am Hatonn.

(Pause)

I am again with this instrument. We do have better contact at this time. We had first attempted to speak through the one known as N, and he is aware of this. However, we will build up his confidence even more as time goes on. We realize that our time is limited this evening. We do wish to answer a question that is in the mind of the instrument. The question has to do with whether you are your brother's keeper.

This instrument is concerned as to whether she is responsible for the spiritual growth of her mate. We would like to speak on this subject, for it is fundamental to an understanding of the true process of spiritual growth as we understand it.

That which is among your peoples known as attraction, or sexual desire, of esthetic appreciation, depending upon the proclivities of those souls involved, is a technique for placing two people in such a position that they are able to be of service to each other. Their free will is not disturbed by this relationship. However, without this natural attraction of polarity, there would be no irresistible reason to sacrifice the pleasures of the moment for a greater or nobler desire to aid another human being. Thus, those among your peoples quite rightly take mates, and thus it is their desire to be of service.

However, let us examine the concept of service. How can you be of service to others, my friends? Can you be of service in an orchard by grafting an apple onto a cherry tree, of a pear onto a peach tree, or by pinning the bloom of a tulip to the leaves of a rose? The only garden that you must cultivate is the garden of your own personality. If you have weeded your own plot, if those things which have been given you are being done to the best of your ability, if you are centered in the love of the Creator, then you can give the only service that is worth giving—yourself.

You may find this easy to give to others beside your mate, for there is an escape. You will leave friends. You cannot leave family, and your family comes to know you; your weeds as well as your crops, your fruit and flowers.

We each have a unique bias. Yes, even we have biases, we of Hatonn, and this is why we take mates as do you, for there are those who are more harmonious to our vibrations than others, those with whom it is well to work out our destinies. But you must remember, my friends, that you cannot change those whom you love; you can only be the best person that you can be. And if your example is an inspiration, then your loved one may change as you desire. You may be seeing quite clearly, but it does not matter, for the free will of your loved one is fundamental to the quality of your relationship. Thus, it cannot change; you can only be. In this way only can you be of true spiritual help to your mate or to anyone else. As we said, it is difficult, for the most part, with one's family. To be—that, my friends, is the essence of difficulty.

When you can look at the pain of a misunderstanding and continue to be yourself in the face of it, then you become as a mirror reflecting that which may help your loved one. Speeches, arguments and inharmonious silences can never be of the help that you can be if you remain yourself.

We answer this question because we feel it is central to all relationships in your illusion, is very active, because you breathe, because you move, because all that you do is in motion. You find virtue in motion. You make lists, get things done. You try to communicate with words and actions. But of all those things, your greatest responsibility is to be yourself. Yes, you are responsible for your mate's spiritual growth, for that is a special and privileged contact among two souls and the Creator. No, you may not change in any way the path of your mate, but only love and be.

If you can remember this simple instruction the terrific confusion that besets the most harmonious of relationships, at times, will vanish. For it is a cliché among your peoples that all are different. Realize only that all are also perfect and that in seeing your own perfection you are allowing your mate to be perfect also. With the pressure gone from a relationship, that which is needed can come naturally. Then and only then can you fulfill your spiritual responsibilities Remember that you are one with all that there is. It is hardest to be one with those to whom you are closest, but it is possible, and it is profitable.

I would like to exercise the channel known as M at this time. We will not attempt to speak words through her but only to briefly contact her. I am Hatonn.

(Pause)

We would now like to condition the one known as J.

(Pause)

I would open the meeting to questions at this time. I am Hatonn. Are there any questions at this time?

(Pause)

J: I have a question. What do you mean by being yourself? How do you know what your … I mean, there are basic things, you know, but *(inaudible)* talk about that?

My brother, we would be delighted to talk on this subject, for it is central. As you know, we have asked you many, many times to spend time daily in meditation. It does not matter how you do it. This instrument has found it best to meditate briefly many times during the day. It works best for her. Other people find it better to spend an extended amount of period in meditation—twenty, thirty minutes, even an hour. This varies from person to person.

However, there is a vibration which is yourself. If you can remember your high school chemistry, you will remember that each metal has a specific spectroscopic color or group of colors which were the identifying colors or vibrations of that substance. The vibrations of a being extend from the physical into what you would call the electrical or astral and, from there, into the more spiritual realms which are called sometimes among your peoples the devachanic. All of these vibratory rates put together give a specific, shall we say, spectroscopic identification.

However, you are not a metal. You are not an element. You are, indeed, an element, that is, but not of Earth. You are an element of consciousness, and your color is one of what you would call relative virtue. You are unique, and your uniqueness is eternal.

In meditation you become one with the Creator and with your higher self, that self which will remain when your physical vehicle is no longer a functioning pile of chemicals, but rather a non-functional pile of chemicals. You will have the same vibration. To get in touch with yourself, it is best to meditate, for to find out who you are by action is a hit and miss proposition, as this instrument would call it. And those who attempt to find themselves this way only find themselves by a process of elimination, by trying something and saying "No, this is not me." Then trying something else and saying, "No, this is not me." And if their analysis is faulty, they may miss that which is themselves. In meditation you become centered in something that is sure, something that is much more permanent than your physical personality, something which is called among your peoples, character.

There are underlying traits that go so deep within your character that you know within yourself that they are not part of your learning experiences. These are clues to who you really are.

Of course, all of us are basically splinters, shall we say, of the great sphere of love that burst into infinite pieces at the beginning of your universe. So you are, in truth, part of love. But which part? Who are you? Who are you really? This is not a question that is prompted by an egoistic search, a selfish desire to know, a narcissistic hunger for selfhood, for selfhood you have, but to truly know that selfhood is the only wisdom. And from that wisdom comes the compassion, the patience, and the grace to love all of those people who are reflections of yourself. Your mate was drawn to you and you to her because you and she are polarized in such a way that you can reflect each other rather accurately and so aid each other in spiritual growth. You can distort that reflection by avoiding the understanding of who you really are, but in your unconscious you know who you really are.

Thus, we ask you meditate. Find not only the love within you but that unique and special love that is within you with all of its unique and special gifts. You know that some can give in one and some in another way. On all levels, some can speak, and some can listen, and some can cook, some can sing, some can hold their arms out to children, some can nurture old people, some have the gift of silence and others that of words. When you know who you are, then your gifts will flow therefrom, and it will be a free-flowing brook, one which is not stopped by the distortion of doubt. This can only be done by daily meditation, seeking the Creator Who is the seed and the source of the love that is you.

Does this answer your question?

J: Yes, thank you.

We thank you, also. Is there another question?

(Pause)

We are being sent love by the one known as Latwii, and he would speak with you but the time is short. He says simply to tell you that he is at this time a beam of light and is concentrating on some difficulties within the Earth's surface in your western American continent. There is some difficulty, and he is sending light to strengthen the weakness of that part of the Earth's crust. However, he sends you a big hello and, as usual, a laughing one. Now, there, my friends, is a perfect example of a planetary culture who knows itself so well that they have become free to be one.

I would at this time like to close through the one known as N. I am Hatonn.

(Pause)

(N channeling)

(Inaudible) … give me and my brothers great joy. We are with this instrument again so we can express certain thoughts and ideas through this instrument.

There is an eternal love ready to be tapped by anyone at any time. It flows, we will say, strictly in love. It is everywhere at all times, even though your illusions can become so strong and complicated that you think that it is not possible.

There is much truth to the saying you have all heard, "Knock and it shall be opened to you; seek and ye shall find." There is little effort involved in finding this eternal, flowing love. You simply desire it, and it is with you. You may not recognize it, for you expect bells to ring and your body to tingle—great excitement happening. It is not like this; sometimes it is, but not often.

Whenever you desire the love of the infinite Creator, it is with you. If you do desire it and think thoughts [that] you desire it, it is with you. You do not have to wonder when it will happen; it is simply with you. You can go on with whatever you are doing and it shall be known to you in one form or another, my friends.

We talk of love of the infinite Creator. Sometimes it is repeated so much it sounds just like words, but, my friends, your language cannot describe the immensity of the love available to you. There are many beings, shall we say, who constantly are projecting love and light to you. It is almost funny to think someone [is] here who has considered themself to be abandoned. It is almost comical to us, because you are never really alone.

I will end this message now, my friends. We love you very much. I am Hatonn. Adonai vasu borragus.

(Pause)

(Carla channeling)

I am Makai. I have not spoken to this group before. I am a member of the Confederation of Planets in the Service of the Infinite Creator and am traveling to a new post and have come across your message being sent. We would like to say that we have enjoyed your vibrations and wish to send you our love, also. We are, shall we say, healers, and we send you our love and healing light as we pass through your skies. We leave you, but we simply wish to say greetings and love. I am Makai. Adonai.

Sunday Meditation
May 20, 1979

(Carla channeling)

I am Hatonn, and I greet you in the love and the light of the One Who is All. It is a great pleasure to be here this evening, and, as always, we greet each of you with much appreciation and *(inaudible)*.

This evening I would tell you a story about a man who was not an ordinary man, but rather a very uncommon one, for within him from childhood was the burning desire to know the love of the Creator.

In his youth this man read widely, feeling extremely frustrated because no one could speak with him deeply enough on the subjects in which he was interested. He found theology a great puzzle, a great confusion of ideas, and wending his way through it was something he did with a burning desire to know the love of the Creator. He did not find it in his books, but he pressed on. He went into what you would call a seminary, and when he graduated he became a minister, preaching the word of his Creator to his flock.

Through the years he listened with interest to the many problems of those who came to his church, drawn by the brilliance of his reasoning and the eloquence of his preaching. And yet, he did not find the love of the Creator.

In time he met and married a woman who gave him children. He spent very little time with them because of his duties but was loved greatly and supported tremendously in his work by a wife who understood much and gave of herself unstintingly in his behalf. Nor, yet, did he find the love of the Creator he sought.

And one day as he walked down the path from the rectory of his church he met a boy that reminded him of himself at a younger age, for now, you see, he was quite old. And falling into conversation with the young man they continued on to the rectory, and he continued his conversation. All of a sudden, something occurred that had never yet occurred in the old man's life.

In this stranger's unlined face, and, burning to know the love of the Creator, the old man saw a person to love; and at the moment he gave his heart to this young man, as a father to a son, he felt the love of God.

This wanderer was never seen by the old man again, for he was on his own journey. The old man fell in love, first with one person, and finally with all mankind.

What had blocked the love of the Creator that he so earnestly sought for a lifetime? We say to you, my friends, that you must love yourself. Not because your personality has any virtue or because your ego, as you call it, needs shoring up by means of a self-indulgent love. No, my friends, we are speaking of a love that is one with the Creator.

Where is the Creator, my friends? Can you touch Him? In your senses, those things which are not seen are not understood. Yet, so it has been always. Had you all been blind you would have thought very differently. But we ask you, my friends, where is the Creator? Is He outside of the world as you know it? Is He unknowable in any way? If so, why would we seek to find Him? My friends, the Creator is in your brothers and your sisters and yourself. Closer to you than your breath, more available to you than reasoning, more heartening to you than your dreams. That which is beyond doing and dreaming is love itself.

It has been written in your holy works that a man who is kind to another is not kind to a man but to the Creator. You cannot be kind to a Creator that is invisible, infinite, untouchable, unknowable; but you can be kind to those about you.

You can allow yourself to be a channel for love, whatever your circumstance. Sometimes the circumstances you face are so difficult that you may wonder if there is such a thing as love. And if there is love, is it given equally to all? If it has a plan is it, shall we say, just?

But we say to you that, as far as we know, the Creator has a plan that has been worked out between love itself and that higher part of yourself which you call your spirit. In meditation you become able to communicate intuitively with that part of the creation that is a combination of the finite and the infinite; in this junction lies the plan. Whatever difficulties you may be having, they can be met with love; and the more deeply committed that you are to finding, feeling and freely giving to others the love that is in every situation, the more quickly you will become what you might call a conscious being, controlling your destiny, improving the harmony, aiding the vibration of your life.

You cannot possess the Creator. You cannot possess yourself. You possess only one thing: consciousness, and you possess it in common with all that there is. That which created this consciousness is love. Thus we ask you, allow love to flow through you. Not your love but the love of the Creator, for yours will run dry very quickly and you will find it reflected all about you. People, themselves, are reflections of you. Allow this reflection to be one of love.

I would leave this instrument at this time, as my friend Laitos desires to work with each of those present. I am Hatonn. Adonai.

At this time I would like to work with each of you. Let me greet you in love and light, as my brother Hatonn. I am known to you as Laitos, and it is my special duty and privilege to work with new channels. My vibration is a broad-beam vibration and more easily received than most of the Confederation vibrations, This has decided our purpose in the great scheme of things among the Confederation, and so we work with the channels who desire to get that service. We also work with each individual who simply wants to improve the strength of spiritual vibration; along with that, that which you may call inspiration or contemplation may flow.

I will attempt now to say a few words through the one known as J, if he would relax and allow himself to speak without analyzing our thoughts. I am Laitos.

(Pause)

(Carla channeling)

I am again with this instrument. I am Laitos, We had partial contact with the one known as J. However, his mind is not totally clear, due to feelings of somewhat conflicting natures about our contact. Consequently, we have, shall we say, a conditioning situation rather than a channeling one, and we are pleased to be of service in this way, for we are always a channel for something.

This particular type of channeling is very specialized, but all of you, my friends, show to the world that which flows through you.

We thank the one known as J and offer our assistance at any time he may require it.

At this time we would like to …

(Pause, as H1 arrives.)

I am again with the instrument. I am Laitos. We would like to pause for a moment while the one known as H1 relaxes, and we greet and welcome her to the meeting.

(Pause)

At this time we would like to say a few words to the one known as G, I am Laitos.

(Pause)

(G channeling)

I am with the instrument.

(Pause)

(Inaudible)

(Pause)

(Carla channeling)

I am again with this instrument. We are pleased to contact the one known as G. And may we say that the one known as G is doing very well in her progress. Although she may not know it consciously, there is a large difference between her conscious desire to be of service channeling and her subconscious feeling that there is perhaps something not quite good about such an activity. This is due to a simple feeling that things may not be what they seem—which is very true in your reality, which is illusory, and has stood the one known as G in good stead in her life—and it is only in this particular instance [that] it is difficult to drop that subconscious bias.

We are faced with a difficult choice. We can either transmit a common and familiar concept to a new instrument, in which case the instrument may block it due to a feeling that such a thought would be one of his own—or we can transmit new information, in which case the instrument might feel that the information was not that of the Confederation, due to its unfamiliarity.

As you can see, channeling is not always easy for those who are intelligent. Thus, we would recommend it for the most intelligent in order that intelligence be set in balance with love and emotions.

At this time we would like to contact the one known as H2 and, if possible, to say a few words with him. I am Laitos.

(Pause)

(Carla channeling)

I am again with this instrument. We thank the one known as H2 and, as always, assure him that at any time he may desire to work on contact we will be with him.

At this time I will leave this instrument, asking you only, as always, to meditate and pray for the good and the peace of humankind, for these are concepts that need to be cherished among your peoples. I leave you in the love and the light Who is the One and the origin of these concepts.

I am Laitos. Adonai.

(Pause)

I am with you. Ah, yes, my friends, I have been awaiting my turn. I am Latwii, and I greet you in the joy and the light of the Creator. It has been my privilege to be asked to join this celestial big league, and we are very happy to play ball with you at this time, as you might say.

We have come for the express purpose of asking if there are any questions, which—as you have noticed—is in itself a question. So you may answer this question with a question if you desire.

G: I have a question. I heard something on the radio, and I heard just the tail end of it. I'm not sure what it was, I don't read the papers much lately. It was something about something up in the air, a satellite or something like that. But the point is that somebody is *(inaudible)* in meditation to do something, and I'd like to know what it is.

We are consulting the group memory of the Confederation at this time, for we also do not know. We know of one item which is in your skies which is desired by your people to remain in orbit, and it is called your Skylab. However, this instrument also does not read the papers, and therefore we are unable to give the specific designation of its arrival into your atmosphere.

The trajectory of physical objects such as this one is unlikely to be altered by meditation, although it would be possible were the meditation powerful. However, among your people there is not the sophistication of other dimensions. Thus, meditating in your dimension would not aid a physical object; but, rather, meditation in the finer or denser dimensions would be much more powerful. However, it is not easy for your peoples to meditate in other dimensions, just as it is not easy for your people to leave their physical bodies and move about freely in their body eternal which is, in a way, a physical body but is physical in another dimension. Thus, we would say that it is likely that an application of, shall we say, government funding rather than group meditation would be the solution to that particular problem.

Does that answer your question, my friend?

G: Well, I had the idea that this was something that was out of control or something that we couldn't do anything about, and there was some group meditating and *(inaudible)*. Never mind. Thank you.

We are sorry that we have not satisfied you, but in our notice of your planet we may have, indeed, missed one of your projects. As we said, the only one of which we are aware of there being a large body of interest in is the one known as Skylab.

Is there another question?

H2: I have a question. I'd also like to comment. I believe the object of interest here is the Skylab. At least, that's my impression from news sources and so on.

My goodness, my brother, we are most pleased, because we were beginning to think that our ability to screen your planet was somehow lacking. Please ask your question.

H2: Yes, according to news sources the Skylab is out of control in a sense, in that it is no longer able to maintain orbit and is expected to enter the atmosphere in some future time.

My question is … I have several. But first, I'm glad you're here, Latwii, because I have a question for you on a subject you brought, and I would like to know in regard to this: if you begin a subject, can Hatonn or Laitos answer questions about it as well?

The reason that we are here tonight is that there was a request for information on a subject which we had previously discussed.

Each of the planetary consciousnesses which speaks to you under some code name, such as Hatonn or Latwii, has a specialty. As we have said before, Hatonn speaks in the vibration of love and has a general fund of information that is perhaps the broadest of any of your contacts at this time. Thus, it is Hatonn that often answers questions.

Our specialty is due to the fact that our form is that of light, and thus we are more able to see the problems involved in the taking on of a physical body, which we do not happen to have at this point in our evolution. Thus, we have a viewpoint on certain questions which Hatonn may not have, specifically, as do we. For there is no, shall we say, party line amongst us, as we are a Confederation of harmony rather than unity of thought. We do not come to group decisions about the truth but only communicate to you our own personal experience of the truth as we know it. Thus, we always repeat that we are, indeed, fallible and, indeed, our views upon a subject which you wish to request information about would be somewhat different from that of Hatonn's, for the ones of Hatonn dwell within a physical body, although in another dimension of space/time.

H2: Thank you. The question I have for you that seems to be in your specialty is about the genetic personality. This was raised in a few sessions back and has aroused my interest.

I believe you said something to the effect that at the time the genetic personality is formed there is a sort of contract made between the entity and the chemical body in the provision of, say, an environment that is best suited for that entity for learning during this incarnation and that it's possible, perhaps, to regress to that point of contract and to review that contract to see if the agreement with the chemical body was suitable for the entire incarnation and purposes of the entity. Is that correct?

This is a properly perceived concept, my brother.

H2: That being to case, then what I'm interested in is knowing how to regress to that point of contract and what procedures could be followed to review it and amend it, if that is possible.

We understand your question, although it is somewhat difficult to answer. What is necessary is that you enter a state of altered consciousness which is somewhat different from your consciousness while dealing in day-to-day experiences. The function of many so-called spiritual healers is that the healer, by giving off tremendous energy vibrating in the spectrum of light creates an environment for the individual in which a momentary dwelling place in which the genetic personality was formed can be maintained by the entity, and in that instant of time, as you know it, a great deal can be accomplished. This is the source of many healings among your peoples.

Other ways of achieving this type of, shall we say, reprogramming are the proper use of your so-called psychedelic drugs. This is a very risky operation, due to the fact that the state in which you will be led to may or may not be in accordance with [the] subject which you wish to cover, due to the fact that your personality may or may not be integrated enough at this time to pursue the course which is desired. Many of those among your peoples who use psychedelic substances to alter the chemical composition of the brain, thus allowing light vibrations to enter into the process of association within your mind, are simply, shall we say, taking short trips which are picnics of the mind but do not have the proper purpose. Thus, as often happens during a picnic, the entity becomes sunburned, bitten by mosquitoes and ants, tired and cranky when be arrives back home and begins to clean the dirt off his bare feet. That is the problem with psychedelic drugs.

Between the spiritual healing type of charismatic energy, as you would call it, and the psychedelic experiences of some, you have the majority of those who have reprogrammed their genetic personality. However, it is possible to do this by means of a carefully conceived program of meditation—meditation for a purpose, which is unlike the meditation which we urge you to do daily in which you are simply listening. In another context we would call this prayer or prayer of pleading or requesting. Even this type of entry into the world where the genetic personality may be reprogrammed will not work unless two conditions are met.

Number one. The entity must have learned that which he decided to learn when he entered into the condition which he now wishes to leave. This is not a partial learning or a majority learning but a complete learning. This learning must have been tested and understood.

Number two. The entity who wishes to reprogram must be able to let go of the circumstance completely. There must be no emotional tie to the previous circumstance. If it is an illness that is to be forgotten, then the person involved must not have a habit of being ill which will then reprogram the reprogramming through continuous, daily, habitual patterns of thinking. If the problem is a wrong relationship, then the person's lessons having been learned, he must be able to forgive completely, and this is very difficult. All wrong circumstances have within them a simple habit which carries an emotional strength. This habit is not at the conscious level, and it is not easily removed. It is for this reason that reprogramming is not more common among your people. However, if you have the desire to change your programming, and if you have learned the lessons that your programming was designed for—in other words, if you are ahead of your program by means of your performance in this incarnation—yes, you may reprogram, and the way to do it is by what many would call intercessory or pleading prayer, saying constantly, "Father, Creator, send your light upon me at this time that I may know the perfection of my being and may drop from my physical form that which is no longer necessary." You may then, if you wish, name that which you feel is no longer necessary, and then you must specifically state your forgiveness and your desire to forget that which has been negative in that experience.

Does this answer your question, my brother?

H2: Yes, very good, thank you. I suspect the question I want to ask now will be answered in the negative, but I would like to ask it anyway. Is it possible to help another in this matter through hypnosis and regression?

May we say that it is, indeed, possible that this be done; but it is a mixed blessing, due to the fact that in regression a person is made aware of the necessary environment for change. However, the person is not consciously aware of the need for releasing all those things which cause the previous programming to continue after the need for it was over. Consequently, the hypnotic approach lacks what we would call staying power, due to the fact that it is part of the mind of the individual's feeling that another entity is necessary for the work to take place. Indeed, this is a dealing of you with yourself, and, if we were to recommend hypnosis or the use of psychedelic drugs, for instance, we would have to say that—unless you are doing hypnosis upon yourself—the psychedelic, clinical type of approach is superior, in that if you have prepared yourself properly, if you go through your programming as you have planned it when you were in an everyday state of consciousness, this remains something you have done for yourself.

However, the most efficacious method is meditation done in addition to the simple meditation of listening. And there are no shortcuts to this. Much patience is usually needed. However, once you have achieved a reprogramming, you have achieved by the strength of your desire, and this is infinitely better for your permanent vibratory personality which has entered into the contract with your physical vehicle and its limitations in the first place. Thus, for the greatest value to your spirit in this eternal quest, we do recommend that type of meditation.

After all, my brother, adjusting your genetic programming is a little more serious than, shall we say, giving up smoking or finding out a previous incarnation, both of which uses we find somewhat frivolous. However, we do not find this reprogramming as frivolous, for it indicates a certain awareness of the way things are, which we do consider more reasonable.

H2: Thank you. You've mentioned psychedelics twice somewhat favorably, if not entirely, but I have determined in my own mind never to touch these kinds of things. Am I wrong in that attitude?

You are perfect and right, as are all beings. Each path is different.

H2: I have one more question, and that is concerning my state of spiritual development at this time. I feel that I'm not progressing as I once believed I was. I seem to have reached a sort of plateau. I'm either bogged down or I'm not advancing somehow. And I wonder if it's possible—because of the kind of relationship I've had in the past—I've gained as much from that as I can and should reprogram for something else holding me back.

We have two things in response to that, my brother. First, no one knows the state of his spiritual development. The opinion which you may have of yourself is quite irrelevant to your actual development spiritually and may, indeed, be quite different from your opinion. The other comment is that we simply cannot answer such questions as you asked in this instance, due to the fact that it is your freedom of will that has brought you here this evening, and we cannot compromise that by giving you specific instructions. We can only ask you to meditate.

Going back to what we said in the beginning: only you are you. Meditation, therefore, is a method whereby you develop an understanding of yourself. When you have meditated the proper amount you will form an opinion about the problem at hand, or the problem at hand will come into harmony without any apparent effort on your part. These are things that occur when one has a prayer or meditation life. It is not something which you can intellectually figure out. Thus, we ask you to invoke the light of the Creator: sit down, meditate and do not worry about your progress, and do not be disappointed or pleased with yourself at any time. Be objective about yourself. In that way you become a channel through which love can flow, for if you are meditating and seeking that which is true and lovely, that is all that is necessary. Your day-to-day problems or, shall we say, your year-to-year problems will become apparent to you.

Because we understand the distress in which you find yourself, we suggest that you go somewhere by yourself each day for a period of a week or two and spend at least ten minutes each day speaking out loud with intensity about your desire to maintain the position in which you find yourself. We then suggest that you spend an equal amount of time speaking intensely out loud about your desire to remove yourself from the same position. We believe that you will find at the end of this indoctrination procedure that you will have burned out the over-concern you feel at this time about this particular problem. And thus, you will be clear and able to catch the signal that you are sending to yourself. Then one day you will know what to do, and you may not be able to explain it to others, but you will feel the rightness of it inside, where it counts. Then you may proceed as you see fit, for that is your free will.

We are aware we have not been terribly helpful, but we have given you the truth as we see it.

H2: Perhaps not helpful from your viewpoint—very—but it's very helpful to me. Thank you.

Oh, we thank you, my brother. Is there another question?

J: Just briefly, what is the … give me some idea of what a soul incarnated in two bodies … or is one soul incarnated in twins?

No, my brother. The way the union works is one body, one soul. However, those who incarnate as twins have met upon the plane of consciousness, which in your inner world precedes incarnation, and have agreed as part of their genetic personalities …

(Tape ends.)

Sunday Meditation
June 10, 1979

(Carla channeling)

I am Hatonn, and I greet you in the love and the light of the infinite Creator. My brothers and I have been silent, for we realized that it was desired that a silent meditation be part of this evening's meeting. We greet each of you and thank you, as always, for the privilege of speaking with you.

There are those among your peoples who are quite concerned at this time as to who we are. It is our fervent wish that your peoples would be more concerned as to who *they* are.

As we look upon your peoples we find half of your population in great hunger and want. We find the other half reeling in the over-abundance of material supplies. Those who are hungry are angry. Those who are over-supplied are defensive. And the great chain of love which should unite you all is continually broken by your failure to understand who you are.

We do not know what to do with your peoples. We continue as we do, speaking with those of you who are on this path, knowing that our words go forth in love, but we are powerless to affect or change the destiny of mankind at the end of this cycle and the beginning of the new one. Only you, my friends, can spread the message of love—the simple message of unity which is our understanding of the truth and in support of which we have come to lend our voices at this time.

It is written in your holy works, "Create in me a new heart and make a right spirit within me." It is one of this instrument's favorite prayers which she will repeat to herself very often. And we share it with you out of her mind at this time, because our message to you this evening is that you cannot deal with your culture, with your surroundings, with your life as it is, with the old heart, with the old spirit, with the human frailties. No, my friends. As if they were skins, you must shed them and allow a transformation to take place within you, which can only take place within the purified atmosphere of meditation in which there is created within you a newness of being, in which you are an instrument for the will of love. We could say the will of God, but, my friends, the culture in which you live does not do well by its God. The master known as Jesus gave you a God of love, but your peoples insist upon remembering that he is the God of judgment in your history. You, my friends, are the God of judgment for yourselves., You, and no other judge, will judge yourself. You, and no other judge, will see that which is needed by the soul, which is yourself. And you will see that it is done, so that you may grow according to your needs.

The transformation that you may feel in meditation is all that can, at this point, harmonize your inharmonious planet.

There are those in this brotherhood that would leave you at this time, for we are no longer in a position to warn you; events themselves are warning you. Many things that have been prophesied are occurring, and it is not necessary for us to speak to you of these things any more. We would scarcely be prophets at this time were we to tell you that you are at the end of a cycle when your scientists are telling you. We bow to your scientists and move on to more important matters.

Create in yourselves, my friends, a new heart And the right spirit within you. Find the peace that accompanies the expanded view of life which you may take as a transformed soul whose horizons have been consciously widened so that the love and the light of the infinite Creator may be seen in every corner, in every task, in every person.

I would at this time attempt to transfer this message to another instrument. I am Hatonn.

(Pause)

I am again with this instrument. I am Hatonn. The conditions are very good this evening, and we are attempting to communicate through the one known as Don. If he would relax and accept our contact, we would desire to speak a few words through him. I am Hatonn.

(Pause)

(Don channeling)

I am Hatonn, *(inaudible)*. It is a privilege to be with this instrument. I have not done so for some time. *(Inaudible)*.

I was speaking of the development of your people of the planet Earth. Unfortunately, development of the general population of your planet has been very slow. It seems it is very difficult for them to become aware of the true nature of creation.

(Pause)

(Carla channeling)

I am again with this instrument. I am Hatonn. We are having good contact with the one known as Don. However, he is somewhat out of practice with our contact and, therefore, is analyzing our message and thus is unable to continue. We will, however, make one more try at exercising this channel, for we do wish to speak through him at this time. I am Hatonn.

(Pause)

(Don channeling)

I am again with this instrument, speaking through him in order to thrust him into my contact. It is somewhat difficult at this time for the instrument to regain the fluidity of contact after a period of *(inaudible)*. He does not practice the technique. I am at this time going to attempt to continue the communication.

It is unfortunate that the people of your planet take so long in becoming aware of the true nature of creation. Everything has been provided upon this planet for them … in order for them to become independently aware of the true nature of the creation.

The process … the necessary process must occur within an illusion such as yours. This [satisfaction] is completed. It's impossible for the individual to progress past that point. As I said, unfortunately a large percentage of the population of your planet at this time has made no progress past that point and is, indeed, not to the point of becoming aware of what I would call their situation in time and space. And they concluded … *(inaudible)* … nothing else is provided … *(inaudible)*.

It is definite. The greatest mystery is unfolded before you in a never-ending array. Clearly *(inaudible)* … people think … they miss the point for the most part. A smaller percentage is discovering *(inaudible)*. A larger percentage is still ignoring it. The real self-disciplined does notice the clues and has done something about them.

I have several suggestions: first, become very active in the application of the knowledge you have received about the mechanics of creation. This is a necessity … *(inaudible)* … be made. Only when this is done can, shall we say, more evidence be provided—the type of evidence that leads closer and closer to a total understanding of that which is true.

(Pause)

(Carla channeling)

I am with this instrument. I am Hatonn. I shall continue through this instrument.

As we were saying, there are suggestions for those who wish to follow the path taken by those who have noticed the clues given them by the Creator.

The second suggestion is that it is very productive to maintain a community of those who wish to follow this discipline together by means of meetings such as yours in as intensive a manner as you can comfortably and willingly fit into your schedules of work and activities.

One candle alone gives off great light in a dark universe, but the power of several of these candles is much greater than the added power. It is multiplied many times, my friends. Therefore, whenever you can, meditate in groups, speak in groups, work in groups along the lines which you feel to be important,

The word "family" has different meanings among different cultures, but you may think of those who are on the path of seeking as a family. And when you have gone down that path together, washed yourself clean in meditation together, and worked to the limit of your ability to help your fellow man, using the knowledge which you have gained together, then you are by far a closer family than can ever be made simply by means of legal and blood relationships.

Thirdly, we would suggest an overriding sense of beauty. We suggest this to you because we feel that it will aid you, even if you are not with a group at the time in which you need help. If you could look about you, the world of the Creator would give you beauty each and every time you look.

Fourthly, we ask you, as always, to maintain that level of detachment which ensures that you are as able to laugh at the comedy of life as it applies to yourself, as you are able to laugh at the comedy of life as it applies to others.

This detachment is a divine sense of humor which will lead you to a knowledge of the oneness of the universe. As you make your errors, so may you laugh and say, "There also am I." Thus, when you see the same error in others, you may nod and say again, "There also am I." Thus, we ask you to practice and share what you know, to constantly rejoin and refresh the inspiration that drives you forward by meeting with those of your own beliefs and pasts. We ask you to see beauty. We ask you to be detached from the folly of existence. These things we would suggest at this time.

We would leave this instrument for a short time, for there is a Confederation member who has not been with us for some time, but he has been requested. And so we will turn this meeting over to him. I am Hatonn.

(Pause)

I am Telonn, and I come to wish you love and light. I will work with you only for a very short time this evening, for I realize that you are somewhat fatigued.

Let us then, my friends, remove ourselves from the heavy physical shell in which we now reside and imagine a pure, brilliant, white glow in the center of the circle in which you now sit. It pulls you towards it, and in your spiritual body you enter it and become one.

(Pause)

I am Telonn, messenger of light. As you travel back to your body, I leave you. And yet I am always with you, and it is hoped by us that our vibration is of help to those who are in pain or are distraught mentally, for we are those of light. I will leave you now.

I am Telonn. Adonai.

(Pause)

I am Hatonn. I am with this instrument. We are attempting to lighten the contact with this instrument, for it is [in] very good condition this evening, and we are sending too strongly for the needs of this instrument. We have adjusted now to this instrument. We will only pause to open the meeting for questions at this time.

(Pause)

If there are no questions we will close. And at this time we would attempt to contact the one known as T, an instrument whom we have not used for some time. If he would appreciate our contact at this time, we would close this meeting through him. I am Hatonn.

(Pause)

(Carla channeling)

I am again with this instrument. We thank the one known as T for the opportunity to condition him. However, we find reservations in his mind at this time and, therefore, would wish to close through this channel.

As you know, we are here in love. We know, my friends, that you are here in love. Attempt, we ask you, to remove from your consciousness the over-mechanization of your culture, which seems to make so many things dead, and know that all things are alive, that the universe speaks with a single harmonious chord, and that each of you is an infinitely beautiful and perfect part of that chord, without which the universe would not be complete.

Vibrate as yourselves, my friends. You can do no more good than that. And love one another.

I leave you in the love and light of the infinite Creator. I am known to you as Hatonn. Adonai vasu borragus. ✣

Sunday Meditation
June 17, 1979

(Carla channeling)

I am Hatonn, and I greet you in the love and the light of the infinite Creator. It is a very great pleasure to greet each of you this evening, and we especially greet those who are new to this group and welcome you to our expression of love for your people.

We are aware that you are somewhat apprehensive, and thus we would like to pause at this time so that we may send you the energy that this instrument has called conditioning in order that you might feel more relaxed. We will pause at this time. I am Hatonn.

(Pause)

I am again with this instrument. We are grateful for your patience in deepening the contact. We now have good contact with this instrument and good harmony in the group.

This evening, we of the Confederation of Planets in Service to the Infinite Creator would like to share with you a little story which you may find interesting.

There are many trees, my friends, but this is the story of only one tree. As a small seed it was carried in the clothing of a not particularly cleanly fellow for several years—you might say in the cuff of his trousers. It was dark, and the seed would have liked to have grown, but it could not; the environment was not correct.

One day at the beach this small, winged seed fell from the cuff of the trousers of the man as he walked, and it lay there on the sand; and again it tried to grow, but it could not, for the conditions were not correct for its blossoming,

And one day a wind picked up the seed and carried it far, far inland, blowing it on the winds of change; and over this the seed had no conscious control. When it landed it saw the sun and felt beneath itself the grass, and the rains came and watered the grass, and the seedling put forth its tiny roots.

With infinite patience and with an instinctual awareness that time fulfills its purposes harmoniously, the small seed became buried, put forth young shoots, dropped its leaves, and began the process of living. As it grew, it gave off oxygen to the air, being of service to those beings who breathed that sweet and healthy substance, who lived nearby. Its harvest was collected. And the beauty of the tree, the delicacy of it in the spring, and the *(inaudible)* richness of its colors in the autumn made many stop to envision the beauty of nature.

We ask you to realize, my friends, that you do not have or should not have pride in your existence or your importance, for that which you are you are because of the winds of change working upon that which is instinctually yours. You, unlike the tree, my friends …

(Telephone rings. Pause while the call is attended to.)

I am with this instrument. I am known to you as Hatonn. We are very sorry for the interruption. However, we felt the one known as Carla would desire to receive the call which was just received; and therefore, we helped her to let her chore of turning off the phone slip from her. Due to her absent-mindedness, we find this very easy to accomplish with this instrument. I will continue at this time.

As we were saying, my friends, you as beings of conscious volition over your destiny are unlike the tree, which has a destiny without free will. Its wisdom is given it freely, and it reaches for the sun and is of service to the creation without hesitation or doubt.

Those of you who enjoy the density which you call Earth and are subject to the emotions and the difficulties of free will are aware that, in many cases, you cannot intellectually know that part of yourself which is the sum of all that you are. You are surrounded by a dense chemical illusion in which your true identity is rather well buried. But you are quite unique, each of you. There is no, shall we say, tree like unto you. And the winds that blow forever changeably must blow each of you to a different spot before it is the proper time for you to grow and come into your own as conscious servers of the creation.

You may think that you do not have the capacity as people to blossom and be of great use to each other; but I say unto you, my friends, it is as instinctual to you to turn towards the light and love of the Creator as it is for the tree. It is simply less easy for you to penetrate the busyness of your daily lives—the limitations and apparent difficulties—and find within yourselves that seed which is very simple; that seed is that part of you which is a unique vibration of love.

In order to reach that part of yourself, we believe that a good method—and surely the quickest method available to you—is daily meditation. Among your peoples this is considered a difficult thing to achieve, for there is, shall we say, no time. May we ask you, my friends, to make the time.

If you knew that there was a reward for an action a million times greater than that of money, or power, or sensual pleasure, would you not indeed then pursue a course of action in that general direction? Yet, this is what we say to your peoples. We ask them to awaken from their journey through power and money and the buffeting of the senses by good and bad feelings. And we ask them to take conscious control of that journey by realizing that they cannot direct their lives but only their selves—their inward and substantial selves—to not give a thought to where you are or to what conditions you may be in. From this point, my friends, seek the one simple truth of the Creator: your identity.

At this point I would like to transfer this contact to the one known as T. I am Hatonn.

(Pause)

(Carla channeling)

I am again with this instrument. We thank you for your patience, and we thank the one known as T for the opportunity to work with him. When an instrument has not practiced for some time, it is sometimes a little while before this type of service becomes easy again.

At this time I would like to open the meeting to questions.

(Pause)

H: I have a question. I keep reading in the literature—metaphysical literature, psychic literature—that there are seven levels, seven states of consciousness, seven heavens, or something of this sort. Is this a valid concept?

We are aware of the question. I am Hatonn. You are no doubt familiar with the concept of quantum mechanics and also with the octave which you may find on any piano.

There are in a major scale, as this instrument would put it, seven different notes, having a relationship to each other which is pleasant. And then there is an octave. In that octave there is an identity—top note with bottom and the tonality begins again. Thus it is with quanta, where you have just so much occurring within a quantum; and then there is a leap, shall we say, to another set of configurations.

There has often been in your culture the term "seventh heaven" heard, and it is only one of many popular beliefs that there is not only a heaven but that there are various heavens for those who have done various things,

Your rather primitive Christian dogma would limit one's heavens to two—one good and one bad—with a rather neutral zone in between for those who have not yet decided whether to be bad or good. This is not accurate.

There are, indeed, seven levels within the realm within the next dimension or quantum—from you. This plane has been called by Theosophists the astral plane. Beyond that quantum there is a further octave of seven, and that plane is sometimes called the devachanic. Beyond that plane there is another octave of seven, which is sometimes called spiritual by your people. Beyond that plane few among your peoples who are incarnate upon your planet have traveled.

There are an infinite number of octaves in the heavenly music. The number seven, however, is the number of completeness, for that is, shall we say, the scale of vibrations within each quantum.

Does this answer your question, my brother?

H: Yes, thank you—except I would like to know now in which octave or in which level of an octave are you?

Well, we are speaking only for ourselves, for we are only one of over 500 civilizations which take part in this operation concerning planet Earth, the planet of sadness, at this time.

We, ourselves, vibrate within the fifth octave. You vibrate within the third. There are many in the Confederation which vibrate in the sixth, and some in the fourth. We have three among our number who, though vibrating in the third dimension, have done so in such harmony that they are able to aid us in spite of the gross physical illusion that they are experiencing and are able to aid us by thought. So you see, my friends, your condition is not hopeless. Your bodies do not pin you down as specimens pinned under a glass table. It is your minds that imprison you by accepting the illusion. We ask you, therefore, to open your minds to the freedom of realizing that there are infinite illusions and that your imagination has the freedom and the right to play among them as at will.

H: Well, what did the Apostle Paul mean when he said he was caught up to the third heaven?

The octave directly above you is the fourth and is called by the one whom you call Paul, the apostle, the spiritual kingdom. There are seven levels to this kingdom and, as we have said, its modern or Theosophical term is astral. In this heavenly universe, that which is not apparent while you are in the physical body—namely, the reality of thought and the illusion of matter—become obvious. Thus, as Paul was caught up—depending on his vibration—into the matching portion of the spiritual kingdom, he was able to do that which in his physical body he desired to do most to do, which was to worship and praise the Creator.

Does this answer your question?

H: Yes, except I have one more. If we are in the third octave, what are the two octaves below us?

As you are well aware, when you have your television set upon channel 3, you cannot see channel 2. Thus, we cannot show you the first and second octaves of existence, except to say to you that in comparison to them yours is a much more interesting and beneficial octave—the second octave of existence being two-dimensional, shall we say, and the first existing as the birth place or point from which the great cycle of being begins.

H: That's all for now. Thank you very much. I'll leave it to others.

As you know, it is always we who are the thankers, for to share our thoughts with you is our only desire. Is there another question at this time?

Questioner: Yes, I have a question about reincarnation. Why is it, when we do not know anything about our former lives, and how, if we do not know these things, can we change direction? We do not know what took place before; we do not know what we have to learn and what we have experienced. So how can we … We are chasing around in the dark without knowing what it's all about. Why are these lives not known to us? Why is there not some light turned on these things?

We will attempt to explain to you the reason for a lack of memory of past experiences. Though it is not an easy concept, you must realize that you are not helpless but are, instead, a person of free will with the opportunity to meditate and to seek the kernel of love that lies within you at this time.

In previous existences, the experiences that you have had have generated within you certain biases. Thus, some people are born with native love, and others without it; some with native goodness, and others without it; some with great native intelligence, others with very little; some with great talent, others who seem quite ordinary.

These biases form the personality which you bring into this world. But other than that, you have the opportunity to begin wherever you are and become a loving being. This is the only test upon your level.

If you knew all that you have done before, your mind would be attempting to carry you through all of the lessons you had learned before. This is too much for the mind to deal with. It is enough that you have this incarnation to deal with. The fruits of former incarnations dwell within your spirit.

Again, we go back to meditation. If you have a difficult relationship or a difficult concept to conquer, meditate and request that light be given to you upon this subject. When you can say, "I have no past, and I have no future, but at this moment I hate no man. I love all beings and all those with whom I may have any score to settle, those things I have settled with," at this point you are beginning to be able to pass the great test of this vibration. It is a difficult one, and it is to show love in the darkness when you seem to be by yourself, not knowing that, in reality, those who love you on other planes of existence are all about you. Those who love you in this life but cannot speak are, without words, supporting you. All these things you cannot know; but, above all, you cannot know by mind alone that which must be given to you by direct intuition of the truth—the one simple truth, my friends, that we are all one and that we must love one another. Many of your masters have spoken to you of this, and we can only repeat it. It is the only lesson worth learning.

Past lifetimes? They are a kaleidoscope; they are you. But so are your future lifetimes. Imagine yourself as part of a great circle where consciousness dwells within this part of it at this time. But all that you must do at this time is meditate and seek the love of the Creator. And then, when you have it, send it forth. As we have said, this is not an easy concept.

Does this, in any way, begin to answer your question?

Questioner: Yes, thank you.

We thank you. Is there another question at this time?

(Pause)

If there are no more questions that you wish to ask at this time, I would like to attempt to close this meeting through the one known as E. I am Hatonn.

(Pause)

(Carla channeling)

I am again with this instrument. We had good contact with the one known as E, but she is very fatigued, and we feel that it is not, at this time, a good idea to use her. Therefore, we shall close through this instrument.

As you know, we are with you at any time that you may request our presence. We ask that you listen to the words of this channel with great discrimination, for we are not much wiser than you—but only a little. We ask that you take what you need.

And we thank you for allowing us to love each of you, for it is only by loving you that we can express our love of the infinite Creator. I leave you in His love, in His light.

I am known to you as Hatonn. It is my privilege to be with this group. Adonai, my friends. Adonai vasu borragus.

Intermediate Meeting
July 5, 1979

(Carla channeling)

I am Hatonn, and I greet each of you, my friends, in the love and the light of the infinite Creator. It is a great pleasure to greet each of you, especially those who are new to this group; for, indeed, it is not only our privilege but our only purpose to share with you our humble thoughts, that you may consider them in the discrimination of your own hearts to accept what is good and to discard that which does not appeal to you.

Tonight I would like to tell you a little story. Once upon a time, my friends, in one of your southern cities there came to be a very unusual creature. This creature had the body of an alligator but the wisdom of a man. Soon, those about him learned to treat him as a man. And he wore special shoes and special clothing and had a hat specially made for him, and learned to sit upright and eat his meals and hold his job and act in every way like a human would act.

One day as he was sitting on a bar stool of his favorite pub, watching the big game on the television set, a rather tipsy man stumbled and stepped upon his tail. Somewhat tipsy himself, the alligator was furious, and he whipped around and made to slay the poor unfortunate who had dared to step on his tail.

"I am sorry," said the drunken man, "but I did not see your tail."

"I do not have a tail," said the alligator with great fury, "for I am a man!" And again he made to lunge furiously at the poor man, who grabbed what he could off the bar, that being a large stick the bartender handed him, and rammed it into the alligator's throat, killing him.

As the alligator lay on the floor, dead, in his shoes and his clothes and his hat, the man said to him, "I may be drunk, but I know an alligator when I see one."

We ask you at this time, my friends, to consider this story in the context of your own personality. You must realize that within your own mind there lives a population of many creatures. Some are saintly—good and pure, kindly and compassionate; others are, perhaps, boring, over-intellectual. Some of your citizens may be too emotional, and a few may actually be beasts that you may not wish to face.

There are many negative emotions, which do not seem so negative on the plane which you now enjoy: greed is explained away as a means whereby produce is generated in the market place; ambition is explained as that which one must do in order to be of service to one's family, to one's children, or to one's best interest; selfishness, jealousy, and envy, all of these things, my friends, can be so easily explained away in your mind. You can clothe them in explanations—the hat, the coat, the shoes.

And so we charge you, in your meditations, first to find your alligator and to remove him, and then to meditate in quiet and humility, knowing that you are not unlike your brothers but very, very much the same. Let the citizens within you which are compassionate grow and spread their wings. This can be done, not by your efforts, my friend, but by meditation; not by conscious thought, my friend, but by intuition.

There is no time to be proud, my friend, to assert yourself as a good person or as a bad person. You are a person … you are the Creator, and you have all of the parts of the creation within you. As that is so, all men are your brothers; from the murderer to the saint, from the fool to the sage. Look past the citizenry of your emotions and find the heart of unity that lies beyond all of the paradoxes of human nature.

You are in this life. Your vision is blurred, and your steps are unsteady and this is for a reason. Come to understand the challenge of this illusion and the possibility of progress. Above all, come to understand that you will never know your progress; you can only continue meditating, seeking the Creator, and attempting to be a channel for His love and His light among men like yourself.

Although we are more advanced than you, we of Hatonn know that our thoughts are varied and are not always harmonious. The difference between us, my friend, is simply that we can see our thoughts. We have a reality in our density. Consequently, we have no chance to quarrel with our alligators. When they arise, we must deal with them without further ado.

We ask you to never fear what is inside yourself, but only to love it, for it, too, is the Creator.

I would at this time pause so that my brother, Laitos, may speak. I am Hatonn.

(Pause)

I am Laitos, and I greet you, as do my brothers and sisters, in the love and the light of the infinite Creator.

If you will be patient with me, I would like to work with some of those among you who desire conditioning at this time. I would like first to work with the one known as E. If she would allow us, we will condition the instrument known as E, and if she desires, we would speak a few words through her. I am Laitos.

(Pause)

(Carla channeling)

I am again with this instrument. I would like to thank the one known as E. We find that, although she is personally a willing and able channel, there are teachers of hers who desire that her tuning be not disturbed at this time, for she is working in other vibrations. Therefore, we will pass on at this time.

We would like to condition the one known as M and allow her to feel our contact. Although we will not attempt to speak to her, we would explain that this vibration may be helpful for healing or for a more peaceful meditation. I am Laitos.

(Pause)

(Carla channeling)

We have a good contact with the one known as K, and we would now attempt to say just a few words through her, if she would desire to be of service in this manner. I am Laitos.

(Pause)

(Carla channeling)

I am again with this instrument. The one known as K is somewhat nervous; however, our contact with her is excellent, and she is a strong channel. In fact, my friends, this is an excellent group and one in which we are most fortunate to work with.

At this time I would like to condition the one known as E, for she is in need of comfort at this time.

(Pause)

(Carla channeling)

We thank our sister, E, and would like now to condition the ones known as T and K, so that they may feel our contact and be strengthened in their meditations. I am Laitos.

(Pause)

(Carla channeling)

I am again with this instrument. At this time, if the one known as G would wish it, we would like to work with her. We are aware that she has some capability of visualizing our truer natures, which is pleasing to us, and we greet the one known as G. We would at this time, if in her free will she would request it, speak a few words through the instrument known as G. I am Laitos.

(Pause)

(Carla channeling)

We thank the one known as G and are aware that she is very fatigued. However, we have greatly appreciated the chance to work with her.

If the instrument known as H will speak freely, without analyzing his thoughts, we would like to close through H. I am Laitos.

(Pause)

(H channeling)

I am Laitos. Latwii was calling on this instrument earlier this evening, but he was afraid to speak.

I am Latwii. I am with this instrument, although he is on the verge of heart failure. I say this humorously. But he is very fearful that I will not give him words to speak. This is the first time he has spoken in this manner in public. However, we have been with this instrument for a long while. Although he was not aware of it, we have worked with him rather intensely subconsciously and in answer to his calls for help. But he was not aware that all he had to do was listen. He would call but not listen. Finally, he got the idea of listening and was able to hear us. Since that time, our messages have been to him directly, and he is doing very well as a receiver.

There is something I would like to say about how to become a channel. All you need do is relax and listen; and when you get an impression of our name or any word or phrase, acknowledge that word or phrase, and we will give you the next word or phrase. Sometimes, if you do not acknowledge, we will give you a brief preview of what is to come, but not usually, because this tends to confuse some [channels] rather than help.

So the key is: relax, be still, listen, acknowledge any impression you get by repeating it to yourself or, as in this case, out loud, and listen for the next impression. That is all there is to it. This channel will acknowledge that now. However, he would have you know something else.

When we were first able to come through to him, he had a tremendous ringing in his right ear. We stopped that. And, also, he had a large hole in his right eardrum, and we healed that. Why did we do this? Because this was interfering with his ability to receive us.

That is all for now. I thank you and wish you all well, and love and light. Adonai. I am Latwii.

(Pause, during which visitors entered the room.)

(Carla channeling)

I am Oxal, and I greet you in love and light. I greet those who have joined us, and I'm here for a specific purpose, for there is a question upon the mind of one who is here which shall not be voiced. But we feel that it is an important question, and, therefore, we would wish to deal with it at this time through this instrument, although we normally do not use this instrument, for she is a little too delicately tuned for our vibration.

It has been said in your holy works that [if] you deal with mediums and spiritists [it] is not good, for it may defile you; and this warning has deterred many from listening to the fount of inspiration within them, which exists for all of us.

May we ask you, then, if to listen to a spirit were to defile, what it was that Saul of Tarsus saw on the road to Damascus? Those about him saw only a light, which blinded the man, but in his blindness, Saul heard a voice.

We do not come to you as gods, as people, as individuals. We come to you as messengers of one consciousness. We hope, and we intend, that that consciousness is that of love, for that, my friends, is what the Creator is and what His Creation is made of: love—divine and perfect.

The words we speak are poor, and we may seem to be speaking through mediums, but we can only assure you, my friends, that far from attempting to defile, degrade, or undermine any sense of self you may have at this time, or any beliefs that you may treasure, we hope only to make available to you a realization of the love of the Creator. We come in love, we speak in love. We look into your hearts, and we see that you are love.

Let your lives be filled with this love, my friends. Let your eyes shine with the light, which is the wisdom engendered by divine love, and the world about you shall be warm in the coldest winter, and those who gather about you shall know not you but the

Creator. This is our hope for us and for you. Join us, my friends, in this place which you may call the heavenly realms, and [be] refreshed at the source of love. Come down again from this place into the world with open hands and open heart.

At this time I would open the meeting to questions. Does anyone have a question at this time? We ask you, please, to feel free to ask anything that you wish at this time.

(Pause)

N: I have a question. Do you have an idea of what percentage of souls on the Earth return—die and are reborn *(inaudible)*?

We are aware of your question, but we will find it less than simple to answer, for the soul which enters this vibration does not enter for one lifetime only, for the most part, but for a cycle of what you would call time, this cycle being approximately 3,000 of your years, according to our best estimates. As you must know, we are somewhat less than perfect in our approximations of your time. Thus, the probability that a person will reincarnate during a cycle is extremely high.

The percentage of those who are in physical bodies, as opposed to denser or more spiritualized bodies, at any given, shall we say, locus in space/time is approximately two percent. Thus, most of the souls in the reincarnational cycle, at any moment during that cycle, will be without a physical body. They will, however, be part of the consciousness of Earth. And it is this unseen and very strong influence which has caused the repetitive actions of your civilization in this cycle. For, unfortunately, your peoples have not made the progress which we had hoped but, instead, have repeated over and over again the cycles of war and intrigue for war which have marred the previous cycle and this one also.

Would you like to continue with your question?

N: Yes, I was wondering, if the cycle is 3,000 years, how many people will be going through the 3,000-year cycle together … or is it just scattered or are there, like, big groups that would start, say, approximately the same time and do a cycle, or just all mixed up as far as … I know you can't get real specific, but I was wondering about that.

I am Oxal. I am with this instrument. I am aware of your question. The pattern of reincarnation changes during a cycle, not only the minor cycle but also the greater cycles—the major cycle and master cycle.

Those of you in this room, for the most part, have met many times before, not simply in the last 3,000 years but prior to that time in the last 25,000 years, and there are a few who have met during the master cycle, which is approximately 76,000 of your years. These are all approximations, you understand.

Now, my friend, what occurs is that as a soul rises from the ignorance of the darkness of the beginning of a cycle, he begins to collect about himself or herself a series of relationships which begin to have a special meaning, due to emotion, which is one of the most powerful words in your language, because it deals with the only reality of your world. Those whom you love, those whom you have wronged in hate or envy—those souls you will meet again to again work out a destiny in which the lessons of love can be learned. Thus, by the end of the cycle, such as this one, you will find quite large groups of people gravitating together for a more or less known and specific purpose, which has been generated due to the lessons learned by each in conjunction with the others over a series of many incarnations.

Does this answer your question?

N: Yes, thank you.

We thank you, my brother. Is there another question at this time?

E: Yes *(inaudible)*. I have noticed with increasing regularity a very unusual phenomenon upon certain peoples' third eye—a symbol—and in particular Jimmy Carter, our president. And I was wondering if you could enlighten me about this symbol that I've seen on various people's foreheads? I started noting this about two years ago, and it's very evident to me, and I think if everyone would look closely they would see the cross that …

(Side one of the tape ends.)

(Carla channeling)

I am Oxal. I am deepening the state of meditation of this instrument so that she may better receive our words. If you will be patient. I am Oxal. I am with this instrument. I am aware of your question.

Yes, my sister, there is indeed a symbol which has begun to appear upon the so-called third-eye chakra of those in your society whose vision is already partially within the world to come. And by this we do not refer to the heavenly world which occurs after death but that which has often been referred to as the Golden Age.

That which seems to be a cross is actually four triangles or pyramids, arranged in such a way that they become a golden wheel which, like the sun, is an entrance into the fourth dimension of being.

There should be increasing changes, not only in this chakra but in the higher, or crown, chakra, and in the auras of many of your peoples at this time as they begin to become aware of what may be called the new vibration or the new age.

The old vibration is, shall we say, not dying an easy death. And in its final illness and decease, it may keep many of your people from seeing the opposite of that which seems so hopeless; for all spiritual truths are opposites.

However, the one known to you as Jimmy Carter, though burdened with great responsibility, is within his heart a true man of a new age, hampered by the realities of his present duties, yet full of an undying hope for the newness of life.

Does this answer your question, my sister?

E: Yes, thank you very much. May I ask you one other short one?

Please do, my sister.

E: What would be the significance of a heart as opposed to a cross on the third-eye chakra?

This normally has to do with the attempt of those among your peoples to be in contact with higher intelligences and, thus, to heal the Earth's brokenness. It is a healing and a loving sign and one which is recognized by many in the heavenly realms as being the sign of sacrifice and, through sacrifice, healing love. Thus, you will find a high vibration in people who carry this sign and, yet, a great desire on their part to deal with the world, as it is at this time, in a healing fashion.

We, ourselves, are attempting through many in the Confederation of Planets in the Service of the Infinite Creator to extend a heart symbol about the entire planet, thus shielding it from itself. And the only way we know to do [this,] without interfering with the free will of your peoples, is simply make this vibration available. Many of the teachers of your inner realms also work with this symbol. The vibration is rosy, warm and good.

Does this answer your question, my sister?

E: Yes, so graciously accepted. Thank you so very much. Thank you.

We are most appreciative that we are able to share our thoughts with you, my sister. Is there another question at this time?

N: I have another question. As far as karma goes, what makes somebody have to turn back, reincarnate again, to work out something that, you know, they didn't work out before? How major a situation does it have to be? Or is it with everything? Would it be as if you stepped on a bug, would you have to come back and make that up, you know, work it out or something, or is it just major things or minor things or … that's the question.

I am Oxal, and we are aware of your question. However, it is best to deal with karma not as your people have dealt with it—as lawyers, attempting to balance the case in court, or accountants attempting to total the debits and credits; for we are dealing here, not with actions, but with thought.

A person is as he thinks. That is reality. His actions are the fruits of his thoughts. There are accidents which do not carry karma, and there are seeming accidents which carry heavy karma, due to the fact that there was thought behind the action not evident to the world.

It is possible for you as a being at this very moment to forgive in your heart all those who have hurt you, with such strength that you may stop the karma forever for them. It is possible, also, for you to take the karma of others, but we do not advise this, for you have your own destiny to work out and that is enough of a job for you.

Thus, you are here to be a loving being. Those whom you meet may be accidents; they may be intentional; it does not matter, for this is the lifetime you are living now, and the actions which are the fruits of your thoughts at this time are the karma that you collect now.

As to canceling out the karma of your own previous mistakes, we can only suggest that you analyze each thought that you may have and find if it is positive, if it is of service to yourself or to another; if it is of disservice to yourself or to another; if it denies the

Creator; if it shuts out the sunlight; if it grasps illusion, unhappiness, want, limitation, need and pain as reality—stop and meditate on love. That is the end of karma, for the law of love is far greater than the law of cause and effect, just as the law of eternity is greater than the law of time and process.

Do not linger in the river of your life, but move onward to the sea, dissolving yourself in love. In this way, karma ceases to become your reality, and your love may be freely taken and freely given, with forgiveness to all men for all things.

Does this answer your question, my brother?

N: Yes, thank you.

Is there another question at this time?

(Pause)

If there are no more questions, we would like to close through the one known as N. I am Oxal.

(Pause)

(N channeling)

I am Oxal. I greet you all once again in love and light.

We feel it has been a great privilege this evening to be with you to answer some questions—some [vocalized] and some not.

My friends, as we view lives and happenings on your planet, we notice some seek love more than others; but in many, many cases the secret being to seek for a while the center more so—feel good, receive some knowledge, taste of oneness—and then become scattered, so to speak, and sidetracked, and then gradually come back to seriously seek again. It is a pattern which, as time goes on, the gaps between the seeking become shorter.

For those of you who have thoughts of oneness and love to surround you, even for a split second, you will never forget it. In that split second of *(inaudible)* is within you at all times. No matter how it may be covered up, eventually it will shine through.

Before I leave you I shall send you a loving vibration with the intention that you may feel the vibration. I leave you now in love and light. I am Oxal.

(Pause)

(Carla channeling)

I am Nona, and I speak only to say hello and farewell. We come, my friends, in love and light. We surround you, and we reach out to you. At any time that you wish us, please ask for the Confederation. We are always there as your guides and all those who are messengers of the Creator.

I am Nona. I bid you farewell and love. Adonai vasu borragus.

Advanced Meeting
July 11, 1979

(Carla channeling)

I am Telonn, and I greet you in the love and the light of the infinite Creator. We are very happy to be with your little group this evening, and we wish to work with you at this time if you would desire to work with us.

Visualize, if you will, a white globe of light that hovers in the center of the room in which you now dwell.

(Pause)

When you can clearly see in your mind's eye this globe of light, transfer your consciousness into the light until you can look back at yourself as you sit in meditation in the dim light of the room.

(Pause)

You may stabilize the globe at this time by realizing that the two of you have become one, and it is your will which will direct the light to wherever you may wish it to go.

(Pause)

With our consciousness protecting you now, slowly move the globe of light through the windows of the room in which you now sit, and up above the roof of the room in which you now sit, and up above the roof of your dwelling.

(Pause)

Look down now upon the quiet house that you have left, and then speed quickly away from the gravity of Earth, through the overcast.

(Pause)

Now you begin to see the rounded shape of the Earth beneath you. Keep your globe stable, and look for a moment at the spinning, beautiful planet which you have now left.

(Pause)

We ask you now to visualize a triangle, moving toward us, away from the Earth. It is green. It seems like a great eye. Move through the eye. Feel the sensation of great speed. You are out the other side. You are in the next dimension.

(Pause)

What do you see, my friends? All that is about you is very bright. The sky is no longer dark. Now you perceive one coming toward you—a watchman of this density.

Remain stable in your globe, and allow him to sense your vibration.

(Pause)

You may greet him now, if you wish, with your thoughts.

(Pause)

Let us travel back now toward the Earth in this density, for we have been cleared for travel in this density at this time.

(Pause)

The Earth is no longer a blue planet with white clouds, is it not, my friends? It is, indeed, a rainbow of colors.

(Pause)

Can you feel any gravitational pull in this density? You should be completely free of movement.

(Pause)

Do not go too close to the darker colors of this environment; they are the dwelling places of thought forms of those among your peoples who are less than fully positive in their thinking. But observe the reality of these thought forms, the activity of the colors, and know that your thoughts are never lost, just as energy can never be lost. Your thoughts are the equation of the next dimension.

(Pause)

Move now into the realms of higher and lovelier light.

(Pause)

We are aware that you are enjoying these realms; for these are the realms of sweet thoughts and kindly deeds, and beings who vibrate in this level dwell therein.

(Pause)

We feel that it is time now for you to return, for we wish to make sure that our protection of you is complete; therefore, we must limit this visit.

Allow yourself to be pulled back through the eye.

(Pause)

You now see the night and the night sky.

(Pause)

Now let the magnetism of your body pull the globe—not too fast—very steadily.

(Pause)

The globe is now with you in the room, and you can see your quiet figures again.

Say goodbye to your unity for now, and partake again of the separation of the physical body.

(Pause)

I am Telonn. I am a messenger of infinity. It is our fervent hope that you and Telonn can enable those of you who desire it to experience higher realms of consciousness and to seek them through your daily life.

I leave you in love and the many varieties and gradations of light—the light of the Creator, my friends. Adonai.

(Pause)

I am Hatonn, and I greet you in love and light. We do not wish to speak for long this evening. We only wish to communicate to this instrument our thanks to you for allowing us to be with you and to send our love.

We have no esoteric message to deliver, for our truth is the same, whether it be said in simplicity or with the greatest of intellectual complexity. We are a portion of the consciousness that is of single-minded determination to speak when asked of the Creator. Many among your peoples have had the same desire, and their information is always distorted. The master, as you call him—the teacher, as we call him—known to you as Jesus, is a perfect example of a man who wished to speak of the Creator, but whose words were so distorted that for a long stretch of your time millions of your people have worshipped a human being instead of the Creator. This was not the will of the one known as Jesus, for he came to fulfill the will of his Father, and so he said time and time again.

What is the will of the Father for your planet? It is very simple, my friends: it is that it may evolve. We do not speak of a Darwinian evolution where the fittest survive, and the weaker are destroyed. Indeed, my friends, it is the very opposite that is true. In spiritual evolution it is the weak that survive and the strong and hard-headed who go down in confusion and must repeat again the cycle of lessons that have to do with loving one another. Loving takes a type of strength that is known among your peoples as weakness. Loving is serving. Loving is not caring what is done to you in return for your love, and such humility is difficult, indeed, to accomplish. In a culture such as yours, where each person demands his rights and each action seems to demand its reward, the act of pure love implies a total disregard of reward. This seems to others to be weakness, You become known as a doormat, as a pushover. Count these things as blessings, my friends. When someone says to you, "You are not liberated," silently give thanks that you are at least trying to be loving rather than demanding.

We are not suggesting that this path is not without its rewards; the rewards are simply personal. The rewards are the satisfaction of seeing an improvement in your state of mind, a raising of your state of contentment and nonchalance about what others may think of you or what you should be doing. You should be doing, my friends, that which in your instantaneous evaluations from moment to moment is of service and of love and of real value to others.

Those who love themselves and love others—those are the rich peoples of your planet. We send you confidence and peace at this time that you may be among those who are in touch with the reality of love, and, experiencing it yourself you share it with others.

We are aware that you will be misunderstood, that you may be found to be cold because you have not given the expected response. We ask that you not allow the vicissitudes of your daily life to influence your attempt to learn to be a loving being.

Love yourself, your circumstances, your troubles, your pleasures, your friends and your enemies, your catastrophes, and your triumphs with a grand and careless equality, and you will find yourself to be on key, on balance, and able to act without selfishness and without foolishness in any situation.

How can you do this, my friends? As always, meditate. And in your daily meditations center yourselves upon that love which, like a gyroscope, keeps you from being tumbled about in this world of illusion that you call Earth.

I am very grateful for the opportunity to have spoken with you this evening. I will pause only to ask if there are any questions.

(Pause)

I am again with this instrument. We caution you once more: in the hierarchy of obedience, be obedient first to that which you feel is correct. If you are meditating each day, your feelings are more trustworthy than the opinions of others.

We are always with you, and we send you our love. I am known to you as Hatonn. Adonai vasu borragus. ❦

Senior Citizens Meeting
July 14, 1979

(E channeling)

A charge to keep I have to serve the present age. God of grace, God of Glory, on Thy people pour Thy power. Crown Thine ancient churches *(inaudible)*. Bring her bud to glorious flower. Grant us wisdom. Grant us courage for the facing of this hour. Amen.

Questioner: *(Inaudible).*

(Carla channeling)

I am Hatonn, and I greet you each in the love and the light of the infinite Creator. It gives me special pleasure to greet the one known as L and the one known as E, for we have not spoken through instruments to these sisters for some time, although, as you know, we are always with you if you desire our vibration.

As we look at the vibration of your world at this time, we are sure that you are aware that we are seeing a darkening of the vibration, due to an increase in negative emotion felt among your peoples toward each other and even toward themselves.

It has sometimes been said that ignorance is bliss; this is a saying among your peoples. And when you are dealing with a spiritual journey, this is very true; for knowledge carries with it a great responsibility. That which is known and not practiced reflects itself upon the knower, so that he must again know that which he has already learned. This is the price of knowledge, my friends—that you practice what you know.

You need several ingredients in order to be able to do this well. In meditation you can deepen several of these ingredients. The first and most important is confidence—the kind of confidence that comes from knowing who you are. Have you ever, my friends, in meditation felt all the parts of yourself finally come into alignment with your highest goals and your deepest beliefs? By centering yourself in meditation, by finding that within you which vibrates in love and seeks the light of the Creator, you can find a quietness and a peacefulness that you can then use in the somewhat hectic and chaotic world that you find about you.

It is true that not all of your problems are large. You do not have to decide the fate of nations, but your vibration on an individual basis is as important, as vital, and as necessary to the salvation of your planetary consciousness as is the vibration of kings and heads of state. You do not move armies with your commands but can you command yourself? My friends, this is perhaps the hardest thing to do of all the tasks that you have been given in this experience. So many things occur which cause you to lose yourself; and instead, you act in a way which you yourself would not approve of, were you in control, were you conscious of your behavior.

As you come out of meditation, then, this confidence that you have gathered therein becomes your armor.

(Telephone rings. Pause while the call is attended to.)

I am with the instrument. I am Hatonn, and again I greet you in love and light. We apologize for the delay. We will continue through this instrument.

As we were saying, the confidence which you have gathered in meditation becomes your armor, and it is as though you are wearing a cloak of light through which no negative vibration may pass. Thus, you do not need to react to irritating, angry and other negative statements from others. Circumstances cannot penetrate the confident one who moves in power. This confidence is, indeed, the most important benefit which you receive from meditation. There are others, and you may find them as you proceed along the path of seeking. You may find yourself deepening as a person, becoming more able to understand the problems of others and finding that you are an ear, which is requested many times by others, for they sense in you a deep understanding. In this way you are of service to your brothers and sisters. You may find the gift of laughter, which is not easy to come by in a daily life which can be so easily filled with difficulties. As your character grows deeper and your knowledge more centered, you begin to see the divine comedy of your existence—the delightful balance of lessons and experience. You cease looking for happiness, and you become divinely happy, whatever your circumstances may be. In short, my friends, you slowly become a generator of your own experience rather than the recipient of other people's experiences of the world view, which is so often negative. In this way only can you aid your planet at this rather dark hour.

We thank you for allowing us to speak to you through this instrument and [for] supporting her and us with your vibrations at this time. It is a great privilege to share our thoughts with you.

At this time we would pause while our brother, Laitos, moves about the room, offering each of you the conditioning wave of our vibration. I am Hatonn.

(Pause)

I am Hatonn, and I am with this instrument only to ask if you have any questions at this time. Please ask them now if you do.

(Pause)

If there are no questions at this time that you would ask, I will leave you in the love and the light of the infinite Creator. I am only a voice through this instrument, known to you as Hatonn; but I and my people send to you the love that we have in abundance from the Creator to you. We leave you in that love and that light, which is not ours but the Creator's, and bless each of you. Adonai, my friends. Adonai vasu. ☥

Intermediate Meeting
July 19, 1979

(Carla channeling)

I am Hatonn, and I am with this instrument through the grace of all present, and we send you blessings and thanks for allowing us in your midst this evening. May we greet each of you and send you our love?

We ask you tonight, my friends, about treasure. We are aware that the treasure that is in your heart is sometimes buried. It has been written in your holy works, "Where your treasure is, there shall your heart be also." And yet we say to you, my friends, that your heart may contain any treasure which you desire. Thus, the question of treasure is far more the question of your buried desire.

We wish to speak with you only for a very short time this evening, but we wish very much, very much to encourage you to desire, with the greatest intensity possible, that which you wish to desire. Have you desired? Have you desired, this day, well, my friends? Have you had small desires easily satisfied? Have you glanced up into the lovely imperium arches of your heavens during this day and sought and dreamt and hoped—those desires which make men into beings who are claiming their birthright? That is what lies between you and the birthright of love and light—which you brought into this illusion—your inability to remember to desire it. That is all that separates you from infinite love, infinite light, and the power of a consciousness which these understandings can coordinate and enable. What have you desired today, my friends? We ask you in the name of the Creator.

At this time we would pause so that the one known as Laitos may pass among you.

(Pause, then the group chants "om.")

I am Laitos, and I am with this instrument, with thanks to my sister of Hatonn. We *(inaudible)*. We should ask this instrument to realign and retune the group, due to the addition of your sister and brother, and we feel most happy with the harmony of your circle at this time.

We would like at this time to condition and send healing to the one known as E. I am Laitos.

(Pause)

I am again with this instrument. We have been working with each of you during the pause. However, we wished especially to work with the one known as E, who is in some discomfort at this time. We would now like to do some more work with the one known as L, if she will relax. I am Laitos.

(Pause)

I am again with this instrument. We would now like to send our vibrations to the one known as H1. I am Laitos.

(Pause)

I am again with this instrument. If the instrument known as N would open his self to our contact, we would like to close through the one known as N. I am Laitos.

(Pause)

(N channeling)

I am Laitos. I am now with this instrument. My friends, as we view the souls on your planet, we yearn sometimes to reach out and aid directly *(inaudible)* to help, but we know we must not; for the will of the infinite Creator does not work that way at this time. We see millions of people evolving, and we know that eventually they will all attain a state of higher consciousness. We are sorrowed by the pain we see, though we know there is a great plan. We know that deep within each of you there is a higher state of consciousness and that each of you, in reality, control your own destiny; for you have willed it so.

My friends, we send you our love. We are with you always. Your time upon this planet is just an instant, as we see it, but it is a valuable … We love you, and we leave you in the light and love. We will attempt to make our vibration known to you at this time, if you will open yourself to it. We would describe it as … a pleasant sort of feeling.

I leave you now in the light and love. I am Laitos. Adonai vasu borragus.

(Pause)

(Carla channeling)

I am Latwii. I greet you in the love and the light of the infinite Creator and am most appreciative of your desire to hear my babbling remarks once again *(humorously)*. Therefore, since you have asked us to be here we are very delighted to be with you this evening; and, indeed, we are most sincere in sending you our love. We have come to answer questions at this time. If there are any among you, we greatly encourage you to ask them.

N: I have a question that I would like you to kind of comment on, but I don't want to say what the question is; so if you feel like attempting that I would appreciate it.

(Pause)

If we would allow our imagination to run free, we would tell you that the answer is no. However, we will attempt to be more responsible than that: we ask that you wait, for in waiting, that plan which our brother has spoken of in this meeting will come to fruition. The forces which surround a moment of time, as you call it, are very questionable and variable, and a simple waiting is often a catalyst for change. Does this answer your question, my brother?

N: Yes, thank you.

We thank you. Is there another question at this time?

(Pause)

H2: Yes, I have a question. Several weeks ago, in response to one of my questions, you said that we or mankind was seeded on this planet, and yet we had nothing to say about that—we had no choice in the matter. Why was that so?

What can I tell you, my brother? None of us have a choice; we are all the Creator. The condition of creation exists; it will exist infinitely. We are in a position in one of the infinite universes of the infinite creation, not due to chance, but due to the cycles with which you have become involved as you pass through the many universes of the Father's creation. You begin in darkness, if beginning is a possibility; of this we are not sure. We are sure, however, that like travelers your eye is caught by a pretty color, and off you go into an illusion that is that color of being. And so you have been attracted to this illusion and ultimately to this incarnation. You are the Creator. You do not have a choice—none of us do. Yet you have infinite choice in the amount of time it takes you and the way in which you wish to articulate your creator-ness. Thus, the paradox which is the necessity of spiritual truth is satisfied. You have no free will, and you have complete free will. You have been seeded by your choice. There is no mysterious and possibly questionable moral gardener who has seeded Earth. The gardeners are you yourselves—not trapped in time and space but delighted, instead, by the color of this creation.

Does this answer your question?

H2: Partially. Paradoxes are a puzzle to me. Do I understand you to say that we had no choice in being created, yet we had a choice in coming here?

That is not precisely correct. You were not created. You are the Creator. You are a portion of all that there is. You are a portion of no time and no space. Consequently, you are not a created being. You are Creator and creation. With that concept under control, we may say to the second part of your question that you do have that portion correctly understood.

Paradoxes, of which you spoke earlier, are an absolute necessity if one is to advance spiritually. If you are not facing a paradox at this time, then you are not trying. Thus, you must at all times be involved in a puzzle. We hope only that the puzzle is worthwhile, that you are pressing ahead from paradox to paradox so that you begin to live what you cannot understand; this, you understand.

How are we doing with you now, my brother?

H2: Better. I also think I have come up against another paradox; and that is, if there is reincarnation, and if there is no time, and all is one, and all is now, then all past lives, present lives, and future lives are now. If this is so, then how is it that in past lives some of us—or at least someone—lived in magnificent structures, ruins of which stand today, and we see them as ruins? If all is now, all in a living instant, how is it that those in centuries past are living there now, yet we see these marvelous structures as ruins?

If you will pardon us, we must take a few seconds to align this instrument, for she is becoming *(inaudible)* to the intensity of our vibrations. I am Latwii. I am Latwii. I am with this instrument. I am with this instrument. We have better contact now. We thank you for your patience.

In answer to your question, my brother, perhaps the most intelligible answer has to do with a rather tired cliché from this instrument's mind; she is familiar with it many times over. Take a piece of living tissue from your thumb and look at it under a microscope—look at it under an intensely strong microscope. Ultimately, under the atomic microscope, you can begin to see the creation—the galaxies, the solar systems, the planets. There are beings on your thumb. How long do you think their lives are, in your time? How many civilizations pass while that cell that is a universe is spending itself as a living part of your being? And when it is sloughed off in a giant nova, when the explosion that ends all life occurs, what infinity do you think has taken place for those beings? What ruins have been built and lost? What Romes, what United States, what Chinas have come and gone?

You yourselves are in time and space that is far less slow, shall we say, relatively speaking, than many universes. The universes of the creation are infinite in their differences. There is one uniting truth, and that is that beyond time and beyond space lies unity. You live in a *(inaudible)*; this is an illusion. The illusion can be manipulated by those who understand it. Thus, we ourselves travel in no time. Some among your peoples have been able to master various dimensions beyond time and space. No one understands this. However, there *is* only now. The problem is that this now is within the understanding only of those who do not have a watch and do not know time. Now is now. You experience now and another now and another. It is as though you were standing on a wheel and going round and round. Could you but stand in the center of the wheel, you might turn, but you would not go anywhere. It is in the state of now that information, such as some of your most famous mediums have had access to, is stored. By some, this place is called, locally, the Akashic Record. This is possible because all times are truly one. You are not living in a straight line; you are living in a circle. The beginning is your ending, and there is no beginning or ending.

Does this even begin to answer your question, my brother?

H2: It doesn't help me understand, and it doesn't help me understand how my camera records this illusion of the Parthenon standing there in ruins, yet at one time Socrates and others were there when it was in all its glory. The thing that bothers me about this … maybe it's unanswerable … is that if all is now, and the Parthenon is now there, Socrates is there and other of his Greek comrades in the living now, and yet I have been there in the living now and it is a ruins, and my camera said it is a ruins also. Does my camera have illusions also?

Your camera is part of the illusion which you now enjoy. We must distinguish between your now now and your other now. You are living in a now now, something like a muu muu, and it is only so so *(said humorously)*. Consequently, in order to understand now you must live in another now, in that other now you may see what you wish to see and really understand what you want to understand, but you cannot be in the now now—you cannot do both. Thus, this illusion is to you a lesson time in which that which is an illusion appears real.

It may be of interest to you to remember that if a physicist were to describe the Parthenon either in ruins or in its original form, he would describe a structure of space. There are great differences among physicists, but it is agreed that there is either almost no mass or no mass at all to any physical structure, including human beings, but rather a series of magnetic fields. Therefore, logically, one could put one's hand through a Parthenon, a person, a table, a building, or whatever one wished to put one's hand through. However, in the now now it is impossible, and your camera is part of the now now. You have many indications in the now now of those who are not within the now now, and those people walk right through everything, thus indicating to you that the now now is not the only now.

Does *this* help, my brother?

H2: *Now* it helps some.

Now we are glad! Is there another question at this time?

H2: I have another question, since you're here, Latwii. It's something you said several weeks ago, when you were talking about the color green and its filling a room in which we dwelled in another part—not here but somewhere else—and you also said that you were enjoying our fifth dimension—I assume the vibration of our fifth dimension. Does that mean that we exist elsewhere as well as here?

It is not a question of location, my brother, for the dimensions are interpenetrating. However, you exist in denser and denser vibrations, according to your abilities. All of you exist into the fourth dimension, and there are adepts among you who are working at this time, actively, in the fifth dimension and are attempting to understand some of the teachings of the inner realms of the sixth dimension. There are a few people who work as far as the eighth, but there are two within this room who have seen it in visions and are aware of its nature, although they could not maintain it for any length of time. This is the octave of your universe, and these are the dimensions of that octave. To go beyond that, you must be free of your chemical body; and therefore we are talking to a roomful of those who are not going to be doing that any time terribly soon; however, there are many, many infinities to explore within those dimensions and much wisdom to learn. Therefore, we urge you onward; for the path becomes lighter, the teachings truer, and the laughter happier.

Did you wish to know about green, or was that the essence of your question?

H2: Green?

Green.

H2: No. You just mentioned the color green, and that was a reference point.

Ah, yes. Green is simply an important color for this particular group, due to the fact that it has healing properties, and there are many in this group who can use them. Therefore, we were attempting to surround you with that vibration.

Is there another question?

H2: Since we were talking about other existences and everything being now, is it possible there is another me living across the street from me or somewhere else on this planet as of now or several other me's?

You are, my brother, in this particular universe, a time traveler but not a space traveler. Thus, you live each of your lives simultaneously, but you are not in the same space with yourself. However, in order to be aware of the past or future you must reach an altered state of consciousness, and this should be done only with the proper respect for knowledge. Knowledge, as we have said to you before, entails responsibility.

H2: Are you trying to give me a message about responsibility?

The message is general, my brother, and not for you alone, and it is simple; that is, if you know it and do not act it, the backlash effect will be hurtful to you; thus, you will begin to know it truly. That is the law of knowledge of the spiritual kind.

H2: Thank you very much, and I also thank the group for my taking this time.

(Pause)

We were drawn here by the one known as E, and thus we would at this time ask her if she would wish to voice her question to us?

(E had left the room.)

I am Latwii. We are sad that our sister is not here to ask the question, for we do not wish to answer in her absence. Are there any other questions at this time?

H1: I have a question. This is about channeling. I have pretty much given up on the idea of being a vocal channel, and I have begun to feel that if I could paint, along with a fellow trying to learn *(inaudible)*. There are certain images and concepts that I get that are in color and form and have movement that I think I could express through those two mediums. I was wondering if I could get any type of conditioning that the verbal channels get.

I am with the instrument. Yes, indeed, my sister. You can get as much conditioning as you need, and to ask for it is to receive it. We would suggest that you request the presence of two of the Confederation whom this group has known for some time: the vibration of Laitos, which is the basic conditioning vibration, and the vibration of Nona, which is an extremely sensitive vibration and one oriented more than most of the Confederation toward that part of love which expresses itself in art and beauty. Thus, this instrument requests the presence of Nona when she wishes to sing, and those who are involved in the arts will do well to request those two vibrations as good underliners to your own natural talent. You understand that we could not work with you did you not already have a good deal of ability in the area of conceptualization, abstract thinking, and the desire to be a channel for the love and the light of the Creator. With these things in your heart and in your character, you can then make full use of the Confederation. We wish you great good fortune, my sister, with your endeavor.

Well, my friends, is there another question at this time?

(Pause)

Questioner: I have one. I am getting ready to open up to a deeper level in my own channeling. I think you can tune in to what I'm referring to. I'm wondering if there is anything that you all might be able to do at this time that would help me to do this.

(Pause)

We would at this time be glad to send you an image which will appear to your inner eye, where it is not infringing upon your free will but only aiding …

(Side one of the tape ends.)

(Carla channeling)

Let us define this image for you now. Make it sharper. This is a key to that level which you may trust. We would also say to you at that time that you may carefully watch the next level beyond that, for this is not necessary for you to enter at this time; and the, shall we say, expansive or … we are giving this instrument a concept she cannot express. We are working with her … Within the next dimension there is a spreading of the personality which we would not recommend. Therefore, if you feel the next vibration beginning to disperse your personality through the universe, we would suggest that you pull yourself back from that realization, for it is not yet time for you to be able to use the knowledge which you would gain in that work.

May we help you further, my sister?

L: I appreciate what you've given. Thank you.

We are most grateful to be of service. Is there another question at this time?

K: I have a question. Is it helpful for us to be aware of other lives and other incarnations from the standpoint of spiritual development? If so, how do we do this?

This is a difficult question for us to answer, because we do not know what triggers the spiritual development of any being. It is usually not at all valuable, as his being spiritually, to know his past incarnations. Normally, what is powerful to the individual is to be in the presence of someone who is happy, who has something that the searcher does not have, who suggests something that the seeker might not know. This is why we speak through these instruments—to attempt to inspire, stretch curiosity, cause you to arouse your own instinct for progress.

Unfortunately, it has become a fad among your people to discover who they were in past lives. If you have a specific personality conflict with another being, it is sometimes helpful—not in the spiritual realm but in the realm of human relationships—to go back to the previous experience and discover what it is that you are reaping in this incarnation as a result of actions in the past, However, if you can learn the art of forgiveness, you do not need to know what it was that somebody did to somebody else. If you can ask forgiveness with all your heart and forgive with all your heart, you have broken the laws of karma. Thus, you have no need of knowledge of an esoteric or occult type.

Unfortunately, this type of information has often been misused, due to the rule we were explaining earlier that knowledge implies responsibility. Thus, if you know what your lesson is and still refrain from learning it, your lesson becomes harder and harder until, as a matter of survival, you must learn it. To make it easy upon yourself, explore the possibilities of love in this incarnation, in this moment, at this time, with these people, in this environment, in this illusion, before you begin working with previous lifetimes. For it is in this life that you have the opportunity, at this moment, to take conscious control of your destiny and to speed yourself on your journey toward the light which you now invoke in this meeting.

Does this answer your question, my brother?

K: Yes, it does. Thank you.

As always, we thank the questioners, for we could not say a word if you did not ask us your questions. Is there another at this time?

(Pause)

K: I have one. During the day, sometimes I'll think about you all. Sometimes I'll ask questions, but I don't … you know … I don't hear the answer, but I can't think of an answer. Are you all listening when I think about you?

We are checking the computers at this time … one moment. The one known as Laitos is with you at all times when you ask your questions. Laitos is the easiest of the Confederation to, shall we say, hear conceptually. At this time you are not picking up the concept. However, if you persist in daily meditations, you will begin to receive impressions. They will not be, or usually are not, in words. You will simply get an impression. Or you may go to sleep and awaken with an impression.

We cannot work more closely with those who seek our advice than the conscious intellect allows. We find your vibration to be one of a strongly logical and commonsense type. This, I am afraid, my sister, is not a very easy vibration to enter, due to the fact that your common sense tells you that you are asking questions of thin air. Thus, we encourage you to ask your questions, and one day you will begin to feel the concept of the presence of the one known as Laitos. We must say, however, that sometimes when the questioner is alone, the answer will simply be a feeling of presence, due to the fact that the power of the individual is not strong enough to warrant a stronger impression. Also, some questions are not answerable, due to our desire not to infringe upon free will. However, the one known as Laitos is there with you when you mentally request his presence. We hope that you will gradually become aware and be comforted by the presence of that kindly vibration.

Does this answer your question, my sister?

K: Yes, thank you.

We thank you. May we ask for another question at this time?

(Pause)

I am going to leave this instrument, for she is becoming fatigued, and if the one known as H2 wishes, we will close the meeting through him. I am Latwii.

(Pause)

(H2 channeling)

I am Latwii. I am with this instrument. I hope he will relax more. I promise not to hurt you.

You have been wondering why I have not talked with you since the last meeting. You are too anxious. You want too much. You must learn to accept what comes to you. Oxal is your main contact.

We would speak to the group about the advisability of learning how to cope with general problems of daily living in a spirit of love. We hope you can keep in mind that we are with you. When I say "with you," I mean someone of us. And we are with you in love, and we will do whatever we can to aid you. By "can," I mean what is lawful for us.

Your hopes for betterment are not in vain. You will evolve in betterment in some time frame, because it is your destiny. You can help it to be now, or—if you must in your own pursuits—it can be any time later. Let it be now, my friends. We do love you. We care for you. We send you love and light.

I am Latwii. Adonai vasu borragus. ☙

L/L Research

L/L Research is a subsidiary of Rock Creek Research & Development Laboratories, Inc.

P.O. Box 5195
Louisville, KY 40255-0195

www.llresearch.org

Rock Creek is a non-profit corporation dedicated to discovering and sharing information which may aid in the spiritual evolution of humankind.

ABOUT THE CONTENTS OF THIS TRANSCRIPT: This telepathic channeling has been taken from transcriptions of the weekly study and meditation meetings of the Rock Creek Research & Development Laboratories and L/L Research. It is offered in the hope that it may be useful to you. As the Confederation entities always make a point of saying, please use your discrimination and judgment in assessing this material. If something rings true to you, fine. If something does not resonate, please leave it behind, for neither we nor those of the Confederation would wish to be a stumbling block for any.

CAVEAT: This transcript is being published by L/L Research in a not yet final form. It has, however, been edited and any obvious errors have been corrected. When it is in a final form, this caveat will be removed.

© 2009 L/L RESEARCH

Advanced Meeting
July 26, 1979

(Carla channeling)

I am Hatonn, and I greet you, my friends, in the love and the light of the infinite Creator. As always, it is our privilege to speak with you, and we thank you for inviting us into the midst of your group.

We share our thoughts with you, insubstantial though they may be, one life speaking to another, one brother speaking to another, for are our lives not like clouds as they cross the moon, visible only for a brief time, before and after lost in the darkness of the eternal heavens? Yet, we are now here, you and we, and it is with deep appreciation that we join our thoughts to yours in this transient moment.

Yes, my friends, your lives are very transient, and yet your spirit is indomitable. There is [nothing] that you cannot seek, nothing that you cannot will to know, if it be done honestly and courageously and without selfishness. And so even though your brief life may sometimes seem to be relatively meaningless, your activities mundane, your thinking confused, we say to you that if you can each day find some moments to meditate, to center your will upon the desire to know the love of the Creator, that wish for the original Thought will be unto you as a beacon, guiding your spirit far into the stormy seas of night when you have crossed the moon and there is no light.

We are sorry that we have had to delay our speaking to you this evening, but there was a desire in one of those present that we not speak. And this[6], my friends, is a perfect example of that which we deal with now: the transience of experience. There is a saying in one of your holy books, "All flesh is grass." We are not being mournful. We are attempting to be emphatic about the direct and important knowledge that you must have that you yourself are not your bodies, your pains and pleasures, or your experiences, but are instead a vibration which is temporarily and transiently housed in a chemical body. That vibration has certain characteristics which show forth to a greater or smaller amount in the physical amount in the physical body. Each characteristic shows forth as the degree of loving kindness of your nature, the degree of generosity, of compassion, of kindliness, that you have within your character. It may show forth in your ability to help people by healing, by the preparation of food, by working with your hands, by singing, or by telling stories, or by raising the young who are entrusted to your care that they, too, may know the Creator as do you. These biases come through from your vibratory personality into the physical illusion. However, you must not take this illusion any more seriously than you would take the passing of a cloud across the moon on a stormy night, such as this one. You know

---
[6] A storm was raging outside.

that there will be other clouds and other nights, other sequences of activities. These are unimportant. Your only important effort should be placed in centering yourself in the knowledge of the original Thought of the Creator, which is that of infinite love expressed in light. This light has formed all of His creatures: the planet in which you live, the skies which surround us in different vibrations. All things are light.

As you begin to have this ability to be detached from the transient experience and to be rooted in the knowledge of the original Thought, your power as a personality will develop, so that those circumstances which may seem to you to be inharmonious will of themselves become more harmonious, for your attitude will become such that nothing can disturb you.

I would pause at this time so that my brother, Laitos, may speak. I am Hatonn.

(Pause)

I am Laitos, and I greet you in the love and the light of the infinite Creator. If you will permit me, it will be my privilege to work with each of you. I would first condition this instrument, for she is experimenting with a deeper, shall we say, meditative state.

(Pause)

We thank the one known as Carla for working with us, and we find that she is more and more capable of working with the light vibration of some of your contacts, such as Latwii, due to her growing ability to deepen her meditative state.

We would now attempt to condition the one known as M. I am Laitos.

(Pause)

We thank the one known as M for working with us, and now we would like to condition the one known as J. I am Laitos.

(Pause)

I am again with this instrument. We thank each of you for being able to work with you. If we can help you to deepen your meditative state, that is our only desire among your peoples, for if we can but help the people of this planet to meditate and feel the oneness of all creation we will, indeed, my friends, have a part in the delivery of a tiny infant. That is the new age dawning upon your planet. At this time it needs all the midwifery that it can get.

Please ask for us at any time that you may wish for us to, shall we say, underscore your own meditative state. I am Laitos. Adonai.

(Pause)

I am Hatonn. I am again with this instrument. We are sorry for the delay, but the one known as Oxal was attempting to contact the instrument known as Carla. However, she was not able to perceive this. Therefore, we will continue for Oxal, saying to this instrument greetings from the one known as Oxal.

The one known as Oxal is concerned lest he be misunderstood in this group, for there has been in this group, shall we say, an impostor using his name. Therefore, the group consciousness of Oxal asks each of you to be in total at-one-ment at any time that the name of Oxal is heard in this group, for it is not wise to allow astral entities to deal with this group in its present configuration. We must explain that there is nothing intrinsically wrong with astral beings in general, but specifically mimicking a Confederation member by an astral being is very confusing to those who would believe the channeling of such beings. Thus, we ask your help in the future, as you call it, and we thank you.

At this time we would open the meeting to questions.

(Pause)

If there are no questions requested of us at this time, we would leave you with only a few thoughts, my friends.

You know that love is all that there is. You may think of it as the great medicine that is needed by your peoples. You may think of yourself as a healer, for the one who loves heals. There are different methods and different levels of healing, peacemaking and calming the troubled waters of your ever turbulent society. Among the millions of you who are incarnate on the planet Earth, some have the power to heal nations through what you call your politics. Some have the ability to heal the hunger for knowledge through what we call teaching. Some have the ability to heal sickness and ill health. Some can heal melancholy, some loneliness, but all work through the vibration of love. There is a great sea of love around you, my friends. Float on it, rest in it.

There is nowhere you can go that is not full of love, if you have but the eyes to see and the heart to understand. In meditation, may your hearts be opened to that understanding.

I leave you in the love and the light of the infinite Creator. I am of the group consciousness of Hatonn. Adonai vasu borragus.

Intermediate Meeting
August 2, 1979

(Carla channeling)

I am Hatonn, and I greet you in the love and the light of the infinite Creator. We, of the Confederation of Planets In the Service of the Infinite Creator, can greet you only with these words, for they describe all that there is, my friend—love and light; for the Creator is love, and it is our understanding that that love, working through motion, or vibration, or, as you may call it, light, has created all that there is in an infinite panoply of beauty and order and unity, so that we are all one divine and unified being, with but one purpose, my friend. And that purpose is to give back that which has been given us so freely.

And what is it that has been given us, my friend? For we are all so different, and so many different things have been given us. Yes, my friends, we are aware that your circumstances differ. Some may have more of a supply of worldly goods than others, some a greater supply of what you on your planet term the intellect, some a greater supply of strength, some a greater supply of courage; and, certainly, all feel they have a greater supply of difficulties and problems. But we are not speaking, my friends, of this one gift, when we speak of any of these, for these are not gifts at all, but limitations that you have chosen for this experience. What you have in common, my friends, is consciousness.

Could you but strip away the layers and layers of concept and illusion that furnish your mind, you would find that the original Thought in which you are molded is that of love made conscious of itself. Each of you, my friends, is love.

How can this be a practical piece of knowledge? How can you use this in your life? That is why we are in your skies at this time. That is why we are attempting to speak through instruments such as this one, to those people of your planet who are hungry for some words that make sense amidst so many words that do not.

All of you [are] aware of the transforming power of love. Each of you has seen it at one time or another—the touch of a hand, the difference a smile or a kind gesture might make to a stranger. And we say to you that there is a method by which you can tap into the infinity of the universal supply of this love. We do not say a great deal [about] the Creator to you, because we do not know about the Creator. We are, as you, fallible, imperfect, unsure—but a little surer than you, my friends, for in the vibration which we now enjoy we can see that our brothers are one with us, so that to do harm to them is only to do harm to ourselves. We cannot lie, for our thoughts are visible to those about us, just as your clothing is obvious to those about you. Our vibrations are visible; thus, there is no deception, and there can be no confusion between people. We no longer even have names, for we do not need them. We were aware of your conversation earlier about names, and it made us smile—for, indeed, in our society we do not need to name an individual, for each individual vibrates in a unique manner and could not possibly be mistaken for another person. Seeing the vibration that is based upon the great octave of love in each person, we thus love each person. But that is easy for us; it is not easy for you.

Through meditation on a daily basis the people of your planet—even though they are in the midst of incredible turmoil of one kind of another—can gradually erode and remove the illusion of that turmoil and discover that which is calm, peaceful and yet ever moving; that which is the fountain of love within each being.

We do not promise you great power, although some souls have been known to find great power through simple meditation. We do not promise great riches, although we can promise you that those who are aware of the moment receive what they need in that moment. We cannot promise you peace of mind, though you will constantly go back into the world. You cannot stay in meditation, unless you wish to stop learning. Coming from meditation with your heart full of love, it is then time to meet the world on its own terms, but with a smile on your lips in the face of that which may make you upset were you not centered in the awareness of yourself in this present moment, safe in a harbor of love that extends throughout the universe.

So many people you meet, my friends—and we are aware of this—are polarized, shall we say, in a negative way. This is not their fault. In their own minds they are trying as hard as they can. In their own minds they are not attempting to be negative, for the most part. They are victims of their own conditioning. And yet, when you meet them you must deal with them, whether they be in stores or in cars or among your friends when they are having a bad day. Even you yourself may be met by you the observer with some horror as you say to yourself, "Can that be me? Can I be this upset, this angry?" Let the part of you that has been found in meditation, that part which is infinite in love, be the self that meets that situation. Find the humor that is hiding in the situation. See the love that is hiding in the person, and make available to that person for the first time the seed of an idea—the idea that it might be possible that there is something that he does not know that he may want to know, that it might change him to know.

We do not say to speak, to testify—as some of your religions call it. No, my friends, you are sent into the world—as it is written in one of your holy works—as sowers to sow a seed here and a seed there. Many will fall where they will not grow. But the seeds of love are the most valuable and precious seeds in your universe. The Creator has sown them all about you; the beauty of the trees breathes with love, the wild life, the flowers, and all of your beautiful grasses, herbs and foods cherish humanity, make it possible for it to live and send it love. The very skies give you wind and rain and sunshine so that you may live and grow your crops and enjoy your existence. This much the Creator can do. Beyond that, you are the Creator, and it is the look in your eye or the touch of your hand or the way you can give love in an unlovely situation that produces the future crop of love in those about you.

And so we say to you, my friends, go into meditation in whatever fashion you may wish. Consciously ask to know the truth. If we have not told you the truth, then find yours, for we tell you only what we know, and we are imperfect. But in all good faith, we ask you to seek for yourself. And then, after you have sought in your daily life, seek then to know the moment—each simple, discreet moment. It will not come again—your chance to be a creature who is a child of love in that moment will not come again—so we ask you to remember from moment to moment what you have learned in the silence.

We are aware that we have outlined a course of action which, were it to be compared to a sea voyage, would be a lifetime voyage. That is all right, my friends. It is our understanding that it is for that voyage that you set out on this incarnation. At least, you are now thinking about taking ship. Some of you have already embarked. You shall become, then, those with the far-away eyes who can touch and help those upon the land who do not yet know that life is a voyage and that there is a purpose: a new world to be found at the end of it.

This experience of yours, my friends, in this illusion will end. Each of you will leave, and then you shall see what you have done in this experience. This is a precious time for you, my friends. This is a time when, under the most difficult of circumstances, you can try to help. That help can be given effectively only from one person to another, in the illusion.

We who are within what you might call the inner planes or the outer planes of existence can only seek to inspire you yourselves to act in such a way as to seek the truth.

At this time we will pause and condition each of those within the group. I am Hatonn.

(Pause)

I am again with this instrument. I am Hatonn, and I greet you once more in love and light. We thank each of you for making yourselves available to us for conditioning, and we ask that if, in any case, our vibration is too strong you simply request mentally that we adjust our vibration.

At this time we would open the meeting for questions.

(Pause)

M: I have a question. I was wondering if you have any insight or comments on any possible reason why I might have such problems getting up physical energy. I feel I exercise regularly and feel like my diet is fairly under control and still I feel almost like it must be some mental or psychic problem more than physical even, maybe.

I am Hatonn. I am aware of your question, my sister. We see in your body no significant difficulty. However, there is a certain amount of indecision at this time which is very deep. We do not specify this, for we do not wish to infringe upon your free will. However, this type of emotional difficulty is very common for those of, shall we say, a certain transitional period which comes and goes within the life span, as you would call it, of beings of your planet. It occurs many times in a lifetime, and we feel strongly in saying that you are, shall we say, all right and should be confident that the problems of transition will run their course as you stay centered, as you have said, physically, mentally and spiritually. Some things simply take time, as you would call it on your sphere, and it is good meanwhile to be very kind to yourself, assuring yourself that to have less energy than at another time is simply a way of conserving the energy that you need to meet an inner source of difficulty.

As for the psychic part of the question, there is a small component of the transitional phase having to do with previous conditioning of a spiritual nature, and we feel that you are making good progress in integrating what was best of that experience with what is best of your present life, which is a more balanced one in many ways. Thus, taking the good from the past and having every hope of the future, we feel that you may balance yourself in a period of what you call time and feel much more energetic when the other problems are resolved. At that point you will feel more *(inaudible)* in an outer way and more serene in an inner way.

As we have said, this is a cycle and, as all things within the illusion, it is part of an experience that you have designed for yourself in order to teach you certain lessons. Again, we would not infringe upon your free will by speaking of the lessons which you have set for yourself. But we know that you are working to understand, and we encourage you and, above all, ask that you be confident and not require more of yourself than you would be able to give at any particular moment. You are doing what you should if you do it with love, however little or however much it may seem to you.

Does this answer your question, my sister?

M: Yes. You've even stated the question better for me than I have; you heard my question better than I said. Thank you.

Oh, we thank you, my sister, as always, for the opportunity to share our thoughts. Is there another question at this time?

(Pause)

This instrument has a question which we will restate for her and answer, for she has been wanting to ask it; we have not had another channel for some time.

The question has to do with the number of UFO movies and television shows which are appearing at this time, and she has been wondering if we are influencing Earth people or if there are extraterrestrials among you.

The answer is, of course, that we are with each of you who ask to hear our thoughts but that there are some among you who have come through incarnation into this illusion, but whose basic personality is, shall we say, extra-terrestrial or extra-dimensional; this would probably be the more accurate term. And, indeed, the generation that is responsible for much of the new activity in these areas within the popular culture of your society is extra-dimensional in nature.

We are not capable, without infringing upon free will, of actually writing, shall we say, television scripts or influencing the minds of people in the business of producing such things to create such scripts as those which have been seen by your peoples. However, we are very pleased that so many of those who came to the Earth sphere during this time have remembered or are beginning subconsciously to remember why they came, for it is very usual in such cases for at least nine out of ten of these incarnated extra-dimensional people to forget for their entire incarnation why it is that they have such a feeling of not belonging, why it is that they do not fit in, why it is that their natures seem so often at odds with society.

We feel that this has answered the instrument's basic question. Is there another question at this time?

(Pause)

D: What could you all … do you see any value in using astrology as a tool to understanding cycles—the sort of cycles you spoke about earlier?

I am with the instrument. I am Hatonn. We are aware of your question. It is a difficult one to answer.

There are many occult sciences, shall we say, such as astrology, which have some use. They have been largely misused among your peoples as a way of prophesying, and this has overtones of infringing upon free will by suggestion. This is not in line with the law of the Creator, which is one of free will and love. Your world is not deterministic, and your stars, shall we say, are merely pointers pointing the way, as you know, to the basic structure of your Earthly personalities. You are also provided with a will which, following the laws of the Creator, can totally transform the basic Earthly personality, if it so desires; most often it does not. Therefore, the system or language, such as astrology, has its purpose in simply helping the aspiring student of himself to begin to understand what it is he is dealing with, what his basic problems are, what his assets might be, etc.

In the determination of cycles, we might compare the value of astrology to the value of an almanac in determining the planting and the reaping of a crop. There is some technical value to knowing what the new moon is, what the full moon is, but you must know what you plan to plant, and this astrology does not tell you any more than the almanac can tell you by a simple explanation of the phases of the moon. The almanac, like astrology, can be mistaken about the precise placement of storms, be they weather storms or storms of emotion that sweep over those in your illusion. Consequently, astrology, just like the almanac, can lead you astray if you are too literal-minded, if you do not rely most completely on your own hunches, on your own intuition, on your own feelings.

Perhaps the best use of astrology and many of the other disciplines, such as tarot, numerology, and the others, is as a focusing point, shall we say, for the psychic power of the individual. It may be quite small to begin with, but by working through this particular system, your own power of intuition begins to develop, and you see more than what is in the stars or in the cards or in the numbers, and you see better. You, unlike the stars, are creatures of compassion and love. The stars in their courses are, indeed, determined. You, my friends, have free will. Thus, we ask you to approach astrology as everything else, in a cautionary manner, trusting most reliably on your own senses, both outer and inner—your common sense and your intuitive sense.

Does this answer your question?

D: *(Inaudible)*.

Is there another question at this time?

(Pause)

We are aware of a couple of unasked questions in the minds of a few of you, but we are unwilling to break into your thoughts, shall we say, and raid the storehouse of your memory. Consequently, we will only say that we are available to you at any time that you may ask for us. We are your very humble companions. But what little help we can give you, we offer you freely.

If at any time we are with you and you request that we leave, we will instantly. And on that note we will close this meeting. We will attempt to transfer this contact to the one known as H. I am Hatonn.

(Tape ends.)

Advanced Meeting
August 9, 1979

(Carla channeling)

I am Hatonn, and I greet you in the love and the light of the infinite Creator. We thank you for summoning us on this evening, and we express our appreciation to you for inviting us into your domicile at this time. We are aware that each of you has had a busy and a trying day, and to know that you are making room for meditation is very heartwarming to us, for to find companions on the spiritual path is, indeed, a great pleasure, as always.

This evening we would talk to you about the strength and the keenness of your desire. We will talk to you about something that you do not think about enough, and that is how complete the illusion is in which you now exist.

Your physical vehicles are, at this point, in what you would call a seated position, held downward by a force which you do not explore but simply take for granted. What would occur, my friends, if suddenly gravity were reversed and you were flying toward the ceiling? Could you think fast enough that your heads would not come into contact with the ceiling before your feet whirl around? Would you land on your feet?

When you walk down the street you expect that no buildings would fall upon you, that people's heads will remain attached to their bodies and will not come hurtling at you. You do not find a high risk in simple actions. Do you realize, my friends, how carefully the illusion has been planned so that you do not have to be aware of the safety of your physical vehicles? You have your gravity, you have your energy fields, you have your physical universe in which your very fragile physical can make its way with a minimum amount of danger.

Why do you think this is, my friends? And why is it that so many people, instead of taking the opportunity of this safety from imminent danger to meditate and to try to penetrate the desire of their lives, simply find more and more comfort to enrich the luxury of their lives, if you would call it that?

There are people that dwell upon your sphere who live in a very high-risk situation at all times. No, my friends, gravity is not reversed, nor do things hurtle at them from others, except in war. But there are other dangers: there is hunger and thirst, being too cold and too hot, and too wet and too dry, passing the parameters of your physical vehicle. And in these high-risk situations many among your species pass from existence in your dimension. But you yourselves, my friends, you are not in such an area. You have incarnated into a physically easy, simple, comfortable number of parameters of existence.

What shall you do with this opportunity, my friends? Much has been taken from your worry that you may turn your will and your desire more deeply into the mystery of who you are and where the truth lies that suffuse your identity. Do you really wish to know? Have you sought in meditation today, even for a few seconds, that link with the Creator that gives you the key that unlocks the door to knowledge of yourself? What do you know of yourself besides the fact that you are comfortable and that you enjoy comfort? You have been placed into this world by yourselves for experience, but you are not to be hungry and at risk by bullets, by tidal waves, by heat, by exhaustion. For what, then, were you put into this world?

Many are the laws of love which you have discovered, and for that we congratulate you. But we tell you that you have only scratched the surface of your own consciousness. We tell you that there is a vast geography beneath the surface of your knowledge of yourself, and in this area of yourself lies an understanding that goes beyond comfort, beyond the physical body, beyond the physical life that you know. How can you seek less, my friends, even for one day?

We do not ask you to lose your sense of humor, to deny yourself any comfort that you may find pleasant. We ask only that you see the place of these things and the importance of these things relative to the real business of your lives: finding and sharing the truth that is within you.

We find within this instrument regret that she has, during this day, failed to be of perfect service to one of her own species. And we say to you in this regard, yes, you must share what you know, but if you cannot share what you know you must not regret your lack. For if what you know is incomprehensible, then to attempt again and again to share it is, as it says in your holy works, to throw pearls before swine. They cannot understand; they will only sicken on such a diet. Thus, allow yourself only to desire to know the Creator in yourself and others. But if the moment has not come for you to be able to demonstrate a teaching, then, my friends, it simply has not come. You were not sent out into the world to change those who were not ready. You must only see in them the possibility that exists for them to, at any time, as you call it, to become aware of that which you may know; thus, never shutting your heart against another, you may bide your time, as you say, and plant those seeds of information, those thoughts of love, when they are asked for, not before.

The important thing, my friends, is to remain untouched by success or failure in contact with others. You do not know in a true sense what your manifestation may have been to another, for that is not in your saying within another's experience. You know only what you feel, and that you have as much control over as you do over yourself as a whole. Therefore, let you heart be glad, let your tongue be honest, and let your thoughts dwell upon the Creator. More than that you cannot do. Less than that you should not do.

(Pause)

I am conditioning each of you, and would like at this time, although the instrument is very fatigued, to say a few words to the one known as Don. I am Hatonn.

(Pause)

(N channeling)

I am Hatonn. I am now with this instrument. Please pardon us. We felt this … would endeavor to speak through this *(inaudible)* at this time, for he is open to our contact with ease.

We of the Confederation have some *(inaudible)* words to be handled. We have been attempting to be of service so that you may speak the truth to those who desire to know the truth. We do not need many words. We use them to aid an understanding; but in reality, my friends, what you seek is very simple. It is so simple, it is not simple. What you desire to know, you already know. The love you yearn to feel surrounds your body and your thoughts at all times; it has never left; it is always here with you.

At this time we will attempt to step up our conditioning rays, so to speak, to bring you closer together as a group during this meditation. We will pause for a moment.

(Pause)

I am Hatonn. Again I am with you. The illusion that you now live, my friends, will distract you very easily, as you know; but in reality it is an illusion.

Your progress spiritually cannot really be intellectually described, but we say only the desire must be there. If you desire truly to know love, you will, my friends, because you already know. Meditation calms you to a point where you can sometimes *(inaudible)* this knowledge and recognize it. It is always available to you.

At this time I will transfer this contact. I am Hatonn.

(Pause)

(Carla channeling)

I am again with this instrument. I am Hatonn. We had again attempted to contact the one known as Don, for we wished to exercise him, due to the fact that he is somewhat out of practice, and it is sometimes a little difficult to regain the fluency one has had in the past immediately. Therefore, we wished to practice just a few sentences with him. We will attempt again a little later.

At this time we would open the meeting to questions.

(Pause)

This instrument has a question, due to the fact that she has been perceiving a concept which is somewhat beyond her abilities, because it is a geographical concept. But we can assure her that we felt that the earthquake activity which was recently felt in California was a great victory for those who do meditate and attempt to lighten the consciousness of your planetary sphere, in that no one was, shall we say, removed from the physical who did not wish to be; and once again some pressure of new transition is eased somewhat. However, due to your continued difficulties in your Middle East and elsewhere in your world, there will be continued difficulties in your oceanic tides and storms. Therefore, we urge you to continue meditating for peace for the worlds, for there is some danger.

We have difficulty giving this instrument the geographical location, but it is west of your nation and south. Thus, we ask your help in your planet's deliverance from a very difficult *(inaudible)* into a new age.

We thank you who have attempted to be messengers of love and light in these times, which do not lend themselves to messengers of that type; and, as we say, we urge you to continue.

Is there another question at this time?

(Pause)

I am again with this instrument. The energy this evening is somewhat low, and thus we are not at our very best contact level, although this is a very good group, as one of your comedians has often said. The energy level of the group is somewhat low; thus, it is less easy for us to make contact, and we thank you for the energy that you give us at the end of such a busy day.

We ask you to remember that in love there is no limitation; there is room for all things to be done in full measure. Thus, if you are physically weary you may draw from an infinite supply of energy which has been called cosmic, but which we tell you is simply the love that created you and that created all that there is.

We will again attempt to contact the one known as Don, that we may close through him. I am Hatonn.

(Pause)

(Carla channeling)

We thank the one known as Don that we are able to work with him, for we are having good success in conditioning him, but we are not making good contact with him, due to the fatigue and his analysis of our thoughts.

Before we leave this group we would condition the one known as G and the one known as M. We are attempting a new, gentler conditioning for the one known as M in hopes that it will be more comfortable for her. I am Hatonn.

(Pause)

I am again with this instrument. I leave you, my friends, in the love and the light of the infinite Creator. Again we bless each of you and assure that at all times we are with you if you wish us. May your days be full of light and your sleep full of comfort. Adonai, my friends. Adonai vasu borragus.

(The tape recorder was stopped and then started again.)

(N channeling)

I am Oxal. I greet you in love and light, my friends. My brothers and I will not detain you, for we know you are tired. But we wish you to feel a higher note, so to speak.

The seriousness that surrounds problems in your individual lives is not so serious as you may think. We ask you to try to view yourself as a grain of sand on the beach of a vast ocean. You are an individual, and you are one of many millions like you forming one great stretch of sand; and every so often the waters of the ocean come in and waves surround you, and the water may be softly turned a little to go back put to sea. As this perpetual motion goes about, you are taken along the path.

My friends, we ask you to think of yourself as a grain of sand, because in the eyes of the Creator you are one of many. But, as with the grains of sand on the beach, not much real harm can come to you, not much can really hurt you, except being bounced around with other grains of sand. If the Creator overlooked creation, it is perfect, and at no time would the Creator let harm come to His creation. The illusion makes it seem that way sometimes, but as a father and mother love their children, they watch and protect us.

It has been a great privilege to speak with you. I am Oxal.

(Pause)

(Carla channeling)

I am Latwii. I greet you. I was afraid I would not get to speak with you before you had not gotten your second wind, but now I will speak only a few sentences to say that I send you love and light in the name of the Creator and, as always since our meeting several of your months ago, watch over you with the greatest of love. I am Latwii.

As you go about your business remember, my friends, whom you serve. Only one thing do you serve, my friends: love. Invoke the light of that love, and all things will come into harmony in their own time. I leave you. I am so glad to have been able to speak with you. I am Latwii. Adonai, my friends.

Intermediate Meeting
August 16, 1979

(Carla channeling)

I am known to you as Telonn, and I come at the special request of your group to lend my vibration to your seeking at this time. We would help to balance and improve the vibration of your group by asking you to join us of the Confederation of Planets in the Service of the Infinite Creator who serve in His love and His light.

In that light at this time picture, my friends, a globe of light that is pure and white, that is in the middle of your circle; and when you see it clearly in your imagination, allow it to grow until it fills the room and has engulfed your consciousness. Within that light which you invoke in the name of the Father we are all one, my brothers and sisters. I am Telonn.

(Pause)

I am again with this instrument. I am Telonn.

We ask now that you maintain a balance of oneness with the universe, and allow your consciousnesses to become seated again in your physical vehicle.

We are aware that a few of you felt a slight sensation that you might describe as a rise in temperature. However, this was not intended, for light and heat are two different things. And in divine light there is no heat, just as in divine love there is all warmth. The sun that is the great star that feeds your race with heat and light has as its attributes the two great attributes of creation. Heat is love, and light is the material that love takes to transmute into all the vibrations that exist in the universe. Thus, we ask you to meditate upon the light and the ever warm love of the Creator of us all.

I am Telonn, and I leave you through this instrument but not in spirit, for you may call upon my vibration by merely requesting it at any time. We are here to serve you. There is no other reason for our mission. Therefore, feel free to call upon us. Adonai, my friends. I am Telonn.

(Pause)

I am Hatonn. I am with this instrument, and I greet you in the love and the light of the infinite Creator.

We of the Confederation of Planets are always happy to greet those who are new to this group, and we greet the one known as P as well as all of those who have been here so faithfully before, for it is a great privilege to speak to each of you and to share our humble thoughts with you.

This evening we would like to tell you a story, for you see, my friends, in stories there are sometimes the seeds of truths that cannot be spoken straight but must be approached through what you would call the parable.

Once there were two sisters. These two sisters were without husbands, for they had both lost them as years went by. Being alone in the world, they sought each other, loved each other, and lived together, taking care of each other and supporting each other in times of distress. As they reached the age of seventy, both of them began to feel the failing senses of old age come upon them. One sister reacted by becoming somewhat bitter. She began to feel that she was, indeed, in a tragic situation and became less and less able to deal with the simple functions of her life and was melancholy indeed, waiting for a death that she did not want, and living a life whose days and nights went slowly and sometimes fearfully.

The other sister reacted in quite a different manner, for even in the same family each individual child is a unique entity. The older sister began to think of the shortness of her remaining years. She began to realize for the first time that, although she had been of great assistance to her husband and to her children and to her sister, in her adult life she had narrowed her world until she was no longer of assistance to those beyond her doorstep, and she determined to crusade beyond her doorstep and see what she could see of the world and do what she could do for the world.

And so this lady began to take a walk—just a short one around the block—and she opened her ears, and she opened her eyes, and within a very few months she had had conversations with many people, had talked about the Creator with confused children, had found from another one that there was a crying need in hospitals for visitors, had found from yet another friend she had met along her way that in prison those who sit in darkness have no visitors and quite often are grateful to speak with anyone, even a 70 year old stranger.

Taking her courage in her hands, as though it were a precious gift, she did that which she had never done before, for she had been a timid woman; and where she was guided, she went. She sat by hospital beds where people were dying and talked to them. She came to prisons once a week and had friends that she made in that unlikely place. And on she walked, and soon the neighborhood began to know of her, and people came to her.

One day, my friends, both women lay dying, for such is the end of the mortal life, and it will certainly happen to you all. And because they had been stricken by the same virus and were dying at the same time, it was possible for them to be in the same room when they went into the hospital for the last time.

The older sister had so many clustered about her bed that she could not possibly count them or speak with them all, for she was very ill. She begged them, "Please, go talk to my sister, for she is in great need of friendship and love." And some would go over to the sister's bed, introduce themselves, and try to speak words of comfort. But the younger sister was very bitter, and she could not accept the love of strangers. "Go back to my sister," she would say. "She is the one you came to see."

In the end the sisters died, and as the older one died she reached out to the youngest, and they were able to hold hands. The last words of the older sister were very simple: "I love you, sister," she said.

The friends still came, though there was an empty bed, and they clustered around the younger sister. And suddenly for the first time the younger sister understood that the legacy of love is an endless repetition and echo of that vibration in others. And as she died, her bitterness left her, and she was able to leave this plane in the vibration of love that her sister had finally been able to share with her.

We ask you, my friends, to be so seated in your hearts that you can do those things which become before you to do in the name of the Creator and in the voice of love. In this vibration were you all made; and this you share, not only with those of your planet but with all sentient beings throughout the universe, in all galaxies of your universe, and in the many universes that fill the dimensions of the great creation. We are all one, my brothers and sisters.

There will come before you things to do. You each have your own talents. They are each different and unique. You cannot be anyone but yourself. Yet, in your own way, you can be one who shows love. There are an infinity of ways to show love. It is your own judgment that will help you to know what your opportunities are, what you can and cannot do. But when you see an opportunity, my friends, turn it not down, but go forward. You will feel in your heart that which is right, and only can know the feelings of your heart.

We ask only one thing. Instead of becoming bitter as the lessons of life hurt you and pain you, physically, emotionally, and mentally—remain open to the healing power of love, which is best done, as we have always said to you, my friends, through daily meditation. It does not matter what type of meditation that you use—you may pray; you may read scripture or other holy works and contemplate the truth of what you read; you may sit in silence in passive meditation; you may engage in magical rituals, such as your so-called holy communion, and by that imagery find peace. But however, my friends, that you can become close to the one original Thought that created all of us, to the one Creator that is love, that is what you should do daily; for you cannot be a loving person by yourself.

Humanity is very limited in its ability to love, for they have not, through the centuries as a planetary consciousness, spent a great deal of time in concentrating upon love but rather in concentrating upon other things, such as the acquisition of goods, the acquisition of geographical territories, the acquisition of peoples, and the disruption of human life in order to gain these goals. Thus, your planetary consciousness does not have love as its strongest suit.

To get into contact with the infinite source of love that may be compared to the star body that is your sun, you must meditate and find within yourself that small part of yourself, which is your real self, and which is part of the original Thought of love.

Once you have found this, you can always deal with situations in such a way as to never betray that within you which is your best. However, my friends, if you fail, do not reproach yourself but go on and try again, for it is expected of a student of life that he will not be perfect in all of his examinations. Thus, encourage yourselves to seek again and yet again the peace of the presence of love.

At this time I would pause so that my brother Laitos may condition each of you in the room, if you will relax and request his presence. He will make himself known to each of you. I am Hatonn.

(Pause)

I am again with this instrument. I am Hatonn. We are deepening this instrument's contact, for we have a very good contact tonight, for which we thank you.

At this time we would open the meeting to questions. If you have a question, please ask it at this time.

(Pause)

I am aware of a question in the mind of this instrument, and thus we will answer her question.

She was asked previous to this meeting by a friend if there was a relation between our planetary consciousness, which is Hatonn, and the deity that was worshipped in Egypt called Aton or Aten.

We are not a deity, and Hatonn is not our real name, due to the fact that we do not have a name. Our planetary consciousness is unique, and we each are unique, and because we dwell in a dimension where these vibrations of thought are visible, we do not need names any more than you need names to distinguish between red and yellow and blue. You would know the colors, whether you could speak or not. Thus, we know each other without the need for names, and we can see the harmonies of each other without the need for names.

However, upon your planet you are very fond of names. They seem very important to you; and therefore, we chose a name when we first came to you planet nearly 30 years ago. We chose a vibration which very closely matches the vibration of love which is the planetary consciousness which we now enjoy. That unity vibrated on your planet by the name Aton. Thus, we adopted that signal for identification for use in speaking with your peoples.

We are aware of the vibratory power of names and are aware, as a matter of fact, that some, having been named in vibration that is unlike their true self, go through life having to deal with the disharmony between their name and themselves. It is too bad that children cannot choose their own names when they are old enough, shall we say, to vote; for by then they know themselves with a fair degree of honesty and can choose the vibration with which they wish to go through life. That is the nature of our name, and that is our connection with the Egyptian name Aton. We are not in any way, shape or form a deity—nor are we Egyptian! However, we did make use of that vibratory name.

Is there another question at this time?

(Pause)

Questioner: I don't know exactly how to ask it, but … one of the meetings you all came to, it seems like I asked Latwii a question, and he had to like switch over so he could consult a computer and found out something … he said Laitos was like the planetary consciousness that dealt with me and *(inaudible)*. Why do they deal with certain people … certain consciousness … I don't know how to explain it. Do you understand what I mean?

Yes, my sister. We are with this instrument, and we do understand your question.

The concept of a computer is very useful to us in describing to you the consciousness that is the collective consciousness of the Confederation of Planets in the Service of the Infinite Creator. We have nearly 600 planetary envoys to your planet at this time. They are from different dimensions, different times, and different universes, but all come because they have heard the cry of "Help!" which is going up into all creation at this time from those upon your planet who greatly desire to know the truth.

We cannot communicate to each other in time, as you would understand it. We must communicate to each other in the condition which you might call *no time*. Thus, we have pooled our thoughts into something which you might best understand by our calling it the computer. It is actually an organized collection of our thoughts to which we have access telepathically in *no time*, as opposed to real time. Thus, if another Confederation group has been working with a person or a group upon the surface of your planet, or if some entity has asked a question that can be answered by reference to the history or the current status of your planet in some way, we do refer to our collective body of knowledge, which we add to each time that we speak with your peoples. We also have those who observe your planet, and whose job it is to feed the current status of your peoples—emotionally and spiritually—into the collective consciousness which you would call a computer. Thus, if we have need of that knowledge, it is there. However, we must pause in our transmission through an instrument, such as this one, for you see, the instruments are living in so-called real time, as a computer person would say, and cannot deal with a no-time transmission. Therefore, we pause—switch gears, shall we say—and then when we have the knowledge that is needed we again transmit through the channel, such as this one.

As to various consciousnesses, such as Laitos working with new instruments who are thinking seriously about attempting to learn to channel, Laitos is almost always the one who works with such new channels, due to the fact that this is his service to your peoples. Thus, when a desire comes for the learning of this service, the call goes to Laitos, and the vibration of Laitos responds by attempting through a conditioning wave to strengthen the new channel's own spiritual vibration. Laitos' vibration is very easy to pick up, in comparison with some of the entities who have spoken through your group. Telonn, for instance, is not at all as strong or, shall we say, a broad band channel, and a new instrument would find it difficult to pick language from such a contact, although she may see vibrations of light, for Telonn is a light vibration, as opposed to a love vibration.

However, your need for Laitos as you attempt to learn to channel is simply shared with all new channels and is not special to you, but is simply the procedure by which we of the Confederation normally go about helping those who wish to channel.

Occasionally we will find a person who vibrates in such a way that another planetary consciousness is more appropriate, and in those cases we use another entity. However, for the most part Laitos is the one to request if you wish to receive conditioning.

Does this answer your question, my sister?

Questioner: Yes, thank you.

We thank you, as always. Is there another question at this time?

(Pause)

Questioner: I'd like to ask if in the near future will there be more people on the Earth that are being more interested in contacting in our other planets in outer space?

There are, my sister, already so many people interested in the possibility of life elsewhere and the possibility of contact that this desire has come into your popular culture. Movies have been made about it, songs have been written, and it is perhaps the most powerful desire among the peoples of your time.

We are the messengers of a transformation that is now taking place upon your planet. In the peoples of your planet, many of them have incarnated for the specific purpose of experiencing this transformation, for during this time of changing vibrations there is an especial intensity of thought and a great polarity of emotions. Thus, those who vibrate in light and love have their work cut out for them, for they must encounter with love both mediocrity, indifference and that which you call evil but which upon greater understanding can be called separation. Many, many of your people are sort of, shall we say, on the fence. They know that there is something that they wish to seek, but they do not know what it is. We are here to attempt to tell them what it is—and that, my friends, is love.

There will increase among the children that are born at this time the knowledge of that love that will become more and more obvious to those who will observe your young peoples that more and more there is an awareness of the life that is in the universe and of the possibilities that abound within the confines of the physical life.

We hope that we can help as many as possible to turn toward the light, to seek love, and to begin to understand their deepest desires; and we are here because there is an increasing of those people, and they will continue to be so.

Does this answer your question, my sister?

Questioner: Yes, thank you.

We very much appreciate the ability to share our thoughts at this time. Is there another question?

(Pause)

If you are ready at this time, my friends, to close the meeting, we will do so.

You, my friends, are in a prison of your own, a prison of your mind. We hope to stimulate your imagination and your emotional commitment to that which is good, true and beautiful, that you may seek that love which opens the door of your prison. There is never a need to be unhappy or distressed, whatever your condition; and we say to you forthrightly—be at peace with yourself. Love will abide.

We leave you in that love, in that light. I am known to you as Hatonn, a messenger of love. Adonai, my friends. Adonai vasu borragus.

Intermediate Meeting
September 6, 1979

(Carla channeling)

I am Latwii, and I greet you in the love and the light of the infinite Creator. It is a great privilege to speak with you this evening, and we have been requested to do so by the group consciousness known to you as Hatonn, who again at this time has been stationed over your Oriental skies, as you would call them, in order to attempt to send vibrations of love and peace to the leaders of those nations, for there is some danger at this time to your peoples that national tempers will rise to the point of armed conflict. Thus, the entity known as Hatonn and we of the Confederation ask that you meditate upon the peace and harmony of the creation of the Father and send those vibrations into the planetary consciousness at the end of each meditation, for the world needs your love at this time very much. The entity known as Hatonn also wishes to thank those in this group who have meditated at times upon the calming of the waters, as it was asked previously that you do. For indeed it has helped to avert even worse disasters in the oceans and storms of those oceans.

The power of what you might call faith or love is so great that even a small group of people, [can be effective if they] are genuinely concerned and give of themselves in prayer and meditation first of all to seek the truth and secondarily to send love and light to those who are in need and to the planet itself. This energy is extremely powerful and we thank those who have lent themselves to this great work at this time.

We are at this time very far from you and speaking through two densities of thought to this instrument. However, the conditions for reception are very good and she is receiving very well, although our contact is causing her to feel a bit electrically stirred; the hair upon her body is somewhat electrically charged. However, we can continue through this instrument and will do so with your permission.

We, as always, are amazed at the serious attempt of your peoples to live by the laws of ethical rightness as you know them. My friends, we would speak to you about these laws for they are sometimes harmful. It has been written in your holy works that when the teacher known as Jesus was asked why his disciples sat to eat without washing their hands, as was the custom among the people of that time, for religious purposes, the teacher answered, "It is not what goes into the mouth of any man that defiles him, but rather those things which come out of the mouth of men." And we would reacquaint you, my friends, with this thought for it is very important in your understanding of the law of the Creator. Yes, my friends, there is a law and that law is love.

Mankind has created many systems of ethical considerations, so that man may live with man without warfare. And this is, of course, to the good of the people. For it is not comforting to know that you might at any time be killed for no reason at all, or dragged before a firing squad, or imprisoned, or the other difficulties facing one who lives in a society which has fallen into the hands of an unscrupulous government. Thus, to the extent that these laws of man, legal and ethical, preserve the common peace and aid the spiritual development of each human being, these laws are to the good. But when they are interpreted literally and rigidly and do not allow for compassion, understanding and the redemption of love then these laws are harmful to the spiritual development of the individual.

How many of your peoples, my friend, have been subjected in their childhood to a long list of things about which they must feel guilty if they not do? These laws cover everything from what one must put on one's body to be well clothed to how one must keep one's dwelling place, how one must speak, who one must speak to, and how one must judge others according to their appearance. All of these ideas of mankind are erroneous, in that the appearance of man, the habits of man, and all of those things which go with a cultural upbringing are merely window dressing for that which is deep within the heart of each man, and that is that spark of love which is the divine Thought which created him.

If you cannot deal with a person because of his differences from you, intellectually, morally, spiritually or simply by appearance or way of speaking, then you have not drawn from your meditation the deeper understanding that all men are the same. That they are all on a path towards the Creator. Some are going at a fast rate of speed, some at a slow rate of speed. Some seem to be taking a vacation from the journey to the Creator or even taking side trips in which they are getting farther away from the love of the Creator. But, my friends, if you take the long view you must realize that it does not matter because if you have eternity in which to develop each soul, and if you understand the inevitability of the progress or, shall we say, the eventual progress of each soul, then you know that each person is either progressing along a spiritual path now or that he will do so in the future. It is this portion of the personality of each being that you meet that must be of importance to you in your dealings with him.

If you are unable to tolerate a person, as understandable as it may be, you must still continue to meditate until you can see that person as the Creator, for that is the law of love. You have upon your planet many who do not understand nor wish to seek the law of love, and it is indeed hard to imagine being able to love some of these people. We would name, for instance, Adolf Hitler, whom it would be difficult to see as a child of the Creator. Yet, my friends, this man is a child of the Creator and this soul, although he has a long, long journey, will in the end become a spiritualized and seeking being. Other political figures of your time, such as the entity this instrument calls the Ayatollah of Iran, seem to be totally lost in totally foolish and shameful acts. But we say to you, my friends, you must see each person as part of the Creator. It is only in doing this that you free yourself to have a right relationship with each person that you meet. These are extreme examples, of course, but in your daily life you meet so many whom you could inspire because of the joy in your heart and your acceptance of them without judgment. They would then wish to know what you had that made you different, my friends. And you would have dropped a seed of love; whether it fall on stony ground or on fertile soil, your service would have been accomplished.

Thus we say to you, know the law of love and understand that it supersedes the laws of mankind. And if you can apply the law of love in any situation, do not hesitate to relax your grip upon the laws of men. For more important than your understanding of the wrongness of others' actions, or even your own, is the understanding that forgiveness is the divine act. And it is within your own heart, through the grace and power of love, that you may forgive yourself and others when you find yourself or the people in error.

How much you people desire to be of service to each other! We appreciate that, my friends, for we wish to be of service to you also. But we are aware that we can only do just so much, and then we must relax and let our thoughts drift towards the golden love and light of the infinite Creator. What we can give you, we do! If we can give you an inspiration, if we can give you a piece of joy from the feelings that we give you in meditation with us, if we can encourage you to meditate in any form whatsoever on a daily basis, we are very pleased. This is what we are here to do. If we fail, we simply wait until we can try again. And we hope that you can develop that kind of patience and understanding of your fellow man.

Life, you see my friends, is truly a humorous condition. If you could look at your life as though it were an old time silent movie with all of the gestures exaggerated and subtitles under each episode, you would then be able to see your life's dream in its true form. It is a movie on your particular screen for your particular understanding and entertainment. You can be an actor, totally lost in the drama of your existence, or you can also be in the audience watching the drama, understanding what there is to understand in each situation and finding the comedy and the laughter that is inherent in the ridiculous assumption that a soul could take on a heavy chemical body and move about and find the importance of things like money, possessions, homes and all of the trappings of your society, when the only important things are love, compassion and service to others. Can you not find the humor of your own thoughts? When you find your mind too much with your worldly goods and ideas, step back, my friends, and watch the action as though it were on a movie screen, have a good laugh and feel refreshed in the knowledge that you are beginning to truly understand the nature of your existence on planet Earth.

At this time we would pause so that my brother may speak. I am Hatonn—we would correct this instrument—I am Latwii. I am speaking for the one known as Hatonn.

I am Laitos, my friends, and again I greet you in love and light. This instrument is somewhat fatigued but we do have a good contact with her and so we will work with each of you at this time. We would like to condition the one known as M, if she would relax and if she wishes it we will send a couple of sentences so that she may speak in order to feel our contact. I am Laitos.

I am again with this instrument. I am Laitos. We had good conditioning contact with the one known as M and we are aware of her reservations on the subject of channeling. We thank the one known as M that we were able to work with her and if she would wish our help in deepening her own meditation at any time, she need only mentally request our presence and we would be glad to send the conditioning ray to her. We would now condition the one known as C. I am Laitos.

(Pause)

I am again with this instrument. I am Laitos. We thank the one known as C for the privilege of working with her also. And along with our brothers and sisters ask you please to meditate as frequently as you can. For it gives you a window upon a world which is more beautiful than this one in which you dwell. And through that window you can see much that is of a higher reality than you can experience in a normal state of consciousness. Thus, we ask you as often as possible to meditate and find your unity with the Creator, and in that unity seek to know the love and the sweetness of that unity. I am Laitos, and I will leave you now. Adonai.

I am Latwii, and I am again with this instrument. I return to this instrument only to ask if you have questions at this time.

(Pause)

If you do not wish to ask questions at this time we will leave you. We leave you, my friends, in a very beautiful creation and we ask that you look at it as you move through it, for the creation of the Father that is all about you is full of lessons of love and of service. For the beauty of the plants and the wisdom of the winds and the rain keep all things in balance and make your lives upon this sphere possible. You must understand that the phrase, "Butterflies are free," is important, my friends. Beauty is another manifestation of truth. Truth is not an intellectual perception but is heartfelt. And if you can feel the beauty of nature or of man's inspiration as co-creator with the Father, such as music, painting, architecture and the written word, you will come that much closer to an understanding of the love that is the original Thought of the infinite Creator.

We leave you nestled like children in the arms of that love. May your path be full of light, my friends. I am known to you as Latwii. Adonai vasu borragus. ♣

L/L Research

Thursday Meditation
September 13, 1979

(Carla channeling)

I am Hatonn, and I greet you in the love and in the light of the infinite Creator. We are sorry for the delay in achieving contact with this instrument. But we are on station elsewhere in your sky and are having to work through a series of what you would call computers in order to relay our thoughts to you. Normally, the one known as Latwii would speak to you, but because of the special group that we have tonight with the presence of the one known as S, we wished to speak to you ourselves.

For there is much that we would say to you that would be inappropriate to say to a larger group. We are able to reach this instrument due to the fact that there are several other members of this group who have not been able to reach your physical domicile at this time but who are meditating with you in their own dwelling places. Thus, we can achieve a good contact.

This instrument has often wondered why the planetary entity that has most often spoken to her from the inner planes, during what you would call séances, was named Moses. We would like to bring out some points about the reason for the one known to your peoples as Moses being one of your inner guides upon the Earthly plane. It was many, many years ago, several thousand of your years to be exact, or more exact shall we say, when you and your little charge of courageous pilgrims, desiring to help the people of this Earth, stood before the Council that governs this solar system and requested permission to incarnate into this solar system in this cycle. Permission was granted. It was not granted to all that applied and to those that won the approval of the Council there still remained mixed feelings, for you knew what you must lose in order to enter such a dense and unloving vibration as the Earth plane.

You have tried through many incarnations to be of service to the people of this planet. It was hoped very much by you before you began this incarnation that this would be the incarnation in which you succeeded in that plan. In other words, my friend, you, like Moses, have been attempting to lead your people through a desert toward a promised land of love and light, which you can see clearly in a distance and know as a reality, but which those around you either doubt or disclaim completely.

And now, my friends, you find yourselves moving through the incarnation, giving of yourself to the best of your ability and to the best of your judgment finding yourself still in the desert. We can only say to you, my friends, that your sacrifice has not been in vain nor will it ever have been for nothing. Even if you do not lead your people into the promised land; even if, as some have rather crudely put it, you cannot save your planet, you have shown by your life and by your works to the best of your ability that love and the light that awaits those who praise the truth of the Creator's love.

Remember that you are not alone in this great effort to heal a planet and its millions and millions of souls. What you have done prepares the way, at the very least, for another generation of those who seek the promised land, as long as your gaze is steady, as long as you know the reality of the eventual goal. The fact that you cannot yourself bring the planet with you to the completion of that goal should not sorrow you, for you must realize that the free will of each soul is supreme. What you must realize for your own sanity is summed up in your holy works, in the parable of Moses and the burning bush. The bush was burned, and yet it was not consumed, and out of the bush a voice addressed the one known as Moses, there in the desert as he stood, foot-weary and dusty and helpless.

"Take off your shoes," said the voice, "for that place whereon you stand is holy ground." You cannot bring people to an understanding. You can only bring yourself to people. And if you have the realization that you are constantly in the holy tabernacle, dwelling in serenity and intimacy with the Creator, which is the spirit of love among men, then you will be able to bring that holiness ever so quietly into the atmosphere about you. We realize that you do not consider yourselves to be saints, that you could not possibly be holy, we realize all this. We can see your hearts and that you quake with the sadness of all of your indiscretions, heated words, wrong feelings, actions which you considered indiscreet and actions which you fear may be indiscreet in the future. But we say to you, my friends, we are not speaking here of the human personality. For there is a level beneath the human personality in which true sainthood and true holiness abides. You do not so much need to tame your human personality as to learn to discard it, to understand the shallowness of its emotions, to understand that as the bedrock of your character lies that with which you came into this solar system, and that which the council of Saturn passed. Yes, my friends, compared to those who dwell upon this planet from a previous age, you are indeed saints, subconsciously.

The longer you spend in meditation the more you will begin to feel comfortable with the fact, not to be proud but only to be able to manifest it in your life by feeling the presence and the power of the Creator Who is with you; no matter how the emotions of your daily life may turn about you; no matter how distracted you may become by the petty concerns of petty people. Yet, you have that to fall back on which they may not, and it is that which makes you a shepherd and it is the lack of that which makes them the sheep. And thus your relationship defined. You will recognize other shepherds when you see them. For you will hear in them the world weariness and yet the total sweetness that comes with the subconscious knowledge that this is truly not reality for you but merely an illusion that you have selected in order to do a job.

We are aware that each of those in your little band has become increasingly desirous of bringing, shall we say, to a head, the business of setting the planet aright. We wish, my friends, that we could give you the personal guarantee of success that you would so like to hear. But you have a planet that's moving rapidly and completely into the new vibration, and its people are not. Its people are becoming more and more polarized, are desiring to stand upon ground which is not holy, are desiring to distract themselves from that which may be of depth and meaning to them, so that they will not have to think of the consequences of being unholy, unkind, ungenerous, unloving.

My friends, you love one another, and you truly try to love those with whom you come in contact. We can only ask that you dig a little deeper into your subconscious, into the knowledge with which you came into this vibration so many long years ago. You have the opportunity to remember the sweetness and the simplicity of constant contact with the oneness of all things. You merely doubt from time to time that these things are so, because you are lost in the wilderness where there are so few shepherds and so many sheep, and the herding of them is almost intolerable.

Therefore we say to you, be of good courage and do not think of goals but only of the mile which you are walking at this time. We do not know how long the wilderness lasts in terms of time. If it lasts past your lifetime, then you will have been a shepherd along the way. You will not be in at the finish, you will not see the end written across the skies. The movie will not be over for you when you leave this incarnation. This is of no concern to you.

Do not be concerned with your accomplishments. Be concerned only with the amount of time that you spend dealing with individuals upon the sturdy and heartfelt basis of the love of the Creator. Be concerned only with the analysis of your own thoughts, that you may reject those thoughts which are not helpful to your spiritual growth or to the growth of others. Most of all, allow your intuition to play the part in your life that it deserves. For with daily meditation, your intuition will point you in a direction that you ought to go. There will always be, to those who pray and meditate, a path that becomes obvious. It is not always what one would desire consciously, but when it becomes obvious, seize it and embrace it, for it is your next lesson. And by learning these lessons and learning them with love, you and your powerful personalities, well schooled in love, are raising the planetary consciousness to a goodly degree.

We are aware that the one known as S has continued to feel isolated, and it is our hope that we have been able to put into the mind of at least one other person in that area the desire to form a meditation group. We do not know if we have been successful. Due to the fact that we do not directly do these things but do them only through instruments, and in this case we used the book written by this entity and the one known as Don, and an inquiry about people in the area of the one known as S, in order that this instrument could write a little note with a telephone number of the one known as S. If this is to be, it will be. We do not know, for it is totally dependent upon the free will of those concerned. But it has always been our desire that the one known as S not be isolated. However, it was felt by us that it was important for the spiritual strength of the one known as S that she be able to go through the wilderness unafraid and without regret.

We are satisfied at this time that she is aware that we are with her, and we feel that her remaining desire to be in touch with us through channels, such as this one, is simply an understandable desire for the closeness of contact. Indeed, this desire is also felt by this instrument who has never tired of these messages. We ask you to realize that we are very grateful to you, for you have been sent into a world that is hostile. And you do not have visible help. You have a great deal of invisible help, but you must always be strengthening your faith in order to be able to lean on this help as you would upon the help of a friend. Not that we or the Creator Himself could ever tell you what to do. But that when you lean upon the spiritual truth of love, love will live your life and you need only follow the path of love. And do to the best of your ability those good works that have been laid out for you to do. They may be as humble as a smile in a crowded supermarket, a sweet thought on a winter's day, the noticing of the beauty of nature. Yes, my friends, these are good works, these things improve the planetary consciousness. There are dramatic good works, yes, but they are far and few between. That which love has for you to do will be governed completely by the capacity of the planetary consciousness to absorb the love which you have to give. If you cannot give it to all, you may give it to some; if you cannot give it to some, you may give it to a few; if you cannot give it to men and women, you may always, my friends, give it to children. For they are simple and open and understand love.

Your tour of duty, shall we say, is almost over and we feel that it would not make you unduly proud to say that you have done well. We wish only that your heartaches could be less and that your joy could be more. For this is what you came into this world to share, the joy of living under the highest law, the law of love. We wish you the greatest of peace and strength and confidence in your day-by-day attempts to express this love in your life, to show this love and this joy in every smile and laugh, in every refusal to be bitter, in every forgiveness and every forgetting of a wrong. In a way you are not special, for you are children of God as are all. It is only that you have more experience and this gives you responsibility. We hope that this responsibility may weigh lightly upon you and that you may find grace.

(Side one of tape ends.)

(Carla channeling)

I am Hatonn. I am again with this instrument. We apologize for the delay, but the noise of the tape recorder which ended lightened this instrument's concentration upon our words, and we felt that she would better finish this message if she were able to turn it and begin another side. We would at this time pause and ask if the one known as S has any questions at this time.

S: *(Inaudible).* Our evolution *(inaudible)* at this time, a great sense of a *(inaudible)* sadness in your words, impression that in fact *(inaudible)* we are not making progress that was once hoped *(inaudible)*.

I am Hatonn. Your impression of the sadness in our voice is correct, my sister. However, it is not sadness because of your failure to be shepherds of the flock. For indeed, there have been many more who remembered the love of the Creator and served that love in their lives than we ever expected or hoped for when this planet was seeded with people such as yourselves who lay down their lives for their brethren, in love. We are very, shall we say, grateful and impressed.

The problem, my sister, lies in a planet which is only with the greatest difficulty avoiding becoming evil. It is holding on to its mixed neutrality only by some effort, and that effort is that which is put out by those such as you.

As we watch the peoples of the world in which you now reside, we do not see any lessening of nationalism and all of the pride and vain glory which that causes, of the desire for war as a tool of diplomacy in order to gain advantage over other nations and ideologies. These things are increasing, in spite of the great tragedies that have happened within the last hundred years. The vibrations are very strong in your planet. It is as though the people were vampires, desirous of blood.

You have tried very hard, and so have we, and individuals among the sheep will pass the graduation test and thus you will have done your job, and for that, you too can be grateful and feel satisfied. But you were fighting against great odds and so are we. We still fight on, and so do you. And we do not consider the situation hopeless; for there is an eternity in which to work it out. However, the fact remains that at this moment we cannot even be on station over your skies, working with groups such as yours, in what you call your United States. It is only through a request to [the] central computer that we have been able to speak with you this evening.

For we are attempting to send [words] of peace and love into the leaders of those in your old world, those in the Orient, those in what you call Russia, those in the Middle East. They seem to be so determined to blow up what they cannot have. And what they do not realize is that they will destroy not only themselves, but souls, if they are allowed to use the nuclear weapons. Thus, we are sad this evening. For we are those who love, and love breeds sadness.

Thus, we too must meditate and remember the joy of the Creator. However, we do not shrink from what we see to be the truth. We simply accept it and realize that all those who at this time are not progressing or progressing very slowly, will simply progress in another time, in another place of their own free will, for the process is inexorable.

We do not then ever despair, for we know that no souls can be lost. They can only be longer in the darkness, and this we wish to help you to avoid on your planet. And we know that you too wish to help your peoples in this way. We are afraid that in the vibration of love as we know it, there is a dynamic of joy and sadness. Joy from the Creator; sadness because of the separation of those who are separated from the Creator. For those who love wish only to serve others, and when you cannot serve, you must then feel sad. Perhaps that is the hardest thing about loving, is to know that you cannot change people, they must come to you, they must be ready, then the seed is planted and joy begins again, in new ground. For this you may hope, for this you may still and always hope. For although this planet will not as a whole successfully enter the next density, there are those who will. And even now, you can help them develop. It does not have to be by the dialectic of spoken word. As we said before, it can be by smiles, by writing, by singing, by touching, by all the ways that you can show love.

We are aware that many times both of you to whom we speak at this time have had the gift of listening. That is a great act of love. We encourage it in you. You may feel that you are not helping by listening, but if you listen with love, you can be the transformative element in the equation. You need not say anything in order for the look in your eye to reflect an attitude, in which the voices of others become aware of what they are saying and so begin to tell the truth, and so begin to find themselves.

But we share our sadness with you at this time, because we want you to know that you are not alone, that we are not without compassion for your feelings. However, we wish you to understand that there is a deeper reality in which you must not and cannot feel sad. For as we said, the place whereon you stand at this very moment, wherever you are, is holy ground. You do not need to reach the promised land, you have the promised land in your heart. Simply because other people cannot see it does not mean that it is not there. You must visit it in meditation and then you will know. Does this answer your question, my sister?

S: Yes. Although I *(inaudible)* active imagination *(inaudible)* broadest transformation *(inaudible)* part of it *(inaudible)* perhaps I may not be part of that *(inaudible)* my *(inaudible)*. Waiting *(inaudible)* problem *(inaudible)* so afraid to do something *(inaudible)* if it's my ego or not *(inaudible)* back and wait *(inaudible)*.

I am Hatonn. I am aware of you sentiments. May we say again, that you are not the only one of your band who feels the intense pressure of action at this time. This was indeed to be the time of movement. And it is possible yet that your little band may be able to do a few things. The one known as M, the one known as K, the one known as B, and especially the one known as Don have all suffered terribly in these last months because of an urgent and continuing feeling that they have not taken hold of their responsibilities. This instrument, who is less susceptible to this pressure, has also felt that this is a critical time, although it has not distressed her as much. Your perception is totally and perfectly correct. This and the years to come, your year 1980 and 1981, 1982, are your critical years in your incarnations. These were the years that you had all set aside to be mature enough and ready enough to work together to aid your planet. The planet which you adopted so bravely.

It will be a measure of the determination of each as to how much of this is realized. However, it is our observation that the outcome of even the most successful campaign on your part is simply questionable. As we said, we have come to the conclusion that we can save individuals and be careful and consciously cautious in beginning their spiritual path by inspiration and so may you be. But we have come to the conclusion that we cannot, as a whole, transform this planetary consciousness. At best, we can simply keep it from tearing up the planet, this very beautiful planet on which you now reside. And that is now our goal and what we continue to ask light groups, such as yours, to pray for. That the weather be asked by your higher selves to be calm, that the leaders of your world be asked by your higher selves to be in peace, in love, and harmony. These may seem to be foolish thoughts in the face of the weather that you are now experiencing and the difficulties that your international scene now presents. But we say to you that each prayer is heard.

What you do can change things on the inner planes. Already, light groups like yours have saved many in California and we ask your help with what you would call earthquakes. At the time that we asked that, rather than one large earthquake, there were several small ones and there was no loss of life. We continue to fight small battles such as this one, in lieu of the important and great battle, which we feel that we have lost, the battle for the planetary consciousness of your people. Many of your people will simply have to repeat the cycle of time which they have just experienced. It is not a true sadness that we feel, for we know that all will be well. It is simply a disappointment, that we cannot share the Creator and the joy of His love with all people who have that joy within them, waiting to be [unblocked,] waiting to be unlocked! But it cannot be if the person does not desire to use the key. So be it!

We shall see, and we will be in touch with your group. You may depend upon it—in the months to come and the years to come—to witness with you and to send our love and support [for] your own program to give love and information to those who desire it on your planet. We know that you will do the best that you can. We do not fear for any ego problems from any of you, for we feel that life itself has taught you enough at this point that you can analyze your own thoughts and work with them yourselves.

Each of you in the group, that has come to planet Earth at this time together, is a highly disciplined person. Ego is useful for being a chemical being upon a chemical planet. To be totally without ego would be somewhat awkward. We do not fear ego or ask you to dismantle it. We ask you to be aware of the way it works in your life. And when you feel that you have become offensive because of it, correct that action. That is all you need to worry about, in ego. If you are giving information to others, you may become tired of the sound of your voice. You may feel that you are showing off your information or your knowledge. But we ask you, why do you think that you had that information? Be humble in your heart and know that you are nothing without the Creator but clay and dust. But know also that you are a perfect created being. Do not be proud of the dust, but be unafraid to share the joy of being a child of God.

We ask you in all sincerity to have confidence and not to worry about your ego, but simply to analyze your actions in each case. And when you have determined whether your ego or your love was working, adjust your behavior accordingly. For you are not in a situation where others will understand you and it would do you no good to speak to others. Thus, you must be your own disciplinarian. You are always able to speak at any time on the physical plane with those others of your group with whom you came. If there is a question that you cannot penetrate, we urge you to speak to the one known as Don or any of the others in your group. And we assure you that we will send you our thoughts, if you ask us. But most of all, you must have the confidence to realize that you know the score, and that you are too much a student of life to allow something that has been a rather beautiful and loving existence up to this point [to] become marred by excessive egoism.

We are aware that you have been egotistic in the past; so has everyone that is incarnate in a chemical universe. Ego is a defense mechanism, it is a separator. Without ego you would become the proverbial doormat.

Know who you are, let your ego speak, but then let it be quiet. Simply see the balance between too little and too much. We are aware that many Eastern religions encourage the total abolishment of ego. This is all very well and good in a culture where the holy are fed. In your particular culture, the holy are normally considered quite insane, thus, retain your protective coloration and your ego [as] part of that. For you cannot function unless the society perceives you as normal. But know in your heart who you are. And let not your ego tell you that you have limitations.

Has this helped you my sister?

S: Yes. *(Inaudible)* I may also pray *(inaudible)* I hope you will send your light *(inaudible)* appear to *(inaudible)*. I guess that goes along *(inaudible)* with incarnating *(inaudible)* physical body. *(Inaudible)* fear of what *(inaudible)* said *(inaudible)* as much as I have tried to tell myself this is an illusion *(inaudible)* and I know there is a greater reality, I still have the fear of my own physical being, the physical being that I have given birth to, and it is sometimes hard to get back to the basics and a *(inaudible)* feel that fear *(inaudible)*. I need all the help I can get *(inaudible)* quiet and get back to reality *(inaudible)* experience.

I am Hatonn. I will give you words of comfort, my sister, by urging you to never look ahead. For one of your singular imagination that is not a profitable activity. The day in which you are living at this point is enough meat for your thoughts to digest. To live in the future is as mistaken as to live in the past. That which you have is only yours for a moment and then is replaced by something else that is only yours for a moment. As you say, in the greater reality all times are one, and you need not fear the future, because it is no longer the future but a great circle of reality, encompassing all that ever was or ever will be. But in this illusion you must train your [mind] …

(Tape ends.)

Tuesday Meditation
September 18, 1979

(Unknown channeling)

I am Hatonn. I greet you, my friends, in love and in light of the infinite Creator. It is a very great privilege, once more …

(Pause)

It is only a short time now till we [meet.]

(Pause)

I am sorry about the delay. We are having some difficulty at this time.

(Pause)

I am sorry about the delay. We will continue. I will sign.

(Pause)

Sorry, this instrument has *(inaudible)*. Conditions are not perfect at this time for contact. I shall start over.

(Pause)

I am Hatonn. I am very privileged to be with you this evening. It is unfortunate that I am unable at this time to contact the rest of your group, for we have something important to tell you this evening.

(Pause)

Carla: May I ask a question?

(Pause)

Carla: Is it possible for you to continue through the instrument known as Don?

I am sorry for the delay. We are having difficulties.

(Pause)

(Carla channeling)

I am Hatonn, and I greet you again in love and light. We are using this instrument, although she is reluctant to channel at this time, due to her desire to hear our channeling through another instrument. Due to the fact that the one known as Carla is often the only channel, shall we say, in a group, she does not have the opportunity to experience the listening to our words, which has been her inspiration for many years. We are aware that she misses this. And, thus, we were attempting to use the instrument known as Don, both to please the one known as Carla and also due to the fact that we have information which could be channeled through a more scientifically-oriented instrument, which this instrument will only be able to touch upon in the most general sense, due to her lack of understanding in these areas.

Before we continue through this instrument, therefore, we shall once again attempt to make once again contact with the one known as Don, if he would refrain from analyzing our words, and if he is willing, we would so desire. I would now try to transfer this contact. I am Hatonn.

(Pause)

(Carla channeling)

I am again with this instrument. We must use this instrument, and so we will attempt to speak as clearly as possible, using her vocabulary and understanding. You are aware, of course, of a situation of your outer illusion, and perhaps you are also aware that—almost unnoticed by the great majorities of your peoples—your entire planet is hurtling headlong into the greatest crisis possible.

The consumption of creative energy has increased the entropy of your planet and its resources and decreased the available creativity and regenerative abilities of the planet itself. Meanwhile, your peoples ignore those forces of nature which cannot be depleted. My friends, your peoples do not deserve the beautiful creation of the Father which constitutes the surface of the sphere on which you dwell.

But this is not the important point, my friends, for with the increased entropy of your physical material there is a corresponding entropy of mental and spiritual creativity; and those who dwell within your culture have more and more become creatures lacking in creativity and imagination, due to the fact that they are one with your planet as they must be, one with the machines that they have created, with the governments that they have created and with the polarities that they have created. Because of their paucity of understanding, you stand at this point at the brink of many disasters.

It is only due to the meditation of those sending love and light to the planetary consciousness, that the many, many natural disasters of recent years have not taken an even greater toll in lives. This will continue to increase as the polarity of your peoples becomes more and more evident. Polarity or separation is indicative, my friends, of one thing—a lack of creativity. For what is creativity, my friends, but an understanding of creation. And what is the creation—but love! And what is love—but unity!

Thus, it is absolutely inevitable that where your peoples have accepted the fundamental dicta of government, society and culture, regarding differences in ideology, religion, social behavior and other artificial walls, you will have endless and proliferating polarities. Thus, we move from natural disaster to manmade disaster. You know already of the small disasters that are taking place gradually. So gradually that people become numbed and do not react to them. The disasters of what you call your inflation and all the many ills of a society, where work is thought of as the lowest form of making a living; and your so called wheeling and dealing where no work is done but only the manipulation of people and money, is thought of as the highest form of work, this disaster and all of its accompanying and corollary problems is breaking your society apart.

For those who actually work are very angry, and they band together and demand more and more and they are locked into a self-defeating and endless struggle for survival. And the same thing, my friends, happens with your governments. Except that with your governments there are many leaders, not a few, but many, who would consider the possibility of planetary annihilation rather than relinquish an ideology, a piece of land, or power whether it be economic or political.

Your people are so unaware that all of these things are not only possible but there is a statistical probability that is growing, that one of your leaders upon your planetary sphere will attempt to use nuclear force to gain an advantage. This, my friends, is the deepest trouble of this cycle upon your planet. You must understand it in terms of what we began with. The spent energy, the unavailability of creative energy of a planet itself being reflected in the habits of the peoples and in the thoughts of your leaders. It is not creative to consider the destruction of a planet as a diplomatic tool; it is indeed suicidal. But your leaders have become numbed to that fact, because they have played the game too long, and because the culture around them is so consistent in its deep sleep of attempting to grab more and more of what is left of the energy of the planet, instead of attempting to restore more and more energy to the planet.

What can you do, my friends? We come to you only through the help of a machine which you would call a small computer. For we are on station at this time over your Oriental skies, as you would call them, attempting to deal with those who govern that part of your planet which you call China. They are watching what is happening in the Middle East with great intent to turn the rather complex diplomatic struggle of several nations to their advantage. Their leaders are completely ruthless and would not hesitate to use nuclear weapons if they thought they could win. Nor would others, which are involved in this conflict at this time.

We may say that your own portion of the planet is to a lesser degree bloody-minded. For it has used nuclear weapons and is correspondingly aware of the ferocity and the horror of using them again. Thus, shall we say, you who are Americans are a strong force spiritually against war. For you do truly desire peace, and the spirit of neighborliness and brotherhood is not dead among you as a people. Thus, we ask you please at this time to include in your meditations a prayer for the peace and the brotherhood of your planet, for it's truly needed at this time.

Again, we apologize for speaking through this instrument, for we could have been much more specific about the relationships between the laws of physics and the laws of men and metaphysics, had we been able to use the vocabulary of the one known as Don. However, we thank the one known as Don and assure him that we understand that when a channel has not been used for some time it is often very difficult to reestablish a good contact due to the fact that an intelligent and analytical mind will inevitably and instinctually analyze our thoughts and thus stop the transmission.

We have not said things through this instrument that we would have to the instrument known as Don, because we cannot. And this, my friends, is the reason that we welcome each and every channel who would be interested in this service. I would leave you now, so that my brother may speak.

Questioner: What … *(inaudible)*.

Yes, my brother.

Questioner: Which country is it that [is possibly endangered] *(inaudible)* nuclear?

We will attempt to answer to this instrument. There is the union of Soviet Socialist Republics. Their leaders are divided, but the majority wishes at this time to roll over Europe much as in your conflict called by you World War II. The one known as Adolph rolled over much of Eastern Europe and well into Russia. They are aware that this is a tactical time to do so, and they have weapons to deploy which are not nuclear, but which they feel would do a fast and furious job, that would annihilate the forces which are called NATO by your peoples. However, they are [unwilling] in the extremity to deploy tactical nuclear weapons.

There is also a desire by the chosen people, as they are called, to ignore their great heritage. For it has been written in your holy work, called the Old Testament, that the Jewish nation should always love the stranger in their midst, for were they not strangers in the land of Egypt? This quotation they have apparently removed from their holy book for they have such fierce hatred for a group of people who are genetically very like them, known as Palestinians, that there are those among those called Israelis that would, if they thought they could, use nuclear weapons.

It is less likely that this would happen due to the fact that the Israelis have a very limited economic stance with the rest of the economic community and are heavily dependent upon the opinion of others for their wellbeing. This is not true of either Russia, as you know it, or China, as you call it.

There are other countries which do not even have nuclear weapons. They are scattered throughout what you know of as the Third World nations. If their leaders were able to lay their hands upon tactical nuclear devices it is very probable that they would do so. It is entirely unpredictable what the result would be, and your espionage world, as you call it, has never been more active, nor more tense, for they know that the stakes are very high at this time.

There are those in almost every nation of the world who are angry enough, if put in the proper position, to consider the use of nuclear weapons. For instance, if the proper people in your continent, among those which are called those of Quebec, could be brought to power and had access to the arsenal of nuclear weapons, it is very possible that they might consider threatening to use them in order to achieve independence.

We are attempting to tell you just how widespread and difficult this situation is, for it is not impossible to build a nuclear device. The greatest difficulty is in formulating what this instrument would call a detonating device to detonate the nuclear device. We are sorry we cannot be more specific through this instrument, but she does not have the knowledge. Thus, among people who have not the ethical and spiritual consideration to think their position through on behalf of all mankind, you have great danger to your planet at this time. And we are working specifically at this time with the leaders of China, for we find their leaders to be quite devoid of scruples.

Is there a further question?

Questioner: Which of this is the greatest threat at this time, nuclear threat?

Your people are not predictable. The most volatile situation is centered about the confrontation between Israel and the rest of the Egyptian community which you may call the oil nations. China is watching this, Russia is watching this. Others of our brothers are sending vibrations of love to the leaders of Russia, to the leaders of each of the countries in Egypt and to Israel. We can only say that the least scrupulous of them, with tactical ability, is China. This ability is not great and [it] is this very lack of supremacy which makes this people the more willing to take risks.

Thus, we are working with them, sending them love and thoughts of peace. However, we do not know what will occur in this situation day-by-day and therefore cannot predict what will happen or when. We can only say that the statistical chances of your planet being destroyed in a war that will truly end all wars for this cycle, due to the fact that it will remove sentient life from the surface of the planet, is growing. We ask for your prayers.

We are attempting to give this instrument another thought, if you will be patient.

The difficulty began many years ago when the homeland of Israel was created. This is a historical and fateful creation and fulfills many prophecies. If you can read these prophecies, you can see the possibility of difficulties in the future. However, my friends, this future has come.

Not too many years ago the world as a whole was not polarized enough to become so intensely involved in the difficulties of Israel and Egypt as a whole, or Arabia perhaps we should say, for that instrument is very weak in geography, but we are attempting to include all of the nations which surround Israel and which do not appreciate Israel's presence. But the polarity between all of your peoples and your peoples' ability to be separated from the love of the Creator has become so marked and noticeable that now those countries with oil have become very strong, for other nations wish to destroy …

(Side one of tape ends.)

(Carla channeling)

I am Hatonn. We are sorry for the interruption; we will begin again. Other nations had a desire to continue the destruction of your planet and its resources by destroying that which is called oil. Thus, suddenly the entire world has become riveted by the conflict between those nations and Israel. There is a fateful significance to this confrontation. And we are sure that you will think upon it deeply, for you may see in the chosen people, as they are called, a great body of good, bad, right and wrong in some the essence of humanity itself. But the role of the oil-producing nations, my friends, that is the question!

It has not been written in stone, shall we say. The future is open and can go along an infinite number of lines. Thus, we ask your prayers in each present moment, at the end of each meditation, for the peace of the world. We would like to see it last long enough to fulfill its journey as a planet into the next vibration. Then those among its people who must repeat again this particular vibration may peacefully leave and do so, leaving the planet for those to rebuild who are ready for the vibration of love. Is there another question?

Questioner: *(Inaudible).*

That is inevitable, my sister. For the seeds have been planted long ago among your peoples. You have been a warlike people. You have not listened to your leaders in the spirit as a people but to your growing polarity, your growing desire to possess territory, money and power.

From the very smallest unit, a person, to the very greatest unit, which in your culture is the multinational corporation, this is true. And it is through many centuries that your tradesmen, and your bankers, and your governments, and your diplomats have forged an ever-growing stream of differences between one people and another. How many times, my sister, have you seen a map in which a mass of land is colored pink and blue and brown and green and yellow? My friends, we ask you sincerely, how can the Creator's land be so divided by men and so fought over?

You see, it's in the hearts of men that this difficulty has been nurtured. Thus, the planet itself and you, as part of the planetary consciousness, become more and more intensely polarized as a new vibration begins to take hold. This has been predicted and is entirely to be expected. It is indeed nothing to worry about, for whether you live a natural and peaceful life or whether you are prematurely removed from the physical, we of the Confederation are here, to make quite sure that no souls will be shattered, even if there is a deployment of nuclear weapons.

We are not concerned with the shadow of death. We are only concerned with the reality of souls, and those we shall protect. We make this vow to you, so that you will know that there is no such thing as death, only the removal of a chemical body, that is not always totally without difficulty in the first place. So it is no tremendous loss to leave such an illusion. That is the worst that can happen, if the vibrations become so intense that nuclear weapons are deployed

Don: Nuclear explosion *(inaudible)* the spiritual body.

That's why we came in the first place, my brother. We came because of the creation of an atomic weapon. This meant that not only would you have a difficult shift into the next cycle, for we knew that already; it meant also that it was possible that your people might actually destroy souls.

Don: What happened in Nagasaki and Hiroshima?

We were there and no one was lost. The effect otherwise would have been to destroy souls. We were able to neutralize the portion of the explosion which disturbed the inner planes of your planet. We did not see fit to remove or neutralize the physical destruction. For, among other things, we felt that your people would then see what they had done and perhaps not do it again. However, we did not lose any souls in those explosions. Our only danger was in not being here in force when the first testing began. It was a matter of luck that we did not lose anyone in the early stages of that development.

Don: How do you go about nullifying the effect?

We are attempting to give information to this channel, but she cannot grasp it. It is technical. We give her the image of a screen which is acting as a filter, but the screen is made up of vibration in the form of light. When the waves of destruction hit this web, they travel along the lines of force of the screen, while the souls of those who leave their physical bodies are not affected by the screen because of their different vibratory rate. The light screen is made up of something which we might call …

(Pause)

We are attempting to give the concept to this instrument. It's very difficult to work with her mind. We would call it negative energy light. The destructive energy of the explosion is attracted to these lines of force like a magnet, and thus removed from the sphere or plane to which souls repair upon leaving their physical vehicles.

I am sorry, we cannot be more specific and as we say, if we could have spoken through an instrument such as you with a knowledge of physics and mechanics, we would be able to be more fluent. However, we think that we have been able to give through this instrument, without undue distortion, the general idea of our mechanism for neutralizing the inner sphere destructive power of nuclear weapons.

(Pause)

Is there another question?

S: *(Inaudible)*.

We are aware of your question, and we would say that your brother, Gandalf, is also somewhat disturbed. We would, with your permission, turn this meeting over to one of our brothers, who has been waiting to brief you and has a message waiting. Would that be satisfactory to you?

S: Yes.

If there are no further questions from the one known as Don, I will then leave you.

S: Actually *(inaudible)* message *(inaudible)* other *(inaudible)* ask *(inaudible)*.

In that case, my sister, we will await your question. We will pause now. In love and light, I am Hatonn.

(Pause)

I am Latwii, and I wish to add my foolish voice to the wise voice of my brother Hatonn in greeting the one known as S who we have not been able to speak to before. Yet, we were aware of her presence, and we are most grateful to be allowed to share a few words with you at this time.

We are aware that things look a little down on planet Earth at this time. But, let us tell you that things do not look so bad from where we are. Because from where we are, you are only where you are for a moment. And in that moment you are working very hard. And after that moment you will play; and before that moment you will play; and what we would like you to do, my sister, is learn how to play during the moment in which you are working very hard.

We ask you simply to release all the burdens of your great responsibilities to the enjoyment of your distinguished feelings of positivity and happiness. Whatever burdens that you may carry, they will become weightless if you put them down. You do not have to carry them, you need only be the best person that you can be; love the Creator with all your heart and let your heart touch others in a spirit of love. If light is shining from your eyes, the light of the Creator, that is your entire responsibility.

You did not come into this world that the world might be entirely altered. You came into this world to display a talent. That talent is to show the love of the Creator. That talent is yours because you have studied and learned and loved through many lifetimes. That talent is yours instantaneously. The talent cannot be employed by worrying or [grief] or realizing with great grief the horrible plight of your planet. It is not that these things are not true. It is that your role in them is to love. No matter what may occur, your role will be to love. It is true that you came into this world to save it, for that was the desire that you had when you volunteered to come and that is true of those in this room.

It depends upon your definition of saving as to whether you have saved the world or not. You have surely made it a better place. You have raised the planetary consciousness through your lifetimes here. You have loved and remembered both the Creator and your mission. So we ask you to pick up your heels and be as loving as you really are.

When you find negativity in yourself, know that that is the world pressing in upon you and that it is not you. It is not what you came into this world with. That is not your personality. You may not be able to shrug it off, for you have had many years of training in your planetary society; and it is thriving on negative feelings all the time. But each time that you can, neutralize a negative feeling and replace it with a conscious love that comes from knowing who you are, what love is, and whence love comes. In each of those times, you have improved not only yourself but the climate of the planet itself.

We ask you to look upon these times as you would a movie. Say you have some inside information. Very well then, use it as such. Nudge somebody on the bus and say, "I told you so"; they won't know what you mean. When the next tidal wave hits, when the next diplomat storms out in anger, you may nod your head knowingly for you have heard it here first. But it is meaningless, my friends, unless you understand it in terms of time.

Time is an illusion in which you are now taking part. And in this illusion of time you are completing a cycle and there are things which are going awry due to difficulties in the vibration of your peoples. And you will do what you can and you will love as best you can. And when it is over, you will look back upon it, and it will be a very interesting movie that you have enjoyed. And it will have lasted the normal movie time and you will have come out of this movie saying, "What did you think of that movie? That was an interesting movie. Did you like the ending? What did you think of the plot? How about the heroes? Did you like the costumes? "This is just how much this will mean to you when you reach reality, or shall we say, comparative reality. It will be in any event the reality of the spirit, as opposed to the reality of the flesh. Both of which are illusions, but one of which is more real and that is the spirit.

Thus, seek always to know who you are in spirit. Seek always to know the heart of the present which is love, and you will not be openly disturbed because your mission is taking a turn you did not expect. Flow with it. Watch the plot develop around you; and soon you would be talking about this movie, which has been your life and the life of those about you. We encourage you to be a good heroine in that movie, to be as wise as you can be, as loving as you can be, as analytical of your own faults and as confident of your own virtues as you can be. What more could you ask from a heroine, my sister?

We are all the heroes and heroines of our own motion pictures, when we have begun a lifetime in an illusion such as yours. Thus, let the movie be one which you will be glad to watch later. Now, you are an actor. But let yourself also be the observer, the director, that keeps your part on an even keel. You are indeed an agent of the Creator's, for you are part of the Creator. And always remember that identity with the Creator and with His creation. Whatever the rest of the planet may be doing, you can be co-creator, yours can be the imagination and the love and the individuality that others may lack.

When the time comes you will be in the company of those who, like you, were attempting to be of help. And we will meet you then! We and our brothers of the Confederation and it will be a grand meeting, and we shall all laugh and rejoice together; for we will have been through quite a bit together. We will look for you there, my sister, in person. And you will see us as light, and we will see you as light. And in the meantime, we are with you in spirit as you deal day-by-day with your illusion. Do not become entrapped in that illusion, but remember always the original Thought of the Creator, which is love. You are a light being. You are not an earth being. Do not be trapped, my sister.

We ask each of you, pray your prayers; do your deeds. But do not be trapped by them. Act only upon your ideals, on your faith, and your love of the Creator in your heart. Let those things be your all in all. The rest of the world and all of its traps, let them go by. They do not cause you to laugh, they do not cause you great joy. But only what is in your heart can cause you to laugh and cause you to have great joy.

We are not saying that it is not right to have possessions, position, power. All these things are neutral, if in your heart you remember the Creator, and you love one another.

What will happen? We of Latwii do not know. We are enjoying the colors of your planet. We are watching them as they vacillate and change in the inner dimensions. Your planet is quite beautiful in these dimensions. And it is in these dimensions that we stay for the most part. Your group is one of the very few which we have spoken to. We thank you for that opportunity. And we urge you to always keep the light touch. Join us in the big belly laugh, for you have a very funny planet, a very silly planet, a very foolish planet. And sometimes, when you are sane and those about you are not, you have a very lonely laughter. But don't forget to laugh even if you laugh alone. This is only a movie. Have a bite of popcorn and keep on. That is all we came to [tell] you, my sister. We are always with you, if you ask us, and we hope you can hear our laughter and our joy when you need it. We leave you all in the light of the infinite Creator and the love that created that light. We will now turn the meeting back to Hatonn. I am Latwii. Adonai.

(Pause)

I am with the instrument. I am Hatonn. We were attempting to contact the one known as Don but he is more fatigued than the one known as Carla. Thus, we will use this instrument. Please go ahead with your questions.

Questioner: I was very flabbergasted when you said that the bombs could destroy souls. *(Inaudible)* forgotten it a great deal *(inaudible)* images as you were saying it *(inaudible)* created *(inaudible)* goes beyond the boundaries of free will *(inaudible)* confusing to me *(inaudible)*. I don't even know how to phrase the question. I hope you can perhaps open my mind *(inaudible)* my confusion *(inaudible)*.

Questioner: *(Inaudible)*.

I will attempt to use this instrument. The classification of the people you see upon this Earth *(inaudible)* is somewhat inherent *(inaudible)*.

Mortals are precisely identical to immortals, if you are assuming these two classifications. What you call a mortal is the chemical appearance of what you call immortal. It is the clothing of the immortal for a short period of time *(inaudible)* physical plane of existence. The immortal is always the active force. The mortal is only temporary *(inaudible)* very intense. Therefore the action of the mortal is always the action of the immortal.

The immortal is the Creator. The mortal is His physical appearance in this particular plane of existence. Is it possible then for the Creator to destroy Himself or cause, shall we say, termination of the continuity for a portion of His experience? This is possible. It is possible through the association of the intelligent configuration *(inaudible)* vibratory nature *(inaudible)* the individualized consciousness which is a portion of the infinite Creator. This is possible with a form of technology which you know of, the nuclear explosive device. This device has effect not only on the physical clothes of the entity, that is, the chemical body, but also the subtle body, which you call the soul.

The reason for this is the very nature of the nuclear device. Energy generated from this device is spinning energy, what you call the atom. The atom is a vibratory arrangement, motion manifested in both what you know as the physical plane and several planes beneath, shall we say, the physical. The spiritual or soul body is composed of, shall we say, a more subtle vibratory arrangement. From your point of view in the chemical body, this vibratory arrangement is highly energetic. A large portion of the energy *(inaudible)* from the nuclear explosion is contained at this level of vibration.

For this reason, the detonation of a nuclear device affects more subtle planes of existence, as you would call it. We were first attracted to your planet in great numbers because of the threat, shall we say, to a portion of the individualized consciousness of the infinite Creator. We were, shall we say, quite *(inaudible)* invading threat. We were successful and shall be successful in the future.

(Tape ends.)

Thursday Meditation
September 27, 1979

(Carla channeling)

I am with this instrument. I greet you in the love and the light of the infinite Creator. I have not previously spoken with this group but have been asked to do so, in the name of the Creator, by the chief teacher of your group, the brothers and sisters of Hatonn.

We are attempting to transmit our name to this instrument, as we have used it before in other groups, but this transmission is, of course, very difficult as this instrument does not know our name.

We are of the constellations of what you know as [Ora,] and we call ourselves [Kasara.] We would like to share with you a little story, my friends, that we offer to you this evening in the humble hope that we might spark a thought or two in your minds that may help you in some way.

Once, my friends, there was a mountaineer and this mountaineer was a wanderer and he wandered up hill and down, many the day and many the night spent he [in] loneliness and enjoying the beauties of his scenery and enduring the hardships of all weathers. This mountaineer had but one desire and that was to find the perfect walking stick. For it was his belief that with a stout stick at his side, he could climb the highest mountain, traverse the longest distance, and always, without fail, keep a sure footing.

For years he tried and tried to find the right stick. He whittled on sticks, he carved on sticks. He traded sticks with others. But somehow, they never seemed to fit his hand just right or to hold him up just right. And one day, after many years of trying to find the right stick, he got tired of looking for something to lean on and decided that if he did not need a roof over his head or walls between himself and the winter, shelter between himself and the rain or anything but a hat between himself and the summer sun, that perhaps he did not need any stick, either.

And once he had found that he had all he needed in himself, then and only then did he become the true wanderer. Then and only then did he become truly happy. Satisfied at last that his purpose was not that of another and his needs not that of another, but that he was complete within himself.

We realize that in your culture it is not acceptable for a man to walk for a living, to live of the land, to have no money, and we do not encourage you to do this. We speak to you allegorically, my friends. What we are encouraging you to do is to leave off looking for the right walking stick in life. You did not come into this world to lean on others, to lean on ideas, to lean on possessions or to lean on preconceived ethics.

You came into this world a perfect creature and that perfection was rapidly overlaid by a complex system of intellectual limitations which were placed upon you by others. You then carefully continued the work of your parents, believed what they told you in good faith, and for your lifetime have been trying in good faith to live according to the precepts of people and ideas and ethics and ways of being that have been taught to you. These are your walking sticks, and none of them fit, do they?

No one else's ideas will carry you through, no one else's ethics can make you feel right if something is wrong, or wrong if something is right to you. Why spend so much of your life confused because of what others think? They may have traded you a walking stick, but you don't have to have it. You don't have to have any!

It is written in your holy works, my friends, "My rod and my staff shall comfort thee." Yes, my friends, even if you walk through the valley of death, you have a rod, you have a staff. You have the Creator within you; you are part of a perfection that is the Creator. And that part of you is the only walking stick you will ever need.

You cannot get in touch with that part of yourself by any outer means; you cannot, even though you think you might, get in touch with that part of yourself by intellectually understanding the means of meditation and service to others. What is a walking stick for, my friends? It is for the steep places. When you need comfort, know that that comfort exists within you. Even if you walk in the valley of death, the Creator is with you. His rod and his staff shall comfort you. Stand on your own two feet, my friends. And in your spiritual path remember that the way of the mountaineer is the true way. Walking, going, journeying, seeking, that is all that there is to living. The rest is illusion!

I am of the consciousness of [Kasara.] I would like to attempt to transfer this contact, if I may, to another instrument.

(Pause)

(Carla channeling)

We have been attempting to contact the one known as B, but our vibration is very light, and we are not finding it easy to use the instrument known as B. We will once again touch with his being and see if he can pick us up, although we are indeed much weaker, shall we say, than the vibration of Hatonn or Laitos. I am [Kasara.]

(B channeling)

I am Kasara. My friends, it is important that you look to your spiritual growth. For, my friends, as I have already stated, *(inaudible)* is illusion. There are many times you will find that, indeed, possessions will help you along your path. But, my friends, I think it is also important to draw the line upon, shall we say, possessions. For, my friends, the pull is so strong that it may in turn engulf you.

As you know, *(inaudible)* meditation you will evolve to a state that you will, shall we say, be able to offer your services to many around you. It is also important that you realize *(inaudible)* of helping a great many people. Therefore, my friends, it is important that you develop yourself to a higher degree. The road is steep and long; but, my friends, well worth the trip!

It has been a great pleasure sharing your meditations, my friends. *(Inaudible)* or shall we say *(inaudible)* we are, shall we say, at your disposal at another time. Continue in your meditation, for it is the path to the Creator. There may be some experiences ahead of you all. I shall leave this instrument now. I am [Kasara.] I leave you in the name of our infinite Creator.

(Pause)

(Carla channeling)

I am Laitos, and I greet you also in the love and the light of the infinite Creator. If you would be patient with me at this time I would like to spend a few moments working with the newer channels. I would like to exercise the channel known as G at this time. I am Laitos.

(Pause)

I am again with this instrument. We will try once more with the one known as G, after requesting that she relax, for she is somewhat tense and therefore is having difficulty receiving our thoughts. Therefore, they are being reflected back into the group. And it is much easier to absorb our thoughts, even if they are not spoken, you each can receive them, as we say, subconsciously. We would once again work with the one known as G and attempt to say a few sentences through her, if she will relax. I am Laitos.

(Pause)

I am again with this instrument. We thank the one known as G and encourage her not to worry, if she has some days when she cannot pick us up, for there are days when one becomes very tense due to the happenings of the day, and therefore one is less able to receive our thoughts. It is a kind of talent which one has a knack for after awhile. But it takes some time to build up, and we will continue to work with her and thank her for the opportunity. We would like now to attempt to speak just a few words through the one known as M, if she would also relax. I am Laitos.

(Pause)

(M channeling)

I am Laitos. *(Inaudible).*

(Pause)

(Carla channeling)

I am again with this instrument. We are having very good contact with the one known as M. We ask that she refrain from analyzing our thoughts. We will tell her what our next two sentences were to be, so that she will know that she had our contact. We would have attempted to say, "What a privilege it was to use each new instrument, and that it is a great honor to welcome each new instrument."

We will again attempt to contact the one known as M and speak just a few words further through her at this time. I am Laitos.

(M channeling)

I am Laitos. *(Inaudible).*

(Pause)

(Carla channeling)

I am again with this instrument. I am Laitos, and again I *(inaudible)* the one known as M. She is very close to making a breakthrough and being able to speak thoughts that she does not expect and that are original to her from us. Her main problem is in analyzing, and it is the breakthrough that we seek that will occur when she is able to speak our thoughts without attempting to discover whether or not they make sense. We are with you in love and love is a universal language, so that it is very difficult not to make sense, no matter what instructions or sentences we may give you. For there is almost no way that we can send you a thought which is not full of love in one way or another. We can only ask you to trust us as we train you in a service which will be more and more needed by your peoples as the new age begins. We thank you so much for your patience and we will close now through this instrument. I am known to you as Laitos, and I leave you in the love and light of the infinite Creator. Adonai.

(Pause)

I am Latwii, and I say to you greetings, my friends, in the love and the light of the infinite Father. As you say upon your planet, "Howdy, and how is everything with you?" We are very glad to see you this evening, and we are just very pleased to be able to speak with you. We have a very strong contact with this instrument, which we are attempting to mediate, so it will not be uncomfortable for this instrument. Unfortunately, we have a somewhat strong vibration. We are with this instrument. We are monitoring this communication. It is more comfortable to the instrument at this time. I am Latwii.

We truly are happy to be with you, and each of your vibrations gives us infinite pleasure as you sit about the room, miniature rainbows in what you think of as darkness but what we see as a beautiful violet glow at this time, due to the basic color of your vibrations, which is of a somewhat amethyst hue. We have come to answer questions at this time and would prefer to speak through the one known as Don, if he is willing to be of service at this time. We will attempt to transfer communications to him. I am known to you as Latwii.

(Don channeling)

I am with the instrument.

Carla: May I ask a couple of questions?

Yes.

Carla: Where is Hatonn now?

Hatonn is in the creation. There has been no change in his location.

Carla: In the configuration of this sphere, in which he assumes the shape of a man and the vehicle of a ship, over what part of our sphere does he now reside?

Southeast Asia.

Carla: Thank you, Latwii. Is it for the same purpose as *(inaudible)*?

Yes.

Carla: I see. Has there been any change?

No.

Carla: I didn't think so. When one has a person who comes to a group such as this one and is overenthusiastic, what is the most safe way of encouraging his ability to meditate and perhaps receive messages without opening him up to the problem of stray astrals which may mimic members of the Confederation?

(Pause)

Carla: Is there a general answer to that?

(Pause)

Information received by a channel is the information the channel desires to receive. The desire is what *(inaudible)* entertaining of the *(inaudible)*. This desire then results in what the channel receives. We in no way wish to modify this process, for it is a natural process.

[If] you find that for your purposes you do not wish some communications to take place, we suggest that you discuss these possibilities with the individual. We have no control over this, for it is a matter of free will.

Carla: I see. Then there is no tried and true method of psychic self-defense that is general. It is completely a function of the honesty of the individual in his desire to seek. Is that correct?

There is no need, from our point of view for what you call self-defense, for all times an individual will bring to themselves *(inaudible)* therefore it's part of a waste of time *(inaudible)* to defend *(inaudible)*.

Carla: What if a person does not know what he seeks?

That does not matter. The individual seeks and finds *(inaudible)*.

Carla: It is a subconscious method then, not a conscious one?

It can be either or both.

Carla: I see.

I shall tell a story. The child and an individual *(inaudible)* TV set seeks that which you don't desire to watch, finds great pleasure in this program and [in] time grows to a state of mind *(inaudible)*. In time, this seeking may become [analogous] to each of you who watch in joy *(inaudible)* program. This condition may exist *(inaudible)*. Or the other type situation that you mentioned as being distasteful to you may exist, which was *(inaudible)* desire different programs than you desire. Which does not mean that programming that he desires *(inaudible)* will not satisfy the desires *(inaudible)*. There is no such thing as bad seeking. There is only seeking. You will find that of what you are *(inaudible)*.

Does this answer your question?

Carla: Fully. There is a problem that's been bothering me for some time, and I really don't know if you can answer it or not. But, crazy as it may seem, I was wondering about gravity. We have always been taught that gravity pulls things together and there has been some scientific evidence now that gravity is actually a repulsive force. Do you have any comments on that? Do we aid our spiritual understanding or is it merely part of the illusion?

I am in consultation for education.

(Pause)

This instrument is being given the impression of an egg partially submerged in liquid. This egg is surrounded by liquid, so is your planet surrounded by material which you know of as space.

(Pause)

Space has different densities. These densities are not a physical property as you know physical property. These densities are condensed out [of] space, and each has its peculiar properties. The thing that you call gravity in your particular density is a function of condensation of your density out of space. It is similar to a bubble being formed below the surface of a window.[7]

(Side one of tape ends.)

(Don channeling)

This bubble is an isolated system and unique in its environment. *(Inaudible)* this is a material of a totally different density. This is how planets are formed out of space. They are formed as submerged bubbles. Submerged planetary bubbles in space. Each has its particular properties because of its

---

[7] Carla: The word represented in the transcript as "window" may have been "meniscus." Don was describing the idea of a bubble caught at the surface layer of a liquid condensate.

[antecedents] which is a function of what you would call its philosophy. Gravitational attraction, as you call it, which you experience, is the result of what you might call planetary philosophy, due to general configuration of mind, the population of your planet, both incarnate and discarnate. Certain level density, what you call physical matter, is condensed out of surrounding space, condensed in such a way, in such an intensity you might say, so as to reduce the intensity of gravity that you experience. All particles are condensed or pushed towards the center. This push or condensing force is philosophical in nature. A less intense philosophy would generate a less intense grip. Gravity is more an emotional thing than it is a physical thing in its origin. Your planet has a uniquely strong gravitation force. This is because of intense philosophical or emotional condensing action. Put in another way, the need for the dense physical experience, of those entities trapped in your vortexian experience, is such that they create the intense gravitational force that they now experience.

You can imagine consciousness being formed because of its like nature *(inaudible)* view *(inaudible)* across space *(inaudible)*. The size and *(inaudible)* being a function of the general state of that consciousness. This then is what you are experiencing, when you experience gravitational force.

Carla: Can I pursue that a little further?

Yes.

Carla: Can we assume then that each planetary entity is conscious or are we to assume that each planetary entity has a consciousness upon it which we would call living, as in living beings?

The consciousness is all the individualized consciousness that originally created the planet. In order to create a planet it is necessary to have condensation, shall we say, of consciousness. If consciousness is infinitely small, an infinitely small planet will be the result of this condensation. If consciousness as a group consciousness is large, shall we say, that numerous birds of a feather flock together so a large group consciousness will be formed, a relatively large planet will be formed. The planet is a result of the consciousness.

Carla: Thus, a large planet may not necessarily have a correspondingly heavy gravity as is thought in science, that the gravity would be dependent then on …

The gravity in your science is dependent on mass. Largeness or smallness is not related to mass, even in your science.

Carla: So you are saying that it is the density of the planet.

The density of the planet is the function of *(inaudible)* nature of the consciousness.

Carla: So when we are dealing with a planet like Saturn, which has been spoken of in other channelings, as well as ours, as being the ruling Council in this solar system, we are speaking of a very high consciousness, although the planet itself is quite large, is this correct?

There is no high or low consciousness! There is only consciousness!

Carla: Shall we say a consciousness more closely aligned with the original Thought of the Creator?

The original Thought of the Creator is that experience be sought. This Thought is being carried out all over the creation. Consciousness develops, anyway.

And this is the Thought of the Creator. It is also the original Thought of the Creator. Since we are at this time at the [earth] as we will be at all times or have at all times, density—shall we say ferocity of experience—is a function of that portion of consciousness, that, shall we say, amalgamates form, a sector of experience in what you call your reality. It is a physical planet. There are many, many planets that are not in your reality.

Carla: You just read my mind, that was my next question.

And exist for experiences at different levels.

Carla: Are they analogs of the physical planets in our system as we know them?

No.

Carla: They are simply infinite?

Yes.

Carla: I believe I am understanding a little more. If you are not too tired, I would like to know what relation that has to the Larsonian System. If you are, please say so.

Mathematical approach, Larson, is not considered a fact of consciousness. Larson's mathematics are useful tools for bottling your physical reality. There will be no explanation total. It does not include formative force of consciousness. It is very difficult to use your language to express this. Consciousness in actuality is the motion of which Larson speaks. *(Inaudible)* of that motion or vibration is the philosophy of the consciousness of which we spoke.

Carla: Then the very basis of the Larsonian system, instead of motion, as he would call it physically, is consciousness metaphysically. Is there an analog to the space/time that motion is equal to physically in the metaphysical understanding of Larsonian work?

There is no space.

Carla: Is it light, perhaps, and love?

There is only consciousness, consciousness which creates the illusion of space and time. There are properties of consciousness. The emotional property called love, the physical property called light. They are one and the same thing, but they are each two representations of the manifestations of consciousness. When this is fully realized, you know everything, there is nothing else to know.

Carla: Do they hold a reciprocal relationship?

You mean more love, less light?

Carla: Is the state of being in unity a love and light in equal portions, forever expanding outward?

(Pause)

Carla: Is less love and more light then the beginning of the great cycle of experience, causing intense vibrations?

I am trying to communicate to the instrument …

(Pause)

Love is light and light is love. They are consciousness. Light … this is difficult to express in your language.

Carla: We understand.

There is no reciprocal relation between love and light. They are identical.

Carla: Is this also true of space and time?

Space and time are mathematically reciprocal. This is meaningless in reality. They are mathematically reciprocal and this is a very useful tool in the building of mathematical molds, what you call your reality.

Carla: When a healer or metal bender uses his ability for action at a distance effect, is he temporarily leaving the mathematical and physical world of space/time and entering the metaphysical world of love?

He was never in the forementioned world but always in the latter, as is everyone.

Carla: What is his tool for bringing …?

His tool is consciousness. It is the only Creator. It is in your language an emotional thing. It may be generated through realization which is a function, usually in your society, of meditation. Meditation is necessary for this, in your society, because of an intense distraction from truth. You become re-linked with truth through meditation. This *(inaudible)* creates what you might call an emotional response. If this can be properly triggered to radiate from the microcosm then this radiating wave can affect physical material as you know it by rearranging basic configuration or vibration. It is not important as to how this mechanism works. What is important is first to understand the state of mind required to create a change. That state is a state of what you would call intense love. That is not necessarily a conscious state. It may be developed very easily by anyone through the process of meditation.

This is a process of cutting yourself off from those distractions you find in your particular section of *(inaudible)* consciousness and realigning your consciousness with that which is in the outer proportions of your sphere of experience. With other words, your planet and those [about] it are condensed from the sea of space which surrounds it. Sea of space is a real solid material, just as solid as your physical world. It just happens to be a different density experience. You may tap this through meditation and use that which is not, shall we say, basic vibration of your planet. It's difficult; the instrument understands it and cannot express it.

Carla: There are then no mathematical ways of describing how consciousness in a state of intense love can enter into the mathematically described universe of space/time. Is that correct?

You can only measure the effects of this.

Carla: You cannot pinpoint its point of entry, is that right?

The point of entry is the photon … is the photon. The intensity of the vibration which you identify as the photon is the point of entry, is the entry, is in fact the state of consciousness.

Carla: Then the link between love and light, love in a sense of consciousness and light in a sense of the reciprocal system, is the photon.

Love is the consciousness that is the vibration

Carla: Yes.

Light is another word for that vibration.

Carla: Yes, I see.

You are looking at the same thing, calling it two different things; it is the photon.

Carla: I am very happy to hear that. Thank you very much.

Are there any other questions?

(Pause)

We apologize for a lack of ability to communicate certain concepts which are very difficult in your language whether *(inaudible)* terminology include these concepts *(inaudible)*. But considerable work might be possible to arrange your language in such a way to make these points very clear. In such a short period of time it's very difficult to do.

If there are no more questions, we will terminate our communication.

Carla: We thank you.

It's been a very great privilege to be of service to you. Adonai vasu.

Thursday Meditation
September 27, 1979

(Carla channeling)

I am Hatonn, and I greet you in the love and in the light of the infinite Creator, in Whose name we come among you peoples to speak to you of the joy and the power that is yours as a birthright. We would like to greet one who is new to our group this evening, one who is known as S, and wish him well. There is some difficulty in transmission this evening due to the necessity of our using relay computers in order to speak with you. However, we hope that you will be patient with us. For we are expending a great deal of energy at this time working with some of the leaders of your world's peoples in hope that we may improve their desires for peace and brotherhood among the nations of your sphere.

We are sure that it has occurred to you, my friends, to ask the same question that has been asked by the one known as David who wrote in your holy works, "Who is man that thou art mindful of him, that thou visiteth him?" Who are you, my friends, and what is your relationship to the Creator? When we can speak to you of the things that are natural in your world, it is so much easier for you to understand your relationship to the Creator. For in your present society, your relationship to the Creator has become very tenuous and very difficult to grasp.

Were you a farmer, as you strew your seeds in the spring you would be doing the creative work given to you by the Creator. And you would be with Him a co-creator, spreading life, being of service, living in such a way that you could see the production of fulfillment which comes as a result of labor. In your present society, my friends, instead of your taking that which the Creator has provided and regenerating it, for the most part your society destroys it. Those of you who can properly understand your relationship with your Creator, you must go to the creation of the Father and study the interrelationships of the various parts of a delicately balanced and infinitely flexible arrangement that that creation constitutes.

Who are you that the Creator may visit you? You, my friends, are part of the Creator. It is as simple as that. You and all those things which are alive constitute a consciousness, the sum of which is the Creator. At any one time, there is a great pool of unconscious love spreading forth from the Creation as brightly and indiscriminately as does your sun spread light to your planet. But you, my friends, are not part of that pool of consciousness that is undifferentiated. You are part of that great circle of learning and evolution which marks the traveling back to the Creator hence you came. Thus, we ask you to appreciate it. Because of the Creator's love of you as that of identity, the Creator loves those parts of Himself, which of their own free will are traveling back towards Him, however slow or fast their trip may be. He loves Himself as He must. And as for you, my friends, what shall you do? In that same poem in your holy works the one known as David exclaims, "How excellent is thy name in all the world."

If you can but feel the closeness of the Creator, the reality of the love of the Creator, so that you too wish to exclaim how excellent are your works, you may feel then a compassion and an understanding for the unhappy creations of man, which have so complicated your picture within your chemical illusion at this time. You as people have a great responsibility for you are part of a planetary consciousness which desperately needs those who can love rather than feel negative feelings, who can feel compassion rather than judgment, who can be a mirror edged with [hope] rather than a black hole, sucking all that is good from the creation by sheer gravity.

In daily meditation [where you] go without a group, you may go into a place where you can be in touch with a place of excellence that is not only within yourself, but is part of an infinite life stream, inhabited by many, many beings of great knowledge and understanding from your own inner planes and from the similar spiritual planes of other dimensions. We ask you to come to that place, using your own judgment and discrimination, not because we advise you. For we do not know the absolute truth, but can only give you the guidance as we understand it to be right, that we know. We tell you these things in the spirit of helpfulness, and because we truly desire that as many of your peoples as possible be found. For many are lost from your flock, and if you can find them and bring them into the fold of understanding of the original Thought of the Creator, there is a joy that will ring in the very heavens, for each soul is precious to the Creator.

And what will happen, my friends, to those who are not to be brought into the fold at this time, to those who indeed desire to be distracted and numbed and removed from all thought of those events which may take place outside the compass of their very circumscribed and short earthly life? Do not worry, my friends, nor pass any judgment, for they will have an infinite amount of time in which to pursue their ultimate destiny. For the road can only go one way and that is towards knowledge of love.

People may learn quickly, they may learn very slowly. They may spend an entire incarnation declining to learn, but they will not lose what they have learned before and there are an infinite number of chances to learn again. For the Creator is truly compassionate. It is only you, my friends, who are so judgmental. We ask you not to build the Creator in your image but to build yourself in the Creator's image insofar as you can. Giving love, giving a kind ear, giving a gentle thought, perhaps simply giving a refraining from negative answers and above all, remembering to sow the seeds that the Creator has given you to sow when you feel that the ground is fertile. Never forcing yourself on stony ground, upon sand, but always responding to the question, to the interest, to the wonder, in such a way that that person may be alerted to the thought that there may be more to the life he is now experiencing than he had previously thought. It is this inspiration, my friends, that we hoped to give you and ask you to share. For each of you has talents. They are not yours, they have been given you by an infinite Creator. Each talent is different and each one creates a responsibility. We ask you to use your talents in love and in compassion. To do this, you must meditate, for there is no other way to remember the excellence of the name of the Creator. Not in the world, my friends, where things are not upon the surface entirely excellent. You must go beneath the surface and find the world of the Creator and the law of love which totally annihilates the world of man and the law of power.

I would pause at this time so that my brother may speak. I am Hatonn.

(Pause)

I am Laitos. I am with this instrument, and I thank you for allowing me to speak with you this evening. I greet you in love and in light. We were attempting to contact the one known as M, and with her permission we will again attempt to say a sentence or two to her. I am Laitos.

(Pause)

(M channeling)

I am …

(Pause)

(Carla channeling)

I am again with this instrument. I am Laitos. We had good contact with the one known as M, for which we thank her very much. We would like to get just one or two more sentences from her, so that she will build her confidence in her ability to give a more extended message, and so if she will be patient with us, we will again attempt to speak just a few sentences to her. I am Laitos.

(Pause)

(M channeling)

I am Laitos. I … I … I … I … *(inaudible).*

(Pause)

(Carla channeling)

I am again with this instrument. I am Laitos. We are most pleased with the one known as M, for we feel we have made a great breakthrough in working with her. Whereas before there was a serious doubt in the instrument's mind as to whether she wished to pursue the service, she is now dealing only with the problem of analyzing our thoughts as they come to her and therefore stopping the flow of ideas. However, we did give this instrument a word-by-word description of what we were going to say through her, and she received correctly until she stopped. This is said to give the instrument confidence that she may continue, shall we say, to let it all hang out, and thereby be of service to others. For when the lock is broken of a fear of speaking without sense, then the instrument will have begun to help in the same way that she herself perhaps feels that she has been helped. And we are very grateful for each channel that we may use.

We thank our sister M, and will continue to work with her in deepening her conditioning wave at any time she would request it. We would at this time like to condition the one who is somewhat near to this group, known as S. And due to the fact that we are not totally familiar with his vibratory pattern, we will be experimenting somewhat with the vibration.

Therefore, if the vibration becomes somewhat intense, we would ask that he mentally request that we moderate the vibration. This vibration's use is twofold. First of all it is intended as a kind of carrier wave for the meditative strength of the individual, so that his own meditation may be more deep. Secondly, if he wishes to become an instrument, it is a vehicle for the conditioning pattern which normally involves the sensation of, the movement of the parts of the mouth and throat which are normally used for speaking. This is to indicate that we are present and that the incident is not occurring only in the instrument's head. We will not attempt to speak to him this evening but only to give him an idea of how our vibration feels. I am Laitos.

(Pause)

I am again with this instrument and would wish to thank the one known as S. We, as we have said, are with those who ask for our presence mentally, at any time that they do so. If at any time you would wish us to leave, you have merely to request mentally that we do so. For it is our desire not to interfere at any time with the free will of those who dwell upon your planet, but only to make available to them our love and our thoughts. I am Laitos. I will leave you now in love and light. Adonai.

(Pause)

I am Latwii. I am very glad to be with you and speak to you in love and light. We were attempting to say hello to you through the one known as M and although we made contact, she was somewhat perplexed due to the fact that we have not spoken to her before and our vibration is quite different from that of Hatonn. We merely wish to say greetings and love as we enjoy understanding the fifth dimension of your planet at this time. We are on watch here cataloguing the various vibrations of that plane and from this point we look upon your peoples with great love. We send you that love. We pass the meeting now back to our brothers of Hatonn, who have waited patiently for us to stick our noses into his meeting. Adonai, my friends. Adonai, in the name of the Creator.

(Pause)

I am Hatonn, and I return to this instrument, as always, with the name of the Creator upon our lips. We will pause only to ask if there are questions at this time. Please feel free to ask about anything about which you may be curious at this time. Are there any questions at this time?

(Pause)

We are aware that there are questions, but we do not feel that we can interrupt the free will of those who would ask but who have decided not to at this time, by answering them. We apologize for the somewhat slow nature of this communication. As we say, it has been through what you would call a machine that we have sent our thoughts. But our brother Latwii is as busy as are we at this time and so we are attempting to speak to you ourselves, although we are not in your skies at this time.

We ask you, my friends, to remember those things which are true and beautiful in your life, in your dreams, in your thoughts, and to refrain from being discouraged at this great reservoir of experience which does not meet the ideal to cherish. You must understand that all upon which you look is a part of yourself. If you are unhappy with what you see, the only alternative is to learn to love it. Not foolishly, but with understanding. Only love can give you that divine understanding and only meditation can give you access to the original Thought of the Creator which is that love.

I leave you, my friends, in that love and the infinite light which it has created throughout this great creation of many universes, many dimensions, and many times. We leave you with the Creator. We are your brothers and sisters, and we are known to you as Hatonn. Adonai, my friends. Adonai vasu borragus. ✣

L/L Research

L/L Research is a subsidiary of Rock Creek Research & Development Laboratories, Inc.

P.O. Box 5195
Louisville, KY 40255-0195

www.llresearch.org

Rock Creek is a non-profit corporation dedicated to discovering and sharing information which may aid in the spiritual evolution of humankind.

ABOUT THE CONTENTS OF THIS TRANSCRIPT: This telepathic channeling has been taken from transcriptions of the weekly study and meditation meetings of the Rock Creek Research & Development Laboratories and L/L Research. It is offered in the hope that it may be useful to you. As the Confederation entities always make a point of saying, please use your discrimination and judgment in assessing this material. If something rings true to you, fine. If something does not resonate, please leave it behind, for neither we nor those of the Confederation would wish to be a stumbling block for any.

CAVEAT: This transcript is being published by L/L Research in a not yet final form. It has, however, been edited and any obvious errors have been corrected. When it is in a final form, this caveat will be removed.

© 2009 L/L Research

Saturday Meditation
November 3, 1979

(Carla channeling)

I am Hatonn, and I greet you, my friends, in the love and the light of the infinite Creator. We were attempting to contact both the instrument known as B and the instrument known as M, so that if either of these instruments felt that they were being contacted, they were correct.

We urge each of you to improve in your self-confidence, and we will again try to contact you later in the meeting. May we say to you, my friends, that it is a great privilege to be with you this evening. For we speak now to those who do not need to hear our words, for you, my friends, are already awake to the consequences of eternity, and do not need our [attempts] at inspiration and the provoking of the [healing] curiosity for more information which we normally need to deal with in our contact with your people through channels such as this one.

Thus, we can speak to you, shall we say, face to face, without shading our words as we so often do and we find this to be an enormous honor. And we thank you for the great privilege of being asked to speak to you, who already are conscious of much that we have to say. Thus, with you we may go a bit further. We have been aware of your conversations this evening, and we send to you our comfort and our blessing that you may not be overly concerned for the future. For eternity exists only in the moment. And prudence is not necessarily an ingredient of spiritual good health

You must of course dwell within your physical vehicles and cope in such a way with your physical existence, that you do not become a stumbling block before others, nor a liar, nor a [dissembler.] This much attention we must give to our daily habits and duties and responsibilities, and we would never encourage anyone to forgo such indicators of a balanced and stable worker along the path. But we say to you, my friends, that you must be mindful of a certain story which has been written in your holy works, and in that story a teacher, known to you as Jesus, was approached by a young man who asked to become a disciple of the great rabbi.

He had listened to the one known as Jesus, and he believed in what he said, and he wished to devote himself to learning more and more. The one known as Jesus turned to him and said: "You are a very good student and you must do only one thing more if you want to follow me; sell all that you have and give it to the poor and come and follow me." You are aware of course, my friends, because you are not introductory students, that this was a parable and not to be taken literally. It is not those things which you have that you must sell; rather, my friends, it's those things which have you, which chain you in some way and block you from understanding yourself and your true desires that you must shed, as a snake would shed an old and faded skin. These things need not necessarily be physical things. They may be nothing more than ideas, attitudes.

You have heard it said this evening—know yourself! That is the most important thing. And we ask you to consider, not for the future, but now, in each moment, what do you desire? It is said of many in the world that they are selfish because they do what they desire. And what they desire may not meet the models of the society in which they live, and yet we say to you, if you do not do what you desire, you will never be content; you will never be secure; you will never know the present moment to its fullest. There is a misconception, that is greatly spread among your peoples, that you are beings who are shaped by circumstance. This is not so, my friend, unless you allow it to be so.

If you are able to remain in contact with the Creator, your life can be totally devoid of circumstance. That is a big "if," my friends, and it requires constant remembrance of your oneness with the original Thought, so that you become full of joy. Not your own joy, my friends, but the joy of creation, the joy that brings things to life. The joy that transfigures death into resurrection. Such a joy is real and is realistic, and can touch all circumstances and all those about you. If you can maintain to any degree this contact with the Creator, the Creator, working through your higher self, will find Its own way to allow you to become aware of what is right for you. You will not know ahead of time; you may not know an instant before. It will not be an intellectual process; it will occur. And there will be an inner conviction and with that conviction, a peace!

We realize, my friends, that you are sad because your clan has not been able to work at full efficiency during your incarnations so far. If you could only see the number of people that you have touched in your work, in your daily contact, in your friendships, you would know that you have not deviated nor forgotten that love which you came to bespeak to the multitudes.

It is possible, and indeed we feel very probable, that the time for drama is over. For your peoples would not accept it. And thus, you could not do it. There were those who would have helped you, but they could not. For they were not ready to pick up the responsibility of the knowledge that they held. Their inability was due to a simple human failing, and that is what we spoke of earlier. And one could sum it up in the word "greed." There was something, an ego problem, a personality problem, a favorite activity. Something as small as that which eliminated them from the life of constant service. But you must remember that the space/time continuum is forever flexible and forever changeable, and in your local world each moment is discreet and separate, thus giving you a nearly infinite number of chances to be of perfect service to the Creator.

We are aware of your great hopes, and we honestly do not know what the future may hold, for there are many futures, and we do not know which one you will choose. But we say unto you, that those who love and seek the Father will find the satisfaction of missions well accomplished, no matter how the plan has evolved, no matter what decisions have led to other decisions, and thus we ask you to live today in a loving way and always to say, "I shall obey the voice of meditation; those thoughts I will weigh."

We would leave you to silence for a few moments, and then we would attempt to transfer this contact to the one known as B. I am Hatonn.

(B channeling)

(Inaudible)

(M channeling)

I am Hatonn. I am with this instrument … *(inaudible)*.

(Carla channeling)

I am Laitos, and I would with your permission work with the instrument known as K for a brief period, for we would like to make contact with her and make her familiar with our conditioning wave. We would attempt to say a few words to her, if she is willing this time. If not, we wish only to make our presence known to her. If she will relax, we will attempt to do so, at this time. I am Laitos.

(Pause)

I am again with this instrument. We were attempting to calibrate our vibration to properly coincide with the basic spiritual vibration of the one known as K. We will continue to work with our sister at any time she may request it. It has been a great privilege to be with you, and we thank you for your patience. I am Laitos. Adonai, my friends.

(Carla makes a tuning sound, twice.)

I greet you in the love and the peace of the infinite Father. I come at your request, and I am known to you as Jesus. Your vibration has reached out to me this evening. And I perceive that you are true disciples, and that you are all too aware of my words, that you must take up your cross and follow me.

It is well, my friends, my beloved children, to meditate upon that which is your cross so that you may the better take it up. But we ask you to remember, that it is through the cross that you can achieve redemption for all those about you, through your great love and sacrifice and ultimate resurrection. What I wish to say to you now is that you will be aware more and more as you grow towards the consciousness, which you choose to call Christ Consciousness, of the endless wonder of existence in the creation of the Father; to live, my friends, in a constellation of beings who are individual, unique and miraculous; to have, through grace and the holy spirit that dwells among you, all power for good and for love. Think you that you are unworthy of wonder and joy?

Shed your unworthiness! You do not need it and it does not need you. Enter then into the kingdom which awaits you. A kingdom that is here, my friends, in this illusion, on this plane of existence. Enter into the kingdom of those who have washed in the waters of healing. Know that which is your cross, and love and accept that which is your cross, and so shall you be healed.

It may not seem so to the world, but it is your soul that is of significance, and it is your soul that must be healed and washed and, once clean, you shall be called holy and you shall be called chosen. Not by others and not by yourself, but by the impersonal and loving judgment of light. For your souls are the stuff of light. Thus, heal your souls by constantly standing in consciousness of love, and wash and wash with that love until you are clean. Let this be private and secret and speak to no man. For the world will not understand that which you do in the name of the Father.

But that which is within will come out. And thus, you will become an instrument for love. What love I have in me is yours, my brothers and sisters. You are my beloved brethren. And you are next to my heart, as are all conscious beings. Know that you can and you will be healed of whatever keeps your soul in bondage.

And seek always that holy ground which lies beneath your feet wherever you stand. I am with you in prayer. I am by your side in meditation. My love goes with you, my peace I give to you. I am known to you as Jesus. My peace to you, my friends.

(Side one of tape ends.)

(Carla channeling)

I am Latwii. I am Latwii. I am Latwii. We are sorry, we always have trouble with this instrument for she is very delicate, and we begin too strongly and have to lighten in our vibration. It is an unusual one, and yet she is very good at receiving it; and we are not used to this because we do not have great success with your peoples in communicating with them. Therefore, we assume that this entity has a certain amount of light vibration in her makeup. That is perhaps due to her weight—ha, ha!

We are aware of the question at hand, and it is somewhat complex. Indeed, due to this instrument's abominable knowledge of very little geography, we will only attempt to speak about the question at hand. The vibrations in the earth are somewhat generalized, however, the one known as Hatonn had been, until very recently, in China, due to an extremely complex situation internationally. We will attempt to sort it out, but you must be aware, that our answer is somewhat simplistic.

The entity known as China is a backward nation with many people. They do not have the monetary strength of their northern neighbor, which is Russia. And although it would seem that they would be natural allies, China has a set of leaders at this time which are in fiercest enmity with the leaders of Russia. You must understand that we consider such things as ideology perfectly ridiculous since all of your peoples fail [to live] out love. Even in your own America you consider the pursuit of happiness and not the pursuit of understanding of love as the most important right of each human being. Thus you have a nation which disports itself instead of becoming disciplined and wise enough to use the great resources that are at your disposal.

There is some wisdom in China but not at this time in its leaders. They seek to undermine the advances of Russia in world events. They seek to do this by many means. They have [started] a conflagration in your Indo-China area which even now is burning out of control. They have attempted to make allies of the United States by offering great incentives to invest capital and technology in China while at the same time planning, at the nearest and most convenient opportunity, to use nuclear tactics to destroy both Russia and the United States.

For in China the leaders believe very closely in the classical ideology of Marx in which there is a worldwide struggle, out of which come the victors, that is, the Chinese. Their hatred of Russia stems from their observation that Russia has relaxed its relentless drive towards world domination and is content simply to be a very powerful communist influence. The Chinese play a more clever game of international politics than their Russian counterparts. And their influence spreads as far towards your West Coast as the Philippines in which there is some unrest which is fomented at times by Chinese encouragement.

Thus, the one known as Hatonn was extremely interested in sending vibrations of love to these leaders. For if pressed too far, if Russia had then realized what China was seriously considering, it in turn might very easily have attacked Western Europe, because at this time, Western Europe lies almost defenseless against their weapons. The great difficulty here, of course, is that it is unlikely that any soldier would allow the nuclear destruction of one side without automatically returning fire and destroying the other side. What would be left would be a maimed and ruined physical illusion, for we do not feel that it is within our rights to violate the free will of those upon your planet if they wish to bomb each other.

As we have said before, we work only to save the soul, not the body. We will and have before successfully neutralized the disintegrating effect of nuclear weapons upon the etheric or electrical body—or as you might call it, the spiritual body or soul—of entities who are subjected to a physical transition due to atom or nuclear bombing. Furthermore, the Chinese are interested in the outcome of Russian interests in Third World countries and have engaged in active espionage which involves the theft of fissionable material for use in unauthorized nuclear devices.

Among nations who are ruled by those who do not have the mental capacity to understand what they might unleash, but only understand the prestige of owning a nuclear device, this so-called nuclear proliferation is very dangerous. And each new source of nuclear attack increases the potential for this becoming a reality. Thus, Hatonn, who is one of our Confederation's most strongly loving entities, has turned its planetary consciousness entirely several times towards these leaders and at times those of Russia.

Does this answer your question, my sister?

Questioner: *(Inaudible).*

We are glad and are sorry that we cannot be more specific through this instrument but her knowledge of geography is truly the pits. Is there another question at this time?

Questioner: *(Inaudible).*

We would be glad to, my sister, for our vibration is a simple one. We have gone through your experiences and we have gone through the experiences of the ones of Hatonn, and our level of experience is one level closer to the original Thought, so that we no longer have bodies as you know them, but are light beings normally moving about as balls of light which can appear to you as UFO's.

We are of a vibration in which many of your so-called angels also move, and therefore we find great delight in singing, laughing, music of all kinds and the great beauty of colors and shapes and harmonies. It is our particular purpose, at this time within the Confederation, to monitor and begin to understand the various vibrations upon your planet in each density, so that we may the better be able to aid those upon your planet. Thus, we spend a great deal of time examining the spectrum of vibration in each of your densities. We enjoy this tremendously, and as we focus on each color we immerse ourselves in it and float about in it as bubbles on a string.

Your planet is very beautiful, and despite many a dark shadow due to negativity, we find it a very beautiful place and put every effort towards preserving that which is beautiful in the thoughts of so many. When you laugh, when you hum, when you think a half a thought, know that we are with you and are joining in your laughter.

Does this answer your question? May we ask you, especially—if you are sad, to call upon us? You cannot be sad when you are full of light, and that is our vibration. Is there another question at this time?

Questioner: *(Inaudible).*

That is correct, my sister. Angels are assigned to people.

Questioner: *(Inaudible).*

That is correct.

Questioner: Does every person have an angel?

Most have more than one angel, depending upon how much of a stinker they really are. The ones who are kindly affectioned, one to another, have as many as twelve, that is normally the complete assortment of angels that one individual will have.

Angels exist as part of the higher personality of each individual in order to give guidance, self confidence and a feeling of support. Very few among your peoples know how to call upon their angels, and yet they are there and they are as full of love and light as are we. But they are members of your planetary sphere, and thus they have the right to do a little bit more for you than we can. In other words they have the right to be with you, whether you request it or not.

Their rights only stop at the point where the person denies that there are such beings, denies the deity, the spirit, and love itself. This does not remove the angel from the person, but it renders the angel completely helpless, and so the angel patiently and consistently will set up again and again a situation, in which the person who does not believe will see something which, if he thinks about it, can open the door to belief. This much an angel may do; we cannot. We can only come when we are specifically called. For we are not of your planetary sphere, and thus must obey the law of Creation, which is total free will.

Questioner: *(Inaudible).*

It depends upon your state of belief as to whether angels can physically aid you. If you believe in their reality, they can do almost anything, for grace is given unto those who believe. And the angels are the ministers of that grace. They are people such as you, who had learned through many lifetimes to glorify and praise the Creator. Thus, having learned, the angel can pass on the power and the invocation of light. There is nothing more powerful than the light of the spirit. Thus, if you pray and hear the rustle of angels' wings, so be it. You have made contact with a part of your personality that links you with the perfection of the Creator.

It is, however, incumbent upon the angel to know the limits of the laws of Creation and the will of the Father. Thus, the angels' laws are not those of your illusion but those of reality, and so it may seem at times that your requests are not being met. And if this is so, it is because it is not the will of your higher self which shares the perfection of the Creator. For remember that you yourself are the co-creator with the Creator and thus a perfect being, who in some part of yourself knows what you must learn, and how you must learn it in this particular experience. Those who make complete use of their meditation, their prayer, and their faith lead the life of harmony that you would expect of one who lives with the knowledge of the love and the plan of the Creator. The angels are simply messengers of his love, as are we.

Does this answer your question?

Questioner: *(Inaudible).*

We thank you, my sister, for without you we would be talking to thin air. Is there another question at this time?

(Pause)

We at this time, before we leave you, would like to share with you a color which we are now experiencing. It is a violet vibration and we find it extremely beautiful and very much in tune with you at this time. If you will pause for a second, we will send this to you. I am Latwii.

(Pause)

I will leave this instrument at this time. It is a great pleasure to be asked to speak with you. We are always surprised to be asked, for we do not speak to many groups but only those who are ready for our somewhat demented attitudes. We hope that we can help with these few foolish words and we leave you in the greatest love and light which is that of the Creator. Adonai, my friends. Adonai vasu borragus. ❦

Special Advanced Meeting
November 18, 1979

(Carla channeling)

I am with the instrument. I am Latwii, and I greet you in the love and light of the infinite Creator. We are sorry for the delay. However, we were attempting to contact the one known as Don. This was for the reason that there are certain questions that we would prefer to use that instrument [for,] due to the fact that the instrument known as Carla has already been exposed to the questions and has formed certain biases in her mind, which will make it more difficult for her to channel without distortion. We do not believe in distortion in communication and therefore prefer a pure source if we can activate it. However, the one known as Don is not easily picking up our signal. And we will pause at this time in order to work with him. If you will be patient we will leave this instrument. I am Latwii.

(Pause)

(Carla channeling)

I am again with this instrument. We are having difficulty with the one known as Don. We would suggest to him a few fast turns around the mental block so that he may be more able to achieve mental contact, because he is a bit rusty. We will attempt once more, suggesting to him that we of Latwii have a gentle ray, which is somewhat unlike the ray of Hatonn. It is to be found in the direction almost perpendicular to the plane of horizontal. If the one known as Don will limber up his capacities, we would like to speak through him. We will give it another shot, at this time. I am Latwii.

(Don channeling)

I am at this time ready for questions.

Carla: Are you familiar with the Australian incident?

[I am Latwii.] I am familiar.

Carla: What happened to the pilot?

Don: Because of the nature of that question—now this is me talking. I would recommend that each of us get an answer, and compare. I've already got my answer. Can you get an answer?

Carla: I think they took him.

Don: Not think. I mean, can you just get an answer.

Carla: Well, I mean that's what I got.

Don: Can you get anything, B?

B: I got an image of his brain turning into light, changing dimension or something … outlined in light around it.

Carla: What did you get?

Don: I got that he was killed, accidentally.

Carla: Well, you were the one with the channel.

Don: See what you get.

Carla: Well, I already did.

Don: Carry on.

Carla: Are you there, Latwii?

(Don channeling)

I am with the instrument.

Carla: There is some fault in our asking the question, is there not? Something that shows our ignorance of how UFOs operate? Am I on the right track?

I am with the instrument. I am sorry for the delay. We have been conditioning the instrument. We will continue. There is insufficient data to explain what has happened. It is difficult for us to explain sometimes.

Carla: Were each of the three images we got correct, or some part of the phenomenon?

They were correct.

Carla: So what we have to do is understand the phenomenon of which those three things were a part. Is that correct?

That is correct.

Carla: Can you help us with that? Or is it for us to know at this time?

Please be patient with this instrument. He is being conditioned. I am with the instrument. I am Hatonn. We are having some difficulty with the other contact. I greet you in the love and the light of our infinite Creator. It is a very great privilege to be with you this evening. Friends, all that you know, your present intellectual condition, is in actuality nothing. Your condition has been chosen by yourselves for a particular type of experience. You are able to manifest a limited ego, in a very limited way, so that you may interact with its environment and itself in such a way as to become aware in greater detail of its shortcomings. This, in actuality, is the only purpose of your present existence.

You ask of a particular situation in which there is a missing individual. The individual was concerned with an encounter with an unidentified object. Well, let's consider your purpose in discovering the fate of this one particular person, when you do not attempt to discover the fate of many who are more closely related to you in time and space. Consider your motives and objectives in determining the location of this particular individual.

We are here to examine, you might say, the entire population of your planet, called Earth. We have removed some of your peoples and will continue to do so. We never act without the consent of the individual being removed. In fact, my friends, we never act in any way without the consent of those involved. For in truth, it is the desire of an individual that brings about a situation in which he finds himself. And only his desire creates this situation. This is true for everything that happens to everyone throughout all space. Each experience that you have is the result of nothing but your own desire for the experience. This is sometimes very difficult to understand. However, it is an absolute truth.

This, my friends, is the way the Creation works: it works on desire. If this were totally understood by the people of the planet Earth you would have immediately a Utopia. For this is obviously the most logical thing to desire. However, the desires of the population of this planet are extremely varied. For this reason you have a rather widely varied experience. You spoke of the fate of the Australian pilot. His fate, my friends, is a complete total function of his desire. He is where he is at this time because of his desire. You are where you are because of your desire.

Speak of the actions of the one known as Ayatollah Khomeini, and how his thinking and actions affect many of the population of your planet. His thinking, his actions, the effect and the effect on the population so involved is a function of his and their desires. You cannot affect or be affected unless you desire it. This is a natural law of the Creation. This may be difficult to understand, but it is in actuality extremely simple.

In the first place, my friends, experience you are not in the physical density of your planet at this particular time. Your desire has created your presence at this particular time in this particular place. When you start with this contact substance, my friends, it immediately becomes obvious that every experience that you have is a function of your desire. Your desire acts in an infinite number of ways in addition to the action that brought you to this planet that you now experience. It acts each waking and each sleeping moment. It brings to you everything that you experience. And it projects all that you project in the way of experience that may be desired by others about you. It is very important, my friends, to understand the mechanism of desire. For this is central to your growth.

Are there any other questions?

Carla: I think that my motivation for asking the question about the Australian pilot was because I had never before seen any evidence whatsoever that UFOs ever did harm to anybody. And I guess I wanted to confirm that hypothesis. Is it possible that the reason you refrained from answering in the earlier meeting was due to the fact that the discussion of beings in UFOs as opposed to beings on Earth was improper, and that we should be thinking of you and we as the same thing?

[I am Hatonn.] You have spoken of harm done to others. In this creation it is quite impossible to administer what you call harm to others. It is only possible to administer harm to yourself. The facts that you see and understand as administering harm to others is total illusion. The harm that is administered is always reflected to those who project it.

Carla: Is this why the information was not made available to the last advanced group?

[I am Hatonn.] This information is sometimes difficult to understand and seems to be nonsense to those who have not progressed intellectually to the point of comprehending what I am giving to you at this time. For this reason certain subjects are not attempted except to those capable of understanding. The points that I have been bringing out about what you call injection of harm in the function of desire are very, very important points. To understand them sometimes requires considerable thought. It seems to you that in the case of a great battle or war there is a negative aggressor, who is able to inject great suffering and pain in those whom he attacks.

My friends, this is the apparent illusion. Everything that he projects he actually instantly receives. All those who feel the effects of his aggression and suffer seemingly from it, are suffering, in actuality, from their own acts of aggression. If a big bomb bursts in the middle of a crowd, some will be severely wounded, some will be killed, some will go unscathed. Your scientists can very accurately predict the probability of casualty for each person, taking into consideration his distance from the center of the blast and his position in the area subtended by his body.

But, my friends, what the scientist does not know is that what he receives in such a situation is what he deserves and desires. He deserves it because of desire. He is here in this particular position, at this particular time, experiencing this particular effect because of desire. He is receiving because of his desire, shall we say, a catalyst in the form of a projector. Your Earth, your planet, your entity vibration is nothing but a training program. It is not a random happening. It is not anything that most of your peoples believe it to be. It has been called by one who knows, one great sleight of hand. This is precisely what has happened. It is happening individually and at all times collectively.

These things can work this way, my friends, because of the nature of space and time. You experience the illusion of a certain amount of freedom and space in a continuing temporal experience that is ruled unbreakable by what you call the stream of time. But this is illusion. This is the key illusion that allows for the precise administration of the physical catalyst for your experience.

All events are, shall we say, programmed for your experience; programmed by your desire, and then experienced in what you understand as sequential time. Every thought that you think programs your experience, no matter how trivial. Every deed that you perform programs your experience, no matter how trivial. For this reason, you must say that we are sometimes amused by questions having to do with the reasons for a particular experience. Because from your point of view in the philosophy of those on the surface of your planet this time there is a completely different reason for everything.

The reason, my friends, is desire. The mechanism is that great sleight of hand that programs your experience. You do not live in a four-dimensional universe. You live in a four-dimensional illusion. You do not exist now at your present age and at an older age in the future, or at a younger age in the past. You exist, my friends, at all ages simultaneously. You experience the illusion of the aging process once more because of that great sleight of hand. You do not live, die and become reborn in that order, or any order, my friends. Because you are. Only the part of you that experiences the present illusion is born, grows through youth to old age and dies. And this, my friends, is a very important part of the illusion. For if the reverse occurred you would not learn. It is necessary in this density to experience the process that you know as aging. It is not necessary if you do not need it. If you need it, it is because you have desired it. No other reason, my friends. It is simply because you have desired it.

Now you experience it. It is illusory and transient. The question having to do with the infringement upon your will in this illusion is also of no consequence. Any infringement is there because you have desired it. My friends, what is the purpose? The purpose, my friends, is education. We give to you what we can to allow you to make greater use of this education. For only you can put knowledge that you receive to use. When you transcend that point, which we shall call the point between awareness of and lack of awareness of the illusion, you then accelerate your understanding at a much, much greater rate than previous to this awareness. You are thinking, my friends, that this is all that there is. Know yourself. And this alone will give you your freedom. Nothing else will do it.

We will transfer this contact to the other instrument. It has been a great pleasure speaking to you through this instrument. I will answer your question.

Carla: *(The gist of the question had to do with whether another group that writes of cosmic awareness is connected to the Confederation of Planets.)*

All groups are connected. There is no other possibility.

(Tape ends.)

Sunday Meditation
November 18, 1979

(Unknown channeling)

I am Hatonn. Greetings, my friends, in the love and in the light of the infinite Creator. It is indeed enjoyable to speak to you, each of you, through this instrument, once again. I and my brothers are great in number, and we gather close to you at this time. For as you are witnessing, day by day, the changes predicted throughout the centuries of your world are occurring more and more rapidly. We draw near to your peoples with the passing of each moment. For love, and our willingness to assist you, increases, as does your willingness to open yourself to the truth of this Creation.

We speak to the best of our ability of the truths and of the laws that govern this universe. But we wish to stress that these truths and laws have been handed down from many sources and introduced into your societies throughout the entire civilization of your planet. We offer nothing new. We have come to give freely of our services, and we of the Confederation are pleased to be invited to speak through an instrument such as this, throughout all of the lands of your planet.

We would speak to you briefly upon the changes which you are witnessing. We of the Confederation have spoken many times of that which is to occur on your planet. We do not wish to deal in particular with precise occurrences, yet, [with their meaning] we wish to speak to you about.

Changes within this universe are beneficial, no matter how grievous they may appear, for as in your life experience, with each change comes a greater understanding of the complexity of not only your life but of the universe. To the best of our knowledge, the universe itself is endless. So therefore are the changes you may experience throughout your travels upon this plane of existence and upon all planes which you may enter into.

You have heard the saying that, "Each cloud has a silver lining." A simple truth! With each appearingly destructive occurrence within your society today, though the activity may be negative in nature, it is presented to mankind, one, because he has created it unknowingly through his own thought processes, and two, so that he may witness that which is undesirable and desire to change once again, and experience that which would be more desirable and of a positive nature.

Yet, mankind, as it is known upon your planet, continually insists upon experiencing the negative aspects of this Creation. Many of your religions have taught you to fear the wrath of your God. It is shameful, in a sense, that man must be taught with fear. For God is not fear and should never be feared by you. God is to be respected; the Creator is divine and all-loving and all-knowledgeable.

Because He has seen your continued stubbornness, shall we say, to learn or progress, as He would wish you to do, He has reluctantly introduced fear into His teachings. Mankind must learn to releases his fears and in so doing, he shall free himself from an intensely negative atmosphere which he has created around himself, thus allowing the energies of the universe, which are all the essence of truth and love, to more evenly penetrate his being. Consider yourself to be as a sponge and the truths of the universe as the liquid of life. You have a cellophane coating about you; remove it without fear, and you shall absorb all the truth that you have so long sought to realize.

Mankind is divine, as is the Creator. The extent of your divinity is unlimited, as long as you choose not to limit that divinity through your own creative abilities, by accepting fear and all things that are associated with it into your life. Know thyself and you shall know thy Creator! Fear thy Creator and you fear thyself! With these words, I pass on this communication to another instrument. I am Hatonn.

(Carla channeling)

I am now with this instrument, and again I greet you in the love and in the light of the infinite Creator, the One Who is that source of us all and that central sun to which we shall return in the fullness of infinite life. We shall continue through this instrument.

When you consider, my friends, what it is that you are, you may then see that there is nothing to fear either outside or within yourself. For you are a being of infinite life, and whatever occurs to your physical envelope which you call your body is but a transitory alteration in your condition of consciousness. However, we realize that at this time, although you have some knowledge of yourself as one with the Creator, although you have a good grasp of the ideals of the ethics of love, but you are at this time enduring difficulties associated with living within the gross or coarse reality which is your Earth plane.

Therefore, we would like to make a distinction for you in order to enhance your understanding of that which you see about you. There are two types of that which you would call negativity.

The first type is extremely beneficial. Night, for example, is the negative of day. Night is very beneficial, giving us rest from our labors and a happy end to the troubles of the day. Cool is the negative of warm and when you have experienced your planet's sunlight for too long a period of time, there is nothing as refreshing to you as the coolness of water as you bathe in it and enjoy its beauty.

You will find these same negatives in people. You will find temper which is the negative of patience, and yet, you will find that temper brings honesty, and honesty brings understanding. You will find illness as the negative of health, and yet, with illness comes the only chance for healing and thus understanding the power of that which you call the holy spirit.

All of these so called negatives are a valuable and gentle necessity of existence. And when they are part of your life, it would be well for you to analyze them and understand the balance that they make for you. For beauty and joy are not one-sided, but occur only because there are gradations of beauty and gradations of joy which extend into their negatives, a lack of beauty and a lack of joy.

When you are sad, realize that you are natural; that you are part of a balancing force. Just as a pendulum will move, so will your spirit seek its balance. Not by standing still, but by rocking. Joy, sadness! Joy, sadness! This is the earthly way.

There is another way, my friends, and that is available to you only through meditation. And when you enter into this [supernal] joy of infinite life and are one with angels and spirits of high divinity, praising the Creator, then there is no balancing necessary. For this is a joy without what you call emotion. It is so wholehearted, as you would call it, that there is no balancing necessary in order to sustain the energy of the feeling. In fact, joy is not a feeling but a creative force. And another word for that is love. And that is what we greet you with, and that is what we always leave you with.

We previously mentioned that there was another kind of negativity, one which you need not fear, but which you might need to understand. And that is an unnatural negativity. One which is not balanced, but is chosen, purposely and perversely by those who would separate themselves from ongoing unity with the Creator. It is a choice of separation, and it is what we would call positive negativity, in that it is positively sought and encouraged.

Yes, my friends, there are those among you who are quite simply unnaturally negative. This is their path and they have chosen it. We do not wish to ask you to have any particular feeling about these people, one of whom is certainly in your mind at this time, for he is in the minds of all those whom we scan in your culture. We refer to the one known as Khomeini. We do not ask you to love, forgive or condone, for these are choices which you must make for yourself. We cannot help you choose your own spiritual reality. But we can hope to enhance your understanding of the fact that although even such a one as he is somewhat negative at this time, by his own choice, you must understand that the path of evolution is ultimately spiritual and is ultimately inevitable.

A negative person may choose at this time to make no progress. He will, however, at a later time have as many choices and opportunities as he needs to choose again. In your holy works there is something called, "The Day of Judgment," and those who are evil, as we have spoken, are to be condemned forever. And yet, it is also written in your holy works, "Yea, though you go to the very doors of hell, I shall be with you."

My friends, you may believe the teacher and not the judgmental statements that follow the teacher. Your heaven and your hell exist within you at this moment. And when you leave your physical body, your existence in the heaven worlds will depend completely upon your vibration in this incarnation. Thus, we ask that you use that balancing act of positive and negative, so that you are constantly learning, constantly moving in an evolutionary spiral that will lead you to a place where in your infinite existence, after this brief life experience in this density, you will be comfortable, comforted and able to give comfort to others.

At this time, I would pause that my brother Laitos may send energy to each of you in this group that desires to know of our presence and wishes to feel the conditioning. That is our basic service to you. I am Hatonn.

(Pause)

I am again with this instrument and would open the meeting at this time for questions.

Questioner: Is there actually a place outside our own? A hell … a place where spirits are cast out as spoken in the Bible *(inaudible)*.

We may answer that in two ways, my sister. There are planets who have completed for themselves a hell, which without outside interference will continue to be totally terrifying.

Carla: *(Commenting about the noise at the door.)* That's S, go ahead and let him in.

(Pause)

Carla: Hi, Scott. Why don't you get the chair by the desk and haul it into the doorway?

(Pause)

(Carla channeling)

I am again with this instrument. I am Hatonn. May we greet the one known as S, and welcome him to our gathering. We will continue through this instrument. As we were saying, there are planets which have no more ability to extricate themselves from a condition of complete terror. They are so frightened that in their soul condition the souls cling to each other with such intensity that they consist of an impenetrable knot of fear, each feeling completely separated from the other and from the Creator. Your planet is not down that road, yet. There are many among your peoples who are very positive. There is no chance at this time that your planet would become one of these. Furthermore, among our ranks there are those whose task it is to release planetary entities such as these from their terror, so that they will let go of each other and be able to be led away to what you would call a hospital for spiritual rest, until they are able to once again take up the task that awaits us all; that of evolving into the original Thought from which we spring.

This is the closest to a hell that exists, to our knowledge, in any of your universes. We, however, are not perfect nor is our information complete. We simply have seen somewhat more than have you. But it is our understanding that the evolutionary process continues onward grade by grade, or octave by octave, and at the end of each grade those who are able proceed to the next. Those who are not able repeat that octave or existence until they have learned the lessons of that existence. Thus, the terms heaven and hell are quite subjective. And what is heaven to you would not seem so to us. And what is heaven to us would be incomprehensible, likewise, to you. For each of us have our own, shall we say, psychological makeup which has been developed through many eons of development in the spirit.

The finality with which heaven and hell occur seemingly in your holy work known as the Bible is the result of a difficulty in speaking to people who cannot easily grasp the fact that they must change their lives. Thus, although it is unfortunate, as we have said before, the one who saves, known to you as the Christ, is also represented as the one who will judge. This is intended to make his followers become worthy of the judgment. It has not succeeded.

The truth that we are saying to you are inner truths which are not obvious, and we do not ask that you believe that which you cannot believe, but only that you listen and take what you need from what we have to say.

Does this answer your question, my sister?

Questioner: Yes.

Is there another question at this time?

Questioner: Can you talk to us about the meaning of the disappearance of the Australian [pilot]? It was claimed he was contacted by a UFO.

No.

Questioner: Can you tell us about the prisoners in Iran, *(inaudible)* or how that will come out *(inaudible)*?

We are aware of your question. The previous question we could not answer due to a spiritual necessity for maintaining silence. This question we cannot answer due to the uncertainty of the movements of those who hold the power of life and death over your fellow countrymen. We do not know what they will do. Our fear, however, is not with the Iranian, as you call them, for they do not wish to kill others as much as to show their bravery by exposing themselves to martyrdom, a concept unfamiliar to you, yet part of their culture. Our concern at this time is for countries such as yours, lest you overreact and cause war. There is that potential in this situation and it is for that reason that we ask you pray, as always, that peace may fill the hearts of those who are in this world. We ask you please to ignore the evidence that such a peace does not fill many a heart. For if it fills your heart,

you have done a tremendous amount for your planet. We do not know what will happen, for many things may still happen, and we can see each of the realities branching off and they will continue to branch off till one path is chosen and completed.

Does this answer your question? We are sorry we cannot do better.

Questioner: Yes, thank you.

Is there another question at this time?

Questioner: *(Inaudible)* I belong to a group *(inaudible)* this afternoon we saw a movie on *(inaudible)* was called *The Long Search (inaudible)* religious trend *(inaudible)* Indonesia, where these people are making animal sacrifices, eating meat, etc. etc. But these people are very innocent beings, not insidious or calculating, *(inaudible)* say of people in our culture *(inaudible)*. I wonder, is it very necessary if you aspire to spiritual truth to be a vegetarian and not be kind of a meat *(inaudible)*?

We are aware of your question, my sister. It is a clear question and we can answer it, however, the answer is not as simple as the question. It is written in your holy books and truthfully that to some eating certain items is very necessary and would be harmful to them did they deviate; to others, anything maybe eaten. It is, you see, a function of the mind. As to the spiritual consequences of eating, you must understand that your bodies are a basic system of electromagnetic fields and they do not function as you believe that they function, but rather because of thought.

Thus, what you think controls a great deal of what you feel and how your body reacts. In general, it is safe to say that if a person feels a calling to become vegetarian, that is precisely what that person should do and will indeed help that person, because that is what that person feels that he shall do. It is as simple as that. Each person will have a different calling. Not all shall be vegetarians and not all shall be meat-eaters. It is totally a matter of your spiritual set, which is part of a thought nexus or system of thinking which you have developed over many lifetimes, giving you certain biases. In other words, you may have spent time in other bodies which were used to a vegetarian diet and thus find yourself in this incarnation quite unable to tolerate or digest the rich diet of your culture. Others find no problem in doing so whatsoever. Thus, the truth simply is it is not that which goes into a man that shows his nature, but rather what comes from him in the way of thoughts, words and deeds.

Can we answer your question further?

Questioner: No, thank you.

Is there another question?

(Pause)

If there are no more questions, I will speak very briefly and close through another instrument. We realize that there are several of you in the room who are wondering about the one known as Jesus. This instrument, for instance, is a confirmed and believing Christian, and while we feel that sometimes her concepts are naive, we do not find her Christianity to be a difficulty to us in using her as a channel. Conversely, she does not find us a threat to her Christianity. However, this understanding is not given to all and they may wonder, if we of the Confederation can speak of all religions and all cultures as being one, who then is the one known as Jesus. And we would answer that question as best we can by discussing with you the concept of karma, with which most of you are quite familiar. Karma being a type of cause and effect in which energies are put into action by former thoughts and deeds which culminate in a present necessity for some kind of atonement or balancing. Thus, if someone or a group of people have been very negative …

(Side one of tape ends.)

(Carla channeling)

I am again with this instrument. As we were saying, my friends, before we were electronically interrupted, when an entire culture has developed a very large amount of negative karma there is an opportunity for a consciousness, such a one as you know as Jesus. This consciousness is a special one and is indeed so close to that of the original Thought that it is almost difficult to understand an incarnation of such a being into your chemical illusion. However, such was the desire of this consciousness and as the supreme transmuter, as the one known as Jesus was upon his cross, he transmuted the collected negative karma of the past so that it was no more.

Two thousand years ago, as you say in your language, your peoples began with a slate that was wiped clean of karma. However, my friends, your peoples have been creating another situation that lies somewhat on the negative side. We hope for your sake as well as for ours that you can curb your instincts towards war. And by remembering the Creator and others in each moment of your life, alleviate that karma, little by little, so that there never need be another crucifixion.

This is our understanding of the one known to you as Jesus. We know him also and feel that as a teacher, as one who is one with the Father, and as one who saved his flock fearlessly, he has no equal. This is our understanding of the one you know as Jesus.

But we must remind you, that worship must be not of a man but of a Creator. As Jesus has said to you in his holy work, "It is not I, but my Father in me, that doeth these things." So let it be with you, my friends, not you but the Creator can live your life also. And each of your days, whatever the external circumstance, may be filled with a special kind of sunshine and love that comes from being at one with the harmony of the creation. I would like to close this contact through the instrument known as B, if she would accept our contact at this time. I am Hatonn.

(B channeling)

I am with this instrument. It has been a great privilege to be with you this evening. We share our thoughts and understandings with you. We of the Confederation are here at this time to be of service to you in any way that we can. You need only to will yourselves to our contact and we will be with you. Meditate, my friends, for this is the way to the Father. And only through meditation and prayer can the negativity which is enveloping your planet be pierced so that the light can neutralize and overcome it. This is still in your power to do. This is part of your service at this critical time for your planet.

We are here to help you in this effort. Our love is with you and our support. You need only avail yourselves to us and we are here. We go in peace, my brothers and sisters. My love is with you each moment of your existences. Adonai vasu borragus.

L/L Research

Sunday Meditation
December 2, 1979

(Carla channeling)

I am Hatonn, and I greet you in the love and the light of the infinite Creator, a Creator Who has given you peace and joy from now until infinity so that all that you have known and all that you will know may be of joy and of peace. We of the Confederation of Planets in the Service of the Infinite Creator are privileged to be with you in thought at this time, speaking through this instrument. And we are well aware that it does not seem to you as you dwell in your illusion of time and space that time is necessarily either joyful or peaceful. We know that there are many questions upon your minds having to do with the great divisions among the peoples of your planet. But what we wish to say to you now has to do with a block which stands in the way of joy and peace on an individual basis. We cannot give peace to nations, my friends, for they will not listen to us. We cannot give joy to a race of men. We can now offer these things only to those individuals who would listen to us. And to you who listen to us tonight, we say that the greatest impediment to joy and peace in your life is a lack of understanding of the true nature of love. It is written in your holy work which you call your *Holy Bible* that the Lord God requires a broken spirit and a contrite heart.

(S enters the room and sits down.)

We will pause for a moment to bring the one known as S into our circle of meditation. We surround you at this time with love and ask you to feel the harmony of your group. We will pause for a moment. I am Hatonn.

(Pause)

I am again with this instrument. I am Hatonn. We will continue through this instrument.

As we were saying, a broken spirit and a contrite heart, my brothers and sisters, seem to be things that would sadden an individual, but in truth, a spirit which is not broken, a heart which is not contrite on its own behalf cannot forgive the infirmities of others, cannot be gracious and kind when compassion is surely needed. How can you break a spirit? With love, so that you do not become sad but rather joyful. How can your heart become sorry for all that it may have done or thought or felt, without feeling guilty, for sadness and guilt were never required by the Creator, only love my friends. But a broken spirit and a contrite heart are the gifts of love. For in love, we know that all things that move and have their being in our illusion and in all illusions are part of us. Whatever you see, whatever you hear, whether it be bad or good, whether it stem from your thinking or the thinking of someone halfway around the circle of your globe, all of these things are part of you. The spirit of love is alive in every man and every woman but its expressions are often distorted.

Thus, the beginnings of freedom is the acknowledgment that your own expression of love may be distorted. When you commit yourself to an examination of your thoughts so that you may more nearly mirror the thought of love which the Creator formed you in, then you begin to have a broken spirit. For you have become a person who is not proud. You have become a person who is not ego-centered, as you would call it, but is, rather, capable of understanding the pain and suffering of those about you. When you walk through a forest, my friends, what does the wind require of you? The grass and the path under your feet, what do they ask of you? The trees as they bend to the breeze, do they require aught of you? The creation of the Father, my friends, is one of service. And it requires nothing from any of its parts but that each part be who that part is. You are becoming yourself in each moment. You are not finished, you are growing constantly and each thing that you learn adds just a bit to the quality of understanding of the original Thought which is harbored in your infinite and ever-living spirit. Your pride and your vanity you will leave behind. These, my friends—pride, vanity, boredom—these are the things that make men sad. When peace and joy are all about you, when heaven surrounds you, there is no need for you to dwell in the tattered rags of a worn-out illusion.

Thus, we ask you to drop your pride, your vanity, your thoughts of self-worth as if they were old garments and take on the armor of light. For you are a creature whose essential nature is love. You were born to serve; it does not matter whether the service is great or small. It does not matter whether you may even feel successful. All that matters, my friends is that you attempt to serve, that you attempt to love. You will make many errors, you will make mistakes, you will find yourself lacking self-confidence and at those times we ask that you call upon us, upon the Creator, upon your own guides, upon your higher self. All of these resources are about you at all times. Comfort yourself and surround yourself with love so that once more you may go your way rejoicing. We want no eye to be sad and no tear to be shed. The illusion is difficult; reality is simple.

We will aid you in invoking the light and I and my brother Laitos will move about the room working with each of you that you may feel our presence. I am Hatonn.

We are having some difficulty with the one known as M because she is fatigued. We will attempt to send her some energy at this time. I am Hatonn.

(Carla channeling)

I am Laitos, and I also greet you in love and light. Before we leave this group we would appreciate the opportunity to attempt to exercise the one known as S. If he would relax, we would condition him at this time and attempt to say just a few words through him. I am Latwii.

(Pause)

(Carla channeling)

I am again with this instrument. I am Laitos. We thank the one known as S. We are aware that we have good contact with him and that he is aware of our contact. The ability to channel is not always easy and will come in time if the desire is there. We would like to make the same experiment at this time with the one known as K. I am Laitos.

(Pause)

(Carla channeling)

We thank the one known as K and would like now to attempt to speak a few words through the one known as R, if she would consent to be used as a channel at this time. I am Laitos.

(Pause)

(Carla channeling)

I am again with this instrument. I am Laitos. If you will be patient we will not attempt to speak through the one known as M but we will attempt to be very specific in making our presence felt to the one known as M.

(Pause)

(Carla channeling)

I am again with this instrument, and I thank you very much for patience. We are sending healing to the one known as R and we thank you all for attempting to learn a service of vocal channeling that will be greatly needed in times to come. We cannot thank you enough for being willing to aid us in attempting to aid your peoples. When you meditate, please ask for our presence if you wish to be conditioned and we will be with you.

I leave you now. I am Laitos. Adonai, my friends.

(Carla channeling)

I am Hatonn. I am again with this instrument, and I greet you again in love and light. As is customary at these meetings, I would at this time ask for questions.

Questioner: You said a moment ago that if we are troubled or do not know, we should appeal to our higher self. Where is this higher self and how would you go about contacting it?

Your higher self, my sister, is in the eternal now and is closer to you than any physical part of your being. In this illusion you are a splinter of your eternal spirit which has been sent into this illusion in order to learn certain lessons and to grow in spirit, and this growth is then added to the higher self, which is eternal. Thus, all that you have learned and all that you will learn are enclosed in your higher self, giving you the benefit of all of your future understanding as well as your past experience. When you are in doubt, if you will pause in meditation and consciously ask that the truth that your higher self knows be made known to you in some way and then release this request, you will find that within the next hours or days through a dream or inner certainty or vision you will be relieved of your problem either by understanding it or by its resolution.

This higher self is not omnipotent, for it is only a splinter itself of the divine Creator, so all true appeals must end at the feet of the Almighty, He Who is the Creator of us all. Your higher self is suggested to you because it is so close to you and your knowledge is so available to you that it can come through to you in a shorter amount of your time. Meditation is always the key; that which you call prayer is always helpful.

Thus, as you spiritually give of your time, the rewards come to you threefold. This is the principle of meditation and the heart of our teaching to you. Using the term higher self is only to identify to you the true nature of yourself, for you can be the sum of all that you are whenever you are dwelling fully in the love of the Creator. That you cannot do this at all times is understandable but by all means, my sister, call upon your higher self by mentally requesting it. For that self is you and it is as easy as talking to yourself to make contact with that which is your deeper, more meaningful, and more knowledgeable self.

Does this answer your question?

Questioner: Yes, very well. Thank you.

Thank you, my sister. Is there another question?

Questioner: I have another question. You indicated to meditate, to having contact with your higher self. I sometimes feel that meditation is such a waste of time when we could be helping others during this time than just sitting there trying to contact your higher self or whatever. Would it not be better to be of service, as in, just say, doing to others during all these hours we spend meditating, or is meditation very essential?

We are aware of your question, my sister. Most people upon your plane of existence do not spend hours in meditation, nor do they spend hours in service. The meditation is advisable to all persons due to the fact that it is in meditation that you are made aware of your true relationship to the Creator and the creation. It is in meditation that you become aware that you and your brothers and sisters are one being and to serve them is to serve yourself. Armed with this understanding of service, you may then go forth and serve, given power by the spirit of love which is infinite.

If, on the other hand, you go forth to be of service to others without taking on the aspect of the spirit of love which is infinite, your ability to be of good cheer in your service will diminish and fail. For that which was given to your personality in this chemical illusion is limited. The only way that you can always be of service is to continually restore your understanding of the holiness of the ground whereon you walk through contemplation of that which is divine.

You must understand that in meditation you are not trying to contact anything. The idea in meditation is one wherein you realize that you are. Not who you are, not where you are, but that you are. That you are aware, that you are in the eternal present. When you feel this you will feel a sweetness and a closeness to the Creator that come from breaking through the illusions of space and time and coming into that place where you can simply be who you are. That person is greatly loved by the Creator. And that person can greatly love others.

Thus, we consider meditation quite essential. We also consider that as you meditate and grow in knowledge you then have a responsibility to share what you know with others in whatever path may seem to be open to you. As we have said, the path may be big or small, it may be dramatic or it may be unnoticed. It may be public or quite private, but whatever it is, it will be your intention to give love and be of service in your little corner of the universe.

You see, meditation and a life of service go hand in hand. We do not suggest meditating for hours each day, for such meditation is valuable only to those who have forsaken the world and have determined to make meditation their life. If you wish to do this, this is permissible. But you were, after all, put into this world to use your hands and your mind and your voice for the good of mankind. See to it, therefore, that you see and do and say that which you have come to understand in the silence of meditation.

May we further answer your question, my sister?

Questioner: I am very, very thankful. You've said just the right thing for me.

We are very happy, my sister. Is there another question now?

Questioner: Can you tell me if my son is going to meet the girl that is right for him soon or if ever?

No. We are sending through this instrument, however, a general thought that may give you comfort. We are aware of your concern and we cannot remove ourselves from our philosophical mission to give you specific advice about matters which have to do with free will, for this we cannot intrude upon in your daily existence. However, may we send you words of comfort and give you to understand that the entity of whom you speak is well-protected and whatever difficulties he may have will be helpful to him. This is not always easy to accept when you wish more than anything to take on another person's difficulties and to make things be well for one whom you love. But this is not the way of the Creator. For each soul has his own path and will follow it. But it is truly written in your holy works that you are not given more than you can bear. It is also truly written that the Creator is always with those who speak of His name. Indeed, He is with all, my friends.

We are sorry we cannot accede to your request for information, but it is outside our guidelines. Please accept our apologies, my sister.

Questioner: Thank you.

Is there another question?

(Pause)

Does the one known as S wish to reserve his question for another time?

S: I will reserve it. Thank you.

We respect your privacy, my brother. My friends, it is a singular joy, as always, to be allowed to share our thoughts with you. We are very grateful for your love and we send you ours unstintingly. For those of you who have needs for healing, we ask that you call upon us, for there are those in the Confederation who work with healing vibrations and we will be happy to work with you. We have no wish to manipulate your peoples, but how we yearn, my friends, to give you rest from your labor and a happy end to your troubles. Meditate, my friends, and these things will not only be possible but will be part of your life. We leave you in a life that is filled with joy and peace. Join us, my friends. It is available to you at any time and we await you with eagerness.

I am Hatonn. I and my brethren leave you in the love and the light of the One Who is All. Adonai vasu borragus. ✣

Intermediate Meditation
December 16, 1979

(Carla channeling)

I am with the instrument. I am known to you as Hatonn, and I greet you in the love and the light of the infinite Creator. Our instructions at this time take us north of you, as you would call it, for we are sending love to those entities who dwell in the area of your planet which many of your peoples call Quebec, and we would ask you to lend your prayers to that region where there is some disturbance in the Earth's aura at that point, as well as others, as you are well aware of. We are, however, close enough to you in your skies to speak to you directly instead of through a transmitter and thus we feel very close to you tonight and greet you each with great appreciation and gratitude, for you are allowing us to share in your meditation.

As you know, we have come to this planet to share with you one simple idea, that is the idea of what has been called the peace which passeth all understanding. It is the original Thought of love that makes all men one. As we look down upon your planet at this time it is as though your peoples are being torn apart from within, and we ask you especially as those who are attempting to lighten the vibrations of your planet to be aware of the influences about you that do not seem harmonious, while allowing yourself to be a channel for compassion, for the inharmony reigns not to harm you, but rather [be] the reflection of the harm that is being self-inflicted by others. You yourselves are creators of your own destiny moment by moment and as you love and give, so your world will reflect that loving and giving back to you.

This is especially apparent among your peoples this time of year which is called by this instrument, Christmas time. It is known by different names and many religions besides the one held dear by this instrument, for it is in truth a basic necessity of man to shake his fist at death and to state the obvious, that winter will not last forever and that spring will inevitably come. It is a greet misfortune of your technological society that your people are not more in touch with the deep elemental feelings of the seasons, for this understanding of the Creator's universe would enable you to understand Christmastide in a much deeper way than the normal person, and you would then not be disheartened by the apparent, shall we say, cheapening of a basic and beautiful truth, that there is no death without birth. Let us look, my friends, at what Christmas in your culture truly means. It is a way of saying to one and all that whatever may happen in the winter of your soul, there is always that which is new that can be worn in the darkness and become your spirit of tomorrow. It is a statement indeed, that this life which seems to end inevitably after a brief sojourn in the grave is only shamming and that indeed this sojourn is only a beginning—only another way of resting in the womb of time, so that your spiritual body may be born. We will go further, my friends, and ask you to look at the implications of the newborn Christ-consciousness which is to be your spiritual home. It carries with it a certain responsibility and in the Christian story as is told in your holy book, those responsibilities are clear to love, to serve, to care for both the Creator and His children whomever they may be. So you see, my friends, although it is true that in your experience at this time, Christmas or Yuletide is little more than a game whereby entities attempt to impress those they may not even like with gifts they cannot afford, and which the recipients do not need, yet you do not need to accept this estimation of the season of Christmas.

Let us look at an image far removed from Christmas, and yet with the same message. A bird called the Phoenix bursts into flames and is consumed in a great fire, and all that are left are ashes. Out of those ashes rises a new and more beautiful Phoenix. As you put a Yule log upon your fire, as you set the star on your tree, let the message of winter, of ashes, and of rebirth fill your heart with the joy of knowing that all joys will be made well because the love that created all things is a perfect love. We wish that your peoples could understand the meaning of Christmas, not only once a year, but throughout the year, for it is a message which we have come to share, the message of love, of unity, of salvation through higher consciousness. You are part of an evolutionary pattern. Those about you may not wish to be part of the evolution that is taking place at this time; so be it. They will have many other chances for advancement, as many as they need, my friends, for all dwell in an infinite realm, for hope truly springs eternal. Meanwhile, you have control consciously of your development; think deeply upon the lessons of creation and rest in the knowledge that even the hardest earth, frozen cold as stone, will soon be crowded with the blossoms of spring, and so will you go on from glory to glory in the creation of the Father. Imagine each of you in your domicile at this time, your hearts beating as one, your breathing, your thinking, and your feeling unified with one great Thought of love. There will come a time when this will be the case among your peoples. We believe that you may be there to witness it, if not in this dimension, then among the inner planes that guard this Earth plane in its fragile path towards knowledge.

I will pause at this time so that my brother, Laitos, may work with you. I am Hatonn.

(Pause)

I am with this instruments. I am Laitos. I am very glad to be here, and I also greet you in the love of the infinite Creator. I hope I have been able to help each of you as you have meditated and I have been very glad to work with each of you and wish only to be of continuing service to you. Because we are in a group situation tonight I will attempt to speak through you rather than simply give you conditioning. I will begin with the one known as M. If she would relax and ask for the contact we will attempt to speak a few words through her.

(M channeling)

I am Laitos …

(Carla channeling)

I am again with the instrument. We will move the direction of our being to a more comfortable angle and again attempt to speak a few words through the one known as M, if she would not analyze but simply speak what she hears.

(Pause)

(Carla channeling)

I am again with this instrument. We are sorry, but we are having some difficulty with the one known as M, both due to some interference, due to mismatching of our vibrations which we are working on, also due to analysis upon the part of the instrument. This is very common among new instruments and is almost inevitable for our thoughts are not distinguishable from your own, and therefore it is necessary simply to say what come to mind without questioning whether it be your thought or our thought. After awhile this practice confirms itself as people inform you they have received messages that you as an instrument could not possibly have known they desired to receive. However, the first step is yours because we do not wish to interrupt your free will by causing you to go into trance or by completely controlling your speech apparatus. We do not feel comfortable with these techniques, although some of our brothers do and have instruments who are willing to be used.

(A knock at the door is heard.)

(Pause)

(Carla channeling)

I am again with this instrument. We thank the one known as M and will continue to work with her. We would like to move on now to the one known as R. If she would avail herself of our contact and, as we have said, refrain from analyzing our thoughts, we would like to speak a few words through her. I am Laitos.

(Pause)

(Carla channeling)

I am again with this instrument. We have good contact with the one known as R. However, we find the instrument to be somewhat unsure and so we will at this time allow her to feel our contact so that she might know of our presence without question that she speak. I am Laitos.

(Carla channeling)

I am again with this instrument. We thank the one known as R and will continue working with her at any time that she desires such contact. We will now attempt to speak through the one known as K, if she would relax and make herself available to our vibrations. I am Laitos.

(Pause)

(Carla channeling)

I am again with this instrument. I am Laitos. The one known as K is analyzing her thought and we understand that completely. Therefore, we will continue to work with her. If she desires our presence she need only ask. If you will be patient we would like to attempt to contact the one known as S, if he will refrain from attempting to discern whether thoughts are his or ours. We feel that he can receive a few words from us at this time. I am Laitos.

(Pause)

(Carla channeling)

I am again with this instrument. We hope that you are not feeling disappointed that you weren't able to, shall we say, channel, but you must understand that we have developed a great deal of energy by means of using the conditioning with each of you and because of your generosity in allowing us to work with you, you will find there are many ways in which you can reach out—we correct this instrument—in which there can be channels for the love and the light of the Creator. Working as this instrument does is only one of the multitude of ways in which you can be of service to your neighbors, to your Creator, and to yourself, thus realizing and feeling the energy that you do [have] at this moment. Lock it in your hearts and refresh it with meditation on a daily basis, so that your movements are always inspired with that love and that light which can come only from the Creator and His humble messengers. I leave you now in the love and in the light of the Father of all of us. I am Laitos.

I am Hatonn, and I am again with this instrument. We have a good contact, which is surprising for the conditions are not atmospheric. However, we are very glad to have such good contact and we return to this instrument to ask you if there are any questions that you would like to ask the Confederation at this time.

Questioner: I would like to thank Hatonn and Laitos for their unselfish service in talking to us and conditioning us and trying to raise our consciousness. I feel every time that I am shot in the arm, pushed up the ladder, learning all these things. Hearing these things can really help us in so many ways, it helped those around us. There is one question I have. Hatonn was talking about the inner planes. Are we able to reach these inner planes in this life, or are we able to reach it after the journey through this life? What are these inner planes, and what will it mean to contact them?

I am Hatonn. I am with the instrument. I am aware of your question. First, we would like to respond to your thanks by explaining to you that we are far from unselfish, for it is our gratitude that must be understood, for without brothers and sisters to help our continued education and growth in understanding of the Father would nearly halt. Therefore, it is in helping you that we help ourselves. It is as though the glass were to thank the window, or the arm the leg, for we are all part of one structure. The triangle of love, light and awareness at the top of the triangle of earth and passion and reflected love at the bottom. We in between, reflect one and nurture the other and in doing so and only in doing so can we further our own understanding of that which is about us on what you have called the ladder of evolution. For us to be able to help you is our deepest hope and our profoundest blessing, and we thank each of you.

As to the inner planes of existence, you must understand that each individual has a singular or particular individual ability to penetrate into the inner planes. Much as you may teach a child to play an instrument but not to be a virtuoso, so you may teach techniques of visualization, concentration and contemplation which will enable one to have all of the techniques available for penetrating the inner planes. This does not mean each person will be able to do so equally. Some are natural penetrates of these planes, some have an enormous amount of difficulty, even with earnest effort. Some fool themselves. This we would guard against and we ask you never to fool yourself, never believe or disbelieve. Simply listen and record that which is happening to you. And when time has passed and other things have occurred which either strengthen or weaken the experience you may then objectively discern whether or not you have had an inner plane experience.

The inner plane theory of your peoples is very old. It is as old as the pyramids and it was a gift to your people by the Confederation from many, many thousands of years ago. The pyramids themselves were used in penetrating into the inner planes of existence. A very simple analogy which this instrument has frequently used is that of the television set. You have at this moment, within your domicile, a television set although it is potentially able to show you a world it is not doing so now because it has not been activated. This instrument or anyone in the room might activate it, and they might choose a channel of existence of which they enjoy the view. They will see one world on one channel, another world on the next, and so on, each channel seemingly coming from the same television set, but each world becoming completely different and completely oblivious to all the other worlds.

So it is with the inner planes. You and all of those things in your world are energy fields and you have energies and certain vibrations we call those vibrations that belong to the third octave of existence. There are also other octaves of existence within your octave of existence. There are seven levels, and some of these levels are not visible, just as one channel would not be visible to another. The skill and art of penetrating into the inner planes is a hidden art. It is hidden for a reason. Each of you is here to learn the lessons of love and as you penetrate into the inner planes, the lessons of love become very obvious and thus your existence here becomes quite changed.

Thus, except for those occasional virtuosos, shall we say, who penetrate into the inner planes without conscious effort, for the most part they are closed to people upon your plane of existence. The method for achieving entrance into higher or, shall we say, denser, more light, more beautiful realms of existence is a mixture of certain disciplines of the person's visualization, applied study, meditation and a constant will to know the truth in order to serve others. If you have this desire you will find people who will help you in your search. For us to give you this information is not necessary for the instrument has within her library volumes which deal with this subject which are available for you to read.

Does this answer your question, my sister?

Questioner: Yes, it does. Thank you.

Does anyone else have any more questions at this time?

S: I have a question. With all the talk of devastation and such, how long before we can unify into service. How soon will this occur?

This phase of your planetary shift, my brother, began approximately ten years ago.

(Side one of tape ends.)

(Carla channeling)

We will continue. Three years ago, according to your timekeeping methods, the second stage of intensified earth changes began. You have two years according to your timekeeping methods before your own continent becomes severely changed. However, these changes, though they will seem devastating, are relatively minor, and we would advise you to concentrate on your love energy upon mankind himself, who is at this time divided against himself in many, many ways. Natural changes with—we must correct this instrument—will cause some depletion of your population, but the population itself will not be significantly reduced, that is to say, the species will easily survive, and find new ways to develop a moral technology that enables mankind to be comfortable while ennobling his purpose to love and serve not only himself but the generations that are to come and the planet on which you dwell.

That which is to be feared is that which mankind may do to mankind. There is nothing in the creation which is called Earth by your peoples that would willingly kill for no apparent reason, but your species is capable of killing as a matter of what you may call policy. This is dangerous, and because your weapons far outrun your morality as a people there is the potential for almost total annihilation. There is no timetable for this for your people are unpredictable. We ask only that in your own way you yourself may love your enemies as best you can, for loving your friends is easy, but to lighten a planet that is torn in discontent, in greed, and in lust for power over others the most important weapon is the unifying strength of love itself.

You do not know what you can do to help your planet but we say to you that we do know and just by your coming together this evening you are part of the raising of the consciousness of the planet. As you meditate, do not try to save the world, for you are the world. Do not try to save yourself because you are perfect. Only be. A tree is a tree; a cloud is a cloud; and you are you. The precious gift of awareness resides in your eyes, in your heart, and in your mind, and no one else thinks your thoughts. Celebrate yourself in meditation, for within you lies the development of the planet, if you can but be. You will be loved, for that is the essence of all that there is. Again we say, yes. We are in the middle of Earth …

(Tape ends.)

Year 1980
January 6, 1980 to June 8, 1980

Intermediate Group
January 6, 1980

(Carla channeling)

I am Latwii. I greet you in the love and the light of the infinite Creator. We of Latwii are extremely happy to be with you this evening and are establishing contact with this instrument. We do not have perfect contact with this instrument and so we will condition this instrument by speaking through her. I am Latwii. I am Latwii. I am with the instrument. The contact is deepening. We are more satisfied now. We will proceed.

We come to you, not for ourselves, but as messengers of love and light. You must know that we come only out of these desires to be of help. It is not because we wish to impose upon you any principle or law which we consider superior.

When you go within, in your meditation, and invoke the light of your Creator you will find the truth, whether we have inspired you to meditate, whether it may be another source of a spiritual nature, or whether it may be simple misfortune which causes you to contemplate the meaning of your existence. The truth is not in our hands nor in the hands of other spiritual guides, nor in the hands of fate. The truth is truth. And it will forever be before you, a beacon of light. And you will forever follow it, learning and sharing with each other that which you gather, harvests of light along a road which leads onward.

We come to encourage you to meditate and to contemplate in that meditation a certain concept. That concept is indescribable, but tonight we would attempt to approach it from the standpoint of what you would call faith. You see, my friends, your illusion in this particular experience of your life cycles is one wherein law rules and is thought to be a good concept. It is often pointed out that without laws the peoples of your planet would become too individualistic, causing pain to each other. Your vehicles would not be able to trustfully, as you would call it, drive down your roadways knowing that no cars would be coming in the opposite direction. For there would be no law. People could not amass possessions. For there would be no law against stealing.

That is the position of your world. It does not seem possible that you could live without law. But we say to you, my friends, that there is a greater law. And it is a law that extends beyond man's concept of law. It is the law of the original Thought. If you could understand the original Thought, you would know what there is to know, and your soul would no longer journey, it would no longer seek, nor harvest, nor share. For it would be one with all seekers, all harvesters, and all sharing. If you could understand the original Thought you would be love. You would not be seeking love. The original Thought is within you. It is not without you. When you look at the world with the original Thought in your heart you can see love. If you look at the world without the original Thought you can only see the illusion of disharmony, and naturally you will desire to ease the situation by using laws. But when you understand the original Thought, you find yourself viewing this same world with eyes that see love.

And thus, without any reason or logic, you discover that you have a faith. It is not a faith that all will work out according to the desires of any one lawmaker. For indeed, in any particular illusion, what can any one person know about the ultimate necessities of each person within that illusion or experience? You cannot have faith that there will be peace. You cannot have faith that there will be harmony. You can only have faith that each person will have what he or she need.

Each entity will experience what they must experience in order to have the opportunity to grow spiritually. There is no other reason for this existence. The rest of your existence is written on the wind and will vanish. As it is written in your holy works, "Like the grass of the field, you will wither." But the soul does not wither. And it uses each moment of your existence in attempting to understand and to grow closer to the original Thought.

We ask you to come with us now and rest. We know that each of you has within your heart a place that is weary of the illusion. Invoke the light, my friends. And come with us to a place that is all light, purely and beautifully lit with the white light of love. And in the center of that light there is a beautiful and loving mother. She is the part of the entity you call God that your culture does not include. She holds out her hands to you and takes you in her arms. And all your weariness can fall away. For you are rocked in the arms of your true mother, the mother of the spirit, who lights your way ever, known in your holy works as the holy spirit. The gentle, nurturing, feminine god always with you, always there to give you grace, grace to understand, grace to accept, grace to endure.

The Creator is neither male nor female. The Creator is infinite and invisible. But as He is manifest into your illusion by faith, in the light and the love which are the materials of your illusion, the Creator develops a polarity of power and wisdom on the one side, and love and compassion on the other. Let this gentle being replace any fear you may have ever had of the Creator and His judgment of you. For the creation is ruled by a law of love. And you can only understand that law by faith.

I would leave this instrument momentarily so that the ones of Laitos may work with you. I am Latwii.

(Pause)

(Carla channeling)

I am Laitos. And I also greet you in love and light.

It would be my pleasure at this time if you would permit me to work with each of you in developing your ability to receive our contact. I would like to begin with the one known as M. If she would relax, we will condition her, and attempt to speak a few words. She must say what she is given without analysis. I am Laitos.

(Pause)

I am again with this instrument. We are adjusting our contact. We have too much intensity around the neck area, and will adjust the contact to the one known as M. We are sorry for any discomfort. I am Laitos.

(Pause)

I am again with this instrument. May we thank the one known as M for the privilege of working with her. We would now work with the one known as K. If she would request our contact, we would condition her. I am Laitos.

(Pause)

We thank the instrument known as K, and are most encouraged. We feel that we are getting a clearer contact with her. And we thank her for working with us. We would now work with the one known as R. If she would relax, we feel we can at this time impress a few words on her. But she must not analyze our words, but simply speak them quickly as she receives them. I am Laitos.

(Pause)

I am again with this instrument. We will send the one known as R a few words in her native tongue, so that she may be made aware of the contact more clearly. I am Laitos.

(R channels two sentences in her native tongue.)

(Carla channeling)

I am again with this instrument. I am Laitos. We sent one more sentence to confirm with the instrument that she was receiving correctly. We were speaking of light. We will continue through this instrument briefly only to urge each of you, if you wish to pursue this particular type of service, we are here for the express purpose of helping you. And if you wish simply to increase your ability to meditate deeply, the conditioning wave may also be used for this. It is yours freely and must be requested by you, as we do not wish to interfere with your free will.

It gives us great pleasure to work with each of you, my sisters. And we thank you. I am Laitos and will turn the meeting back to Latwii, who is attempting to be serious, and has succeeded admirably so far, although we mistrust his ability to continue seriously. I am Laitos, and we will leave this instrument at this time. We leave you in love and light. Adonai.

(Pause)

I am Latwii. I am again with this instrument. We are certainly being serious and do not need to be reminded of our efforts by our friends of Laitos. We will continue to be serious. We are being serious. We have not made one single joke. We are learning to be proper, so that we may best aid our beloved sisters of the saddened planet.

There. You see, my friends, we can be serious.

Now. We at this time would like to open the meeting to questions. Do you have any at this time?

We will answer a question that this instrument has while you are considering whether to ask a question. This instrument would like to know why we are speaking instead of Hatonn.

We are speaking to you, instead of Hatonn, due to the difficulties of your planet at this time. The situation in many areas is very tense. And Hatonn is again doing his best to speak to the leaders of Russia and of China and send them vibrations of love and peace. And his feeling at this time is not that this group is in need of introductory material on the uses of daily meditation, which messages are stored in computers and can be given to groups of an introductory level without Hatonn personally working with the group consciousness. Therefore, he has asked us to monitor this group and deal with your individual needs along the spiritual path. For he feels that you are individualized enough in your search for love that you need a little bit more advanced counseling to the best of our poor ability to give it to you.

The one known as Hatonn sends you his love as always. And the part of the planetary consciousness that is not involved in this very great effort to send love to that part of the planet always keeps you each in the group consciousness in love, so that you need only think of the one known as Hatonn and that presence will be with you and love surround you.

This instrument is requesting more information on the crisis, as you call it. But we are sorry, we do not feel that this information is spiritual in nature. Nor do we feel that you can do anything specific about it. For it is almost a planetary problem, at this point. Thus, you must look to your own vibration and pray for the wholeness and the health of the planet itself, and not any particular region of it. There is a sickness that has invaded your planet and it is called greed. This is unfortunate, but this is what is. Thus, we ask you in your personal life to be aware of the many blessings of each day, so that you will not be part of the greediness of the planet, so that you will realize the luck that you have in being fed and clothed and warm and dry. For there are a great many in this world of yours who are not so lucky, and that is what creates greed. If you are thankful, if you send out vibrations of light to the Creator and to your brothers and sisters you will do far more for your planet than you realize. And we thank you, for we know that you will attempt to do as we have asked. And we appreciate your faithfulness.

Is there another question at this time?

Questioner: I have a question about our solar system … *(The question is mostly inaudible; it is about whether the Earth is getting nearer to the sun, and what are the consequences of this.)*

We are measuring the light spectra of your octave of existence. That is our primary function. Indeed, you are our first group with whom we have spoken. And we are not aware of a mad rushing of your planets toward your planetary sun. However, your entire solar system is moving very quickly into a new area of space/time, which is somewhat closer to what occultists, as you would call it, have called the central sun.

However, we do not believe that this is what your source meant. It is our understanding that the measurements you spoke of are not proper or correct, and are the result of, what you might call, relativistic error. The actual tendency in the long run is for inertia to gradually lose its power as the planetary sun body, at the center of its system, loses its heat. The aspects of gravitation which this involves are not understood by your scientists. And they are attempting to explain the so-called black hole. However, the formation of black holes is not understood by your scientists, and through this instrument we would not be able to be at all clear. At a meeting of which the channel known as Don is present we would be happy to attempt to answer through him, for his mind is furnished with the proper vocabulary for dealing with questions of this nature, whereas this instrument has about as much scientific knowledge as your average 12-year-old. We won't get very far with her. We are sorry that we can not answer your question further.

Is there another aspect of this question, or another question that we may attempt to answer?

Questioner: I was going to ask you about the black holes. Did you mean that you wouldn't be able to tell us about them? Or was that referring to the measurement of the distance from the planet to the sun?

Through this instrument we would be unable to tell you the physics involved in the black hole. However, the understanding of the black hole as a transformational point from dimension to dimension is a proper understanding arrived at intuitively by several of your scientists. Is this what you wish to know, or would you like to question further?

Questioner: I guess I probably wouldn't know what they were if you explained it to me.

That is the problem of this instrument. The physics is fascinating and we believe that the instrument known as Don could explain, for he has the ability to picture what we are speaking of. However, this instrument has a mind which somewhat resembles a black hole when we attempt to transmit this information to her, although her particular black hole is blank. We are fond of this instrument but must say that she is better equipped to deal with philosophy than physics.

Is there another question at this time? We will try anything, my friends.

Questioner: Well, what about the center of the Earth, are there any inhabitants, or anything going on in the center of the Earth that you can tell us about?

We are able to tell you of what was, but not what is, because what is, is no more. There was a civilization which survived a deluge, many, many thousands of years ago. It was an advanced civilization. And it was not a positively-oriented civilization. Eventually, it destroyed itself. And for long years there remained the remnants of that civilization, which were machines, some of them destructive. Through timeless years, as you would call them, these machines no longer function. As you can see, your planet has had a difficult time of it, for many, many cycles, battling the tendency to become negative, yet never truly becoming negative, always clinging to an ideal of the good, which continually saves it from becoming a dark planet. However, it causes this planet to be a saddened and tortured planet, uncertain of its destiny and desirous of that which is better. And that is why we are here. For in your peoples, there is hope to be had. There are people to be saved. All is not dark on your planet. And we will be here through the coming years to aid those of you who seek the light.

No, to answer a question that this instrument had, we were not part in any attempt to help that particular civilization, due to the fact that it did have a desire for negativity. And we are not allowed to infringe upon free will. However, as the civilization was dying, and it could see the results of its negativity, borne in upon themselves, destroying themselves, they repented and thus again your planet was saved. You, my friends, as a planet have far more hope than they. For you have never embraced the darkness. It is simply that you have never, as a people, totally embraced the light.

Is there another question, my friends?

Questioner: Can you tell me, years ago when we saw a big light follow us, do you know what that was?

We are seeing it in your memory. Yes, my sister, we can tell you what that is because this will not interfere with your spiritual growth. There was at that time in your existence a learning. And your higher self was very near, taking the form of an angel, traveling in a light body, giving you a sign. This is not what you would understand to be a UFO. In other words it …

(Tape ends.) ♣

Intermediate Meeting
January 20, 1980

(Carla channeling)

I am Hatonn. And I greet you in the love and the light of the infinite Creator. I and my brother Oxal were attempting to speak through the one known as N in order to increase his confidence for times when he might be the solitary channel for a group meditation. And we will attempt again at this time to begin this meditation through the instrument known as N. I am Hatonn.

(N channeling)

I am Hatonn. Greetings, my friends, in the *(inaudible)*. My brothers and I are greatly pleased that you have gathered here this evening to seek truth. We know there are many ways to do this. And it is *(inaudible)* that, my friends, we always seek the truth *(inaudible)* they will *(inaudible)* for it is a wall, so to speak. Many paths have led up to this particular [form] where the paths cross. Let this time be a time to gather each of your vibrations together so that in this group effort you may feel more easily this light of the Creator which is in each of you. You may branch out seemingly far away from your true desire to know truth and love but you cannot go far enough away to escape the love of the Creator, for He forgets no one, for He is everyone. Deep beneath your layers of illusion runs the true life. All the knowledge you wish to receive is within you already, my friends. You only have to discover this as you have already done so. We of the Confederation of Planets in Service to the Infinite Creator know of the troubles upon your planet happening *(inaudible)*.

Remember for each problem, my friends, there is a solution. And through the practice of meditation answers to these problems will be made aware to you. No matter who you are, how obscure you may seem to feel, the love and light is in you and you will shine forth. You only have to desire this for it to happen. It may happen overnight while you sleep or take a longer time. But the time is not important in this respect. For if you truly seek love for your effort you shall be rewarded.

At this time I will transfer this contact. I am Oxal. I leave you in the light and love of the infinite Creator.

(Carla channeling)

I am with this instrument. I am Oxal. I will continue through this instrument, if you will be patient, for we must condition this instrument briefly for she is attempting to balance our contact. We believe we have better contact now; we will continue.

Your minds are full of many things, my friends. As we were saying, your world is full of words, full of guns, full of negativity at this moment in your space/time continuum in your illusion. All of you are at this time obeying the only wisdom known to man. And that is you are silent and [in search] of the single Thought that created all of you, to which all of you belong, your original Thought, the Creator, my friends, which is love.

We will tell you a small story to see if we can inspire you with a greater respect for meditation and the art of silence.

It was winter and beneath the cold *(inaudible)* the pine cone gave up a seed to the soil. And when Spring loosened the earth the *(inaudible)* blessed it. The seedling became a sprout. The years passed and the small pine tree began to grow. Many things occurred about the pine tree, There was a forest fire not far from him and he felt the agony of many of his brothers. There were woodsmen who killed others of his older brothers and again he felt their pain. But they did not speak, but always stretched living fingers to the sky as if to touch the sun. For all things in Nature know to turn to the sun, although they do not call it love, for they have no words. They do not die but the great Sun-body, symbolic of love and light, is to them their source.

Eventually a little boy moved close to this forest, and he cared about this tree and became very fond of it, and one Christmas he dragged his father to the tree and begged him to bring it home as a Christmas tree. And the Father, very fond of the young boy, dutifully dug the tree up, put it in a bag and after Christmas planted it by the old family house. The boy and the tree grew together and the boy, first so childish, became grown. He became wiser and wiser and he asked many questions of the tree. For he felt very close to this tree that had grown nearly as tall as his house while he had grown to be a man. And at each question the tree would lift his fingers to heaven and point toward the Kingdom of the Creator.

And as an old man, this person found finally that all of his questions had but one answer, and that was in the Kingdom of Heaven; not the kingdom of man, for there are words. And he had found there are no answers but only that which is.

And as he died, he asked of his family only one thing. He said to them, "I am ready to say good-bye to all things on this plane, for I love you all and I have no enemies. And I have nothing more that I wish, but I would that you would bury me near my friend. And they looked puzzled, for they did not know he had a friend. And he said to them, "The tree—the silent tree beside the house." And so it was that in eternity, he and the tree became one.

Anything that we can say to you, my friends, is folly. For words cannot reveal anything of importance. We speak through these instruments to hopefully give you the encouragement and the inspiration to seek through meditation the truth, the Creation. We, well grounded in the love and the light of the infinite Creator, are as helpless before you as trees pointing their fingers to the Kingdom of Heaven. We can show you the way but we cannot give you the desire to seek. You are here tonight because of that desire. Have that desire on a daily basis, my friends. Continue in your seeking; and you will find that your path becomes ever more light and that your questions become ever more few.

I will leave this instrument now so that one of my brothers may address the meeting. I am Oxal. Adonai, my friends. I leave you in the love and light of the infinite Creator.

(N channeling)

I am Hatonn. I am with this instrument. Greetings again from …

Many of your peoples sometimes feel they have no purpose in living besides the seemingly unimportant things on this planet. When we tell you you live in an illusion and this is true. As you know, these objects that you see from your planet are not the same things; are not really what they appear to be. They are comprised of much smaller units you call atoms which come together, form the illusion of being solid.

You may wonder why you are here to begin with in this illusionary world. My friends, we say to you that if you did not truly desire to be here, you would not be. We can compare your planet to a school: many lessons to be learned through your experiences. The only difference is with your schools on Earth you receive grades, but in the plan of the infinite Creator you receive not grades but the experience of learning and when you have learned something, my friends, you evolve.

At this time, my brothers and I would like to send you what we call a conditioning wave. We will attempt to make known to you our presence by intensifying our vibrations, so to speak. And at this time we pause for a moment. In order to do this, if you desire this, we will attempt to make ourselves known to you.

(Pause)

(N channeling)

I am again with this instrument. I am Hatonn. It has been a very great honor and privilege to speak through this instrument to you this evening. My friends, we sincerely hope you have benefited from this meditation. And if you desire *(inaudible)* our presence you only have to make it known and we are with you wherever you may be. We send you our love. I will leave you now. I am Hatonn. Adonai vasu borragus.

(Carla channeling)

I am Latwii. And I greet you in the love and the light of the infinite Creator, as we do all of us of the Confederation. We have no choice, for that is all that there is.

My friends, I come to you only to offer my services in case you may have a question for us at this time. If you do, please ask now.

We have a question from one who is not present at this time. But we would wish to address to the one known as S our love and constant devotion to her as she is physically very alone in her seeking at this time. We are aware that she has again become comforted by our presence and it makes us very happy that we have been able to reestablish contact with her. Along with the one known as Hatonn, we of Latwii have been requested to monitor the desires of the one known as S so that she may draw comfort from our presence whenever it is necessary. We cannot say the words that she wishes at this time. However, we are aware that she will understand that this has to do with her own free will and therefore our metaphysical hands are tied. Again, to sister S we send our love.

Is there a question among those in this group at this time?

(Pause)

I am Latwii. My friends, I think I am losing my touch, for I cannot answer any of your questions this evening. However, I offer my love and my thanks for your patience, for the one known as S was much desirous of our speaking. I will leave you this time, as always, in love and light. And may you find some laughter along the way. Adonai, my friends. I am known to you as [Latwii]. ✣

Intermediate Meeting
February 3, 1980

(H channeling)

[I am Hatonn.] Greetings, my friends, in the love and the light of our infinite Creator. It is indeed a privilege, as always, to speak to you. We of the Federation of the Planets in Service to the Infinite Creator have come to you to share with you our thoughts this evening. You have gathered for this purpose and for this we are grateful. For this is our greatest means of touching with your people and serving them in this manner as it is at the present time our best means of relaying our thoughts, our energy, and our love to your civilization.

We speak through many instruments such as this one around your planet. And we of the Confederation wish to grow closer to your people. For as all of you may witness, your peoples, which are divided into segments called countries are driving down what you might call the darkest avenue of their experience. Yet at the end of this avenue they shall find the love and the light of the Creator.

Your planet is experiencing great turmoil. Yet if you had the ability to look into what you would call your future, as in some extent we do, you could see the great benefit that can be derived from your present difficulties. Your planet must grow. It must grow rapidly. And with this growth there shall be the accompanied pains of growth.

As you travel throughout your life, you hold dear to many concepts. Many of these concepts as you grow older are altered. And many times you are separated from them for you have seen an alternative. And the people upon the planet Earth now must learn to expand their awareness. And they must be willing to separate themselves from many of the concepts that they hold so dearly. For in holding to a fixed concept, allowing for no variation, as your people seem to do, you limit your ability to grow. Yet, indeed, the growth shall occur for the planet on which you reside grows in spirit as do you. Its growth is undeniable by any of your peoples. You may share in it or you may be consumed by it. The choice is yours.

Many of your people are focusing their energies at this precise moment on the concept of what you would term as war. We must say that as things stand we do not foresee an immediate large scale warfare. Yet farther down the road it looms largely in the possibilities. And it is indeed brought even closer to happening by the present thoughts of each of your peoples. For every one of you that consider this concept, in doing so, you add energy. And with enough energy added to the concept, it will indeed be created. For all of you upon this planet, as all of your brothers throughout the galaxies, were as your Bible states, "created in the image and likeness of your Creator," thus meaning that you have the ability to create also.

The creation itself is a magnificent thought energy, to the best of our realization. Your thoughts are energy, and indeed shall materialize on one plane of life. Therefore, we urge your peoples to turn from this concept. And consider not the warfare that may loom so largely in your future, but concentrate on the dawning of awareness and the coming of your so-called messiah.

We of the Confederation wish to assist your people in utilizing their thought energies to the greater benefit of all civilizations. By speaking through instruments such as this one we are doing the greatest amount of good that we can do at this time. We hope that in the future we can work with you, amongst you, and grow with you, if this is the choice of your people. When you are ready, we shall come to you.

We of the Confederation are weary, for we have waited a long time, as you would consider years. We are weary because we have watched over your people. And we have seen them struggle, struggle beyond that which is imaginable by any of us, searching for the answers to your existence, the meaning of your life. And we have grown weary because the answers are so simple. In fact, each of you already know them if you would but look within yourself and discover your own reality. The purpose of your life on this particular planet, or shall we say, in this particular classroom, the greatest purpose is to learn to love one another without any vice, without any stipulation, without any envy or regret. If your peoples learn even half of this lesson they shall advance into a civilization which is compatible to ours. And they shall grow to work with us and to travel with us throughout the universe, and to spread what they have learned to their unfortunate brothers on other planets who have yet to come to these realizations. The simplicity of your existence, the meaning of your existence, the reason for your existence is love. Love encompasses all things. For it is the ingredient upon which all things were created.

I shall transfer this communication to another instrument. I am Hatonn.

(Carla channeling)

I am with this instrument. I am Hatonn. We are sorry for the interruption and greet the instrument known as Don. We again greet you in love and light.

And what is that subject of which we speak, my friends? What is that strange and much sought after thing that is called love among your peoples? It is not what you think it is, my friends. We ask you to visualize in your mind's eye an individual whom you admire, an individual whom you would be like. What is the nature of this individual, my friends? What in this individual inspires you in this admiration? The answer is something different in each person's experience. But we suggest that the one thing that there is in common is that people who are loved and admired are themselves the open channels for that which is truly love. Not love as it is known among your people. Not something that is done or said or spoken or thought. But something that is.

There are some people that you know that have the gift of being. And whoever they are, and whoever type of being that they show, they show it in such a way that the love of the Creator shines through. And they become windows in which is reflected the fire of love. Yes, my friends, love is a very intense fire. Love is that which you experience, when you experience all that you experience. You yourself are love. All that you experience is love. The creation is a creation of love, love impressed upon waves of light in many, infinitely many, combinations giving the universes infinite densities, and giving the entities that dwell in those universes their infinite varieties. But all, my friends, all are varieties of love. Who are you, my friends? What variety of love have you experienced this particular day? What love did you see today? What love showed through you today? We ask you these questions.

We ask you these questions because there is a point in your seeking at which these questions will become very, very important. And that is the point at which you decide that you want to take responsibility for yourself. Your life in this particular experience is short. And each experience that you have is fleeting. And if you know that each experience is one of love, you then, my friends, are in command over that experience. You know what to look for. You know what you are seeking. You are seeking to understand the love that created the observer in yourself that is observing the experience. And you are seeking through that observer to find the love in your experience. You are love and you are waiting to be reflected.

When you see that love distorted around you, when you see anger, when you see global anger, or when you see personal anger, when you see fear, trepidation, unhappiness, all of the negative emotions, be they small or great, if you are looking with the knowledge that all things are love then you can see that all these things are distortions of a basic vibration of love. And that which is unlovely you can have compassion for. And that which is difficult you can surround with your own desire to give comfort and rest to those things around you which need comfort and rest. You cannot do this from the stores of your own love, for they are but limited, my friends. You can only do this when you make contact with the source of all that is. We are speaking of that one experience which is the source of all experience, that one love which is the source of all love, that one Thought which is the source of you and this channel and we ourselves as we speak through this channel.

Seek the Creator, my friends, in meditation. For it is the Creator's love that is infinite and can carry you through all those experiences of your days, giving you the sweet and precious understanding of the truth, the fine and lovely contentment that only love can bring, and the happiness that the divine laughter of joy in love will produce. We speak to you from a place which you would call the kingdom of heaven, for it is a place where love is visible. We wish that you could join us here. And you can join us in thought. And that is why we ask you to call upon us whenever you might be ready. For we would gladly assist you with our conditioning wave so that you will find it easy to meditate.

At this time I will leave this channel, briefly, so that one of my brothers may work with the conditioning wave. I am Hatonn.

(Pause)

(Carla channeling)

I am Laitos. And I have been working with each of you. I greet you in love and light. And wish to tell the instrument known as H, the instrument known as W, that we have been attempting to speak through each of them. However, they were not properly conditioned to accept our words and thus we simply conditioned each of you, attempting to make our presence known to each of you. We thank you for your grateful attention and we will leave you at this time. As always, we leave you in the love and light of the infinite Creator. I am known to you as Laitos. Adonai, my friends.

I am again with this instrument. I am Hatonn. And I return to this instrument to ask that if you have any questions at this time you ask them of this instrument. Is there a question at this time?

(Pause)

We are aware that there are two questions, but we prefer to wait until the questioner decides to ask them of us, rather than speak before we are specifically invited. If there are no more questions we will leave you.

We are sorry, my friends, for any and all difficulties that may face you this day. We know that your illusion is a difficult one. And we send you our love and support, as always. You must remember the value of insubstantial things. For the rainbow that was the promise in the covenant of Abraham was only a bridge of light. Take that bridge, my friends. It cannot be felt. It cannot be touched. It cannot be weighed. But you can see it and know it. And there is promise for you in each moment. For you too have a covenant and birthright, for you are children of the Creator. And in that Creator resides all love. Desire then, my friends, to experience that love, and to know that one original Thought. Knowing that simple thing, you then have access to all that there is.

We leave you with these few pitiful words, knowing that we cannot touch you in any important way, but that only you can choose your own spiritual path. We hope that we can encourage you along that path. Adonai, my friends. We leave you in the love and the light of our infinite Creator. I am Hatonn. ☥

L/L Research

Intermediate Meditation
March 23, 1980

(The recording is barely audible. Inaudible sections are marked with ellipses.)

(Carla channeling)

I am Hatonn, and I greet you in the love and the light of the infinite Creator. We are very happy to be able to serve you … for we of the Confederation of Planets in the Service of the Infinite Creator have no other wish except to share our thoughts with you for whatever aid they may be to you in your isolation for the path that you most desire to walk in this most dense illusion that you call Earth. You walk in darkness. It is now dark about your dwelling place but through this instrument's ears she hears a branch of your … into a sort … nourishing plants that have also borne your darkness will now come … We would suggest that you remember that your entire life as you now perceive it is only … You will see that which is truly light as you leave this earthly … which you call. And yet you have that light within you just as the caterpillar has the butterfly, for you see, to fly … We ask you to think this night, my friends, of … It is written in your holy work that the master whom you call Jesus the Christ was come into the world by leaving so much darkness … and … He was an example of light. That, is he was an example of realized consciousness. You yourselves take for granted many limitations but find you are imprisoned in a kind of spiritual darkness which separates you from the light. What you accept as reality, those things about you … to you are less than … as we are … for yours is a world of illusion. That is why we wish to speak to you about light. For only the warmth … light from darkness has borne … to take for granted that … all those things which … The lesson that you learn while you are within this creation of darkness you learn by choosing one … the light. Reaching toward … Yet how difficult it is to do that for … It would seem … that evil … that the … it is to … But we would take you into a country … We would take you into … where all offices are the same for that which is justice is … We would take you beyond … beyond … all … Just as … will not. So your, finally … a paradox which is an ultimate … Thus while you are lonely … the age-old … thoughts what country while your spirit … and you … of light … I am conditioning this instrument … We are with you … We … are called … but we dwell … standing … We are not … We would now at this time transfer … you would feel … I am again with this instrument. We ask that … it is … strengthen your … We encourage you in your meditation … and assure you that we will be with you … We will … another member of the Confederation to speak with you. I am known to you as …

(Carla channeling)

I am Laitos, and I too greet you in the love and light of the infinite Creator. It is my especial privilege to work with those who wish to become instruments and to help each of you with the conditioning process. So if you will be patient with the new instruments we would like to work with each of you. We would like to send energy to the one known as C. We are aware that he is fatigued but we would like to attempt to let him be aware of our vibrations if he would.

(Carla channeling)

I am again with this instrument. We can feel a great deal of, shall we say, improvement in the reception of the one known as C. We understand that he is … by questions and doubts as to our basic origin and … This is entirely proper. We hope that as time goes on he will in addition to … allow the process of opening … will requestion information and pursue his attempts to understand at any level he may desire. … At this time we would like to attempt to speak a few words through the one known as … if she would relax … I am Laitos.

(Carla channeling)

I am again with this instrument. We would like to adjust the energy which we have given to … adjust our vibrations and again attempt to speak a few words through the one known as … if she would …

We thank the one known … We ask you, my sister, not to feel badly because we … for our thoughts … but it does take time … we are aware … greatly desire to we … We would like to now work with the one known … if she would … she would … herself that which she thinks without attempting analysis as to whether it is her thought or simply learn a concept into the instrument's …

(Carla channeling)

I am again with this instrument. We are aware that the instrument known as M … next time we attempt to make our presence known to her by …

(Carla channeling)

I am again with this instrument. We thank the one known as M and offer ourselves to her any time that she wishes to receive the particular service of … only one of … times that … so much of the wisdom … other sources for a relief from … of your … If you will be patient we would like to work with the instrument known … We have difficulty … would like to attempt … she would relax … I will transfer to the one known as K. I am Laitos.

(Carla channeling)

I am again with this instrument. To the one known as K we would say you have just received a … that was ours and will again send it and ask that … be brave … speak forth you will discover that if your thoughts …

(Carla channeling)

I am again with this instrument. We thank our sister K for working with us. We know that it is difficult for you to allow your mind to … hear … contact … through this type of overture. We know that it takes practice and confidence … And with time as you call it … We are glad … Thank you … our love … If wish to receive … simply mentally request … If you are receiving conditioning … I am Laitos … Adonai.

(Carla channeling)

I am Latwii. I come to this group only to wish you well for I do not have a great deal to say to you at this time. This instrument is expecting me to give her some wise and inspirational thought but, my friends, you are the inspiration. It is your understanding of this that will save you, not our words. You must think of yourselves as the fence that intertwines one strand with another, forming great strength so that flowers may grow over it and winds may never blow it over. Alone you are only a … seeing the cosmos and the cosmos seeing you. Hold out your hand to your brother, my friend.

What an inspiration. We cannot give you that inspiration for you are the inspiration. You are the Creator. We are only a voice given through a channel coming from a dimension that is not distant. We are like thoughts that you may think yourself. You must understand that we of the Confederation in no way wish that you become champions of the so-called UFO's. For we do not think of our philosophy as being the truth of the Creator, for we as you and all the beings that there are are the Creator. We are speaking to ourselves … But you are living in a density in which you have tremendous capacity to learn. You learn from sorrow, you learn from … you can learn from any means … always remember, the inspiration, the answers are within you. There is no outside input. Like you … by becoming conscious are truly one …

We ask you to do this, my friends, of course in meditation, but we feel that you are an advanced group to the point where you have realized that meditation is not a … You can meditate and then five minutes later … The next lesson, my friends, is not … The next lesson, my friends, is that you realize who you are. To be in such a state that you are the inspiration to the outer world that you truly are … Let yourself be free, to be joyful, to share that joy with others. You have something to give that is so precious that it cannot be described. … For you will never be alone for you are on a path which is shared by many, many … There is a kind of interweaving … so that you can never be alone. You walk with the Creator and with all those who seek the Creator. Imagine, my friends, the loneliness of those … who do not know that they are the child of the Creator. Yet they are. They are part of the great and perfect union that is …

Well, my friends, I speak a long time for someone who has nothing to say and I apologize if I speak too long. But I come basically to ask if there are questions, for I would be very happy to attempt to help you understand … Questions?

Questioner: *(Inaudible).*

(Carla channeling)

My friend, we understand your question, however, it is very easy to speak of … it is in fact something that you do very well. However, due to your analyzing … Therefore let us say a bit about the condition … no entirely … Conditioning acts as a kind of a carrier wave which strengthens the signal of your own so-called alpha wave … It is a basic meditative frequency … to … shall we say brain … although … But this instrument would … channel information. When you meditate … wish to seek conditioning, simply ask for … This job is given to our brother Laitos and it is felt in various ways. For those who do not wish to channel … electricity, shall we say … some part of the body. … you can see … If someone wishes to use the conditioning in order to become a vocal channel, simply mention … mentally to us and Laitos will then work with more intensity … on your vocal … into your muscle … exercising you … objective evidence that there is an entity that is not yourself that is … activity. When you have become sufficiently conditioned to, shall we say, believe in us, which is an almost literal thing, then your belief that there is something to receive has given you enough confidence to allow you to speak thoughts as they are given to you without analyzing … then … will … vocal channel … we will be gone as quickly as … Some develop very quickly, some develop slowly. It is usually the analysis of our thoughts that keeps the instrument from developing more rapidly. Thus, as you receive conditioning, if you will refrain from analysis, then simply accept whatever … you are feeling, when the vibration is transferred to you, you will be in much better position to have the confidence … to speak without knowing what is to come next. For this is … not knowing what they are going to say next, they do not say what they are feeling … thus they are not able to receive … Do you understand what we are speaking …? How may we help you?

Questioner: *(Inaudible).*

(Carla channeling)

That is indeed correct, my brother. And yet if you have ever watched … you know that every … respond with … For … surrounds all … We will give you another image which may help you. … is something … there is no … All of those things … Perhaps this will aid you … sincerely …

(Tape ends.)

Intermediate Meeting
March 30, 1980

(Unknown channeling)

I am known to you as Hatonn, and I greet you in the love and the light of the infinite Creator. It is a great privilege to blend our thoughts with yours at this time and through this instrument, and we thank you for the opportunity. This evening we would speak to you in a small parable, for often that which is true can be seen better when it is seen as a part of a story, and so for you, my friends, we write a story of a prince who had a kingdom.

Standing upon the turrets of his castle, the prince gazed over the great domain over which he reigned, and he was very glad, for was he not prince, and did not all he saw belong to him? He was by nature a kindly man, much given to good deeds, and merciful in action, living at peace with his neighbors, skilled in diplomacy, and without any blemish that could be seen.

How he loved his kingdom. He loved his fields and his forests, his farmlands, his villages and towns, and the lovely castle which had been improved and added to over centuries until it was indeed a glorious sight, with spires and castellations, towers and watchtowers. And once every year in the castle keep came all of his people rejoicing that their king was so just, so mighty, and so powerful.

One day the winds of change came upon the kingdom—boats of a foreign and strange creation landed upon the shore, and within a very short time the peace-loving king was removed quite utterly from his reign. The joy of centuries diminished, the ownership of land, field and forest changed. The king escaped because of the love of his people, for they took him in as one of them and he began life anew as an humble cottager toiling in the fields, carefully guarding the forests, and serving the new lord of the land.

And once a year the people, fewer each year for fewer remembered, would come to visit one small village, and they would kneel before one old cottager, humble and full of years. And he, well adjusted to his new life, would say as if in ritual, "Do not bow your knee to me, for I have no fields and no forests. I have neither land nor estate." And his people would remain on their knees and say, "We praise you as our king, because you have taught us goodness and peace."

This cottager who had been king died quietly and the kingdom remained, unhappy now, scourged by heavy taxes and unfair practices of all kinds that reduced the villagers and the townsmen to near slavery, and in the length and breadth of time came there those with books and knowledge. And slowly, very slowly, the kingdom again changed so that it began to balance between total peace and total aggression.

Amidst all these experiences, my friends, amidst all those who were loved and those who were unloved, the creation of the Father grew and flourished in its season. Fields and forests, birds, animals, fish, nothing of man truly upset the creation of the Father, for there is a love in such balance and of such power that its ability to heal itself, given enough time, is perfect.

We are aware, my friends, that each of you are in a different situation with different perspectives. Some of you dwell under a good and peaceful ruler, either yourself, another being, or a great ideal that you seek. And so love rules your life and all of your movements are graceful, and that is well. Those of you to whom we speak, we ask that you meditate upon the meaning of your fortune, and upon how you can share your love. Some of you dwell under the angry queen—we correct this instrument—Some of you dwell under the angry king. You are in slavery or bondage to yourself, a habit, a possession, another person, or a false ideal. We ask you in your meditation to ponder the reason for your slavery, and how, through sharing your difficulties with the Creator and with your friends, you may free yourself from all addictions, limitations and difficulties, and be healed. But those who are fortunate and those who are not are often one and the same person in different moods and at different times. And so we speak to all of you when we ask you to look up, outside your windows, outside your world, into the world of the Creator. Try not to miss one single day of the creation, for your days are numbered. And as it is written in your holy works: all flesh is grass that blooms for a day, and then it withers and is no more.

In your season of blooming watch the creation of the Father, for it too has its cycles and they are quick. And the understanding and the healing in your watching of that creation is very great. All of those things in the creation of the Father are designed to be of service, one component to the other. As you pass along beneath your trees, remember that they are breathing oxygen to you, and cleaning your air. Think of the gentle rain as it falls upon the thirsty earth, producing your food. And the wind that spreads the beautiful clouds and the gentle rain. Watch the insects as they create fertile fruit and flowers. In the creation of the Father, each thing is a mystery that cannot be known, can only be loved and appreciated.

And if you spend some time with the creation of the Father you will find that it asks only one thing of you—it only asks that it may love you just as you are. The rain and the sun shine on all of you, criminal and saint, fool and wise man, the trees shade all of you, and the presence and the consciousness of the Earth is one of total acceptance of you. It is a great sorrow of ours that many among the peoples do not reciprocate this feeling. But we are aware that many of the peoples are now becoming aware that their planet loves them, and that it is deserving of love in return.

Your fortunes will pass, good and bad, the kings of your life will change, but the fields and the forests will be there for you. When your internal lessons are not audible to you in the silence of your meditation, walk out into the incredible beauty of the creation of the Father. And open yourself to communion with that which only desires to be of service and to love.

We are aware that this instrument has reservations about what we have just said, and she is doing well about not analyzing our thoughts, and we would answer her reservation because we do feel that it would be of service to others also. There are those elements in the creation of the Father which seem very competitive and warlike. As one of your poets has written, "Nature red in tooth and claw …" But this, my friends, although it may seem destructive, is a means of balancing the species so that each may live according to their best strength. For instance, you may perhaps be aware that wolves, as they are known among your people, are considered vicious because they kill the caribou in the northern country, and the caribou are a threatened species. However, if you will look more deeply you will find that the wolves are removing from the pack of the caribou those who are sick and old and would hinder the caribou from reaching winter pasture land. Thus, the wolves strengthen the caribou while they themselves are surviving in their own way.

We are aware that this does not seem altogether without violence; however, the creation of the Father includes that which is known to you as violence. The difference between the violence in nature and that in man is that in nature there is a purpose to be fulfilled which is helpful.

At this time we will pause and allow our brother Laitos to work with each of you. I am Hatonn.

Intermediate Meeting, March 30, 1980

(Unknown channeling)

I am Laitos, and I also greet you in love and light, my friends. I am very happy to be with you and if you will be patient we would like to work with some of the newer channels. I would like to begin with the instrument known as D. If she would relax, we would like to attempt to make contact with her and say just a few words to her at this time. I am Laitos.

(Unknown channeling)

I am Laitos. I am again with this instrument. We will remove the conditioning from S at this time so that he may be more comfortable. He is making a great breakthrough in hearing our concepts and has difficulty only because of an emotional reaction to doing something which he has desired to do for quite a while. As he becomes used to this contact, it will smooth out and the feeling which could be described by this instrument as "the rush" will no longer incapacitate him from being able to speak.

We are profoundly grateful to you for any spending this time with us, and we will be with you at any time that you request it, either for conditioning, or the meditation, or for conditioning for vocal channeling such as this instrument is doing at this time. The choice, my friends, is up to you, and we have no prejudice, for it is not everyone who desires to become a vocal channel. But indeed, you are all channels in your way, and we believe that the conditioning which enables you to meditate can help each of you. And we in turn have great need of vocal channels for, as we have said many times, there are those who will be asking questions, and we cannot come among you without interfering with your free will, for there are those among you who do not wish us to be here. And so we must speak through people such as you, to share with you what knowledge we do have. It is no knowledge you cannot have, for this knowledge is your birthright. It is simply that the forgetting is so great among your peoples that it amounts to a deep sleep. You who are awake are greatly welcomed. We will join you in meditation, my friends. For now, I leave you in the love and the light of the infinite Creator. I am Laitos. Adonai.

(Unknown channeling)

I am Hatonn, and again I greet you, my brothers and sisters. Our friends of Latwii send you greetings. They are very taken up at this moment with observations, and so we will attempt to aid you in answering any questions that you might have. Is there a question at this time, my friends?

Questioner: As we are now moving into the fourth density, what does that hold for us? What changes will there be? It's called the age of understanding, so explain what this all means.

I am Hatonn. We are aware of your question, but it is somewhat complex. Not because you meant it to be, but because the information comes from several different levels. This planet, in this density, is moving into a more pleasant aspect of this density. There will be, on this density of this planet, another cycle of third density following the conclusion of that which even now is occurring, having to do with the end of the cycle. Namely, the weather changes, the natural changes in geography, and the possible armed disputes and economic disasters that will be part of this change. Some of the people now dwelling upon your planet at this time will repeat that great cycle which, depending upon the various gravitational changes and electromagnetic variations, lasts somewhere between seventy-five and seventy-eight thousand years.

Such a cycle you have already gone through, and the harvest is at hand. You are being harvested as you leave the physical plane. Those of you who love yourself more than your neighbors will go through this particular classroom again, learning how to love. That is not called the Golden Age, that is called repeating the grade, or that is what this particular channel would call it. However, there will be a harvest, and this harvest of people in a body finer—or shall we say, more dense than the spiritual body, a body which we could almost call the angelic body, but we will simply call it the spiritual body for that is the name you know—in this new body, those who graduate, those who love others more than themselves, will enter the Golden Age and will become of a part of the inner plane system of this planetary sphere, or will have the opportunity to go on to do work in other spheres, depending upon their vibration.

For the most part, those of the Golden Age will remain upon the inner spheres of the planet Earth, for in the vibration of those who are sensitive to the higher love and light vibration, there dwells a calling to service, a great desire to help those who have gone before, and in the realization that a fourth-density personality does not yet have the ability to project through thought in time, through the dimensions, such entities will choose to be of service in their own backyard, shall we say.

In the Golden Age love will be seen. It will be a highly creative and a highly satisfying change, for when thoughts are visible, then no deception is possible, and thus, if love does not abide it can be approached through communication and understanding.

Would you like to question us further about this Golden Age, my brother?

Questioner: After we pass into this next phase, will we be helping other people of our own race achieve the level we've reached?

That is correct.

Questioner: Will it be a time of more love in our race as a whole?

Those who have not graduated will begin where they left off. Those who have graduated will be given such a glimpse of truth and love that there will be a great explosion of love in your inner spheres. And thus the vibration of the planet as a whole will be greatly enhanced as more and more of your peoples join those who dwell in love and light. Thus, we must answer you, yes, it will be a time of greater love. However, you will always find there are those who, of their own free will, choose to take a long, sad and lonely path through darkness, and this you, and we, must allow them to do until of their own free will they turn to the sunlight and seek love.

Does this answer your question, my brother?

Questioner: Yes. Can I ask some more?

You certainly may, my brother.

Questioner: Will our civilization still have government the way it is? Our present society creates a lot of resistance to the love in our race. Will this be the case then?

At the beginning of the next cycle there will be a breakdown of your government as you know it in the third density, and a type of dark ages, shall we say, as it may well be called in the future, will descend upon your peoples due to the fact that you have built a very fragile society in your, shall we say, civilized culture. Things will become more simple, and it is only a matter of conjecture as to what the free choice of those entities at the time will choose.

However, in the fourth density there is no need for government as you know it, for the rule is freedom in love, which means that no one obstructs the freedom of another, nor would wish to harm another, and since that which is needed can be created by thought, there is no need for the labor on a cooperative basis of your society.

However, in order for you to help, your work will be of a collective nature, melding and becoming one with each other so that you may, as a group consciousness, work for the good of the planet which nurtured you and which you now wish to nurture. Therefore, although you will not have government, you will be working as a unit in attempting to grow ever closer together.

As we are talking about two different dimensions, you can see that each density will have its own culture and society.

Questioner: My last question. Will we maintain our physical existence along with our spiritual self the way it is now, or will it be just the spiritual self?

My brother, we did not say that anything was "just" the spiritual self. We think that's the star attraction here. However, we understand the meaning of your question. You will have what will seem to you to be a physical body in the fourth dimension and in the fifth dimension. In the sixth dimension, which is a light dimension, and from which our brothers and sisters of Latwii come, there …

(Side one of tape ends.)

Questioner: Is our evolution to become a ball of light and lose the body altogether?

We are aware of your question, my sister. The goal of spiritual evolution is the transformation of consciousness. The Creator has given a proper shape and configuration to each level of consciousness, so that each transformation is accompanied by a transformation of the vehicle, so that the consciousness may be housed in the most appropriate vehicle for further learning and growth. To attempt to grow spiritually in order to become a ball of light would be like attempting to, shall we say, become a flower or a cloud. The form of consciousness is not within the power or provenance of an evolving entity. It is not anything for that entity to be concerned with. The only concern of the seeker is that he seek. To be a seeker is the basic drive of the nature of all mankind. The basic question of your life is, "What do you seek?" When you understand what your most basic desire is, the priorities of your existence arrange themselves accordingly and you set about your path, seeking as you go, using each minute as a vehicle for learning about that which you seek.

Thus, instead of nullifying desire in removing oneself from acts of will and desire and longing, we ask that you become intimately familiar and totally honest with all of your desires on whatever level they may be, denying none of them, understanding them, and appreciating that the Creator has made you with these desires. The question is in how you order them, and how you moderate them according to your most basic desire. In this way, you begin, and continue, on the road of spiritual transformation. You are attempting a mutation of the mind and spirit. You can do this only by opening yourself to that which is true. If you call it "good," if you call it "God," if you call it "love," if you call it "Buddha," if you call it "Jesus," we do not object. You may call it the unnamable. Whatever it is, we ask you to seek it and to know yourself as a seeker.

The prize goes not to any form or design, but to the man with the greatest heart and the greatest will to know. We are not speaking of true believers who attempt to win the world to their ways. We are speaking instead of people who realize, finally, that their greatest single endeavor in life is to be themselves. This we offer you from what knowledge we have. Seek not any form, seek not to become a ball of light. Seek to be yourself, seek to know yourself, seek to share yourself, for it is you yourself who contain the essence of all that there is.

It is written, "As above, so below," and we say to you, each cell of your body knows the body. If you take a cell from your arm, will it produce an arm? No. We say to you it will produce a body. If you take a cell from your leg will it produce a leg? No, my friends, it will produce a body. Thus, know yourself in all your parts. Know all of your thoughts: those which are basic, those which have to do with existence, with security, with power, with things with which you may not approve. Know all the good things. Know all the things that you had forgotten about yourself that are quite lovely. And to know most of all your inner true and perfect self, that self that changes only very slowly and through many life experiences, growing ever closer to the Creator, sparked by the Creator and returning to the Creator.

Does this answer your question, my sister?

Questioner: *(Inaudible).*

As always, we thank you, and are grateful for your questions. Is there another question at this time?

Questioner: *(The question is mostly inaudible; essentially, it was, "We cannot be objective in this life, in this body. Will all be understood when we are in spirit?")*

We are aware of your confusion, my sister, and we ask only that you relax, for the truth is so simple that it is almost always missed. We give you a very simple truth, and it is so simple that the intellect rejects it. But we tell you all that we know of the truth, and that is that you are a being created in love, that you walk in love, and that you may at any time choose to act with love, thus maximizing the effects of learning in this dense and sometimes difficult life, as you call it, that is so [brute].

It is a very common and everyday affair for those who seek, to slip, by habit, into old patterns of thought which are negative. This is understood and should not be a source for self-blame or any sort of guilt upon the part of the seeker. You are simply adding two plus two and receiving the answer of five. There is no guilt, there is a simple error involved. The illusion is very strong among the peoples, and in order for you to be able to control your reactions to those things about you which cause you to initiate patterns of behavior that are negative, we can only suggest that you meditate daily and seek to ground yourself in what we may call a tabernacle of yourself and the Creator, a holy place within your own breast in which the Creator may dwell, as in a tent, as in an oasis, so that you too may repair to your own heart and to the Creator. And from that gentle and well-watered garden, thereby remember not to react to circumstances which cause the negative feelings of which you are speaking. It is nothing more than a habit of mind, and when recognized as such by the use of daily meditation, and by the constant reminder of the Creator within, can by slowly eliminated so that eventually, in one area of your life and then in another, two plus two will begin to equal four.

When you are dealing with habits of very long standing, the error is sometimes very difficult to catch before it has begun. Thus, above all, do not blame yourself, or feel less than confident, or less than spiritual, because you have made an error. Simply begin again, for in the Creator all things are new, and at any moment you may begin anew, and each time that you find yourself in negativity, simply begin anew. And that is the beginning of a new life, for the Creator is such that once two plus two is four, He does not remember the error, and nor should you.

We hope that this helps you, my sister.

Questioner: Yes, thank you, it is very, very reassuring.

We are very glad. Is there another question at this time?

H: About the volcanic action in the state of Washington. Does it have any particular significance for Earth changes at this time?

Yes, my brother H. It is one of many volcanic actions that have begun to take place beginning in 1976. And these volcanic actions will continue, along with other Earth changes, for some time to come.

H: Is it possible that other volcanic eruptions could occur along the coast of this continent, the west coast?

We can speak only in probabilities. There is a great deal of positive energy being sent to California and this is aiding the situation in more ways than one. Consequently, the outlook there is better than it would have been had not people been working on the earthquake situation there for some time. However, the probability is approximately 35 percent that volcanic actions in Alaska and Hawaii will occur.

H: Thank you.

You understand, my brother, that this is only a probability, and can change.

H: *(Inaudible)*.

Yes, my brother, we are aware of your familiarity with statistics, so we need not have asked that question. However, there are others in the room who were not as familiar with probabilities and how they may change in time.

Is there another question?

(Pause)

My friends, it has been a great pleasure to us to speak with you. We wish for you to realize that our speaking is not perfect and our knowledge is far from perfect, but that our love for you is as great as our being and our desire to serve you in any way that we can. We thank you for reaching out to us and we encourage you in your own seeking.

I am Hatonn. I will leave this instrument in the love and the light of the infinite Creator. Adonai vasu borragus. ✣

Intermediate Meeting
May 4, 1980

(Carla channeling)

I am Latwii, and I greet you in the love and the light of our infinite Creator, and give you the blessing of the Confederation of the Planets in the Service of the Infinite Creator.

It is our privilege to work with you this evening. We have not spoken to this group as the, shall we say, keynote speaker for some time now, for this is not our usual task, as you know. But your teachers of Hatonn, because they are of the vibration of love, are at this moment very, very busy elsewhere upon your planet, for there are many in your Middle East and in that country which you call Russia, who would like to make war at this time. Our fear is not for your physical bodies, but simply for the timing of this global conflict, for such it would be if those in Russia, as you call this land mass, had their way, for at this time they are capable of superiority in weaponry of a type which is not part of the normal repertoire of armaments among the people of your culture. They are what you call mind control weapons and your peoples do not have a defense for them. Therefore, there is a clear advantage at this time to a global conflict.

We do not wish to stay the conflict forever, if that is the will of your peoples, but we wish to send as much love as possible to your leaders of all nations, of all beliefs, and of all polarities, in the hopes that we can for just a little while longer continue to offer the pathways of observation, convocation and evolution to your peoples. We are trying to offer to your peoples—those who wish to seek—an understanding of the true nature of observation. For to see with eyes of love is to see for the first time that which is real. For those few sheep among your peoples who wish to be saved, and who seek a group of like-minded people, we offer them the principle of convocation and give them the knowledge that they may find such groups and raise their voices as one in their desire to know the truth. And above all, we find each moment in which we can speak to your peoples of evolution an infinitely precious moment, because, although your peoples cannot go backwards, they can certainly drag their heels. And the majority of your peoples have dug in their heels and are resisting with a great deal of effort the relentless march of evolution towards the light.

Yes, my friends, you can resist. There are a few planets who have resisted so completely that there is no light. But evolution is inevitable, even upon such lost planets. Yours is just in the middle, my friends. There are not so many who would be evil, but my friends, there are not so many who would be good. The great majority of your peoples would be neither good nor evil, but do not seem to have a predisposition to either. Hence, they are as pawns in a game which they know not of.

You, my friends, have begun to understand the game, and have begun to aid in your own evolution by understanding the value of being polarized toward love. This is not an easy polarization and that teacher named Jesus would never have promised that it was easy. For he said, "If you would be my disciple, take up your cross and follow me." Did he mean, my friends, that all of you must go through life in some kind of terrible martyrdom, suffering in order to be wholesome? No, my friends. Your teacher laughed at weddings and changed water into wine so that his friends might make merry and rejoice. He had a very deep sense of humor and rarely felt sorry for himself. He knew the ways of love and he knew that the path involved is a stony path. The path of evolution is a rocky path.

The reason for this is very simple, my friends. Say that you are not aware of the process of evolution. You are therefore not responsible for your lessons. You react in a completely instinctual manor and through the catalyst of many, many lifetimes' experience you begin very slowly to develop. You may have a hard life, but the aspect of learning lessons will not seem a great part of it. However, when this student takes on the responsibility of the path towards truth, he will be given small quizzes along the way.

Now, everyone is given these quizzes, but most do not recognize them. The student recognizes them, and therefore has the responsibility for meeting them. If you are having difficulty loving an enemy, you will be faced with that problem until you have conquered it. If you have trouble with one enemy, that enemy may go away, but you will have another. If you are having trouble with some addiction either in thought, in action, or in temperance, the source of that addiction may go away but you will be challenged again. Each time that you have the choice between anger or some other negative emotion and calm acceptance and creative understanding and you choose the release of anger or some other negative emotion, you know—those of you who are on the path—that you must do it again, you have made an error, and that it will meet you, most surely.

Your entire planet, as a planetary consciousness, has not yet reached the level of conscious development. It is simply reacting as it has reacted for many thousands of years in a warlike and somewhat negative fashion.

It would be well, my friends, if you would meditate briefly for the success of our brothers and sisters of Hatonn, and for peace in the world, for there are very critical occurrences at this time. We wish we could tell you how this will all come out because we like a good story as well as you, but we do not know the answer, we do not know the timetable, we do know the final outcome—for there is only one final outcome. In the battle between good and evil, that which survives will be neither good nor evil—but love. Good and evil are the light and the shadow of love. Love will prevail, but we do not know when and we do not know what will occur during these days while good and evil struggle upon your land.

We ask you especially to understand that in such a situation as you face now, each side is convinced of his own rightness and goodness, no one in this particular situation feels evil. No one accepts the role of the bad guy. Each feels that God, Allah or history is on his side. You may ponder that, my friends, for it will give you an insight into the true meaning of love, into the true nature of the Creator, and into the true oneness of all mankind upon your planet. You are fighting a civil war, my friends, for you are all planetary brothers and your national feelings and tribulation, difficulties, secret missions, secret weapons, and all the rest, remind us of a finger plotting against its hand, or one foot plotting against the other knee. We do not understand totally why you would wish to mutilate yourself. However, we accept that it is so. Nor do we judge you, for you are not unlike many of our brothers who have gone through similar sections of learning in their own evolution.

We ask you to lift up your hearts now, my friends, for we vibrate in the light and in the light there is no disharmony. We ask you to let these things drop away and to cleanse your soul as you would a garment, rinsing it in the cool, clear waters of a mountain stream until it is completely and utterly cleansed of nationalism, pride, glory and righteousness. We ask you to see those who you think are your enemies. Lift them up into the light, my friends, for they are your brothers. They are sad, they are puzzled, they do not know the light, they cannot recognize the light. Your own leader, my friends, knows the light and in his own way, is of a very pure nature. Many of your peoples do not understand the quality of light in the one who is your president at this time. We are aware, my friends, that it is not a practical or a prosperous characteristic, nevertheless it is inspiring to us to find anyone in a position of authority who is in the light. Lift him up also, my friends, for he knows where he is.

Feel the peace of this place which exists, my friends, inside yourselves. The light is white, but is not blinding and so may your understanding be to you. Keep that white light in your heart, my friends. Release all of the thoughts which we have given you, and settle back into your bodies now. You are of the light. You have understanding available to you. It will not blind you to action, however, it will make you more thoughtful. It will make you less understood, but it will make you more understanding.

I will pause at this time, that you may rest for a moment in silent meditation.

(Pause)

I am Laitos, my friends, and I greet you in the love and the light of the infinite Creator. It is my privilege to join our brothers and sisters of Latwii in sharing our thoughts with you. We would like to pass among you at this time to work with each of you in the conditioning wave. If you would relax, we will be with each of you for a few moments.

(Pause)

I am with this instrument and I thank you for your help in opening yourself to us.

We very much enjoy working with each of your vibrations and find them most enjoyable. We are always with you. We ask you to think of us not as a wiser source than yourself, but only as a more experienced brother or sister, for we never know which you will get when you request our presence. We are more experienced and we share it with you just as your older brother might do. That is what we are here for, that is our mission here.

We can do so little for you, my friends, and we are so filled with the fire of love, and wish so dearly to give it to your peoples. As we dwell above you in our ship, we spend much time in prayer for your peoples, for we have heard your call for help and we are here, and yet we can do so little. We ask those of you who meditate to meditate just a bit more, we ask you to be on fire with love, for the Creator has made a mighty and beautiful creation and it is one with you and you are one with it, and all divisions are nothing but illusion. Reach out, my friends, when you feel that it is in you to do so, reach out in love. Feel that inner glow, the warmth of that fire that is within you. It is real, it is not an illusion. That is who you are, that glow, that spark, that power created you from nothing and you are eternal.

Before this world rolled in a circle, you existed. A soul on a long path. Here you are, my friends, in this place, in this time, on your path. Your Creator can only speak through you. His hands can only reach through you. The words of love are only spoken through you. Thus, be open to inspiration, be open to kindness, to cheerfulness, to the simple actions, the smiles, the courtesies, the gentle touch, that make the people around you know, not that you are such a fine fellow, not that you are such a wonderful girl; no, my friends, that is not it. But that the Creator has created a marvelous and wonderful creation. One in which gladness is the total truth. Love is the total truth. Love is the total reality. Meditate, my friends, and feel this, and then let it shine forth in your eyes, through your lips, and by the service that you do.

I am Laitos, and I thank you for listening to me. But I felt that you had a desire to hear this this evening, and though I do not usually spend so much time speaking of philosophy, this evening I felt that while I was giving the conditioning wave, I would speak to you about love. I thank you for listening to me, and I will at this time pause and say adonai so that my brother may again speak with you. I leave you in love and light. I am Laitos.

(Pause)

I am Latwii. I am again with this instrument. We are having trouble with this instrument, for she smells food and her concentration is wandering. We will work with this instrument, if you will have patience. I have a better contact with this instrument at this time, and would wish at this time to open the meeting to questions. Is there a question?

Questioner: *(A question is asked about nationalism.)*

I am with the instrument. That is a very good question, my brother, and we must answer it not in your terms but in ours. There is no should or shouldn't to evolution. There is only the inevitable. At a certain point in your evolution you will no longer have groups that are smaller than the planetary consciousness, for you will have discovered that you are all men and women of Earth, as you call your planet. We call your planet Sorrows. There are many names depending upon the quarter of the sky from which our ships have come. When that occurs, there will not be a feeling "nationalism," there will be a feeling of planetary oneness due to the fact that the true geographical entity upon your planet is the planet.

You will notice upon the maps that you have of your states and countries that say, for instance, you may have the state in which you reside colored pink, while the state called Indiana by your peoples colored yellow and the state called Ohio by your peoples colored blue. However, if you take off in what you call your airplane and achieve an altitude sufficient for you to see parts of those three states which is possible even in a small plane, you will notice that there is no obvious demarcation between your Kentucky, your Indiana, your Ohio, and moreover you will notice that they are not pink, yellow and blue, but are indeed all of a camouflage color of brown and green and some black, with ponds sparkling and rivers flowing here and there, knowing no boundaries other than the natural boundaries of altitude.

This is true of your entire planet. The feelings of nationalism are proper to your situation at this time. However, it is good for you and for all those who wish to live a loving and thoughtful life, to be aware that nationalism, while appropriate to the circumstance [in] which you find yourself, is part of an illusion. This illusion is taking place that you may grow. We are not speaking of physical growth but spiritual growth or, as we have said before, the evolution of spirit. Thus, if you can view the situation which you call political which demands nationalism at this time, in a light which includes the understanding that this is not the ultimate reality, only an illusion, then you may observe the illusion and attempt to understand the lessons which this particular illusion at this particular time is attempting to show you.

We earlier brought you to a place of light and specifically brought rulers, leaders of three nations deadlocked in a near war with each other, so that you could feel in your heart that the reality was that they and you are brothers, are one being. How can you serve the Creator with nationalist feelings? My friends, you will; you will serve the Creator, and it is not inappropriate to have the feelings that you have, however it is appropriate to both to respond as the situation in the illusion requires you to respond, and to know beyond a shadow of a doubt that it is an illusion, and that you are, in truth, a child of the Creator. That whatever actions are necessary, you will do, but you will not do them with hate, with obsession, with pride, with righteousness, but only with compassion, both for yourself, for those who are of other nations, and for your Earth in its tribulation.

Have we made this clear to you, my brother?

Questioner: Yes.

Is there another question at this time?

Questioner: *(A question is asked about Russia's mind control weapons.)*

We are aware of your question and are examining this instrument's mind. However, as in the past, we find this instrument lacks many of the virtues of a scientific training. However, we will attempt to speak through her.

The mind has an electrical field and so does the Earth and so does every living thing. Weapons of a psychic or psychotronic nature—may we correct this instrument, she is not familiar with this subject matter. The pronunciation is "psy-ca-tronic." Those weapons know as psychic or psychotronic weapons are capable of sending a wave or electrical field through the Earth in any direction they may wish and at any power that they may wish, so that the minds of those in the field of that particular weapon are no longer capable of functioning normally. Various physical disabilities will occur, such as nausea, blinding headaches, rage, fury, and other extreme emotions which are finally turned to self-destruction, so that you have those who would fight the enemy instead fighting themselves, and, at the extreme, dying.

This is one type of weapon; there are others. However, this is the most generally effective and the one best tested by their scientists. The USSR has also spent many years developing what seem to be random psychic powers among certain gifted individuals, so that [they] may be used by the state, alone, in groups, and in conjunction with machines. Those of your scientists in the early '60s debated the use of such weapons, but decided not to spend a large amount of revenue upon that type of research.

As this instrument would say, they dropped the ball. There is now what you call a definite gap in the efficiency of the weapons deployed by Russia, as you call this country, and your own country. Both of you have weapons to destroy each other with physical means, but only one country has the ability to destroy through energy.

You can well imagine the possibilities of this in balance or grace. However, Russia is vulnerable to determined and prolonged attacks upon power sources for the great machine that developed the psychotronic devices. Therefore, they are not quite bold enough to move in the face of world opinion at this time. However, you will have observed that they are becoming more and more bold, and are very, very seriously thinking of increasing that boldness beyond the level of open warfare.

Have we been able to explain through this instrument that which you wish to know, my sister?

Questioner: Yes, thank you.

We thank you. Is there another question?

Questioner: Is there any way of escaping the psychotronic weapons?

No, my sister, not at the level of vibration you find yourself. If you could all leave your bodies, it would be just fine.

(Side one of tape ends.)

(Carla channeling)

[I am Latwii.] I am again with this instrument. We apologize for the delay but this instrument desired to change the tape. We do not wish to speak long upon this question for this instrument knows of some of the experiments that have been done by those you call Russians, with the instruments you call psychotronic. Therefore, it is not necessary for us to channel this information through her, she will be able to speak to you herself. However, in simplicity we will say, "no." There is not any shield, not earth, not stone, not metal, not any shield whatsoever, that can block the extremely low frequencies of the psychotronic weapons.

Is there another question?

(Pause)

If there is no question, we would like to answer a question that has not been asked, but which we feel is general enough that we may answer it without embarrassing anyone.

My friends, we realize that there is a great deal to worry about and we do not blame any of you in this illusion for being concerned and worried about situations which seem beyond your control. We ask you to have faith in the great continuum of love and light, and to know that if your heart desires truly, that heart's desire will one day come true. Thus, take time out from your worry, let it slip from your shoulders, and envision what you need, what you desire and what you wish to be so. It is the Creator's good pleasure to give you His kingdom. Thus it is said in your holy work called the Bible, "The Creator is not far from you," and He knows your worry, and He must let you have that worry until such time, if you are through with that particular worry, as long as you worry.

No matter what happens in your life you will find something about which to worry. Think instead of that which is good, let the solutions appear, in time, and meanwhile view all of those connected with the situation with as much love as you can muster in very difficult circumstances. That which is broken will be healed, and that which is unbroken is so precious, we ask you to put it first. Seek out the lovely, the living, and the good. We hope that this has helped you and we will leave you in your privacy. We will pause to see if there is another question at this time.

(Pause)

I am with this instrument. I am Latwii. I feel that your group is at peace, and we join you in that peace and that serenity. We ask you to carry it with you in memory and know that we love you as brothers and sisters. May you enjoy yourselves, my friends, to the fullest in the week ahead. May you laugh and be joyful and know that all things in the creation are the Father's. They are distorted, they are shadowed. Look through, my friends, look through the distortion and see love.

I will leave this instrument now in great thanksgiving for our time together. It has truly blessed me and my brothers. I leave you in the infinite love and the light of the infinite Creator. I am known to you as Latwii. Adonai, my friends. Adonai vasu. ♣

L/L Research

Intermediate Meeting
May 11, 1980

(Unknown channeling)

I am Latwii, and I greet you, my friends, in the love and the light of the One Who is All. We send you the love and the infinite regard of our brothers and sisters of Hatonn, and assure you that they are conscious of this group's prayers for them in this past period of your time, which you call a week. It is most appreciated and we ask your continued support and Hatonn continues his work of love.

We are very glad to be with you, although as this instrument well knows, we are not the smooth talking professors of Hatonn and are not nearly as used to delivering the inspiration that is in our hearts. However, we ask that you feel about you at this time that which is in our hearts and mind. That is, my friends, the great love and light of the Creator which, burning like a fire, removes all before it that is [gross] and encourages the bloomings of all those things that [are good].

Which things in your life, my friends, turn towards this light? How long have you spent in the shade of things? We ask each of you. Each moment that you spend with your face away from the sun, the great central sun of your existence, love of the Creator, is a moment lost, my friends. The faces of love are infinite. There is a face in every problem, in every situation.

You may consider it like a game, my friends. You may consider this a game. Find the hidden picture. You will remember this game. There is a picture of a tree and hidden in the branches of the tree there is a picture of a kangaroo. So it is with your life, my friends. Hidden in every picture is a picture of love. Love distorted, love undistorted. Love strained by your own misunderstandings, but nevertheless, my friends, that thing which we call love creates the changes and incarnates all that there is.

We know, my friends, that you are on a path and we would help you on this path, but we cannot [be] your walking stick. All we can do is say to you, yes, my friends, there is a path; No, my friends, you are not foolish. Yes, my friends, hidden in the tree there is a kangaroo. For many of those about you will not understand. Many of those about you will only see that which is on the surface of any situation. You must not allow yourselves the self-indulgence of wasting time, as you call it, moments of your consciousness in this incarnation. Meandering through a thicket of details without remembering the great detailer that drew up the great plans. And who is this great detailer, my friends? Someone far off to whom you may pray, someone with a name? This great detailer, my friends, is yourself! This fine creator is yourself! Yourself in an alternate form! Yourself with all of your parts put back together in harmony!

(Tape ends.)

Intermediate Meeting
May 18, 1980

(Carla channeling)

I am Oxal, and I greet you in the love and the light of the infinite Creator. We are most grateful for the opportunity to share our thoughts with you at this time and are very pleased to greet the one known as E and each of you. As you are probably aware, I and my brothers and sisters of Laitos have been working with you to balance the circle, for there has been some imbalance of energy and we are more happy now with the unity of this group. We ask your kind permission to join you in your meditation and to share with you some thoughts on the subject of love.

If you can picture with me now, my friends, a field distant from any neighboring settlements or domestic dwellings, a field, my friends in which butterflies fly freely and clover lies beneath the wildflowers. We ask you to go to that place which you have imagined and to feel the sun of a warm day down upon you. Feel your body, my friends, as you stand in this field, your senses completely filled with the love of the Creator. You can hear the wind whispering its ever-changing song through the trees and grasses and weaving the sounds like ribbons through the air or birds who call to each other in hunger and pleasure. The flowers smell sweetly, my friends, and you can touch the fragrant petals of the wild and rambling roses. As you view all these things and feel the heat and light of the sun, you are experiencing the creation. You are part of the creation and you are a rightful dweller in what is truly paradise. Allow your consciousness to sink deeply within that body, standing in that warm field, until you are aware of that bird song and the sweet smell of the wild flowers and the lovely colors of the field and the touch of the grasses about your bare skin are all a part.

This, my friends, is the simplicity of that which we have to give to you. It is a simplicity that has proved fatal for us, for you in your complexity desire complex answers and you feel that were we advanced we would have advanced in complexity. However, my friends, that extrapolation is [not true.] I am Oxal not because I am of greater intellect than you who sit in meditation; I am Oxal because I love. I and my brothers know this love, see this love, and feel this love. We ask you to come out of the field now, my friends, and enter another field of existence that is much more difficult to dwell within, that is, the field of life, in which the flowers that you touch are papers[8] and people.

And often, my friends, you cannot touch but must instead grapple with difficult communications because you cannot understand each other's

---

[8] Carla: With regard to the use of word "papers," I think perhaps this referred to correspondence—certainly we have had a lot of writing with various folks over the years, so perhaps it was literally paperwork they meant.

creations completely. The ever changing wind gives way to the creations of man. And even near your dwellings, my friends, have you not seen entities who bring their noise with them and drown out the wind, and know not the message it whispers through the branches of the trees? Can you see the Creator, my friends, as you look at the distorted creation of man? We would be very amazed if indeed you were fully able to see the Creator in every man and every woman. There is a reason for this, my friends. We have free will and so do you. We are not the clay, we are the potter. The clay consists of our actions and our thoughts but we are the potter that forms these actions and these thoughts. We are the potters of our existence. And if our thoughts are seemly and lovely to behold, then it will be more possible for us to be a person through whom the Creator may work the magic of love. But most of you, my friends, have dwelt ever so long in an environment in which love is not understood and in which, therefore, the free will of each of your associates has caused them to distort that magic of love into shapes that are almost indiscernible as love.

And yet, my friends, there is no place that love does not go. There is no action that love does not allow. It is written in your holy works, "If a man go to the depths of Hell, he cannot escape the Creator." We ask you to begin with yourself and to end with yourself in your attempts to discover love. We ask you to forgive yourself of any and all errors that you may commit. We ask you to love yourself in whatever imperfect state you may judge yourself to be. We ask you to release from yourself the responsibility for your nights and days, for your tasks and responsibilities. For those responsibilities belong to a part of yourself but not to your whole self. They belong to a shell of yourself that is dwelling in this experience. And of course, my friends, you will do the best that you can. Were this not so, you would not be in this room at this time, in this dwelling, seeking the truth in this manner. But an infinitely greater part of you is not dwelling within your experience at this time, it is one with the Creator and you may draw upon it as you will.

If you were in a drunken stupor and you tripped, would you not forgive yourself in the morning? That is your situation, my friends. You dwell in a very heavy chemical illusion. It is a difficult and challenging experience. However, in it you learn quickly and that is why you have put yourself in this experience. So learn what you can, my friends, but above all, allow that great portion of yourself that dwells with the Creator to indwell within you consciously each day in meditation so that you may bring it forth into manifestation, into whatever area you need its magic worked within. For, my friends, you are all magical, as the greatest miracle that you might ever imagine. Each of you has an infinite history and yet here you are, my friends, through an extremely amazing set of circumstances, dwelling in one room, pondering a set of thoughts, and experiencing the love and the unity of the group in which you sit. Let that love be as a candle to you, my friends, a very bright taper that has no end but burns mightily as does the sun. Desire to know that love.

I will leave this instrument at this time. It has been a great privilege to share my humble thoughts with you and if you have a use for them we urge you to use them. If not, we urge you to forgive them, for as this instrument has said many times on our behalf, we are indeed like yourselves, those who seek the truth. We are not those who can speak the truth without error. We send our love, and through us, the love and the light of the infinite Creator. I am Oxal. Adonai, my friends.

I am Laitos, and I greet you also, as does my brother. I am delighted to be with you and send you love and light. We wish for the one known as Jim to know that we were working with him before this instrument began to speak, in order to build up his confidence. We say this in confirmation, so that in future times when there may not be a confirming channel, you will have had an experience of knowing that we were indeed contacting you.

At this time we would like to condition and say a few words through the one known as C, if he would relax and speak each word as it comes to his mind. I will transfer now. I am Laitos.

(Carla channeling)

We are aware that the one known as C is somewhat fatigued and therefore we will adjust the conditioning wave a slight amount and work a little bit further with him. I am Laitos.

(Carla channeling)

I am again with this instrument. We would thank the one known as C and assure him that at any time that he wishes, we will be with him. At this time we would like to exercise the instrument known as Jim, if he would also relax and completely refrain from analyzing any concepts that he might receive. Simply speak forth one concept at a time, as they enter. I am Laitos.

(Carla channeling)

I am again with this instrument. I am Laitos. We have a good contact with the one known as Jim but he requires a bit more of the conditioning and we will therefore adjust our contact so that he may have more confidence. I will again attempt to speak a few words through the one known as Jim. I am Laitos.

(Carla channeling)

I am again with this instrument. We are aware that the one known as Jim is having some difficulty due to analysis and therefore we will simply continue to work with him, through his own desire to experience conditioning. We may say that perhaps one of the greatest stumbling blocks to a new channel is that the first concept he receives is the identification of the so-called channel. And since the instrument already knows who the channel is going to be, it sets up the conditions for analysis. We could trick you by saying, "I am Herbie," or "I am Hillary," but we do not think that would be in the interest of genuine work such as you desire to do.

For those humans who have need of our thoughts, therefore, it is simply a matter of overcoming the desire to make sure that you are being contacted and that you are not speaking for yourself. Perhaps the best way to achieve this is simple practice. And, as this instrument always does, a prayer of intent is very useful in tuning and protecting the instrument from stray channels, as you would call them, who might attempt to speak through you. These stray channels would include portions of your own consciousness and entities who are of this planetary sphere but have nothing particularly informative to offer to you. Thus, the tuning is important in channeling the work.

We thank each of you for your patience as we work with the newer channels. And we will pause for just a moment and condition each one of you as it may aid you in achieving a more deep meditative state.

I am Laitos and I would leave this instrument at this time. But, if in your daily meditations you desire our help in achieving a good meditative state or in working on conditioning, you have only to ask and we will be glad to work with you. I bid you peace and love, in the name of the Creator of all things, my friends. I am Laitos.

(Carla channeling)

I am Latwii, and I am very glad to greet you in the love and the light of the infinite Creator. I am very glad that it is my turn for I have waited patiently in order to speak to you this evening.

I have been enjoying the spectacle that your planetary disturbances have had in some of the spheres of color, which are beyond that which can be seen by your eyes. It is very beautiful, my friends. Although, we are, of course, sorry for any grief that you may feel at the rearrangement of certain molecules of some of the entities which now dwell in another plane of existence, due to this colorful display. We were waiting in the wings, as you might say, so that we could answer any questions that you might have at this time. Does anyone have any questions at this time?

Questioner: *(Inaudible).*

We are aware of your question, my brother. This instrument will have a hard time answering this question because her mind is not furnished properly. However, we will attempt through this instrument, since we do not have a proper one. The use of humor in altering the genetic personality is only now beginning to be appreciated by some of those among your researchers, whom this instrument would call, "holistic health experts." There are many secretions of the brain, as you call it, which will control and reprogram the self-healing of the physical, emotional and spiritual bodies. They do not have as much luck with mental body difficulty due to the fact that in mental problems it is more difficult to achieve mental breakthroughs. However, the brain being relatively unimpaired, we can then say that the possibility of using humor is excellent.

The ability to remove one's consciousness from one's little tiny area is very important in the reprogramming of the genetic personality. In order for this to occur there must be some agent. Most often in your recent years, those who have experimented in this area used chemical substances, such as that which you call LSD. These are also those who have used meditation and other less, shall we say, outward going therapies, in order to achieve reprogramming. There is a plethora of pseudo-reprogramming effects which may or may not last, depending on the sincerity of the individual. However, if a person once discovers how to laugh, this person will have a good chance of reprogramming basic metaprograms, which affect the life essences of the personality as it is manifesting in the genetic mode, in any given incarnation.

In order to release oneself completely through laughter, it is necessary to be able to feel that one is in a safe or trusted place; this is a prerequisite. What occurs when one is able to trigger the mechanism of laughter is that the secretions of the brain, having to do with metaprogramming, do the work of LSD or other powerful chemicals, but do it in ways already arranged by your very kindly Creator. Thus, you do not have to go outside your own being for the remedies for your difficulties.

We realize that we have not covered the subject adequately and therefore, if you wish to ask further questions we will attempt through this instrument to answer them.

Questioner: *(Inaudible).*

This is not a correct concept which you have generated within your mind. We are not sure that the true reprogramming concept can be generated intellectually. You can, for instance, decide what you wish to reprogram. But, you will never know in your normal, shall we say, work-a-day state of mind, the mechanics of this reprogramming. It is not so much a state of objectivity that you need to reach, as a state of freedom, and this is not a freedom from yourself. It is a freedom to yourself.

For in reality, in the physical illusion, you are separated from yourself by all the concepts which have been generated in your mind as distortions of the truth, by those about you whom you trusted since your early childhood. These distortions are many and varied, and at a very young age you chose which distortions you felt comfortable in living with. Therefore, various people have various distortions. So, the laughter releases you not to objectivity but to yourself, which is the ultimate subjectivity, since each person's universe is unique and unreplicable.

Does this answer your question?

Questioner: *(Inaudible).*

May we answer you further?

Questioner: *(Inaudible).*

We thank you and certainly hope so. Working with this instrument on some subjects is like chewing rye bread.

May we ask if there is another question at this time?

Questioner: *(Inaudible).*

Are you referring to the life-forms which are so-called test tube babies, or life-forms which are the constructions of scientists having to do with the computer design of life-like beings?

Questioner: The second. The latter.

Both governments are attempting to do various things, The most basic is to achieve an interface between a computer—this instrument does not have the word; the closest we can come to it is terminal—within the head or brain of an individual, thus allowing a living being, not a man-made being, to interface with all the bits of information which could be stored in a computer. This has not been successfully accomplished yet, due to the extreme delicacy of the synapses involved, so that the interface is difficult. There are already many mechanical and computer-led devices upon both sides, especially since it is part of the scenario of both governments that there may be necessity for beings which are not affected by radiation to perform certain tasks, in order to preserve the lives of the more fragile humans who exist in the same ecosphere.

To run through the number of experiments on each side would take some doing. Is there some specific category that you would like this instrument to channel information upon?

Questioner: I was thinking specifically of our leadership and the leadership of Russia and what it all amounts to *(inaudible)* on what they are … on whether or not they are artificial life forms?

I am Latwii. I am again with this instrument. The question that you ask is answerable upon two levels. In the first level, the leaders of Russia and the United States are people; they live and die. There is however, another level which is equally important to those who are attempting a serious study of this particular time in the evolution of man. The battle that is waged upon this other level has been called Armageddon. Must we terrify you by such a flagrantly biased word? Let us assure you that we mean the war of polarity. The polarity which you may call good and evil has little to do with national boundaries, although the vibrations of the land mass which you call North America are much more positive in nature than those of the land mass which you may call Russia.

This battle is not in the physical and is certainly not fought with people but with thoughts. Moreover, there are, from previous cycles of civilization upon this sphere, machines which have intelligence, which dwell within some of the deeper rock formations of your planet, the product of a civilization which long ago ended. They are not positive but rather, negative in nature, and therefore are the pawns of the thought forms that are strong enough to penetrate this particular form of machine.

Thus, as you see, we are speaking of two levels here. The level of your own daily life is peopled with humans, but underlying this drama which you are witnessing, is a deeper and age-long struggle between good and evil, light and darkness. And although there is no question of the ultimate outcome, there are, shall we say, some dicey moments. Certainly you are experiencing the transitional period, in which these moments may come rapidly, for some time to come. We are glad that you did not ask about the Chinese, for that is another subject, and one which we would rather not go into at this time, since that situation has passed.

Does this answer your question?

Questioner: It gives me food for thought.

We are always glad to give someone a mental snack. Is there another question at this time?

Questioner: *(Inaudible)*.

I am with this instrument. I am Latwii. We must decline to answer this question. We are sorry for that but we feel that attempting to channel that particular information at this time would be premature.

Questioner: *(Inaudible)*.

We are checking the computer. I am Latwii. The one known as Hatonn is working hard and doing fairly well. The prayers of many have joined the entities of that planetary society. There are gains registered [on] both sides. The probability of the most serious consequences is down somewhat. However, there is, shall we say, a semi-critical situation and we continue to ask for your love and support, of Hatonn and of those leaders with whom Hatonn is working.

Is there another question?

Questioner: How can we help people to get through these heavy times we are going through?

I am aware of your question, my brother, but it is so general that we have to go back to "Go" and collect $200.00. You can only help those people who ask you for help. That eliminates a large number of people. Thus, you must not worry when you cannot help people. Help is only appreciated if it is requested. Unwanted help is unnecessary help, and it will not help but only interfere, for all have a sovereign free will, and no matter what occurs in this physical illusion there is an infinity of time for each entity to learn and understand the truth.

Thus, abandon your desire to help everybody. We realize this is not a conscious desire, but it is a common subconscious desire, due to the fact that those who seek to know the truth are also those who have a love for other beings with whom they share this planetary surface of yours. There are a few whom you may help and they will ask you for that help. There are as many ways to help as there are requests. Some people may require a smile, some may require food. There are endless ways to share the bounty and the love of the Creator. If you are able to offer seed thoughts for the promotion of change for the individual who requests it, then, you have done the greatest help of all. For the greatest help is a spiritual help. And, the spiritual help can only be truly accomplished by the person himself, with you acting as a catalyst. Thus, think of yourself as a watershed, over which many will flow. There a few whom you may help with a word, a few with a touch, a few with generosity of food, or speech. Whatever is needed, it will be asked for and it will be a matter of your own understanding as to what you can do to fulfill the needs of those who ask.

We ask you to remember that the Creator's supply of love, whether it be food, caring, thought, words or any deed, is completely and totally infinite. So that, if you are a channel for the love of the Creator, you do not have to worry about running out of steam or being unable to help in one way or another. You need only to work upon yourself, so that you are a clear channel, unmoved by the ridiculousness of many situations, and in great humor when others find a situation quite grim. For you see, you dwell in the midst of a great cosmic joke and a great cosmic tragedy. And the ability to see both polarities of this truth equally is a very helpful one in dealing with yourself. And when you have dealt with this polarity within yourself, laughing at your grief and solemn in your joy, you may be of balanced help to others, for you may not then be touched by their difficulties to the point where you will be unable to respond in the way the Creator within you would respond.

There are many who make the mistake of caring without asking how to care of their higher self. Ask that, my brother, and that will be a greater source of information than any arbitrary way of helping that we could give you. You know, the one known as Jesus said, "If you do these things to the least of these, my brother, you do them unto me." That is the secret, my brothers: you and your brothers are one. You are the Creator and he is the Creator. Your brothers and sisters, and you, and we, and the Creator, are one being, the cells of which sometimes get themselves all mixed up. Let your cell of existence be calm, be joyful, and be one body of the creation.

Does this answer your question, my brother?

Questioner: Yes.

We are truly enjoying ourselves for we have developed a great affection for this group, and we thank you for allowing us to talk to you, for we do not have any other groups upon this planet who we can talk to. You are our first and we are really enjoying this a great deal. So, we hope that you have another question.

Questioner: *(Inaudible).*

That is correct. We are observing in your northern hemisphere at this time. And also in your southern hemisphere there is another buildup at this time which is creating very beautiful colors in your spectrum. However, these are not the same precise vibration as the colors of your sun and do not have the same properties. So, we are very busy cataloguing them all. And we thank the Creator for allowing us to see a transition in action. It is a very awe inspiring thing and we are specialists in what you would call spectroscopic analysis in many dimensions of space/time. Therefore, we are especially appreciative of the vibratory nature of your transition.

Questioner: *(Inaudible).*

Yes, my brother. This instrument does not know geography. We are having difficulty. The *(inaudible).*

Questioner: *(Inaudible).*

The chain of disturbance that we are showing this instrument occurs south of your country and to the east, in the ocean, with not very much land. There will be difficulties. We cannot see yet from the *(inaudible)* of the color whether it will be of what you would call of a volcanic nature or an earthquake. However, there will be an adjustment of the plates, as you call then, of the planetary *(inaudible).* If you would desire for this to be less violent you may, of course, send …

(The rest of the tape is inaudible.) ❧

Intermediate Meeting
May 25, 1980

(Carla channeling)

I am Hatonn, and I greet you in the love and the light of the infinite Creator. It is a very great pleasure for us to be with you again. We have missed our chances to speak with you very much. But we are afraid that at your present level of planetary intensity of political feelings we may well be absent from time to time, as you would say. We come to you upon the winds of love and are very honored to take a small part in your meditation. This evening we would talk to you of freedom, my friends.

There was once a young man who desired freedom, for he was a young man of great sensitivity. And when he saw the poverty, the hunger, the suffering in the world about him, he could not understand how these people could be bound to their suffering. This young man spent years working actively to alleviate suffering and promote personal freedom for his brothers and sisters, wherever he found the need. But ultimately he was betrayed by his own bitterness, for he knew that no matter what he did, it would never be enough to alleviate prison, which hunger and poverty had caused for so many upon your sphere.

And so he set all his daily work aside and went upon a journey, to seek an understanding of the reason why men must be bound by suffering, and why they could not be free. And he asked many people and received many answers. For there are those who believe many different things upon your planetary sphere, my friends. And each of those believes that they are the percipience of the truth. Some believe there is no such thing as freedom. Others believe that some must pay a price and are bound by their own previous errors. But with none of these answers was he satisfied.

One day he stopped upon an isle, for his ship needed supplies. And he was free to roam about this small tropical place. And he saw poverty again and conditions which were not conducive to health. And he found a native upon the island who spoke his language. And he told this native of his great dilemma. The native was a large man and his laugh was equally loud. And his laughter rang through the small room in which they sat. And the native man tapped his forehead, "Freedom," he said, "Here is freedom, nowhere else." And the young man cried, "But what about all of those who are starving, or ill, or poor?" And the big man reached out and tapped the seeker upon the forehead, "Their freedom is in your head," he said, "You must let them go, then, their freedom will be in their heads."

My friends, you do not live in an objective universe. All those things which you see about you are in fact not what they seem, as you are well aware. Any limitation which you might experience is a limitation only because of your perception of the way things should be as opposed to the way things are. If you desire to be what you are, and if in that being you discover that you seek the truth by nature, then, my friends, you will have achieved a type of personal freedom that is not known by those who are swayed by their perceptions of what should be but is not.

If you are fully grounded in your knowledge of who you are, then, my friends, you are free to fulfill your desire to know the truth and to express that truth in any way that you may need. There are as many different works as there are people. The great secret, my friends, is that there is only one spirit, and that is love, that provides all works for all people who dwell in love. If you try to change the world, if you try to help others, if you only modestly try to help one person, and try to do it upon your own, thinking and puzzling and perception, you will almost surely fail. For your perceptions are not their perceptions. And indeed, my friends, unless you allow yourself to flow into the channel of love, your help will often be unpalatable to the ones you seek to help. You are free only when you snap the cords of your own desire to be somebody in this world and to do things in this world as your own person. When you have accomplished the dismantling of your desire for reputation, then, you have no more bonds or limitations and you are free.

There are still those who are hungry, who are poor, and who suffer. This is so, my friends. We would never attempt to cause you confusion by stating that we do not know that your planetary influence is a difficult one. But each man is free if he desires to be. And you yourself are free of whatever limitations you may chose to have brought upon yourself [in] the moment in which you allow yourself to be one who desires to know the truth, one who seeks to know the love of the Creation, for this love, my friends, is a very powerful thing. Those who need you will be drawn to you, for you are not responsible for the world. You are responsible for yourself and in yourself dwells the world. Those who are drawn to you will ask and as you open yourself to love, you will know that which is of help. We urge you never to volunteer esoteric information to those who have not asked, nor to withhold it from any serious student.

But pay attention, my friends, always, to the only person who can be free, and that is yourself. A desire for freedom is an impossible desire, for you dwell in the prison of a body, of a gravity well, of an illusion that is heavy. And yet, you are willing prisoners of the catalyst of the experience of this planetary sphere. The way to freedom lies in accepting the conditions of your particular incarnation and in asking to know the truth. It is written in your holy works, my friends, "Seek and know the truth, for the truth shall make you free." Freedom does not come without a commitment, not to self, not to what you would call ego, but to the truth and to service in the name of that truth.

We are aware that you have a great desire to be of service and that you feel a responsibility to your kind, especially in these days that you face now in the unfoldment of your planetary experience. But, you must work on yourself, and know that as you achieve a state of true desire to know the love of the Creator, a burning desire to feel the spirit of that love which created you, you will then find all else that you seek added unto you. It is not an easy path, my friends, but it is a fruitful one.

(Pause)

We thank you for having patience during this pause, and we greet our brother S. Therefore, my friends, we ask you to be at peace with the world as it is, knowing that it is in each man's grasp to perceive his world in any way in which he sees fit. This is difficult for you to imagine, for you have never starved or suffered in the way some of your brothers and sisters have. But you must take stock of how you came to be where you are, what advantages this has given you as a channel for the love and the light of the Creator. And then you must seek to do the will of that love that created you, and set you in this particular place at this particular time. We all, my friends, have work to do. Ours is to be available to you and to those upon your planet who desire or require our love. Yours is whatever you make it. For indeed, my friends, you are free. You have only to break the tiny chains that keep you from your desire.

At this time my sister Laitos will pass among you and work with each of you, while we attempt to continue this contact through the one known as Jim. I am Hatonn.

(Carla channeling)

I am again with this instrument. I am Hatonn. We are aware that the one known as Jim is the recipient of a great deal of energy, and this group is a well-charged one. And therefore, we will attempt to focus this energy in a more manageable way, in order to facilitate the contact. We will again transfer to the one known as Jim, if he will simply speak without analyzing that which he receives. I am Hatonn.

(Jim channeling)

(Inaudible)

(Carla channeling)

I am again with this instrument. I am Hatonn. We may say, for the sake of his confidence, that we do confirm that the next thought was to thank him for the privilege of using him as an instrument. We are aware of the problem of analyzing thoughts and we are very sympathetic, for it is not easy to speak when you do not know what the end of your sentence will be, much less what the thought will contain. However, once the one known as Jim achieves a better state of confidence, may we say that he will be a very good channel. We would like to transfer now to another instrument, while Laitos continues to work with you on your conditioning. We would now transfer to the one known as S. I am Hatonn.

(S channeling)

I am Hatonn. I am with this instrument. We have a very strong contact. You must stop analyzing *(inaudible)*. I am Hatonn. We thank you for this contact, for it is a privilege to work with each of you *(inaudible)*. I will transfer to the one known as Carla. I am Hatonn.

(Carla channeling)

I am again with this instrument. We are aware that the one known as M would like the experience of feeling the contact and as Laitos concentrates upon him, we will attempt to *(inaudible)* him, so that he may feel what our contact is like. I am Hatonn.

(Carla channeling)

I am again with this instrument. I am Hatonn. Thank you, my friends, for your patience. It is one of our desires to develop as many channels as we can of the vocal type, because there are so many who desire to hear the type of information which we share. But, we assure each of you that in your own way all that you do is your way of channeling the Creator. Each time that you serve your brother or your sister, you serve the Creator. Therefore, let your mind be at rest and let your heart be happy. We leave you in the temple of the creation. We leave you in the present, for there is no time. And we cannot even leave you, for there is no place, for all of creation is here. And the Creator is you, and your brothers and your sisters and all those things that live that consciousness of love. We leave you in that love and that light. I am known to you as Hatonn. I thank you for the opportunity to speak. Adonai, my friends.

(Carla channeling)

I am Latwii. I also greet you in the love and the light of the infinite Creator. As a member of the Confederation of Planets in the Service of the Creator, I am always at your disposal. We have been having a great time here, watching the spectra of your planetary energies as your Earth changes take place. You have a very beautiful planet, my friends. We enjoy the one known as Hatonn and are very glad to be here with you. We come to answer any questions that you might have at this time, if this instrument might by any chance be able to channel them. Is there a question at this time?

M: I have a question. Since I was a young age, I felt I saw a UFO. Can you tell me why I have been searching ever since then? I have studied and tried to understand what it was that I saw and the related fields that I studied. Can you tell me why, or what, lies in the future for me? Why the purpose besides trying to get people more awake to the greater? But I feel I'm singled out.

I am aware of your question, my brother. Much of it we cannot answer due to the necessity for your will to be free, However, you answer your own question. If you have not thought it through, I will attempt to help you. You are not to help others, given the phenomenon you describe, but did it not awaken you? What, my friend, is the purpose of what this instrument would call the two-by-four applied to the forehead of the mule, is this not to get his attention? That is why we are here. We are attempting to engage the planetary attention and to, shall we say, give a soft sell, that is not provable but is subjectively available to the people, that will catch their attention and make them begin to seek. That is the reason for this experience, my friend. Your life experience has to do with your evolution as a spirit. You now have your attention upon this fact. Do you now see the place of that experience in your early life, in what has happened to you subsequently?

M: Yes.

Does this answer your question, my brother?

M: Yes, it does, but I feel that, could there be another reason besides *(inaudible)*. Do you understand?

We understand what you wish to hear but we will not speak what you wish to hear. But rather, admonish you to remember that the creation waits for no man. Nor should man wait for the creation. You are a part of all that is. That which you do is a part of all that is. Each of those who sit in this circle has a purpose in life or perhaps more than one purpose in life. And the road upon which that purpose lies is a many-branched road, so that you cannot stray from your purpose. You can take a longer or a shorter road. You can only go slowly or quickly or sit down; the purpose remains. However, the purpose of each of you is simple, my friends and has to do with knowing the love of the Creator. As our brother said earlier, once you have established contact with the Creator and the creation, you are then one with the flow that will bring to you that which you need, and will give you the opportunity to do the work that your higher self has prepared for you. Thus, worry not about your purpose in life, but instead, desire to know love. And in that love, to share that love with others. In this way alone will your purpose become evident and its termination final. Does this answer your question?

M: Yes.

Is there another question?

Jim: I have a question. Ruth Montgomery *(inaudible)*.

I am Latwii. I am establishing contact with this instrument. If you will be patient we must deepen contact for she lost her state of calmness for a moment. I am Latwii. I am, I am, I am. I am aware of your question, my brother.

The number of people, or as you would call them, planetary entities or societies in our Confederation varies, but the number is between five and six hundred. However, they are broken down into various subgroups and these are the groups a channel known as Ruth was speaking of. Those of Latwii have only begun to work with the teaching branch of the Confederation with your group. Previously we had been what you might term scientists, and that is still our primary duty. But we were attracted to your group, for we have found that although it is not, shall we say, a greatly advanced or tremendously bright group, it is amazingly consistent in its desire to seek the truth and this has attracted our interest, for we have a turn of mind which is similar. And therefore, we asked permission of the teaching branch of the Confederation to speak to this group. You may have noticed that we are not entirely smooth, but we hope we are getting a little better. However, the information about the sixty subgroups is basically correct, although you must understand this number does vary, depending upon the needs of the planet and the terms of stay, shall we say, of the various members of the Confederation. Some are here for the duration, some are here for less time.

May we in any way enlarge upon this question for you?

Jim: Yes. I would like to know if this Confederation is of this galaxy or of more galaxies than our own?

My brother, this instrument is not particularly well equipped to answer this question but we will do our best through her. Your contemplation of the galaxy is somewhat humorous to us, for we realize that we see that which you cannot, that is, the many planes of existence. That is our specialty, that is the study of vibrations. We are not only an intergalactic Confederation but also interdimensional.

For instance, your group speaker who has been with you since your beginnings as a group is from, what you would call, Andromeda. Were you to go to that dimension you would not find Hatonn, for it vibrates in a dimension which is two octaves above your own. We have many here from various parts of your skies, some in your density but not very many, most are from a density beyond yours, because in our densities we are able to accomplish what you would call travel by thought, and without the experience of duration which you are bound to in your illusion.

Does this answer your question?

Jim: Yes.

May we help you further, my friend?

Questioner: Yeah, I'd like to know if you cover the entire known universe or just a portion of it?

This instrument has trouble relaying the concept we gave her. We must learn to curb our levity. We showed her the picture of us as paint being tossed over the galaxy and dripping down on the sides, what covers the, as you put it, known galaxy. What covers the infinity, that is, the creation, is love. We have, shall we say, arrived at a vibration of experience in which we are conscious of that love, in which we can see that love, and therefore, are desirous only of following that love, wherever it may lead us. When we are needed, we hear that call, regardless of the so-called distance and those who call, and we come and give what aid we can.

And meanwhile, we study what is occurring in the creation. For at this particular point in our own evolution of spirit, we do not fully understand the plan of the Creator, and we collect all the information that we can to further our understanding of this plan. Our basic understanding is that there is indeed a plan, and with this, shall we say, article of faith, we go forth and do our work, while the teaching branch sends forth its love and its light to the individual entities dwelling upon spheres such as yours who have cried out so greatly that we could not help but hear you. Were you in the farthest reaches of the farthest density in this infinite creation, we would hear you, for our ears are only those receptors which hear the cry of the child in need of love, and that is your planet.

Your planet is fearful and is in great need of what it does not have. And we are not able to give to your planet that which it truly desires, that is, a sign which shall be obvious to all man. For we cannot interfere with the free will of your planet. Therefore, we remain somewhat hidden, somewhat questionable, and available only to those who are lead to hear us by their own desires. In that way, we do not infringe upon the free will of any who may wish not to hear what we have to say.

Does this answer your question, my brother?

Questioner: Yes.

We are so happy, and hope that it is not a "TV dinner," as this instrument would call it. Is there another question at this time?

M: Yes. *(Inaudible).*

I am aware of your question. I am Latwii. We are having trouble with our solemnity, if you will pardon us. Sometime you people are very serious and we find that hilarious.

May we say to you that all things in your experience are very useful for your understanding, and this definitely includes dreams, for one third of your life, if you are lucky, is spent in garnering these messages from parts of your mind and spirit that are forced into quietude during your active, daily work-a-day world. Sometimes your dreams will simply attempt to work out frustrations in your daily life and are simply a means of helping you to adjust to a situation which is less than perfect. However, if you become a student of your own dreams, that is, if you begin to write them down as soon as you awaken, you will begin to understand things about yourself that you did not understand before. For you are, in your dreams, conversing with parts of yourself that are in touch with your higher self and with those whom we would call your angels or your guides.

Once you have begun to pay attention to your dreams, you will begin to have memories of being instructed or even of instructing others, depending upon your particular vibratory pattern as a personality coming into this incarnation. Eventually, you will be able to use faculties of your consciousness in dreams, so that you will have a much better communication with yourself in your deeper or subconscious, as this instrument would call it, mode of being.

Therefore, we would of course encourage you to pay attention to your dreams, just as you would pay attention to those things that occur when you are awake. It is widely known among your peoples that sleep is necessary only because of dreaming. If sleep occurs without dreaming, the entity becomes ill. In your dreams you are in contact with your higher self and with the Creator. This is your spiritual rest. There are many, many of your peoples to whom this is the only comfort, for whom this is the only contact. Thus, the more that you meditate or pray, the less that you will need sleep. If you were to totally spend your time in an inspired or loving state, conscious of the Creator, and in ecstasy with the joy of the creation and love, you would not need your sleep. And, there have been those among your peoples who have achieved this level of contact with love. However, for the rest of those upon your planet, as this instrument, for instance, you will continue to need a sufficient amount of sleep, so that you can make contact with those deeper parts of your being.

Does this answer your question my brother?

M: *(Inaudible).*

We certainly hope so. We would hope so for everyone because there is so much beauty in your world, it is a shame to miss the night with all of its sparkling splendor.

Is there another question, my friends?

Questioner: *(Inaudible)* Although I know on a deep level *(inaudible)* relationship to the planet, to a new civilization. I would like insight from you of *(inaudible)* my relationship *(inaudible)*.

I am with this instrument. We are aware that you desire this information but there are things which we can not share with you, due to our desire for your unimpaired free will. The information that you request is within you, as you stated and we do not wish to influence any life decisions or understandings that you might obtain. Remember that the information that we give you is basically quite meaningless. The information that you truly need comes from within yourself. You have the information that is necessary for you. We are here, as the one known as E said, to give you food for thought, never, ever to influence your decisions. We are sorry that we cannot speak freely upon this but we do not wish to become advisors, but only friends along the way. Can you understand our position, my friend?

Questioner: Yes. *(Inaudible) (Laughter)* Thank you.

Now, my brother, you are beginning to enjoy yourself. We are very glad. We were afraid that you would get mad at us.

Questioner: That would be impossible.

We will take a little break here while we are getting ourselves sober again. We are very much enjoying the mood of this session, for it is a very good one this evening. Thank you for your beautiful vibrations. Is there another question at this time?

Questioner: *(Inaudible)* … mentioned … eruption of Mount St. Helen … in the future some sort of activity somewhere to the south …

I am Latwii. We are aware of your question and due to the fact that someone has informed this dull instrument of the Ring of Fire, we now are able to give her a much clearer picture than we could last week. The probability of a problem occurring in an arc of approximately twenty minutes, starting out to sea and crossing land near South America, but north, is greater than it was last week. The probability at this time is approximately two one *(21 percent)*. This is a significant rise in probability. This is due to the fact that there are pressures generated by heat within the planetary sphere, which must come into balance.

We are showing this instrument fire. We are having difficulty pinpointing our concept.

(Pause)

I am with this instrument. I am Latwii. We were unable to give this instrument the precise information she needs, due to the fact that we know that she would be interrupted. You must realize that it is very difficult for us to give precise information through a channel such as this one. And in this case we do not speak of her particular educational and life experience, which have prepared her more to channel philosophy and words of beauty than to speak words of specific information. Rather, it is due to the type of contact which we of the Confederation prefer to use with our channels, for the amount of control that is necessary for a perfect contact is very uncomfortable in the conscious state. We do not like to work with trance, due to the fact that we wish the entity at all times to be able to reject or accept our thoughts. Thus, we do not infringe upon the free will of our channels. Therefore, we will attempt to give information but you must understand that these are simply probabilities.

The greatest probability of an occurrence is that of another eruption upon an island which will be fiery. There are probabilities of earthquakes on land or under the ocean which would cause tidal waves. However, as the land shifts, these probabilities will also shift and we do not know for certain how the Earth will release the pressure which has built up within it.

If you wish to send your love to the planet, it will use it to release pressure on the inner planes, and perhaps you would like to do this. This is acceptable, for you have the right to aid your planet, because you are incarnated upon it. We can send love to it but cannot directly influence it, for we are not of your planetary being. Does this answer your question?

Questioner: Yes.

Questioner: *(Inaudible)*.

Yes, my brother. The greatest probability would be off into the—we must search this instrument's mind—off to the north-east of that area, where there are islands. However, there is also some probabilities of adjustments in the Earth's crust occurring along the line that you mentioned. We are still looking for the name of the waters of your planet.

Questioner: Could it be the Caribbean Sea?

We thank you, my brother. This is what we were attempting to pull out of this instrument's mind, for it was in there, but she does not use the word very frequently. That is correct.

Is there another question?

Questioner: I have another question about that area. Could this be near the area that the continent of Atlantis is supposed to be?

We are consulting the computer. I am Latwii. The continent of Atlantis was, in fact, several bodies of land, which stretched over a large body of water. Therefore, the question that you ask is confusing. However, part of Atlantis is near the area, yes, my brother.

Questioner: Will this activity uncover any of the remains of the part of Atlantis that is in that area or will it destroy it even more?

We are with this instrument and have a picture of what you ask, from the computer. We do not have knowledge of this particular part of your planetary experience. However, computer knowledge indicates that your peoples have already rediscovered parts of Atlantis. However, there are many who doubt everything, and therefore, evidence which should be quite apparent is not. For some reason there are people upon your planet who wish to be the only ones who are upon your planet. It is an interesting phenomenon, my friends. Perhaps, in their incarnations in Atlantis, before the end of the last cycle, when they failed to go on and were forced to repeat over another cycle of experience, they had experiences that they would rather not remember. Therefore, they deny Atlantis.

However, there are those among your people who can show you artifacts and places that the shifting sands uncover that are quite definitely made by man, and quite definitely too old to be of this civilization. Thus, Atlantis is with you already and will continue to rise, as other parts of your planetary land masses sink. The water, my friends must go somewhere. However, all things eventually become less whole than they were, due to the nature of magnetic fields. So, as time passes there will be less undisturbed evidence of Atlantis.

Does this answer your question?

Questioner: Yes, it does. It brings some other questions to mind too. In that area, as it settled, a crystal was found there inside a pyramid, in a shaft of metal. Is this a storage device for energy or could it have been an energy source?

Are you familiar, my brother, of the person with power who works with a crystal? You think of this person perhaps as a gypsy, who gazes into the crystal ball. Are you familiar with this concept?

Questioner: Yes.

You must understand that as one disciplines the personality and becomes aware of one's true nature, one begins to achieve powers and can come into attunement with crystals, for weal or for woe, to heal or to destroy. The crystals were used to a very large extent in the civilization which you know of as Atlantis. They were also misused in the end. As you proceed with your own seeking and as you find yourself becoming a more powerful personality, keep in mind the responsibility for good or for evil that you carry within you, for you must always make that choice. This may sound simple but it is not, unless you let the Creator move you as the wind blows the trees.

We realize we have gotten a bit off the subject of crystals. However, there was a lot of trouble because of those crystals and we ask you to take that to heart.

Does this answer your question, my brother?

Questioner: Yes, thank you.

We thank all of you for allowing us to speak to you.

Is there another question at this time?

Questioner: *(Inaudible)* advanced civilization *(inaudible)*. Had they achieved higher level of consciousness *(inaudible)*.

That is correct, my brother.

Questioner: Is that similar to what happened between *(inaudible)*.

No, my brother, it is not similar. The name we have for that planet is Maldek. That particular planet chose consciously the evil way. Thus, it destroyed itself. In the case of Atlantis, there were, even at the end, very advanced beings on the side of light. They escaped and helped to form very advanced civilizations in South America and in the region which you call Tibet. Thus, the two situations are not alike. Maldek was a pure planet, and if you can appreciate evil as the polarity of good, you can appreciate the dark magnificence of that planet as it destroyed itself.

We do not have the sentimental hatred for evil, as you call it, that those among your peoples do when they speak of evil, that which Lucifer has become, that is, the devil. We find evil useful, because it delineates the good, giving you the choice that makes you learn. You have only to be conscious that you have that choice in order to have a great head start upon vibrating always towards the positive, towards love. Because of this you may well suffer. However, each tear that you let fall is gold, for you learn as you grow. And with each trial you become more able to be above good and evil, so that you seek only the Creator.

(Transcript ends.)

Intermediate Meeting
June 1, 1980

(Carla channeling)

I am Latwii, and I greet you, my friends, in the love and the light of our infinite Creator. I am having to use a somewhat stronger control with this instrument this evening due to her condition, which is somewhat fatiguing to her. However, she is willing for this to happen and we will speak to this group, for we are very appreciative of your coming together to seek the truth and realize that you have a desire for the words of the Confederation through an instrument such as this one, no matter how imperfect or desultory they may be.

The brothers and sisters of Hatonn send you their love and light also. They are again on duty, again in the Middle East. They have become regular Henry Kissingers these days and regret their being unable to be with you, for they are by nature those who desire to teach. And, it is always their desire to have a student who wishes to learn rather than a student who wishes to leave the classroom and go about other business. Unfortunately, my friends, the classroom upon your planet is your entire life, so that you cannot play hooky. You can only experience the gradations of feelings that you call emotions and states of happiness and sadness that are part of the catalyst of experience, which bring about thought and a greater understanding of the process which you as a soul are growing and evolving.

There is always one important point that we wish to make to those who meditate and truly seek the way of the pilgrim. That point may perhaps be illustrated rather than explained. Let us say, my friends, that you all have known an explorer, a treasure hunter, whose desire in life was to seek out the greatest and the best treasure of all time. Your friend sought out old maps and read old stories and talked to many archaeologists and experts, seeking a good trail to the best treasure of all time, a treasure that was priceless, a treasure that would be his.

Because all desires become reality, this young man found an old man who knew of the greatest treasure. "But," he said, "this great treasure is guarded by a three-headed dragon, and you must go down into dark caves to find this treasure. If you can get past the dragon you will have the only priceless treasure upon your planet."

So, my friends, our explorer sold all that he had and set out to find the cave, and after traveling in every conceivable hardship he reached a part of a great wilderness in which he found the deep, dark grotto in which the treasure lay. Bravely, he proceeded, tracking down many meaningless dead ends, retracing his steps, moving in the dark but with a remarkable tenacity of purpose. Finally, he heard the hiss of the dragon and saw it, as it glowed an unearthly green in the great vault where the dragon had its nest, and there was a great battle. Finally, the explorer had slain the three-headed dragon, and the beast had poured its green life-fluids upon the damp dark stone of the cave's floor. There was no more hissing and the explorer could move onward.

Onward he moved in total darkness again, now that the dragon-light had been extinguished, and came he then to the treasure chamber. Upon a pedestal stood a beautiful filigree box, locked with an intricate lock. He felt of it in the darkness and knew that it was the treasure, or it contained the treasure, he knew not which.

Painfully, slowly, he retraced his steps until he came again unto the light of day. He was starved, for he had not eaten since he entered the grotto. The light blinded him, but days passed and he recovered. He set about to try the lock, with the infinite patience of those who truly desire the priceless. He tried every combination until he found how to open that lock, and lo, he opened the box. In the box lay a brown leather book, or so it seemed. He picked up the book and opened it and saw his own face, for the insides of the book, my friends, were two twin mirrors.

We ask that you think of this story as you proceed upon your path. Spiritual friends and guides have a function in your life. They may tell you where to find the cave, and they may warn you of the dragon. They may assure you that there is a treasure, but once you have found the treasure, what have you found?

You, my friends, are the treasure, the one priceless treasure of the universe, for you are life and this pricelessness you share with all who have life and consciousness. If you look at yourself in the mirror you may see many surface faults in your appearance, but if you look in your inward mirror, what do you see? Deeply buried is treasure that lies within you. How much love, how much patience do you need to uncover yourself to yourself, for yourself, and for the world in which you live?

We ask you to trust not any outer garment of word, idea, thought, fact, message, dream or action but to go instead into meditation. Leave all of these things as if you were cleansed of them. If you make a habit of this, you will find the treasure that you seek, the knowledge that you seek. The more that you know, the less you will be able to speak. Until finally, you will become one who shows people the map and warns people of the dragon and assures them of the treasure. That is the path upon your particular sphere at this time.

May we ask anyone in this room what you perceive the treasure as being?

Questioner: Man and angel.

The blending of those two answers, my friend, is the Amen of existence. We thank you for allowing us to tell our poor tale to you and will leave this instrument momentarily in order that our brother Laitos may pass among you. I am Latwii.

I am Latwii. I am with this instrument. We also greet in love and light and would like to exercise those who desire to become channels at this time. If the one known as Jim would relax and not attempt to analyze his thinking processes. We would at this time transfer our contact to him and Laitos.

(Jim channeling)

I am Laitos, and I would like to express my appreciation for the privilege of exercising this instrument. It is always a joy to be able to say a few words through this instrument. I am Laitos.

(Carla channeling)

We were attempting to transfer our contact to the one known as E without speaking that thought. And we wish to confirm that he was receiving a contact. Now that we have confirmed it, we would like to transfer to the one known as E, that he may have the experience of vocalizing our thoughts. I am Laitos.

(Carla channeling)

I am again with this instrument. We thank the one known as E and are aware that we got as far as the first word. That is the first step, my brother. Please feel very free and know that we are grateful to be working with you. At this time we would like to transfer contact to the one known as C. I am Laitos.

(C channeling)

I am Laitos. *(Inaudible).*

(Carla channeling)

I am again with this instrument. I am Laitos and we are very, very glad to make contact with our brother, C. We are sorry about the phenomenon which you might call a "rush," which causes one to blank out. However, as one continues to work with the group this will become very manageable, for it is only the energy of a group as it is directed to you with the contact.

We are somewhat concerned about the brother who is going too deep. We will attempt to bring him back to a more conscious state at this time. If you will be patient, we will work with him. We ask you now, our brother, do you feel that you wish to work with us this time?

Questioner: Yes.

We feel that you are very sensitive and therefore we wish you to be very conscious as we work with you. For you have a capacity for other types of mediumship and we do not wish to interfere with your studies. If at any time we trouble you, we ask that you mentally request that we leave. Do you understand, my brother?

Questioner: I understand.

In that case, we feel that we need only ask if your guides would wish us to work with you. If you will be patient we will speak with them at this time.

I am Laitos. We have permission and at this time we will attempt to transfer to the one known as M.

(M channeling)

I am Laitos. *(Inaudible).*

(Carla channeling)

I am Laitos. I thank the one known as M. We will continue working with him as we talk through this instrument to bring him up to a more conscious level. We continue to be concerned that he will go into a more trancelike state. This is not desirable, for we do not wish to interfere with his free will or the work of his other teachers on other planes.

We have greatly appreciated all of your patience and we thank each of you. To our sisters, we give our love and will continue to send our conditioning ray at any time that you may request it, not only to become channels, as you call it, but to enhance your own meditations. We will be with all of you if you request it. And if you find yourself in a situation in which you wish that we not be with you, please simply mentally request us to go, for our greatest desire is for your free will. For you are citizens of the universe of the Father and freedom is your birthright, that is the law of creation.

I will leave this instrument at this time. You know, my friends, that I can only leave you in love and in light. It may seem an impossible feat upon a planet that is torn with strife, but it also seems impossible that a hummingbird can fly, for you cannot see his wings. Yet, you live upon a world fashioned completely of love. And there is nothing that you do not look at that is not part of your self.

I leave you in the wholeness and the unity of all that there is, the love and the light of the infinite Creator. I am Laitos. Adonai, my friends.

(Carla channeling)

I am Latwii, and am now establishing contact again with this instrument. I again greet you in love and light. I realize there is some thought in this room that now all philosophy is over, we can get down to business. But, my friends, let me tell you, all of the questions about the world as you see it are questions about illusion. Our philosophy, as flimsy as it is, is much more to the point and much more "survival oriented," as you people are fond of saying, than knowledge of a specific type. However, we are glad to share with you whatever information we do have, on any subject about which we can answer without interfering with your free will. Therefore, at this time we will open the meeting to questions, if you have any. Is there a question at this time?

Questioner: *(Inaudible).*

(Carla channeling)

I am Latwii. I am with this instrument and I am aware of your question. We answer you very simply. You are not able to use this information at this time due to your lack of purity of thought. This is the problem not only of yourself but of many highly evolved persons upon your plane of existence, and it is, shall we say, a touchy one. Therefore, it may take years for you to work toward a purity of thought that understands that there is something beyond good uses and bad uses and something beyond the vices. And when you get to the place where you wish only to serve the Creator in purity, then the information that you are now concerned about will have a free passage into your awareness.

Do you understand, my brother?

Questioner: *(Inaudible).*

Is there another question at this time?

C: *(Inaudible).*

(Carla channeling)

I am with the instrument. That is a question that is less easy to answer. There is a clear answer, so we will tackle it through this instrument. In the first place there is nothing but illusion until you get to a level in which words are not used at all, not telepathically, nor vocally. We are dwelling in an illusion. Our illusion is much denser than yours. And, we have the facility to move into other illusions and vary our experience. Most of all we have the facility of moving into dimensions higher than our own at will. We can work with our teachers at a conscious level. We are at a dimension called six. Our teachers are higher and they too live in illusion. We do not know where illusion stops. However, we can say that reality is like a carrot that is dangled in front of the nose of the donkey, as this instrument would put it. Each reality, once gained, becomes the illusion and a new reality is seen. Once again, that becomes the illusion. We know that the path is infinite but suspect that it is also circular, that in the end we do dwell completely in reality, but without individual consciousness and then are sent forth again to complete the circle. This is only a suspicion on our part, as even our teachers do not know that this is so.

Some of our teachers are stars and have lived a long time in …

(Tape ends.)

L/L Research

Saturday Meditation
June 7, 1980

(Carla channeling)

I am *(inaudible)*, and I greet you in the love and the light of the Creator. I have been given special dispensation to be with you this evening, for it was the wish of our planetary consciousness that we be here to speak, those members of our Confederation whose work is the Father's, whose grief is the most difficult to bear. For you, my sisters, have been sent into the *(inaudible)* and although you freely *(inaudible)* for the sake of the planet. We love you and you know that we do not flatter you when we say this, for you are doing *(inaudible)*. We are grateful that you have *(inaudible)* forgotten.

(Several minutes of recording are inaudible.)

I am Latwii, and I greet you in the love and the light of the infinite Creator. We are sorry we are disturbing your cat. However, we are most privileged to be able to add our voice to the sister who was speaking from the planetary confluence of *(inaudible)*. We thought that she was a bit gloomy, but that is understandable considering the duty that Hatonn is doing at this time, working with those in the Middle East would make anyone gloomy.

My friends, we ask you at this time to look at the road ahead of you and accept it with joy. You do not know what the road will bring. It bends, it curves, it will have branches; accept it now. When you have eased your mind, then you will be able to be free in the present moment. We are aware that you are becoming conscious of the times to come. Those are parts of a road that has not yet turned up in your experience. We ask that you experience the road of today.

Your people are very nice for the most part and sincerely want to help, but they are very serious. And we feel that healing lies in a true understanding of joy. If a person has never felt joy it can cause tremendous damage, for it is a profound emotion. You will find people who have been overjoyed in tears very often. For this is the expression among your peoples of sorrow and yet it is also the expression of joy. That is how unused your people are to joy.

We ask you to remember your heritage. Invest this portion of your [life] with the full power of yourselves, for you are joyous people who dwell on a sad, dark planet. There is no need for you to hide, as your holy work says, your life under the bushel. In whatever your situation, be yourself. And in being yourself, your joy will flow from you like wine from a new bottle, for each of you has within you the spring of eternal joy. We do not understand why you allow so many insignificant details to clutter up the mind and keep you from radiating this joy. You are aware that this is your primary function in altering the planetary consciousness. And yet it is a continual difficulty within each of your lives to allow the minor difficulties of the day to be as they are and to allow your native joy to shine forth.

We ask you to consider how you feel, each about the other. Each of you finds the other to be beautiful and joyful and most adored. If all of you feel that way there must be something to it. Therefore, we ask you to have confidence in yourself as well as in each other.

At this time I would open the meeting to questions.

Questioner: *(Inaudible).*

I am Latwii. I am with this instrument. In two parts, the defense against the psychic is metaphysically another psychic. That is, if you vibrate in love and light that is the best defense you can offer. It is a generalized one but unless you wish to engage in metaphysical warfare, thus stooping to the level of those who *(inaudible)*, and becoming adept at certain kinds of magic that are not without taint. There is nothing specific that you can do. It is, to be simply stated, a matter of somewhere between five and twenty years of research that the United States has not done because it was pure research and that the Russians have done because they have a long view of *(inaudible).*

To answer the second part of the question, you must understand that each entity upon your planet is the Creator. And, each Creator has complete free will to [mold] his own universe. Those who wish to use their psychic powers in a negative capacity are completely able to do so, unless they are greedy. If they simply use them for the supposed good of their world, as they understand it, they are able to maintain their gifts; this is their birthright.

Negativity is a very viable alternative to the people on Earth and it is not denied by the infinite Creator to His children, the choice is theirs. The only thing that is denied at this time, by us, is the murdering of souls on the inner planes by nuclear devices.

We are aware of the possibility of nuclear war and have no intention of stopping it, for that is not our right. However, your peoples do not understand that the emanations from such devices penetrate into the finer densities of existence in your sphere and can disrupt vibratory patterns and personalities so that they must revert back to the very beginning of the cycle of existence. This is not understood by your people. Therefore, it is not against their free will if we do not allow this to happen. Therefore, we are able to prevent it.

Do you wish to question us further, my sister?

Questioner: *(Inaudible).*

My sister, by the time your peoples become aware of the finer dimensions they will not want to use nuclear devices *(inaudible)* themselves.

We are here for the transition. We expect the transition to take some more time of your years. We are terrible at naming your years but we believe that it is approximately thirty of your years. The effects will be complete and the new vibration will be established. Once this is done, those who are not able to stand the higher vibrations will have perished, either by war or by natural calamity or by the simple maturation of old age, as your physical beings have such a short life span. Those who remain in the higher vibration will not want to part from each other. They will be able to see the brotherhood of man as a reality and not a [phase.]

Do you wish to question further?

Questioner: *(Inaudible).*

We cannot speak in any certainty now. There are so many possibilities that it is as if a teacup had two hundred cracks in it and you knew it was going to break but you did not know which one would go first and how it would fall, or if, when it fell, how it would hit.

There are probabilities due to the fact that some of the faults that run through your Earth's crust are very unstable. By that, of course, we refer to the fault that runs from California to what you call Alaska. And also the fault that runs through what you call England. These are somewhat unstable. There are many, many other unstable areas in the country but we do not know, shall we say, how the dice will fall.

The forces of light upon your planet have so far done a tremendous amount of alleviation of destruction. So that those natural changes that have taken place have been much less difficult and dangerous to human entities than they might have been, had not light centers such as yours been *(inaudible)*. Thus, we of course urge you to continue to send love to your troubled planet as we *(inaudible)*. We feel that you are already aware of some of the dangers of your dwelling place. Is this not true, my sisters?

Questioner: *(Inaudible)*.

That is correct. That is also correct.

Questioner: *(Inaudible)*.

You are extremely correct.

Questioner: *(Inaudible)*.

Those would be good.

Questioner: *(Inaudible)*.

Less good. There are places in the east which are very stable but those places in the west which are in your mind have great potential for not only being stable but for attracting those of like mind. So that those who dwell there will be able to work together. That is *(inaudible)*. There is less possibility of stability as we head towards the west coast. You must not place too much emphasis upon our words, for we are looking at a probability sheet and, as you know, long shots do come in. However, the favorite at this point is not the mountains of the east or the mountains of Canada but rather, those mountains called the Rocky Mountains.

Questioner: *(Inaudible)*.

I am Latwii. I do not know my sister, that will be up to you. You may not yet be tested. However, we would advise you to practice, as this instrument would call it, [being] cool. The only way to present yourself to destiny is with the knowledge that if you live, you live, and if you die, you die. And since you are an eternal being it does not matter. With this attitude you can work your way through most situations with a minimal of disquiet. It may sound cold-hearted but believe me, the time to sit on your emotions is the time when you most want to express them.

You must realize that in the creation of the Father, there are many distortions of love. When you view a distortion of love, you may not intellectually realize in that moment that this distortion will eventually begin its positive evolution towards love in its true state. But, if you train yourself from time to time, the muscle memory, shall we say, will give you strength.

As you know, we are with you. And, although we cannot keep your from losing your physical vehicle, if a mountain falls upon you or sea washes over you, we can certainly guard your infinitely precious soul. That will never be in any danger. We hope that this gives you some comfort. We realize also, this will not stop you from being afraid but we like to point out that most brave people are afraid.

Is there another question?

Questioner: *(Inaudible)*.

I am Latwii. You are correct in a sense. Do you wish any further information?

Questioner: *(Inaudible)*.

You are coming in contact with your teacher, who has been dealing with you for some time. Your lessons do not have any connection with your physical life in this density, at this time, rather, with the continuing evolution of your true self in its whole capacity. This part of your education is something that you could not do without. Nor could most of those who are called "apples" or "wanderers" by this instrument. The vibrations of your adopted dwelling place are such that it is very difficult for most of you to receive consciously the continuing lessons that you desire in your spirit self. Therefore, they must take place when your spirit is released through sleep.

Does this answer your question, my sister?

Questioner: *(Inaudible)*.

No, my sister, that is not precisely the reason for the separation. You were brave and desired to help the planet in which you now dwell. However, you were extremely reluctant to leave the very concentrated study, it was your whole existence previously. Thus, you did not invest your Earthly personality with a giant helping of your true personality but reserved a generous portion of it for continuing your study. This has caused you to feel as you described.

The possibility of uniting the astral or ethereal self and the S self, as you may put it, is quite good and would only require that both the S self and the astral or spiritual self requested the adjustment. However, we find that you are doing very well in aiding the planet, just as you intended. And therefore, any changes that you make in your personality are entirely up to your own personal discretion. For you are doing what you came to do. And, we realize, that is your answer.

Does this aid you, my sister?

Questioner: *(Inaudible).*

I am Latwii. We believe that you are describing the sphere known as Earth *(inaudible)*. We have to agree with you. It is a difficult place at best. Now, let us seriously address your question.

As we said before, there is no need for you to feel that you are shirking your responsibilities to your adopted planet. For you have invested your personality with a tenacity towards helping the planet. There is nothing lacking in that part of your personality. Also, you have not cut your ties with your teachers but are continuing your education. This was a prerequisite to your coming here, for you could not have survived or you could not have taken the vibrations. Therefore, your fears are groundless. And you do not have to feel guilty about yearning to go back home. For you have made arrangement to bring a little bit of home with you. And we repeat, those who are fond of the man-made creation upon your planet are either not paying attention or are somewhat negatively polarized.

You have a beautiful sphere upon which to live in. It is unfortunate that the entities upon that sphere are not as beautiful in their manifestations of love and service to others. We would find it very, very unusual that a wanderer could feel at home in such an atmosphere. The instrument through which we speak, for instance, has never been able to live well in this atmosphere of distrust and hostility and the vibrations have affected her body, although her spirit is very brave.

The one known as B is the most serene soul of the three of you. However, she too would give anything to be at home again. Therefore, rest easily, for each of you having made the sacrifice and followed through with your decision are doing what you came to do. And there is nothing more to be said and not guilt to be felt because you do not like some of the excesses of negativity in this sphere. We ourselves have spent most of our time working in the inner dimensions and *(inaudible)* …

(Tape ends.)

Intermediate Meeting
June 8, 1980

(The entire tape is difficult to hear.)

(Carla channeling

I am Latwii, and I greet you in the love and the light of the infinite Creator. *(Inaudible)* We of the Confederation *(inaudible)* and especially welcome those who are new to this group. We are very honored to have [this opportunity] and wish to express our happiness at being able to share our thoughts with you, but always with the understanding that we are your brothers and are not all-wise or all-knowing but only beings who can make errors. Thus, we attempt to tell you the truth as we understand it but do not ask for your complete [belief] but rather your careful consideration, for yourself are the, shall we say, master *(inaudible)*, the creator of your destiny and whatever information you may get from any source is nothing unless you make it *(inaudible)*.

We were aware of your chanting this evening as you polarized yourselves toward the unity of God. In the religion which fostered the birth of that *(inaudible)* a central prayer is the prayer, "Hear, O Israel, the Lord your God is One." Listen, my friend. What can you hear? This instrument can hear voices, birds, the humming of the machine. That is one way. What can you feel, my friends as you enter into meditation? You feel a fullness enter *(inaudible)*. All of you are One. Here are One. What can you see with your eyes closed? It is not the invocation of the light, but the one light, my friends, the light of love. See, my children. The light is One. You are the gate through which all of these things pass from the outside to the inside, from the inside to the outside. That is your true position within this illusion. You allow in what you choose, you allow the manifestation of what you choose.

Now, my friends, let us consider all of the great serious issues of the past *(inaudible)*. What of that great reputation that you had hoped for, what of your good looks, what of success, what [of cutting the grass right,] what of doing the right thing? Let us consider all these things and then let us consider *(inaudible)*.

We are all one, my brothers and sisters. Cut your grass, pursue your goal. It is for this that you came into this environment, to attach importance to the simple doing day by day. The importance must be attached to the awareness that you have in the doing of it. Are you aware of the unity and the love involved in what you do? When you take out your garbage, my friends, when you flatter your boss, my friends, when you are angry at someone, you are learning spiritual lessons. But not from garbage, not from your boss, not from anger—from the love that in its infinite wisdom created you in individual consciousness, able to choose one gate that you would open from the outside to the inside for the inside, from the inside to the outside.

Your consciousness, my friends, is a permeable membrane. It can keep nothing out that belongs to you. And what you create within you cannot be kept from manifestation. So we ask you to turn your heads away from ambition, from pride, towards love and the oneness that links you to your brothers and sisters, to the world in which you live. It is very difficult to do these things on your own. It is even difficult to do them with us, and it is certainly *(inaudible)*.

However, my friends, *(inaudible)* is ever near to the seeker. The help lies within the seeker and the method used to discover this source of love is meditation. In quiet, simple meditation, when used on a daily basis, will do more to center and untangle your thoughts than any amount of self-understanding, self-analysis, or intellectual decision, for there are many parts of yourself that are not intellectual but which belong in the decision-making process. In the processes *(inaudible)*. These parts of you dwell beneath the totally conscious, totally articulate self and to meditate is, among other things, to get back in touch with those different parts. There is much more to meditation than this, but this will be discovered as progress in meditation continues by each person who on a daily basis seeks the Creator *(inaudible)*.

We realize that we do not have as articulate a way of speaking as our brothers of Hatonn, who, by the way, send you all of their love. But we can only emphasize to you that although your world seems complex and your actions in it therefore also complex, reality is in fact a very simple thing, consisting completely of the love of the Creator which has formed from light all of the vibrations of being that manifest of their magnetic field in your illusion. Thus, we welcome you in love and light and we leave you in love and light, for that is all that there are. Two components which are, in fact, one, for love is light. Light is simply the vehicle through which love manifests itself.

So, the next time that you become angry, remember that love has become angry with love. We will allow you to draw your own conclusions about [love.] I can see that we do not have a very risible audience tonight because nobody is laughing. We would like to exercise one or two channels before we leave so that Laitos may *(inaudible)*. We would transfer to the one known as B. I am Latwii.

(Carla channeling)

I am Laitos, and I greet you in the love and the light. We are very happy to work with this group, and as we exercise each of the newer channels we will also be working with the vibrations of each of you in order that we may aid you in your meditation. If you become aware of our presence through some physical sensation, do not be at all alarmed, but if for some reason we are causing any discomfort at all, mentally ask us to adjust our vibrations.

We would like at this time to transfer to the instrument known as Jim McCarty, if he would, as always, speak the words that we give him without *(inaudible)*. I am Laitos.

(Jim channeling)

I am Laitos. We greet you in the love and light of the infinite Creator. It is again our pleasure and privilege to speak with you briefly through this instrument. It is necessary for the instrument to refrain from judgment or analysis.

(Carla channeling)

I am Latwii, and find that the one known as Jim *(inaudible)*. It is extremely good to be present with this group *(inaudible)* and we realize that here and there are the difficulties with analysis and *(inaudible)*. Of course, my friends, as listeners we do not want you to suspend judgment or discipline yourselves against analysis. However, for the verbal contact to be as precise as possible it is necessary for the instrument who offers himself or his service to totally suspend the analytical portion of the mind so that he may hear our concepts. We do not use the word "hear" in an auditory sense but in an inner sense. Just as you hear your own thoughts, so you hear ours and it takes a passive mind in order to accept the suppression. They feel precisely like your own thoughts. That is the reason that the instruments have a great deal of trouble at first, for they have no confidence that they are not simply *(inaudible)*. Often what will happen is that they will channel something that someone needed to hear and *(inaudible)* so they would know within themselves …

(The rest of the tape is inaudible.)

www.ingramcontent.com/pod-product-compliance
Lightning Source LLC
Chambersburg PA
CBHW080420230426
43662CB00015B/2162